VISIONARY FILM

VISIONARY FILM

THE AMERICAN AVANT-GARDE

P. ADAMS SITNEY

NEW YORK OXFORD UNIVERSITY PRESS ♔ 1974

Parts of chapter eight appeared in *Artforum* and parts of chapter nine appeared in *Film Culture*. They are reprinted by permission of the publishers.

"Salutation the Second" by Ezra Pound is reprinted from *Personae*. Copyright 1926 by Ezra Pound. Reprinted by permission of New Directions Publishing Corporation.

The excerpt from "Miss Furr and Miss Skeene" is from *Selected Writings of Gertrude Stein*. Copyright 1946 by Random House, Inc. Reprinted by permission of the publisher.

The numerous quotations from *Film Culture*, The Film-makers' Cooperative Catalogue, and the publications of the Film-makers' Cinematheque are reprinted by permission of the publisher of *Film Culture* and Film Culture Non-Profit Corporation.

Illustration credits:

René Magritte, "Le Soir qui Tombe," 1964, Private collection, USA
René Magritte, "Les Promenades d'Euclide," The Minneapolis Institute of Arts.
Willem de Kooning, "Woman with a Green and Beige Background," Private collection.
Jackson Pollock, "Cutout," Private collection.
Wassily Kandinsky, "Loosely Bound," Pasedena Museum of Modern Art, Galka E. Scheyer Blue Four Collection.
Joseph Cornell, "Medici Boy Box," Fort Worth Art Museum.

To Jay Leyda and Jacques Ledoux
and to the memory of Adam Parry

PREFACE

When I first conceived of this book in 1968, it was to have been a short collection of interpretations of a selected number of films made by American independent film-makers. At that time I was taking the International Exhibition of the New American Cinema to a number of European film archives and universities. In the repeated screenings of a large collection of films I was able to become very familiar with the works I wanted to interpret, and in my lectures on those occasions I had an opportunity to refine my ideas. Yet when it came to writing a book, two years later, that original plan expanded into this lengthy study.

The interpretation of individual films spread to the consideration of the whole career of their makers. Then the question of the relationship of one film-maker to another arose. Soon I found my work moving in a direction that could lead to a life-long enterprise, a history and analysis of the American avant-garde film in several volumes, continually to be revised to encompass new films. At that point I had to clarify my aspirations and define my topic.

The earliest American films discussed here were called "film poems" or "experimental films" when they were first seen. Both names, like all the subsequent ones, are inaccurate and limiting. Of the two, the term "film poem" has the advantage of underlining a useful analogy: the relationship of the type of film discussed in this book to the commercial narrative cinema is in many ways like that of poetry to fiction in our times. The film-makers in question, like poets, produce their work without financial reward, often making great personal sacrifices to do so. The films themselves will always have a more limited audience than commercial features because they are so much more demanding. The analogy is also useful in that it does not put a value on the films in question. Poetry is not by essence better than prose. "Experimental" cinema, on the other hand, implies a tentative and secondary relationship to a more stable cinema.

Both terms fell out of use in the late fifties. In their places arose the "New American Cinema" on the model of the French Nouvelle Vague, and the "underground" film, in response to an increased social commitment on the part of certain newly emerging film-makers. Very few film-makers were ever satisfied with any of these labels. "Avant-garde" is itself unfortunate. On the one hand, it implies a privileged relationship to a norm which I do not wish to affirm, and on the other hand it has been used to describe thousands of films which fall outside the scope of this book, some of which are excellent and many of which are very bad. I have chosen to use the term "avant-garde" cinema throughout the book simply because it is the one name which is not associated with a particular phase of the thirty-year span I attempt to cover.

The precise relationship of the avant-garde cinema to American commercial film is one of radical otherness. They operate in different realms with next to no significant influence on each other. In the forties when the first generation of native independent film-makers learned their art, young people could not make films freely within the industry. A long apprenticeship was required and the division of functions (writer, producer, director, cameraman) was jealously protected. In reaction the young American film-makers turned to the European avant-garde tradition. But unlike the painters and poets who had made films in the twenties, they did not stop film-making after one or two efforts when they did not find commercial support. They continued to make films, responding to each other's work and to the forces that were active in American painting, poetry, and dance around them.

The commercial film industry was in fact so conservative that in France a new critical theory was developing in response to the loss of directorial authority in American films. The followers of André Bazin enunciated "la politique des auteurs," which sought out the stylistic constants in the films of directors who had to work under factory-like conditions. This critical method was later imported into America as the "auteur theory." However there have always been two independent strains in the theory of cinema. One goes back to the psychologist Hugo Munsterberg and includes the writings of other psychologists, sociologists, and philosophers such as Arnheim, Kracauer, and Merleau-Ponty, as well as Bazin, and has tried to understand what constitutes the whole cinematic experience. The other strain includes the theories of film-makers themselves from Delluc and Epstein in France through the great Soviet theoreticians Kuleshov, Vertov, Pudovkin, and Eisenstein. They have sought the ideal essence of cinema and their theories have been concerned with how films should be made. While French and American critics were propounding the auteur theory for the cinema of the forties and fifties, major theoretical writing was being produced by the film-makers within the American avant-garde. Deren, Brakhage, Markopoulos, and Kubelka were defining new potentials for the cinema.

American avant-garde film theory has received even less critical attention than the films. Therefore I have assumed the task of commenting on the major theoretical works of the period and I have tried to analyze the theoretical stance of those film-makers who have responded in their films if not in their writings to these issues. The selection of film-makers to be discussed here has been guided as much by their commitment to the major theoretical concerns as by my original list of films to interpret.

Just as the chief works of French film theory must be seen in the light of Cubist and Surrealist thought, and Soviet theory in the context of formalism and constructivism, the preoccupations of the American avant-garde film-makers coincide with those of our post-Romantic poets and Abstract Expressionist painters. Behind them lies a potent tradition of Romantic poetics. Wherever possible, both in my interpretation of films and discussion of theory, I have attempted to trace the heritage of Romanticism. I have found this approach consistently more useful and more generative of a unified view of these films and film-makers than the Freudian hermeneutics and sexual analyses which have dominated much of the previous criticism of the American avant-garde film.

In the course of writing, historical patterns emerged which I have allowed to control the structure of the book. I have had to invent a series of terms—the trance film, the mythopoeic film, the structural film, and the participatory film—in order to describe this historical morphology. It is almost too obvious to point out that the film-makers themselves did not think in these categories when they made their films. Many of them will, of course, resist my categorizing them at all.

The thirty-year period which this book covers has seen vast changes in the incidental circumstances of avant-garde film-making and distribution. Many of the film-makers discussed here have been able to earn their living in the past few years as professors of film theory and film-making. This is a function of the increasing interest in this mode of film-making

shown by the academic community. Hundreds of colleges now regularly
screen avant-garde films; they have become an essential part of the program of the nation's few film archives. Literally hundreds of new independent films are made and distributed every year. All this has occurred
without any significant influence on the programming of commercial
theaters.

Naturally the vast majority of independent films produced in any year
are of very low quality, as is the year's poetry, painting, or music by and
large. This book does not pretend to be exhaustive of American avant-
garde film-making. Nor does it discuss the work of all the most famous
and important film-makers. Major figures such as Ed Emshwiller, Stan
VanDerBeek, Storm De Hirsch, and Shirley Clarke, to name a few, are
not discussed here. This book attempts to isolate and describe the visionary strain within the complex manifold of the American avant-garde film.

P.A.S.

New York
January 1974

ACKNOWLEDGMENTS

I began writing *The Visionary Film* in 1969 for a series of books on cinema conceived and edited by Annette Michelson. Even though its ultimate publication was not in that series, she has consistently encouraged and aided me in every stage of its production. I am deeply grateful for the advice she has given me over the past four years which concerns both the general structure and the details of the book.

Over the same span of time Ken Kelman has been a sounding board for many of the ideas and observations that I had during the time of writing. His responses are often reflected in this work. Willard Van Dyke and the Film Department of the Museum of Modern Art invited me to give a series of lectures in the Spring of 1971 where I was able to give the first public presentation of the central theses of the book.

I cannot imagine how this work would have been possible were it not for Anthology Film Archives. In its theater I was able to re-see numerous times the films discussed here and its vast library of books and documents on the avant-garde cinema was the foundation of my research. My assistants there, Caroline Angell and Kate Manheim, spent many hours helping me prepare detailed screening notes from which much of the book was written.

Cecily Coddington who typed most of the manuscript suggested many stylistic changes that were incorporated. Jonas Mekas and Steven Koch read and commented on the typed text. For their insights I am grateful. At Oxford University Press my editor, James Raimes, and Leona Capeless have been uncommonly helpful common readers of this specialized book. My particular thanks go to Robert Pattison who worked with me through the more than seven hundred page typescript with exceptional patience.

The more elaborate and complex stills reprinted here were made by

Babette Mangolte; other illustrations were provided by Anthology Film Archives, The Stills Archive of the Film Department of the Museum of Modern Art, and *Artforum* magazine. Tom Hopkins kindly helped me through the proofreading and Nora Manheim made the index. Georges Borchardt, my agent, helped me in numerous ways.

My wife, Julie, convinced me, in 1968 on a train in Norway, that this book should be written. Since then she has been consistently encouraging, especially in my most desperate moments.

The intellectual debts of *The Visionary Film* are numerous. There were no times during the writing of it that I was not coventously reading or rereading articles and books by Maurice Blanchot, Geoffrey Hartman, and Paul de Man. But my debt to Harold Bloom must be singled out. While I was at my typewriter at least one of his books was always on my desk and in continual use.

P.A.S.

CONTENTS

1. Meshes of the Afternoon, 3
2. Ritual and Nature, 20
3. The Potted Psalm, 47
4. The Magus, 93
5. From Trance to Myth, 136
6. The Lyrical Film, 174
7. Major Mythopoeia, 211
8. Absolute Animation, 266
9. The Graphic Cinema: European Perspectives, 313
10. Apocalypses and Picaresques, 343
11. Recovered Innocence, 368
12. Structural Film, 407
   Notes, 437
   Index, 445

MESHES OF THE AFTERNOON

The collaboration of Maya Deren and Alexander Hammid shortly after their marriage in 1942 recalls in its broad outline and its aspiration the earlier collaboration of Salvador Dali and Luis Buñuel on *Un Chien Andalou* (1928). By a surrealistic principle, Dali and Buñuel sought to combine images so that one would bear no logical or rational connection to the next. This principle was not original to the authors of *Un Chien Andalou*, although it never had so rigorous an application in cinema before them. Others, of course, had extended the mechanics of "the Exquisite Corpse" into literature and painting. The Exquisite Corpse, in its purest form, is drawn by a number of persons upon a piece of paper folded so that one can draw the head, another the neck and shoulders, another the trunk, and so on, without any one contributor's seeing the work of the others. The unfolded paper reveals the synthetic, radically malformed figure—the Exquisite Corpse.

In his first autobiography Dali describes the effect of the film:

> The film produced the effect that I wanted, and it plunged like a dagger into the heart of Paris as I had foretold. Our film ruined in a single evening ten years of pseudo-intellectual post-war advance-guardism.
>
> That foul thing which is figuratively called abstract art fell at our feet, wounded to the death, never to rise again, after having seen "a girl's eye cut by a razor blade"—this was how the film began. There was no longer room in Europe for the little maniacal lozenges of Monsieur Mondrian.[1]

Perhaps in 1928 *Un Chien Andalou* looked as indecipherable and shocking as Dali's account would suggest. I doubt it. Buñuel too has written a note on the film:

In the working out of the plot every idea of a rational, esthetic or other preoccupation with technical matters was rejected as irrelevant. The result is a film deliberately anti-plastic, anti-artistic, considered by traditional canons. The plot is the result of a CONSCIOUS *psychic automatism*, and, to that extent, it does not attempt to recount a dream, although it profits by a mechanism analogous to that of dreams.

The producer-director of the film, Buñuel, wrote the scenario in collaboration with the painter Dali. For it, both took their point of view from a dream image, which, in its turn, probed others by the same process until the whole took form as a continuity. It should be noted that when an image or idea appeared the collaborators discarded it immediately if it was derived from remembrance, or from their cultural pattern or if, simply, it had a conscious association with another earlier idea. They accepted only those representations as valid which, though they moved them profoundly, had no possible explanation. Naturally, they dispensed with the restraints of customary morality and of reason. The motivation of the images was, or meant to be, purely irrational! They are as mysterious and inexplicable to the two collaborators as to the spectator. NOTHING, in the film, SYMBOLIZES ANYTHING. The only method of investigation of the symbols would be, perhaps, psychoanalysis.[2]

What Dali and Buñuel achieved through this method of compiling a scenario was the liberation of their material from the demands of narrative continuity. Far from being puzzling, the film achieves the clarity of a dream. The extremity of the violence and the calculated abruptness of changes of time, place, and mood intensify the viewing experience without satisfying the conventional narrative demands of cause and effect. The concentration on only two actors, male and female, and the insistence on tactile imagery set up a situation of identification that more randomly organized films do not have. The strength of the identification in the context of the abrupt dislocations and discontinuities provides us with a vivid metaphor for the dream experience. Had Dali and Buñuel set about to study their own dreams and clinically re-create a dream on film, they could not have surpassed *Un Chien Andalou*.

The film begins with a cliché and then a paroxysm of violence. After the title "Once Upon a Time," a man, played by Buñuel himself, slowly and carefully sharpens a straight razor and slices the eye of the heroine. The horror of this opening is intensified by an extended visual metaphor. As he is sharpening the razor, Buñuel looks with entranced madness at the moon just as a sliver of cloud is about to cross it. At the moment of cutting the eyeball, the film shows the cloud slicing across the moon's circle.

The image is both a reflected horror and a relief: horrible in the precision with which it suggests the cutting of the eye, and a relief in that the viewer for a moment thinks that the metaphor has spared him the actual slicing. But immediately we see the razor finishing its work and the interior of the eye pouring out.

The title which follows, "Eight Years Later," seems to promise a causal account. The action disappoints the expectation. A man dressed as a clown, with a striped box held by a thong around his neck, rides his bicycle through city streets. When he falls from it a young woman rushes out of her house, embraces him on the ground, and removes the box around his neck. Back in her room, she lays out the articles of his clothing and the box as if to reconstruct the man from these mute objects. But suddenly she sees that he is at the other end of the room, now dressed in a suit, and staring at the palm of his hand, out of which ants are crawling.

In a series of dissolves the ants become a woman's armpit, which in turn becomes a sea urchin and then the top of an androgynous head. The head belongs to a character who stands in the street where the bicyclist had fallen, poking a dismembered hand with a long stick. A crowd gathers around her like ants around the hole in the hand. The police intervene; they push back the crowd; and one of them picks up the hand, places it in the striped box, and gives it to her. As she clutches it to her breast, an automobile runs her down.

The young woman and the cyclist watch this episode from their upstairs window. He is excited to madness. As blood trickles from his mouth, he feels the bare breasts and buttocks of his companion. She tries to escape him, but he pursues her, pulling after him two grand pianos loaded with dead donkeys. She rushes into the next room and slams the door, but she catches his hand in the process. The palm, caught in the door and crawling with ants, horrifies her. Then she notices that he is in the same room with her, although he is now dressed in the clown suit and lying on the bed.

The next episode begins with the title "Around Three in the Morning." A new character, seen from the back for a long time, rushes in on them. He punishes the protagonist by throwing his collar, frills, box, and thong out the window and making him stand in the corner. The title "Sixteen Years Before" appears without a change of scene, but now the action is in slow motion. The features of the newly arrived man look remarkably like the protagonist's. He seems to be instructing the cyclist as he would a schoolboy. The books he gives him turn to guns in his hands. With them the cyclist shoots his tormentor, who falls, not in the room, but in an open field against the back of a naked woman. Strollers in the field are indifferent to his corpse.

Back in the room, the cyclist and the young woman again confront each other. He has lost his mouth. Hair grows in its place. Annoyed by what she sees, she looks under her arm to find the hair there missing. She sticks her tongue out at him, opens the door behind her and finds herself on a windy beach with a new man. They laugh at the remnants of the cyclist —his collar, box, and thong—washed up by the waves. Arm in arm they stroll away.

Finally there is the title "In the Spring" followed by a still shot of the central couple, buried in sand, blinded, and covered with insects.

I have passed over many details of this very intricate film. The outline presented here preserves the abrupt changes of location, the basic action, and all the titles. Let us postpone for a moment further comment on this film, in order to present *Meshes of the Afternoon* and lay the basis for a comparison.

The fifteen years between *Un Chien Andalou* and *Meshes of the After-noon* were not without scattered avant-garde film production. In America, the outstanding works of this period sought their inspiration from Expressionism or from the achievements of still photography. The sort of dream narrative that the Dali-Buñuel film offered as a new cinematic possibility was not explored.

When Maya Deren and Alexander Hammid made their film, they worked against a background of more than a decade of scattered expressionistic, impressionistic, and realistic films. They did not consider themselves surrealists.

Maya Deren's background had been literary and choric. She was born in Kiev in the year of the revolution, emigrated with her parents in 1922 to America, where her father, Dr. Alexander Deren, a psychiatrist, worked for and eventually directed the State Institute for the Feeble-minded in Syracuse, New York. After secondary schooling at the League of Nations School in Geneva, Switzerland, she attended the University of Syracuse as a student of journalism until she married. She and her husband moved to New York, where they were both active in the American Socialist Party. She took her Bachelor of Arts from New York University and divorced soon after.

During her first years in New York and until she began to make films, Maya Deren wrote poetry, but she was never satisfied with it. At the same time she developed an interest in modern dance. She was not a dancer herself—at least not a trained dancer. Her mother and friends recall the sudden, inspired, but undisciplined dances she would privately perform, especially in later years after her field work in Haiti and her initiation into voodoo. In the early forties she conceived the idea of writing a theoretical book on modern dance and looked for a professional dancer to work with her. She interested Catherine Dunham in her project and traveled with her on her tour of 1941-2. The book never materialized, but Catherine Dunham had introduced her to Alexander Hammid when her company was in Los Angeles. They married in 1942.

Alexander Hackenschmied, who later changed his name to Hammid, was a professional film-maker born in 1907 in Prague, Czechoslovakia, then working on a minor Hollywood project. He was well known in film-making circles as a cameraman, editor, and director. The best-known films he had worked on by that time were the documentaries *Zem Spieva* (*The Earth Sings*, 1933), *Crisis* (1938), *Lights Out in Europe* (1939), and *Forgotten Village* (1941).

They shot *Meshes of the Afternoon* in two and a half weeks in their own home with borrowed 16mm equipment. They played in the film themselves. There was no script. They worked out the overall outline together and talked over the shooting details while making the film.

It has an intricate spiral structure based on the repetition, with variations, of the initial sequence of the film, and it has a double ending. In the opening shot a long, thin hand reaches down from the top of the screen to leave a flower on a road. A young woman, played by Maya Deren, walks along the road, picks up the flower, and glimpses the back of a figure turning the bend ahead of her.

She goes to the door of a house, knocks, tries the locked door, then takes out her key. She drops it and pursues it as it bounces in slow motion down the stairs. When she finally enters the house, the camera pans a disordered room and ends in a dolly up to the dining room table. There is a loaf of bread, with a knife in it, on top of the table, but as the camera approaches, the knife pops out.

She climbs the stairs, passing a telephone with the receiver off. In the upper bedroom the wind is blowing a curtain. She turns off an unattended record player and returns downstairs to relax in an easy chair by the window. She slowly caresses herself as a shot of her eye and the window are intercut until they are both clouded over. This is the basic movement of the film. In the initial presentation there are no full-figure shots. We see first the shadow of the protagonist, then her hand picking up the flower. Within the house, the camera moves subjectively, imitating her field of vision and her movements. This is a clear-cut formulation of the idea of first person in cinema. In the initial sequence we only see what the heroine herself sees, including glimpses of her own body.

As this basic movement is repeated the transitions between the variations are fluid, so that the viewer finds himself in the midst of a recurrence before it is expected. The first person switches to third.

From the window in front of the easy chair, we can see the initial setting of the film, the road. Now a black figure, like a nun, with a mirror for a face, walks slowly in the same direction as the young woman had in the beginning. She is followed by the young woman again, who is running after her. As fast as she runs she cannot gain on the walking figure, so she gives up and climbs the stairs to the house. For the first time we see her face. She enters without a key and looks around the room, noticing the knife is now on the stairs where the telephone had been. She climbs up in slow motion, then slowly falls through a black gauze curtain into the bedroom. The phone is on the bed. She pulls down the covers, again revealing the knife, and sees the distorted image of her face reflected in its blade. She quickly pulls back the covers, replaces the receiver on the telephone, and glides backwards through the veil down the stairs as the camera does a somersault to dislocate her motions in space. Once downstairs, she sees herself sleeping in an easy chair. With a long stretch she reaches across the room to turn off the phonograph next to her own sleeping figure.

The pace of the events accelerates with each variation. The terror increases as well. After turning off the record player, the second Maya Deren goes to the window from which she sees yet a third version of herself chasing the black figure, who again disappears beyond the bend. She presses her hand against the window and looks wonderingly. The third girl takes her key from her mouth and enters the house where she catches sight of the black figure again. She follows the figure up the stairs and sees it disappear (through stop-motion photography) after placing the flower on the bed. The knife is there too. A quick pan from it brings us back to the sleeper in the easy chair.

This time the camera looks out the window without the mediation of a woman through whose eyes or over whose shoulder the action is seen. We see the same pursuit and its frustrations. Again the key comes from the mouth, but this time it turns immediately into the knife in her hand. She passes through the unlocked door holding it. Within are two Maya

Derens seated at the dining room table. She joins them, as a third, placing the key on the table. The first woman feels her own neck, reaches for the key, and holds it in her palm for a moment. The second does the same. The third reaches without feeling her neck; her palm is black; the key turns into the knife when she holds it. Wearing goggles, she rises from the table, holding the knife aggressively. We see her feet step on beach sand, grass, mud, pavement, the rug—five shots in all. Then, as she is about to stab her sleeping self, the sleeper's eyes open to see a man who is waking her. They go upstairs. Just to reassure herself she glances at the table, which is perfectly in order. The man picks up the flower and puts the phone, which had been left on the stairs, back on its receiver.

Upstairs he lays the flower on the bed and she lies down beside it. His face is reflected in a shaving mirror. He sits next to her and caresses her body. The flower suddenly becomes the knife. She grabs it and stabs him in the face, which turns out to be a mirror. The glass breaks and falls, not to the floor, but on a beach. The tide approaches and touches it.

Without transition we see the same man walking on the original road. He picks up the flower, takes out his key, enters the house, and finds the young woman lying in the easy chair with a slit throat amid broken glass. That is the end.

"This film is concerned," Maya Deren wrote,

> with the interior experiences of an individual. It does not record an event which could be witnessed by other persons. Rather, it reproduces the way in which the sub-conscious of an individual will develop, interpret and elaborate an apparently simply and casual incident into a critical emotional experience.   . . .

> This film . . . is still based on a strong literary-dramatic line as a core, and rests heavily upon the symbolic value of objects and situations. The very first sequence of the film concerns the incident, but the girl falls asleep and the dream consists of the manipulation of the elements of the incident. Everything which happens in the dream has its basis in a suggestion in the first sequence—the knife, the key, the repetition of stairs, the figure disappearing around the curve of the road. Part of the achievement of this film consists in the manner in which cinematic techniques are employed to give a malevolent vitality to inanimate objects. The film is culminated by a double-ending in which it would seem that the imagined achieved, for her, such force that it became reality.[3]

In recent years commentators on this film have tended to neglect the collaboration of Alexander Hammid, to consider him a technical assistant rather than an author. We should remember that he photographed the whole film. Maya Deren simply pushed the button on the camera for the two scenes in which he appeared. The general fluidity of the camera style, the free movements, and the surrealistic effects, from slow motion to the simultaneous appearance of three Maya Derens in the same shot, are his contribution. If *Meshes of the Afternoon* is, in the words of Parker Tyler, the most important critic of the American avant-garde film in the forties and fifties, "the death of her narcissistic youth," it is also Hammid's portrait of his young wife.

Before he came to America and worked in the documentary tradition, Hammid had made some independent films. His first, *Bezucelna Prochazka* (*Aimless Walk*, 1930), is particularly relevant here. In that film, which I have not seen, a young man observes himself in his daily activities. Hammid, unfamiliar with montage or superimposition techniques in this first film, created the effect of self-observation without montage by having the protagonist quickly run behind the camera and take up another position while the camera was panning between his two selves. His subsequent films display a professional handling of the materials and an awareness of the achievements of the Russian and British documentary schools.

One looks at Maya Deren's subsequent films, noticing the broad similarities to *Meshes*, and tends to decide that the first film must have been primarily hers. Hammid has done nothing to contradict this. The mildness and acquiescence of his personality are the opposite of Maya Deren's persistence and dynamism. Furthermore, his subsequent films veer far away from *Meshes*. It is to his earlier films that we must look for a more accurate index of his share in that collaboration.

The visual style of *Meshes of the Afternoon* is particularly smooth, with cutting on movements and elisions to extend the continuity of gesture and action. From the very opening, there is a constant alternation of perspectives from synecdochic representation of the action to subjective views of what the protagonist sees, usually through the moving camera. Although the rhetorical figure synecdoche, the part for the whole, is an essential characteristic of all cinema, where the act of framing a picture can bring into play a potential field outside of the frame of which the filmic image is a small part (e.g., any close-up of a part of the body), I refer in this book to the deliberate and extreme use of framing portions of an action as synecdochic. For instance, in the first cycle of *Meshes of the Afternoon*, there is no establishing shot, no view of the whole figure in her environment; toward the middle of the film, as the situation takes on more symbolic dimensions, the camera tends to compensate by stasis and wider views.

The transitions between cycles are subtly achieved. In the first transition between waking and sleeping, the film uses the wavy shadow over both the eye and the window. That sequence is interrupted by a view of the original road, where the black figure is about to appear. But before it does, there is a dolly back from the window, now masked by a cylindrical pipe which emphasizes the transition.

The division between the second and third cycles has the same fluidity. The first shots of the new cycle are cut in before the last of the old one is seen. In this case, after looking at the sleeper, the protagonist goes to the window to see herself running after the black figure. Even after she disappears around the bend and the pursuer begins to climb the stairs, we see another shot of the protagonist in the window, peering out, her hand pressed against the pane.

When we compare the image of Maya Deren, framed by the window where the reflections of trees blend with the mass of her hair, with the parallel image of Pierre Batcheff, sadistically watching the androgyne and the dismembered hand from his window in *Un Chien Andalou*, one contrast between the two films becomes clear. It is, in fact, a difference which obtains between the early American avant-garde "trance film" (as I will call this type of film in general) and its surrealistic precursors. In *Meshes of the Afternoon*, the heroine undertakes an interior quest. She encounters objects and sights as if they were capable of revealing the erotic mystery of the self. The surrealistic cinema, on the other hand, depends upon the power of film to evoke a mad voyeurism and to imitate the very discontinuity, the horror, and the irrationality of the unconscious. Batcheff, leering out of the window, is an icon of repressed sexual energy. Deren, with her hands lightly pressed against the window pane, embodies the reflective experience, which is emphasized by the consistent imagery of mirrors in the film.

The next cycle, the third, ends with a spectacular pan from the knife, in whose blade her face is reflected, on the bed upstairs, to the sleeper in the easy chair a floor below. It is achieved in a single, quick movement, followed by a direct view from the window, framed so that the right sash is in view as well as about half of the window. The black figure walks completely past and out of frame, followed by the protagonist, running,

(A) The window as a repressive barrier in Dali and Buñuel's *Un Chien Andalou*.
(B) The window as a reflector of the self in Hammid and Deren's *Meshes of the Afternoon*.

also out of frame to the left. The next shot is almost identically framed; it shows the left sash and perhaps two-thirds of the window, so that the two views overlap, but not completely. In this shot the black figure walks from screen right to screen left and disappears again, but the protagonist stops mid-frame, gives up, and turns to the house, so we see her begin her climb.

The rapid succession of these two carefully framed and skillfully directed shots presents the illusion of an immediate continuity of action with the equally potent illusion of an irrational discontinuity of space. Similar skillful manipulation of virtual continuities appears throughout the film.

Meshes explicitly simulates the dream experience, first in the transition from waking to sleeping (the shadow covers the eye and the window at the end of the first cycle) and later in an ambiguous scene of waking. The film-makers have observed with accuracy the way in which the events and objects of the day become potent, then transfigured, in dream as well as the way in which a dreamer may realize that he dreams and may dream that he wakes. They have telescoped the experience of an obsessive, recurrent series of dreams into a single one by substituting variations on the original dream for what would conventionally be complete transitions of subject within a single dream.

In the program notes for a screening of her complete works at the Bleecker Street Theater in 1960, Maya Deren warned, as was her custom, against a psychoanalytical reading of this film: "The intent of this first film, as of the subsequent films, is to create a mythological experience. When it was made, however, there was no anticipation of the general audience and no experience of how the dominant cultural tendency toward personalized psychological interpretation could impede the understanding of the film." Within the film itself, the double ending mitigates against interpretation, showing the makers' preference for sustaining the dream-like ambivalence over the formal neatness of a rounded sleep.

A comparison can be made between this film and *Un Chien Andalou*, while suspending any question of influence. The Deren-Hammid film consciously uses much of what was beyond the intention of Buñuel and Dali. Buñuel and Dali did not set out to create a film dream; the dream-like quality of their work derives from the strength of their sources, from the ferocity with which they dispelled the rational while keeping the structural components of narrative. They show us neither sleep nor waking, but simply a disjunctive, athematic chain of situations with the same characters. The startling changes of place, the violence, the eroticism, the tactility, and above all the consistent use of surrealistic imagery, suggest the dream experience.

Meshes of the Afternoon is not a surrealistic film. It was made possible through a Freudian insight into the processes of the surrealistic film-makers. Nor is it a Freudian film. Surrealism and Freud were the vehicles, either latent or conscious, behind the mechanics of the film. Thus some of its methods seem to derive from *Un Chien Andalou*. In the first place, both films have a "frame" and a double ending. In the case of the Dali-Buñuel film, the frame—the opening sequence of the eye slashing followed by the title "Eight Years Later" as if a causal flashback were about to occur—diverts the narrative. The two endings—the beach scene, followed by the title "In the Spring" and a still of the two figures grotesquely buried in the sand—likewise confound our expectations. Deren and Hammid also made imaginative use of the convention of a frame. Had their film ended with the scene of the girl awakened by the man, that frame would have fulfilled the standard function of dividing imagination from actuality. But the continuation of the violence of the dream, and its dislocations, in the scene between man and woman, which is suggestive of waking, then lapsing back into sleep, changes the film's dimension by its affirmation of dream over actuality.

Un Chien Andalou attempts to present us with a broken, violent, spatially and temporally unstable world, without final reference to a more conventional actuality. *Meshes of the Afternoon*, on the other hand, offers us an extended view of a mind in which there is a terrible ambivalence between stable actuality and subconscious violence. Many of the means of presenting this mind are the same as those of the earlier, more radical film. For instance, in *Un Chien Andalou* a door which we expect to open on a corridor opens on a windy beach, just as the broken glass from the mirror in *Meshes* falls not on the floor but on the lip of the ocean. In *Un Chien Andalou*, when the man is shot by a gun, he starts falling inside the apartment and ends in an open field with his hands clawing the back of a naked lady. The transition is smoothly made through the continuity of action. All through *Meshes* there is similar cutting on action across disjunctive spaces.

In the original shooting script for *Un Chien Andalou*, the man who enters the house to chastise the protagonist is his double:

> At that instant the shot goes out of focus. The stranger moves in slow motion and we see that his features are identical to those of the first man.

They are the same person, except that the stranger is younger, more full of pathos, rather like the man must have been many years earlier.[4]

In the actual production, this identity is obscure. They are not played by the same actor, though their similarity and the dream-like structure of their confrontation do suggest the idea of a double.

This coincidence of the theme of the double can provide us with a clue to the real relationship between the two films. It is possible that neither Hammid nor Deren had seen the Dali-Buñuel film before they made theirs. They could have seen it; and they could have read Dali's book, published just a year before *Meshes*, and learned of it indirectly. If she had seen it, Maya Deren does not mention it in her subsequent writings. In speaking of Surrealism she is not enthusiastic. However, in the construction of the scene in which the stabbed face turns out to be a mirror, they pay homage, perhaps unknowingly, to a motif of the painter René Magritte. In several of his paintings a broken window gapes out upon a void, while the illusory image that one had seen while looking through it lies shattered among the glass on the floor.

In all likelihood Deren and Hammid were more conscious of the influence, however indirect, of Orson Welles's then recent *Citizen Kane*, with its regular shifts of perspective, than of *Un Chien Andalou*. But regardless of the question of influence, it is true that the mechanics of *Un Chien Andalou* and of *Meshes* result from a theoretical application of the principles of cinema to the experience of the dream. The theme of the double, an archetype in dreams, could find two completely different treatments in the two films, yet the abrupt changes of location, so common in dreams, have the same cinematic meaning for both sets of collaborators.

The difference between the films is instructive. *Un Chien Andalou* is filled with metaphors—the eye and the moon, a drink shaker as a doorbell, the sea urchin, and underarm hair—but *Meshes* has none. Objects in the earlier film recur, especially the box of the clown figure, but without the symbolic dimensions of the knife, key, and flower in *Meshes*, which accumulate their deadly charge through repeated use in slightly different circumstances.

Finally, the space of the two films is quite different. *Un Chien Andalou* takes place in a deep space with axial co-ordinates in all four lateral directions and up and down. The virtual space behind doors and walls is much used, as in most surrealistic films. The space projected by *Meshes of the Afternoon* is more rounded and linear, less cubic than the earlier film.

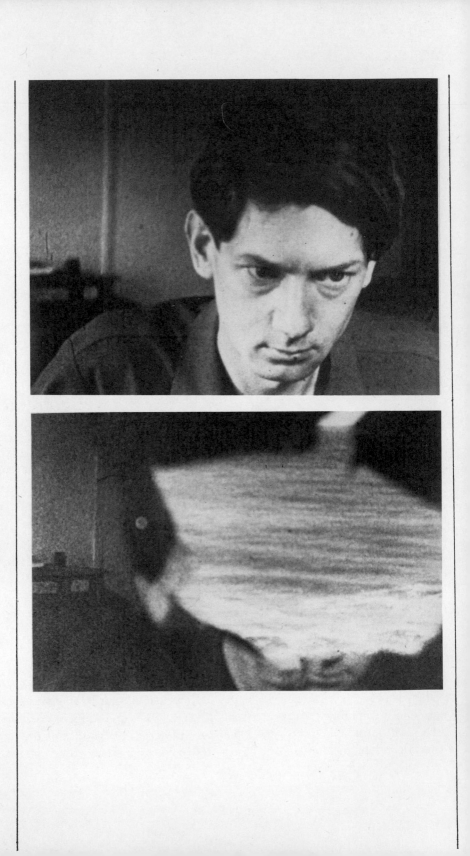

The surrealistic shattered image: Hammid in *Meshes of the Afternoon* before and after the knifing of the mirror. Magritte's "Le Soir qui Tombe."

There is little movement into or out from the space of the images. Actors tend to move across the screen. There is a sense of depth only when the hand-held camera is moved in the subjective shots.

The articulation of space in avant-garde films is often unconscious. The conscious decisions about movement, fixity of camera, choice of sets, imply an inflection of space that the film-maker is often unaware of. We can in fact often observe a common attitude toward space among filmmakers who have deliberately tried to distinguish themselves from each other.

A fluid linear space is just one characteristic that this particular film shares with many of the American films which were to follow it. Another is the evocation of the dream state. And a final characteristic of many avant-garde films from this period (most of them trance films as well) is the film-maker's use of himself as a protagonist. There are many reasons for this, and they vary with the film-maker. Obviously, there is a strong autobiographical element in these films. But beyond that, if the film-maker has neither the ability to command amateur actors to do precisely what he wants nor the money to hire trained actors, it is logical that he attempt to play the role himself, thus completely eliminating the process of "directing." There is also another, more subtle reason which accounts for the number of self-acted films, particularly at the beginning of the avant-garde film movement in America: film becomes a process of self-realization. Many film-makers seem to have been unable to project the highly personal psychological drama that these films reveal into other characters' minds. They were realizing the themes of their films through making and acting them. These were true psycho-dramas.

As psycho-drama, *Meshes of the Afternoon* is the inward exploration of both Deren and Hammid. The central theme of all the psycho-dramas that marked the first stage of the American avant-garde cinema is the quest for sexual identity; in their film, unlike those that follow in this book, it is two people, the makers of the film, who participate in this quest. With the exception of the surrealistic film, *Le Sang d'un Poète*, which will be discussed in the next chapter, the avant-garde film of the twenties had no psycho-drama, even in a rudimentary form. The explosion of erotic and irrational imagery that we encounter in many of these earlier films evokes the raw quality of the dream itself, not the mediation of the dreamer.

If we turn from the Dali-Buñuel collaboration to another, but somewhat less successful, example of the period, Man Ray's *Étoile de Mer*

(1928) based on a poem by Robert Desnos, there are a number of remarkable coincidences of imagery and structure between it and *Meshes*.
Yet the same essential difference of orientation obtains. *Étoile de Mer*
opens with the encounter of a man and a woman on a road. They go to
the woman's apartment where she strips and he immediately bids her
adieu. Twice again in the course of this elliptical and highly disjunctive
film, the same man and woman encounter each other at the same spot.
The last meeting might even be a dream, since it immediately follows a
scene of her going to sleep.

Then consider the use of the image of the starfish in Man Ray's film.
The hero first finds the glass-enclosed creature during his second meeting
with the woman. Alone in his room, he contemplates it. Yet during two
mysterious and completely unexplained scenes—one in which the woman
mounts the stairs of her apartment brandishing a knife, another in which
she steps barefoot from her bed onto the pages of a book—the starfish unexpectedly appears in the scene—on the staircase, and next to the bed—
like the knife and the telephone of the Deren-Hammid film.

Most of *Étoile de Mer* is photographed through a stippled glass which
distorts its imagery and flattens its space. In the use of this distortion
we see the first major difference from *Meshes*. The transitions between
distorted and normal views are not psychologically motivated. They appear random, in fact. In *Meshes*, as I pointed out, the wavy field of vision
indicated the transition to sleep. Like *Un Chien Andalou*, *Étoile de Mer*
is full of metaphors, many of which are introduced by the titles which
Desnos wrote. They are deliberately jarring. After an allusion to "les
dents des femmes" we see a shot of the heroine's legs, not her teeth. In
the central section of Man Ray's film all action seems to disappear, in
order to be replaced by a series of verbal and visual similes comparing
the starfish to the lines on the palm of a hand, to glass, and to fire. Narrative itself seems to exist within *Étoile de Mer* only to be fractured or
foiled.

The central tradition of the American avant-garde film begins with a
dream unfolded within shifting perspectives. Much of the subsequent
history of that tradition will move toward a metaphysics of cinematic
perspective itself.

2

RITUAL AND NATURE

Since I have chosen to begin this book with a discussion of the films of Maya Deren, by herself and in collaboration, it will be useful to analyze them generally. Even though formal innovation has always been an aspiration of the avant-garde film-maker, he has at times allowed his formal inventions to become collectively accepted forms. In the first place the genres have tended to emerge independently in the works of artists out of touch with one another; secondly they have survived precisely as long as they were vital and necessary to contain what was most pertinent to the film artist at the time.

Naturally, imaginative works tend to overstep the boundaries of generic classification. The genres are fluid; they merge; they admit bastard forms. Yet an awareness of some classifications can bring into focus the ambitions and achievements of individual film-makers and of the avant-garde cinema as a whole, as a nexus of related aspirations and reactions.

The elements of dream, ritual, dance, and sexual metaphor abound in the avant-garde films made in America in the late 1940s and early 1950s. For a time the dream generated a form of its own, occurring simultaneously in the films of several independent artists. I have called this the trance film. Its history is an extension of the initial discussions of the American avant-garde film in Parker Tyler's book *The Three Faces of the Film*.

In his captions to the illustrations for that volume, Tyler offers a brilliant and succinct analysis of the form and history of the genre. Under a still from Brakhage's *Reflections on Black* he writes:

> The chief imaginative trend among Experimental or avant-garde film-makers is action as a *dream* and the actor as a *somnambulist*. This film

shot employs actual scratching on the reel to convey the magic of seeing while "dreaming awake"; the world in view becomes that of poetic action pure and simple: action without the restraints of single level consciousness, everyday reason, and so-called realism.[1]

Then, between stills from *The Cabinet of Dr. Caligari* and *Meshes of the Afternoon*, he writes:

> Cesare, the Somnambulist of *The Cabinet of Dr. Caligari*, has been an arch symbol for subsequent avant-garde film-making, one of whose heroines is seen below. Art is the action which knits the passive dreamer, as it knits the passive spectator, to realms of experience beyond his conscious and unconscious control. In such realms, wild excitement is often found by way of the movies. But rarely, except in avant-garde films, does the strict pulse of beauty govern the engines of "wild excitement."[2]

If Cesare is the archetypal protagonist of the trance film, then the form of Jean Cocteau's *Le Sang d'un Poète* is the model for its development. The trance film as it emerged in America has fairly strict boundaries. It deals with visionary experience. Its protagonists are somnambulists, priests, initiates of rituals, and the possessed, whose stylized movements the camera, with its slow and fast motions, can re-create so aptly. The protagonist wanders through a potent environment toward a climactic scene of self-realization. The stages of his progress are often marked by what he sees along his path rather than what he does. The landscapes, both natural and architectural, through which he passes are usually chosen with naïve aesthetic considerations, and they often intensify the texture of the film to the point of emphasizing a specific line of symbolism. It is part of the nature of the trance that the protagonist remains isolated from what he confronts; no interaction of characters is possible in these films. This extremely linear form has several pure examples: Curtis Harrington's *Fragment of Seeking* (1946) and *Picnic* (1948), Gregory Markopoulos' *Swain* (1950), Kenneth Anger's *Fireworks* (1947), Stan Brakhage's *The Way to Shadow Garden* (1955), and Maya Deren's *At Land* (1944), her first film after *Meshes of the Afternoon*. The genre naturally has had many variations, transformations, and mixed uses. These I will discuss later.

At Land is the earliest of the pure American trance films. In it, the heroine, again played by Maya Deren, is washed out of the backward-rolling waves of the sea; she rises, crawls over logs and rocks until she finds herself in the middle of a banquet table, crawls down it without being noticed by the banqueters, and steals a chess figure from a board at the end of the table on which the pieces seem to move by themselves. The middle of the film records her pursuit of the chess man through other similar landscapes: beach, tree, rocks, and interior. No one seems to notice her. At one point, she loses the chase and finds herself talking with a man who is constantly being replaced by other men. Then, finding another chess game in progress, she steals again. This time, as she flees with the chess man, she is watched by images of herself from the rocks, the beach, the banquet, and the tree. In a series of dramatic temporal ellipses, she disappears among sand dunes.

Here is the classic trance film: the protagonist who passes invisibly among people; the dramatic landscapes; the climactic confrontation with one's self and one's past. *Meshes of the Afternoon* had some of these elements, but its intricate, coiled form gave a more personal, less archetypal tone to its narrative. The form of *At Land* is completely open. The camera is generally static. This time Hella Heyman photographed and Maya Deren set up the compositions. The principle of the editing, whereby every scene seems magically continuous with the previous, must have been planned in advance. For instance, as the protagonist crawls from the dead tree to the banquet table, we see her head disappear beyond the top of the frame in one scene, and in the next, now in the banquet hall, it rises from the bottom of the frame. As she pulls herself up into the hall, we see a final shot of the tree as her dangling leg passes through the top of the frame. This kind of montage must be provided for in advance, and, in fact, is the basis of the structure of this film.

In *Meshes*, Hammid and Deren had employed a number of montage illusions which created spatial elisions or temporal ellipses for the sake of the psychological reality which informed their vision. In *At Land*, Deren, now on her own, conceives from the beginning that the film should continually use these figures of cinematography as formal or stylistic devices. Indeed, they are essential principles of her film. She says as much in a letter to James Card:

> Anyway, *Meshes* was the point of departure. There is a very, very short sequence in that film—right after the three images of the girl sit around the table and draw the key until it comes up knife—when the girl with the knife rises from the table to go towards the self which is sleeping in the chair. As the girl with the knife rises, there is a close-up of her foot as she begins striding. The first step is in sand (with suggestion of sea behind), the second stride (cut in) is in grass, third is on pavement, and

the fourth is on the rug, and then the camera cuts up to her head with the hand with the knife descending towards the sleeping girl. What I meant when I planned that four stride sequence was that you have to come a long way—from the very beginning of time—to kill yourself, like the first life emerging from the primeval waters. Those four strides, in my intention, span all time. Now, I don't think it gets all that across—it's a real big idea if you start thinking about it, and it happens so quickly that all you get is a suggestion of a strange kind of distance traversed . . . which is all right, and as much as the film required there. But the important thing for me is that, as I used to sit there and watch the film when it was projected for friends in those early days, that one short sequence always rang a bell or buzzed a buzzer in my head. It was like a crack letting the light of another world gleam through. I kept saying to myself, "The walls of this room are solid except right there. That leads to something. There's a door there leading to something. I've got to get it open because through there I can go through to someplace instead of leaving here by the same way that I came in."[3]

Hammid remembers that the original conception of that scene in *Meshes* was specifically Maya Deren's.

Nevertheless, in her first solo film she is still very much under the influence of her collaborator. The denouement, in which the protagonist is seen by images of herself, comes right out of the center of the earlier film, which may derive from Hammid's own first film. The fluid, rounded space of *Meshes* is echoed in the linear style of *At Land*, with its soft cutting on motion and illusory elisions. But the rich texture of interlocking alternations of subjective camera and synedochic framing of elaborate and dramatic pans, which *Meshes* owed to the creative involvement of Hammid, disappears here, as the photographer worked under the direction of the author-actress.

Trance films in general, and *At Land* in particular, tend to resist specific interpretation. In the case of *At Land*, one could point out the allusions to sexual encounter—the moustached man in bed, and the caressing of the girl's hair by the beach—or interpret the banquet scene in terms of the individual's resistance to the social organism, but it would be difficult to extend such an interpretation to all the actions of the film.

Deren is a good critic of her own work when she writes in her notes for this film:

> The universe was once conceived almost as a vast preserve, landscaped for heroes, plotted to provide them the appropriate adventures. The rules were known and respected, the adversaries honorable, the oracles as

articulate and as precise as the directives of a six-lane parkway. Errors of weakness or vanity led, with measured momentum, to the tragedy which resolved everything. Today the rules are ambiguous, the adversary is concealed in aliases, the oracles broadcast a babble of contradictions.

Adventure is no longer reserved for heroes and challengers. The universe itself imposes its challenges upon the meek and the brave indiscriminately. One does not so much act upon such a universe as re-act to its volatile variety. Struggling to preserve, in the midst of such relentless metamorphosis a constancy of personal identity.[4]

As Maya Deren began to move more confidently from writing to film, her interest in form became clearer. She has left us six films. In each one of them she explored a new formal option. I have already suggested that her interest in the overlapping of space and time arose as a result of the editing of *Meshes in the Afternoon*. That interest never flagged during her film career. In *At Land* she pursued an open-ended narrative form based on her initial discoveries. In her next film, *A Study in Choreography for Camera* (1945), she returned to her old interest in dance to make a completely new kind of film.

It is clear that even in the first two films her concern with dance was not suppressed. The plastic space of both films, which cutting on motion makes possible, is closely akin to the dancer's art of connecting motions.

Even before her collaboration with Hammid on *Meshes of the Afternoon*, she had spoken casually with dancers about recording ethnic dances on film. After the making of *Meshes* and her revelation that the space and time of film was a *made* space and time, a creative function and not a universal given, she was no longer interested in the camera as a simple recording device for the preservation of dances. *A Study in Choreography for Camera* was a dance film with equal participation by both arts. She subtitled it "Pas de Deux," referring to the one dancer and the one camera.

She did not herself appear in this film. Since she had no formal training, she enlisted the help of a dancer, Talley Beatty, as her one performer. The film they made is extraordinarily simple—a single gesture combining a run, a pirouette, and a leap. It lasts no more than three minutes.

The opening shots recall the ending of *At Land;* in both instances she used one pan movement of the camera to encompass several temporal ellipses. It is as if she were panning through time as well as over space. She ended *At Land* with one sweeping shot, actually made up of a series of carefully joined shots, of herself walking away over sand dunes. As the camera in its leftward motion sees each successive dune, she crosses over the top and disappears on the other side. Thus in the evocation of a very short time (the time of moving the camera on its tripod) we see the illusions of long periods of time, the walking between dunes having been eliminated.

Choreography begins with a circular pan in a clearing in the woods. In making the one circle the camera periodically passes the dancer; at each encounter he is further along in his slow, up-stretching movement. At the end of this camera movement, he extends his foot out of the frame and brings it down in a different place; this time, inside a room. The dance continues through rooms, woods, and the courtyard of a museum until he begins a pirouette, which changes, without a stopping of the camera, from very slow motion to very fast. Then he leaps, slowly, very slowly, floating through the air, in several rising, then several descending shots, to land in a speculative pose back in the wood clearing.

The dance movement provides a continuity through a space that is severely telescoped and a time that is elongated. The film has a perfection which none of Maya Deren's other films has ever achieved.

There are two aspects of this film that deserve consideration. One is formal, concerning the emergence of a new way of composing films; the other is synthetic, concerning the possible use of dance in film, and more broadly the problem of prestylization, which Erwin Panofsky, in his essay "Style and Medium in the Motion Pictures" (1934), identified as the failure of all films like *The Cabinet of Dr. Caligari* (his example) which use aesthetic objects such as expressionistically-painted sets or ballet movement instead of natural gestures and real scenes as raw material.

Choreography for Camera forecasts the shift from narrative to imagistic structures within the avant-garde film movement. Before it, there had been several ways of putting together such films. Narrative had been the most common. By this I do not mean simple story-telling, but abstracted narrative forms such as *Un Chien Andalou, Meshes of the Afternoon*, and the trance films. Thematic composition was another possibility: the city symphonies, usually describing a day in the life of a city; or tone poems about a season, a place, or a form of matter, such as Steiner's H_2O about water patterns. The sophisticated thematic structures were extended metaphors—one thinks primarily of Léger's *Le Ballet Mécanique*, in which graphic abstraction, repetitive human actions, and machines in operation are synthesized into an image of a gigantic social supermachine.

Maya Deren introduced the possibility of isolating a single gesture as a complete film form. In its concentrated distillation of both the narrative and the thematic principles, this form comes to resemble the movement in poetry called Imagism, and for this reason I have elsewhere called a film using this device an imagist film.[5] There I concentrated on pure examples and described the inevitable inflation of the simple gesture to contain more and more aesthetic matter. Kenneth Anger's *Eaux d'Artifice*, Charles Boultenhouse's *Handwritten*, and Stan Brakhage's *Dog Star Man: Part One* provided the examples.

In brief, all of these films describe a simple action like the leap of *Choreography*. In Anger's film it is the walk of a heroine through a baroque maze of fountains in pursuit of a flickering moth. Boultenhouse's film revolves around the slamming of a fist on a glass table top, and Brakhage's describes a man climbing a mountain. Each example represents a progressive stage of inflation, whereby lateral or foreign material is introduced around the essential action without completely disrupting its unity or continuity.

Maya Deren herself returned to the imagist film to make *Meditation on*

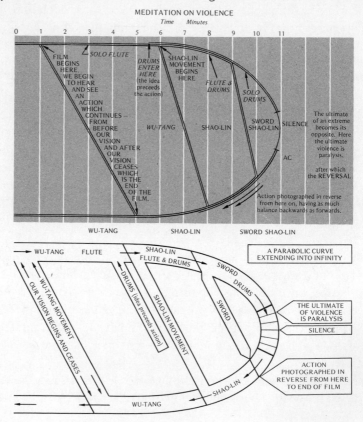

Violence in 1948, and again just before she died when she conceived
the idea of the haiku film. The structure of *Meditation on Violence* almost duplicates that of *Choreography for Camera* on a larger scale, with
a proportionate loss of tension. Deren's own notes for the shooting of the
film employ two parabolic arcs. Theoretically, the film describes in
a single continuous movement three degrees of traditional Chinese boxing
—Wu-tang, Shao-lin, and Shao-lin with a sword. A long sequence of the
ballet-like, sinuous Wu-tang becomes the more erratic Shao-lin; then for
two or three minutes in the middle of the film there is an abrupt change
to leaping sword movements, in the center of which, at the apogee of the
leap, there is a long-held freeze-frame; finally we see the boxer move back
through Shao-lin to the original Wu-tang. For each transition there is a
change of background and filmic style. We see the Wu-tang against a
curved, unbroken black wall; the Shao-lin takes place in a room with
alternate black and white walls to emphasize its angularity. The montage,
which had been very fluid with elided joining, becomes appropriately pronounced and angular. The sword play occurs outside, with jump cuts, slow
motion, and the freeze-frame. The last portion of the film is printed
in reverse motion, but the continuity of the movement disguises this from
the spectator.

So much for its abstract plan. In the notes for this film, Maya Deren
makes some extravagant intellectual claims for it, which are interesting
because the film fails to live up to them:

> The film consists not only of photographing these movements, but
> attempts an equivalent conversion, into filmic terms, of these metaphysi-
> cal principles. The film begins in the middle of a movement and ends in
> the middle of a movement, so that the film is a period of vision upon
> life, with the life continuing before and after, into infinity. The rhythm
> of the negative-positive breathing is preserved in the rhythm at which the
> boxer approaches and recedes from the camera. Both the photography
> and the cutting of the Wu-Tang sections are deliberately smooth and
> flowing, so that no "striking" shots or abrupt cuts occur in these sections.
> This whole approach is further amplified in the diagram and notes.
> Moreover, it seemed significant that not only were these movements re-
> lated to metaphysical principles (an inner concept) but that they were
> *training* movements—the self-contained *idea* of violence, not the actual
> act. Training is a physical meditation on violence. So, too, the film is a
> meditation. Its location is an inner space, not an outer place. And just
> as a meditation turns around an idea, goes forward, returns to examine it
> from another angle, so here the camera, in the WU-TANG section, re-
> volves around the movements of the figure, returns to some previous move-

ment to examine it from another angle altogether, to achieve a "cubism in time."

However, meditations investigate extremes, and life, while ongoing and non-climactic in the infinite sense, contains within it varieties and waves of intensity. So this film, as a meditation, proceeded beyond the WU-TANG School, to examine where the SHAO-LIN concepts of aggression would lead. This school, called "exterior," is based on exterior conditions of opportunity. Its emphasis is upon strength, impact, sudden rhythms, and the body is not treated as a whole. Rather, the sharp strength of the arms and legs is emphasized for independent action. The logic conclusion is to even *implement* this sharpness with a sword. And so, in the film, the increasing violence bursts into an extension: the arm sprouts a sword.

Even this is carried forward. The climax of this meditation on violence is a paralysis. From which point the return is a reversal. The movements are actually photographed in reverse from this point on.[6]

Meditation on Violence, from a theoretical point of view, is a film overloaded by its philosophical burden.

Maya Deren's initial creative period extended from the completion of *Meshes of the Afternoon* in 1943 through the making of *At Land*, *Choreography for Camera*, and *Ritual in Transfigured Time*, the discussion of which I have postponed for a few pages—three years of almost uninterrupted film production. At the end of that period she published a book of theory, *An Anagram of Ideas on Art, Form, and Film*, and left for Haiti, initially to make a film, but eventually to write her study of Haitian mythology, *The Divine Horsemen*. *Meditation on Violence* was the first film she completed after this period. It bears the full burden of her theoretical and philosophical thought in the intervening years. It suffers, as does her subsequent film, *The Very Eye of Night*, made after a silence of ten years, from excessive stylization, both intellectual and graphical. Yet her aspiration to use film to imitate the processes of the mind was exalted and certainly has been felt by other film-makers within the American avant-garde sphere.

In her program notes she clarifies her attempt to represent mental processes cinematically:

> The camera can create dance, movement and action which transcend geography and take place anywhere and everywhere; it can also, as in this film, be the meditating mind turned inwards upon the idea of movement, and this idea, being an abstraction, takes place nowhere or, as it were, in the very center of space.
>   . . .

> There the inner eye meditates upon it at leisure, investigates its possi-
> bilities, considers first this aspect and angle, and that one, and once more
> reconsiders, as one might plumb and examine an image or an idea, turn-
> ing it over and over in one's mind.[7]

The spectator is confronted with something more restricted than this.
There is the boxer, moving before a painfully artificial black wall; then
comes a change of boxing style before an equally contrived, angular set of
walls, and ultimately, in open space, the boxer is costumed and leaping
with a sword. In *Choreography for Camera*, speed was the key to the
unity and tension of the image. By elongating the action in *Meditation on
Violence*, the fusion of spaces, costumes, boxing modes, and cinematic
styles dissolved; it fragmented into vague sections. In principle, such an
elongation is not impossible. We shall see later how Stan Brakhage successfully elongated the imagist film in *Dog Star Man: Part One* without
losing its essential tension.

The intellectual framework of the film, however, and its philosophical
aspirations indicate a continuation of Deren's vision of a cinema capable
of abstract meditation. That vision had reached an initial peak in the
theories which Jean Epstein, Dziga Vertov, and above all Sergei Eisenstein put into practice in the 1920s and the early 1930s and which they
continued to develop in their writings while Maya Deren was making her
films. In fact, in the 1940s, before the emergence of the American avant-
garde, the sole locus of radical innovation in the cinema had been within
theoretical articles and books by men who had made their most ambitious
films almost two decades earlier.

One of the major contributions of three decades of independent film-
making and theoretical speculation by avant-garde film-makers to the
evolution of film theory has been an elaborate exploration of the uses and
the limits of perspective. This exploration was initiated by the "meditations" of *Meshes of the Afternoon* and was extended and tested in all of
Maya Deren's other films. The potential for a phenomenology of cinema,
which is implied in the notes on *Meditations on Violence*, later came to
be realized by Stan Brakhage and Michael Snow, among others, whose
achievements can, in part, be traced back to Maya Deren's vision.

In *Ritual in Transfigured Time*, the film which immediately followed
Choreography, Deren openly grappled with the problem of using dancers
in a film. The result is her most complex film, and the one that most fully
contains her achievements, her theories, and her failures.

Formally, *Ritual in Transfigured Time* is a radical extension of the

trance film in the direction of a more complex form. That form, the architectonic film, which was to emerge in the early 1960s after other ambitious
efforts, aspired toward myth and ritual.

The pure trance film has a single protagonist—all other human figures
being distinctly background elements—and a linear development. *Ritual*
has two principal figures (although ultimately the film reduces itself to
the initiation of a single persona, the female) and utilizes several others
more dynamically than does the trance film. Despite the attempt at a
continual and gradual movement from trance into dance, *Ritual in Transfigured Time* has three parts: an opening, a party, and a dance in the
open air.

The images of this film, unlike any of her others, evoke traditional interpretations. They are not so much symbolic as archetypal, drawn primarily
from the visual vocabulary of ancient mythology. The images of Norns,
of Fates, and of Graces adorn a film which, in its center, describes a sexual
rite of passage. In her notes Maya Deren called this rite the passage of the
"widow into bride."

Beyond the classic images, we see the same enigmatic, obsessive totems
of her other films. The confrontation of the self takes a new form here.
In *Meshes of the Afternoon* we saw, through a camera trick, three simultaneous, juxtaposed images of the heroine in a single shot; in *At Land*,
the editing of shots of her looking off-screen, followed by a shot of her in a
different location as if filmed from the angle of vision of the previous
glance, created the illusion of meeting with the self. Now, here, the self
is composed of different bodies; their metamorphosis occurs through
cutting on motion. The gesture begun by one is continued by the other.
The result is an evocative ambivalence of identity and a sense of mysterious, perpetual metamorphosis.

The form of *Ritual in Transfigured Time* anticipates the even more
complex architectonic films of Gregory Markopoulos and Stan Brakhage,
in the early sixties, though it lacks their precision of proportions, and
their overall evenness of execution. Because of her dedicated interest in
form and her reluctance to repeat her previous achievements in that dimension, Deren tended to over-extend her formal ambitions at times; as a
result she came to cinematic forms earlier than she could handle them
well.

Thus her first four films (including *Meshes of the Afternoon*) rehearse
in general outline the subsequent evolution of forms within the American
avant-garde cinema over the following two decades. Her summary of her

achievements in the letter to James Card, previously excerpted, takes on a prophetic tone:

> *Meshes* is, one might say, almost expressionist; it externalizes an inner world to the point where it is confounded with the external one. *At Land* has little to do with the inner world of the protagonist, it externalizes the hidden dynamics of the external world, and here the drama results from the activity of the external world. It is as if I had moved from a concern with the life of a fish, to a concern with the sea which accounts for the character of the fish and its life. And *Ritual* pulls back even further, to a point of view from which the external world itself is but an element in the entire structure and scheme of metamorphosis: the sea itself changes because of the larger changes of the earth. *Ritual* is about the nature and process of change. And just as *Choreography* was an effort to isolate and celebrate the principle of the power of movement, which was contained in *At Land*, so I made, after *Ritual*, the film, *Meditation on Violence*, which tried to abstract the principle of ongoing metamorphosis and change which was in *Ritual*.[8]

I will show in this book how the trance film gradually developed into the architectonic, mythopoeic film, with a corresponding shift from Freudian preoccupations to those of Jung; and then how the decline of the mythological film was attended by the simultaneous rise of both the diary and the structural film. The latter are extensions of the imagist form in the direction of visual haiku, epiphanies, and diaries. They are static, epistemologically oriented films in which duration and structure determine, rather than follow, content.

In the opening scene of *Ritual in Transfigured Time*, a woman played by Maya Deren stands in a double doorway. She passes from one of the two visible rooms into the other to get a scarf, then returns to the first room with a swatch of yarn. With her head she signals another woman, "the widow," in from the darkness. Like the first woman, the widow is dressed in black, but she is more mournful and she walks with her hand out before her like a somnambulist. She comes in and sits before her, making a ball from her yarn. The first woman, "the invoker," sings, laughs, and chants while she juggles the wool between her hands in gradually slower and slower motion. The widow, hypnotized and enchanted, continues to wind the wool in a ball.

With another turn of her head the invoker indicates that a third woman has entered the room by yet another door. We can call her "the initiator" or "the guide." She beckons the widow while at the same time the invoker hieratically raises her arms, dropping the yarn and thus releasing her from the spell. When the widow looks back, the invoker's chair is empty.

This opening episode is distinguished by compositions-in-depth of more sophistication than anywhere else in Maya Deren's films. A geometrical sense of the relative placement of the three women determines the editing sequence, which is accented by rapid alterations in the speed of recording, causing sudden shifts from slow to normal motion. The composition-in-depth and the handling of a large group of actors in the subsequent scene indicate an advance in Maya Deren's conception of cinematic form and in her powers as a director.

The form of the opening passage is that of the trance film; slow motion was one of its chief cinematic means of expression. In the party scene, the trance is replaced by a collective choreomania, as the entire crowd moves again and again in a half-dozen repetitive patterns; they stop short, suspended in a frozen frame. The means of achieving this effect were simple. Maya Deren printed several copies of a few complex movements, showing the wanderings of the guide, the hesitant movements of the widow, and the pursuit of her by a young man, presumably seeking to meet her. Then she simply repeated the very same shots at fixed intervals and punctuated them with the freezes. The result was the highly successful rendering of dance movement from elements outside the dance. It is this middle passage that makes one think that Maya Deren was openly trying to deal with the problem of the prestylization of dance in film, although she never stated it as such in her highly articulate writings.

When the young man meets the widow—they literally "bump into one another"—the scene cuts away to an open field in which the performers are posed, faces just about touching, exactly as they were at the party. They occupy the same portion of the film frame. Thus the transition is sudden and clean, even though the young man is no longer fully dressed but bare-chested, and the widow now has bare legs and feet.

Then they dance. Behind them three female figures from the party, resembling drawings of the Graces, dance before neo-classic columns. The guide is one of the Graces. The dance of the couple becomes one of flight and pursuit. As she runs, the widow turns into the invoker, then back again. In the transition there is a change of scarfs, from mourning black to bridal white.

It is the widow again who enters a gate to find her pursuer transformed into a statue on a pedestal. In slow motion with several freeze frames he gradually comes to life, and after some instantaneous petrifications in mid-air, he leaps to the ground. As the pursuit continues, the heroine runs full speed, while the young man follows in graceful ballet leaps in slow motion. Physically, the situation of *Meshes of the Afternoon* is here reversed, as the fleeing runner cannot make gains on the slow-motion pursuer.

They pass by the guide in their chase. Just as he reaches for her, there is a metamorphosis from widow to invoker, and she runs into the sea. As she sinks we see her in negative, her black gown now white while she changes again from invoker to widow, now prepared as a bride for the young man who has not followed her into the water.

Ritual in Transfigured Time is Maya Deren's great effort at synthesis. There is, on the one hand, the transformation of somnambulistic movement to repetitive, cyclic movement; that is, to dance. There is also the fusion of traditional mythological elements—the Graces, Pygmalion, the Fates—with private psycho-drama (the film-maker herself plays the invoker); and an attempt to present a complete ritual in terms of the camera techniques she had utilized in her earlier films—slow motion, freeze-frame, repetition of shots, and variations on continuity of identity and movement.

Nowhere are the cinematic co-ordinates of ritual and myth as clearly stated as in the first film of Jean Cocteau; and nowhere has Cocteau found so enthusiastic a reception for his films as among the pioneers of the American avant-garde cinema. In France, where the avant-garde had maintained a social front, a violent repudiation of bourgeois aesthetic values, *Le Sang d'un Poète* (1930), Cocteau's first film, was accused of being a parasite on the body of Surrealism, while perverting surrealistic ferocity into dilettantism. Cocteau made his films at a time when French art eschewed myth and ritual. Yet these were precisely the concerns of the American avant-garde artists who were beginning to make films in the late forties and early fifties. The result has been an over-estimation of Cocteau's films in America, equivalent to the under-examination he has received in Europe.

Maya Deren had not seen his films before she started making her own. It was in the forties, perhaps even after *Ritual in Transfigured Time*, that she first saw *Le Sang d'un Poète* or so Alexander Hammid remembers, and she was struck by similarities to her own work.

In that film Cocteau explicitly places the events of his film either outside time or within an instant of time. The first image of a crumbling tower, interrupted mid-air, recurs at the very end of the film so that the

The cinematic Pygmalion:
The poet of Jean Cocteau's *Le Sang d'un Poète* leaves
the statue-muse and dives through the mirror of water.

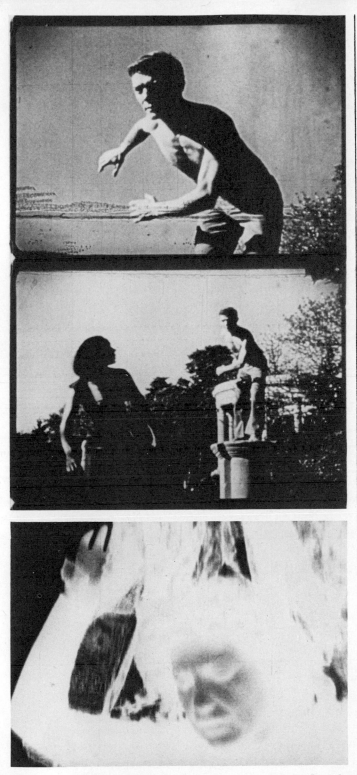

The widow of Maya Deren's *Ritual in Transfigured Time* flees the living statue and "marries" the sea, drowning in negative.

tower can continue its collapse to the ground. By bracketing his film this way, Cocteau wants the viewer to understand that his mythic ritual occurs in "transfigured time."

The events of Le Sang d'un Poète bear a general resemblance to the trance film: a single hero, the poet, finds that the painted mouth he wiped from a canvas continues to live in his hand. It talks to him; it stimulates him sexually as he runs his hand along his body. Finally, with great effort, he transfers the mouth to a statue, which comes alive. The metamorphosis of statue into muse is attended by an alteration of the space in which it occurs; for in this process the door and window of the poet's chamber disappear. His sole exit is through the mirror. So he plunges into a realm of fantastic tableaux which seem to exist solely for his inner education. Two of the four tableaux in the Hotel des Folies-Dramatiques depend upon the mechanics of the camera for their magic: reverse motion and illusory defiance of gravity. His initiation into these mysteries leads to a symbolic suicide.

Back in the chamber, the poet destroys the statue and in so doing is changed into one himself. In the subsequent episode, a group of young students break up the statue to use as fatal ammunition in a snowball fight. Over the bleeding body of a slain student, the muse and the poet, both in the flesh, play a game of cards which culminates, again, in his suicide.

In its climax, where the imagined death becomes reality, and in the complexity of its episodic variations on the trance film type, Le Sang d'un Poète forecasts Meshes of the Afternoon; in the mixture of allegory and ritual, with its enigmatic images, it anticipates Ritual in Transfigured Time. Ultimately it is closer to the later Deren film in its conception; both are theoretical films in which a vision of the fusion of arts (poetry and film for Cocteau, dance and film for Deren) becomes the subject of the invented ritual.

Parker Tyler has pointed out, again in the captions to the illustrations of The Three Faces of the Film, the persistence of the motif of the statue within the avant-garde film tradition. Willard Maas, a contemporary of Maya Deren who began making films in 1943 with his wife Marie Menken and the poet George Barker (Geography of the Body), invoked this motif on a grand scale in his most ambitious project, Narcissus (1956). The hero, played by his collaborator Ben Moore, wanders in desolation through an outdoor corridor formed by two rows of busts of the Roman emperors. Unlike Cocteau's or Maya Deren's statues, these do not come alive, yet in Maas's film their animation is potential, and the pathos of that fragment of the trance derives from the refusal of the statues to live and advise.

Behind all the employments of the statue in the trance film, however obliquely, is the myth of Pygmalion. In his revival of that myth in the terms of a "magical" illusionism of cinema, Cocteau initiated a cinematic ritual that a whole generation of American film-makers felt sufficiently vital to restate in their own terms.

Ritual in Transfigured Time was meant to be first of several cinematic investigations of ritual. In a request for a Guggenheim foundation grant, Maya Deren proposed a complex film correlating the ritual aspect of children's games with traditional rites as they survive in Bali and Haiti. She had enlisted the aid of Margaret Mead and Gregory Bateson, whose exhibition and catalogue of South Seas ritual objects at the Museum of Modern Art at that time influenced the conception of the film. In her request for the grant she appended the following chart of ritual parallels and wrote as an example for the project:

> When a child hopes to be given a bicycle for Christmas, it may resolve to walk all the way home from school without stepping on a crack in the sidewalk. Not only is the form of this little ritual completely unrelated to its objective, but that separateness may be frequently reinforced by secrecy: one of the conditions being that no one, and especially the parents, be aware of the performance.[9]

Under the title "Cinematics," she outlined some of the means of achieving her aim, which she had previously stated as "stating the almost fixed constancy of the idea of ritual action":[10]

RITUALS INVOLVING MINIMIZATION OF PERSONAL IDENTITY

(This column descends in degree from highly individual, animate identity to inanimate.)	*Religious* Bali and Haiti	*Secular* (games)
1. *Displacement of performer's identity by another identity and the actions originate rather freely from the assumed character.*	Haitian Possession Some Balinese Trances	Animal impersonations Blind man's bluff, etc. Playing house, engineer, etc. Improvised theatricals
2. *Representation of Another Identity*, with action deriving either from the actual performance or the mask	Various masked ceremonies.	Masquerades

identity or from a
play between them.

3. Identity, either original, displaced or represented, subordinated to relatively prescribed action pattern.	Communal ceremonies. Pre-puberty Balinese trance dancing.	Formalized theatricals. Group games such as Farmer in the Dell.
4. Representational Images (X *is* so and so)	Deity Images	Dolls Puppets
5. Manipulation of symbolizations (X *stands for* so and so)	Cabalistic symbols and others. Fetish objects.	Chess Cards

RITUALS INVOLVING COMPACTS OF BEHAVIOR

(Since the degree of skill is here often critical, the identity of the performer is either retained, or at most on an anonymous or collective level. Where it is greatly minimized, it overlaps with Category three of the Identity Rituals.)
(The specific work on Bali and Haiti in this connection still remains to be done.)

	Religious	*Secular*
Personal: Ordealistic; Undefined maximum. Failure to achieve prescribed degree represents not only a failure of the form, but a critical effect upon the performer.	Haitian Ordeals	Acrobatics Gymnastics Follow the Leader
Impersonal: maximum defined within reasonable limits of normal achievement.	Simple religious ceremonies, Offerings	hop-scotch jump-rope marbles

In 1947 the Guggenheim Foundation granted her their first fellowship for work in creative motion pictures and she went to Haiti to film rituals and dances. That film was never finished. As late as 1955 she had written that she did not have sufficient footage for a documentary film about Haitian ritual. Presumably, the plan for the cross-sectional ritual film was quickly abandoned. While in Haiti, her career as a film-maker was radically deflected. The film she planned to make became a book about Haitian cults, published as *The Divine Horsemen*.

In the preface to her book, she speaks of being "defeated" in her attempt to make the cross-sectional ritual film by the revelation of the mythic integrity of the Haitian cults:

> This disposition of the objects related to my original Haitian project—
> evidence that this book was written not because I had so intended but in

spite of my intentions—is, to me, the most eloquent tribute to the irref-
utable reality and impact of Voudoun mythology. I had begun as an
artist, as one who would manipulate the elements of a reality into a
work of art in the image of my creative integrity; I end by recording, as
humbly and accurately as I can, the logics of a reality which had forced
me to recognize its integrity, and to abandon my manipulations.[11]

At this time her initial productive spurt had exhausted itself. After returning from Haiti she considered still another ritual film, this time based
upon athletic contests. In her search for the appropriate sport, she discovered Chinese boxing, and that inspiration was transformed into *Meditation on Violence*. Apparently she was not content with the film. By the
middle of the 1950s she was "getting a real strong itch to re-edit it, short-
ening it, and this will improve it, I think." She never did.

The film involving children's games and the initial conception of a
ritualistic sports film give evidence of the success with which she regarded
the central party episode of *Ritual in Transfigured Time*, in which she
had raised familiar gestures to the level of ceremony. Throughout the fifties she continued to conceive of films which would choreograph skilled
but familiar maneuvers. Each new subject entailed formal evolution. If
the film of children's games combined with Balinese and Haitian rituals,
even in its speculative form, represented another stage in the evolution of
architectonic form, then a film that she was planning to make in 1954
marks an advance over that. In a letter, she describes her idea of a film
involving various circus acts:

> Each of the circus acts which occurred to me—the trapeze, the jugglers,
> the tumblers, the bare-back acts—is composed of sort of suspended TIME
> phrases. And the form as a whole of the film, which is beginning to
> emerge, is a kind of series of interlocking time spans—a kind of necklace
> chain of time-phrases. For example, the tumblers begin their time phrase;
> about half-way through we are led to the juggler as he begins his time-
> phrase; as the tumblers complete their time phrase we are already in the
> middle of the juggler's phrase and, before he is finished, we have been
> started on the aerialists' phrase, which is already carrying us by the time
> the juggler finishes. Actually it would be constructed somewhat like a
> singing round, so that once the song is started, it never ends, being always
> carried forward by successive voices. The idea fascinated me as a concept
> of structure, and as being able somehow to convey the whole sense of tim-
> ing which, as I had always felt, and as you re-affirmed it, is absolutely basic
> to all of these activities. Filmically speaking, it means building the whole
> film in terms of staggered simultaneities.[12]

Here is the first clear hint of the form by which the architectonic or mythopoeic film would emerge—through "staggered simultaneities"—for in the epic films of Markopoulos, Brakhage, and Harry Smith, the narrative pulse, which normally accents temporal development with climaxes and modulates its rhythm by creating scenic comportments, gives way to a sense of simultaneity, over which a broad narrative development may, or may not, occur.

The ironies of Maya Deren's later career are almost tragic. Before her death in 1961, she completed only one more film, *The Very Eye of Night*. It does not aspire to the same formal innovations as the projected outlines from which I have quoted; her concern was with plastic development, conflict of scale, and dimensional illusion rather than with total structure.

The most pointed irony concerns the circumstances of her death. At the turn of the decade she was living on a pittance from the Creative Film Foundation in return for her energetic work as its secretary (it was a one-person operation, with nominal officers) and on her husband Teiji Ito's income as an enlisted private in the army. Just before his discharge, the death of a relative raised hopes of an inheritance for Ito. After a disappointing meeting concerning this inheritance, Maya Deren came down with a terrific headache which led to a paralyzing seizure the next day. Within a week she had suffered her third cerebral hemorrhage and died after three days in a coma. Not long after that the elusive inheritance came through.

She died before she could see the fruit of her work as an apologist and propagandist for the avant-garde film. Yet friends who remember her rages qualify this last irony; she might have found more to oppose than to acclaim in the explosion of film-making and theorizing of the 1960s.

Nevertheless, despite some grievances and voodoo curses against her fellow avant-garde film-makers, Maya Deren worked hard to better the position of the independent film artist and to further the cause of what she called the "creative film" in general. That effort is an important aspect of the visionary tradition within the American avant-garde film. Not only have there been artists making films in the spiritual wake of Poe, Melville, Emerson, Whitman, and Dickinson; there has been a movement among these artists to advance the cause of cinema in general. Such unions have been part of all the arts in this century. This is true, especially in the United States, where a literary tradition grew out of next to nothing in the last century and where a new tradition in the plastic arts was forged less than thirty years ago. Yet one would be at a loss to discover among painters or writers, dramatists or dancers, an effort as intense or as sustained as that made by independent film-makers for the security of their art. There are obvious reasons for this: the medium is very expensive; its aspirants were relatively few in number until the 1960s; and success in independent film-making is considerably less rewarded than in painting, writing, or drama.

Maya Deren's vision of a better situation for the film-maker developed out of her experiences as a lecturer and theorist of the medium. In the latter capacity, she has left, in addition to the illuminating notes and articles on her completed films, a coherent body of theoretical writings. They include relatively technical essays for amateur trade publications—"Efficient or Effective," "Creating Movies with a New Dimension," "Creative Cutting," "Adventures in Creative Film Making," two widely circulated essays on the possibilities of the cinema, "Cinema as an Art Form" and "Cinematography: The Creative Use of Reality," and a pamphlet, written as early as 1946 and published privately by the Alicat Book Shop in Yonkers, New York, *An Anagram of Ideas on Art, Form, and Film.* Just before her death, she did a number of guest columns for Jonas Mekas in the *Village Voice* which assume more a critical than a theoretical stance. The technical articles are essentially autobiographical and offer encouragement to amateurs without money or expensive equipment. They reaffirm the principles of the more general essays without amplifying them.

The basic tenets of her theories can be simply stated. She takes for granted the indexical relationship between reality and the photographic image. In each of her three major articles she insists upon grounding the cinema in photographic realism. Perhaps her experience as a still photographer (she did portraits for *Vogue, Harper's Bazaar, Mademoiselle,* and several art magazines) prejudiced her against photographic distortions.

She analyzed the two functions of the film camera as "discovery" and "invention," the former referring to visions of space and time beyond the capabilities of the human eye, including telescopic or microscopic cinematography on the one hand and slow motion, freeze-frame, or time lapse photography on the other. Among these methods she would continually admit her predilection for slow motion. As an instrument of "invention," the camera records imaginative constructs in reality and reconstructs them through the illusions of editing. She insists on the principle of recognition rather than graphic composition within the photographic image:

> In a photograph, then, we begin by recognizing a reality, and our attendant knowledges and attitudes are brought into play; only then does the

aspect become meaningful in reference to it. The abstract shadow shape in a night scene is not understood at all until revealed and identified as a person; the bright red shape on a pale ground which might, in an abstract, graphic context, communicate a sense of gaiety, conveys something altogether different when recognized as a wound. As we watch a film, the continuous act of recognition in which we are involved is like a strip of memory unrolling beneath the images of the film itself, to form the invisible underlayer of an implicit double exposure.[13]

The elemental authority of the photographic image lends reality even to the most artificial events recorded by it.

From these observations she makes an interesting inductive leap:

Inasmuch as the other art forms are not constituted of reality itself, they create metaphors for reality. But photography, being itself the reality or the equivalent thereof, can use its own reality as a metaphor for ideas and abstractions. In painting, the image is an abstraction of the aspect; in photography, the abstraction of an idea produces the archetypal image.[14]

As an example of the archetypal function, she lists film stars.

A series of lectures she gave at a Woodstock, New York, summer workshop in 1959 (she was beginning to work on her haiku-inspired film then) began with the polemical statement "Art must be artificial." Her emphasis then, as always before, was on form. Twelve years earlier she had defined form:

Art is distinguished from other human activities and expression by this organic function of form in the projection of imaginative experience into reality. This function of form is characterized by two essential qualities: first, that it incorporates in itself the philosophy and emotions which relate to the experience which is being projected; and second, that it derives from the instrument by which that projection is accomplished.[15]

She finds it highly significant that the age which produced the theory of relativity produced in the film camera an instrument capable of synthetic constructions across space and time. Speaking of "the twentieth century art form" in her last theoretical essay, she raises a concluding question and answers it:

How can we justify the fact that it is the art instrument, among all that fraternity of twentieth-century inventions, which is still the least explored and exploited; and that it is the artist—of whom, traditionally, the culture expects the most prophetic and visionary statements—who is the most laggard in recognizing that the formal and philosophical concepts of his age are implicit in the actual structure of his instrument and the techniques of his medium?

If cinema is to take its place beside the others as a full-fledged art form, it must cease merely to record realities that owe nothing of their actual existence to the film instrument. Instead, it must create a total experience so much out of the very nature of the instrument as to be inseparable from its means.[16]

Her major essays all take shape through a series of negative reductions; she rejects the graphic cinema and animation for their refusal to accept the reality of the photographic image and for their use of painterly forms in film; she criticizes the documentary for its exclusion of the imagination and its passive dependence on accidental phenomena; and she calls the narrative cinema to task for its imitation of literary modes.

Nevertheless in each of these highly critical essays, the dance creeps in as an acceptable part of cinematic synthesis. In "Cinema as an Art Form," she makes this parenthetical observation:

(Dance, for example, which, of all art forms would seem to profit most by cinematic treatment, actually suffers miserably. The more successful it is as a theatrical expression, conceived in terms of a stable, stage-front audience, the more its carefully wrought choreographic patterns suffer from the restiveness of a camera which bobs about in the wings, on-stage for a close-up, etc. . . . There is a potential filmic dance form, in which the choreography and movements would be designed, precisely, for the mobility and other attributes of the camera, but this, too, requires an independence from theatrical dance conceptions.)[17]

The densest and most interesting of her theoretical writings is the earliest, *An Anagram of Ideas on Art, Form, and Film*. Even the form of the book reflects her obsession with structures; here she brings together her views on science, anthropology, metaphysics, and religion with the attacks on the conventional modes of film-making which I observed in her other writings. In trying to define an aesthetic and ethical world view, she launches into an attack upon Surrealism, which she finds as deficient as realism in providing images of human consciousness. "Consciousness" is her key word in this essay, and she approaches it historically, claiming a fundamental change in human mentality took place around the seventeenth century. "In the course of displacing deity-consciousness as the motive power of reality, by a concept of logical causation, man inevitably relocated himself in terms of the new scheme," she wrote in the opening section.

The Surrealists, according to her, hark back to a world before this absolute change.

> Their "art" is dedicated to the manifestations of an organism which antecedes all consciousness. It is not even merely primitive; it is primeval. But even in this effort, man the scientist has, through the exercise of rational faculties, become more competent than the modern artist. That which the sur-realists labor and sweat to achieve, and end by only simulating, can be accomplished in full reality, by the atom bomb.[18]

She sees the artist's role as reconciling the need for an integral world view, strongest in primitive societies, with the fragmentation of the contemporary scientific outlook. She rejects the option of the contemporary primitive artist, arguing that in ancient or static societies the artist made full and sophisticated use of the tools at his disposal. She confers the same responsibility on contemporary creators.

In the subsequent discussions of art and form she proceeds to clarify definitions, to make distinctions in usage, and so to select from the past a sense of art appropriate to the present. She would have us bear in mind that the classicism of the early eighteenth century was a function of the shift from an absolute to a human ideal in the previous century. Furthermore she considers the psychological orientation and the cult of personality in contemporary art to be a degeneration from this successful period.

There is some discrepancy between her theory and her films. In the preface to the *Anagram*, she warns us of the danger of expecting a perfect continuity between them:

> In my case I have found it necessary, each time, to ignore any of my previous statements. After the first film was completed, when someone asked me to define the principle which it embodied, I answered that the function of film, like that of other art forms, was to create experience—in this case a semi-psychological reality. But the actual creation of the second film caused me to subsequently answer a similar question with an entirely different emphasis. This time that reality must exploit the capacity of film to manipulate Time and Space. By the end of the third film, I had again shifted the emphasis—insisting this time on a filmically visual integrity, which would create a dramatic necessity of itself, rather than be dependent upon or derive from an underlying dramatic development. Now, on the basis of the fourth, I feel that all the other elements must be retained, but that special attention must be given to the creative possibilities of Time, and that the form as a whole should be ritualistic (as I define this later in the essay). I believe of course that some kind of development has taken place; and I feel that one symptom of the con-

tinuation of such a development would be that the actual creation of each film would not so much illustrate previous conclusions as it would necessitate new ones—and thus the theory would remain dynamic and volatile.[19]

Her intense rejection of the cult of the personality, of the psychoanalytic approach to art, and of explicit symbolism ignores the privacy of the sources of *Meshes of the Afternnon, At Land,* and *Ritual in Transfigured Time.* That intimacy, which her films share with the painting of their time, although they share little else, is to their credit. When she moved further from the powerful element of psycho-drama, in *Meditation on Violence* and much later in *The Very Eye of Night,* her art diminished.

In the text she distinguished between imagery and symbolism:

> When an image induces a generalization and gives rise to an emotion or idea, it bears towards that emotion or idea the same relationship which an exemplary demonstration bears to some chemical principle; and that is entirely different from the relationship between that principle and the written chemical formula by which it is symbolized. *In the first case the principle functions actively; in the second case its action is symbolically described in lieu of the action itself.* An understanding of this distinction seems to me to be of primary importance.[20]

But she interpreted imagery very literally if she could describe the footsteps on water, grass, pavement, and rug of *Meshes of the Afternoon* in this way: "What I meant when I planned that four stride sequence was that you have to come a long way—from the very beginning of time—to kill yourself, like life first emerging from primeval waters."[21]

She makes an interesting connection between the quality of classical art and ritualistic form:

> The romantic and the sur-realist differ only in the degree of their naturalism. But between naturalism and the formal character of primitive, oriental and Greek art there is a vast ideological distance. For want of a better term which can refer to the quality which the art forms of various civilizations have in common, I suggest the word ritualistic. I am profoundly aware of the dangers in the use of this term, and of the misunderstandings which may arise, but I fail, at the moment, to find a better word. Its primary weakness is that, in strictly anthropological usage, it refers to an activity of a primitive society which has certain specific conditions: a ritual is anonymously evolved; it functions as an obligatory tradition; and finally, it has a specific magical purpose. None of these three conditions apply, for example, to Greek tragedy.[22]

The ritualistic form reflects also the conviction that such ideas are best advanced when they are abstracted from the immediate conditions of reality and incorporated into a contrived, created whole, stylized in terms of the utmost effectiveness.[23]

Above all, the ritualistic form treats the human being not as the source of the dramatic action, but as a somewhat depersonalized element in a dramatic whole.[24]

In several other places Maya Deren refers to her art as "classical" and to her films as "classicist," yet there is little to justify this description in her works unless it is the conservative quality of the dance movements or the occasional references to Greek myth.

Classicists looked on the arts of Greece and Rome as paradigms of logical and moral order. The revision of this perspective resulted from a late Romantic investigation of Greek irrationality, initiated by Friedrich Nietzsche in *The Birth of Tragedy from the Spirit of Music* (1871), which affirmed the primitive and ritualistic elements in all the arts, using Greek tragedy as the pivotal example. In calling her art "classical," Maya Deren seems to have wanted to point out the chastening of Dionysian elements in her employment of ritual. She also seems to have perceived that the American art of her time in painting, poetry, and potentially in film was deeply committed to an elaboration of its Romantic origins. By calling herself a classicist she was trying to disassociate her work from the excesses of that tendency. The disassociation was never complete, nor did she want it to be. What she could not know was that in its future evolution the American avant-garde film would plunge into a dialogue with the major issues of Romantic thought and art and that the mythic inwardness of her early films would be used as springboards for that plunge.

3

THE POTTED PSALM

There have been many collaborations in the history of the radical cinema. Before Maya Deren and Alexander Hammid made *Meshes of the Afternoon,* Dali and Buñuel had collaborated, as had James Sibley Watson and Melville Webber on *The Fall of the House of Usher* (1928) and *Lot in Sodom* (1933). René Clair, Francis Picabia, and Erik Satie joined forces to make *Entr'Acte,* which I shall discuss shortly. Film-making has been, and remains most often, a group activity, with specialized divisions of labor. It is not an extraordinary situation, then, when artists from other media, complaining of the poverty of imagination in existing films, set out together to make a virgin attack on the cinema. And it often happens that a writer or painter works with someone who already knows the mechanics of the camera and the editing machine.

At the end of the Second World War, film was a potentially fertile field for American visionaries. Maya Deren had made her first films, although few people were aware of them until late in the forties when she had begun to lecture and the two great film societies, Cinema 16 in New York and Art in Cinema in San Francisco, had been formed and showed them. It was possible, however, to see "the boiler plate of the Museum of Modern Art," as Sidney Peterson called the widely distributed prints of *Potemkin, Un Chien Andalou, Entr'Acte, Symphonie Diagonale, Rhythmus 21,* and the numerous other classic films available from New York. These works opened up the area of cinema without establishing a constricting tradition for the artists who saw them.

When Peterson himself began to make films, he was fully conscious of the strategies of Buñuel and Dali. He applied them to his own situation. When he met the poet and playwright James Broughton, they had decided to collaborate on a play. They worked out an outline and began to write the dialogue together (it was to have been about George Sutter's old age) when the project shifted into film. The play and its ideas were abandoned.

Peterson had shot some footage with a friend on a camping trip and had assembled it in his living room. This gave him sufficient knowledge of the mechanics to dare a more ambitious film. A discussion in Peterson's house one evening in 1946 initiated the film. Four people were there, including Broughton and Peterson. One happened to own a camera, another had some money. They decided to begin a film rather than just talk about one.

It was not long before the angel, unhappy in the role of sponsor, dropped out. The man with the camera lent his equipment but stayed out of the project. With no money, they could only shoot one reel of film at a time. That meant one hundred feet—or about three minutes of film—during each session. Thus the shooting, spread out over three months, was highly discontinuous. That discontinuity was accented by the disappearance of the young man they had chosen as their protagonist.

Unlike Maya Deren, Peterson and Broughton preferred to use their friends as actors in their first films, not themselves. In their choice of a leading player they followed a tactic of *Un Chien Andalou* by selecting a type who projected a quality of madness. Shortly after the completion of the Dali-Buñuel film, Pierre Batcheff killed himself; not too long after that, the leading lady also killed herself. In the case of *The Potted Psalm*, Harry Honig simply disappeared after one shooting session. The rest of the film had to deal with this contingency.

From the reports of both creators, the collaboration went smoothly. Peterson operated the camera, and they both agreed on the choice of shots. When it came to the editing, they worked together "over one another's shoulders" according to Peterson.

When the film was first shown during the initial season of Art in Cinema, Peterson wrote the following note:

> *The Potted Psalm* was shot during the summer of 1946. The original scenario and shooting script were discarded on the first day. Thereafter fresh scenarios and scripts were prepared at least once a week for a period of about three months. The surviving film was cut into 148 parts and the parts numbered—one to one forty-eight. The scenarios then read like stock market reports.
>
> This pullulation of literary material, finally taking a numerical form, was deliberate. What was already literary had no need to become cine-

matic. The resulting procedure corresponded to the making of a sketch in which, after an enormous preliminary labor of simplification, the essential forms are developed in accordance with the requirements of a specific medium.

. . .

The necessary ambiguity of the specific image is the starting point. From a field of dry grass to the city, to the grave stone marked "Mother" and made specific by the accident ("objective hazard") of a crawling caterpillar, to the form of a spiral, thence to a tattered palm and a bust of a male on a tomb, the camera, after a series of movements parodic of the sign of the cross, fastens on the profile of a young man looking into a store window. All these scenes are susceptible of a dozen different interpretations based on visual connections. The restatement of shapes serves the general purpose of increasing the meanings of the initial statements. The connections may or may not be rational. In an intentionally realistic work the question of rationality is not a consideration. What is being stated has its roots in myth and strives through the chaos of commonplace data toward the kind of inconstant allegory which is the only substitute for myth in a world too lacking in such symbolic formulations. And the statement itself is at least as important as what is being stated. The quality, for example, of rectangularity in the maternal tomb is a primary consideration. Psychologically it constitutes a negation of the uterine principle. Aesthetically it derives its force from what has been called the geometric as opposed to the biologic spirit. The definition and unification of these opposing spirits is one of the functions of a visual work. Nor is it necessary for an audience to analyze these functions. It is enough to know that they exist. At least they may be presumed to exist. Having made the assumption, it is possible to go on from there.

Unfortunately, where we go is by no means certain. The replacement of observation by intuition in a work of art, of analysis by synthesis and of reality by symbolism, do not constitute a roadmap. It is perhaps wanting too much of art to expect it to perform the kinds of miracles ordinarily demanded of world statesmen. Not a roadmap possibly but the beginnings of a method. A method of statement, in a medium sufficiently fluid to resolve both the myth and the allegory in a complete affirmation.[1]

By design and by necessity *The Potted Psalm* evolves disjunctively; the various women of the film (there are six in the credits) form a virtually continuous spectrum from innocent girl to savage old lady, but at any given moment of the film it is difficult to tell the middle figures apart; the mixture of motifs and styles, styles which in later films are typical of either Peterson or Broughton, makes it difficult to bring the film into focus as a totality.

The overall plan is quite straightforward: a graveyard episode is followed by an interior scene and ends again outdoors near the graveyard.

Brief exterior scenes punctuate the middle sections. At times the film seems to proceed narratively, though with radical ellipses, and at times it seems to be a thematic construction, cutting away from narrative time. The themes of schizophrenia and the bifurcated male, in addition to being an obsession of Peterson's, fit the fact of the collaboration and its helter-skelter method.

The film opens with a pan from deep weeds to a hilltop view of San Francisco. We are immediately confronted with a metaphor which determines much of the movement and montage of the film. Ever since this film, San Francisco has inspired avant-garde film-makers to portray it as a paradise of fools. Peterson himself, turned writer, has spent the last decade on a book about the philosophy and eccentricity of the city itself.

From the weeds, the camera sweeps sideways over a grave marked "Mother" while a snail or caterpillar creeps one way as the camera moves in the opposite direction. Another pan moves left. Then from the top of a palm tree the image descends to an overgrown grave. In the program note I have quoted, Peterson speaks of making the sign of the cross with the camera. This simple sight gag does not work: the opening of *The Potted Psalm* is an exhilarating liberation of the camera in which sectors of space are combined into a dynamic portrayal of a static and serene area.

The camera settles on the granite head of a man carved on a gravestone. A cut shows us the protagonist's face in a similar profile; his pimples are highlighted. His face twitches. Throughout this film almost everything else twitches—feet, thumbs, eyes—in a spasmic response to spastic construction.

He stands before a shop. When he looks in the window he sees, amid collected junk, a nude female figure, the first indication of the theme of adolescent sexuality which pervades the film. Shortly he makes his way to a house which might be a madhouse or a bordello, or both. Inside he undergoes a metamorphosis into a headless man in a navy jacket. There he sees an old lady eating the leaves of a plant; when he lifts the skirt of another woman seated beside him, he finds she has a carved table leg; later both her legs are of flesh, but the foot of one is stuck in a glass beaker.

Intercutting between this interior and the grave suggests that these madwomen or whores might be ghouls or that their house might open into the realm of death. Once he is inside, narrative causality disappears. The headless man pours a drink down his neck. In a closeup, someone picks at a plate of broken glass with a knife and fork. From the perspective of the subjective camera, a drink is drunk and a cigarette smoked as if the camera itself were consuming them. Other women appear and dance with the camera, which may stand in for the protagonist, and with a reflecting tube wearing a hat.

Suddenly we are back outside, in the graveyard and amid ruins, watching a snail, or the carcass of a dead animal, or the twitching eye of the hero. Back inside, one of the women kisses an anamorphic mirror. From that point onward, distorted and reflected images increase in frequency. The twitching, scratching, tongue flicking, and dancing accelerate as well. We come to see more and more of a female mannequin, dipped in water, and an androgynous statue caressed by the young man. Eventually he flees from the house, and the semblance of narrative begins again.

Violence dominates the next images. The mannequin is broken and bloody. The hero, at times headless and at times the pimply youth, takes up a knife, kicks away the dead carcass, and cuts through meat, but only a snail falls away. Now we are back at the scene of the film's opening, by "Mother's" grave. From here a woman runs away in slow motion. The camera follows her, superimposing several images of her flight. The speed changes from very slow to very fast. Then, when she passes over a hill, the film ends.

This rough synopsis ignores half the images in the film. Another viewer, selecting different material, might construe the film much differently. The film has all the sudden changes and the metaphors of dreams without the essential spatial and temporal orientation. The use of distorted imagery, outrageously contrived effects such as the navy jacket pulled up over a man's head, wild camera movements, and a montage that suggests free association, are the signposts of still another cinematic form, the picaresque, which emerged through the collaboration and later the individual films of Peterson and Broughton, and remained curiously centered in San Francisco, in certain films of Christopher MacLaine, Ron Rice, and Robert Nelson (see Chapter 9). It is a form that comes from the comic side of Surrealism, with a debt to the great slap-stick tradition of Max Sennett, through Chaplin, Keaton, Lloyd, Langdon, and Laurel and Hardy.

In their subsequent films Peterson and Broughton draw heavily on the experience and material of The Potted Psalm, but with more successful formal organization. Perhaps that film, which was made on a lark, might have been its makers' last were it not for its success at the opening season of the Art in Cinema film society. As a result of the near riot at its opening, Douglas MacAgy, then the director of the California School of Fine

Arts, conceived the idea of including avant-garde film-making in the curriculum of his school.

At the end of the war the students of the art school, somewhat older than usual, tended to be more proficient than inspired. The film-making course offered more involvement in the experience of art-making. Peterson was hired to teach it. Each of the students paid a small fee for materials and to finance their collective film. Peterson used the situation with consummate skill to pursue his film-making. The films he made between 1947 and 1949, *The Cage, The Petrified Dog, Mr. Frenhofer and the Minotaur,* and *The Lead Shoes*—the totality of his avant-garde work—were all workshop projects. In each of them the students acted, constructed sets, or supplied the basic themes.

The evolution of the first of these films, *The Cage* (1947), shows the vicissitudes of the situation in which Peterson found himself, but also his ability to turn it into an aesthetic triumph. To begin with, he engaged his friend Hy Hirsch as a cameraman. Hirsch had not yet made any of his own films, but he had experience with a motion picture camera, access to equipment, and a sincere interest in the project. Peterson decided not to operate the camera himself because he had to lecture while he was in the process of making the film.

Peterson's talent lies in synthesizing. He begins with a few themes and a few stylistic principles. The film then emerges spontaneously. He shoots with the idea in mind that the structural cohesion of film comes in the editing. Looking at the whole of his work, we can see how he challenges his own aesthetic by providing himself with radically different components to synthesize. This becomes more obvious in the later films.

The Cage begins with a picaresque theme, the adventures of a loose eyeball. This was to be filmed "with every trick in the book and a few that weren't." He used all the camera times: slow, fast, normal, and reverse. Superimposition and stop-motion disappearances are employed. To these he added a few tricks of his own, such as a cut-out collage which moves to reveal the actual scene or the counterpoint of forward and backward motions (he filmed his actors running backwards through a crowd and had the film reversed so the crowd runs backwards and the actors forward).

He chose the student with the maddest expression as the protagonist. He could not have been very surprised, after the making of *The Potted Psalm,* when this schizophrenic-looking young man dropped out of school and deserted the film midway through shooting. Peterson employed the same tactic he had earlier: find a double and deflect the theme of the film. This time he could do it with more control.

He already had a shot of the first young man sitting on a chair, bent over thinking, with a patch on his eye. He put his new hero in the same position and had the laboratory make a dissolve of the two shots, so that one blends into the other. A concave anamorphic image shows the two fusing together (achieved by joining two different images at the point of maximal distortion so that the clear image of the first blurs, and out of the blur comes the second). When, later, the second man wears the patch, the transfer is complete.

The construction of the film is so continuous that, unless told by the film-maker, the viewer could not guess that the film did not proceed completely according to plan. In its final version *The Cage* describes the adventures of a "mad" artist. In a symbolic or real self-mutilation, he takes out his own eye, which immediately escapes from his studio into an open field and then meanders through San Francisco. His blinding is accompanied by complete schizophrenia. He alternates with his double throughout the film.

His girlfriend, who is also his model, frightened by his mad groping around his studio for the lost eye, gets a doctor. The girl, the doctor, and one of the two protagonists then chase around the city after the eye. Throughout the film the perspective alternates between that of the pursuers and that of the eye itself. The eye's vision is filmed through an anamorphic lens.

The strategy of the doctor is to catch the eye and destroy it. To save the eye, the double continually has to thwart the doctor's attacks with darts and rifles. Eventually the eye is recovered, and the schizophrenic becomes the original young man. His first act as a reunited man is to knock out the doctor who otherwise would have ruined his recovery and, presumably, taken the girl.

In a deliberately parodic ending, the artist and girl walk off hand in hand. He embraces her in a field, and she flies out of his arms into a tree.

As the comparison of outlines would suggest, *The Cage* develops much of the material rehearsed in *The Potted Psalm*. At times the imagery coincides. We see a snail crawling over the eyeball, just as we had seen one repeatedly in the earlier film. In *The Potted Psalm*, the carcass, the eating of glass, and the cutting through meat function as visual jolts. They are reminiscent of the sliced eye in *Un Chien Andalou*. In *The Cage* the tactile horror is greater, though still not on a level with the Dali-Buñuel film.

The snail crawling over the eye; the eye rolling in the mouth of a sleeping man, or onto the hatpin of a shoplifter; the eye caught in a wet mop; these are all images that create a virtually tactile response. The most vivid of them, the hatpin, fuses horror and humor in the best surrealistic style.

The Cage also has within it a mad "city symphony" of San Francisco as seen from the rolling eye. When Peterson eventually gave up film-making and concentrated on writing, he published a novel, *The Fly in the Pigment*, elaborating on the picaresque adventures of the eyeball in *The Cage*. In the novel a fly escapes from a Dutch flower painting in the Louvre and explores the human comedy of Paris before dying by being accidentally slammed between the pages of a book.

The images and movements of the camera we see in *The Cage* are Peterson's. Hy Hirsch executed them well, kept the focus, and balanced the darks and lights. There is nothing in the dozen later Hirsch films like the camera work of *The Cage*; it recurs in all of Peterson's work.

To begin with, there is the anamorphosis, the lateral and vertical distortion of images emphasized by a twisting movement of the lens which shifts the axis of contraction and elongation. The distortions of *The Potted Psalm* seem to have been done with a mirror or a crude mask over the lens. With *The Cage* and thereafter, Peterson uses an optically distorting lens. The device is simple and has been attacked as too "easy," yet Peterson used it more intelligently and creatively than any of the numerous other film-makers who have tried before and after him. In his films the anamorphic lens opens an Abstract Expressionist space. Even though structurally he related anamorphosis to various forms of madness, his distorting lens offers an alternative to haptic perspectives.

In *The Cage* the distorted imagery clearly represents the perspective of the liberated eye. The other perspective, that of the viewer, has its own spectacular disorientations. Early in the film a collage appears on the screen. When its elements move away through animation, the actual room, the studio of the painter, can be seen. The cut-out parts of the collage room, especially its window, hang in the deep space of the actual room, creating a dialogue of depths and scale.

After the eye is dislodged, it remains for a while in the room. The protagonist chases after it while all the furniture flies over and at him in slow motion. Peterson skillfully pivots the camera in a circular movement. The flying furniture and the spinning camera are intercut and subvert our gravitational orientation. The episode ends, effectively, with a reverse motion shot of the flying furniture as the floor and the eye are mopped up.

The illusion makes the fallen chairs, tables, easel, etc., return to their places through the action of the mop.

Peterson attempted so many things that the film is much more interesting than it is successful. Yet where it is successful, as in the dialogue of perspectives and their spaces, it is breaking new ground for a subjectivist cinema. It is specifically his use of radical techniques as metaphors for perception and consciousness (which is intimately bound up with the Romantic theme of the divided man) that elaborates upon Deren's central contribution and paves the way for future refinements of cinematic perspective in the avant-garde.

There is a section in the film where the dialectic is especially effective. Just after the eyeball floats out the window, there is a shot of the girl sleeping on the couch in the studio, fully dressed, with the doctor's foot by her head. The double of the hero lifts his patch and we see, presumably, what he perceives: his alter ego rushing through the streets of San Francisco with a cage over his head. The people of the city all walk backwards; the cars too run backwards. Then the shot of the sleeping girl returns.

This small episode attracts our attention because of its ambiguity. In the first place, it suggests a dream; what follows, or perhaps the whole film, might be the vision of the girl's afternoon sleep, as in *Meshes of the Afternoon*. Then, within the dream, comes the set of shots which suggests that the episode is the interior reflection of the double.

The bird cage which gives the film its title appears first just after the dissolve connecting the double protagonist. The first is wearing it over his head. From then on, until he is made whole again and his caged self is buried in the sand on a beach (reverse motion), he wears it as a symbol of his schizophrenia. Obviously these scenes were shot before the theme of the alter ego entered the film, since it is the actor who disappeared who wears the cage. The specific use of the symbolism is simply a result of the film's ultimate construction. Here then is the clearest example of the process of film creation that Peterson described in his note to *The Potted Psalm*.

The second appearance of the cage comes at the end of a wild camera movement during the first scramble after the rolling eye when the cage lands on the head of a statue, that persistent archetype of the early avant-garde film. The statue emerges in the most ambitious subjectivist films as a desperate surrogate for basic human needs.

A discussion of *The Cage* would not be complete without referring to

The cage as an icon of the discontinuity of the self: Sidney Peterson's *The Cage*;
Anaïs Nin in Kenneth Anger's *Inauguration of the Pleasure Dome*.

Entr'Acte (1924), the exemplary film of the Dada movement. *Entr'Acte* stands in the same relationship to *The Potted Psalm* and *The Cage* as *Un Chien Andalou* does to *Meshes of the Afternoon*. Its conception resembles that of Peterson's collaboration with Broughton; as a finished film, it is more like his first solitary exercise. The ways that they differ point up the differences between the American avant-garde film of the 1940s and the French of the 1920s.

Entr'Acte was made to be shown between the acts of a ballet, called *Relâche*, or *No Show Today*. The negative titling was the work of Francis Picabia, the Dadaist painter, who wrote the film scenario and made the sets for the ballet itself; Erik Satie provided music for both. When he decided that the performance should have a filmed curtain raiser and a movie intermission, the task of production was given to René Clair.

Clair modestly describes the circumstances: "When I met him he explained to me that he wanted to show a film between the two acts of his ballet, as had been done, before 1914, during the intermissions of café-concerts. And since I was the only one in the house involved with the cinema, I was called upon."[2] There is no reason to doubt him. For Picabia the film was a casual affair. He jotted down the most schematic of scenarios on stationery from Maxim's. One can imagine him writing as he finished his coffee:

At the rising of the curtain: cannon charges in slow motion performed by Satie and Picabia; the shot will have to make as much noise as possible. Length: 1 minute.

During the intermission:
1. Boxing assault by white gloves, on black screen: length 15 seconds. Written slide for explanation: 10 seconds.
2. Chess game between Duchamp and Man Ray. Waterspout maneuvered by Picabia sweeps over the game: length 30 seconds.
3. Juggler and Père Lacolique: length 30 seconds.
4. Hunter shooting at the egg of an ostrich on waterspout; a dove comes out of the egg and lands on the hunter's head; a second hunter shooting at it (the head) kills the first hunter: he falls, the bird flies away: length 1 minute. Written slide 20 seconds.
5. 21 persons lying on their backs, showing the bottom of their feet. 10 seconds, handwritten slide 15 seconds.
6. Female dancer on transparent glass filmed from underneath: length 1 minute, written slide, 5 seconds.
7. Blowing up of balloons and rubber screens, on which figures will be drawn along with inscriptions: length 35 seconds.

8. A funeral: hearse drawn by a camel, etc., length 6 minutes, written
slide 1 minute.[3]

Satie was more meticulous; he pressed Clair for a shot by shot breakdown
of the finished film, with timing, so that he could carefully synchronize a
score for it. This was before sound projection, and the orchestra of the
ballet played along with the film.

Clair had a free hand. The artists named in the scenario all played their
parts. He omitted the third and fifth sections, and freely improvised on
the sixth and eighth.

Two years after the ballet, *Entr'Acte* went into distribution without
sound and with the curtain raiser attached to the front of the film as a
prologue. That was how Peterson and Broughton first saw it. In this form
the film opens with a cannon moving by itself around the roof of a building in Paris. In slow motion, Satie and Picabia leap into the frame. They
discuss a plan, which at first shocks Picabia, but he soon agrees to fire the
cannon into the buildings where Satie has pointed. They do it. Then they
fire it in the direction of the camera and audience.

A series of superimpositions establishes the roofs of Paris, while images
of balloon dolls being inflated and a ballerina, seen from below dancing
on a glass floor, are intercut.

The flames of matches dance in superimposition in the hair of a man
whose face cannot be seen. He scratches his head, then lifts it, revealing
surprised eyes. Repeatedly throughout this scene and through most of the
film we see glimpses of the ballerina, until a change of camera angle eventually reveals her not to be a ballerina at all, but a bearded man dressed
as one.

An off-screen jet of water ruins a game of checkers, played by Marcel
Duchamp and Man Ray. Then, after a series of superimpositions involving water, a paper boat, and the pseudo-ballerina, we see an ostrich egg
held in the air by a vertical jet of water. A hunter spots it, but every time
he lifts his rifle, the egg multiplies into two, four, eleven dancing eggs.
Finally it becomes singular again, and he fires. To his happy surprise a
pigeon falls from the sky and lands on his head.

Picabia, on a nearby roof with a rifle, has spotted the hunter with the
pigeon on his head. He tries to shoot the bird off, but he kills the man instead. The scene jumps to his funeral. Yet the water still holds up the egg
and the dancer dances. A ridiculous burial procession is led by a camel-
drawn hearse. As they pass an amusement park the hearse comes loose
and the whole party, including the widow and numerous old men, chase

after it. As the hearse picks up speed, the camera movements become wilder and scenes from a roller-coaster are intercut with the chase.

Eventually the coffin flies off the hearse, rolls through a field, and pops open. Out comes a stage magician. With his magic wand he makes the assembled mourners disappear; then he performs the same trick on himself.

When the title "Fin" appears, a man jumps through the paper upon which it is written; then the shot is reversed so that he leaps back, the paper heals its rip, and the film ends.

In its round-about manner of narrative, its slapstick chase, its exploitation of camera tricks both as metaphors and as developments of the "plot," and the comic violence of its shooting scenes, *Entr'Acte* prefigures *The Cage*. It anticipates *The Potted Psalm*, on the other hand, with repeated interruptions of the picaresque development by fragments of continuous scenes which bear no direct relation to the main chain of events. Behind all three films, of course, lies the comedy style of Max Sennett.

The differences among *Entr'Acte, The Potted Psalm, The Cage,* and the slapstick comedy are more interesting than their similarities. The avant-garde films which owe their inspiration, in part at least, to slapstick comedy tend to exhibit a shift of rhythm away from comic punctuation (for the humor of the great film comedians is a rhythmic function) toward the abstract. This displacement reveals the irrationality and the unconscious dynamic behind the previously funny archetype, the chase. In an effective silent comedy there is no time for metaphors. The comic film-maker can only deviate from the main line of comic action when the point to which he deviates extends the humor by prolonging it. The periodic recurrences of the pseudo-ballerina in Clair's film relieve the tension of the funeral chase.

Yet when we compare *Entr'Acte* with either *The Potted Psalm* or *The Cage,* it seems a much more comical film. Satire was the film-makers' inspiration. Remember the circumstances which motivated its creation: the bearded ballerina mocks the expectation of a ballet audience, and the members of the funeral procession mock the audience itself. In the prologue and in the murder of the hunter, Picabia and Satie flippantly disregard the most potent taboo of modern times—murder for its own sake. In the same spirit of provocation, Satie had announced that his music for the ballet would be "pornographic."

In *The Potted Psalm* and *The Cage,* the slapstick sources are at a greater remove. Everything moves in an aesthetic direction. The film-makers of the 1940s in America, unlike their Parisian predecessors, were not mocking the sacred cows of the bourgeoisie. The Second World War had obliterated much of what Picabia was attacking. In the films Peterson made, either as collaborator or sole maker, what had previously been social is made aesthetic.

Broughton, however, had a more classically comic sensibility. While Peterson's humor resided in his sense of the irrational and in the collision of ideas, Broughton's focused on character. The childlike man is Broughton's favorite metaphor. "Mother's" grave, the bordello aroma of the interior scenes, and a shot of the hero on a kiddymobile must surely have been among Broughton's contributions to *The Potted Psalm*.

In a recent interview Peterson remembered how Broughton used to roar with laughter at the rushes of the film, while he was, if anything, disappointed. But when the editing was completed it was Peterson who felt the magic of the whole, while Broughton was apprehensive. Peterson was the synthesizing Surrealist; Broughton, the comedian of archetypes. His humor turns on the universal rather than the peculiar; the emblem he has taken for himself, and wears on a stickpin, is the alchemical sign for essence.

In 1948 Broughton made his first film by himself. He employed a cameraman (in this case, Frank Stauffacher) as he has done on almost all his subsequent films. Broughton's experience, aside from. *The Potted Psalm*, had been as a poet and playwright. It is out of his early plays and poems that the theme of this first film, *Mother's Day*, emerged.

His own notes are an articulate introduction to the film:

> From the beginning I accepted the camera's sharply accurate eye as a value rather than a limitation. The camera's challenge to the poet is that his images must be as definite as possible: the magic of his persons, landscapes, and actions occurring in an apparent reality. At this point something approaching choreography must enter in: the finding of meaningful gesture and movement. And from the beginning I decided to make things happen head on, happen within the frame, without vagueness, without camera trickery—so that it would be how the scenes were made to happen in front of the lens, and then how they were organized in the montage, that would evoke the world I wanted to explore.
>
> The subject matter of *Mother's Day* cannot, certainly, be considered specialized. Most of us have had some experience of childhood, either by participation or by observation. But do we remember that children are often incomprehensibly terror-stricken, are always ready to slip over into some private nonsense-ritual, or into behavior based upon their misconception of the adult world? Furthermore, what about the "childish be-

havior" of grown-ups, their refusal to relinquish childhood misconcep-
tions, or to confront the world they inhabit?

Although this film is, then, by its very nature, a nostalgic comedy, it
eschews chronological accuracy in either the period details or the dramatic events. It has been one of the clichés of cinema since the days of
cubism that the medium allows the artist to manipulate time: to cut it
up, retard or accelerate it, and so forth. In *Mother's Day* historical time
may be said to stand still. Periods and fashions are gently scrambled. The
device is deliberate: for with this film we are in the country of emotional
memory, where everything may happen simultaneously.

This is because the basic point of vision of the film is that of an adult
remembering the past (and the past within the past): projecting himself
back *as he is now*, and seeing his family and his playmates at his present
age-level, regarding them with adult feelings and knowledge, and even
projecting them forward into his present-day concerns.

In *Mother's Day* I deliberately used adults acting as children, to evoke
the sense of projecting oneself as an adult back into memory, to suggest
the impossible borderline between when one is child and when one is
grown-up, and to implicate Mother in the world of the child fantasies as
being, perhaps, the biggest child of them all—since she, in this case, has
never freed herself from narcissistic daydreams.

Since this is a film about mothers and children, about families and
forms of social experience, it is dominated by the circle, and—as Parker
Tyler pointed out—by the object revolving on a fixed axis.[4]

A series of six ironic subtitles divide the sections of the film. It opens
with a young man sleeping in the arms of a statue, an evocation of the
opening of Chaplin's *City Lights*, and another instance of this ubiquitous
motif in the early American avant-garde film. Then we read "Mother was
the loveliest woman in the world. And Mother wanted everything to be
lovely." A number of brief, enigmatic shots follow in what the film-maker
calls a "formal prelude." There is an elegant middle-aged woman, a spinning medallion, a young couple sitting at opposite sides of a statue of
Cupid, and a scene in depth of the ruins of a building with a formally
dressed man in the background and Mother up close to the camera.

This basically abstract passage introduces a number of typical elements
in the film without explicitly delineating the main ironic structure. The
impression of an animated family album, heightened by the nostalgic
music of Howard Brubeck, written for the film, is immediately apparent.
In this brief passage, the mother has at least four changes of costume. In
the remainder of the film there is a minor or major change of this sort in
nearly every one of her appearances on the screen. These changes involve

an intentional mixture of periods and styles. At one point in the prologue gauze in front of the camera modifies the image.

The effect of the alternations of costume, the short shots, the occasionally unusual angles, and the gauze is to create a scintillating image which seems to weave randomly through time. The music, the rhythmic intercutting between images, and the concentric movements within the frame—such as the spinning medallion—give a fluid cast to the continuous metamorphosis. The dialectic of tensions, the smooth rhythm, and the staccato imagery make for formal strength which is reinforced by a play on scale and foreshortening related to the dominant themes of the film. The montage in the ruins of the building uses depth and angles to suggest the dominance of the female over the male.

In the next section, entitled "Mother always said she could have had her pick," foreshortening makes the same statement. We see Mother at her upstairs window, shot from below to magnify her stature. Her suitors, filmed from high above, are diminished by the perspective of the camera.

The first shot of this episode is as brilliant an example of both metaphor and ellipsis as can be found anywhere in the avant-garde film. The camera pans up the stairs of a wooden house to its façade, at which moment we see that the house has been destroyed. There is *only* the façade. Next we see Mother smiling from the second-story window of a different house. The montage simultaneously suggests that Mother's house is now destroyed (in other words, the ruin is proleptic), and that Mother herself is a façade (a visual metaphor). This is a rather simple example of cinematic prolepsis. In its more radical employment by Broughton in *Dreamwood* and by Brakhage and Markopoulos in several films, a shot may first seem to function in a simple relationship to the previous shots and only later, sometimes much later, is it grounded in a context more appropriate to the manifold of its aspects.

Broughton constructed the entire episode around the image of Mother scanning her suitors from the window. In each of her appearances, as I have mentioned, she changes a hat, an ornament, or her dress. The use of ellipsis is extreme and highly original. First, one suitor presents himself. We see mother from below; when the camera cuts back to the suitor, there are now two of them, holding gifts. The exchange continues until there are four. At the end of the sequence, there is a man in her room.

With the changes of shots in the interior scenes, there are changes of background comparable to the alternation of costumes. The sets themselves are in the theatrical tradition: screens, plants, pictures on the walls;

a minimum of objects and furniture necessary to give the impression of a cluttered, turn-of-the-century interior. The basically static camera creates a sense of composition-in-depth out of these stage backgrounds. Mirrors are frequently used. In the third episode, "And she picked father," we see the bearded father for the first time, reflected in an oval hand mirror into which Mother had been looking as she combed her hair. He is next seen, with his eyes bulging, posed in a frame on the wall as if he were a portrait.

The image, at the end of that section, of her playing with a doll introduces the next part, "Then Mother always said she wanted little boys and girls to be lovely." We see her children. Although they are grown up, they play the games of children. In this and the remaining two sections of the film, the concentration on Mother is gradually replaced by that on the children. The progress of their games involves disguised rituals of the passage into adolescence. At the same time, their satiric mimicry of their parents reflects the adult world. As Broughton pointed out in the note I have quoted, the use of adults to play children is not solely ironic; it re-creates the psychological superimposition of the past and childhood upon the adult.

In their games, each "child" plays alone, though several may appear simultaneously in a single shot. One waves her dolls; another devours a box of candies; another chalks a naked lady on the wall. They tease, fight, and cry. While they play, Mother stays at her dressing table, and the father, with his straw hat on his knee, watches them, tapping with his cane. The elements of this section are held together by a strong internal rhythm created by the tapping cane, the moving swings, a bowling pin rolling in water, and hopscotch steps—all in time with each other and with the music.

The thought or sight of the children makes Mother envision her old age. In the first shot of the next episode, "Because ladies and gentlemen were the loveliest thing in the world," we see the face of an old lady who whispers to a man, so that the children cannot hear. But they have their own party. We see a homely girl sitting on a couch with a man. Another girl enters the room. Then we see the first one on the same couch with two men. The very same entrance shot is repeated four times. In each instance another man joins the girl on the couch. Thus the children use a parody of Mother's courtship for their own sexual initiation.

The sixth and final title, "And so we learned how to be lovely too," completes the ironic definition of loveliness. In a series of flashes, six bowls, each larger than the previous one, appear on the screen with a tape-measure indicating their diameters. Like the spinning medallion, and later the spinning mandolin, they are hermetic images. These can be taken as metaphors for growth, to be sure; their function in the film is primarily irrational, rhythmic, and textural. They recall a sequence in *The Potted Psalm*, in which a nut is cracked and bread is broken in rapid succession. The sudden and unexplained deployment of a series of close-up details enriches the texture of *Mother's Day* by intensifying its unpredictability.

The last episode begins when Mother leaves the house for a ride in an antique car. The children symbolically take over the house. A girl tries on her mother's hats; a boy, his father's. The straw hat is destroyed. They pull off the father's beard. Out of a window fly the straw hat and the cane. Finally we see the living portrait of the father, only now upside-down. The mother, seen as usual at her mirror, is "left behind in a empty room, still dressed to go out but with nowhere to go" (Broughton's note).

Mother's Day is a masterpiece of its genre. Nothing Broughton has done since has surpassed it. The film vibrates with witty imagery in a rapid succession of metaphors and visual surprises.

The inventiveness of *Mother's Day* has had no imitators and therefore little influence on the subsequent development of the avant-garde film in America. It remains a unique cinematic object without predecessors or heirs. Simpler films by Broughton, with less radical formal ambitions, have had more influence; Christopher MacLaine, in *The End*, made a black version of *Four in the Afternoon* and Ron Rice extended *Loony Tom, the Happy Lover* into *The Flower Thief*, though neither were aware that they were so close to Broughton. Broughton's intense interest in comic types turned his films away from the trance film inspirations in a way that neither he nor his critics could see at the time. The trance film was predicated upon the transparency of the somnambulistic protagonist within the dream landscape. The perspective of the camera, inflected by montage, directly imitated his consciousness. Broughton invested too much in the individuality of his protagonists and too little in the cinematic representation of perception to contribute substantially to the trance film. It was only much later with the making of *Dreamwood* (1971) that the debts to Cocteau and Deren, which he had always readily acknowledged, surfaced visibly in his work. Even when he touched upon psycho-drama by playing the chief role in his second film, a version of the quest for sexual self-discovery so central to the early American avant-garde film, he saw himself with such irony, and so clearly as a psychological type, that *The*

Adventures of Jimmy (1950) is as far from *Fireworks, Swain,* or *Flesh of Morning*—the psycho-dramas of Kenneth Anger, Gregory Markopoulos, and Stan Brakhage—as *Mother's Day* was from *The Cage* or Deren's films.

The Adventures of Jimmy is an autobiographical picaresque in which a mountain boy looks for companionship in the big city. The episodes are highly elliptical. Jimmy climbs into a canoe on a small stream in one shot and finds himself in a busy bay in the next; he wanders into a boarding house looking for a room and is followed by a prostitute, only to rush out and away, comically horrified, an instant later. In rapid succession he seeks love in an artist's rendezvous, a dance hall, and a Turkish bath; he tries religion and psychoanalysis.

With every episode he changes his hat, from farmer's cap, to sailor's crew, to underworld fedora, to a ceremonial top hat. The last is the emblem of his final solution, marriage, as he walks out of church with his bride.

The irony, the ellipses, the symbolic changes of costume, that we found in *Mother's Day,* recur here. Yet they are less ironical, less elliptical, and the transformations not as radical. But above all, the difference between the two films lies in their respective rhythms. The former is as calculated and modulated as the latter is casual.

By the time that Broughton made this film, Peterson, now deeply involved in the use of sound in cinema, had made his last avant-garde film, although he probably didn't realize it at the time. In 1948 and 1949 he produced three sound films with his Workshop 20 at the California School of Fine Arts, the last two of which are his greatest achievements. *The Petrified Dog, Mr. Frenhofer and the Minotaur,* and *The Lead Shoes* were made in successive semesters as group projects with student participation.

The Petrified Dog takes its title from the statue of a lion seen repeatedly throughout the film and from an allusion to the freezing of the camera's motion, which we see first in the background of the film's titles. In theme, it might be called the further adventures of Alice in Wonderland. The heroine Alice climbs out of a hole in a park with her characteristic broad Victorian child's hat into a world where we have already seen a painter working within an empty frame, a slow motion runner hardly getting anywhere, a lady in fast motion eating her lipstick, and a photographer who sets his camera up with a delayed shutter so that he can stand on pedestals and be snapped as a statue. Into this Wonderland she crawls, in slow motion, at first.

The events of the film are essentially disconnected. We see them in the order in which Alice, continually blinking (as the hero of *The Potted Psalm* continually twitched), turns her shutter-like gaze on them. Like Maya Deren's first heroine, she also sees herself in the mad landscape. The sole example of distorted imagery in this film is a brief shot of Alice looking at her reflection in the hubcap of a car. Peterson operated the camera himself this time. He eschewed the dynamic movements that characterize all his other films except for a few timid pans and some brief moving shots of the lion statue, both normal and upside-down. The stasis of the camera functions organically within the film: there is a sense that the episodes and gags are eternal, contiguous realities, not progressive events, and the camera style emphasizes the discreteness and fixity of the separate scenes, while the use of slow and fast motion brackets them.

I have deliberately neglected the climactic scene of the film. A terrified young man wanders over a statue of Abraham Lincoln and into a massage parlor where two men are fighting; a skeleton decides to take advantage of him, prone on the massage table. As the skeleton wrestles with him and possibly rapes him, in normal and slow motion, the camera is liberated from its tripod and joins in the frenzy. From this point on, the episodes show signs of internal development. A bum approaches the painter with an empty frame, sticks his head through, and demands a hand-out. When the artist finally pulls a full cup of hot coffee out of his pocket, the bum is thankless; he throws it down and kicks it away. The lipstick-eating lady eventually finishes her pasty lunch and walks away dropping several handkerchiefs. The painter follows her collecting the droppings, which eventually include a bra and a slip. He pursues her through her door, only to be thrust out and attacked by her husband. Alice also sees herself in a chase: she eludes her nanny.

The most interesting episode in the film is the one involving the painter and the bum, and it is interesting precisely insofar as it alludes to the art of René Magritte. The empty frame which makes a painting out of whatever rectangle of reality it faces recalls a number of Magritte paintings in which a canvas, resting on an easel fixed in a landscape or interior, transfigures, in an illusionary way, the space in which it is placed.

If there is a single theme which pervades the early American avant-garde film, it is the *primacy of the imagination*. In Peterson's films this theme is wedded to his own interest in the irrational sensibility of the artist. Yet despite the shift from the anarchistic themes of *Entr'Acte* to the psychological and aesthetic themes of Peterson's first three efforts, those films are closer to the sensibility of Dada than Surrealism.

The surrealistic frame in Peterson's *The Petrified Dog* and Magritte's "Les Promenades d'Euclide."

The sound track of *The Petrified Dog* is a primitive, and early, example of *musique concrete*. Peterson used four non-musicians, a couple of traditional instruments, including an open piano so that the strings could be plucked or beaten, and anything at hand, even slapping oneself before the microphone of Hy Hirsch's wire recorder. After a few run-throughs, they recorded the entire soundtrack in one long take. Clyfford Still, who was also teaching at the California School of Fine Arts, was so taken with the music that he offered to pay for the transfer to film if he could have a copy of the wire recording.

The soundtrack of *The Petrified Dog* is as free and as wild as the camera movements of Peterson's two earlier films. It is also functional within the experience of the film. The problems of the formal use of sound in film (synchronism, asynchronism, montage, or picture with sound) have no place in a discussion of *The Petrified Dog*. There have been two consistent approaches to sound within the American avant-garde: the functional and the formal. The extreme formal position, which Stan Brakhage propounds and Peter Kubelka practices, and which we shall consider in detail in the portions of this book devoted to their works, holds that no sound should be employed in a film except where it is absolutely necessary, that is, where the film has been conceived as a careful audio-visual synthesis. The functional position rests on the assumption that music (or words) intensify the cinematic experience, even when the film has been shot and edited without consideration for the sound. The functionalist hires a composer after his film has been edited; at his most casual, he finds a piece of recorded music that "fits" his work. In the catalogue of *Art in Cinema* (1947), considerable space is devoted to the editors' researches on the original musical sound tracks for many early French and German avant-garde films, and when research produced no results, they suggested a record which they had found, by experimentation, "fit" the older films.

Broughton and Peterson had asked Francean Campbell, a relative of the man who first lent them a camera, to compose music for *The Potted Psalm*. They did not like the result; they never used it. Peterson noted in his discussion of this experiment that a soundtrack was not necessary then because Art in Cinema (the only place where they conceived the film could be shown) had been so active in finding records to play with silent films. It is true that live or recorded music usually accompanied the silent avant-garde films when they were shown in the 1920s. But the difference between the speed of projection at that time (between 16 and 18 frames per second) and the speed standardized in 1929 for sound (24 frames per second) made it next to impossible to put sound on those films even after the invention and popular use of optical sound tracks. The distribution of early silent films through the library of the Museum of Modern Art created a new aesthetic of *silence* within the American film experience. Thus Maya Deren made her first three films intentionally silent, as Brakhage has made most of his films after 1958.

As collaborators, and later separately, Peterson and Broughton began with a functional conception of sound and moved toward a formal one. (Broughton has returned to the employment of a composer in his most recent films.) In both cases the formalization of the soundtrack occurred through a displacement of narrative information from visual images to voice, resulting in an elliptical treatment of the montage and an oblique method of conveying essential information through poems, songs, or a stream-of-consciousness monologue. The simultaneous displacement of the narrative principle in both sound and picture necessarily provides for a new synthesis in their combination and for the possibility of a formal interplay through asynchronism, as one anticipates or reiterates the other.

It was Peterson rather than Broughton who made the most of these formal possibilities. His step toward the integration of the visual and the aural coincided with the development of his general conception of cinematic structure. *Mr. Frenhofer and the Minotaur* and *The Lead Shoes* recall the complex fusion of trance film, myth, and allusion in the kind of spherical mould that we found in Maya Deren's *Ritual in Transfigured Time*. Peterson has an irony that Maya Deren totally lacked; these two films are more mandarin, more allusive than hers.

The elements of Peterson's synthesis in these films are easily isolated: for *Mr. Frenhofer and the Minotaur* they are Balzac's story, *Le Chef-d'Oeuvre Inconnu*, Pablo Picasso's engraving *Minotauromachia*, and a monologue in James Joyce's style. The visual unification is achieved simply and elegantly by the nearly absolute use of anamorphic photography and either fluid camera movements responding to the movements of the actors or almost choreographic movements of the actors within the static frame. Slow motion, especially at the beginning of the film, contributes to its gracefulness. There is almost no fast motion, superimposition, or wild movement of the camera. Peterson operated the camera himself.

The film-maker treated Balzac's story as the framework for continuing his investigation of the artistic sensibility, which had been the theme of all of his earlier films. It was a theme especially suited to the situation out of which these films emerged—a workshop designed to infuse somewhat

uninspired painters and sculptors with an excitement for the making of
art through a collective film-making experience.

Balzac's short story, from his *Contes Philosophiques* of 1831, involves
two real painters of the seventeenth century and one imaginary one. The
mature Porbus and the novice Poussin meet Balzac's creation, Frenhofer,
who subjects Porbus' latest work to a scathing critique, shows him how
to bring life and depth to it with a few brush strokes, and then proceeds to
tell them about the masterpiece he has been working on for the past decade, *La Belle Noiseuse,* a portrait without a model of the courtesan Catherine Lescault. They are desperate to see the work in progress. Frenhofer
refuses to show it.

Porbus conceives a plan for bringing Poussin's beautiful young mistress
to Frenhofer as a model so that he may compare perfect living beauty
with his idealization. This had been Frenhofer's dream, and after much
persuasion Gilette is talked into modeling for the old master. Shocked
when he finally sees the picture, Poussin cannot help exclaiming that there
is nothing there but a wall of chaotic colors and formless masses. All the
two painters can see on the other's canvas is a foot, an absolutely perfect
realistic foot buried beneath the accumulated revisions of the painting.

For Balzac, there is no question but that Frenhofer in his Pygmalion-
like desire to perfect his idealized women has obliterated his masterpiece.
The thrust of the story, in any case, is not only aesthetic but moral: a par-
allelism and antithesis between the love of Gilette for Poussin and of
Frenhofer for his painting, between the model in the flesh and the illusion
on canvas, and ultimately between a man's work and his love.

Peterson transferred the character of Gilette from an innocent and devoted mistress to a garrulous, flighty art student; the reluctance and fore-
boding of the original become the narcissistic fantasies of the girl in the
film. If we could consider the film without its soundtrack, it would be elliptical, involuted, and schematic. The interior monologue, which has subtleties and reversals of its own, provides the narrative coherence.

The anamorphic imagery congests the space, isolates the images, and
suggests the realm of dream, memory, or a visionary state. The opening
distortion of a cat with a dead mouse, followed by the slow fainting scream
of Gilette accompanied by a violin whine, sets the tone for the whole film.
It is one of several framing devices which initiate a dialogue of perspectives within the work.

There is a fade; the brief image of a fencer; and then we are thrust into
the middle of a scene complicated by the beginning of an interior mono-

logue of associations. Gilette and a young man (Poussin) are dancing in
slow motion on a mattress. The hand-held camera, gracefully following
the bouncing of the bodies and the swaying of the hem of her dress, accents the erotic metaphor. A change of camera distance reveals that an old
man (Porbus) has been watching their dance. Poussin formally introduces
him, and he kisses Gilette's hand. They dance together on the bed. Another shot of the fencer, followed by a little girl carrying a candle (two
images based on Picasso's etching), marks the transition from this scene to
the next.

In that scene, on the same bed and without the men, Gilette repeatedly
pets her cat, intercut with recurrent images of the two figures from the
Minotauromachia. These parallel scenes remain independent of each
other, never appearing in the same frame, until the climax of the film.
Yet in the monologue the elements from Balzac and Picasso are intertwined from the beginning. As she plays with the cat, she speaks the following monologue:

> So much for nature mortified. And it doesn't run very deep anyway.
> Better never than too early. It's ever a question of how or ever. And no
> wonder the tired eye is a bird who sees something worked over for ten
> years. And no wonder too, it's a plot to bribe the mater so chere with a
> modele, so to louvre to then chef d'œuvre. And in this dream I too,
> caught like a spittle girl, immersed all in a stirry, a silly story: to pose or
> not to pose. I love him; I love him not. Or rather, since I love him less,
> already, why not?
> An old man, mad about paint, Frenhofer and Gilette, boquet and
> med, me and Minotaur. Cats are carnivorous. Somewhere there lies a
> man's head and the leftover part of a bull. God save us. Was that really
> a threat to Greek maidens?

The introduction of elements from the *Minotauromachia* occurs gradually. The minotaur itself, like Picasso's, obviously a man with a beast
headpiece, enters while Gilette is petting her cat. Poussin has come to
visit her, to sit with her on the mattress, and to read aloud to her from a
book, Balzac's *Le Chef-d'Oeuvre Inconnu*. Although we have already seen
in schematic form and heard in fragmentary allusions almost half of the
story, the reading begins at the beginning, in Gilette's voice. "On a cold
December morning in the year 1512, a young man whose clothing was
somewhat of the thinnest. . . ."

Another transition comes with the image of a hand winding a music
box, its gears and wheels exposed, and jumps elliptically in mid-action to

the first scene in a location other than Gilette's bedroom. Two drinks are on a café table, fingers are drawing in the wetness of the surface. The sudden interjection of this shot represents the extreme of ellipsis and synecdoche in Peterson's style. He does not show the faces of the men. From the next shot, of the back of a head, we know one of the men is Porbus. The other must be Poussin, whose hands are fiddling with a wine glass. After a brief interplay of these close-ups, the repetition of the music box marks the end of the episode. Back in the bedroom, we see that the reading continues, but at this juncture the narrative returns to stream of consciousness ("Why not? Ham on rye, cheese and salad. If I'm ruined it's a question of pride or games. There's nothing in it for him. If he showed his wife, it's because he loved her not in order to see something better. Or because.")

Again the monologue switches from Gilette's thoughts to Balzac's prose. Yet here, in the longest quotation of the film, Peterson has chosen a passage that does nothing to further the narrative; it is Balzac's reflection, his philosophizing.

From this point on the scrambling of Balzac and Picasso, of music box and reading aloud, accelerates with elliptical leaps. Another image of the young man winding the music box leads to a shot of Gilette nude, her back to the camera, with Frenhofer in the background, facing us, comparing her to his canvas. True to the elliptical style, we come in on the end of the scene. In the same shot, after an interruption of images of the Minotaur, she puts on her dress. The posing has ended.

By this point in the film, the images of the *Minotauromachia* occupy as much screen time as those from the story, and subsequently the proportions shift in favor of Picasso-like material with the narrative elements coming to function as an interruption of the etching come to life, just as the fencer and the little girl had previously been formal interruptions of the story. In this way the short scenes in Frenhofer's studio become progressively elliptical. Against a total of six shots in the studio, Peterson uses twenty-four shots of the *Minotauromachia* and one of the music box. The twenty-four shots are joined by rhythmic rather than narrative connections. A contrast is established between the fast motion, jump-cut, repetitive runs up and down a ladder by a new figure, a man in a loincloth, and the lady in the window calmly petting her dove.

The last six shots of the sequence I have been describing bring the two worlds of the film's title together. A lunge from the fencer strikes Frenhofer in the heart. He falls to the ground and the fencer wipes the blood from the foil. Just before the last image of the dying painter's head, Peterson shows the Minotaur looking at the miraculous canvas, which of course we never get to see. The death occurs without a passage of monologue or reading.

Balzac's portrayal of the death of Frenhofer is an appendix to his story; it is the pitiful conclusion to a tragedy of failure. For Peterson and for us, after the experience of the past seventy years of painting, Frenhofer's canvas is not a failure but a prophecy. The climax of the film—the death of the artist—calls up the myth of Pygmalion and invokes in explicit terms the central theme of the visionary cinema: the triumph of the imagination.

It is not the artist who brings his work to life, although that is his aspiration as reflected in the paraphrases from Balzac in the monologue: "Where is art? It's absolutely invisible. It is the curve of a loving girl, and what fields of light! what spirit of living line that surrounds the flesh and defines the figure, that stands out so that if you wanted to you could pass your hand along the back." It is the work, represented by the elements of the *Minotauromachia*, that engulf the man.

The elements of *Mr. Frenhofer and the Minotaur* gravitate toward the idea of abstraction. By choosing to incorporate a painting from Picasso's classical period, rather than, say, an example of analytical Cubism, Peterson approaches the prophetic facet of Frenhofer's painting through indirection. In a recent interview he has described his intention:

> It was my decision to do a thing about the Balzac story, taking seriously as the theme of the story the conflict between Poussin's Classicism and its opposite. So as strained through my mind it became, really a way of exploring the conflict state in Rousseau's remark to Picasso: "We are the two greatest painters: you in the Egyptian manner; and I in the modern." In a sense, [I was] taking the quest for absolute beauty in the Balzac character and contrasting that with Picassoidal Classicism, the imitation of the *Minotauromachia*. It was not necessarily thought out clearly as though one were writing an essay; this was thematic material. Then the chips fell, partly again, in response to the curious limitations of doing this kind of thing with people who were not even "anti-actors."[5]

Peterson provides the material for a dream-like interpretation of the whole film. The opening and ending sequences contribute to the circularity of a dream; Gilette's trauma of seeing her cat with a dead mouse may become, in the dream, an image of the minotauromachia (scratching the cat, she calls him, "mini-mini-mini-tower"). By another train of association, reflected in the monologue, she connects "Kitty" with Catherine Lescault of Balzac's story, which her lover may have read to her.

Nevertheless, the composition of the film is not a simple chain of associations. Its structure pivots on the narrative from Balzac and the allusion to Picasso. The film evolves by means of the disintegration of the narrative and a progressive emphasis on the ritualistic elements of the minotaur tableau. Eventually the narrative factors integrate with the plastic, making a single ritual of two classical myths, Ariadne and Pygmalion.

Peterson was never completely satisfied with *Mr. Frenhofer and the Minotaur* because he had originally conceived of a more serious rendering of the monologue. He tried it himself, but found the recording incomprehensible. The girl who eventually recited it, was perhaps too glib and heavy of emphasis for Peterson's liking, but in his intimation of the film's failure, he ironically impersonates his protagonist.

When the magazine *Dance Perspectives* published a special issue on dance in films, Peterson contributed a characteristically witty article. He begins with a reference to slow motion, more revealing of his Workshop 20 films than his attempts at filming dance:

> So far as I know, no one has ever shot even a fragment of ballet at 100,000 frames per second, even though by this simple device one minute of shooting would be extended to more than 69 hours of performance. It would be like watching the hour hand of a clock move. The only possible audience would be the performers themselves, and not even the most narcissistic would be able to take all 69 hours.
>
> I mention this fantastic possibility only because slow motion has, almost from the beginning, been the most obvious technical device (instant lyricism) for producing results that have gratified dancers and pleased cameramen.[6]

In *Mr. Frenhofer and the Minotaur* slow motion, along with anamorphosis and ellipsis, solves the problem posed by bad actors. The dancing on the bed, and later the gestures of the old painter as he throws out his guests and then sits to admire his painting, shifting his chair and folding his arms, have an elegance and emphasis in slow motion that they would not otherwise have. He writes:

> If dancing were basket-weaving, there would be no problem about its being relegated to the role of subject matter in a cinematic or televised message. The main difficulty arises, I believe, because dance too is an art of the moving image. It does not relate to film as, for example, scene painting relates to theatre. It is, in effect, a competing medium.
>
> The important thing here is the realization that the art of the moving image did not commence with Fred Ott sneezing for Thomas Edison

with the help of a jar of red pepper, any more than it commenced with
Loie Fuller doing her famous *Bat Dance* in somebody's back yard for an
anonymous cameraman. Both were practitioners of an art as old as hu-
manity, if not older.[7]

We are at the crux of Peterson's genius: his ability to formulate a new
perspective and to test its implications.

Film has the problem of divesting itself of much that it has accomplished; of, in effect, starting over from scratch, returning to a time when
it still had choices in the directions it might take, when it had not yet
discovered its potentiality as a narrative or dramatic medium.
The stupendous past and a Pisgah future are clearly in the hands of
experimentalists, who have nothing to lose by their pains. The traditions
of the art of the moving image are as broad as they are long.[8]

The example he uses to illustrate his new conceptual orientation for film
as an aspect of "the art of the moving image" is Maya Deren's *Choreography for Camera:*

Beatty's celebrated leap had its origins, not in film, but in the so-
called Dumb Ballet of the English stage, of which *Fun in a Bakehouse*
and *Ki Ko Kookeeree* were examples. *The Oxford Companion to the
Theatre* calls the leap "the supreme test of the trick player" throughout
all that part of the nineteenth century when it flourished. In this sense,
Miss Deren (whose leap Beatty's really was) with her leap joined Méliès
and a company that included—not Taglioni, Grisi, or Cerrito—but
Grimaldi, the Lupinos, the Conquests, and those extraordinary "entortil-
lationists" and "zampillerostationists," the Hanlon-Lees.[9]

In the first three films from Workshop 20 the students participated as
actors and observers. In the summer semester of 1949, Peterson decided to
let them participate in the conception of the film. A couple from Virginia
(the Johnsons, as Peterson recalls) suggested that they film a traditional
ballad. Mr. Johnson had just been studying the relationship of old English ballads to their American counterparts. Another student volunteered
a diving suit, and still another her hamsters. The sheer incongruity of the
materials must have awakened the best of the film-maker's problem-
solving and synthetic instincts. An instinct for the synthetic is normally
the gift of a film editor, who is often faced with the task of making a coherent whole out of disparate and insufficient materials; Peterson, however, carried the editing principle into the very conception of his films.

The anthropological principle of Johnson's thesis, that the ballads take on irrational and disjunctive aspects after translocation and the passage of time, became the deliberate aesthetic of Peterson's new film; he would accelerate the disintegration by scrambling two ballads and by employing the type of cinematic ellipsis and association he had developed in his previous film.

The titles of the film mention "The Three Edwards and A Raven," a reference to the mixture within the film of the ballads, "The Three Ravens," and "Edward." Parker Tyler's notes on the Cinema 16 screening of the film in 1950 are particularly fine:

> Peterson came upon two old ballads, "Edward" and "The Three Ravens," the first a Colonial popularization of the Cain-and-Abel legend, and the second concerning three birds that witnessed a fallow-deer carry off a dying knight from the field of battle. In Peterson's film, the mother's passionate hysteria when she learns of "Abel's" murder indicates that at least a symbolic incest is present, a point given more weight when we consider that "Edward" is a variation of an older Scotch ballad, "Lord Randall," about a son who confesses to his mother that he killed his *father*.
>
> In that timeless time in which the true creator does preliminary work —perhaps in a twinkle—Peterson visualized Edward, the murderous "Cain," in kilts and the corpse of "Abel" in a diving suit; thus the two ballads are fused because the diving suit substitutes for the knight's armor in "The Three Ravens." Then he must have felt the violence of a complex insight: a diver's lead shoes keep him on the seabottom, which seems equivalent to that abysmal level of instinct where anything is possible.
>
> When the frantic mother digs up her son from the sand on the shore, she is performing again the labor she had on giving birth to him; the suit itself becomes a sort of coffin. Once more, before he is consigned to the grave, she must hold him close to her. If we can assume all this, as I believe we can, we may go further to note that the tragic emotion is ingeniously modified by two devices: one is the hopscotch game seen parallel with the main action. Every mother of two sons has the problem of balancing her affections, which must be divided between them. This moral action was once anticipated in the physical terms of the hopscotch which she played as a girl: the player must straddle a line between two squares without falling or going outside them. The second device, the boogie-woogie accompaniment with its clamorous chorus, like the first, may have been instinctively rather than consciously calculated by Peterson. It operates unmistakeably: the voices and music supply a savage rhythm for the ecstatic if accursed performers of the domestic catastrophe. It is the lyrical interpretation of the tragedy and suggests the

historical fact that Greek tragedy derived from the Dionysian revel. Lastly we have the sinister implement and symbol of the castration rite, the knife and the bread—perhaps representing the murderer's afterthought rather than part of his deed.[10]

A confusion in Tyler's interpretation reveals the essential ambivalence with which the ritual film is organized and by which it can be interpreted. The three credits in the titles of the film are "Mother," "Father," and "Edward." Furthermore, there is nothing on the soundtrack to indicate a conflict of brothers. What the film does do is reduce the primitive antagonism to abstract absolutes, so that a father-son and brother-brother conflict are equivalent.

The Lead Shoes opens with the hopscotch game. In a film of approximately one hundred shots, this image occurs fifteen times. Its repetition contributes to the frenetic pulse of the work; like the dancing on the mattress in the earlier film, it sets the tone and rhythm of the whole; in this case, fast, jumpy, hysterical movement, often filmed backwards. And like the images from the *Minotauromachia,* it divides the episodes and provides the middle terms of some of its ellipses; yet inversely its appearances are more frequent in the first part of *The Lead Shoes*—for the first two sequences it virtually amounts to parallel montage.

At first, the narrative elements of the film occur strictly as intervals in the hopscotch game. In the subsequent episode the regularity of the intercutting begins to diminish. We see more and more of the mother who runs through the streets (in fast motion), then across the beach (in slow motion), to exhume the diver (in reverse motion).

The complexities begin with the next scene (introduced by another hopscotch image). The mother pulls off the diver's helmet. Then she opens the helmet window and takes out what appear to be three rats. While she is doing this, a barefoot man in kilts enters the frame; blood drips on his feet. Thus is the condensed and elliptical introduction of Edward. We see the helmet become bloody; then we see his bloody hands on his mother's nightgown, and he leaves.

The mother finds a laundry cart and dumps the diver into it so that she can maneuver him more easily. At one point she stops to read a letter. From whom? How did she get it? We do not know.

The penultimate repetition of the hopscotch game (the final occurrence is the last image of the film) introduces the longest and most intricate episode of the film. With the help of strangers whom she had accosted on the street, the mother manages to hoist the diver in his suit up to her balcony and drags him across the floor and onto the bed. She strips him of his suit; and then, in the film's most enigmatic image, lowers the body rather than the suit into the street. The instant the dead man's head hits the sidewalk, Peterson cuts to a bounding loaf of bread, suggesting a ghoulish transubstantiation. Edward picks up the bread. In a series of jump-cuts we see him eating it in an outdoor cafe. In his hands, the loaf becomes a bone. He puts it down; suddenly there is a dog in his chair munching on the bone. These shots occur one after the other without any intercutting.

Here is the point of maximum hysteria on the soundtrack. Peterson put together a jazz band, made up of the faculty of the art school where he taught. His students sing, howl, and chant, with the repetitiousness of a broken phonograph, phrases from the two ballads. He credits the Johnsons, with their experience of ejaculatory singing, for some of the intensity of the soundtrack.

The mother, at the height of her hysteria, accented by a twisting of the anamorphic lens, begins to writhe sexually on top of the empty, prone diving suit. We return to the dog at the table. In a reverse sequence, without actually reversing the photography, the bone becomes bread again, and Edward breaks it. Blood drips onto his plate, and he eats with fiendish relish as the scene fades out and then in on the last shot of the hopscotch game.

In addition to the transference that Tyler notes of diving suit to coffin to knight's armor, Peterson has short-circuited the ballads so that the scavenging mother assumes the role of the fallow deer in "The Three Ravens" who carries off the body of the dead knight; Edward becomes the ravaging ravens, a symbolic cannibal. One of his responses, in the ballad and on the soundtrack, to the endlessly repeated question, "How came that blood on the point of your sword, my son?" was that it was the blood of his dog. Here the dog also crosses over his role to become one of the ravens, eating the bone from the bread.

The Lead Shoes and *Mr. Frenhofer and the Minotaur* are spherical forms with a narrative drift. The narration, such as it is, suggests eternally fixed cycles of behavior; it is aligned with ritual and myth. In both films the vital clues to the visual action are buried in the soundtrack, which also has functions altogether separate from conveying information. The soundtracks dislocate the sequence of events, and through their anticipations of what is to be seen, they magnify the sense of the eternal and the cyclic.

These two films are complementary in another way, using the Apollonian myth of Pygmalion and the Dionysian myth of Pentheus in disguised forms.

One can see in the careers of Peterson and Maya Deren, after their initial bursts of film-making, similar problems for the visionary film-maker twenty years ago. Maya Deren tried to establish a foundation to support the avant-garde film-maker. That work spilled over into an effort to promote the cause of independent film-making and encourage—or sometimes discourage—new film-makers. It was an effort she did not live to see fulfilled. Peterson attempted to channel his radicalism in more conventional directions—the documentary, television, the animated cartoon—and encountered all the well-known problems. With a naive oversimplification that is unusual for him, he has said, "I was trying to solve all those problems, which have subsequently been solved by a *movement.*"

Speaking of James Broughton, Peterson has defined the difference between their sensibilities and their works as that between visual orientation and *mise en scène.* Broughton wrote a brief autobiographical sketch in which he says, "Sidney Peterson introduced me to the magic of experimental film." They are both unusually generous for one-time collaborators when referring to each other's work.

In an essay for *Film Culture 29,* reprinted in the *Film Culture Reader,* "A Note on Comedy in the Experimental Film," written thirteen years after *The Lead Shoes,* Peterson explores the comic roots of the entire avant-garde film movement; what he says scarcely applies to most of the avant-garde film activity between *The Lead Shoes* and the time of writing; naturally, he is referring to himself more than to anyone else. His reflections on the comic lead him to postulate a *dynamiteur* who must start the laughter when there is an ambivalence between the serious and the ridiculous; then he distinguishes between the audience who sees a finished film and the audience of its makers seeing the rushes and rough cuts. The feeling for participation, the sense of the making, the work behind the scenes, reveals his experimentalism in the late forties and early fifties; there is no film-maker for whom that term is more fitting than Peterson. Married to his idea of both experimentation and modernism is the notion of *blague.* He has pointed out the importance of Edmond and Jules de Goncourt's *Mannette Salomon,* a novel about pre-Impressionist studio painting in France, as a central text of the sensibility of modern art, with its distinction between work for friends and for oneself, work to be seen in the studio and work destined for the salons. Out of this distinction emerges a rhetoric of authenticity, an attention to the working process, and a new sequence of myths of the artist.

The myth of the visual sensibility prevails now. Since the Second World War a synthesis has bound the "visual" and the "dynamic" in a supposed opposition to the "literary." Peterson's position toward film-making, like that of Maya Deren, draws energy from that emergent synthesis, although to subsequent "dynamic visualists" in the dialectic of abstraction their works will look "literary." Roughly stated, that position holds that the film-maker should be his own cameraman and editor. The visualist approach implies the synthetic unity of functions which the film industry has jealously separated. A corollary to the same proposition often demands that the film-maker appropriate the whole visual field, leading ultimately to an expressionistic employment of anamorphosis, superimposition, painting on film, and numerous other ramifications of the images as they come out of the camera "factory perfect." The emergence of this aesthetic during the reign of Abstract Expressionism is not a coincidence.

Peterson's distinction between visual organization and *mise-en-scène* boils down to a twin observation about Broughton: that he has a pronounced feeling for the dramatic and that he does not usually operate his own camera. He makes the kind of film where it is possible to employ a cameraman. The theatrical component in Broughton's cinema actually owes its greatest debts to the popular stage of the turn of the century, especially to *tableaux vivants*, mimes, and variety shows. This was a theater which was brought over into the first films. A nostalgia for the origins of cinema vitalizes much of Broughton's film-making.

If Peterson and Deren purified cinema and used its perspectives to imitate the human mind, Broughton took cinema back to the time before the elaborate narratives of the early century in order to recapture the excitement of seeing and showing human bodies in action, apparitions, and sudden disappearances, and to imbue that cinema of action with a more profound sense of the cyclical rhythms of life and the feeling for the essential he equates with poetry. In "What Magic in the Lanterns?" he wrote:

> Modern poetry has been deeply influenced by film. Modern film has
> not sufficiently returned the compliment. . . . Let us be quite clear. To
> ask for poetry in cinema does not mean that one is asking for verse plays
> transferred dutifully to celluloid. . . . No, one is asking rather for the
> heart of the matter. For the essence of experience, and the sense of the

whole of it. For the effort and the absurdity, the song and the touch. For how we really feel and dream—grasped and visualized afresh.

Memorable poetry has always been a dramatic ritual. The coliseum. The cathedral. The theatre. The bullring. For us, the cinema. . . .

Lumiere and Freud: fellow workers. They have given the Absolute a rough time and may have bashed it for good. The single picture is no longer the total picture. The modern mind thinks in associations and relativities, knowing the world's complex merry-go-round is a mixed up truth.[11]

Broughton's deepest feelings are for physical types, for costume and the naked human body, for cyclical rituals, and above all, for the comic. His capacity for laughter is extraordinary. I cannot help thinking that Peterson is writing about him in "A Note on Comedy in the Experimental Film":

I remember once being involved in the production of a film that was made to the accompaniment of howls that would have put the most callous laugh-track to shame. Every bit of film that came back from the lab was enjoyed I won't say hysterically but with remarkable thoroughness.[12]

In that same essay, Peterson writes, "the best introductions to the extravagances of experimental cinema are not the works of Ford, Eisenstein or de Mille. They are those silent comedies, first French, then American, in which people used to experience, until their ribs ached, the ferocity and heartiness of the farcical view of things." What he is saying here is even truer of Broughton's work than of his own. They both share the ferocious aspect of the comic, although it is much more on the surface in Peterson's rituals of destructive self-realization, dismemberment, and *omophagia*.* Yet the credit for reviving the methods of the silent comedians—the crew and a group of performers ready for anything, free to romp and spontaneously create a comic situation—belongs to Broughton. In his quest for the origins of cinema it is natural that he would feel an affinity for slapstick

---

* The Greek terms *sparagmos* and *omophagia* refer to stages in obscure Orphic rites as attested in Plutarch and early Church fathers and discussed in E. R. Dodds' *The Greeks and the Irrational*. The terms literally mean the "ripping apart" and the "eating of flesh." This rite surfaces in literary history with *The Bacchae* of Euripides, in which Dionysiac rites of animal *sparagmos* culminate in the cannibalistic death of Pentheus. In this book I have used the term *sparagmos* to underline the ritual origins of the numerous scenes of dismemberment in the American avant-garde cinema. I have also used it for both explicit thematic manifestations of the rite and for those cinematic tropes which more obliquely allude to it.

comedy, the genre which preserved the original vitalism of cinema the longest, certainly into his childhood. His transformation of the silent comedy into an avant-garde picaresque influenced much of what Ron Rice did and what Robert Nelson still does, following him with increased liberation, even anarchy.

Broughton is no anarchist. It is significant that he links the names of Freud and the Lumières; for, although he is deeply committed to Jungian, rather than Freudian psychoanalysis, the nostalgia for the origins of cinema is fused in his work with an ironic quest for the origin of his own psychic development. His films are all tempered with a view of the cyclic and ritualistic nature of human events and antagonisms, but one must see his works of the late sixties and early seventies, where ritual becomes explicit, elliptical shifts become extreme, and the sexual quest becomes more immediate, to isolate these elements in the earlier films. In *Four in the Afternoon* (1951), he showed four vignettes, each built around a single image with a verse soundtrack. He outlined the organization in a note:

> A quartet for poems moving
> A film in four movements
> Each movement is a variation on the same theme
> The movements are at four ages and four stages
>   1. the girl of 10
>   2. the lad of 20
>   3. the woman of 30
>   4. the man of 40
> Each movement is in itself a poetic movement
> Each movement blends its movement with music and verse.[13]

In a more elaborate series of notes he assigned musical terms to the four parts: "Game Little Gladys," *Allegro;* "The Gardener's Son," *Adagio;* "Princess Printemps," *Scherzo;* "The Aging Balletomane," *Lento.* The entire film derives from his book of poems, *Musical Chairs.*

For each of the four film poems there is a distinctive cinematic trope; with "Game Little Gladys" it is stop-motion manifestation and disappearance of possible lovers; in the case of "The Gardener's Son" it is a composition-in-depth with the boy in the foreground and the women he desires in the background. At one point he comes towards the camera, walking barefoot almost in slow motion, as a blonde girl passes him walking in the opposite direction. We never see her face. As she recedes, he turns to watch her go. A statue of Venus is cut into this scene. Later we see him in the foreground spying on three girls in a clearing, dancing like the Graces.

The success of this episode, like the weakness of the subsequent one, "Princess Printemps," is a matter of *mise-en-scène*. It is the successful organization of movement with an emotional vector. In the autobiographical sketch I have already quoted from, he says, "I have learned more about the writing of poetry from music than from literature. And more about the making of films from dance than from cinema." The difficulty with "Princess Printemps" is that it is too much dance, or too much theater, and not filmic enough.

The final section, "The Aging Balletomane," may be the finest. In a rocking chair looking out upon a lower class backyard with tiers of laundry hanging out to dry, the has-been dancer, who seems much older than the forty years the film-maker assigns to him for the symmetry of his outline, rocks in slow motion conjuring up a magical reverie with opera glasses instead of a wand. Reverse motion is the trope of this episode, a natural choice of mechanics for unrolling the past. So in a backward leap a ballerina floats onto the pedestal before him; she performs the reverse of a series of classic movements, as the old man, in a series of slow motion leaps following the trajectory of his rocking, tries to approach her. She dissolves away before he can touch her. Then we see him running backwards into his chair twice, either to reinvoke her or to taste the sweetness of his apparition.

This film is a crucial case of the fusion of verse and film within the American avant-garde. It is unfortunate that Broughton himself was not present at the famous Cinema 16 discussion of the fusion of these two modes on October 28, 1953. The text of the discussion between Willard Maas, Maya Deren, Parker Tyler, Arthur Miller, and Dylan Thomas has been printed in *Film Culture* and in the *Film Culture Reader*. Thomas and Miller were not prepared to contribute significantly; but for Maya Deren it was an occasion to make a theoretical statement which throws a great deal of light on the aspirations of poets making cinema in the 1950s. She set out to define the essence of poetry:

> The distinction of poetry is its construction (what I mean by "a poetic structure"), and the poetic construct arises from the fact, if you will, that it is a "vertical" investigation of a situation, in that it probes the ramifications of the moment, and is concerned with its qualities and its depth, so that you have poetry concerned, in a sense, not with what is occurring but with what it feels like or what it means. A poem, to my mind, creates visible or auditory forms for something that is invisible, which is the feeling, or the emotion, or the metaphysical content of the movement. Now it also may include action, but its attack is what I would

call the "vertical" attack, and this may be a little bit clearer if you will
contrast it to what I would call the "horizontal" attack of drama, which
is concerned with the development, let's say, within a very small situation
from feeling to feeling. Perhaps it would be made most clear if you take
a Shakespearean work that combines the two movements. In Shakespeare, you have the drama moving forward on a "horizontal" plane of
development, of one circumstance—one action—leading to another, and
this delineates the character. Every once and a while, however, he arrives at a point of action where he wants to illuminate the meaning to
this moment of drama, and, at that moment, he builds a pyramid or in-
vestigates it "vertically," if you will, so that you have a "horizontal" development with periodic "vertical" investigations, which are the poems,
which are the monologues.[14]

Her examples within the avant-garde film were both from Willard Maas's
films:

It's things of this sort that, I believe, occur in the work of Mr. Maas,
who has done that to a certain extent in his last film, *Image in the Snow*,
where the development of the film is very largely "horizontal," that is,
there is a story line, but this is illuminated constantly by the poetic commentary so that you have two actions going on simultaneously. Now this,
I think, is one of the great potentials of film and something that could
very well be carried and developed much further, and I think that one of
the distinctions of that film and also of *Geography of the Body*, is that
it combines these principles. I think that this is a way of handling poetry
and film, and poetry *in* film.[15]

In the earlier of these two films, *Geography of the Body* (1943), Maas,
his wife Marie Menken, and the poet George Barker filmed details of each
other's bodies with dime-store magnifying glasses taped to a 16mm camera that the animator Francis Lee had left with them when he entered the
army. Barker wrote and recited a surrealistic poem for the film. Its allusions to exotic and mystical travels suggest, with the synchronized con-
currence of images from ambiguously defined zones of the body, the image of the body as a landscape and as a continent.

A few simple observations can be made now, in the light of historical
perspective, on the emergence of the film with poetic commentary in the
forties and fifties, and its disappearance in the late sixties. In the first
place, the idea of a complex rendering of the momentary experience provides us with a central clue. By 1953 Maya Deren had started to use sound
in her films and was considering cross-cultural visual analogies as a means
of probing the moment in depth. As usual, she was forecasting what

would happen years later, as will be evident in my discussions of Kenneth Anger and Stan Brakhage in the 1960s. At another point in the same discussion she gave the following example about sound:

> And so, in that sense, they would be redundant in film if they were used as a further projection from the image. However, if they were brought in on a different level, not issuing from the image, which should be complete in itself, but as another dimension relating to it, then it is the two things together that make the poem. It's almost as if you were standing at a window and looking out into the street, and there are children playing hopscotch. Well, that's your visual experience. Behind you, in the room, are women discussing hats or something, and that's your auditory experience. You stand at the place where these two come together by virtue of your presence. What relates these two moments is your position in relation to the two of them. They don't know about each other, and so you stand by the window and have a sense of afternoon, which is neither the children in the street nor the women talking behind you but a curious combination of both, and that is your resultant image, do you see?[16]

Was she actually considering the equivalent of a *Meshes of the Afternoon* in sound? Her example shows a sophistication beyond the present discussion, since vertical montage of separate realms is formally quite different from poetic commentary. Her ideas during this panel are both an indication of the way the poetic film was viewed by its makers in the early fifties and of future developments.

In Broughton's next film, *Loony Tom, the Happy Lover*, a Chaplinesque elf-man skips through fields, farms, and estates, kissing and chasing the girls and bringing lovers together. Tom's sing-song poem bursts in on the film as an ecstatic nursery rhyme, a subjective hallelujah where gesture cannot reach. This film is an appendix to *Four in the Afternoon* and a homage to the silent comedy.

The visionary film-maker in America does not go on quietly doing his work indifferent to considerations of exhibition, distribution, and response, even though that may be his goal. The crisis that Peterson faced in 1950, when he decided to try to make a documentary, Broughton encountered two years later. It took a form traditional to American artists—extended exile in Europe. One can say that the deflection of Art in Cinema away from the exhibition of "experimental" films in the early 1950s accelerated the break-up of the film-making nucleus in San Francisco. But beyond the local factors, there was the sheer economic struggle of raising even enough money for the most minimal productions, which made it next to impossible for aspiring film-makers to see a future of self-produced work.

In England, with the help of his friends Lindsay Anderson and Basil Wright, Broughton obtained financing for a 35mm feature film, *The Pleasure Garden* (1953), based on the materials of his earlier films but with an obvious dramatic structure. The success and failure of *The Pleasure Garden* itself is a topic beyond the scope of this book. What interests us is the effect it had on the film-maker. It almost ended his career. In his own words, it "spoiled" him for any low-budget production after that.

In 1961 Broughton married. It was an extravagant, eclectic ceremony performed by the writer and onetime priest Alan Watts, following a civil service in San Francisco's City Hall, and preceding a sea ritual of Broughton's invention. He asked Stan Brakhage to record all the ceremonies on film as a keepsake. At that time Broughton had definitively given up film-making. Two years later, when he was at Knokke-le-Zoute, Belgium, as a judge for the third International Festival of the Experimental Film, he still had no plans to edit the wedding footage or to make a new film, unless by a stroke of good fortune he were to receive one of fifteen grants of ten thousand dollars which the Ford Foundation was offering film-makers that year. He did not get one. Only Kenneth Anger, of those film-makers discussed here, received one, although almost all applied.

When Jacques Ledoux, the director of the Cinémathèque Royale de Belgique and organizer of the Experimental Film Festival, came to the United States in 1967 to seek films for the next festival, he conceived the idea of giving a small amount of color film stock to a number of previous participants in the hope that they would make new films for his festival. Broughton responded to the challenge. He engaged William Desloge as a cameraman and made *The Bed* (1967).

In form it is another picaresque romp, asking, "What can happen to and on a bed?," with overtones of the short cycle of man's life as opposed to the life of the human species. The first of many naked people to occupy the wandering bed represents Adam; through stop motion, Eve is born at his side. In slow motion they chase each other. Jump cuts breaking their graceful motion—this is the most balletic of his films and is very diversified in terms of its internal motions compared with his earlier works—they move off-screen, to return just before the end. Pan appears; he plays a saxophone in a tree to charm the bed. Then Broughton himself sits on the mattress in a lotus position contemplating a snake. Another man, in slow motion, leaps over the bed, with a movement that recalls *Choreog-*

raphy for Camera and makes explicit the debt that he had been acknowl-
edging for years.

The tableaux and brief scenes are extensive: a wedding party, a cowboy
sleeping in his boots, an ancient couple, a naked girl and a motorcyclist, a
somnambulist who rides off on a horse, a ball game, a card game, pot
smoking, faun and satyr, a black odalisque, a doctor who becomes a priest
to administer last rites, Death; numerous sexual arrangements, men and
women together, men and men, two men and a girl, an androgyne. At the
end of the film Adam and Eve return; the film-maker and his snake appear again; then the empty bed departs across the field as it came.

There are no words with this film; only the music of Warner Japsus.
The poem had disappeared as a possible soundtrack for avant-garde films
in the late 1950s. One of its functions, the presentation of the first person,
had been usurped by camera perspectives and associational montage. The
most ardent exponent of contemporary poetry as a guide to film construction, Stan Brakhage, argued that cinema should elaborate its poetics in
the field of the visual.

Broughton himself is one of the exceptions who continued to use the
poetic voice into the seventies. *The Bed* had been unusual for him. In
Nuptiae (1969) he utilized fragments of the marriage service and a song
he wrote for the occasion. *The Golden Positions* (1970) combines spoken
text with songs and choral odes; *This Is It* (1971), more than any other
film of Broughton's, depends fundamentally on the interactions of visual
images and the ironic cosmological poem on its soundtrack; and finally,
Dreamwood (1972) opens with a brief poem, defining the quest of that
remarkable work, the last of the trance films.

Broughton's productivity since 1967 attests to his complete rebirth as a
film-maker. Although *The Bed* did not gain a prize at the festival for
which it had been made, it had an unusual success for an avant-garde film,
in part because of its nudity and in part because of its gaiety. Its reception,
which included some festival prizes and a brief commercial distribution,
inspired and encouraged Broughton. He accepted a post teaching film and
concentrated on the medium in a way that he had never done before. The
fourteen years between *The Pleasure Garden* and *The Bed* had been a
time of radical change in the situation of visionary film-makers. They were
now teaching; they were distributing their films in cooperatives; some were
receiving grants from major foundations; they were making more films
than before; the film-maker had become the artist as hero, a role previously reserved for poets and painters in this country.

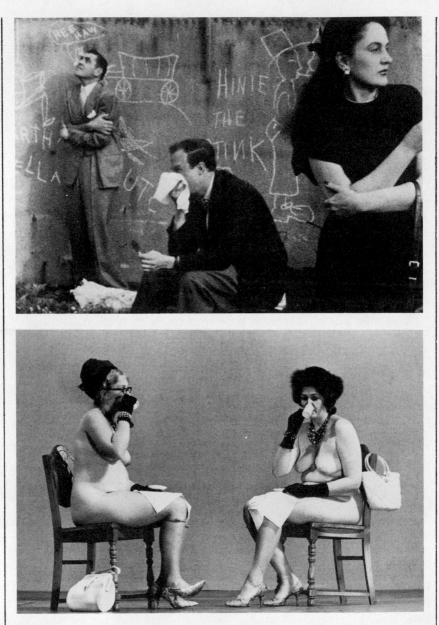

Tableaux from James Broughton's *Mother's Day* and *The Golden Positions*.

In *The Golden Positions* Broughton refined the format of *The Bed* by increasing the number and the variety of the tableaux, by exploiting the tension between scenes of movement and of stillness, by organizing the brief scenes into thematic movements, and above all, by giving the whole film a rigorous structure—his most rigorous and complex since *Mother's Day*. As that first film had played with the form of the family album, *The Golden Positions* imitates the Mass, opening with a Gospel reading, which the film-maker calls "The Lesson" in his script, describing the three essential positions of "standing, sitting, and lying." The film begins with a navel in close-up. "Let us contemplate," Broughton speaks in liturgical tone as the camera zooms back to frame the whole naked male form. In the subsequent sections, "Anthem," "Creation of the Body," "A Short History of Art and Religion (Adam and Eve to Pieta)," "Secular Life," "Domestic Eroticon," and "Finale: The Positions of the Gods," Broughton playfully exhausts his repertoire of parodies of the human cycles.

This Is It is more concise and direct in its parody of cosmology than *The Golden Positions* had been of the Mass. Broughton's vehicle is a "home movie" of his son, Orion, playing naked with a large red ball in a yard. The camera first isolates the ball amid grass. "In the beginning it was already there," Broughton says on the soundtrack, and he continues his parody cosmology with other shots of the isolated ball, withholding the introduction of the child until the voice of God proclaims, "It needs something that looks more like Me." *This Is It* refuses to identify the camera's perspective with the child's vision. It insists, in words and chants, on the absolute resignation of metaphysics to the present moment.

> This is it.
> This is really it.
> This is all there is.
> And it's perfect as it is.

As such, it is gently subversive of his friend, Stan Brakhage's, Romantic struggle with the loss of the primal vision of childhood and his subsequent attempt to reconcile that loss with imagination in a new cosmological and epistemological epic in his films from *Anticipation of the Night* (1958) to *Dog Star Man* (1961-65). Broughton's strong attachment to Brakhage's work, a decisive factor in his return to film-making, leaves room for fundamental poetic disagreement.

In editing the footage that Brakhage shot of his wedding, Broughton steeped the work in ritual. He intercut drawings, paintings, and symbols of marriage and union from oriental and alchemical sources in a network of images corresponding to the three phases of the wedding. He constructed the sequence of the film in a conscious movement into and out of the flat space of these insertions by rhythmically incorporating flattened perspectives of the rituals themselves. First he uses a classical montage technique, cutting from a close-up marble figure in the frieze of the city hall to a series of deeper shots of the whole facade of the building, including the frieze; in that suddenly deepened space, the Broughtons walk toward the camera. Then he flattens the space again by freezing the frame. Later in the film he uses other freeze-frames, superimpositions, and distorted shots to sustain the interplay and equate images from the actual wedding with the traditional flat pictures of the alchemical wedding, Orpheus, Buddha, and the revolving Taeguk.

The project he submitted to the Ford Foundation in his unsuccessful bid for a grant in 1963 had been a cycle of four films to be called *Unclassifiable Wonders*. The four films he completed over five years approximate his plan for that project. They are *The Water Circle, The Golden Positions, The Dance of Shiva,* and *The Sacred Marriage:*

> The first of these is a hallelujah ode to nature. The second is a little documentary on mankind. The third is a cinematic dance of the Holy Spirit. The fourth is a mystical love rhapsody. . . .
>
> These four films I conceive as a kind of mandala, which attempts to give some illuminating experience of the unclassifiable wonders that are the mysteries of life.
>
> They represent my urgent vision of what I would next like to realize in cinema: a vision of our world and our humanity as a participation in a divine entertainment, equally compounded of beauty, folly, grief and joy.[17]

At least as far back as the time of making *The Bed,* Broughton contemplated a serious attempt at mythopoeia. "The subject of *Dreamwood* had obsessed me for years," he wrote. "I first conceived shaping it as a variation on the Theseus myth." But once he started the film, with the help of a Guggenheim Foundation grant, he quickly replaced the scheme of the traditional myth with a quest of his own invention. *Dreamwood* alludes to several myths—Hippolytus, Apollo, Sisyphus, and Narcissus are seen passing in the background of different scenes, but these allusions become witty intrusions into the otherwise thoroughly personalized vision; they are, in fact, the only vestiges of ironic self-mockery which abound in all of Broughton's earlier films. As a total work, *Dreamwood* occupies the space between the trance film and the mythopoeic cinema, much as Maya Deren's *Ritual in Transfigured Time* had, but from the retrospective rather than the anticipatory position. No single film in the whole of the American avant-garde comes as close as this one to the source of the trance film, Cocteau's *Le Sang d'un Poète*.

The film begins with its hero in a spiritual crisis in his tower room. In pursuit of his vision of a female presence, he leaps from the tower. He follows an ominous couple to the end of a pier, and then is ferried alone across an expanse of water to an enchanted island where he endures terrible trials and undergoes a series of sexual initiations. Broughton's note on the film elaborates upon the events, but it also obscures the direct linearity of the film:

DREAMWOOD: SCHEMATA

The Poet in his tower, at an impasse.
Out of dreams comes the Call to Adventure: his anima abducted by the First Parents.
Beginning of the Quest: the Night Sea Journey.
The Other Shore: a strange bare island.
Before he can enter the Forest of Dreamwood he must pass three guardians of the mysteries:
> the helpful Crone,
> the Terrible Father-Mother of his past who would hold him back,
> the Mother Superior of the forest who prepares him for entry.

FIRST INITIATION: the vision of the green chapel of the Goddess is disturbed by manifestations of nymphs & children, culminating in the encounter with Artemis bathing. For approaching her, he pays a price. Wakes up outside.

SECOND INITIATION: returning to the wood, he overcomes the Amazon guardian (Hippolyta). In the forest Alchemina has sport with him, to lead him deeper. Finally he encounters Lilith who takes her pleasure with him. Out of the cold frenzy he wakes again outside the forest.

THIRD INITIATION: the guardian of the gate this time is a woodsman. In their encounter they discover they are "brothers." The woodsman takes the poet to the place where he may climb up to where the Old Queen Hecate dwells. Overcoming his fear, he enters her to be reborn. He survives this ordeal and this time awakens inside the forest.

FOURTH INITIATION: he finds himself again in the green chapel. This time it is welcoming and the presence of the Goddess is felt. She calls to him as to a lover. He disrobes and makes offerings to her, from his body. These are accepted, and he then makes love to her body, the Earth itself.

CODA: thanks to this union, his anima soul is contained within him. And this sacred marriage is blessed by sun and moon.[18]

The naming of the deities might suggest a complex mythography such as I shall describe in Kenneth Anger's *Inauguration of the Pleasure Dome* or Gregory Markopoulos' *The Illiac Passion*. In fact, the identification of the figures in Broughton's film is almost unimportant. The three sexual initiations are performed by a single actress in slightly different costumes. The axe murder of the hermaphrodite, the *sparagmos* of the hero by naked children, the love making, the rebirth, the offerings of saliva, urine, feces, and sperm, and the final incorporation of the sun and the moon are so vividly and directly depicted in the film that their mythological analogues are superfluous.

Broughton employs a rhetoric of apparitions throughout the film. He generally achieves them by dissolving a new figure into a scene that has already been set up. When the protagonist reaches the end of a pier, a rowboat and a Charon-like oarsman suddenly appear at his feet. The female presence, which the film-maker calls his "anima," sometimes appears through such a dissolve, but for the most part she is seen in sudden superimpositions. The apparitional quality is furthermore affirmed by the continual references to him as a dreamer. At the end of each major trial of initiation, as at the very beginning of the film and in the prelude to the tower episode, we suddenly find him waking from sleep. In those waking moments he is clothed, although just before we had seen him naked.

Cocteau froze time by showing his entire vision between two frames of a tower's collapse. Broughton undermines sequential time by dwelling on a black-and-white photograph during the initial scene in the tower where the hero lives. We discover at the end of the film that that photograph—of him in the nude leaping with arms spread—was a still of the final image, his ecstatic leap commemorating the conclusion of his quest, the union of male and female within him. When he made his version of the trance film with such vitality in 1972, the film-maker too folded time and created the work which most clearly illuminates his films of twenty-five years earlier.

4

THE MAGUS

Kenneth Anger, more than any other avant-garde film-maker, is the conscious artificer of his own myth. He is also the author of *Hollywood-Babylon*, a slander catalogue amounting to a phenomenology of the myth of the scandal in Hollywood. On October 26, 1967, the *Village Voice* carried a full black page with this in white: "In Memoriam Kenneth Anger 1947-1967." Some readers presumably must have thought the maker of the well-known *Scorpio Rising* had died. Others who had been watching his films for more than twenty years must have been puzzled.

A few days before that, Anger had arrived in New York, after a catastrophe in San Francisco, on his way to the massive March on the Pentagon that year. He showed Jonas Mekas and Leslie Trumbull, the Secretary of the Film-Makers Cooperative, the cans of his unreleased films, some made before *Fireworks* (1947) and some, primarily unfinished, made afterwards. As he unreeled the yards of film for burning, Mekas tried to persuade him to allow a copy of everything to be saved for scholars. When his arguments failed, Mekas left, unable to bear the sight of that much destruction. How much and what Anger burned that day I do not know. He said that he would make no more films, would change his name, and would leave America for ever.

The dates that Anger gave for his obituary corresponded at that time to his public career as a film-maker. He had been making films since he was eleven: *Who Has Been Rocking My Dream Boat* (1941), *Tinsel Tree* (1941-42), *Prisoner of Mars* (1942), *The Nest* (1943), *Escape Episode* (1944), *Drastic Demise* (1945), *Escape Episode* (shorter sound version, 1946); but his first work to be released and remain in distribution was *Fireworks*. Claiming that he would make no more films, he left a corpus of four essential works—*Fireworks* (1947), *Eaux D'Artifice* (1953), *Inauguration of the Pleasure Dome* (1954, revised 1966), and *Scorpio Rising* (1962-63)—plus a fragment of *Kustom Kar Kommandos* (1965). In this chapter I shall consider these works as comprising a distinct phase of Anger's career, for he has gone on to make new films and to revise old ones.

The catastrophe which had generated the obituary occurred on September 21 of that year at the Straight Theater in Malachi, California, when 1600 feet of his work in progress, *Lucifer Rising*, had been stolen from a locked trunk. The film was to have been projected as part of a benefit toward its completion at an event called The Equinox of the Gods. There was no other copy of that footage; the stolen film was an original.

The news of the theft, reports of his destruction of films at the Film-Makers Cooperative, the appearance of the death notice, his expatriation, the change of name, and the statement that he would make no more films seemed at that time like a simple cause and effect: the loss of his work in progress had taken its emotional toll on the film-maker. So that when one suddenly saw *Invocation of My Demon Brother* in 1969, it was easy to think that he had gotten over his trauma and was back at work.

Seen from the perspective of three more years, it is clear that Anger was not reacting to the loss of his film with public hysteria, but that the theft precipitated a change which Anger himself would describe as "magickal," the spelling preferred by his master in matters occult, Aleister Crowley. At the time of the Straight Theater theft or shortly afterwards, Anger must have had the kind of experience which ritual magicians describe as "a change of order," the initiation into a higher degree. In his autobiography, Crowley describes several such changes, which involve the death of the previous personality, a change of name, and a rebirth. Thus the perplexities of the death notice become clearer; and clearer too when we take into consideration the reports that "Kenneth Anger" is a taken, rather than a given name. Crowley also chose the Aleister, and kept it for convenience even after his rebirths and new names. The events of the fall of 1967 were, for Anger, of a major religious scope, and they will be significant in my interpretation of the subsequent changes in his work.

He was born in southern California in 1930. According to his interviews, he played the role of the child prince in Max Reinhardt's movie of *A Midsummer Night's Dream* and had Shirley Temple for a dancing partner at cotillions of the Maurice Kossloff Dancing School. For him more than for any other avant-garde film-maker Hollywood is both his matrix and

the adversary. In his excellent article on Anger's films,[1] Tony Rayns cites
the Olympian analogy from Anger's *Hollywood-Babylon:* "There was
Venus and Adonis only called Clara and Rudy; there was Pan called
Charlie; there was even old Bacchus named Fatty and maimed Vulcan
named Lon. It was an illusion, a tease, a fraud; it was almost as much fun
as the 'old-time religion'—without blood on the altars. But the blood
would come." The ambivalent mixture of satire and homage with which
that book is written amounts to an exercise in fascination characteristic of
everything to which Anger devotes himself. Scandal, evil, violence, and
Fascism, like Hollywood, are centers of fascination for Anger, and his
films are the fields in which the dialectic of that fascination is played and
fought.

Of Anger's very early films there are no descriptions in print. Lewis
Jacobs, in his contribution to *Experiment in the Film,* is our sole source
of information about *Escape Episode:*

> Less concerned with cinematic form and more with human conflict
> are the pictures of Kenneth Anger. *Escape Episode* (1946) begins with
> a boy and girl parting at the edge of the sea. As the girl walks away she
> is watched by a woman from a plaster castle. The castle turns out to be
> a spiritualists' temple, the woman a medium and the girl's aunt. Both
> dominate and twist the girl's life until she is in despair. Finally in a ges-
> ture of defiance the girl invites the boy to the castle to sleep with her.
> The aunt informed by spirits becomes enraged and threatens divine retri-
> bution. The girl is frustrated, becomes bitter and resolves to escape.
>
> The quality of the film is unique and shows an extreme sensitivity to
> personal relationships. But because the thoughts, feelings and ideas of
> the film-maker are superior to his command of the medium, the effect is
> often fumbling and incomplete, with parts superior to the whole.[2]

Anger's notes on his films are often the best guide to their mysteries; in
every case they are interesting. In *Film Culture* 31, he provided the following filmography of his work before *Fireworks:*

WHO HAS BEEN ROCKING MY DREAMBOAT (1941)

7 min. 16mm B&W. Silent. Filmed in Santa Monica, California. *Credits:*
Conceived, Directed, Photographed and Edited by Kenneth Anger. *Cast:*
A dozen contemporaries recruited from the neighborhood. *Synopsis:* A
montage of American children at play, drifting and dreaming, in the last
summer before Pearl Harbor. Flash cuts of newsreel holocaust dart across
their reverie. Fog invades the playground; the children dropping in mock
death to make a misty landscape of dreamers.

TINSEL TREE (1941-42)

3 min. 16mm B&W. Hand-tinted. Silent. Filmed in Santa Monica. *Credits:* Conceived, Directed, Photographed and Edited by Kenneth Anger. *Cast:* A Christmas Tree. *Synopsis:* The ritual dressing and destruction of the Christmas Tree. Close-ups as the branches are laden with baubles, draped with garlands, tossed with tinsel. Cut to the stripped discarded tree as it bursts into brief furious flame (hand-tinted gold-scarlet) to leave a charred skeleton.

PRISONER OF MARS (1942)

11 min. 16mm B&W. Silent. Filmed in Santa Monica. *Credits:* Conceived, Directed, Photographed and Edited by Kenneth Anger. Camera Assistant: Charles Vreeland. Settings, Miniatures, and Costume Designed and Executed by Kenneth Anger. *Cast:* Kenneth Anger (The Boy-Elect from Earth). *Synopsis:* Science-Fiction rendering of the Minotaur myth. A "chosen" adolescent of the future is rocketed to Mars where he awakens in a labyrinth littered with the bones of his predecessors. Formal use of "serial chapter" aesthetic: begins and ends in a predicament.

THE NEST (1943)

20 min. 16mm B&W. Silent. Filmed in Santa Monica, Westwood and Beverly Hills. *Credits:* Conceived, Directed, Photographed and Edited by Kenneth Anger. *Cast:* Bob Jones (Brother); Jo Whittaker (Sister); Dare Harris—later known as John Derek in Hollywood—(Boy Friend). *Synopsis:* A brother and sister relate to mirrors and each other until a third party breaks the balance; seducing both into violence. Ablutions and the acts of dressing and making-up observed as magic rite. The binding spell of the sister-sorceress is banished by the brother who walks out.

ESCAPE EPISODE (1944)

35 min. 16mm B&W. Silent. Filmed in Santa Monica and Hollywood. *Credits:* Conceived, Directed, Photographed and Edited by Kenneth Anger. *Cast:* Marilyn Granas (The Girl); Bob Jones (The Boy); Nora Watson (The Guardian). *Synopsis:* Free rendering of the Andromeda myth. A crumbling, stucco-gothic sea-side monstrosity, serving as a Spiritualist Church. Imprisoned within, a girl at the mercy of a religious fanatic "dragon" awaits her deliverance by a beach-boy Perseus. Ultimately it is her own defiance which snaps the chain.

DRASTIC DEMISE (1945)

5 min. B&W. Silent. Filmed in Hollywood on V-J Day. *Credits:* Photographed and Edited by Kenneth Anger. *Cast:* Anonymous street crowds. *Synopsis:* A free-wheeling hand-held camera-plunge into the hallucinatory reality of a hysterical Hollywood Boulevard crowd celebrating War's End. A mushrooming cloud makes a final commentary.

ESCAPE EPISODE (SOUND VERSION) (1946)

27 min. Music by Scriabin.

This shorter edition makes non-realistic use of bird wind and surf sounds, as well as Scriabin's "Poem of Ecstasy" to heighten mood.[3]

The corpus of Anger's work I have selected begins with *Fireworks*. His note on it is cryptic; it assumes the viewer already knows the film!

FIREWORKS (1947)

15 min. 16mm B&W. Sound (Music by Respighi). Filmed in Hollywood. *Credits:* Conceived, Directed, Photographed and Edited by Kenneth Anger. Camera Assistant: Chester Kessler. *Cast:* Kenneth Anger (The Dreamer); Bill Seltzer (Bare-Chested Sailor); Gordon Gray (Body-Bearing Sailor); crowd of sailors. *Synopsis:* A dissatisfied dreamer awakes, goes out in the night seeking 'a light' and is drawn through the needle's eye. A dream of a dream, he returns to a bed less empty than before.[4]

As we watch the film we hear Anger speaking a prologue: "In *Fireworks* I released all the explosive pyrotechnics of a dream. Inflammable desires dampened by day under the cold water of consciousness are ignited that night by the libertarian matches of sleep, and burst forth in showers of shimmering incandescence. These imaginary displays provide a temporary relief."

The opening image is of water; a burning torch is dipped into it. Then there is a close-up of a sailor. As the camera dollies back from his face we see in flashes of illumination, like lightning, that he is holding the protagonist, the dreamer, in his arms. After a fade-out, the camera observes the same dreamer in bed. Another dolly movement shows he is alone. He stirs, wakes. A pan of the room reveals a marble or plaster hand with a broken finger. Images of the dreamer's hands moving on his own body suggest masturbation. We see in a long shot of the whole room that he has a monstrous erection under the covers. Then he takes out an African statue which breaks the phallic illusion. Photographs are scattered on the floor of the earlier shot of the sailor holding him. From these photographs it is clear that he is bruised and bloody.

Once he is out of bed, the camera pans up the dreamer's pants; he zips his fly just as the camera eye passes by; then to his face, framing a composition with the broken hand in the background. The camera follows him fluidly as he picks up the photos, throws them into the cold fireplace, and puts on his shirt. Another composition in depth frames the dreamer between the primitive phallic statue in the foreground and mirror in the far back as he takes out U.S. Navy matches. He leaves his room through a door marked GENTS in grotesquely large print.

The scene shifts as he passes through the door from compositions-in-depth, with regular camera movements, to fixed shots of the protagonist highlighted in black, formless space. A muscle-bound sailor appears before the painted backdrop of a bar. The dreamer approaches him and watches as he flexes his bare arm and chest muscles in close-ups. When the dreamer asks him for a light, the sailor punches him, knocks him off the screen, then twists his arm behind him. Suddenly, they are before the fireplace in the original room. The sailor takes a torch of sticks out of the fire and lights the cigarette for the dreamer. Then he picks up his cap and leaves.

Again the scene shifts to the dreamer highlighted against black. From above, the camera looks down on the hero, smoking. He turns abruptly and, in the next shot, sees a gang of sailors. They come at him, passing from light through darkness into light again. The camera follows their shadows. They rush him, carrying chains.

The following scene of orgasmic violence is constructed out of close-ups of the dreamer's body isolated in darkness and shots of the sailors performing violent acts just off screen. From above we see fingers shoved into the dreamer's nostrils, and blood shoots out of his nose and mouth. A sailor twists his arm, and he screams hysterically. A bottle of cream is smashed on the floor. With a broken piece a cut is made in his chest; hands separate the pudding-like flesh to reveal a heart like a gas meter. His chin is framed in the bottom of the black screen like a frozen wave. Cream poured from above flows over it into his mouth. Cream washes his bloody face; then it flows down his chest. There is a pan of empty urinals. The GENTS door opens, but no one is behind it. Then the sailor of the opening sequence appears; the camera dollies to his face in the reverse of its initial movement. In the next shot, he opens his fly and lights a roman candle phallus which shoots out burning sparks.

The fire of the roman candle becomes the flame of a wax candle on the tip of a Christmas tree which the dreamer wears like a giant hieratic helmet. He bows toward the camera, enters his room, and lights the photographs in the fireplace with the burning tree. We see him sleeping again, as in the opening. But now there is a fire in the fireplace; and a pan of the bed shows someone in it beside him. Scratches over the filmed images hide his face from us. The pan continues to the plaster hand, now

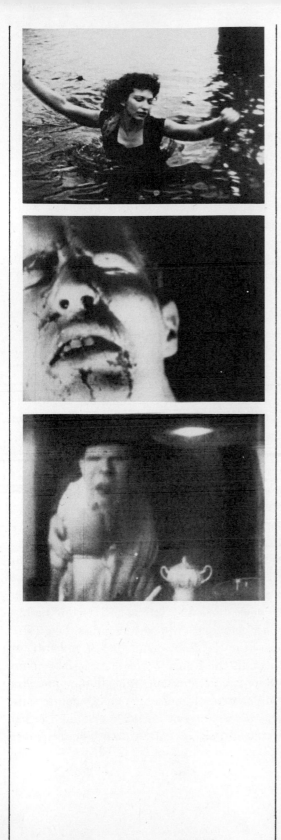

The psychodramatic trance film: Maya
Deren in *Ritual in Transfigured Time;*
Kenneth Anger in *Fireworks:* Stan Brakhage
reflected in the metal of a toaster in
Flesh of Morning.

repaired so that all its fingers are whole. The hand falls into the water, where the torch had been quenched in the first shot. "The End" appears in superimposition over the water.

Fireworks is a pure example of the psycho-dramatic trance film: the film-maker himself plays out a drama of psychological revelation; it is cast in the form of a dream beginning and ending with images of its hero as a sleeper; finally, the protagonist is the passive victim of the action of the film. Actually, there are two dreams in *Fireworks*. The first is the brief disjointed opening couplet of fiery images—the extinguishing of the torch in water and the dolly shot of the sailor holding the beaten dreamer amid flashes of lightning and peals of thunder. A slow fade-out, the only one in the film, marks the end of this sequence, which we can presume to be a dream, because the subsequent image is of a sleeper; this is further confirmed a minute later when we see the pictures of the sailor and the dreamer scattered beside the bed, as if they were the objects of a masturbation fantasy before sleeping.

The day and night of the falsely wakened dreamer betray a dream structure before the final confirmation that the whole film has been a dream in the last images of the sleeper. The exaggerated GENTS sign; the substitution of a gas meter for a heart; the repeated sudden changes of locale from barroom to fireside, from men's room back to bedroom are standard in the cinematic vocabulary of the dream. Finally, the dramatic substitution of a roman candle for a penis, from which the film derives its title, suggests that we have entered the mind of the sleeper rather than that the sleeper has awakened to the causal world.

There is a comic or satiric element in the hyperbolic symbolism of this film, as in almost everything Anger makes. The roots of Anger's aesthetic lie in French Romantic decadence of the late nineteenth century. Like his predecessors, he favors an art which argues with itself. For him it is not a matter of vacillation. Anger makes his films with an intense involvement in his subject and often an equally intense criticism of their limitations. The simultaneity of the prophetic and the satiric distinguishes the greatest Romantic art, and the failure of the classically-oriented taste and criticism of our times has been not to credit the Romantics with a sense of humor and to ridicule their achievements with the same ridicule they practiced on themselves. The crucial difference, of course, is that Romantic satire measures the limitations of its heroes in their quest for absolute freedom while classical taste calls even the limited movement toward those ends grotesque.

In *Fireworks*, poetic irony plays considerably less of a part than in all of Anger's later films. In *Scorpio Rising* it reaches its climax, as I shall show. *Fireworks* may be the strongest of the trance films. It is truly remarkable that a seventeen-year-old film-maker could make so intense an analysis of himself at a time when any allusion to homosexuality was taboo in the American cinema. But it is all the more remarkable that he invested his film with the critical humor of the false erection, the gas meter heart, the firecracker penis, and the Christmas tree miter. In 1947 Anger had not yet developed his feeling for the opposition of contraries or for total ambivalence as a structural principle in cinema. But the ironic sensibility had begun to manifest itself.

Later Anger wrote, "This flick is all I have to say about being seventeen, the United States Navy, American Christmas, and the Fourth of July."

Before we go on to consider his later films, I would like to call attention to certain textural properties of *Fireworks*. The opposition between scenes in depth, with prominent foreground and background objects, and scenes of figures isolated in blackness has been indicated in my synopsis. There is a considerable amount of camera movement early in the film. Each movement is very steady and is punctuated so as to distinguish two visual facts. The opening dolly shot shows first the sailor, then reveals that he is holding a bloody body in his arms. The dolly across the bed shows first that the dreamer is asleep, then that he is alone. The pan up his pants as he is getting dressed shows him zipping up his fly, then fixes his torso in relation to the broken hand in the background. The dolly at the end of the film has three phases; first the dreamer is back in bed; then there is someone beside him; and finally the broken hand is repaired.

In the sequence between the hero and the sailors, there is no camera movement. All the figures are in white within black spaces. Anger arranged lights so that the gang of sailors comes forward and passes from light through darkness into another light. For the most part the shots of the sailors and of the hero are separate and their interaction is created through montage. Once from above we see them surround him in a circle. In another shot the sailors twist an arm, but we know it is the hero's only through the editing. In order to reinforce the logic of his montage, Anger makes careful use of off-screen looks and movements. By coordinating one with the other he creates a sense of the continuity of space outside the film frame. This becomes particularly important to him in creating illusions of extreme violence.

It was a long time before he finished and released his next film, *Eaux D'Artifice* (1953). Its title might be translated "Water Works" ("Fireworks" would be "Feux d'Artifice" in French), suggesting the dialectical relation it has to the earlier film. Here we see the first mature development of the ironic sensibility and the balancing of contraries as a formal endeavor. One must not forget that although these two films are six years apart, Anger thinks of his films as a whole rather than as totally independent works. He is constantly revising them, subtly altering their relationships to one another. For the special program of his complete works at the Spring Equinox of 1966, he hand-tinted the candle atop the Christmas tree in *Fireworks* and the scratched-out face of the man in bed beside the dreamer to underline the relationship with *Eaux d'Artifice*, which ends soon after the appearance of a hand-tinted fan.

In *Eaux D'Artifice* we see a baroque maze of staircases, fountains, gargoyles, and balustrades. A figure in eighteenth century costume, flowing dress, and high headpiece hurries through this environment while the camera zooms into and away from the mask-like faces water spirits carved in stone or studies in slow motion the fall of fountains and sprays. Just before the end of the film, the heroine flashes a fan, then turns into a fountain, and her silhouetted form dissolves into an identical fountain arrangement.

The entire film has a deep blue color, achieved in the printing through the use of a filter. The sole exception is the brief flashing of the fan which the film-maker tinted green by hand. The whole film is successfully tuned to a fugue by Vivaldi. Unlike *Fireworks*, its interest is not narrative, but primarily rhythmic, and its elements are the pace of the heroine, the speed of the zooms, the slowness of the retarded waterfalls, and above all, the montage in relation to the music.

In his early notes for the Cinema 16 catalogue, Anger describes this film as "the evocation of a Firbank heroine," and her flight as "the pursuit of the night moth." His new note is:

EAUX D'ARTIFICE: SUMMER SOLSTICE 1953
"Pour water on thyself: thus shalt thou be a Fountain to the universe. Find thou thyself in every Star! Achieve thou every possibility!" *Khaled Khan, The Heart of the Master, Theorem* V. Hide and seek in a nighttime labyrinth of levels, cascades, balustrades, grottoes, and ever-gushing, leaping fountains, until the Water Witch and the Fountain become One. Dedicated to Pavel Tchelitchev. *Credits:* Conceived, Directed, Photographed, and Edited by Kenneth Anger. *Cast:* Carmillo Salvatorelli

(The Water Witch). *Music:* Vivaldi. Filmed in the gardens of the Villa D'Este, Tivoli, by special permission of the Italian Department of Antiquities, on Ferrania Infra-Red. Printed on Ektachrome through a Cyan filter. The Fan of Exorcism hand tinted by Kenneth Anger with Spectra Color.[5]

An earlier version of this note adds that Thad Lovett was the camera assistant and that the heroine's costume was designed by Anger.

Anger has said that he chose Carmillo Salvatorelli, a midget, for the part in order to create a play of scale. The allusion to Firbank in the earlier note can be traced to the end of Ronald Firbank's novel, *Valmouth*, where Niki-Esther, at the time of her marriage, went into the garden in pursuit of a butterfly, dressed in her wedding gown and carrying her bouquet.

According to Tony Rayns:

> Anger's grandmother was a costume mistress in silent films, and it was she who, working with Reinhardt, got Kenneth into the 1935 *Midsummer Night's Dream*. In his early youth Anger used to love dressing up in her costumes ("my transvestite period") and it was this that inspired the costume in *Eaux d'Artifice*, worn there by a circus dwarf Anger met in Italy. The Lady ("a Firbank heroine in pursuit of a nightmoth") owes her plumes to Anger's Reinhardt costume, and her light-headedness to her past in Anger's childhood.[6]

Eaux D'Artifice plays the same role in the evolution of Anger's style that *Choreography for Camera* played in Deren's. Both films are what I have labeled the single-image film, and both culminate in a union between protagonist and landscape. That Deren and Anger, as well as Curtis Harrington and Stan Brakhage in their generation of film-makers, should follow the same course of formal invention is not an indication that one copied the other; it shows, however, the options open to serious, independent film-makers. Furthermore, the achievement of one artist in a given form—say the trance film—did not exhaust that form for the others. Many of the film-makers of that generation went in similar directions in their work at different times. The sequence of forms discovered by Maya Deren in her six films between 1943 and 1958 started a pattern that extended from the late 1940s through the 1960s. To this parallel evolution of different film-makers I shall return repeatedly in this book.

Between the completion of *Fireworks* and of *Eaux D'Artifice* Anger had initiated many projects. In 1948 he attempted to make a feature-length color film about faded Hollywood stars and their fantasy mansions.

Soon after that the footage for *The Love That Whirls*, with simulated Mexican rituals in the nude, was destroyed by the laboratory to which it was sent for processing because they deemed it obscene.

He moved to Paris in 1950, where he stayed on and off for the whole of that decade. There he began to shoot a 35mm black and white film called *La Lune des Lapins*, which he called "a lunar dream utilizing the classic pantomime figure of Pierrot in an encounter with a prankish, enchanted Magic Lantern," but he ran out of money. The next year, 1951, he filmed in 16mm a version of Cocteau's ballet, *Le Jeune Homme et La Mort*, in the hope of raising money to make a 35mm film of the whole ballet. That financial endeavor also failed.

For two years after that he prepared to film Lautréamont's *Les Chants de Maldoror*, again incorporating professional dancers from the Marquis de Cuevas's and Roland Petit's companies. He got no further in the production than rehearsals and tests. It was following the collapse of *Maldoror* that he made *Eaux D'Artifice*. A year later, in 1954, he returned to California to settle a family inheritance and made *Inauguration of the Pleasure Dome* with the money.

There have been at least four versions of *Inauguration of the Pleasure Dome* at different times. The first, which no one to my knowledge has seen, was edited to a soundtrack by Harry Partch, the American composer and inventor of several exotic instruments. The version that was in distribution in the late 1950s and up to 1966 had Janáček's *Glagolithic Mass* for a soundtrack. For the second Experimental Film Festival, held during the Brussels World's Fair of 1958, he made a version of the film with three-screen synchronous projection for the climactic final two-thirds of its forty minutes. In 1966 he issued his Sacred Mushroom version of the film, subtitled "Lord Shiva's Dream," at the occasion of his Spring Equinox program at the Film-Makers Cinemathèque in New York. This version began with a reading of the whole of Coleridge's *Kubla Khan*, from which Anger derived the original title of the film, while still pictures of Aleister Crowley and images from the repertory of occult symbols and talismans appeared on the screen. To the first part of the film Anger had added some more photographs of Crowley in superimposition and images of the moon at strategic points. It was in the final third of the film, where once the images on two flanking screens had appeared, that he made his major changes. Superimposition, sometimes many layers deep, replaced the earlier linear development and montage. To the multiplication of his characters he added shots from Harry Lachman's *Dante's In-*

ferno, mainly crowd scenes of burning, printed in red, and most of *Puce Moment*, a fragment of the unmade *Puce Women*, which Anger had completed in 1949, distributed until 1963, and then withdrew from the public. He also mixed sounds of screaming with the music of Janaček, which he otherwise retained entirely. It is this version only which is in distribution today.

The opening sequence of *Inauguration of the Pleasure Dome* is one of Anger's finest cinematic achievements. A slow pan up the title card, with gold letters and lines against black, blends into a slow pan up over the edge of a bed, suggesting the breaking of dawn. The camera passes a constellation of glittering crystalline objects too close to be in focus. As the pan continues to ascend we perceive that it is a string of jewels we have been looking at. Now they are being slowly raised and wrapped around the hands of a yet unseen figure on the bed.

A slow dissolve brings us closer to the hands, and the camera pans past them to the right to reveal a table with a pipe and several rings. This sequence continues for several minutes; most of the separate shots are joined by dissolves which underline the slow and hieratic quality of the gestures of the waking figure who, Anger tells us, is called Lord Shiva. He swallows the string of jewels, rises from the bed before an elaborate dragon mirror, passes through several doors and then beyond a Japanese curtain to perform his ritual cleansing before a three-sided mirror. It is here, as he leans forward to the mirror, that we see his first transformation: his face fades out, and we see a man-like beast with long fingernails filmed in red light. From Anger's notes, we know this is the hero's metamorphosis as Beast 666 of the Apocalypse, or simply the Great Beast. After this brief interjection, the image fades out again and the film returns to Lord Shiva at his prayers. A few moments later, the Great Beast reappears, this time in a yellow light. Shiva finishes his preparations and retraces his steps through the labyrinth of doors he had previously entered.

The lavish color of the rooms; their exquisite ornamentation; the slow movements of the camera and of Shiva; his sensual handling of objects; and the slightly elliptical sequence of dissolves which both cuts short each action and blends it into the next combine with the opening of Janaček's *Mass* to create a sequence of excessive richness and to set an intense expectation for the film.

Another upward pan, somewhat faster than the opening shot, reveals a woman in brilliant white clothes and make-up with flaming red hair isolated in blackness. She is Kali and the Scarlet Woman, according to

Anger's notes. She turns her head to the right, then to the left, looking off-screen. In *Inauguration of the Pleasure Dome* the off-screen glance has the crucial function of relating the positions of the film's numerous characters to the central figures of Shiva and Kali. To a great extent the revisions of the Sacred Mushroom version have obscured this principle in the final third of the film, where superimposition has assumed the structural burden formerly based upon the geometry of off-screen looks and movements.

With the turn of her head the Scarlet Woman sees Shiva at his door. She turns again, and he has become the Great Beast. In a series of dissolves she discloses a tiny statue of a devil in her hands and offers it to him. In his hands it turns to fire. With that fire the Great Beast lights her cigarette, or "joint," for her. As she puffs it, we see a superimposed photograph in blue tint of Aleister Crowley smoking a pipe.

In the opening passage of the film, Anger used drapery, painted walls, and rich costumes as the instruments of color control and color rhythm. In the following scenes, in which Shiva in his several guises receives the gifts of the gods, Anger gets his essential color alterations from filtered lights with which he spotlights his figures in black space. This recalls the two kinds of lighting and evocation of space in *Fireworks* and the color control of *Eaux D'Artifice* achieved through filtering (in that case, in the printing of the film, not in the lighting of the scene as in *Inauguration*).

At this point in analyzing the film it would be useful to quote Anger's notes:

INAUGURATION OF THE PLEASURE DOME
Sacred Mushroom Edition   Spring Equinox   1966
otherwise known as 'Lord Shiva's Dream'

"A Eucharist of some sort should most assuredly be consumed daily by every magician, and he should regard it as the main sustenance of his magical life. It is of more importance than any other magical ceremony, because it is a complete circle. The whole of the force expended is completely re-absorbed; yet the virtue is that vast gain represented by the abyss between Man and God.

"The magician becomes filled with God, fed upon God, intoxicated with God. Little by little his body will become purified by the internal lustration of God; day by day his mortal frame, shedding its earthly elements, will become the very truth of the Temple of the Holy Ghost. Day by day matter is replaced by Spirit, the human by the divine; ultimately the change will be complete; God manifest in the flesh will be his name."—*The Master Therion (Aleister Crowley), Magick in Theory and Practice*.

Lord Shiva, The Magician, wakes. A convocation of Theurgists in the
guise of figures from mythology bearing gifts: The Scarlet Woman,
Whore of Heaven, smokes a big fat joint; Astarte of the Moon brings
the wings of snow; Pan bestows the bunch of Bacchus; Hecate offers the
Sacred Mushroom, Yage, Wormwood Brew. The vintage of Hecate is
poured: Pan's cup is poisoned by Lord Shiva. The *Orgia* ensues; a
Magick masquerade party at which Pan is the prize. Lady Kali blesses
the rites of the Children of the Light as Lord Shiva invokes the Godhead
with the formula, *"Force and Fire."* Dedicated to the Few, and to
Aleister Crowley; and to the Crowned and Conquering Child. *Credits:*
Conceived, Directed, Photographed and Edited by Kenneth Anger. Cos-
tumes, Lighting and Make-up by Kenneth Anger. Properties and Setting
courtesy Samson De Brier. *Cast:* Samson De Brier (Lord Shiva, Osiris,
Cagliostro, Nero, The Great Beast 666); Cameron (The Scarlet Woman,
Lady Kali); Kathryn Kadell (Isis); Renata Loome (Lilith); Anais Nin
(Astarte); Kenneth Anger (Hecate); the late Peter Loome (Ganymede).
Music: Janáček. Filmed at Shiva's house, Hollywood, California, and an-
other place. Printed by Kenneth Anger in Hand Lithography System on
A, B, C, D, and E rolls, on Ektachrome 7387.[7]

A note from the Cinema 16 New York premiere in 1956 gives a somewhat
different synopsis of the same action:

The Abbey of Thelema, the evening of the "sunset" of Crowleyanity.
Lord Shiva wakes. Madam Satan presents the mandragore, and a glamor
is cast. A convocation of enchantresses and theurgists. The idol is fed.
Aphrodite presents the apple; Isis presents the serpent. Astarte descends
with the witch-ball, the Fairy Geffe takes wing. The gesture of the Juggler invokes the Tarot Cups. The Elixir of Hecate is served by the Somnambulist. Pan's drink is venomed by Lord Shiva. The enchantment of
Pan. Astarte withdraws with the glistering net of Love. The arrival of the
Secret Chief. The Ceremonies of Consummation are presided over by
the Great Beast-Shiva and the Scarlet Woman-Kali.[8]

In that cast of characters Aphrodite is played by Joan Whitney, the
Somnambulist by Curtis Harrington, Renata Loome is called Sekmet
(rather than Lilith), and Pan is listed as Paul Andre, although still other
credits identify him as Paul Mathison, who also painted the title card.

The ambiguity of roles and synopses points out the inessential nature
of the identifications. *Inauguration of the Pleasure Dome*, like Deren's
The Very Eye of Night and Markopoulos' *The Illiac Passion,* both made
after it, is a mythographic film in its aspiration to visualize a plurality of
gods. What is more important than the identification of characters in
each of these difficult films is the way in which the film-maker sustains a

A

B

C

D

Anger's *Inauguration of the Pleasure Dome:*

(A) Lord Shiva eats the jewels.

(B) The Great Beast lights the "joint" of the Scarlet Woman, with a super-imposition of Aleister Crowley.

(C) The arrival of Pan.

(D) Drinking the elixir.

E

F

G

H

(E) Pan poisoned.

(F) A mirror image superimposition from the *orgia*.

(G) Lady Kali blesses the rites before the fires of Hell.

(H) Lord Shiva invokes the godhead.

vision of the divine in cinematic terms. Both *Inauguration of the Pleasure Dome* and *The Illiac Passion*, with their multiplication of divinities and their resolution through a central figure, present versions of the primary Romantic myth of the fall of a unitary Man into separate, conflicting figures, a myth that dominates the prophetic writings of Blake and finds expression in the *Prometheus Unbound* of Shelley.

Each of the divine figures of the film offers a gift to Shiva in one of his forms after the lighting of the Scarlet Woman's "joint." Aphrodite passes from pink to orange light bearing a golden apple, which she gives to the hero in his toga costume as Nero. The Scarlet Woman turns to see Isis feeding Shiva a snake as he wears his Egyptian costume of Osiris. They are both bathed in a yellow light. When the Scarlet Woman next turns she watches Lilith pass candles and artificial butterflies (in orange tints) to offer a jewel to Cagliostro (so I take his fur-capped metamorphosis). This passage is made up of sixteen shots and eight dissolves.

The subsequent sequence, which parallels the dramatic entrances of Pan and Astarte, has a more complex structure. We see for the first time at this point the preview of a kind of superimposition that Anger employs repeatedly: two images, mirror inversions of each other, seen together. Later in his employment of this kind of superimposition of the Scarlet Woman, she will be seen looking both left and right, Janus-like. Here it is an abstract pattern created by placing a balcony backdrop over its inversion. When the superimposition ends, we see Astarte on a swing in the foreground and Shiva in the background near the balcony.

Astarte leaves her swing and Pan enters the frame carrying grapes, which he gives to Shiva. Shiva eats one and tosses the bunch out of frame; in the connecting shot the flying grapes land on Nero's foot as he lies on a couch. The Scarlet Woman, Lilith, and Aphrodite watch Pan lustfully as he comes forward. A slow series of dissolves cuts between Pan's boots, as he crosses the patterned floor, and tableaux of the other gods; when he passes him, Nero bats his eyelashes seductively.

With a gradual shift of interest, the emphatic entrance of Pan becomes the equally emphatic entrance of Astarte. She lowers her mesh-stockinged feet on to a fur cushion; Shiva unwinds her blue dress; as she lifts her arms over her head in a circular motion, passing momentarily out of screen, a pearl in her hand changes first into a silver ball, and then, with another revolution, into a silver globe suggesting the moon. She gives it to Shiva. In two dissolves the globe shrinks again into a pearl, and he

swallows it like a pill. Suddenly he sprouts tiny wings and smiles effemi-
nately.

In a scenic breakdown originally in French, presumably by Anger himself, of the three-screen version of the film, the action I have so far described represents the first act ("The Talisman") in three scenes:

scene 1 In the Abbey of Thelema, Lord Shiva wakes.
scene 2 The Goddess Kali presents the mandragore, and the enchantment begins.
scene 3 An assembly of magicians and theurgists transformed into
Saints: Aphrodite, Isis, Lilith, Astarte offer their talisman,
potent with the Powers of the Age of Horus: the God of Ecstasy
and Violence, the God of Fire and Flame. Pan arrives bearing
Hermes' gift.

That much of the film was to be on a single screen. The following two
acts, of three and two scenes respectively, were on a triptych.

What Anger called the second act ("The Banquet of Poisons") begins
as the Great Beast, with the Scarlet Woman beside him, snaps his fingers
and Cesare, the Somnambulist, taken from Weine's *The Cabinet of Dr.
Caligari*, appears behind his hand. The film-maker Curtis Harrington
plays this role in white make-up and black tights. Like his prototype in the
1919 film, he walks stiffly with arms outstretched. The Beast points and
the sleepwalker leaves the frame. The next shot, joined to the previous one
by a dissolve, is one of the most impressive in the film: the Somnambulist
passes a row of candles and approaches a black wall, upon which are
drawn Egyptian cats. As he nears the wall a passage opens in it, and he
passes into a bright and silken sanctum where his zigzag movements are
only occasionally glimpsed by the camera. In the present version of the
film, Anger has superimposed a cartoon of Crowley's face over the image
so that the door opens not only to the sanctum but into Crowley's head.

Another dissolve brings us into the sanctum where Cesare takes an
amphora from the masked figure of Hecate. He pours a powder-like substance from the amphora for the Beast and the Scarlet Woman. Shiva
makes a magical gesture (Anger identified it as the Tarot of the Juggler)
and two chalices rise by his sides. Aphrodite holds one, Isis the other.
They drink, toast Shiva, and laugh. The first of the Janus-like superimpositions of the Scarlet Woman appears here. In this passage, the montage
returns again and again to Shiva's eyes, glancing demonically from his
green-tinted face. Soon the child Ganymede makes his first appearance,

pouring drinks for Shiva, Pan, and Lilith, who are gathered in a single composition with three different tints—Shiva, purple, Pan, yellow, Lilith, red. Shiva pours poison into Pan's drink from the hidden chamber in his ring. Pan drinks and clutches his neck.

At this point the linear development of the film evaporates; the multiple superimposition begins. There are no more dissolves; the pace changes from slow to frenzied. Only at strategic moments, as will be pointed out, does a single image appear on the screen without superimposition. Up to this point there have been 114 different shots, according to my working synopsis taken while screening the film. Of these, 61 have been joined by dissolves which tend to retard the force of montage. There have been ten instances of superimposition.

In the remaining portion of the film, there are alternations between two, often three, and sometimes even more layers of images. A change in one layer is not necessarily synchronous with a change in any of the others. Therefore a fugal pattern develops which escapes accurate analysis because of its speed and complexity.

After the poisoning of Pan we see the gods wearing masks and laughing in triple superimposition. In all, there are a dozen different guises. When the Scarlet Woman takes off her skeleton mask, there is another one underneath it, and still another skeleton image painted on her face. We now see as a new layer of imagery the parade of fancy dresses that opens *Puce Moment*. At this time Hecate makes her first appearance. One version of Anger's synopsis says the elixir was stolen from Hecate, which accounts for her sometimes violent gestures. Another synopsis has Hecate offering the potion.

The drinking continues, the ringed hand reappears, and the parade of costumes ends. The single image of Shiva's face, now with a violet coloring, punctuates the clusters of doubling and tripling images. From now until the end of the film he is in absolute control of the orgy.

Astarte unfolds her net over the changing images of gods and goddesses. Suddenly we see Pan, without superimposition, possessed by the poison. There is a fade-out. We return to a triple superimposition of Astarte dancing with her net over the images of the revelers. Then a veiled figure emerges from the sanctum over the superimposition of the gold and black title card. Again the action returns to Astarte's dance, sometimes seen from three different camera depths simultaneously. Pan is attacked and beaten with feathers. The goddesses' feet kick and press his chest, while the first images of the hell fire of *Dante's Inferno* enter the texture of the film. This is the fated *sparagmos* for which the orgy was convened.

Then the Scarlet Woman appears in her manifestation as Kali, seated on a throne with one breast bare. The superimposition ceases as she surveys the scene. The hell fires shoot up behind her. Sometimes her image appears over that of Shiva whose hand gestures control the orgy; other times we see three different views of her at once.

The camera dollies in on the single image of the veiled figure dancing wildly. The pace of the zooms on the masked dancer increases with the intensity of Pan's *sparagmos* until, at the end of the film, Kali raises her hand in benediction, and Shiva smiles and gestures with his hands. After a montage of occult symbols, including a pentacle and the eye of Horus, the image fades out on a single shot of Shiva bringing his hands together.

Even with the introduction of superimposition, the disjunctive editing of the dances of Astarte and the masked figure and the introduction of material from two completely different films, the scenario of the Sacred Mushroom version is not so different from the outline of the three-screen projection, in which the three scenes of the second act ("The Banquet of Poisons") are,

scene 1 The Somnambulist brings the Elixir of Hecate. Communion of the Saints: "You are Holy; whose nature is unformed; You are holy, the great and powerful Master of light and darkness."

scene 2 The drink of Pan is poisoned by an aphrodisiac-initiatory powder that Shiva had hidden in a chamber of his ring. The intoxication of Pan.

scene 3 Astarte's return with the net of Love.

The third act ("The Ceremonies of Consummation") has two scenes:

scene 1 The arrival of the Secret Chief. The invocation of the Holy Fire. The Infinite Ritual.

scene 2 The ceremonies of consummation are presided over by Shiva and Kali, The Whore of Babylon and The Great Beast of the Apocalypse.

Anger told *Take One* magazine about the sources of this film in the work of Crowley:

The film is derived from one of Crowley's dramatic rituals where people in the cult assume the identity of a god or a goddess. In other words, it's the equivalent of a masquerade party—they plan this for a whole year and on All Sabbaths Eve they come as the gods and goddesses that they have identified with and the whole thing is like an improvised happening.

This is the actual thing the film is based on. In which the gods and goddesses interact and in *The Inauguration of the Pleasure Dome* it's the legend of Bacchus that's the pivotal thing and it ends with the God being torn to pieces by the Bacchantes. This is the underlying thing. But rather than using a specific ritual, which would entail quite a lot of the spoken word as ritual does, I wanted to create a feeling of being carried into a world of wonder. And the use of color and phantasy is progressive; in other words, it expands, it becomes completely subjective—like when people take communion; and one sees it through their eyes.[9]

In a British newspaper, *Friends*, he spoke of the costumes of *Scorpio Rising*, with a relevance to the concerns here:

Even in fancy dress films the people are still as I see them and how they see themselves. In Rio you have people who live in shanty towns and save up all year for the fab costume that they will wear for the Carnival, and that's what they live for the whole year. For that spangled moment: and during the Carnival when they're all dressed up, that's really them, it's not them when they are working, sweeping the street or doing somebody's washing.[10]

In a film of the complexity of *Inauguration of the Pleasure Dome* one has to turn from the film-maker's program notes to the myth of the film itself. Everything in the film, as it is now available in the Sacred Mushroom edition, must be measured in terms of the figure of the Magus. The essential tension of the film rests on the resolution of the Magus' several aspects into a unified, redeemed man, or man made god, to use Anger's terms. The final shot of the film is the turbanned Shiva completing the semi-circular hand gesture he had been making throughout the climax of the film; the Magus' apotheosis, the Great Beast, Nero, Cagliostro, and the winged Geffe are reunited. Not only they, but all the actors of the film are subsumed in his power and glory. If, as Anger's remarks suggest, these characters are most themselves when assuming the *personae* of gods, they sacrifice their "spangled moment" to the central energy of the Magus; for *Inauguration of the Pleasure Dome* is not an apocalypse of liberated gods or chaotic demons, nor is it a perversion of the myth of Pentheus and Dionysus, in which the god is devoured, although Pan is as much the "eucharist" in this film as the potion of Hecate. What divinity the others obtain comes through the Magus.

For the spectator, the Sacred Mushroom version fuses the perspectives

of Shiva with Pan. The opening of the film, with a solemnity and slowness of action suggestive of the traditional Japanese Noh and Kabuki
theaters, dramatizes the hierophant's point of view. Immediately after the
poisoning of Pan, the style switches to the delirium of the intoxicated
god, with a punctuation of shots of Kali and Shiva from the sober perspective of control. Disregarding the notes again, we see that Shiva's most
spectacular act is the transformation of the Scarlet Woman into Kali
when she reappears as the diabolic female in the superimposition sequence
over the flames of hell. Ultimately, she too must be subsumed into the
Magus.

The recurrent theme of the American avant-garde film is the triumph
of the imagination. Nowhere is this clearer than in the films of Anger.
Here it triumphs over the superficiality of the masquerade, the campiness
of the actors, and the shabbiness of Hollywood's reconstruction of Dante's
hell. The opposition of the reality principle and the imagination, which I
mentioned in discussing *Fireworks*, operates more covertly in this film. It
is in his next completed work, *Scorpio Rising*, that this dialectical process
reaches its maturity and becomes the organizing principle of the film.

There is nearly a decade between the two works. We do not know what
formal evolution might have been shown in his version of *The Story of
O*, which he prepared in the late fifties but never shot. In a history of
ruined projects, stolen films, and works aborted due to insufficient funds,
the abandonment of *The Story of O*, in part because one of the actors
turned out to be involved in a kidnapping, reaches outrageous dimensions.
In 1955 Anger managed to complete a documentary film of the erotic
paintings Crowley made for his Thelema Abbey in Sicily, but that film is
either lost or Anger does not want to show it. In 1960 J. J. Pauvert published his *Hollywood-Babylon*. In 1962 Anger returned to the United
States, and while living in the Brooklyn apartment of the film-makers
Willard Maas and Marie Menken, began to make *Scorpio Rising*.

Scorpio Rising is built around the ironic interaction of thirteen popular
songs with the same number of schematic episodes in the life of a motorcycle gang. The quotation from Crowley with which Anger prefaces his
note to the film refers to his use of the songs:

> It may be conceded in any case that *the long strings of formidable words
> which roar and moan through so many conjurations have a real effect in
> exalting the consciousness of the magician to the proper pitch*—that they
> should do so is no more extraordinary than music of any kind should do
> so.

Magicians have not confined themselves to the use of the human voice. The pan-pipe with its seven stops, corresponding to the seven planets, the bull-roarer, the tom-tom, and even the violin, have all been used, as well as many others, of which the most important is the bell, though this is used not so much for actual conjuration as to mark stages in the ceremony. Of all these the tom-tom will be found the most generally useful. (*The Master Therion, Magick in Theory and Practice.*)

The body of the note divides the film into four parts:

A conjuration of the Presiding Princes, Angels, and Spirits of the Sphere of MARS, formed as a "high" view of the Myth of the American Motorcyclist. The Power Machine seen as tribal totem, from toy to terror. Thanatos in chrome and black leather and bursting jeans. *Part I:* Boys & Bolts: (masculine fascination with the Thing that Goes). *Part II:* Image Maker (getting high on heroes: Dean's Rebel and Brando's Johnny: the True View of J.C.). *Part III:* Walpurgis Party (J.C. wallflower at cycler's Sabbath). *Part IV:* Rebel Rouser (The Gathering of the Dark Legions, with a message from Our Sponsor). Dedicated to Jack Parsons, Victor Childe, Jim Powers, James Dean, T. E. Lawrence, Hart Crane, Kurt Mann, The Society of Spartans, The Hell's Angels, and all overgrown boys who will ever follow the whistle of Love's brother. *Credits:* Conceived, Directed, Photographed, and Edited by Kenneth Anger. *Cast:* Bruce Byron (Scorpio); Johnny Sapienza (Taurus); Frank Carifi (Leo); John Palone (Pinstripe); Ernie Allo (The Life of the Party); Barry Rubin (Pledge); Steve Crandell (The Sissy Cyclist). *Music:* Songs interpreted by Ricky Nelson, Little Peggy March, The Angels, Bobby Vinton, Elvis Presley, Ray Charles, The Crystals, The Ron-Dells, Kris Jensen, Claudine Clark, Gene McDaniels, The Surfaris. Filmed in Brooklyn, Manhattan, and Walden's Pond, New York, on Ektachrome ER.[11]

With *Scorpio Rising* Anger began to refer to his films as "Puck Productions." A credit with that name appears before anything else in the film. On it we see a Bottom-like ass with a banner reading, "What Fools these Mortals Be," a reference not only to *A Midsummer Night's Dream* but also to Anger's own childhood performance in the Max Reinhardt film version. In the penultimate section of *Scorpio*, as the motorcycle race is in full swing, we see a brief shot of Mickey Rooney, as Reinhardt's Puck, cut into the film as if he were cheering on the riders. Several critics have pointed out how Anger subscribes to Eisenstein's concept of intellectual montage in this film. In this brief instance of the injection of the image from the Hollywood film into the action of his own film, Anger establishes a series of intellectual vibrations which reach to the core of his dialectical vision. Anger's collage, like the quotations in Eliot's poetry, compounds ironies. In the present case, we are struck first by the wit of the juncture; then, as we remember the antics of Shakespeare's Puck, we realize that he is cheering them on to their deaths; and finally, we recognize the ironic loss of intensity implicit in the use of Hollywood's, not Shakespeare's, Puck, Mickey Rooney.

Lengthy analysis diffuses the strength of rapid montage. The importance of Anger's film is the clarity and depth of his vision and the skill with which he can present complex ideas and sudden qualifications through the editing of tiny bits of film. Another aspect of this Eisenstein-ian approach is the vertical montage or the interaction of sound and picture as the lyrics of the songs—ironic because they are "found objects" from popular culture—comment upon and qualify our thoughts about the visual images. The intensity and complexity of the ironies vary greatly from song to song; nevertheless, the end of one song and the beginning of another is a dramatic highlight at every transition, and the spectator awaits eagerly the detonating image which will fuse the song to the episode.

Each of the thirteen sections has a comic highlight or a dramatic surprise. Often the very first shot of a new sequence marks a visual collision with what we have been watching; often too Anger holds his punch shot half a minute until the central phrase of the song's lyrics has been uttered so that the interaction of picture and sound will be synchronous. The force with which he achieves this is concentrated in the central episodes of the film.

The relative autonomy of the different song-and-picture sections calls to mind a serial form. In many of his interviews, and in his autobiographical schema for the Anger Magick Lantern Cycle of Spring 1966, he names Flash Gordon as one of his central heroes. For Anger, the Flash Gordon serials seem to function on a level of inspiration similar to that which the Surrealists derived from the serials of Louis Feuillade (*Les Vampires, Fantomas, Judex*). By releasing the first segment of his new version of *Lucifer Rising* (1972) separately, Anger has moved further into the form of the serial.

The first four sections of *Scorpio Rising* form an introduction to the film. From the very first shots—the unveiling of a motorcycle in a garage, then a series of horizontal and vertical pans of bike parts, lights, shining chrome fenders, young men oiling gears—it is clear that the texture of the

film is unlike anything Anger has done before. This is a film without
superimpositions, filtered lights, or isolated figures in blackness. Anger
still uses the coordination of the off-screen look, especially in collaging
foreign material. The low-key lighting makes possible a lush pastel view of
motorcycle cushions, lights, and portions of chrome with stars of light
reflecting off them. As usual the camera movements are steady and slow,
but the rhythm of the film as a whole is much quicker than anything
Anger had ever made before.

The comic moment of the first scene comes at its end. Framed by
quick zooms in on a plaster scorpion, the back of a cyclist rises before a
red wall, and as he ascends, we can gradually read the title *Scorpio Rising*
spelled out in silver studs on the back of his leather jacket. When he is
standing erect, we see "Kenneth Anger" studded at the belt line. He
turns around, revealing his bare chest and navel as the song and episode
end. The subsequent segment simply prolongs a single metaphor: the
montage compares motorcyclists tightening bolts to a child winding up
three toy cycles and letting them roll at the camera. The song "Wind-Up
Doll" underlines the comparison.

The unveiling, greasing, shining, and completing of the motorcycles in
the introductory series of episodes exaggerate the preparatory stage of the
film, a stage which has always been important for Anger, as in the waking
and costuming sections of *Fireworks* and *Inauguration*, and suggest that a
climactic show-down is forthcoming. The first intimation of disaster occurs in the third episode, also of motorcycle polishing and fitting, which
opens and closes with views of a Grim Reaper skeleton in a black velvet
hood surveying the cyclist and his machine. We hear the threatening
lyrics of the song, "My boyfriend's back and there's gonna be trouble. . . ."

Anger once described his finding the fourth song as an example of
"magick." He said that he had completed the selection for all the other
songs and needed something to go with this episode, in which three
cyclists at different locations ritually dress themselves in leather and
chains with the montage continually jumping from one to the other.
Anger turned on his radio and exercised his will. Out came Bobby Vinton's "She wore blue velvet," which when joined to the episode created
precisely the sexual ambiguity Anger wanted in this scene. In fact, there
is a brief cut in the middle of the episode as one bare-chested cyclist leans
forward toward the camera and the image switches to the crotch of another as he zips his pants, suggesting fellatio. Similar eroticized montages
occur later in the film, as when the hero kisses the plaster scorpion, his

totem, for good luck, and the image quickly cuts to the bare navel of another cyclist.

The next four song-episodes, forming the second part of the film or
"The Image Maker," as the notes call it, comprise its core and culminate
in the "Heat Wave" and "He's a Rebel" episodes which represent Anger's
clearest and most intricate thought on the dialectics of reality and imagination. The previous part had ended as a fully-dressed cyclist wheeled his
bike out of the garage. The sudden appearance on the screen of a frame
of Li'l Abner comics introduces Scorpio, the hero of the film. We see him
lying in bed reading the funnies as Elvis Presley sings "You look like an
angel, but you're the devil in disguise." His room is a vast metaphor; its
walls exhibit a virtual catalogue of his unconscious, in the same way that
the cluttered walls of many American adolescents, where everything
meaningful to them is tacked and pasted, represent their unconsciouses.
Thus, without resorting to expressionism, as in the GENTS room of *Fireworks*, Anger shows us an iconographic space that is also a real space.
On the walls are pictures of James Dean, Marlon Brando, and a Nazi
swastika. There is also a television, turned on through the series of episodes in this room. It functions as an aesthetic reactor. Whatever we
glimpse on it is always a metaphor for what is happening within the hero
of the film. Its metaphoric level extends simultaneously as an aesthetic
dimension of Scorpio's thought and action in the realm of plastic illusion and as an icon of contemporary life—the source as well as the reflection of the unconscious. It is from the images on this television that Anger
gets his most interesting collage effects.

After his own ritual costuming to the sound of "Hit the Road, Jack,"
ending in his putting on rings quite like the opening of *Inauguration*,
Scorpio takes a sniff of cocaine. Here we have an exultant image of Romantic liberation when the most interiorized of the songs in the film,
"Heat Wave," is combined with an image on the television of birds escaping from a cage, and then, amid two frame flashes of bright red, a
gaudy, purple picture of Dracula. We see in one or two seconds of cinema
the re-creation of a high Romantic, or Byronic myth of the paradox of
liberation. This brief montage evokes both tremendous liberation and
tremendous limitation; the liberation inherent in the exuberant enthusiasm of the editing and the ecstatic pace of the music, and the simultaneous limitation in that the sudden "ace of light," as Michael McClure
calls the sniff of cocaine, comes from a bottle and a powder; it is exterior.
The image of the monster is just a gaudy photograph, and the freed birds

are in the end just a couple of pigeons on television. Although I have to describe these contradictory aspects of the cinematic experience sequentially, they occur simultaneously in watching the film.

From this point on, the entire film is structured around the interaction of contraries. In the "Heat Wave" episode the initial flash from the cocaine blends into images of his heroes. Scorpio is intercut with photos of James Dean. Marlon Brando appears on the television, in his motorcycle film *The Wild One*. When we catch sight of him he has an interiorized smile, his eyes are closed, and he too seems to have just sniffed the cocaine. When Scorpio puts on his jacket, we see the skull on the back of Brando's.

At the end of the scene, Scorpio repudiates his heroes, for Anger's vision of the myth of the American motorcyclist argues passionately with the tepid social morality of Brando's and Dean's films. Next to the Promethean Scorpio, they are "bad boys" from Boys' Town. So Scorpio draws his gun on a still of Gary Cooper from the show-down in *High Noon*, and he points it into the television, but Brando is no longer there; instead we see first a Hebrew menorah and then a crucifix as the objects of his attack. At this point he kisses the scorpion and leaves his room.

In the course of the film there is a transition from minor to major heroes, from movie stars to the charismatic powers who have shaken the world. The first example, which we meet in the coming episode, is Christ; the second later is Hitler. The gunning of the menorah and the crucifix established the context of interpretation for the following sequence. As the camera follows the boots of the hero through the street to the music of "He's a rebel, and we'll never know the reason why," we are prepared for the comic highlight of the film. From Cecil B. DeMille's silent *King of Kings* we see Christ parading past his followers. Like the heroes in photographs and on television, this Christ comes to us at one remove. The space abruptly shifts from the colored scenes of Anger's photography to a flat, blue-tinted black-and-white image in the intercuttings. True to the high Romantic tradition, of which Anger himself may be only dimly aware, the heroic Christ is wrenched from the traditional Christian interpretation. Through the montage we learn what Scorpio would do if he were Christ, or perhaps what he thinks Christ really must have done: when Christ approaches the blind beggar, Scorpio would have kicked him, as he kicks the wheel of his motorcycle, and would have given him a ticket for loitering, as a cop places a parking violation on the bike; Christ touches the blind man's eyes; through a very quick intercut we see that Scorpio would have shown him a "dirty picture"; and when the beggar goes down on his knees before Christ, Scorpio offers him his stiff penis.

Scorpio Rising is a mythographic film. It self-consciously creates its own myth of the motorcyclist by comparison with other myths: the dead movie star, Dean; the live one, Brando; the savior of men, Christ; the villain of men, Hitler. Each of these myths is evoked in ambiguity, without moralizing. From the photos of Hitler and a Nazi soldier and from the use of swastikas and other Nazi impedimenta, Scorpio derives a Nietzschean ecstasy of will and power. *Scorpio Rising* is a more sophisticated version than Anger had ever before achieved of the erotic dialogue. In this film he is no longer describing the visionary search for the self, as he had in *Inauguration*, but presenting an erotic version of the contraries of the self.

In all but the last of the remaining five song-episodes, Anger continues to compare the motorcyclists to DeMille's Christ. Flashing red lights in the spokes of a motorcycle introduce the "Walpurgis Party." Here, to the music of "Party Lights," the cyclists come in costume. One wears a skeleton suit through which his penis protrudes. Their entry is meshed with a procession of DeMille's disciples obsequiously accepting the invitation to enter a house. When Christ himself is seated the song changes to "Torture" and his off-screen looks are intercut with the party to give the impression that he is supervising the members of the gang who have started to smear hot mustard on the bare crotch of one of their comrades. Scorpio has arrived at the party, but he quickly leaves to explore, with a phallically placed flashlight, a church altar, draped with a Nazi flag.

In the party episodes the camera movement is looser and faster than anywhere else in Anger's work. In hand-held sweeps, it follows the pranks of the cyclists—dropping their pants, poking a woman with a bare penis, slapping each others' asses like a tom-tom, sending someone pantsless on his cycle out into the night, and pouring on the mustard. Toward the end of the "Torture" section, the camera regains its calm horizontal and vertical panning. A ceramic of Christ's face passes the screen. Scorpio points downward from the altar, and the camera, following his finger, shows us quivering buttocks brutally beaten. In the initial version of the film, which has undergone very few important changes, a shot of a plastic bottle of "Leather Queen" stood where the sadistic image now appears.

In the final three sections of the film, Scorpio, still standing on the altar which he progressively desecrates, directs a motorcycle race in an open field. As the cyclists rev up their bikes at the starting line, Christ is hoisted onto a donkey side-saddle. It is "The Point of No Return," as the accompanying song tells us. The hero, in a black leather mask with a Luger in one hand and a skull and crossbones flag in the other, signals the riders on. The one superimposition of the film occurs when the image of the scorpion hovers behind the waving death flag. In the second part of the race, to the song, "I will follow him," Scorpio reaches the height of his demonic possession. The montage suggests that he is a diabolical Puck in a collage previously discussed. Before pictures of Hitler and pans over Nazi parade troops, he urinates in his helmet and holds it high on the altar as his offering. Then he kicks books off the altar and leaves in the night.

A pastel sketch opens the final scene. It is a skeleton head smoking a cigarette labeled "Youth." At the sound of a cash register or a slot machine, a picture of Christ guiding a clean-cut young man appears in the skeleton's eye socket. "Wipe Out" is the last song. The images are the most abstract of the film: a montage of Nazi pictures, flags, even swastika checkers. Briefly we see Scorpio with a sub-machine gun shouting orders. A cyclist crashes in the race and presumably dies. The final images of the film show a red flickering police car light rhythmically intercut with the face of a cyclist filmed in infra-red so that he too is red against a black background. The end title is written in studs on a leather belt.

Tony Rayns, in his analysis of the film,[12] says that Scorpio is the motorcyclist who dies. I see no evidence for this. The death is the sacrifice that Scorpio demands. It, and not the winning of a race, has been the obvious culmination of the film from the beginning, as Pan's *sparagmos* had been needed to inaugurate the pleasure dome.

In Anger's booklet of notes on the Magick Lantern Cycle of 1966 he provided the following schematic autobiography:

> Sun Sign   Aquarian
> Rising Sign   Scorpio
> Ruling Planet   Uranus
> Energy Component   Mars in Taurus
> Type   Fixed Air
> Lifework   MAGICK
> Magical Weapon   Cinematograph
> Religion   Thelemite
> Deity   Horus the Avenger; The Crowned and Conquering Child
> Magical Motto   "Force and Fire"
> Holy Guardian Angel   MI-CA-EL

Affinity   Geburah
Familiar   Mongoose
Antipathy   Saturn and all His Works
Characteristic   Left-handed fanatic craftsman
Politics   Reunion with England
Hobbies   Hexing enemies; tap dancing; Astral projection; travel; talis-
man manufacture; Astrology; Tarot Cards; Collage
Heroes   Flash Gordon; Lautreamont; William Beckford; Méliès; Al-
fred C. Kinsey; Aleister Crowley
Library   Big Little Books; L. Frank Baum; M. P. Shiel; Aleister Crowley
Sightings   Several saucers; the most recent a lode-craft over Hayes and
Harlington, England, February 1966
Ambitions   Many, many, many more films; Space travel
Magical numbers   11; 31; 93[13]

Formally, *Scorpio Rising*'s precursor (by a few years at most) was
Bruce Conner's second film, *Cosmic Ray*. Whether or not Anger has seen
the film is hardly relevant here, as I can hardly believe it had a direct influence upon him. Nevertheless, Conner should be credited as the first
film-maker to employ ironically a popular song as the structural unit in a
collage film. The title of his film is a pun, referring both to Ray Charles,
whose song "Tell me what I say" forms the soundtrack of the film, as
well as to atomic particles from outer space. Conner intercut material
which is primarily the irreverent dance of a naked girl, which he photographed himself, with stock shots from old war films, advertisements, a
western, a Mickey Mouse cartoon, etc., ridiculing warfare as a sexual
sublimation. The structure of the ideas evoked by Conner's collage is
straightforward; unlike Anger's film, there is no room for ambiguity in
Cosmic Ray.

In the sequence of Anger's films, there is an evolution of forms from
the late forties through the sixties which will recur again and again in
the works of his contemporaries. The shift is from the trance film to the
mythopoeic film. Both forms assert the primacy of the imagination; the
first through dream, the second through ritual and myth. Almost all of
the film-makers discussed in this book have moved through these two
stages at almost the same time. The development of Maya Deren's formal
concern with cinema had been from dream (*Meshes of the Afternoon*)
to ritual (*Ritual in Transfigured Time*) and myth (*The Very Eye of
Night*). Had she lived longer, the contours of her evolution would doubt-
less be as clear as Anger's. The cases of Peterson and Broughton are ex-

ceptional; they do not fit the pattern neatly, but that is because the former stopped making films in 1949 and the latter left the medium for so long before returning to it.

Inauguration of the Pleasure Dome was the first major work to herald the emerging mythic form in the American avant-garde film. In its initial form, in 1954, it was closer to Maya Deren's concept of a cinematic ritual than to what would emerge in the 1960s as the mythopoeic cinema— *Scorpio Rising*, Markopoulos' *Twice a Man* (1963) and *The Illiac Passion* (1968), Brakhage's *Dog Star Man* (1961-66), Harry Smith's *Heaven and Earth Magic* (approx. 1950-60). In that early version the Kabuki-like pace of the opening part extended throughout the film; its formal operation was like the choreography in *Ritual in Transfigured Time*. After *Inauguration of the Pleasure Dome*, the mythic form emerged in Deren's *The Very Eye of Night* (1958) and Maas' *Narcissus* (1958). In all three instances the film-makers sought to represent specific myths and mythological figures. The triumph of the mythopoeic film in the early sixties sprang from the film-makers' liberation from the repetition of traditional mythology and the enthusiasm with which they forged a cinematic form for the creation or revelation of new myths. *Scorpio Rising* is an excellent example of this new vitality.

Immediately after the success of *Scorpio Rising*, Anger tried to apply the very same formal invention to a similar theme, the custom car builder. Early in 1964 the Ford Foundation experimented with giving a few independent film-makers grants of ten thousand dollars. After their initial grants, they discontinued the experiment. Anger was fortunate enough to be among the recipients. With his money he made some slight revision of *Scorpio Rising*, created the Sacred Mushroom version of *Inauguration*, and began *Kustom Kar Kommandos*. The film was never completed. In 1965 he showed an episode, similar to some of the opening scenes of *Scorpio*, in which a young man polishes his finished car with a giant powder puff. The pastel colors and the fluid movement (the car seems to be turning on a giant turntable) are even richer than similar effects in his previous film. Like *Scorpio*, too, this episode had as its soundtrack a single rock and roll song, "Dream Lover." At the end of the sequence as he showed it, Anger appended an appeal for funds to finish the film. Those funds never appeared and *Kustom Kar Kommandos* has been abandoned. Anger has left its one episode, resuscitating the form of the fragment as he had done when he distributed *Puce Moment* from *Puce Women*.

Fortunately a prospectus survives for the complete *KKK*. It is reproduced here in its entirety. It is interesting to note that the "Dream Lover" segment is not to be found within it:

"KUSTOM"
(KUSTOM KAR KOMMANDOS—FILM PROJECT)

Film project by Kenneth Anger utilizing the Eastman rapid color emulsion Ektachrome ER, whose ASA rating of 125 opens up hitherto inaccessible realms of investigation in low-key color location work for the independent creative film-maker. Running time 30 minutes, track composed of pop music fragments combined with sync location-recorded sound effects and dialog.

KUSTOM is an oneiric vision of a contemporary American (and specifically Californian) teenage phenomenon, the world of the hot-rod and customized car. I emphasize the word *oneiric*, as KUSTOM will *not* be a "documentary" covering the mechanical hopping-up and esthetic customizing of cars, but rather a dream-like probe into the psyche of the teenager for whom the *unique* aspect of the power-potentialized customized car represents a poetic extension of personality, an accessible means of wish-fulfillment. I will treat the custom cars created by the teenager and his adult mentors (such customizers as Ed Roth, Bill Cushenberry and George Barris, whose Kustom City in North Hollywood is a mecca of this world) as the objects of art—folk art if you prefer—that I consider them to be.

The aforementioned adult "mentors," most of whom are located in the periphery of Los Angeles and hence readily accessible for filming, will be shown at work in their body shops on various cars-in-the-process-of-becoming, in the role of "arch-priests" to the teen-agers whose commission they are fulfilling. (The locales of body shops and garages will be presented uniquely in gleaming highlighted low-key, in a manner already essayed for the motorcycle garage locations of SCORPIO RISING); the idolized customizers (the only adults seen in the film) will be represented as shadowy, mysterious personages (priests or witch-doctors) while the objects of their creation, the cars, will bathe in a pool of multi-sourced (strictly non-realistic) light, an eye-magnet of nacreous color and gleaming curvilinear surfaces.

The treatment of the teenager in relation to his hot-rod or custom car (whether patiently and ingeniously fashioned by himself, as is usually the case, or commissioned according to his fantasy, for the economically favored) will bring out what I see as a definite *eroticization* of the automobile, in its dual aspect of narcissistic identification as virile power symbol and its more elusive role: seductive, attention-grabbing, gaudy or glittering mechanical mistress paraded for the benefit of his peers. (I am irresistably drawn to the comparison of these machines with an American cult-object of an earlier era, Mae West in her "Diamond Lil" impersonations of the Thirties.)

The formal filmic construct of KUSTOM is planned as follows: (The division into titled "sections" is uniquely for working convenience; these divisions will be "erased" in the finished work.) The dominant pop record is indicated in capitals.

1 HAVE MONEY (The Young Conformers.) An introduction insinuating the spectator into the teen-dream. A fast-shifting visual reverie utilizing the linking device of the lap-dissolve and the wipe to establish patterns of convention followed by the teenage (and sub-teen) group: similarity of hair-styling, style of dress, of language, attitude or manner, taste in dance patterns and pop music; the omniscience of certain popular heroes or ever-shifting masks on Archetypal Images.

2 DAWN (Crystalization.) The concept of individual "style" dawns upon the Teenager. The carefully composed aerodynamics of a crested coiffure as it is formed. The love-lock. Racked sideburns. The embroidered, self-identifying jacket or painted T-shirt. The "far-out" color combinations in stove-pipe pants, shock-effect shirts and socks. The Grail: the vision of the Teenager as Owner of his own, screamingly individualistic, unique and personalized custom car. (These images of the Grail, "the goal," will be floated across the mirrored image of the Teenager as he arranges his coiffure or clothes.) Subliminal flashes as thumbs through hot-rod magazines or plays juke-box. Closeups of high-school desk tops showing open text books (Science or History) while adolescent hands doodle, first crudely, then with increasing refinement, silhouettes of hot-rod and custom "dream" cars.

3 THE NITTY-GRITTY (Realization.) The Teenager attacks. Dream into action. Abrupt change in formal construct: sharp cuts, swift pans, darting dollies. The night-lit junk-yard, weird derelict cemetery: lifting a "goodie." The first jalopie: a rusty junked car pushed into the dark initiatory cave of the garage. Series of car-frames in the process of being stripped: an almost savage dismantling (analogy to wild animals dismembering a carcass).

4 MY GUY (The Rite.) Under the occult guidance of the shadowy, mysterious adult customizers performing as Arch-Priest, the Teenager's Dream Car is born (allusion to obstetrics). The alchemical elements come into play: phosphorescent blue tongue of the welding flame, cherry glow of joins, spark shower of the buffer. Major operation: dropping the front, raising the back of the car, "channeling" and "chopping." The Priest-Surgeon (customizer) perfects the metal modulations from cardboard mock-ups; plunges in with blowtorch and mallet. The swooping sculpted forms (blackened and rough) materialize in closeups and their intent is perceived.

5 IN HIS KISS (The Adorning.) Sudden darting color: the rainbow array as cans are opened, stirred dripping gaudy sticks held up for the

Teenager's contemplation and approval. The iridescent "candy-flake" colors and shock-jewel tones in vogue. The Teenager chooses *his* color: tension, decision, joyful release. The cult-object—the shaping-up car body —in the swirl of colored spray-gun mists: rose and turquoise fluorescent fogs as coat upon carefully-stroked, glittering coat, the car-body emerges as a radiant, gem-hued object of adoration. A reflected color-bath splashes over the absorbed faces of the watching teenagers: a whoop of triumph, a jungle-stomp of joy as the custom car is "born."

6 WONDERFUL ONE (Possession.) The Teenager takes possession of his own completed custom or hot-rod car: the painted finish is caressed, the line admired (as would be the line of a girl friend) the chromed shift fondled, firmly grasped. (For this kaleidoscopic montage involving scores of custom and hot-rod cars, it is hoped to include the outstanding examples of customizing currently touring America in the Ford Custom Car Caravan, which could well represent the ideal Dream Cars of America's custom-conscious teenagers. However, for their appearance in KUSTOM, it will be necessary to film them *in movement* against unified black or nocturnal backgrounds—an effect that can be accomplished by camera or optical artifice if it proves impractical to night-drive these valuable machines.)

7 THE FUGITIVE (Flight and Freedom.) The Teenage hot-rodders "rev up" (The Syndrome of the Shift) and take off for a nocturnal drag race (irreal colored light-sources throughout). A lone hot-rodder races down a curving mountain road (Dead Man's Curve). The Custom Boys, *in slow motion,* take command of the controls of their Dream Cars. (This concluding sequence of KUSTOM operates exclusively in the realm of "dream logic": it is intended to create a Science-Fictional atmosphere.) The hot-rodders experience the erotic power-ecstasy of the Shift (the Hurst shift will be employed) to the magnified accompaniment of motor and exhaust. The Custom Boys resemble Astronauts at their controls: their vari-hued craft seem to lift into space. (If possible, a prototype of an actual "air-car" by a noted West Coast designer will be utilized in this section.) The Dragsters streak down the search-light stabbed runway (ideally seen by helicopter) as in cross-cutting the Custom Boys are liberated into weightlessness with their strange craft, and plunge star-ward.

8 SHANGRI-LA (Apotheosis.) The Dragsters streak towards an imposing podium (by montage inference) piled high with towering, animated trophies of glittering gold; the Custom Boys range above the golden mountain high and free. A nocturnal jostling cheering crowd of teenagers (lit by swinging stabbing searchlights) swing up on their shoulders The Winner—Mr. Hot-Rod, his glowing triumph-filled countenance streaming sweat, his bare arms bearing his Golden Trophy Tower—he exults as The Conqueror, drinks in the adulation of the ado-

lescent sea around him; he is startled by the sky-borne vroom of the
upward-sweeping Dream Cars, his beaming face swiftly mirroring, in the
moment of his triumph, a greater wonder, a greater goal.

END

Anticipation of KKK gradually faded in the late sixties as Anger made
statements about his new project, *Lucifer Rising*, which was to be his
"first religious film." Before the theft of his footage in 1967, Anger had
faced two major crises while he was trying to make the film in California.
His first "Lucifer," a five-year-old boy, killed himself trying to fly off a
roof; his second, Bobby Beausoleil, was convicted of murder. In addition
to this, there was the perpetual financial struggle.

In several interviews he contrasted the project for *Lucifer Rising* with
Scorpio Rising as films about the life force and the death force respectively. "It's about the angel-demon of light and beauty named Lucifer.
And it's about the solar deity. The Christian ethos has turned Lucifer
into Satan. But I show it in the gnostic and pagan sense. . . . Lucifer
is the Rebel Angel behind what's happening in the world today. His message is that the Key of Joy is disobedience." Anger has also described his
encounter with a demon, Joe, who got him to sign a contract in blood and
disappeared after providing him with information that would help him
to make the film. According to the early reports, *Lucifer Rising* was to be
about the "Love Generation" in California, hippies, and the magical aspects of the child's universe.

In a career as littered as Anger's has been with aborted projects, scan-
dals, and disasters, one can imagine that to some extent the destructive-
ness is self-generated. His recent productivity indicates that Anger is now
determined to complete his projects and to make many new films.

The first sign of this was his completion of *Invocation of My Demon
Brother*, which includes material from the original *Lucifer Rising*. Then
he rereleased *Puce Moment*, synchronized to a new song, and finally he
finished *La Lune des Lapins*, having re-edited the material after twenty
years, added a set of songs, and translated the title to *Rabbit's Moon*. As
was mentioned before, the first chapter of *Lucifer Rising* is also in distribution, and recent British newspaper reports indicate that the film is
still in progress. All of this activity marks the early 1970s as Anger's most
productive period.

Invocation of My Demon Brother also marks a stylistic change and a
refinement of Anger's Romanticism. Stylistically he shifts from the closed
form of his earlier films to a more open form. The terms "closed" and

"open form" denote degrees, not absolutes. The early films of Anger
observe for the most part the classical unities of time and space and tend
to have clearly defined beginnings, middles, and ends. Allowing for its
dream transitions, *Fireworks* has a simple narrative continuity. The images
of *Eaux D'Artifice* also follow a simple temporal progression and never
move from one locale. The original version of *Inauguration of the Pleasure Dome* also has a strict temporal and spatial cohesion. The introduction of superimposition and above all the addition of hermetic insignia
opened that form somewhat, but even then those foreign elements always
had a more direct, literal relation to the central action. Even in *Scorpio
Rising* the various elements of collage specifically comment upon the episodes Anger photographed, and they are edited to suggest the illusion of
spatial and temporal continuity (Christ looking at the mustard torture,
Puck cheering the racers on to death). In *Invocation of My Demon
Brother* Anger still utilizes the off-screen look as a formal fixture; one can
distinguish an introduction and a conclusion. But nevertheless the film
marks a radical step for him in the direction of open form, where montage does not depend on the illusion or the suggestion of spatial and
temporal relationship between shots. The editing of images in Bruce
Conner's *Cosmic Ray* exemplifies an open form. We see a naked girl
dancing, an Indian chief from a Western, an African beating a drum, the
Iwo Jima flag raising, many shots of armies, guns firing, explosions, a
Mickey Mouse cartoon, and an academy leader. The transition between
shots follows a pattern of rhythm and shock.

The intellectual coordinate involved in this change is more subtle. I
have already referred to the Romantic tradition which informs all of
Anger's films and which is especially clear in *Inauguration* and *Scorpio
Rising*. In the subsequent chapters of this book I shall explore the variations of the Romantic heritage in relation to the works of other major
American film-makers. These variations are almost as complex and discontinuous as the Romantic movement itself in Europe and America
since the beginning of the nineteenth century. But the term remains useful. With admirable condensation, René Wellek defined the English
and German tradition of Romanticism as "the glorification of creative
imagination, a rhetoric of metamorphoses and universal analogy."[14] In
Invocation of My Demon Brother, Anger continues to glorify the creative imagination as he does in all of his films, but he extends the rhetoric
of metamorphoses and universal analogy beyond the transformations of
Inauguration and the dialectical metaphors of *Scorpio Rising* into a "web

of correspondences, a rhetoric of metamorphoses in which everything reflects everything else," to quote Wellek again on the movement within
Romanticism called Symbolism.

In *Invocation* Anger combines material from the original *Lucifer Rising,* a document of the Equinox of the Gods ritual he performed the
night the film was stolen, a helicopter landing in Vietnam, footage of
the Rolling Stones, alchemical tattoos. For the first time he uses anamorphic photography.

As with his other films, our description will follow the outline of his
program note:

> INVOCATION OF MY DEMON BROTHER (1969)
>
> Directed, Photographed, and Edited by Kenneth Anger. Filmed in San
> Francisco. Track composed by Mick Jagger on the Moog Synthesizer.
> *Cast:* Speed Hacker (Wand Bearer); Lenore Kandel and William (Dea-
> coness and Deacon); Kenneth Anger (The Magus); Van Leuven (Aco-
> lyte); Harvey Bialy and Timotha (Brother and Sister of the Rainbow);
> Anton Szandor La Vey (His Satanic Majesty); Bobby Beausoleil (Lu-
> cifer). *Synopsis:* Invocation of My Demon Brother (Arrangement in
> Black and Gold). The shadowing forth of Our Lord Lucifer, as the
> Powers of Darkness gather at a midnight mass. The dance of the Magus
> widdershins around the Swirling Spiral Force, the solar swastika, until the
> Bringer of Light—Lucifer—breaks through. "The true Magick of Horus re-
> quires the passionate union of opposites."—Aleister Crowley.[15]

Anger's subtitle of the film ("Arrangement in Black and Gold") ironically recalls the titles Whistler gave to his paintings, such as "Nocturne
in Black and Gold: The Falling Rocket," or the famous portrait of his
mother, "Arrangement in Gray and Black." Of course, the blackness is
also metaphorical: the spiritual matrix from which Lucifer, whose wings
are golden in this film, emerges.

The titles of the film are printed in golden letters over a painting of a
black Lucifer with a Cyclopean eye and flaming stars surrounding his
head. The first shot of the film is a parody of the painting. A white-
haired man, whose head is flanked by stars from a flag, opens his eyes.
(Again Anger begins a film with an image of waking.) He sees a naked
torso. When he turns to the right, then the left, he sees two different
shots of the same two naked boys on a sofa. Before he lifts and lowers a
long transparent wand, we see images of an occult tattoo.

The tattoo, like the costume in *Inauguration,* is central to the structure
of *Invocation.* The film moves among levels of reality, suggesting that one

image is the signature of another. It is Anger's most metaphysical film; here he eschews literal connections, makes the images jar against one another, and does not create a center of gravity through which the collage is to be interpreted, as the images of Christ could be interpreted through the actions of the motorcyclists in *Scorpio*, or as the images of Crowley could be interpreted through the ritual of *Inauguration*. Thus deprived of a center of gravity, every image has equal weight in the film; and more than ever before in an Anger film, the burden of synthesis falls upon the viewer.

When the Wand Bearer looks up, we see the first of two shots of a helicopter letting out American Marines. The image is tinted red. Anger told Tony Rayns that he printed this image on a C roll over the entire film, but so faintly that it emerged to the naked eye only twice. He suggested that with infra-red glasses it might be seen throughout.

Gradually the center of attention shifts from the Wand Bearer to a hashish party in which the Deacon and Deaconess are smoking with a friend. Before the first appearance of this threesome, the camera pans a band of jazz musicians. With the first puff of hashish, Anger cuts to a hand-held movement back and up from a skull. As the hashish pipe is passed back and forth, he cuts to the skull again and then to a cat pawing at a table and a dog sinking to the floor. From behind a plant someone seems to be spying.

Suddenly, at the end of the hashish episode, as if the smoke had dramatically worked its power, the Magus, Anger himself in the costume of an Egyptian god, appears before a fountain of fire (out of *Dante's Inferno* again, recalling the spectacular appearance of Kali in *Inauguration of the Pleasure Dome*). Then we see him rushing around a stage, waving a wand, pouring potions, and performing his Autumn Equinox ritual, often in superimposition and always with an accelerated speed. The film-maker Ben Van Meter filmed this section for Anger the night of his rite at the Straight Theater. In the early stages of the ritual center of the film, Anger interjects shots of himself reading Crowley's novel of witchcraft, *Moonchild*, and then of arachnid—or spider-like—tattoos.

The more we see of the ritual, the more often it is interrupted by other shots. There is an eye behind a fishbowl; then the first of many superimpositions suggestive of playing cards appears—an image is superimposed over itself with a reversal of top and bottom, so that the picture resembles the face-cards in the deck. The first of these images shows a young man, naked above the waist and with many moving arms like the traditional

Kali of Indian iconography. The progress of the ritual seems to engender a greater degree of abstraction and anamorphosis in the film.

During the bombardment of superimposed and abstracted images, we catch a first glimpse of a horned and bearded devil who at the end of the rite will fuse with the Magus in a rapid montage of similar body and facial gestures. This is his Demon Brother. Yet before this culmination of the ceremony, a door with a Tarot skeleton on it opens and His Satanic Majesty enters and ceremoniously places a skull on the floor. The Magus burns a document, then a cat.

As the cat is burned, a shot of a group of Hell's Angels standing around in their leather gear fades in over the image of the flames. This combination of images is particularly evocative of the interpenetration of levels of reality mentioned earlier. The opposition of filmic textures reinforces this impression as the thin, somewhat murky, superimposed images of the rite seem about to melt into a rich, sunlit view of the Hell's Angels in their black leather and silver studs. But the image is only momentary. The Magus becomes his Demon Brother. Then he carries a Nazi swastika around the stage as the film cuts to another bare-chested boy with a swastika pattern projected over him. The scene shifts again, in texture as well as image, to a group of ecstatic dancers in the audience of a rock festival. The force is precisely that of the Hell's Angels shot, of suddenly wrenching the film out of the realm of rite and occult signs into a more familiar realm. In a complementary but converse way, we simultaneously see the Hell's Angels and the rock festival as aspects of an occult system.

Immediately after that, the second image of the Vietnam helicopter landing recurs. The nude boys we saw in the beginning reappear, wrestling in a card-like superimposition. The Wand Bearer also returns, superimposed over tattooed flesh. Suddenly, but with less flourish than the entrance of the Magus, Lucifer appears for an instant as a handsome young man in black top hat with golden wings. Immediately afterwards, the Deacon and Deaconess and the members of the jazz band begin to descend a staircase, perhaps a dozen figures in all. Lucifer pops up again, this time under the superimposition of a playing card with a top hat on it. Mick Jagger, his earthly manifestation, appears on stage at a festival.

The film comes quickly to an end as a series of shots interrupts the repeated image of a bare-chested youth with a moiré pattern projected over him. We see the Magus on the stage for the last time, then a final shot of Jagger performing. Finally, a tiny mummy (more in the South American than the Egyptian style) rushes down the empty staircase in a cloud of smoke with the sign "Zap You're Pregnant. That's Witchcraft."

The last time I met Anger was on a boat going from England to Holland. He had just emigrated from America. In our brief conversation he doubted if he would ever distribute his films again. He was dissatisfied with the basic materials of cinema. After having made a film with vertical, rather than the traditional horizontal elongation in Egypt, he had destroyed it by projecting it with the projector turned on its side. The leaking of oil caused a fire which burned the film. He said he would much rather "project the images directly into people's heads." It is very much a part of the aspiration of *Invocation of My Demon Brother* to get beyond the limitations of cinema and directly into the head. In the curious message of the mummy, we have an attempt to do magic directly through cinema. Rayns opens his excellent study of Anger with a statement by Anger of his attitude toward film:

> "I have always considered movies evil; the day that cinema was invented was a black day for mankind. Centuries before photography there were talismans, which actually anticipated photographs, since the dyes they used on the cheap vellum produced patterns when they faded in light. A talisman was a sticky fly-paper trying to trap a spirit—cunningly you printed on it a 'photograph' of the demon you wanted to capture in it. Photography is a blatant attempt to steal the soul. The astral body is always just latent in a person, and certain cunning and gifted photographers can take an image of the astral body. The whole thing is having an image of someone to *control* them. If you're out of your mind with love it becomes understandable. *Any* crime is justifiable in the name of Love. In fact, it shouldn't have to be a 'crime': *Anything* is justifiable in the name of Love.
>
> "My films are primarily concerned with sexuality in people. My reason for filming has nothing to do with 'cinema' at all; it's a transparent excuse for capturing people, the equivalent of saying 'Come up and see my etchings'. . . . It's wearing a little thin now. . . . So I consider myself as working Evil in an evil medium."[16]

In Anger's films his image of himself, of the self, is as a Magus, never as a film-maker. He continues the tradition of Jean Cocteau, a film-maker dear to him, who in *Le Sang d'un Poète* first made the aesthetic quest legitimate as a subject for cinema. Interestingly, Cocteau used film to examine the workings of poetry, refraining from the absolute reflexive of a film about cinema. Anger and other American avant-garde film-makers took from Cocteau both his fascination with the traditional means of art —poetry, music, sculpture—as opposed to cinema itself and his fusion of the aesthetic and the erotic quests. We have already seen how Sidney

Peterson in both *The Cage* and *Mr. Frenhofer and the Minotaur* continued in that track. Deren too, though less directly, defined the self in
terms of the fusion of erotic and aesthetic; and we shall shortly see the
same is true of Markopoulos, who unlike them has posited the film-
maker as his central artist.

For Anger the aesthetic endeavor is a category of magick. His image
of the self is particularly complex because it involves as many distinctions
as there are grades for the magician. Like *Inauguration of the Pleasure
Dome,* the vision of the self in *Invocation* has its foundation in the Romantic idea of the unitary man whose one character is made up of different individuals in opposition. But the magician of *Invocation* is of a
higher order than Shiva of *Inauguration,* and the range of the film is both
wider and more diffuse. The central act of the film is described in its
title, but the cinematic context in which this manifestation occurs is a
meditation on Anger's art and its place in the world. The first part of
Lucifer Rising was to be called, for reasons not entirely clear to me, "The
Magic House of Oz." The document which the Magus ritually burns is a
text by Crowley, of which the first word, "oz," is all that can be seen on
the screen. The reference must also extend to the books of L. Frank
Baum, which Anger has said he admires. The scenes of smoking hashish
and the descent of the staircase probably take place in "the magic house
of Oz."

It has already been pointed out that the appearance of Lucifer does
not compete in dramatic or visual intensity with the first shot of the
Magus in *Invocation.* Nor does Lucifer sustain his appearance in the film
for more than a few seconds. *Invocation of My Demon Brother* is neither
a substitute for nor a salvaging of *Lucifer Rising,* as some may have
thought when it first appeared. It is an investigation of the aesthetic quest
through occult rhetoric. What makes this film more difficult than any
previous Anger film is the film-maker's new use of his art as an instrument of discovery. The film is about the concentration of the imagination
and indirectly about the power of art to achieve it. The montage compares the trance of music—the jazz band, Jagger and his audience at a
rock festival—and the trance of drugs—smoking hashish—with possession
by war—the helicopter scenes—suicide—the Saturnian torso—and with
sexuality—the wrestling naked boys—as the dynamics of imaginary initiation. The eventual glimpses of Lucifer are the first tastes of its achievement.

By describing the cinematography of *Invocation* as an instrument of discovery one assigns to Anger the modernist principle of presenting the process of making as the central fact of the artifact. Watching this film, one feels that the film-maker did not know what the film was to be until it was finished. Obviously, the element of discovery exists in all film-making and in the making of all art. Yet there is a point for the artist when revelation becomes the most important aspect of his work. Anger reached that point with *Invocation of My Demon Brother*.

5

FROM TRANCE TO MYTH

In Los Angeles in 1947, while Kenneth Anger was editing *Fireworks,*
Gregory Markopoulos began to shoot *Psyche,* the first film of his trilogy,
Du Sang de la Volupté et de la Mort. He was at the time a film student at
the University of Southern California, and he had made films before.
A short and rather charming version of Dickens's A *Christmas Carol,*
which he made when he was twelve, was exhibited briefly in the mid-
1960s, and an autobiographical outline from 1954 says, "Upon entering
Woodward High School I began making some very bad 8mm films. . . .
During my second semester at USC I made a short film in experimental
form based on Hudson's very handsome tale, *Green Mansions.*" Markopoulos' filmography nevertheless begins with *Psyche,* his first 16mm
film and the first film he put into distribution.

A few months before he began shooting *Psyche,* he had assisted Curtis
Harrington in making his first film, *Fragment of Seeking,* where a young
man pursues an elusive blonde girl through a maze of corridors reminiscent of Maya Deren's pursuit of the mirror-faced figure in *Meshes of the
Afternoon,* to discover in the end that she is a skeleton with a wig. In
this pure example of the trance film, Harrington wanted to play the
young man himself. He enlisted Markopoulos to help him. Markopoulos
has always scrupulously declined any credit for the film: "I photographed
the film, exactly following his directions. Everything was done by him:
all I did was to push the camera starter. Curtis took all the exposures."
Three years later, when Markopoulos was to make his own version of the
psycho-dramatic trance film, *Swain,* he would enlist the aid of his friend
Robert Freeman to do precisely the same for him.

Psyche has no parallel among early American avant-garde films. For

Markopoulos is at once the film-maker most attracted to narrative of his generation (he has adapted several literary works to film) and one of the most radical narrative film-makers in the world. He took such extreme liberties with Pierre Louys's unfinished novella, *Psyche*, that one would hardly recognize it as the source of his film. Nevertheless, he took just enough to give his film a cohesion and a tension that make it a continually fascinating work.

In *Psyche*, as in his later, narrative-based films, Markopoulos dispenses with speech without giving up the intricacy normally found only in the talking film; although he absolutely relies upon visual means—his sound-tracks, even in the rare cases where words are involved, never explain the visual dimension—he does not simplify. Three interrelated characteristics define Markopoulos' style: color, rhythm, and atemporal construction. Color, rather than story, has been the emotional vehicle of his films. Although his control of rhythm and of atemporal construction has gradually evolved from *Psyche* in 1947 to *Gammelion* in 1968, his handling of color has been sure and consistent from the beginning. As Markopoulos made more films, the complexity and scope of his rhythmic invention increased. In his later films, his shots are either much shorter or much longer than in his early works; his rhythm becomes progressively more independent of the subject. What I have called his atemporal construction can be more amply described as a dialectic of time, where the shots of a film sometimes fall into a temporal order and sometimes cluster together in a plastic unity divorced from sequence and causality. As Markopoulos' art developed, the distinction between imagination and actuality dissolved completely and several "shimmering threads" of continuity began to appear simultaneously, sometimes interweaving into a fine net. Nevertheless, the extent to which *Psyche* forecasts one whole line of Markopoulos' evolution, as the second film of his trilogy, *Lysis*, does another, is extraordinary.

Psyche opens with a statue of Mercury pointing upward and toward a field as if beckoning the spectator into the film. A door opens on a figure shrouded in black, whom the film-maker has called both "a specter" and "the unknown" in his paraphrases of the film. There are blossoms scattered on the floor, and a hand offers flowers to the figure. This specter will reappear at crucial moments in the film. In a lecture delivered in Athens in 1955, the film-maker publicly rejoiced in the ambiguities of his film: "A hand offers flowers. The film spectator may assume what he will. The shrouded figure may be Psyche."[1]

The sudden intrusion of a hand-held shot looking down at walking legs introduces the meeting of the male and female protagonists. They pass each other in the street; they then turn around and begin to talk and laugh familiarly. "Why should the words be supplied?" the film-maker asks. "The film spectator, thrust into the film by the film creator, supplies the thoughts and feelings which make up the dialogue."

Markopoulos frames his shots just behind the head, or over the shoulder of the listener, so that with the intercutting of faces in this unheard conversation, he maintains a view of both speaker and hearer and a sense of their relative distances from the camera. Throughout *Psyche* the framing and moving of the camera are dynamic and interesting. Markopoulos paid particular attention to compositions-in-depth, with details both in the foreground and background of his image. His awareness of the composition of the individual frame was the most acute of the avant-gardists of his generation, save perhaps for Broughton's in *Mother's Day*. Markopoulos' life-long devotion to Josef von Sternberg, who taught at USC while Markopoulos was studying there, centers perhaps upon that director's attention to the frame. Yet the photography of *Psyche*, especially in its play of depth and movement, seems to owe more to Welles's *Citizen Kane* than to anything in von Sternberg.

Together the couple climb an outdoor staircase to a terrace from which he points out a house and in particular a window with its blinds half-closed. As she stares up at the window the wind blows her hair. In his lecture, Markopoulos speculates about this moment: "It is, perhaps, Eros being born again from the West Wind? Who knows? Let us not forget, though, that the West Wind is of a jealous nature." Then, just as suddenly as the man's legs appeared, Psyche is seen standing on a beach dressed in a long white gown; then, kneeling near the camera, she moulds a mound of sand, seaweed, and rocks, until a shadow falls across it and her. She looks terrified as a male hand touches and twists her hair as the wind had a few moments earlier in the film. Into the montage of this caressing and terror the film-maker weaves his first atemporal construction, mixing flashbacks in a stream of consciousness that suggests the whole beach episode was a dream, a fantasy, or perhaps an archetypal memory triggered by the movement of wind through her hair.

Immediately after the shot of his hand touching her hair comes an image of his face, not on the beach but on the terrace before the window. Their exchange of looks, hers from the beach and his from the terrace, initiates a brief recapitulation in which two strains—one of their meeting, climbing the stairs, and pointing to the window, the other of Psyche's run, building the mound, and the sea itself—are both scrambled out of sequence and intermeshed in checkerboard fashion. For a moment this abstract cascade of images halts with both figures again on the terrace. Then the first reappearance of the specter serves as a buffer shot in a transition to a new scene.

This montage of abstraction and recapitulation is an essential of the Markopoulos style. In *Psyche* there is another, longer, such sequence at the end of the film. Similar constructions are crucial to the structures of the later films *Swain, Serenity,* and *Twice a Man.* In the films made after that, particularly *Himself as Herself, The Illiac Passion,* and *Gammelion,* temporal order becomes so ambivalent that recapitulation ceases to be meaningful in the world Markopoulos evokes. Yet even in the late works brief clusters of images are used to execute the secondary function they have here: making a graceful and abstract transition of scenes.

At the end of the section just described, after the shot of the specter, we find ourselves in Psyche's bedroom. A slow dolly toward her sleeping on her couch is interrupted twice by images of the hero in a costume suggesting his transformation into Eros. In this dream he embraces her. When he caresses her black gloves, she laughs in her sleep and awakens.

She examines a marble bust, which Markopoulos tells us is of "Psyche herself," touches her face, then kisses the statue. She spins around gaily, the twirl of her dress intercut six times with a hummingbird buzzing at a flower. Her happiness seems to extend through the beginning of the next scene in which we find her at the end of her twirl. She and the man are walking hand in hand through an exotic garden, smiling, and giving each other flowers to smell. When they come to a hilltop, she walks forward to the camera, while he remains behind, framed over her shoulder in the background. Her gaiety is gone. A shot at the level of their knees shows him approach her from the distance. The wind has caught her hair. When he touches her shoulder and gently sniffs at her hair, she turns to him in fear and recoils back out of his reach, falling out of frame. The music of the soundtrack stops. We are plunged into a blue-tinted superimposition of waves, seagulls, the rays of the sun, palm leaves, and two indistinct figures on a beach. Markopoulos described this elusive episode in his article, "Psyche's Search for the Herb of Invulnerability": "The erotic nightmare continues. A hand is placed on Psyche's shoulder. She shudders, for she is in that other country and it is cold. The fingers of Eros are like frost. Unsuspectedly the film spectator and the silver screen, bathed in blue, become submerged with Psyche upon the borderline of her fears."

From a pure blue the color switches to orange. It is sunset as she re-gains consciousness. As she breaks away from the man, the specter ap-proaches the camera and the image is flooded with an orange sunburst. The startling transition to blue and its resolution in orange are examples of the emotional use of color in this, as well as in all of Markopoulos' films. The orchestration of color is by no means limited to solid screen dominants; it operates in his choice of setting and clothing for his charac-ters as well. For example, in the scene immediately following the appear-ance of the specter, Psyche descends the steps of a church wearing black; she is obviously very upset. She momentarily and vainly seeks comfort and steadiness by caressing the base of a black metal lamp-post. She reads a letter, crumples it, and thrusts it into the camera lens. The sudden change of scene, the omission of what led her to the church or of what happened in it, and the withholding of the text of the letter, make this the most enigmatic and elliptical episode in the film. But the choice of color and the heroine's reaction to the letter provide enough information for us to assimilate the scene into the highly ambiguous context of the film as it has been evolving.

The reader of Louys's novel will have an advantage over the untutored spectator of the film at this point, although that advantage might just as easily be called a hindrance within the logic of the film experience. In the novelette, Psyche asks her priest's advice about whether or not she should accept her lover's invitation to visit his estate. He tells her not to go, but she goes nonetheless. It would be futile here to embark upon a discussion of the relative merits of psychological clarity (the novella) and poetic ambiguity (the film). The essence of Markopoulos' skill as an abstract, narrative film-maker resides in his ability to present events in a richly am-biguous context without sacrificing the illusion that there is a fictive scheme, however elusive, holding them together. This discretion is the aesthetic justification for his cavalier treatment of literary works.

Returning to the film itself, at the end of a transitional passage, we see Psyche in red in a Japanese garden, before a red bridge. She seems very happy. As she strikes a large gong, there is a brief montage of a path, the gong, an eye, an ear, and the closing of a door. A passage of darkness ends with a moving shot of a row of candles being snuffed out by an unknown hand. The camera moves in on Psyche naked on a bed. The bare legs of a man come forward. As they embrace we see clouds shift from blue, green, yellow, to red. An image of water dripping into a pool suggests the climax of the lovemaking. A stone shoulder and a stone foot are intercut with the final images of their embrace. A clock appears. Then the man, dressed in a suit, appears smoking in the Japanese garden. An oriental or Negro woman walks through the garden, smiling at him. He smiles back at the woman; then he tosses his cigar into the pool (the camera set-up is the same as at the end of their lovemaking) and follows her. The specter appears again. Psyche, lonely in a white dress, presses her face to the large window of a hallway. At night, in the next shot, there is a man, perhaps the hero, sitting at supper.

In the final montage the specter nods its head; then, in quick succession, images appear of an old lady who glared at the couple when they first met, the laughing pair, their kiss at the train station, statues, Psyche naked in bed, the laughing pair. After a final image of the specter, the door closes, and the film ends.

Markopoulos made *Psyche* under conditions of incredible austerity. He borrowed a camera, used money that was sent for his school tuition to buy film, and when it came to editing, he put the film together with Scotch tape because he had no rewinding or splicing equipment. That he had to shoot only 1200 feet of film for a work that runs 835 feet when edited is another testament to his economy.

In the years since the film was made he has offered many and even contradictory clues to the film's interpretation. The lecture of 1955 which I have quoted frequently here returns again and again to an Orphic interpretation of the film as a rite of initiation both for its heroine and for the film spectator. In reference to Psyche's dream he writes, "Day and Night no longer exist. Like Hercules, Psyche has begun her search for the *herb of invulnerability*. In order to discover this *herb of invulnerability*, she must journey to another country, she leaves behind her body, and now travels boldly into the unknown with the film spectator." About the meeting at the train station, he adds, "Psyche actually believes that through Eros she will be able to discover the *herb of invulnerability*." He implies her search was in vain. The climax of his lecture is deliberately obscure: "Swiftly, with the furious symbols of the stone foot, the stone shoulders, the film reveals the theme of *Psyche* and rushes like the *psyche* towards its completion. Events appear in retrospect, until once again the spectator realizes that he has returned to the original point of departure." The most evocative, and perhaps the most helpful idea of Markopoulos' article, appears in the second paragraph: "Color is Eros."[2]

An earlier document from 1952 again raises both useful and baffling points. Like the later lecture, he couches his analysis in ambivalent phrases:

> The specter throughout is what Pierre Louys meant by "the unknown," perhaps it is the young film creator, who did not know the film's final outcome, similar to Jung writing one of his books and spending years deciding exactly what he said. Or it may be the author Louys, who never finished the book *Psyche*. But I would like to think that it is all three of the above. Fourthly, it is the clue to my cutting technique and film construction.

In elaboration on the last point, Markopoulos recently wrote that the veiled figure in *Psyche* functioned like a fade-out.

Other statements in this text are more puzzling, such as one that the film is "a study in stream-of-consciousness narration of a *Lesbian Soul*, who in abandoning her own *psyche* destroys herself." He asks us to notice how in the train station episode the color is drab before they kiss and with the meeting of their lips becomes bright.

Markopoulos' notes equate the film *Psyche* with the human psyche. The source of Markopoulos' distinctive montage, and hence of the structure of his films, is not a literary tradition of stream-of-consciousness writing, but the source shared with that tradition, his study of how the mind thinks. The ultimate aspiration of Markopoulos' form has been the mimesis of the human mind. In different degrees and different ways this might be the aim of the American avant-garde film-maker in general. In that case the realm of Markopoulos' distinction has been the investigation of memory, personal and archetypal. His films lay bare a way of visionary thinking affirming the perpetual present tense, in which causality and linear time are secondary discontinuous modes of experience.

After completing *Psyche*, Markopoulos left Los Angeles for his home town, Toledo, Ohio, where he completed his trilogy. He called *Lysis* "a study in stream-of-consciousness poetry of a lost, wandering, homosexual soul. There is a symbolic birth in the opening scene; the wanderings; the reincarnations of one soul into a still greater soul, until in the final cycle the soul of immortality or of UNDERSTANDING is given to the wanderer; we see him going toward the far city."[3]

The film's title comes from a Platonic dialogue on the nature of friendship. Set to Honegger and Claudel's oratorio, *Dance of Death*, the film begins with a rapid succession of static images (Chinese figurines before a tapestry, a photograph of mother and child, a painting), which may be read as the thoughts of the artist as he stands by a river. After a second burst of mementos, in which the juxtaposition of childhood photographs with delicate toys and laces suggests a formative period under strong feminine influences, the rhythm of the film evens out to an almost metronomic pace. A series of tableaux form the body of the film: an ugly woman pops from one tree to another in jump cuts; a young man lying in bed rubs his feet against streamers; the artist, played by the film-maker himself, wanders through a graveyard; a nude man, hanging by his wrists, is stabbed in the back; a Negress plays with a swan; a boy in toga jumps, through stop photography, among the columns of a neo-classical building; another youth sleeps in a tree. At the end of this series the artist follows railroad tracks away from the camera.

Markopoulos' note for *Charmides* includes a virtually complete synopsis of that brief film:

> A concluding cinematic statement to the film trilogy. By no means, though, the final statement of the film author on the major theme employed in the trilogy. The locale is a midwestern college campus. A lone youth on the campus green is scrutinizing a tiny ceramic horse whose one leg is broken. Next a walk into the woods, but where? Nowhere. Two coffins, one right after the other, appear, a superimposed cemetery, a young child running to her grandmother by a grave. The trilogy is at an end. The spectator's mind keeps probing . . . what?[4]

The title again comes from Plato. In this particular dialogue Socrates inquires who is the most beautiful boy in Athens, and then gives his views on temperance. If the toga-clad youth and the allusion to the classical myth of Leda and the Swan gave *Lysis* a tenuous connection to its Platonic source, the relation between *Charmides* and the original dialogue is even more ephemeral. The three parts of the trilogy *Du Sang de la Volupté et de la Mort* show a diminishing intensity. The play of nearness and depth, the orchestration of colors, and the complexity of montage which distinguished *Psyche* are gone in the two subsequent films, and the formal invention of *Lysis* and *Charmides* was not to mature in Markopoulos' work until the mid-sixties.

The film-maker edited his film in the process of shooting. The only splices occur at the joining of the one hundred-foot rolls of film which fit into the camera he borrowed from Carter Wolff, in gratitude for which he dedicated the whole trilogy to him. The experimental eschewing of post-photography editing and the idea that a film could be shot and constructed at the same time show Markopoulos' commitment to cinema as an instrument of discovery.

Throughout his entire career, even when he prepared elaborate scenarios, he approached his materials with an extraordinary freedom from preconception, so that the first complete print returned from the laboratory would always be a revelation to him. Furthermore, no Markopoulos film has ended up looking like its original outline. Even when he undertook the commission of recording the play of his friend George Christopoulos, *The Death of Hemingway*, he completely restructured it in the editing (which he tends to do sequentially, from the beginning of the film to the end, without revisions) by incorporating in that color film a black-and-white ice floe, which happened to be left over at the editing table from Adolfas Mekas' *Hallelujah the Hills*.

It was in 1950, again in Toledo, that he made his version of the trance film, *Swain*. His collaborator Robert C. Freeman, Jr., chose the locations and mechanically operated the camera, as Markopoulos himself had once done for Curtis Harrington.

Swain is a film in three parts or movements with an elusive frame. It is part of what was to have been a much longer film called either *Rain Black, My Love,* or *Poème Onerique,* and it is a remarkably oblique distillation of Nathaniel Hawthorne's first novel, *Fanshawe.* The transformation is so drastic that no one could guess the source. In the first part of the film, the protagonist, played by the film-maker, rushes through the woods, climbs an embankment, discovers and then enters a mysterious house. In the middle section, a woman appears. Following the path of the hero, she pursues him through the house and subsequently disturbs his reverie in a greenhouse. As before, he flees from her. In the final part of the film, they meet briefly and awkwardly before a climactic recapitulation of images. The frame of the film appears piece-meal, first in the opening shots of the hero studying himself in a mirror. It is forecasted, though we cannot realize it at the time, in a series of architectural shots in the middle of the film, and again in a brief cut very late in the work, from the hero discovering a woman's stocking to a different view of him, dressed in pajamas, ripping up decorations or flowers. At the end of the film these elements are resolved: the hero in his pajamas opens his curtains, which disguise a windowless brick wall; the architectural details were those of an insane asylum, and we see his pursuer leaving it after paying him a visit. Like *The Cabinet of Dr. Caligari*, the whole of *Swain* is framed within the mind of the inmate of an institution, but unlike

Weine's film, there is no great overhanging question. We can infer that the patient is institutionalized only because of his refusal to accept a sexuality he finds foreign and gross and which society insists upon as a norm.

In an essay which Markopoulos has called "perhaps the only perceptive article concerning my work," Donald Weinstein says, "*Swain* is an evocation in gentle images and visual symbols of a subconscious rejection of the stereotyped masculine role that society and women insist upon. This rejection takes the form of escape: flight in fantasy from what is visually conceived as crude, repelling sexuality into the purity of creative activity, of nature, and of individual personality left inviolate."[5]

Swain is rich in metaphors. In the run of the hero through the woods and up a hill, quick interjections, first of a worm crawling on the wing of a dead bird, then of an alligator trying to mount another in a mud wallow, provide the first suggestion that his running might be a flight. The precise nature of that flight is further hinted at by his encounter with the marble head of a satyr on the road to the house. Inside the house, the woman encounters the hero sleeping on a bed. As she leans over to kiss him, the montage shows a black bug crawling within an exquisite white flower, a metaphor which also forecasts the scene in the greenhouse. Later the image is reversed: the bug crawls back out of the center of the flower when the heroine continues her pursuit into his floral sanctuary. The last in this series of animal and statuary metaphors is the image of a ram gargoyle intercut repeatedly with the heroine during her meeting with the hero in the last part of the film.

As in *Psyche*, costume plays an important function in *Swain*. The hero's elegant robe in the opening shots at the mirror and his pajamas at the end are the uniforms of his narcissistic imprisonment. The woman first appears in a white wedding dress, following the trail of the hero. When she encounters him in the house, he is asleep in a military uniform. At their final encounter, both are dressed in suits, suggestive in this context of the formality and the strain of their meeting. Sudden changes of clothes give the linearity of the film an elliptical texture. The hero alternates between a gray and a brown suit in the final section without apparent purpose.

A simple contrast is made throughout the film between the handsomeness of the hero and the homeliness of the heroine. Their comparative sensitivities are measured by his gentleness and curiosity in the greenhouse and her rough brushing of her hand over the flowers as she rushes through in pursuit of him. But as Weinstein has observed, there are visions which are hers, not his. When he first looks in the window of the house, he sees only his own image in the glass. Looking in the same window, she sees the face of a senile man—another forecast of the climax. "Mirrors," Weinstein writes, "rather than windows are [the hero's] interest."

At the end of the film, while the heroine and hero are talking before a small colonnade, a rapid recapitulation moves the film to its conclusion. Forty very quick shots, ranging from three to eight frames long and each, on the average, on the screen for a quarter of a second, recapitulate the whole film, mixing shots of the hero from various points in the film with buildings, statues, and the gargoyle. This spectacular summary of the film changes to images of the hero confined and of the heroine walking away from the institution.

In terms of its speed and scope of images, the clustered recapitulation of *Swain* is a great advance over that of *Psyche*, where the shots were for the most part a second and a half in length (the shortest being twenty-seven frames, or just over a second). The image cluster does not figure in the construction of the two short films Markopoulos completed in the early 1950s, *Flowers of Asphalt* (1951) and *Eldora* (1952). Between 1954 and 1961, he worked in Greece, Italy, and America on *Serenity*. The film had only a half-dozen screenings before it was stolen by its producer and disappeared. I did not see it and do not know the pace or form of the final montage, where the film is said to end "with a clip from every scene in the picture following each other in lightning sequence."[6] Thus the technique of *Swain* extends through *Serenity* to *Twice a Man*.

Swain, with the title *Rain Black, My Love*, ran for about an hour when Markopoulos left in 1950 for his first trip to Europe. When he returned, Brandon Films offered to distribute it if he would cut out half an hour. Markopoulos removed a long section in which the hero wandered within the house, which Amos Vogel of Cinema 16 once considered the most exciting scene in the film. Unfortunately, he destroyed what he removed.

Swain was not so much based on Hawthorne's *Fanshawe* as a project that originally began as an adaptation of *Fanshawe*. Hawthorne's novel describes the adventures of three college students—two men, Walcott and Fanshawe, and a girl, Ellen Langton. The first radical alteration of Hawthorne came when Markopoulos decided to combine the two males. In an interesting article on the film, "From *Fanshawe* to *Swain*," he admits it was the early description of Fanshawe that inspired him, not the plot: "a ruler in a world of his own and independent of the beings that surrounded him." That article continues with a set of quotations from the journal of Freeman, his collaborator, who writes: "Early we dropped this and gradually most traces of Fanshawe."[7] Unlike *Psyche*, *Swain* does not yield a literal paraphrase when compared closely with the novel; Hawthorne illuminates none of the difficulties in the film, although one might have wished for an insight into the enigmatic meeting of pursuer and pursued near the end of the film.

Nor does the film-maker use a novelistic form or novelistic intricacy in *Swain*. The complexity of *Psyche* derives, in part at least, from the artist's desire to condense the events of a novella into a short cinematic form and create a network of associations in portraying the affair of two active participants. *Swain*, on the other hand, is a trance film. Its hero is passive; its development is linear, with elaboration by metaphor rather than by the interaction of events. The trance film is by nature an erotic quest, and its quest figure is either a dreamer or in a mad or visionary state. In *Swain* the search through the imagination for a sexual identity takes a negative form; flight replaces quest, and the film resolves itself in narcissism and in a portrait of society's imprisonment of the self.

Twice a Man loosely follows the myth of Hippolytus. In Euripides' play, his stepmother, Phaedra, tries to seduce him. When he spurns her, she falsely accuses him to his father, by whose curse he is driven into the sea and drowned. In the opening of Frazer's monumental study, *The Golden Bough*, we find the subsequent legend that through the aid of the goddess Artemis and the physician Asclepius, he was resurrected and lived immortally in the sacred grove of Nemi. Frazer says he was called "Twice Born" there, and it is from this legend that Markopoulos adapts his title.

In the film, Paul, a contemporary Hippolytus, makes a visit to his mother's house after crossing New York Harbor to Staten Island. As he wanders through the house, mixing memory with prophecy, he envisions scenes of his life with his mother and with a male lover, whom the film-maker calls the Artist-Physician, a representation of the creative self.

The montage of the film interweaves the thoughts and memories of four people—Paul, his lover, and two versions of his mother, one as a young woman, the other very old. The point of reference shifts from one *persona* to another in an interlocking set of framing structures. The specificity of the reference point looms at one time and fades away at others. Paul exists both before and after his death; once, when entering the house, he sees glimpses of the young men come to mourn his death.

The film opens with an imageless screen. For a long time, it is totally

black and only the sound of rain is heard. The first shot we see is of the
Artist-Physician sitting sadly on the deck of the slowly moving ferry. One
could view the film as if it had evolved entirely through his mind. The
opening shot is interrupted six times by split-second flashes of the New
York skyline. The interruptions grow longer and more frequent until the
skyline is the dominant shot, and a single very short echo of the first shot
punctuates it. This form of cinematic enjambment distinguishes the
change of shots throughout most of *Twice a Man*. It offers the film-maker
nearly infinite variations for telegraphing his next image and for sustaining the overtones of the previous one. To the eye quickly trained by a few
minutes of watching *Twice a Man*, a direct cut, without forecast or recall,
is a visual shock.

A second shot of the Artist-Physician on the ferry prepares us, through
its interruptions, for the introduction of the hero, Paul. In the first elaborated sequence of the film, Paul seems to contemplate suicide. He stands
at the very edge of a roof looking down. His isolation is emphasized by
a rhythmic intercutting of his ascent to the roof by climbing a ladder, as
seen through a slowly following zoom lens mixed with shots of the movements of dancers at the party he has just left, shot from above. The Artist-
Physician, his lover, appears on the roof, framed in the distance behind
Paul. He places his hand on Paul's shoulder in a shimmering montage of
intercut close-ups of hand, shoulder, and lips. In his article on the production and the structure of the film, "The Driving Rhythm," Markopoulos
refers to this episode as the earliest meeting of Paul and his lover.

Paul, too, leaves Manhattan and embarks on the ferry. His trip moves
through day and night simultaneously, combining sunset, moonlight, and
dawn, and includes such shadowy images of other passengers that it distinctly suggests Hades and the crossing of the Styx. Within the course of
the crossing several brief episodes occur, for the reference has shifted now
from the mind of the lover to that of Paul. The interspersed events are
social gatherings—two unresolved scenes with different girls and a group
listening to a man recite—of which Markopoulous writes, "These are the
nameless who are without destination." Their sudden occurrence elec-
trifies the texture of *Twice a Man*, and the spectator is continually led to
expect new developments and to retain in his mind fragmentary scenes for
a possible resolution later in the film.

After the ferry lands, Markopoulos gives us another scene of rhythmic
and intellectual counterpoint before Paul goes to his mother's house. In
the episode in question, he cuts between Paul sitting among giant marble

slabs of a public monument and his lover pacing on the marble terrace of a museum as the sun fades and shines again in synchronization with his movements. The montage contrasts the calm waiting of one and the anxiety of the other, but still more interesting is the atemporal juxtaposition of the two scenes.

The house of Paul's mother is the climax in a line of mysterious or enchanted houses in Markopoulos' work—the house which the couple in *Psyche* point at and observe, the house in *Swain*, whose exploration the film-maker unfortunately removed—and in other early American avant-garde films. The ultimate source and most fabulous example of this motif was the Hotel des Folies-Dramatiques in Jean Cocteau's *Le Sang d'un Poète*. As Paul wanders through the rooms, scenes with his mother as a young woman inside the house and scenes with his lover outside take shape. The mother as an aged woman remains throughout *Twice a Man* an indistinct figure. She incarnates the spirit of memory and of loss which pervades the film.

Alternately, the house is empty and inhabited. As Paul first enters he sees, almost as if they were mirages, two young men crying. They are his mourners. He calls out, and we see quick flashes of the young and the old mother and hear a human voice for the first time in the film. Although we might expect to hear the hero at this point, each time he calls it is a young woman's voice that calls his name.

In the early digressions from the action in the house, Markopoulos gives us three scenes of the Frazerian Hippolytus in inverted order. In one we see him ritually cut a lock of his hair while kneeling on a city street and "offer" it in a mailbox. The second, through a breath-taking cut from the purple and rose interior of the living room to the yellows and oranges of a forest in autumn, shows us Paul caressing the trunk of a tree, presumably in his sacred grove.

The last of the three, which by chronology would be the first, shows his rebirth in the heavens. This episode is fused with the interior action, while the other two had been sudden ruptures. The reincarnation comes at the climax of a scene in the kitchen where the young mother seems entranced. She speaks through billows of smoke. The words that she speaks on the soundtrack are physically fragmented by the film-maker's cutting into the sound tape and deleting parts of the utterance: "Our air/ sent thro . . . sun's golden/ por . . . and descended/ invi . . . move . . . lea. . . ." The words "through," "pores," "invisible," "movement," and "leaves" have been fragmented. First we see brief flashes of his navel (two frames) and of the Milky Way (two frames). Very gradually the length of these shots increases, and they vary so that in superimposition Paul unravels from a fetal position in the Milky Way and in Saturn. His chest and back appear in the disk of the sun, then his head. The images of astronomical rebirth are scattered through the scenes of the mother in smoke, so that they appear as illustrations of her prophecy.

Before the scene of the hero's heavenly regeneration, the voice of the mother had asked him why he kept seeing the Physician. The remaining digressions, or framed episodes as he wanders through the house, are, as if in response to the question, a review of the encounters of the two men meeting in the rain, walking together, and visiting the classical sculpture gallery of a museum.

Within the house the numerous murals, richly painted walls, velvet and elegant wooden and straw furniture, golden cupids in relief, and other decorations of a visually lush nature form the background for the hero's wanderings. The transitions to bright exterior scenes or to subdued interiors, such as his lover's blue apartment, create a dynamic visual counterpoint.

At one point we see Paul asleep in a chair. A book, *Prince of Darkness*, lies in his hand. What follows may be his dream: his young mother in a white wedding dress hovers over his dead body, which is stretched out on a rock beside the sea. Part of her dress covers his naked loins. At the point when her lips touch his face in a kiss, the film-maker cuts to an extreme close-up of a white cat licking his chops. The death by sea is one specific reference to the imagery of Euripides. On the other hand, the presence of his mother in her wedding dress recalls the pursuer of *Swain*. In the next scene, we find Paul stretched out on a bed, stroking the cat; a further indication that the previous image was his dream. Yet in *Twice a Man*, past, present, and future, dream and waking, are so fused that they dissolve as distinct categories of experience or thought; they exist within the perspectives of the film as flavors of experience.

From the scene in the bedroom to the end of the film, the center of reference oscillates between the Artist-Physician and the two mothers. The old one appears more frequently now. At one point both mothers even appear on the bed with Paul.

That shot is interrupted by a spectacular recapitulation of seventy-seven shots, each only two frames long, of clips from the beginning of the film up to that point, more or less in the order they had first appeared. The entire passage blazes by in less than seven seconds. This sudden explosion of images initiates the drive toward the climax of the film. At the end of it, the montage slows down for a moment, briefly reorienting itself in the house as Paul comes out of a bath, but within a few seconds the scene shifts again to the corridor of an opera house or theater, where Paul sits at the top of a staircase, his lover beside him. As the lover's finger traces the line of the hero's profile, from his forehead past his nose, a second recapitulation occurs, this time of thirty two-frame elements in a somewhat more scrambled order. His lover takes his hand. While a new sequence from the mother's house begins to assert itself, we see Paul simultaneously standing up and collapsing to the ground, as bits of each movement are intercut.

Back in the house, the bathroom episode is intercut with a complex scene of the two mothers, seen individually, and reflected through a mirror, reaching out to touch the hero's cheek as he shaves. The scene gradually shifts from the mirror to a final location, an empty ballroom. Here we see Paul dancing by himself, with a superimposition of shimmering crystals as if from a chandelier above his head. His lover is reflected in the glass of a mirror column. He dances until he collapses. His lover comes to kiss him, as his mother had done. As he lowers his head toward the protagonist, whom we assume to be dead now, his face completely intermeshes with his in superimposition, so that we see two people but one face. He kisses him. When the Artist-Physician lifts his head away, the image of the hero's face cracks, like broken glass, and the pieces fall away leaving a white screen, where at first there had been only black.

Markopoulos conceived *Twice a Man* as a film with synchronous dialogue. Throughout the film we see people talking, but cannot hear them. In *Film Culture 29* he wrote up some of his notes from the shooting in the form of a tentative script. Here is part of the scene of the two mothers by the mirror:

> Cut to the young Olympia and her son seen through a magnificent mirror. We see the son's face and Olympia is a hazy image in the background. We hear her ask:
> Why do you keep seeing the physician?
> The son, Paul, in the same composition, turns and looks towards the sun's rays—a long ray glistens to one edge of the film frame, and we hear him say:
> When you get to like a man's face,
> There's nothing you can do about it.
> The scene changes to the aged mother before the mirror. Now she is seen through her mirror. Slowly, exquisitely, in profile she raises her hand as if

to touch Paul—he falls into frame. In the mirrored shot we see his face covered with shaving cream. The aged mother's hand touches his face, and draws away. Cut to the young Olympia. There is cream on her finger-tips. Paul is by her side. Slowly she goes to touch his lips. As she turns her hand away towards the rays of the sun, Paul grabs it, and as if in a dream, tilts it toward the camera lens. He holds her outstretched hand, saying:

Mother!

Cut to Olympia, the younger. She raises her hand. Cut to the aged Olympia. She is alone before the mirror, her hand held high in the air. There is no one there.[8]

He edited the film sequentially from beginning to end without revision. Markopoulos had the cosmic rebirth scene printed first "to see if it would work." Then he ordered the whole silent print. By this time, he had decided to discard synchronous sound and use the voices of Paul, his young mother, and perhaps his lover. When his protagonist failed to show up for a recording session, he decided to use only the single woman's voice. Finally he hit upon the idea of fragmenting her words. In "The Driving Rhythm" he describes this process more dramatically: "Originally dialogue was to be utilized, until I decided in favor of the more powerful motif of thunder."[9]

He does use several claps of thunder in the film, as well as bursts of rain, and the sound of shattering, cracking ice in the final image. He also placed snatches from the third movement of Tchaikovsky's *Manfred* at several points in the film. Earlier in *Psyche*, he balanced silence and sound by stopping the music for the blue reverie; in *Swain* he keeps the film silent until the hero approaches the house, and then the music begins.

The words of *Twice a Man* begin as Paul enters his mother's house. They continue through the various scenes in the house as if it were haunted by fragmentary echoes. Rather than making the words meaning-less, the fragmentation creates new ambiguities and an aural tension. The ear rapidly reconstructs the broken words.

Markopoulos completed *Twice a Man* in 1963, just in time to enter the third Experimental Film Festival at Knokke-le-Zoute in Belgium, where he won a $2000 prize. The film came at the high point of the mythopoeic development within the American avant-garde. Brakhage had finished and was exhibiting the first two sections of *Dog Star Man* by then; Jack Smith was still exhibiting the year-old *Flaming Creatures*; *Scorpio Rising* appeared almost simultaneously with *Twice a Man*. As I have written else-where, the shift from trance film to the mythopoeic film can be viewed as a shift from a cinema rooted in Freudian psychology to one related to Jung. I do not mean to imply that these film-makers all read Freud at one time, then read Jung and changed their films. The shift from an interest in dreams and the erotic quest for the self to mythopoeia, and a wider interest in the collective unconscious occurred in the films of a number of major and independent artists. The mythopoeic film need not evoke a classical myth or compare different myths, although it may do either or both. Mythopoeia is the making of a new myth or the reinterpretation of an old one. In the world of myth, which all these films share, imagination triumphs over actuality, and this imagination is unqualified by the perimeters of dream or delusion, as it is qualified in the trance film.

So strong was the impulse to create a mythic cinema that all the artists I have just mentioned immediately plunged into new myth films after completing the films named. Brakhage continued to work on the three remaining sections of *Dog Star Man* until 1966; Jack Smith shot *Normal Love*; Anger sought to repeat *Scorpio Rising*'s form in *Kustom Kar Kommandos*. Finally Markopoulos, now confident in the maturity of his form, began the Prometheus project which he had wanted to make since his U.S.C. days.

During the making of *Twice a Man*, Markopoulos began publishing his most important theoretical articles. He had written and published on film throughout his career, but it has been the articles since the early 1960s that embody his mature vision of cinema; he has tacitly recognized this himself by including nothing written before 1962 in his collected articles, *Chaos Phaos* (Temenos, Florence, 1971).

In "Towards a New Narrative Film Form," he discusses the montage system of *Twice a Man*. After criticizing the conventional sound cinema for its neglect of the "film frame" and for its failure to achieve a "poetic unity" of word and picture, he speaks of his newly-created editing style:

> I propose a new narrative form through the fusion of the classic montage technique with a more abstract system. This system involves the use of short film phrases which evoke thought-images. Each film phrase is composed of certain select frames that are similar to the harmonic units found in musical composition. The film phrases establish ulterior relationships among themselves; in classic montage technique there is a constant reference to the continuing shot; in my abstract system there is a complex of different frames being repeated.[10]

Earlier in the article he had rejected the use of filters, anamorphic lenses, laboratory effects, and even costumes as significant elements in the formal organization of films. Thus he grounds his polemic in the central theoretical dialectic of the American avant-garde film. Deren, as we have shown in the second chapter, sought the essence of cinema in the very mechanics of the filmic materials and equipment. She defined the art of cinema as the manipulation of space and time as it was recorded by the camera. For her, fast and slow motion and the use of negative were legitimate tactics, while graphic imagery and anamorphosis were not, because the former were tied directly to the conventions of the camera and the latter were expressionistic or surrealistic distortions of its function.

Although he did not elaborate his opposition to this position in theoretical articles, Sidney Peterson in practice made a cinema in which the representation of space was purely a function of the will and the imagination of the film-maker rather than a given of the lens. Polemically, Stan Brakhage became the theoretical expositor of this position, as we shall see in the next two chapters. For Brakhage, indeed, one primary responsibility of the film-maker as an artist is to overcome imaginatively the built-in predispositions of the equipment as it is standardized and manufactured.

The argument about the ontological status of the spatial image in cinema has animated most of the theory of the American avant-garde. For instance, when James Broughton wrote, in his note to *Mother's Day*, that "from the beginning I accepted the camera's sharply accurate eye as a value rather than a limitation . . . I decided to make things happen head on, happen within the frame, without vagueness, without camera trickery . . ." he aligned himself with Deren's position and implicitly distinguished himself from his former collaborator, Peterson. Anger never took a public stance on this issue, but his films, through *Scorpio Rising*, depend upon a spatiality that originates with Deren. In fact his most Deren-like construction, *Inauguration of the Pleasure Dome*, marks a turning point in his practice. In the original version from 1954, montage and the correlation of offscreen vectors perform the whole work of synthesis; but when he re-edited it in 1966, the elaborate use of superimposition introduced a new type of synthesis, within the spatial dimension, which he continued to explore in his later film, *Invocation of My Demon Brother*.

Markopoulos has always focused his energies on the reconstruction of time in his films, and has tended to accept the givenness of cinematic space even when his work on single-frame montage within the camera led him to superimposition. His theoretical exploration of the operation of the single frame begins with the investigation of its representation of psychological complexities and subtleties, but it quickly moves beyond that. In the later essays he assigns it an hieroglyphic significance which puts into question the authority of cinema's representation of movement itself. For instance, when he introduces the category of the "Invisible" into his theories, in "The Event Within the Camera," he is reviving, consciously or not, the theory of the *Interval* of Dziga Vertov. Vertov called attention to the differential between film shots (not frames) as the most significant element of montage. He was, of course, arguing with Eisenstein's concept of synthesis between shots. Markopoulos would have had access to Vertov's speculations on the *Interval* when a collection of Vertov's writings was printed in *Film Culture* while *Twice a Man* was being shot.

Unfortunately, Markopoulos' theoretical formulations have not received the degree of attention they deserve, even from the critics most sympathetic to his films. This is due in part to their elliptical and often hyperbolic style. A considerable hermeneutic effort is often required to isolate his insights and set them within their proper context in the history of film theory.

The evolution of his thought on the function of the single frame corresponds to a change of its function within his work. In *Twice a Man* the single-frame montage grows out of the recapitulatory passages in *Psyche, Swain,* and *Serenity.* Since the whole film is inscribed within the memory of the Artist-Physician, the single-frame clusters tend to represent complexes of his remembered past, while the variations which mark the transitions between shots can be interpreted as proleptic movements in the mind's narration to itself of its own history. In the later films this psychological representationalism disappears. In *Himself as Herself* and *The Illiac Passion* this method of montage will undercut the illusion of the temporal autonomy of a scene or the narrative autonomy of a single mythological episode. In *Gammelion,* Markopoulos abolishes the "continuing shot" as a matrix for the single-frame cluster and invests totally in the "hieroglyphic" power of the static frames. In these later works the film-maker continues to see cinematic structures as a model for the human mind but he no longer accords a privileged place to the category of memory within that model.

Among the polemic reductions common to the film-makers of the American avant-garde, although not universally true of them, a new attention to the single frame, the one twenty-fourth of a second unit of cinematic experience, is foremost. As early as the mid-1950s, Peter Kubelka, in Austria and then unknown to any of the American film-makers, was affirming the dominance of the single frame in his films and in his utterances on cinema. Markopoulos is correct when he writes that for the commercial film-maker the fact that cinema is a rapid succession of still pictures "has been understood only as a photographic necessity." The illusionism of conventional cinema depends upon the obscuring and erasing of the single frame to heighten the novelistic identification of the viewer with the characters filmed.

In forthcoming discussions of Stan Brakhage, Peter Kubelka, Robert Breer, and Hollis Frampton, the question of the approach to the single frame will be considered more fully. What is interesting and unique in Markopoulos' formulation is not so much the attention to the frame that he shares with others, but his attack on the classical notion of the "shot," which must be defined as a given camera take whose length is determined by the number of its frames before the interruption of a splice. In its place, he substitutes the more elaborate notion of the "complex of frames," or the conventional shot together with its echoes of the previous images and its forecast of the next. In Markopoulos' system the change of elements would not occur at a precisely defined instant—the appearance of a splice—but at the more diffused moment when the previously interrupting image becomes the dominant one. Thus he replaces the concept of editing as a "collision" of images, to use Eisenstein's phrase, with the more musical notion of a sequence of accented shots. He need not give up the sense and power of "collision" montage in so doing, since it remains one option of the joining of frames in the interruptions or the meeting of the dominant with its minor images.

Markopoulos continues his essay with a discussion of the visibility of the single frame. Then he enumerates its advantages:

> Limitless change in rhythm, or the sudden interjection of alliteration, metaphor, symbol, or any discontinuity introduced into the structure of the motion picture, makes possible the arrest of the film spectator's attention, as the film-maker gradually convinces the spectator not only to see and to hear, but to participate in what is being created on the screen on both the narrative and introspective levels.[11]

In "The Filmmaker as the Physician of the Future," he suggests a spiritual force within the avant-garde film movement tantamount to its having curative effects: "the New American Cinema Film-maker is a physician of images, the first of his kind." The characterization of the lover in *Twice a Man* as the Artist-Physician comes to mean more in this context than the fusion of the idea of the film-maker with the myth of Asclepius. "From film to film," Markopoulos writes, emphasizing the continuous process of the artist's work, "the creative film-maker as opposed to the commercial film-maker, offers to the creative film spectator (a recently realized species) with each film conception that murmuring vibration which after a time, from film work to film work (I think of Brakhage, of Harrington, of Stroheim, of [Jack] Smith) becomes the congeries which reveal this self-same film spectator's Being."[12] He offers two instructions for the audience in viewing his films (this essay was read as a lecture before a screening of *Through a Lens Brightly: Mark Turbyfill* and *Himself as Herself*):

> A—Do not attempt to single out any one film frame or series of film frames passing across the screen, and thus neglect others. Such abstraction would lead to a total misunderstanding of either film.
>
> B—To view the film as image composed to image, regardless if it is only a single frame. It is the Invisible that the film spectator must seek. This Invisible will lead him forwards and backwards and ultimately towards the Future: the future in this case is the understanding of the films.[13]

The application of his confidence in the montage of *Twice a Man* came with the making of *The Illiac Passion* and *Himself as Herself*. Although the latter film was made and edited after the former, it was printed and released first. Before either film was released, the film-maker finished and showed *Galaxie*, a collection of thirty portraits, and *Ming Green*, a study of his apartment.

In *Himself as Herself* Markopoulos offers a tour-de-force concentration for one hour of film on a single character, who manifests alternately a male and a female *persona*. Perhaps the limitation to a single figure was a reaction to the handling of almost thirty characters in *The Illiac Passion*.

Himself as Herself takes Balzac's *Seraphita* as its source, reducing the five characters to one and transferring the action from the Norwegian coast to an elegant quarter of Boston. Balzac's novel, his most occult work, describes the union of Seraphita and Seraphitus in a single body, feminine and masculine, and his eventual ascension into a Swedenborgian heaven.

The film proceeds statically with some thirteen major scenes, or locations, edited in the same way as *Twice a Man*, but without any recapitulation or framing devices. It opens with the protagonist dressed in a tuxedo, as he is through most of the film, and operating an electron microscope. The repeated and puzzling alternation of a beautiful fan and a gilded human foot punctuates the scene. The interior scenes of *Himself as Herself* are as elegant as those of *Twice a Man*, but they suggest much greater wealth. We first see the hero inside, beside a fireplace, where he finds a ring and reaches out as if to embrace someone who isn't there. Our first view of his female manifestation occurs next when his intercut ascent and descent in a hand-operated elevator shows him alternately in his tuxedo and in a woman's sari. He lightly touches stuffed birds and cowers in fear as a live parrot looks on. Then, in a central and revealing scene, the protagonist crawls undressed under a fur piece to sleep. A mysterious hand strokes his hair; unidentified lips kiss him.

The transition from one episode to another is gradual. The use of single frames prolongs the change of scene which by contrast had been relatively rapid in *Twice a Man*. The occasional choice of close-ups, such as the foot and the fan near the beginning, as the central shots of a scene, further separates the significant actions of the protagonist and gives the film a static quality despite the flickering of its montage. A fine glass is broken on the rug, and a bobby pin appears in one such scene of close-ups. Furthermore, the sensual attention to objects by both the camera and the protagonist reinforces the stasis. He sits next to a glass cabinet in which a wedding dress (again!) is displayed. He is handling a woman's white shoe.

Markopoulos makes more use of the off-screen look and gesture as a force unifying the different locations in this film than in any other. The protagonist finishes writing a letter, signs it with the pressing of a flower on the page, and reaches out off-screen, as if to the single-frame echoes of his female self in the previous scene in the garden. In the climax of the film, both male and female *personae* seem to come together and embrace on a staircase. Markopoulos achieves this while maintaining a sense of their individuality by very rapidly intercutting from the masculine to the feminine as they move toward the same point on the staircase. A final scene brings the hero to a religious ecstasy as he falls to his knees, beating his heart and apparently crying, in New York's Trinity Church. The *Gloria* of Poulenc, heard before and during the titles, accompanies this scene.

Robert Lamberton has found sources for the images of *Himself as Herself* in Balzac's novel, from which he offered the following excerpts:

It always hurts me to see you use the monstrous wisdom [science] with which you strip all human things of the properties conferred on them by time, space and form, to consider them mathematically under I don't know what pure expression, just as geometry acts upon bodies whose solidity it abstracts from them.

.   .   .

Seraphitus undid his sable-lined cloak, rolled himself in it, and slept. . . . To see him thus, wrapped in his usual garment, which bore as much resemblance to a woman's peignoir as to a man's coat, it was impossible not to see the delicate feet which hung below as those of a girl . . . but the profile of his head must have seemed the expression of human force brought to its highest degree.[14]

In a note for the Film-Makers Cooperative catalogue, the film-maker refers to the theme of the film:

The film's point of departure and inspiration is from de Balzac's famous novel *Seraphita*. While de Balzac's novel depicts with grave Swedenborgian overtones the ecstasies of a hermaphrodite, Markopoulos' own *Himself as Herself* depicts the tragic situation, typical to the day, and one might say especially of the American scene of that black-tie Athenianism that is prevalent on the Eastern Seaboard. Indeed, a denial of one's self. *Himself as Herself* begins in the laboratory which contains an electronic microscope at Boston University and ends at Trinity Church.[15]

And in an interview with Jonas Mekas he says, "The clue to the whole film is the tuxedo that the protagonist wears. You see, it's a certain strata of society. That's my first social comment." *Himself as Herself* is Markopoulos' most mysterious film. These clues hardly clarify the mystery. They refer, I believe, to a level of the film which can be paraphrased as the spiritual crisis and revelation of a man who at the beginning lived and thought superficially. The film moves from science (the electron microscope) to religion (the church), and its turning point is a scene of ambiguous love-making (the fur piece). Markopoulos once contrasted the revelations of American avant-garde films with those of science, saying that the viewing of certain films "becomes an inevitable religious act: containing all that the Sciences, various as they are, very often do not contain, and often as not do not communicate to the average spectator."

The "clue" to *Himself as Herself*, despite what its maker has said, is not the tuxedo or the social status of its hero. Its mystery is more fundamental than that and rests in the end upon Markopoulos' unique conception of the relation of cinema to literature. When asked, for what must have been the thousandth time, about the relation of his films to the French *nouveau roman* by the Voice of America he answered:

I don't think it's the film-makers that are being inspired by the latest gimmickry of the French novel, such as Robbe-Grillet and company. I think what is happening is the image which, you know, for thousands of years was trying to replace the use of the word has done that, and the novelists just have no way out. They have to imitate film. . . . You have to go all the way back, you know, to hieroglyphics. We're back at that interesting stage, and I think that's where vital communication can come into effect. . . . A film is made up of a series of frames. These frames can be used to a psychological purpose. I mean, literally, the single frame—and they do not become subliminal. You can actually see a single frame on the screen. It's just a matter of, you know, even the theatre-going film spectator becoming accustomed to this sort of thing. But, you see, in my kind of work, in about . . . two seconds, I can release how many frames and reveal an emotion, an idea, or anything you can think of.[16]

In his references to hieroglyphics, Markopoulos is suggesting that picture narrative ontologically and historically precedes verbal narrative and that the invention of the motion picture camera made possible a revival of this ancient and fundamental form of expression. The novel, then, would be a secondary attempt to translate cinema, even before its mechanical invention, into words.

In *Himself as Herself* Markopoulos has relied more than in any other film on the "hieroglyphics" of cinematic imagery to assume the burden of narrative. Its companion piece, *Eros, O Basileus* (Eros, The King), was made shortly after *Himself as Herself* and released at the same time. Although the film-maker has never formally coupled the two films, they complement one another. *Eros, O Basileus*, too, has only one character, who appears naked in most of the film's nine tableaux. His sexual presence and confidence on the screen are very much the opposite of the introspective androgyne of the other film. The objects he touches—books and paintings—are the icons of the creative spirit; there is also a camera and rewinding equipment in the film. When the protagonist slowly strikes the pose of Eros and shoots imaginary arrows from an invisible bow, one feels not so much the presence of the god as a Mannerist tension between the naked youth and his role, a tension reminiscent of the grinning nude San Giovanni Battista of Caravaggio.

Before he shot *Himself as Herself* Markopoulos said it would be edited in the camera. Later he changed his mind. *Eros, O Basileus* was constructed while shooting with a small amount of editing afterwards. The formal innovation of that film for Markopoulos is its punctuation by fade-outs made in the camera, not as terminal points, but as phrase-markers within a single camera set-up or shot.

The film-maker resurrected the discipline of making films without post-editing in 1966 when he shot his collection of portraits, *Galaxie*. The previous year Stan Brakhage had completed and screened a series of portraits of his family, other artists, poets, and ending with a portrait of the film-maker Jonas Mekas—all in 8mm. That collection of portraits, called *15 Song Traits*, was incorporated within his serial film, *Songs*. Somewhat earlier Andy Warhol had put together two sets of short facial portraits—one take to a person—called *13 Most Beautiful Boys*, and *13 Most Beautiful Girls*; he had also done a feature-length, full-size portrait of Henry Geldzahler, the art critic and curator, smoking a cigar. Of the forty portraits Markopoulos shot, thirty were incorporated into his finished film. A year later he did a single portrait, about twice as long as the others, called *Through a Lens Brightly: Mark Turbyfill* (1967).

In making the portraits his method had been to select an object or an activity with personal significance to the subject. Carefully watching the frame-counter on his camera, he would expose a number of takes of one image interspersed with blackness, achieved by simply covering the lens for as long as he wanted. He would then rewind the film and expose the units of the next view, detail, or object. In the finished portraits, each of which lasts for three and a half minutes, or the time of projecting 100 feet of film, each image has its own metrical pace, which alternates with or is superimposed upon the others. By gradually increasing the length of an image from a single frame to a long take, and then diminishing it correspondingly, he could create an effect similar to the editing junctures in *Twice a Man* and *Himself as Herself*. Three factors determine that a film made this way will have a texture more muted and less marked by "collision" montage than the post-edited films. First, a certain calculus of change is inherent in the method; its limits are controllable, but as the control gets more and more precise, the subject must become more static and the intervals more regular. Second, the inevitable superimposition of junctures makes for softer transitions. Third, the method from the first implies a stationary subject, while it absolutely excludes such radical collisions as change of film stock, mixing black and white with color, and switching to negative, all of which Markopoulos has done at one time or another in his career.

In *Ming Green* (1966) Markopoulos gives us a portrait of his apartment. Through the window we see trees. After a short moment of blackness we see the trees again, with still other trees superimposed. Then a view looking down at the garden below is intercut with blackness (eleven frames of the garden eight times, with a variation of nine to thirteen frames of black in each interval), giving the impression of a winking image. On the eighth view of the garden the trees reappear in super-imposition.

Within the room, a close-up of the buds of a flower in a vase quickly fades in and out. A bright red chair at a typing table alternates in flashes, at times in superimposition, with books on the window sill. Then several views of the window appear at the same time in a flood of light. A composition with record jackets, two red chairs, and a lamp alternates with a rose. The rhythm varies in overlapping waves from long holds to quick flashes. Several compositions of the full room show the ming green walls from which the film takes its title. A bookshelf, a red drum, and an orange drape "wink" in syncopation on the screen. Then a different bookshelf appears with superimpositions of the plaster texture of the wall and a close-up of a casually thrown white shirt. Finally, over recurrent flashes of the orange drape, a framed photograph of the film-maker's father appears. The white shirt appears in eight-frame-long flashes over a dim photograph of the film-maker's mother. The superimpositions end; there is a clear hold on this photograph. When it goes out of focus, the film ends.

Ming Green is silent until the final photographs. At that point Wagnerian music can be heard. The orchestration of color, the controlled metrics of the flashing and superimposing images, and the sureness of the compositions, make this film one of Markopoulos' most successful achievements of in-the-camera editing. With unusual structural control he builds the intensity of his images from the opening with trees and garden, through the pivotal introduction of the red chair, to a sentimental but in no way maudlin climax with the shirt and photographs.

In his article, "The Event Inside the Camera," he reminds us of the technical achievements of George Méliès and D. W. Griffith in creating effects within the camera. He lists the advantages of this method of working:

> The event inside the camera leads, according to the technical and aesthetic skills of the filmmaker, to: (a) editing; editing directly in the camera; (b) creating effects, filmic nuances, with the camera itself. The advantages of editing in the camera have economic and aesthetic values; for by editing in the camera one must be more and more exact; the idea

and the image more concentrated; the result a more brilliant appeal to the mind and dormant senses.[17]

As Markopoulos indicates, one cannot discount the economic advantage of editing within the camera. By comparison to any other genre, school, or period of film-making, the new American film artist creates his works with an astounding economy. Still, if one is faced with the burden of paying laboratories to print films (and Markopoulos had his splicing for *Twice a Man*, *Himself as Herself*, and *The Illiac Passion* done in a laboratory according to his precise indications on the frame) and after the expense of raw materials, developing, and renewal of equipment, the financial burden on an individual without outside aid is enormous and often defeating. Thus for the prolific artist, editing within the camera has a decided financial advantage; particularly for Markopoulos, who had first used this method in *Lysis* and *Charmides*. He revived this method after editing *The Illiac Passion* and while that film was sitting in the laboratory awaiting splicing and a complex form of printing that would have cost tens of thousands of dollars if he had not reformulated his conception and relinquished his desire for certain special effects.

The Illiac Passion culminates fifteen years of successive projects for a film based on the Prometheus myth. The first script the film-maker prepared for it appeared as early as *Swain*. At the beginning of that film the hero picks up the script in a field and dances with it in fast motion, just before the intercutting of the dead bird and mating alligators.

In a text written around 1949, he speaks of his aspiration toward "my ultimate universal films":

> "Prometheus" would be in color. In the opening scene a figure of "Prom" would appear alone in a great valley and there he would symbolically nail himself to the "world" by raising his hands to the sky— many figures would come to see him—Poseidon, Io, Hermes, etc. "Prometheus" scenes would be filmed in one locale—the various other sections would be filmed in various countries. Io in Egypt, Hermes as a medieval figure in England, etc. All of these would be spliced together and we would have a truly "universal" film. There would be no dialogue except at the end, when the camera sinks into the ocean. Prometheus will say, "Behold me, I am wronged." Not only would he say it in English but other voices would be heard as if echoes in other languages.[18]

The title goes back to the mid-1950s, to the section title of his long poem, *Angelica Clamores*. There it was spelled "The Iliac Passion." It refers, of course, to the iliac region of the body where the liver is found, the source of Prometheus' "passion" and the object of Zeus' torture.

His note for the New York premiere of the film will be the starting point of my analysis:

> The Illiac Passion is the odyssean journey of a film-maker amongst the characters of his imagination. That is to say, Markopoulos used as his point of departure the Greek myths, universal in essence, even to the present day, and from these was inspired to discover the various personalities inherent in these mythic themes from everyday life. For his characterizations he selected the exciting personalities which were in the scene, circa 1964-66 in New York City.
>
> The Illiac Passion retells the passions of one man, the figure who crosses Brooklyn Bridge at the beginning of the film, comes to the Mother Muse, then proceeds to the forest in the tradition of, say, all heroes, perhaps, Zarathustra, and there under an apple tree communes with his selves. These selves are recreated by some twenty-five characters; and each character or set of characters relate a complete situation. Yet each situation is summed up as the very Being of the only protagonist in the true sense of the word, the hero of The Illiac Passion, who is without name. It is as if the characters were the very molecules which made up the protagonist. It should be noted that Markopoulos continues his intricate and basic compliment to classic editing, in his further use of the single frame, as an equally important component in editing: better yet, in telling his story to the New Cinema Film Spectator. As for the narrative: it is taken from the translation of the play Prometheus Bound by Aeschylus. Not only is the text read by Markopoulos in a highly original manner which enhances the theme of the film, but he also, at the same time, frequently appears in the film himself. Always urging the film to its natural conclusion. It is like Andre Gide in his most famous novel, Les Faux Monnayeurs, reviewing his characters.
>
> Richard Beauvais—Prometheus; David Beauvais—his conscience; Robert Alvarez—Narcissus; Taylor Mead—the Demon or Sprite; Sheila Gary—Echo; Mrs. Peggy Murray—The Muse; Tom Venturi—Hyacinthus; Tally Brown—Venus; Kenneth King—Adonis; Margot Brier—Pandora; Paul Swan—Zeus; Wayne Weber—Icarus; Carlos Anduze—Hades; Stella Dundas—The Moon Goddess; John Dowd—Endymion; Philip Merker—Apollo; Beverly Grant—Persephone and Demeter; Clara Hoover—Io; Gregory Battcock—Phaeton; and the Film-maker Markopoulos.[19]

Like Anger in his notes for Inauguration of the Pleasure Dome, Markopoulos has several figures in his film whom he does not identify in this note. This may be only marginally successful because, again like Anger, he has sometimes changed the identification from one god to another during the shooting or editing. Finally, in a film with so many characters flashing on the screen in simultaneous groupings, it is not easy to be confident one has correctly identified each figure every time he appears.

One should say at this point that the sorting of the pantheon is not essential to the experiencing of the film. In fact, as the note suggests, the fusion of the gods is more significant than their separate characters, and the form of the film promotes that fusion. Nevertheless, in a descriptive analysis, the individual identifications save lengthy paraphrases and follow the plan of the film-maker.

The whole film is rounded by an image of an iron fence at dusk, which appears at the very beginning and the very end. The permutation of characters in between is the most complex of Markopoulos' career and one of the most elaborate in all of the cinema.

Like *Himself as Herself*, *The Illiac Passion* has no recapitulation; instead, Markopoulos created several brief scenes in which sets of figures come together in the same frame although their myths are not related. One such scene in the middle of the film shows several characters crossing paths in Central Park; another shows Pandora, Orpheus, the Muse, Adonis, Phaeton, and others doing a slow, circular dance.

For the most part the film presents each myth individually, sometimes intercut with one or two others. In waves all the way through the film, parts of several myths come together, then separate. The action of the myths is continually punctuated by images ranging from very brief to whole episodes of Prometheus and his counterpart, his naked, writhing "Conscience." To a lesser but still great extent, it is also punctuated by the recurrence of the Muse or Sprite (a composite for Markopoulos of Aeschylus' Force and Might); and finally the film-maker makes sudden incursions into the film: disentangling Persephone's scarves; taking a light-meter reading on a grand staircase; filming in a broken mirror; or tapping a lamp to give it a pendular swing.

After the initial shot of the fence at dusk, a series of fades introduces many of the pantheon as they walk through New York's Central Park in a montage that uses imagery interwoven from all the seasons. In flashes, the costumed Persephone runs through the landscape with flowing crepe scarves. Markopoulos decided to introduce the fades after he saw how they worked in *Eros, O Basileus*. The fading continues to the end of the film and assumes a formal role almost equal to that of the single-frame transitions of images.

On the soundtrack we hear the film-maker's voice reading from Thoreau's translation of Aeschylus' *Prometheus Bound*. He selects words for repetition as he reads, making the literal sense of the text thoroughly abstract. Markopoulos' rendering begins: "I, I, I, I contemplate far bounding earth, earth, earth, earth unapproached, approached, unapproached, approached solitude, solitude unapproached, solitude, to the unapproached solitude." The primitive, incantatory quality suggests the mysterious reception of the gift of language which Prometheus gave to man more than the complex word formation and periphrasis of Aeschylus' style.

A figure crosses Brooklyn Bridge, whose "adamantine structure" of stone and cable suggests to the film-maker the binding of Prometheus. In a transition of quickly intercut flames (recalling another of the god's gifts to man, fire) the figure encounters the Muse, a middle-aged, benevolent-looking lady posed on a rock. Prometheus himself appears in a three-piece suit and assumes a position as if bound to a tree, strikingly reminiscent of the Proustian "Prometheus" in Max Ernst's collage novel, *La Femme 100 Têtes*. The Sprite, or Demon, the most humorous character in the whole of Markopoulos' work, appears on a rock, hooting and gesturing; then he descends to taunt Prometheus at his tree.

Some of the characters of *The Illiac Passion* dress conventionally, while others assume exotic costumes or appear primarily in the nude. The costumes, such as the Sprite's streaming red tassels, Icarus' mosaic wings with encrusted film strips, Poseidon's silver suit, or Io's hieratic dress, were created by Jerome Hiler in close collaboration with the film-maker.

I do not have the space in this book to begin an extensive analysis of *The Illiac Passion*. As an index of its complexity, I shall simply enumerate the mythic allusions in the order in which they occur in the film and the montage of parallels, anticipations, and returns by which they are joined.

The first of the myths to be elaborated is that of Narcissus. Here, as with most but not all of the other myths, the presentation is schematic, with narrative dependence on both explicable and inexplicable objects. Narcissus is seen in a bath. A bronze bug appears on his body. He studies his face in a mirror of mica. Narcissus shares his cinematic time with another young man (Hyacinthus?), who is first seen eating an egg. For a few moments the rush of myths runs together; there are flashes of Orpheus, Persephone, and the Muse within the continuation of Narcissus' self-contemplation. Persephone and Hades making love gives way quickly to the introduction of Daedalus, an artisan with a goatee, who first appears smoking. The last stage of the Narcissus myth occurs with a superimposition of several views of his nude form dancing and writhing against a background of newspapers. The presentation of his body here, as elsewhere in the film with other figures, conforms to the postures of mannerist painting.

Between scenes of Daedalus in his workshop and a somewhat later scene of him collapsing in the snow as he looks up and off-screen, presumably first at the flight and then at the fall of his son Icarus—between these fragments there are flashes of the female figure Markopoulos calls Echo, wandering in a yard among piles of desks and chairs, and of the Sprite confronting Prometheus. After Daedalus' scene in the snow, we see the body of Icarus lying on a beach as a storm whips up the waves in breakers and foam. Another juncture of myths brings Daedalus, Icarus, Persephone, and Hyacinthus, who is throwing a pencil instead of the traditional quoits, together with a figure of Eros stretching red ribbons like a bow. Out of this cluster, scenes of Icarus come to dominate. We see his wings; then an apple is rolled over his naked body.

The image of the apple found its way into the film through an interesting set of associations, rather typical of the aesthetic transition from literary to cinematic in Markopoulos's work. A friend told him of the Propertius poem (*Book I, Elegy* 3) in which the drunken poet returns home to find his mistress asleep. He playfully rolls an apple over her torso until she awakens and immediately begins to criticize him. In Markopoulos' use of this image, the apple is sensually rolled over the body of Icarus by the filmmaker himself. In "The Adamantine Bridge" he miscredits it to Catullus. Before beginning almost every film, Markopoulos undertakes an extensive reading, spends weeks in the library, researching sources, versions, analyses. Perhaps he never did so as extensively as for *The Illiac Passion*. An alchemy such as the incident above suggests has been the typical fruit of his researches.

Like *Twice a Man, The Illiac Passion* has scenes shot for synchronous sound and later used silently. The nude figure of Prometheus' Conscience writhes and speaks, punctuated in the film by the droll image of the Sprite swaying and hollering at the top of a tree. At this pivot, which is the psychological as well as the temporal center of the film, the figure of Prometheus is replaced more and more by that of his Conscience. We see no more of Narcissus, Daedalus, Icarus, Echo, Hyacinthus, or Apollo. New figures are introduced, and some who briefly appeared before, such as Persephone, are elaborated later.

Switching between her earthly role as Demeter and her subterranean guise as Persephone (Markopoulos compounded the two), the twin goddess appears superimposed under a fountain. Dressed in brown, she wanders through a forest, makes love with Hades, and feels her way through the mist. Her unearthly movements continue into and through the several scenes of Aphrodite and Adonis, which are the longest in the film. Aphrodite, with obese sensuality, was inspired, Markopoulos has said, by Shakespeare's version of the myth in his poem "Venus and Adonis." Adonis is by contrast a thin youth. We see them in bed, in a quarry where Adonis is sun-bathing, performing a ritual marriage in an empty church, and smoking a hookah. When she kisses him, the film-maker intercuts the colored flares that occur at the end of a roll of film from overexposure to the light. It is in the midst of their story that we see several figures as if dancing on the beach—the Muse, Pandora, Adonis, Orpheus, Eurydice, and Phaeton. The conclusion of Aphrodite and Adonis coincides with the end of Persephone/Demeter's appearance on the screen.

The recurring image of Prometheus' Conscience at this phase suggests a painting by Magritte: fire is superimposed as if in the foreground and deep through the outline of his nude back a street receding into the night can be seen. Briefly, an aged Zeus accepts a cup from the naked Ganymede. Poseidon, played by Andy Warhol before a backdrop of two of his large flower paintings, furiously pumps an Exercycle and talks to the naked Conscience of Prometheus on the floor in front of him.

With the introduction of his hieratic Io, the film moves toward its end. The scenes of Orpheus and Eurydice are intercut with her unheard speech. Orpheus walks out of a tavern in a panic. He and Eurydice appear walking as if out of Hades, with black veils over their heads; when they prematurely remove them, she disappears from his embrace in a series of jump cuts. Io and the Conscience of Prometheus meet at a lighthouse in the winter, while Orpheus and Eurydice appear in a kitchen eating melon. A hand rests on the fence of the opening shot; when it leaves the frame, the film comes to its end.

The Illiac Passion is clearly Markopoulos' most ambitious achievement so far. To sustain and control such a large and diversified form he called upon all his powers of formal invention. Numerous plans, techniques, and strategies were tested and discarded. Early in the planning of the film he wrote:

> *Prometheus*, that project of many years, seems to be growing heavily. I think of making each of the characters in *Prometheus*, creating them out of single frames. The Character of *Prometheus* would appear at such a rapid pace that the audience might sit through the filmic movement of the character for an hour and not realize it! Then would follow the move-

ments of the other characters; and finally the final movement, the emotions, interrelated of all the characters, that is the theme, visually, cinematic with sound, would be expounded.[20]

During the first weeks of shooting, he collected leaves, rocks, objects from the scene, which he planned to collage into the film stock as Stan Brakhage had done in *Mothlight* and *Dog Star Man: Part Two*, but the plan was dropped.

All through the editing he wanted to print the film on 35mm with different screen portions assigned to Prometheus and to the myths around him. This plan underwent its own variations, and I do not know what version of it the laboratory was instructed to execute. In a letter of June 26, 1964, long before the shooting was complete, the film-maker drew me the following plan for the printing which will suggest the complexity and expense involved:

> Now, I am so pressed for time; but I do want to show you a diagram of how my film will look on the screen; and hope you will be able to figure it out. Here it is:

* The 35mm. will at times appear as single or longer shots: sometimes superimposed. Both color and black and white. At times the 16mm. frame will be enlarged: and at times the 8mm. frame which will make it grainy: the 8mm.
** The 16mm. will be in color and the heart of the film with the greatest variations occurring in that section of the screen.
*** The 8mm. will be like the most inner consciousness which probably is unreachable.

The laboratory told the film-maker that his plan would cost tens of thousands of dollars to realize. He tried to raise the money. Then, at the end of 1967, just before the fourth Experimental Film Festival in Belgium, he returned to the United States—he had left after making *Eros, O Basileus* —and very quickly got the footage into shape for conventional printing. In this last-minute change, a film that went to the laboratory originally as three hours long came out lasting ninety minutes. The difference between the film as now seen and the staggeringly ambitious montage that went to the laboratory in 1966 will always be a mystery.

When Markopoulos obliquely writes in his introductory note that "each situation is summed up as the very Being of the only protagonist in the true sense of the word," he identifies himself with the Romantic tradition. That tradition, as I have already stated, and will continue to amplify throughout this book, dominates the aesthetics of the American avant-garde film. It manifests itself differently in the works of the different artists (Anger and Markopoulos are less reluctant than others to embrace Romanticism without reconstruction), but it manifests itself persistently. As Harold Bloom observed of the twentieth century tradition in English poetry, "every fresh attempt of Modernism to go beyond Romanticism ends in the gradual realization of the Romantic's continued priority."[21] Even in his approach to Hellenic mythology Markopoulos follows the strategies the Romantics found most successful; *The Illiac Passion* has less in common with Aeschylus' play than with Shelley's vision in *Prometheus Unbound*, particularly with the symphonic rapture of its apocalyptic final act. Shelley too saw Prometheus as the unitary man tormented by his divided selves, and he interiorized the Aeschylean conflict. In Markopoulos' modernist inflection of the Romantic Prometheus, the whole struggle with Zeus (Aeschylus' one surviving play of the trilogy; Shelley's First Act) disappears. In the vacuum he has supplied a new dimension: the relation of the film-maker to his film.

The Romantic posture did not rest well with Maya Deren. She struggled against it in her own films, and labeled them "classicist." She opposed Anger and later Brakhage when his work veered toward Romanticism. Her contact with Markopoulos, though, was minimal. When she was exercising some limited power through the Creative Film Foundation, he was in Greece making *Serenity*; she died soon after he returned. They, more than any other two film-makers I shall be considering, attacked the dialectics of narrative time in their films. Maya Deren devoted meticulous attention to the subversion of sequence and space-time connections. But ultimately her aesthetic of transfiguration is an affirmation of the presence of time in its logical order. Markopoulos cut the Gordian knot; the simultaneity of his narrative structures abolished or at least scorned time. The first approach is a modified classicism, the other purely Romantic.

Harold Bloom has used Hart Crane's phrase "the visionary company" to call attention to the confidence of the major English Romantic poets of the nineteenth century that they were the inspired prophets of a tradition stemming from the Bible and continuing through Spenser, Shakespeare, and Milton to them. In Markopoulos' article, "Projection of Thoughts," one finds the following enthusiastic appraisals of the role of the American avant-garde film-maker:

> The film-makers who have banded together under the auspices of the Film-Makers Cooperative have each and every one of them that divine fire and confidence which the ancient Greeks called *thrasos*. . . . Furthermore, I would venture to suggest that only in the motion picture as an art form and that means immediate and continued experimentation/ creativity/inspiration while at work, is there the truth of what we enjoy naming Reality.[22]

Taken as a whole his writings are a continued ode to the process of film-making in itself and as a source of revelation to the film-maker. Everything else, from the audience's comprehension to the finished work of film, is secondary. One is reminded of Sidney Peterson's "A Note on Comedy in the Experimental Film," when Markopoulos describes in "Institutions, Customs, Landscapes" the projection of the rushes of *The Illiac Passion* for the cast and friends:

> This festival of the emotions of the spirit, of the mind, continues week after week. Its intention is perhaps Dionysian, and the New Cinema Spectators enter as freely into it as the ancients entered into their Dionysian revels. . . . Often, when the footage projected is a work in progress . . . the New Cinema Spectator finds himself engulfed with a divine frenzy or enthusiasm, sharing the excitement of the film-maker himself.[23]

The first film Markopoulos made after moving to Europe was *Bliss* (1967), a study of a small church in Greece, edited in the camera and reminiscent of *Ming Green*. His next was a long film, *Gammelion* (1968). That film had its origin in a visit he paid to Caresse Crosby's castle Roccasinabalda in 1961 while *Serenity* was being shown as part of a New American Cinema Exposition at the Spoleto Festival. Soon after visiting the castle he prepared a meticulous adaptation of Julien Gracq's novel, *Le Château d'Argol*, with Roccasinabalda in mind. Like all of his detailed scripts, of which this was the last, the film was never made. He wanted to shoot *Eros, O Basileus* there before he settled upon a New York loft as the location.

In the summer of 1967, with enough money for only two rolls of color film—about seven minutes' running time—he went to the castle and shot very short shots of the surrounding valley, the walls, ramparts, gardens, corridors, a red spot that might be blood on the road, the frescoes, etc. Out of that material he made one of his major works.

Gammelion takes its title from the ancient Greek month suitable for marriage. The film is structured by a thousand slow fades in and out of black-and-white leader, which extend its time to 59 minutes. As the screen slowly winks from light to dark and the reverse, tiny shots—sometimes just single frames—are interjected of the landscape around the castle. We gradually move closer and closer to it, view the corridors, glimpse a nude couple in the frescoes, and then move outside again. On the soundtrack there are snatches of music from Roussel, the sound of horses' hooves over pavement, and the voice of the film-maker reading Rilke's lines: "To be loved means to be consumed. To love means to radiate with inexhaustible light. To be loved is to pass away, to love is to endure."

The impression of *Gammelion* is unlike that of any other Markopoulos film. It is at once terribly spare and very rich. The unmoving images (there may be a slight flutter in the castle's flag, but that would be all), the lack of figures other than the couple in the fresco, who first appear so quickly they might be actual, and the total lack of incident in the film create the aura of a fiction without elaborating any specific fiction. Markopoulos wrote that before going to Roccasinabalda he thought he would make a film that suggested in pictures the sense of smell (as his and other silent films have suggested sounds), but that he gave the idea up before shooting. *Gammelion* does not evoke odors and perfumes; yet it reverberates with a vitality beyond what it explicitly shows. It suggests, through the possibility of blood on the road, through the very emptiness of the castle which is obviously not abandoned, and above all through the sound, a permutation of novelistic situations as the film progresses. Again the artist seems to have returned, always in fresh ways, to the enchanted house of *Psyche, Swain, Twice a Man,* and *Himself as Herself.*

The making of *Gammelion* in Italy coincided with the emergence in America of a new form, the structural film. In that form the over-all shape of a film is its predominant characteristic, as the even sequence of fades is the overriding formal principle of *Gammelion.* The structural film represents in the history of the American avant-garde film as important a development as either the trance film or the mythopoeic film.

In the late 1960s the structural film, and its derivative, the participatory film, followed the mythopoeic form. The causes of this evolutionary shift are too complex to pinpoint. It is certainly not a case of one artist creating something which others imitate. The emergence has been too general and has been manifest in the works of too many otherwise opposed film-makers for that to be the case, although the question of temporal priorities seems to be an obsession of the film-makers themselves. Regardless of the cultural factors causing these shifts, we can see in the films of Gregory Markopoulos both an internal consistency and an evolution parallel to the general evolution of the avant-garde tradition.

Gregory Markopoulos has been, from the beginning of his film-making career, an erotic poet of the cinema. If we consider his long films in the order of their making (not their release)—*Twice a Man, The Illiac Passion, Himself as Herself, Eros, O Basileus, Galaxie*—leaving a question mark for the unseen *The Divine Damnation*—, and finally *Gammelion*, we can trace the gradual diminution of narrative, but we see (with the portraits as an exception) a sustained dedication to the definition of physical and spiritual love in cinema.

6

THE LYRICAL FILM

The previous chapter concluded with the proposition that the important stations of the evolution of the American avant-garde film were collective, and not the invention of any individual film-maker. The major exception has been the forging of the lyrical film by Stan Brakhage. The pervasiveness of the lyric voice in cinema among the works of neophytes in the late 1960s, a decade after Brakhage's formative works in that mode, was so great that it seemed that that way of film-making was completely natural and must have existed *ab origine*. Harold Bloom's observation about Wordsworth's achievement could be applied to Brakhage:

> Nor can I find a modern lyric, however happily ignorant its writer, which develops beyond or surmounts its debt to Wordsworth's great trinity of *Tintern Abbey, Resolution and Independence*, and the *Intimations of Immortality* ode. The dreadful paradox of Wordsworth's greatness is that his uncanny originality, still the most astonishing break with tradition in the language, has been so influential that we have lost sight of its audacity and its arbitrariness.[1]

In this chapter I shall retrace the history of the lyrical film through the early evolution of Brakhage's cinema and observe its influence where it has been most fruitful, in the films of Bruce Baillie.

Stan Brakhage is so prolific that it would be impossible to give even a cursory analysis of all of his films in this book. At the time of writing, they number either 49 or 78, depending on whether one counts *Songs* as one or thirty films.[2] Several of those 49 works are made up of separable parts, edited to be complete films in themselves. Five or six years younger than Anger, Markopoulos, and Harrington, he made his first film five years after they started. As an energetic and candid film-maker still in his teens,

Brakhage assumed their discarded reputations as the *enfants terribles* of the avant-garde film. Unlike Anger and Markopoulos he did not begin brilliantly; it was only after many films that his work began to approach the intensity of *Fireworks* and *Psyche*.

The 1950s were quiet years within the American avant-garde cinema. The enthusiastic surge of the late 1940s had ended; Peterson had stopped making films; Broughton was in retirement; Deren produced only one film; and I have just shown how Anger and Markopoulos spent most of that decade on frustrated projects. Nor was there a significant influx of new artists until the very end of the decade. Thus the figure of Stan Brakhage, making between one and five films every year from 1952 to 1958 and struggling to create a new form for himself, dominates the history of the radical film during that time.

The version of the erotic quest in all of his early films affirms again and again an unredeemed pessimism, not even momentarily relieved. Freud has never meant as much to any other film-maker. Brakhage even initiated an ambitious *Freudfilm*, but failed to bring it off. He was unwilling to accept the trance film as a suitable form until he had reconstructed it on his own terms. These early works vacillate between a dramatic realism and Expressionism.

In his third work, *Desistfilm* (1954), he liberated his camera from its tripod and filmed a teen-age party, with five boys and only one girl. He successfully objectified the argument between Realism and Expressionism that was informing his art. From a beginning in which each of the characters is painfully isolated, though cramped in a small room (one plays guitar, another builds a house of cards, still others smoke solipsistically, pull lint from the navel, or make a fan of burning matches), the film moves to the teasing of a Pan-like youth, glimpsed at times in the nude. The boys toss him in a blanket and chase him through the woods at night, while a couple remains behind; their discreet lovemaking is seen from behind distorting windows. That distortion is removed with the sudden reappearance of the group, who glare at the lovers in clear focus.

While Brakhage was making his early films he was also directing a theater company composed of the actors who appeared in his films. The company undertook ambitious projects for summer tourists in Central City, Colorado. After dropping out of Dartmouth College, Brakhage had gone to San Francisco in the hope of studying with Peterson at the California School of Fine Arts. But that year the film program had just been terminated. He returned to San Francisco a couple of years later and took the room of James Broughton, who had left for Europe, in the house of the poet Robert Duncan and the painter Jess Collins, who is known by his first name. His fifth film, *In Between* (1955), his one essay in explicit dream structure, uses Jess as an actor and attempts to translate into cinema the dream world of his art.

In Between takes its title from the space of fantasy in between the film's framing images of the protagonist sleeping and waking. The dream moves from a neo-classical cloister to an abstract montage of colors, flowers, and cats, ending in a nightmare as a carved animal menaces the dreamer. *In Between* is distinctly minor Brakhage, even when compared to his early achievements. Yet like *Desistfilm* it shows a formal advance: here for the first time Brakhage develops what he called "plastic cutting," or the joining of shots at points of movement, close-up, or abstraction to soften the brunt of montage. Ostensibly this method was first used here to render dream changes, but in later Brakhage films it becomes a formal characteristic of his work.

Brakhage's final version of the trance film appears in four works—*The Way to Shadow Garden* (1955), *Reflections on Black* (1955), *Flesh of Morning* (1956), and *Daybreak and Whiteye* (1957). After these, the form ceased to have significance for emerging avant-garde film-makers. Of the four, *Reflections on Black* is the most complex. *The Way to Shadow Garden*, the most orthodox trance film of the other three, contains the first of Brakhage's "metaphors on vision" in the final minutes, when its hero, overwhelmed by adolescent frustrations, gouges out both his eyes and the film plunges into negative, showing him feeling his way through a garden of brilliant white flowers in an illusionary night. In *Flesh of Morning* Brakhage managed to film himself in a masturbation fantasy. The twin film *Daybreak and Whiteye* opposes a closely-held jump-cut view of a girl waking, dressing, and walking out to a bridge—presumably to kill herself—with a subjective view of someone trying to write a love letter and pacing back and forth in a room which looks out on a barren snow scene; the camera is held as if from the subject's position; we only see his hand in the film.

Reflections on Black is a trance film striving for a new form that has not yet been born. The "visions" of a blind man give the film its shape. On a street, he passes a prostitute, ignores her, then enters a tenement. He climbs three stories, at each of which he "sees," in a visionary sense where fantasy and sight mingle together, three different incidents of erotic frustration. By the time Brakhage made this film, he had begun to transcend the distinction between fantasy and actuality, moving into the cinema of triumphant imagination. The crossing of that threshold came later and at greater cost for Brakhage than for others, but once he had achieved it, the scope of his investigation of the perimeters of the imagination extended wider than that of any of his contemporaries.

Brakhage tried to reach beyond singular and personal agony by comparing three episodes in *Reflections on Black*. At the same time he tentatively proposed his version of the identity of erotic and aesthetic quests. He affirmed the physicality of the film material within the context of the blind man's "vision." Flashes or film flares—the stippled black-and-white effects that appear at the end of a roll of film because of exposure to and leaking of light—are intercut with the first walk of the blind man. Like the negative in *The Way to Shadow Garden*, they are metaphors of vision. Later, more emphatically, the film-maker has scratched with a sharp instrument on the film stock itself, so that a set of brilliant white stars shimmers over the blind man's eyes, changing slightly from frame to frame. By attacking the surface of the film and by using materials which reflect back on the conditions of film-making, Brakhage begins to formulate an equation between the process of making film and the search for consciousness which will become more clearly established in his later work as he has greater confidence in the truth of the imagination.

In the first of the scenes which the blind man witnesses within his limited imagination, a clear line is drawn between hallucination and actuality. A woman whose love for her husband is frustrated by his bitterness hallucinates that he embraces her while he is shaving, but a puzzled look from him brings her out of her daydream. Next, she thinks he had hanged himself as she sees his shadow in the next room, but he is merely changing an overhead light bulb. We leave her dropping dish after dish (jump-cuts) in her neurosis. At the second story, the voyeur himself takes part in the sexual quest. His eyes see again, and he begins to make love to a woman. When he rests her on a couch, her husband enters, and the white stars appear instantly in his eyes. The final episode is introduced by scratches of stars bursting on black leader, as if we too were seeing through the blind man's eyes. Here the masturbation of a woman is recorded symbolically by an intercutting of her twitching fingers with a pot of water on her stove that boils over.

Reflections on Black was the first film Brakhage made after moving to New York. While he was there, he initiated a new direction in his work almost by accident. Joseph Cornell, the collagist and Surrealist box maker,

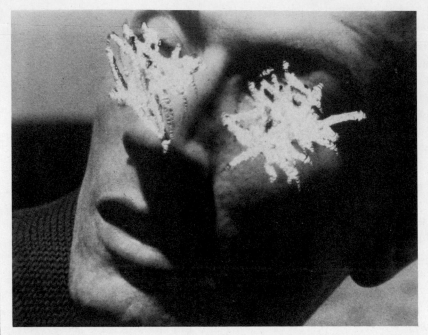

Scratching on film as a "metaphor on vision" in Stan Brakhage's *Reflections on Black*.

wanted someone to film the Third Avenue El before its destruction. Parker Tyler gave him Brakhage's telephone number. When Cornell called, according to Brakhage's account, the young film-maker had to admit he had never been on the El. That ended the conversation and, he thought, his election to make the film. But the next day he received in the mail two tokens for the El. Cornell supplied the materials, and Brakhage made *Wonder Ring* (1955).

Faced for the first time with the need to make a film without any skeletal drama or even an actor, Brakhage called upon and amplified the repertory of technical strategies he had used in his earlier work. The free-wheeling camera movement of *Desistfilm*, however, is notably absent. *Wonder Ring* records a trip on the El as if it were a round dance. Its formal texture springs from an alternation of plastic cutting with collision montage, the repetition of shots and of slow panning camera movements, and rippling distortions from an imperfect window in the car. Brakhage assembled the minute parts of his film in a continual flow of movements; not only of the train itself, whose forward motion is inferred from the passing sights outside the window, but also of reflections moving in the opposite direction within the car, and of the bouncing patches of sunlight intersecting both the movement of the train and the inverted movement of its reflection. A continual, lateral rocking motion suggests the rattling of the train to the ear's imagination in this silent film. Finally, the rhythmic structure follows the slowing down and speeding up of the train as it enters and leaves stations; for in those moments all the elements (passing view, reflection, and sun play) reduce, then pick up speed.

The same year Cornell asked Brakhage to photograph a film for him of an old house that he liked which was about to be torn down. The film he made was called *Tower House* until Cornell edited it and renamed it with a phrase of Emily Dickinson's, *Centuries of June*.

The encounter with Joseph Cornell opened a new direction for Brakhage's work. The shooting of *Tower House* and the editing of *Wonder Ring* were his first experiences with the sensuous handling of a camera and the purely formalistic execution of montage. In his works of the following two years we see side by side the purging of the black-and-white trance film—*Flesh of Morning* (1956), *Daybreak and Whiteye* (1957)— and the growth of a more abstract color form—*Nightcats* (1956) and *Loving* (1957). Brakhage was striving in those years to bring into the abstract form the intensity of experience and the complexity of ideas he had achieved in his modified trance films, and he extended that effort toward synthesis into his theoretical formulations as well. With the making of *Anticipation of the Night* (1958), he forged the new form for which he had been searching: the lyrical film. At approximately the same time, he began writing *Metaphors on Vision*.

The lyrical film postulates the film-maker behind the camera as the first-person protagonist of the film. The images of the film are what he sees, filmed in such a way that we never forget his presence and we know how he is reacting to his vision. In the lyrical form there is no longer a hero; instead, the screen is filled with movement, and that movement, both of the camera and the editing, reverberates with the idea of a man looking. As viewers we see this man's intense experience of seeing. In the lyrical film, the space of the trance film, that long receding diagonal which the film-makers inherited from the Lumières, transforms itself into the flattened space of Abstract Expressionist painting. In that field of vision, depth and vanishing point become possible, but exceptional, options. Through superimposition, several perspectives can occupy that space at one time (although it was only after *Anticipation of the Night* that Brakhage began to explore superimposition). Finally, the film-maker working in the lyrical mode affirms the actual flatness and whiteness of the screen, rejecting for the most part its traditional use as a window into illusion.

Joseph Cornell was not the sole influence in Brakhage's creation of the lyrical film. Ten years before *Wonder Ring*, Marie Menken had made her first film, *Visual Variations on Noguchi* (1945). Noguchi had asked her to look after his studio while he was away, and she decided to make an abstract film of her views of his sculpture. With a freely swinging camera, she shot rhythmic movements around the smooth, curved forms. Menken and her husband, Willard Maas, were among the first people to treat Brakhage kindly when he came to New York. They were responsible for his first public screening at the Living Theater. Several of the strategies of *Anticipation of the Night* can be found in Menken's *Notebook*, which contained fragments of films she had been saving since the late 1940s. In 1962 she gave it a definitive form. Within that work the sections "Raindrops" (thin rain hitting a pool, a drop slowly forming and falling from the tip of a leaf), "Greek Epiphany" (an Easter procession at night with only the lights of candles and lights of the church visible), "Night writing" (neon lights filmed with such quick movement that they appear to be brilliant calligraphy on the screen), and "Moon Play " (in which the moon seems to dance and jump about in the sky), all prefigure tactics employed in *Anticipation of the Night*.

Both *Whiteye* and *Loving* prepare the way for *Anticipation of the Night*. The subjective posture of *Whiteye* reappears with a new richness in the later film. Again we can only see those parts of himself that the man looking out at the world sees without the aid of a mirror: his arm, and, repeatedly, his shadow. From *Loving* Brakhage takes for his subsequent work a Modernist musical structure; in that film he perfected the rhythmic and contrapuntal premises of *Wonder Ring*. The camera sweeps past a couple making love in the grass. No long shot definitely establishes them in an "actual" space. Within the screen's space, they appear so close and in such a network of swift movements that often the viewer cannot separate male from female, decide if it is the lovers or the camera that is moving, or in which direction the movement is going.

The camera finds its way through leaves and branches before spotting the lovers, but once its sweeping motions catch them, the point of view shifts, and we see the sun, the sky in motion, and the trees as if from the eyes of the active lovers. When a foot presses against pine needles on the ground, the flowing imagery is arrested by a quick series of static shots of other needles, as if to suggest by the abrupt, staccato editing the tickling pain of the foot in contact with them. Brakhage freely mixes upside-down shots with his other material, and we again become aware of the blended perspectives—film-maker's and lovers'—when he uses a montage of short flares at the orgasmic climax of the short film. In *Loving* the editing is faster than anything Brakhage had done before; there are chains of shots, two, three, four, and five frames long, and often as many as twenty of them form one complex movement.

Brakhage's poetic paraphrase of *Anticipation of the Night* follows the sequence and evokes the spirit of the film:

> The daylight shadow of a man in its movement evokes lights in the night. A rose bowl, held in hand, reflects both sun and moon-like illumination. The opening of a doorway onto trees anticipates the twilight into the night. A child is born on the lawn, born of water, with promissory rainbow, and the wild rose. It becomes the moon and the source of all night light. Lights of the night become young children playing a circular game. The moon moves over a pillared temple to which all lights return. There is seen the sleep of the innocents and their animal dreams, becoming their amusement, their circular game, becoming the morning. The trees change color and lose their leaves for the morn, become the complexity of branches on which the shadow man hangs himself.[3]

The great achievement of *Anticipation of the Night* is the distillation of an intense and complex interior crisis into an orchestration of sights and associations which cohere in a new formal rhetoric of camera movement and montage. The first images of the film counterpoint the soft brown shadow of the protagonist passing through a beam of light coming from an open door and a window with the jittery dance of fast-moving lights at night. In a series of variations the shadows of the protagonist are joined by the shadow of a rose floating in a glass bowl, and the night-lights, continuing their rhythmic opposition, fuse with flares from the ends of film rolls. In the course of the repetition, inversion, and variation of the sequence of shadows, the film proceeds from inside the house outward. The closing of the door recurs again and again throughout the whole first third of the film, marking the transition alternately with a shot of the slowly swinging wood of the door and with the moving reflection in its window.

The retracing of phrases which gradually move forward reminds one of the syntax of Gertrude Stein's prose, a major influence on him:

> The voice Helen Furr was cultivating was quite a pleasant one. The voice Georgine Skeene was cultivating was, some said, a better one. The voice Helen Furr was cultivating she cultivated and it was quite completely a pleasant enough one then, a cultivated enough one then. The voice Georgine Skeene was cultivating she did not cultivate too much. She cultivated it quite some. She cultivated and she would sometime go on cultivating it and it was not then an unpleasant one, it would not be then an unpleasant one, it would be a quite richly enough cultivated one, it would be quite richly enough to be a pleasant enough one.[4]

In describing the sequence of scenes Brakhage accurately chooses the verb "to become." Although the film plays with the counterpoint of hard and soft montage, as indicated in the opening collision of night and day shots, the major scenes blend into one another in a rhetoric of becoming. The significant transitions of large areas of film, unlike the counterpoint, are forecast in advance by a pattern of camera movement, a drift of colors, or the "soft" preview of a forthcoming image. Like the single-frame montage of Markopoulos' mature style, the editing of *Anticipation of the Night* challenges the integrity of the shot as the primary unit of cinema. In its place, unlike *Twice a Man*, it proposes camera movement as the elementary figure of filmic structure (the static being a rare and special case of movement). By artfully eliding shots with plastic cutting, Brakhage can present a complicated movement spanning actually disconnected spaces as a single unit. The elimination of depth inherent in shadows, night photography, and fast panning motions enhances the concentration of camera movement as a formal unifier. Nowhere in this film do we find the deliberate use of foreground or background figures.

From the intercutting of trees reflected in the closing door with trees photographed directly, the film proceeds through fast, blurred shots of overexposed foliage to fast panning movements, each ending in a sudden "hold" on leaves. Then circular pans of the garden become continuous with circular sweeps of nightscapes. Out of the circles emerges a series of complex camera maneuvers in which a single shot seems to reverse its direction at the point of maximal speed. Brakhage creates this illusion, of course, through plastic cutting.

A recapitulation of the initial shadows shows them in inverted order (door, window, doorway). Outside again, the camera catches the rainbow in the spray of a garden hose and blends it, at times harshly, at times softly, with night-lights and flares.

In the course of the subsequent return to the day and night alternation, the sweeping camera passes the arm of a crawling baby. He returns to the infant's motions (again, as in *Loving*, "discovering" him in the garden) until the screen goes white in a close-up of his clothes. The intercutting of the baby's face entering the screen from different directions with wild circular and irregular pans of the flora, calls to mind the opening of *Metaphors on Vision*:

> Imagine an eye unruled by man-made laws of perspective, an eye unprejudiced by compositional logic, an eye which does not respond to the name of everything but which must know each object encountered in life through an adventure of perception. How many colors are there in a field of grass to the crawling baby unaware of "Green?" How many rainbows can light create for the untutored eye?[5]

As the street lamps alternately proceed toward and recede from the camera, the views of the baby become more aerial and distanced. We see him in the context of his garden arena as we never saw the lovers of *Loving*. But here the perspective is clearly the film-maker's, and for him, the attempt to capture the vision of the child was a failure.

A short mixture of what Marie Menken called both "Moonplay" and "Night Writing," here intercut, prepares the transition to an amusement park, where older children take rides in the night. In this passage the dominant range of colors tends to orange. Previously the street lamp images centered in blue, the garden in green, and the shadow-play brown and rose.

Even the shots of the children whirling on rides in the foreground with the lights of the park behind them have next to no depth on the screen. He intercuts the rides on the ferris wheel with those on the whip. The shots of these amusements grow shorter and less frequent as the nervous, jumping images first of the moon, then of the moon over a columned building called "the temple" in Brakhage's working notes for the film, assume the center of attention.

The brown and yellow temple scenes blend with the blue street lamps, photographed in the rain. In this juxtaposition the first shots appear of children asleep, and as the changes grow quicker, the first quick glimpses of exotic animals are seen. The theme of the temple and the moon falls out of this fugue-like structure, leaving a montage of street lamps and sleeping children punctuated by dark passages and red neon flashes.

In this context the close movements following the curved contour of a swan seem like part of a child's dream. The wings flap menacingly. Often in this part of the film the movements of the camera over the sleeping children appear on the screen upside-down.

The street lamps have changed from blue to red. The first images of trees at dawn, intertwined with the children at sleep, indicate that the film is moving to its end. The light grows brighter; the rainy green-blue street lamps pass for the final time; and in the cloudy dawn the protagonist reappears. His hand ties a rope to a tree. Slowly, mixed with moving shots of trees, his bright shadow swings, like a pendulum, as he hangs himself.

By the rigid standard of his subsequent aesthetic, Brakhage has criticized this ending as artificial and therefore wrong. Yet he hastens to add that while making the film (he edited it as he went along) he said to himself and others that he might hang himself for the finale, leaving a note to attach the footage of him hanging to the end of what he had already edited. He almost did kill himself by accident while filming that episode, he claims, although as a Freudian he interprets the "accident" as willful.

Despite the film-maker's repudiation, *Anticipation of the Night* works beautifully in its totality. It describes the doomed quest for an absolutely authentic, renewed, and untutored vision. The tender rendering of the crawling baby, the riding, and finally the dreaming children offer only momentary solace—and a more profound despair in the recognition of the impossibility of regaining that kind of innocence—to the visionary protagonist, who is seeking a cure to heal the irreconcilable divorce between consciousness and nature that he dreads. In his subsequent films through *Songs* (1964-1970), the estrangement from nature does not lessen; it may even become more acute, if that is possible. In any case, it becomes more explicit, but the film-maker responds less despairingly, with dialectical revisions of that fundamental crisis.

While he was making *Anticipation of the Night*, he married one of his students, Jane Collum. Nearly all of his films from that point focus on the modalities of married life, with the significant exception of *Dog Star Man*. In the interview which introduces *Metaphors on Vision*, Brakhage attacks what he calls "one of the most dominant [myths] of this century," that an artist cannot be meaningfully married, with a sketch of how his wife has inspired and helped to make all of his films from the time of his marriage to the publication of that book.

In the interview, the film-maker described the crucial decision for his work after *Anticipation of the Night* as the uprooting of drama from his films. Drama seems to be equated with a superficial view of external actuality for him, and his rejection of it is couched in terms of the Romantic discovery of the instability of the self:

> I would say I grew very quickly as a film artist once I got rid of drama as prime source of inspiration. I began to feel all history, all life, all that I would have as material with which to work, would have to come from the inside of me out rather than as some form imposed from the outside in. I had the concept of everything radiating out of me, and that the more personal and egocentric I would become, the deeper I would reach and the more I could touch those universal concerns which would involve all man. What seems to have happened since marriage is that I no longer sense ego as the greatest source for what can touch on the universal. I now feel that there is some other concrete center where love from one person to another meets; and that the more total view arises from there. . . . First I had the sense of the center radiating out. Now I have become concerned with the rays. You follow? It's in the action of moving out that the great concerns can be struck off continually. Now the films are being struck off, not in the gesture, but in the very real action of moving out. Where I take action strongest and most immediately is in reaching through the power of all that love toward my wife, (and she toward me) and somewhere where those actions meet and cross, and bring forth children and films and inspire concerns with plants and rocks and all sights seen, a new center, composed of action, is made.[6]

The idea of the multiple self is also reflected in the working notes for *Anticipation of the Night* which Brakhage published as the fifth chapter of *Metaphors on Vision*, "Notes of Anticipation." There we find the following fragment of a scenario:

Sequence Order for Shooting the Night Film

The rose as it may pertain to self.
The self reflective among tree shadows.
The self as a force of water.
The dance of the twilight children.
The children's faces in the night backed by artificial lighting.
The water spots as fallen stars.
The self reflected in black pools.
The fires of night.
The self afire.
The passage of night events, shifts of scene, explosions.
The self in a perpetual turn.
The drunkenness becoming perpetual night.
The self as God.
The passages of memory as blocks of light suddenly thrown open.
The self in parts played out as on a stage.
The avalanches of white sheets.[7]

This passage is quoted as an index to the mentality of the film-maker, not as a guide to the finished film. Brakhage has repeated in all of his writings and in speeches that his films arose from visions and needs that could not be verbalized. For the chapter "His Story" in his book, he offers a brief preface, "being entirely composed of script and scenario fragments so liter-realized that the necessity to visualize them never compulsioned the filming of them." The paradox of all of *Metaphors on Vision* is that it is a film-maker's book about the antagonism of language and vision. The penultimate chapter, "Margin Alien," in which the artist lists the literary, painterly, and musical influences he had to overcome in order to make films, ends "I am thru writing, thru writing. It is only as of use as useless."

In his aesthetics Brakhage has revived and revised the Romantic dialectics of sight and imagination which had been refocused in American abstract expressionistic painting and American poetry (particularly in the work of Wallace Stevens) during the film-maker's intellectual formation. The history of that argument is worth consideration at this time. William Blake championed the imagination against the prevailing epistemology of John Locke, who maintained that both thought and imagination were additive aspects of the verbal and visual memory. Blake wrote, "I assert for My Self that I do not behold the outward Creation & that to me it is a hindrance & not Action"—a forecast of the phraseology of Abstract Expressionism. "It is as the dirt upon my feet, No part of me. . . . I question not my Corporeal or Vegative Eye any more than I would Question a Window concerning a Sight. I look thro' it & not with it." Wordsworth too writes of the tyranny of sight:

> I speak in recollection of a time
> When the bodily eye, in every stage of life
> The most despotic of our senses, gained
> Such strength in me as often held my mind
> In absolute dominion.
>   (*Prelude*, XII, 127ff.)

Our philosophies and psychologies have shifted from the naturalism of Locke and his confidence in the senses. For some artists in the tradition of Blake and Wordsworth the eye now had a renewed and redemptive value. As Wallace Stevens puts it,

> The eye's plain version is a Thing apart,
> The vulgate of experience.
>   ("An Ordinary Evening in New
>   Haven," 1-2)

Harold Bloom has observed that "Modernist poetry in English has organized itself, to an excessive extent, as a supposed revolt against Romanticism, in the mistaken hope of escaping [Romanticism's] inwardness (though it was unconscious of this as its prime motive)."[8] The eye which both Stevens and Brakhage enlist in the service of the imagination confirms while striving to reconcile, as Bloom's view would have it, the Romantic divorce of consciousness and nature.

Brakhage claims to see through his eyes, with his eyes, and even the electrical patterns on the surface of his eyes. When he decided to become a film-maker he threw away his eyeglasses. At the beginning of his book he argues with the way language constricts vision and with the idea of sight built into the film-maker's tools. In "The Camera Eye," he writes:

> And here, somewhere, we have an eye (I'll speak for myself) capable of any imagining (the only reality). And there (right there) we have the camera eye (the limitation of the original liar) . . . its lenses ground to achieve 19th Century Western compositional perspective (as best exemplified by the 'classic' ruin) . . . its standard camera and projector speed for recording movement geared to the feeling of the ideal slow Viennese waltz, and even its tripod head . . . balled with bearings to permit it that Les Sylphides motion (ideal to the contemplative romantic and virtually restricted to horizontal and vertical movements) . . . and its color film manufactured, to produce that picture post card effect (salon painting) exemplified by those oh so blue skies and peachy skins.[9]

He proceeds with a program for bringing the camera into the twentieth century by distorting its lens, obliterating perspective, discarding the tripod, altering camera speeds, and changing film stocks. He calls for these home-made modifications in the name of the eye, demanding of the film-maker (actually of himself) a dedication to what he actually sees, not what he has been taught to see or thinks he should see. That the resulting version of space corresponds to that of Abstract Expressionism, whose motivations are away from the physical eye, seems not to have occurred to Brakhage. His sense of vision presumes that we have been taught to be unconscious of most of what we see. For him, seeing includes what the open eyes view, including the essential movements and dilations involved in that primary mode of seeing, as well as the shifts of focus, what the mind's eye sees in visual memory and in dreams (he calls them "brain movies"), and the perpetual play of shapes and colors on the closed eye-lid and occasionally on the eye surface ("closed-eye vision"). The imagination, as he seems to define it, includes the simultaneous functioning of all these modes. Thus Brakhage argues both with Blake and Locke, but his sympathies are with the former. Like the Romantics themselves, Brakhage's work attempts to refine the visionary tradition by correcting its errors.

The Romantic strain in Brakhage emerges with the creation of the lyrical film and culminates in his essay in mythopoeia, *Dog Star Man*, and its extended version, *The Art of Vision*, which will be discussed in the following chapter. Brakhage began to shoot his epic two years after finishing *Anticipation of the Night*. In the meantime, and through the shooting of that long film, he continued to make short lyrical films that mark one of the great periods in American avant-garde film. In this series of films— *Window Water Baby Moving* (1959), *Cat's Cradle* (1959), *Sirius Remembered* (1959), *The Dead* (1960), *Thigh Line Lyre Triangular* (1961), *Mothlight* (1963), *Vein* (1964), *Fire of Waters* (1965), *Pasht* (1965)— Brakhage invented a form in which the film-maker could compress his thoughts and feelings while recording his direct confrontation with intense experiences of birth, death, sexuality, and the terror of nature. These works have transformed the idea of film-making for most avant-garde artists who began to make films in the late sixties.

Window Water Baby Moving and *Thigh Line Lyre Triangular* record the births of the film-maker's first and third children respectively. Between the two, finished only two years apart, there is a great shift in style: the former treats the occasion almost dramatically, although the montage attempts to relieve the drama which Brakhage obviously felt while shooting the film and seeing his first child born; the latter film centers itself more fully in the eyes of the film-maker as a visual and visionary experience. The difference between them is not simply a measure of experience (seeing a third child born as opposed to the first), but that is part of it.

There is an interplay between the film-maker and his wife in *Window Water Baby Moving* that disappears in *Thigh Line Lyre Triangular*. The poetic fulfillment of that interplay comes at the moment late in the film when we see the excited face of Brakhage just after the child has been born. His wife, still on the delivery table, took the camera from him to get these shots. Earlier, they had photographed each other during an argument, which Brakhage intercut with negative images of them making love in the film *Wedlock House: An Intercourse* (1959).

In no other film does Brakhage make as much of the reorganization of chronological time; for the most part, his lyrical films exist outside sequential time in a realm of simultaneity or of disconnected time spans of isolated events. *Window Water Baby Moving* begins with images of late pregnancy. The first shots are of a window, framed diagonally, intercut with flashes of blackness. Throughout the film Brakhage uses black and white leader to affirm the screen and the cinematic illusion as one of several tactics for relieving the dramatic tension built up as the moment of birth approaches.

A rhythmic montage moves from the window to the light cast on the water in a bathtub where the pregnant wife is bathing. The camera is static, and the shots remain on the screen longer here than in other films of the same period. After a longish pause of blackness, we see Jane for the first time on the delivery table. At a painful moment in her labor, he cuts from her screams to her smiling face from the earlier episode and follows it with a recapitulation of the window and water shots. He flashes back to the earlier scene nine times, always showing it in a group of shots and always passing from one scene to the other on a plastic cut, as the glimpse of a window behind the held-up placenta, near the end of the film, initiates another cut to the window of the opening and a recapitulation of the sunlit images that follow it. *Window Water Baby Moving* ends with shots of the parents and the baby spaced amid flashes of white leader following the rhythmic pattern at the film's opening.

In *Thigh Line Lyre Triangular* we see a radically transformed space. The passages of black and white leader are more insistent; there are twisting, anamorphic shots of Jane in labor; the montage mixes the birth with

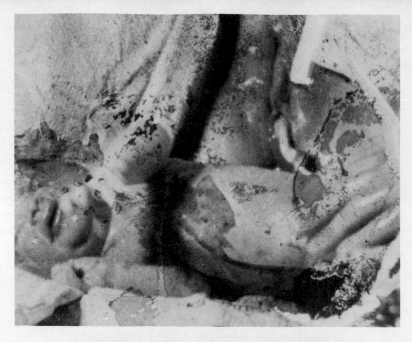

Abstract Expressionist space in Stan Brakhage's *Thigh Line Lyre Triangular* and Willem de Kooning's "Woman with a Green and Beige Background."

flaring shots of animals, a flamingo, and a polar bear from the out-takes of *Anticipation of the Night*. The entire film is painted over with colored dots, smears, and lines. The film begins with a painted stripe which seems to open up on a scene of childbirth with labor already under way. Underneath the rapidly changing, painted surface, we see the doctor, the birth, the placenta, the smiling mother, but in an elliptical flow completely devoid of the suspense of the earlier film. Where Brakhage used plastic cutting to switch from present to past or future in his first birth film, he uses the painted surface to smooth out and elide the transitions from the birth to the strange upside-down appearance of the polar bear or the shot of the flamingo.

Although we do not see him in this film there is no doubt that we are looking at the birth through the eyes of the artist, whose eccentric vision is ecstatic to the point of being possessed. At the time of the birth he was sufficiently self-composed to pay close attention to the subtleties of his seeing while watching his wife give birth. In the interview at the beginning of *Metaphors on Vision*, he explains that

> only at a crisis do I see both the scene as I've been trained to see it (that is, with Renaissance perspective, three-dimensional logic—colors as we've been trained to call a color a color, and so forth) and patterns that move straight out from the inside of the mind through the optic nerves. In other words, in intensive crisis I can see from the inside out and the outside in. . . . I see patterns moving that are the same patterns I see when I close my eyes; and can also see the same kind of scene I see when my eyes are open. . . . What I was seeing at the birth of Neowyn most clearly, in terms of this "brain movie" recall process, were symbolic structures of an animal nature.[10]

In the first chapter of his book Brakhage observes, "This is an age which has no symbol for death other than the skull and bones of one stage of decomposition . . . and it is an age which lives in total fear of annihilation." In *Sirius Remembered* and *The Dead* he searches for a deeper image of death. When his family's dog Sirius died, his wife did not want it buried. They left the body in the woods where it froze in the winter and rotted in the spring. Brakhage made periodic visits to it and filmed the stages of its decomposition. The title of his film puns on the memory and the reconstruction of the dog's members.

Formally, *Sirius Remembered* is the densest of his films in the repetitive, Steinian style of *Anticipation of the Night*, and it introduces a new style, which finds its purest expression in *The Dead*. The opening passage resembles a fugue, as one sweep of the camera is followed by another, beginning a little earlier and going a little further, while the third carries on from the first. The speed of these alternations and the sudden changes they make by a reversal of direction, the injection of a brighter still image, or the occurrence of a long pan suggest that the fugue has been transposed to the micro-rhythms of post-Stravinskian music. The similarity of the shots and their reduction through movement to two-dimensional abstractions fixes the attention on their rhythmic structure.

The pattern of rhythms established in the opening shots continues throughout the film as its visual material becomes more complex. The film proceeds through fall to winter to spring, with some reversals and overlapping of the seasons. Brakhage arrests the movement of the winter scenes with flashes of whiteness when the dog is covered by a layer of snow, to affirm the flat screen and puncture the illusion, but here also to suggest an emanation from the dog of pure white light.

Midway the already complex rhythmic structure becomes compounded by superimposition. The second half of the film elaborates an intricate harmonics as the two layers of fugue-like rhythms play against one another.

In this film Brakhage views death as the conquest of the antagonist, nature, over consciousness. He illustrated this antagonism with a story of the visit of two friends during the making of the film:

> Suddenly I was faced in the center of my life with the death of a loved being which tended to undermine all my abstract thoughts of death.
>
> I remember one marvelous time which gave me the sense of how others could avoid it. [P.T.] and [C.B.] came to visit us and C. wanted to go out into the fields "to gather a little nature," as he put it. "Nature" was such a crisis to me at this time that I was shocked at that statement. [C.] made some martinis, handed me one; and [P. and C.], and I all went out into Happy Valley where they toasted the new buds of spring that were beginning to come up, etc., and marched right straight past the body of Sirius either without seeing it at all (any more than they can see my film *Sirius Remembered*) or else they saw it and refused to recognize it. [C.] was envaled in the ideal of toasting the budding spring and here was this decaying, stinking corpse right beside the path where we had to walk, and he literally did not, could not, or would not see it.[11]

In the same interview he describes in detail how a mystical illumination helped him edit the film.

The skeletal head of the dog in *Sirius Remembered* was the first of several conventional images which Brakhage has attempted to redeem from the realm of the cliché by looking at them freshly and presenting them in a novel form. Others are the image of the tombstone as a significant image of death (*The Dead*), the heart as an image of love (*Dog Star Man: Part Three*), and flowers as an image of sexuality (*Song XVI*).

While passing through Paris to work on a commercial project (for a long time Brakhage supported himself and his art by taking commercial assignments), he sneaked his camera into the Père-Lachaise cemetery to film the monumental tombs in black-and-white. During the same trip he filmed people walking along the Seine in color from a slow-moving tourist boat on the river. At the end of a black-and-white roll, he took a shot of Kenneth Anger sitting in a café.

When he returned to America, Brakhage associated Europe, Anger, and the two traditional images, the river and the tomb, with his thoughts on death. He says:

> I was again faced with death as a concept; not watching death as physical decay, or dealing with the pain of the death of a loved one, but with the concept of death as something that man casts into the future by asking, "What is death like?" And the limitation of finding the images for a concept of death only in life itself is a terrible torture, i.e., Wittgenstein's *Tractatus Logico-Philosophicus* 6.4311: "Death is not an event of life. Death is not lived through. If by eternity is understood not endless temporal duration but timelessness, then he lives eternally who lives in the present. Our life is endless in the way that our visual field is without limit."[12]

He put the three images together—Anger, the tombs, and the Seine—to make *The Dead*.

Nearly every image in the film appears in superimposition, which serves several formal functions which I shall enumerate as they appear, and one poetic function: to make a spectral light emanate from people and things, as if the spirit showed through the flesh and burst through the cracks in marble tombs. Visually, Brakhage relates this effect to a thermal light sometimes visible to the trained eye, and to the Anglo-Saxon allusions to *aelf-scin*, a fairy light that hovers on the horizon at dusk.

The film opens with a pan up a Gothic statue, interrupted by flashes of negative. The black-and-white positive and negative have been printed on color stock, giving them a green-gray tint. From the color footage, only the blues of the water and occasional reds (sweaters, the oars of a rowboat) registered on the composite film. A quick image of Anger in the café changes to a double image of him as the negative is placed over the posi-

tive with left/right orientation reversed. The camera moves with fragments of rocking pans among gravestones and crypts upon which sporadic
superimpositions briefly appear. This part of the film contains frequent
sudden solarizations (the simultaneous printing of negative and positive,
causing an instant flash or leap of the image on the screen).

A quick movement toward a crypt blackens the screen. Out of that
darkness come deep blue images of the Seine, in a rapid montage; followed by a leisurely pan of the cemetery in tinted black-and-white. Another variation on the opening passage (Anger, Gothic ornamentation,
the statue) ends in a white-out.

People, in blue and red, strolling along the banks of the river, appear
over pans, sometimes upside-down, of the tombs. In this introduction of
the theme of "the walking dead," as Brakhage calls these strollers, the
tempo changes from slow, to staccato, to slow again, to staccato again, until the scene almost imperceptibly shifts from the superimposition of people with graves to a flow of superimposed cemetery images, a few frames
out of synchronization, with its solarizing negative. The negative echoes
the slow rocking of the positive images and pursues them like a ghost.

The shifting of visual themes and their gradual evolution through synthesis and elaboration constitute a meditation on death and the spirit in
which thoughts, in the form of images, are tested, then refined, and finally
passed over. A persistent idea of the light behind the objects of sight
haunts the mind's eye of the film-maker and the structure of his film.
Through the medium of the river, the stress shifts from positive to negative.

By overexposure of the film the graves appear almost washed out by
the light of day. Another montage of water shots introduces a multiple-
layered positive shot of the graves so white that only faint images in the
corners of the screen indicate what they are. The movement on the river is
contrasted with that of the cemetery through intercutting and superimposition until flashes, then long holds of pure white, break up the river
shots.

The climax of the film is its breakthrough into negative following the
flashes of whiteness. Brilliant, pure white trees in a black sky and dark
crypts with cracks of brightness rock across the screen, paced with black
leader. The long rocking motions move first in one direction, then another, shifting with the black shots. There is a long movement containing
four black pauses as the camera passes so close to large tombs that the
light is completely cut off. The second of these is so long that one thinks
the film might have ended. But sudden flashes of solarization revive the

ending structure, like final optimistic surges of sound before the end of many symphonies. A short finale brings us back to the Seine and the film ends on a slow movement across the shadow-marked marble wall of the river bank.

Like *Sirius Remembered*, some of the rhythmic texture of *The Dead* comes from the opposition, repetition, and superimposition of different movements of the camera. But here, rhythmic intricacy is less essential to the form of the film. *The Dead* uses superimposition organically, eliding the transitions from theme to theme or from one tempo to another. The abrupt element in the film is solarization. Finally the passages of pure whiteness and blackness act as poles in the spectrum from positive to negative and from black and white to color; they seldom interrupt the texture of the meditation. The best example of this is the long black passage in the pan of graves. The viewer can imagine the continuity of movement as he believes the camera is passing behind a large tomb. The shot a few seconds earlier prepared him for this. But gradually the overtone of movement evaporates, and the viewer is confronted with the presence of the black screen—another, most pessimistic, image of death. That too is denied the authority of a final image as the movement does eventually continue after this unnatural pause.

In *The Dead* Brakhage uses the vicissitudes of his raw materials—different kinds of film stock, the imperfect printing of black-and-white on color material, the washout effect of certain bright superimpositions—as metaphysical illuminations. Out of the specifically cinematic quality of light as it passes through these materials, he moulds his vision of the light of death. In *The Dead* Brakhage mastered the strategy he had employed limitedly in *Anticipation of the Night* of presenting and rejecting tentative images of the essence he seeks to penetrate. The traditional symbols of the tombs and river and the absolute poles of blackness, whiteness, and negativity are the primary metaphors for death which he tests, varies, and rejects. In the course of the film the process of testing, contemplating, and rejecting becomes more important than the images in themselves.

His most radical exploration into the inflection of light through his raw materials initially occurred in response to his oppressive economic situation. When he had no money to buy film stock, he conceived the idea of making a film out of natural material through which light could pass. The clue to this came from his observing the quantity of glue and paint which Stephen Lovi had put on his film *A Portrait of the Lady in the Yellow Hat* (1962). Brakhage collected dead moths, flowers, leaves, and seeds. By placing them between two layers of Mylar editing tape, a transparent, thin strip of 16mm celluloid with sprocket holes and glue on one side, he made *Mothlight* (1963), "as a moth might see from birth to death if black were white."

The passing of light through, rather than reflecting off, the plants and moth wings reveals a fascinating and sometimes terrifying intricacy of veins and netlike structures, which replaces the sense of depth in the film with an elaborate lateral complexity, flashing by at the extreme speed of almost one natural object to each frame of the three-minute film. The original title of this visual lyric, when the film-maker began to construct it, had been *Dead Spring*. True to that original but inferior title the film incarnates the sense of the indomitable division between consciousness and nature, which was taking a narrative form at the same time in Brakhage's epic, *Dog Star Man*.

The structure of *Mothlight*, as the film maker observes in a remarkable letter to Robert Kelly printed in "Respond Dance," the final chapter of *Metaphors on Vision*, is built around three "round-dances" and a coda. Three times the materials of the moths and plants are introduced on the screen, gain speed as if moving into wild flight, and move toward calm and separation; then in the coda a series of bursts of moth wings occurs in diminishing power, interspersed with passages of white (the whole film is fixed in a matrix of whiteness as the wings and flora seldom fill the whole screen). The penultimate burst regains the grandeur of the first in the series, but it is a last gasp, and a single wing, after the longest of the white passages, ends the film.

Significantly, in Brakhage's description of his interest in the moth's flight, sight, and functioning as oracular events in his life, he attributes to the appearance of a moth during the editing of an earlier film a liberation from a slump into self-consciousness that stalled his work:

> I was sty-my-eyed sinking into sty-*me*ed in all self possession when suddenly Jane appeared holding a small dried plant which she put down on the working table, and without a word, left me—I soon began working again . . . in the midst of attempts to work, what must surely have been the year's last moth . . . began fluttering about me and along the work table, the wind of its wings shifting the plant from time to time and blowing away all speculations in my mind as to movements of dead plants and to enable me to continue working.[13]

For Brakhage, extreme self-consciousness and the seduction of natural objects are equivalents (which can, as in the present case, cancel each other) since they both inhibit the working process, which is his ultimate value.

In "Respond Dance," Brakhage, adapting Robert Duncan's view of the poet's role as a medium working for the Poet to the situation of the film-maker, writes:

OF NECESSITY I BECOME INSTRUMENT FOR THE PASSAGE OF INNER VISION, THRU ALL MY SENSIBILITIES, INTO ITS EXTERNAL FORM. My most active part in this process is to increase all my sensibilities (so that all films arise out of some total area of being or full life) AND, at the given moment of possible creation to act only out of necessity. In other words, I am principally concerned with revelation. My sensibilities are art-oriented to the extent that revelation takes place, naturally, within the given historical context of specifically Western aesthetics. If my sensi-bilities were otherwise oriented, revelation would take an other external form—perhaps a purely personal one. As most of what is revealed, thru my given sensibilities clarifies itself in relationship to previous (and fu-ture, possible) works of art, I offer the given external form WHEN COM-PLETED for public viewing. As you should very well know, even when I lecture at showing of past Brakhage films I emphasize the fact that I am not artist except when involved in the creative process AND that I speak as viewer of my own (NO—DAMN that "my own" which is JUST what I'm trying, DO try in all lectures, letters, self-senses-of, etc., to weed out)—I speak (when speaking, writing, well—that, is with respect to deep con-siderations) as viewer of The Work (NOT of , , , but By-Way-Of Art), and I speak specifically to the point of What has been revealed to me AND, by way of describing the work-process, what I, as artist-viewer, un-derstand of Revelation—that is: how to be revealed and how to be re-vealed TO (or 2, step 2 and/or—the viewing process.) [14]

What he reveals in the introductory interview, as the critic and expli-cator of his own work, is always illuminating and usually pertinent to our analysis of his films. But in the case of *Cat's Cradle*, the film does not support his expression of its theme. Brakhage recounts there how shortly after his marriage he took his wife to visit two friends, James Tenney and Carolee Schneemann, whom he had filmed in *Loving*. The film he shot of that encounter was to contain his observations on the tensions, identi-fications, and jealousies that it engendered. Yet the film itself effaces psychology and develops through its lightning montage of flat surfaces and gestures in virtually two-dimensional space an almost cubistic suggestion of the three-dimensional arena in which the four characters and one cat might interact, if only the furious pace of editing could be retarded and the synecdochic framing expanded.

The camera does not move. Like the montage at the opening of *Win-*

dow Water Baby Moving, the cutting at times follows an imaginary path of sunlight from the back of the cat, to a bedspread, to a bowl of flowers, to the opening of a door, etc. When there is movement within the frame, its direction and pace influence how it is cut. The various gestures of the film (a bare foot on the bedspread, Brakhage walking while buttoning his shirt, Carolee Schneemann painting and washing dishes, Tenney writing, Jane undressing) never seem complete; they are spread out evenly and often seen upside-down or simultaneously through the whole film without sequence or internal development. For the most part these activities are framed to obscure who the performer is so that together with the speed of the editing they tend to fuse the two men and two women together and even to create one androgynous being out of all four.

Floral wallpaper, an embroidered pillow, an amber bottle, and the cat's fur mix freely with the human gestures and with recurrent flashes of white leader and emphasize the flatness of the images. Off-screen looks of the human figures and changes of angle in a single subject establish axes of geometrical positioning, but with the rapidity of shot changes these axes spin wildly and eccentrically. The 700 shots in this five-minute film (remember there were some 3000 in the fifty minutes of the highly-edited *Twice a Man*) vary from two frames ($\frac{1}{12}$ of a second) to 48 (two seconds) with by far the greater number of images under half a second screen time.

Cat's Cradle suggests statis through, and despite, the speed of the colliding shots. In *Pasht*, made six years later, he again used a very rapid montage (one frame to sixty frame shots—mostly five or six frames), in a five-minute film for an even more stationary impression. In his blurb for the film in the catalogue of the Film-Makers Cooperative Brakhage tells us that the title comes from the name of a pet cat, named for the Egyptian goddess ruling cats. He shot the film while she was giving birth and edited it after her death. Without this guide the viewer would not know specifically what is happening in the film. It begins in black and soon shows a red furry image in the center of the screen—edgeless, undefined, and not filling the entire screen rectangle. Bits of black leader intercut with it make the image flicker like hot coals. The movement within the frame is slight, except for fragmentary glimpses of the discontinuous twisting of the fur by an anamorphic lens. The montage unites tiny bits of very similar images. Sometimes a moving orange spot of light appears, reminding the viewer of the cat in *Cat's Cradle*.

The whole screen seems to pulse with variations in the light intensity of the image, the degree of movement, the clarity of the fur, the time of a shot on the screen, and the number of elements in burst-of-image between passages of blackness. A typical passage has one black frame followed by six of soft focused fur, another frame of black, three of focused fur, six of blurred fur ending in a flash of light, another black, one bright orange, and three black. As the film nears its end the bursts become longer and the hairs of fur more clearly focused and at times larger images fill the borders of the screen, almost identifiable as very close views or anamorphic views of a cat scratching or giving birth.

Pasht presents a vision of an organism simultaneously seeming to die and regenerate. It is clearly animal but liberated from the specifics of species and character. The difference in rhythm between *Pasht* and the lyrical films of 1959 and 1960 indicates the general, but not absolute, shift in the film-maker's approach to the lyrical film before and after the making of *Dog Star Man*. *Pasht* and many of the films that follow it substitute an organic, retarded pulse for the earlier counterpoint and microrhythmic dynamics. In this later phase of the lyrical form, Brakhage seems to want to still the filmic image and catch the shimmering vibrations of the forces that inspire and terrify him.

Fire of Waters operates within a structure similar to that of *Pasht*. Here the matrix is gray instead of black, and its black-and-white images are grainy and thin, with an ascetic denial of visual contrast. The film begins with static lights at night—for again the camera does not move—and flares toward whiteness. The image seems to wait, while a house light or a streetlamp sits on the depthless surface of the screen, for single-frame occurrences of summer lightning. With these flashes the silhouettes of trees, house, and clouds appear. At times only a portion of the screen is dimly lit by the lightning, and at other times the whole screen flashes. The duration of the illuminations varies from one to five frames toward the middle of the film, and when the lightning explosion extends beyond the single frame, there is always a slight variation in each of the frames in which it occurs.

The change of streetlamps, car light, or house lights prefigures each new flash and makes the viewer expectant. A flare introduces a scene of suburban houses in the quivering daylight of a gray sky. Three slow tones are heard on the soundtrack, which had previously been silent. When the film reverts to night, the lightning flashes are edited to follow one another more quickly than in the first section. A final change to daylight accompanies the sound of fast panting.

In a previously unpublished interview with the author, Brakhage describes his thematic and formal concerns in making this film:

> *Fire of Waters*, as its title suggests, is inspired by a little postcard that Robert Kelly sent me when we were searching into the concerns of Being, Matter and Subject Matter, and Source. He sent a card which cut through all my German windiness about it. It said, "The truth of the matter is this, that man lives in a fire of waters and will live eternally in the first taste." That haunted me. First I couldn't make any sense out of it at all, other than that "fire of waters" would refer to cells, in that the body is mostly water and is firing constantly to keep itself going.
>
> That summer we were living at that abandoned theater. I had got a lot of lightning and streetlights on black-and-white film. I took a lot of daytime shots of the houses that surrounded us. There seemed to be an awful foreboding about that kind of neighborhood in which we were then living, which was a typical suburban neighborhood. I remember referring to it and saying "These houses look like inverted bomb craters." I had a sense of imminent disaster which I always seem to get more mysteriously and in a more sinister way in an American suburban area than I do even in New York City.
>
> When I finally came to edit that, which was just before Christmas '64, I was inspired by Kelly's card and I had the sense that the opening shot would come out of pure white leader and then be a streetlight blinking. The blink of the streetlight would set a rhythm which then I could repeat in flashes of both other streetlights and of lightning flashes, and that blink would be source for the whole rhythm structure of the film. I wanted to see how far I could depart from that rhythm exactly and still retain that rhythm as source.
>
> Then, as the whole concept deepened, I showed the actual source of those night house lights and house shadows by showing the daylight scenes of them. Then I could throw it back into the night with a build-up of the night structure, and then finally end with that one single house that dominated most of my concerns, directly across the street from us.
>
> Then I felt the need for sound. For years I had imposed the discipline on myself that if ever a single sound was needed anywhere on a track to go with an image I would put that sound in even if no other sound was needed in the whole film. That permitted me when I felt the need of slowed-down bird sounds (that is a bird's cry slowed down so that it became like a western musical instrument), to put it in where I felt it was needed. Then that caused me to feel the need of a sound of wind rising to a certain pitch at the very beginning. At the end then the speeded-up sound of Jane giving birth to Myrenna occurs on two levels in the last

shot of the house. It definitely sounds like a dog in somebody's backyard in the drama sense of that scene, yelping in pain. It does actually carry the sense of a terror beyond that. That's how the sound came into it and balanced out.[15]

Brakhage had made one other sound film since *Anticipation of the Night. Blue Moses* (1962) uses strategies from the lyrical film without itself being a meditation firmly postulated in the eye of the film-maker. For this one time in his career he employed synchronous speech. The existence of this film within Brakhage's filmography is very curious; there is nothing else like it in his work. It explicitly postulates an epistemological principle: that there can be no cinematic image without a film-maker to take it and that the presence, or even the existence, of the film-maker transforms what he films. Formally, *Blue Moses* anticipates the participatory film that calls upon or addresses itself directly to the audience, a form that emerged in the early 1970s on the tail of the structural film. We have encountered its embryonic manifestation already in Anger's *Invocation of My Demon Brother*.

The single actor of *Blue Moses* hollers to the audience when he first appears from his cave. He is the merchant of metaphysical fear Melville knew as "The Lightning Rod Man." He tries to scare us by proposing to quiet our fears: "Don't be afraid. We're not alone. There's the cameraman . . . or was . . . once." Then in an elliptical way he informs us of what we should be afraid of. He points to mysterious tracks, in a desolate place, left by a man who must have been running. That narrative hint, recurring throughout the film, hovers on the edge of parody of the devices used in novels and films to draw us into illusionism and suspense. In a fugal structure of leap-frogging episodes interrupted by dissolves to the same actor in different costumes, Brakhage lets his actor assume different guises from the history of acting (a classical Greek mask is painted on his face, in robes he strikes "Shakespearean" postures), and his language, usually that of the confidence man, veers to sing-song and melodrama.

The leap-frogging counterpoint of scenes at the beginning of the film is recapitulated in superimposition, both of picture and sound, near the end. The actor pulls off a false beard and, in a Pirandelloistic cliché, reveals himself to the audience. "Look," he says, "this is ridiculous. I'm an actor. You see what I mean? . . . You're my audience, my captive audience. I'm your entertainment, your player. This whole film is about us." In the course of the speech, the superimposition becomes footage from

earlier in the film, projected over his chest. When he turns his back to
the projector, the film images cease, and he is framed in a white rectangle
of the projector operating without film.

In the middle of his speech in front of the interior film screen he repeats his consolation: "But don't be afraid. There's a film-maker behind
every scene, in back of every word I speak, behind you, too, so to speak."
When the camera suddenly swings around into the darkness, glimpsing
the hand signals of the director, he adds, as if a spectator had turned his
head to the projection booth: "No. Don't turn around. It's useless." It is
at this point that he himself turns toward his screen and the images
change to pure white light on his body.

Blue Moses ends as it began with a series of dissolves of the protagonist
returning to his cave and gesturing ceremonially. In its form and substance *Blue Moses* attacks the dramatic film as an untenable convention.
Brakhage temporarily accepts the principles of the realists of film theory
who argue that cinema arises from the interaction of the artist with exterior reality in front of the camera. But he rebuts them with a demonstration of how fragile their sense of exterior reality is. At one point the actor
of *Blue Moses* gestures to the sun and cries, "an eclipse," at which point
an obvious, messy splice throws the image into blackness, and he adds,
"manufactured, but not yet patented, for your pleasure." *Blue Moses* is a
negative polemic, an attack on the modified Realism of the European
cinema of the early sixties (Godard, Resnais, Fellini, Antonioni, etc.).
In its place he proposed the investigation of the consciousness confronting
(and constructing) external nature in the form of the lyrical film.

Of the many film-makers of the sixties working in the lyrical mode
after Brakhage's initial work, Bruce Baillie has had the surest voice of
his own.

In his lyrical films, Baillie turns from the uneasy inwardness of Brakhage's work to a problematic study of the heroic. *Mr. Hayashi* (1961),
Have You Thought of Talking to the Director? (1962), *A Hurrah for
Soldiers* (1962-63), and *To Parsifal* (1963) prepared the ground for his
major extended lyrics, *Mass for the Dakota Sioux* (1964) and *Quixote*
(1965, revised 1967). The first of these films was made as a newsreel advertisement to be shown at Baillie's film society, Canyon Cinema, in the
second year of its existence. It shows a Japanese gardener, Mr. Hayashi,
performing his daily tasks in a few black and white shots. The form is intentionally brief, minor, and occasional; although there is no metaphor or
conflict of images, it reminds one of the aspiration first voiced by Maya

Deren and later echoed by Brakhage to create a cinematic haiku. The plastic and formal tradition indigenous to San Francisco, the center of Baillie's activity, owes something to oriental, and specifically Japanese, aesthetics. The oriental "saint" in a fusion of Zen, Tao, and Confucian traditions is the first of the heroes proposed by Baillie's cinema. The second, Parsifal, logically prefigures the first; his quest seeks the reconciliation of nature and mind that makes the oriental saint possible.

In *Mass* and *Quixote* he subtly blends glimpses of the heroic *personae* with despairing reflections on violence and ecological disaster. In the earlier films those poles were explored in separate, and much weaker works. *Have You Thought of Talking to the Director?* casually articulates an image of sexual loss and paranoia by combining an interview-like monologue about girlfriends in a moving car and on the streets of a small California town with a frame story derived from *The Cabinet of Dr. Caligari*; that is, Baillie repeatedly cuts from the speaker to him sitting silently in the corridor of a hospital, and the sinister doctor who whispers near him appears—no longer as a doctor—at significant points in the events outside the hospital. In *A Hurrah for Soldiers* Baillie naively attempted to illuminate an elliptical and rhythmically edited scene of imagined violence—a man attacked by a gang of girls—with photographs of actual violence from a newspaper. He is more successful in the mixing of sounds in this film than in the cutting of images. In his major lyrical films he extended his natural talent for sound fusion to a textured visual surface which uses superimposition and often mixtures of negative and positive black-and-white with color, in a rhetoric of slow transformations. His notes for *Mass* give a clear picture of its structure:

> A film Mass, dedicated to that which is vigorous, intelligent, lovely, the-best-in-Man; that which work suggests is nearly dead.
> Brief guide to the structure of the film:
> INTROIT: A long, lightly exposed section composed in the camera.
> KYRIE: A motorcyclist crossing the San Francisco Bay Bridge accompanied by the sound of the Gregorian Chant. The EPISTLE is in several sections. In this central part, the film becomes gradually more outrageous, the material being either television or the movies, photographed directly from the screen. The sounds of the "mass" rise and fall throughout the EPISTLE.
> GLORIA: The sound of a siren and a short sequence with a '33 Cadillac proceeding over the Bay Bridge and disappearing into a tunnel.
> The final section of the COMMUNION begins with the OFFERTORY in a procession of lights and figures in the second chant.

The anonymous figure from the introduction is discovered again, dead on the pavement. The touring car arrives, with the celebrants; the body is consecrated and taken away past an indifferent, isolated people accompanied by the final chant.[16]

At the very beginning he shows a man struggling and dying on a city street at night, ignored by passers-by as if he were a drunk collapsed in the street. In the subsequent weaving of moving camera shots, in counterpointed superimpositions of factories, expanses of prefabricated houses, traffic, parades, and markets, all complemented by a soundtrack that blends Gregorian chant with street noises in shifting degrees of priority, the viewer tends to forget the dying man or to see him as the forecast of the section of the film that enjambs bits of war films with advertisements shot directly off a television without kinescopic rectification so that the images continually show bands and jump.

Contrasted to the images of waste and violence, a motorcyclist appears in the traffic and Baillie follows him, shooting from a moving car for a very long time. He is the tentative vehicle of the heroic in this film. But when he too disappears in the welter of superimposition, we do not expect his return. Instead the movement shifts to the grill of a 1933 Cadillac as it cruises the highway. As the second part of the film circles back on itself, the Cadillac turns out to be the ambulance/hearse which brings doctors to the man on the street and which carries away his dead body. Then when it reenters the highway, Baillie again shifts the emphasis to the motorcyclist, whose second disappearance concludes the film.

Two images demonstrate the ironic pessimism with which Baillie views the American landscape at the center of the film. Over the sprawl of identical prefabricated houses he prints the words of Black Elk: "Behold, a good nation walking in a sacred manner in a good land!" Then he pans to an American flag waving on a tall pole in the distance. By changing the focus without cutting from the shot, he brings to view a previously unseen barbed wire fence between the camera and the flag. "The Mass is traditionally a celebration of Life," he wrote in the Film-Makers Cooperative catalogue, "thus the contradiction between the form of the Mass and the theme of Death. The dedication is to the religious people who were destroyed by the civilization which evolved the Mass."

In *To Parsifal* Baillie began to elaborate his equivocal relationship to technology by employing the train both as a symbol of the waste land and the heroic thrust of the Grail quester. The motorcyclist of *Mass* possesses some of that ambivalence. But it is in *Quixote* that Baillie utilizes the tension between the heroics and the blindness of technology as a generative principle for the organization of the whole film. He told Richard White-hall:

> Quixote was my last western-hero form. I summarized a lot of things. I pretty much emphasized the picture of an American as a conquistador. A conquering man. For example, up in Montana there's a bridge being put up, driving straight through the mountains, and it was half made when I got there.
>
> They're chopping their way right through. And, to me, that was the best explanation of what western man was up to.[17]

In many ways Quixote restates the structural principles of Mass with increased irony and ambiguity. For instance, the tentative protagonist of the earlier film, the motorcyclist who appears near the beginning and the end, becomes a flying man, a movie version of Superman, at both ends of the later film. Despite his sophistication, Baillie remains an innocent; the whole of his cinema exhibits an alternation between two irreconcilable themes: the sheer beauty of the phenomenal world (few films are as graceful to the eye as his, few are as sure of their colors) and the utter despair of forgotten men. It is in Quixote alone that these two themes emerge into a dialectical form, an antithesis of grace and disgrace.

The incessant forward movement of Mass leads to the meandering journey, of which Quixote is the diary, of a film-maker in search of a hero who can be his mediator without irony. But the series of agents he finds cannot sustain that burden: they are tired Indians in a luncheonette, an old farmer, a prizefighter reduced to Bowery life, a naked girl, the artificial Superman, and even animals (a turtle, horses). In their impotence, the lyrical film-maker, himself a Quixotic observer without Anger's confidence that the cinema is a magical weapon, becomes the hero of his own film as he descends through a nostalgia for the lost Indian civilizations (manifested in the intercutting of contemporary chiefs with turn-of-the-century photographs of the tribes) to a vision of New York streets meshed with a collage of old films and footage of the war in Vietnam.

With Baillie we return to an aspect of the visionary film-maker suspended since our discussion of Maya Deren: his role as a champion of reform for the film-makers' plight. In 1961 he founded Canyon Cinema, the first permanent showcase for the avant-garde film in the San Francisco area since the collapse of Art in Cinema more than a decade earlier. The next year it moved from the town of Canyon, still keeping the name, to

Berkeley and initiated a newspaper, *The Canyon Cinema News*. Shortly afterward he founded the Canyon Cinema Cooperative, following the example of Jonas Mekas and the original Film-Makers Cooperative in New York. Although Baillie soon retired as the chief administrator of the Canyon Cinema functions, they continue today much in the spirit in which they were founded. The visionary inspiration which informs the work of the American avant-garde film-maker has in many instances spread to the creation of his institutions.

Stan Brakhage, too, has been influential in the formation and promotion of organizations to benefit the film-maker. He was one of the founding members of Mekas' Cooperative, and in its early years he acted as an informal ambassador, uniting factions in different parts of the country whom he encountered in his lecture tours. One of his major concerns has been the encouragement of private libraries of 8 mm and 16mm films. To promote this idea and promote careful and repeated viewing of films, he has been uncomfortable in his alliances with the community of film-makers and has on several occasions withdrawn his films from cooperatives and attacked them. His motives have been for the most part aesthetic, not economic; and within the politics of aesthetics he has fought, with all the polemical means at his disposal, tendencies he felt were contrary to the making and reception of films as revelation. Repeatedly he has invoked the myth of Faust in his periodic attacks on other film-makers and ideas, reserving for himself a Prometheanism, wherein the commitment to aesthetic perfection and prophetic revelation triumphs over seduction. His repeated reconciliations with film-makers' institutions are usually attended by confessions that his dramatic response was personally essential to the rooting out of drama from his films. Markopoulos, too, and in spite of his enthusiastic appraisal of the inspired work of the cooperatives, has withdrawn, returned, and then withdrawn his films again without the public histrionics of Brakhage.

But Baillie has eschewed the polemical struggle in the ten years he has been making films. His rare interviews reflect his pacific personality, generosity, and disinterest in theory. Since the mid-sixties, he has traveled continually, living out of his Volkswagen bus, in a tent in the California commune of Morning Star, or in a cabin by the ocean in Fort Bragg. A persistent struggle with serious hepatitis since 1967 has circumscribed his activities and generated a meditation on death in his longest film so far, *Quick Billy* (1971), which will be discussed in the next chapter.

In the end, the argument between consciousness and nature is as cru-

cial to Baillie's cinema as it is to Brakhage's. But it is problematic because
the weight of the dialogue seems to rest outside of the film, especially in
the prolific stream of films from the late sixties—*Tung* (1966), *Castro
Street* (1966), *All My Life* (1966), *Still Life* (1966), and *Valentin de las
Sierras* (1967). In these, the eye of the film-maker quiets his mind with
images of reconciliation; the dialectics of cinematic thought become calm
in the filming of the privileged moment of reconciliation. In an interview
with Richard Corliss, he describes his achievement as a film-maker and
the fundamental shortcoming of that achievement:

> Now, I can answer a little bit just for myself, as having been a film
> artist. I always felt that I brought as much truth out of the environment
> as I could, but I'm tired of coming *out of.* . . . I want everybody really
> lost, and I want us all to be at home there. Something like that. Actually
> I am not interested in that, but I mean that's what you could do. Lots of
> people would like it. I have to say finally what I *am* interested in, like
> Socrates: peace . . . rest . . . nothing.[18]

Baillie's two versions of the structural film, coinciding with the general
emergence of that form, draw upon his lyrical films and point toward the
consecration of the privileged moment. By replacing a form which has internal evolution with a monomorphic shape and by affirming the priority
of the mechanics of the tools over the eye of the film-maker, the structural film terminates the dialectics of the lyrical and mythopoeic forms.
Baillie comes to it in the apparent hope of subduing the reflective ego
and, at least tentatively, exploring deep space and unquestioned natural
objects. In *All My Life* (1966) he pans along a fence lined with rose
bushes. Then in the same slow movement of the unstopping camera, he
switches from the horizontal to the vertical, rising above the fence into
the sky, resting in a composition of two telephone lines trisecting the
blue field. The movement lasts as long as it takes Ella Fitzgerald to sing
"All My Life" on the soundtrack. Its complement, *Still Life* (1966),
fixes an interior view with an unmoving camera, which I shall discuss in
the last chapter. The voices on its soundtrack suggest that the dim figures by the far window are looking at a series of photographs of shrines
devoted to Ramakrishna. Baillie refers to this in the Film-Makers Cooperative catalogue as "A film on efforts toward a new American religion."

Castro Street returns to the lyrical form with a renewed lushness of texture and color. His note for it is typically gnomic and tantalizing in its
guarded hints about his working process:

Inspired by a lesson from Erik Satie; a film in the form of a street—
Castro Street running by the Standard Oil Refinery in Richmond, California . . . switch engines on one side and refinery tanks, stacks and
buildings on the other—the street and film, ending at a red lumber company. All visual and sound elements from the street, progressing from the
beginning to the end of the street, one side is black-and-white (secondary), and one side is color—like male and female elements. The emergence of a long switch-engine shot (black-and-white solo) is to the film-
maker the essential of *consciousness*.[19]

A different note subtitles it "The Coming of Consciousness."

The film begins slowly and gradually changes pace several times. Its
fusion of black-and-white negative with color, often moving in opposite
directions, recalls Brakhage's micro-rhythms. The superimposition tends
to destroy depth and to reduce foreground and background to two hover-
ing planes, one slightly in front of the other. The opening movement,
accompanied by the sound of a train in slow motion, occurs on the back
plane. An iris isolates a smokestack, then slowly wanders on the screen,
drifting toward the upper right corner. The first dynamic image is of a
negative, high-contrast power line moving in the superimposition.

Baillie occasionally uses slightly distorted images of the trains and the
railroad yard with prismatic colors around the border of distinct shapes.
He also uses images which were recorded by an improperly threaded
camera so that they appear to jump or waver up and down on the screen.
A ghost image of a man and the numbers from the side of a boxcar jump
in this way on the foreground layer early in the film. Soon afterward part
of the screen clears to show a red filament inside a tube; for Baillie not
only uses superimpositions but soft masking devices so that parts of the
screen will be single-layered, while the rest is double, or will contain a
third element which appears on neither one of the superimposition layers,
as if melted into the picture.

As the trains move faster, the pace of the film changes. The smokestack
in the iris returns, now red-filtered and occupying the center of the screen.
Another central iris replaces it, looking out on violets in a yellow field;
slowly an old Southern Pacific engine pulls into the iris beyond the violets,
recalling the later movements of *To Parsifal*. A yellow car crosses almost
pure white negative cars.

At this point in the film we hear whistles, muted voices, and the tinkling
of a piano. A curtain is drawn open to show the blue of the sky, and then
it closes, blending immediately into the superimpositions, which become
progressively anamorphic. To the sound of clangs, negative and color

Bruce Baillie's *Castro Street:* "the images of *Consciousness*."

trains move in opposite directions across the screen, ending in the dominance of a silhouetted negative engine with a man in it, slowly crossing the field of vision. This is the image Baillie refers to as the "essential of consciousness."

Just before the film ends another negative figure takes over the film. The camera follows the blazing white pants of a walking workman, then shows his polka-dot shirt. His appearance crowns the passing negative of the engine and its conductor. Then a red, dome-like barn appears while a sign, saying "Castro Street," pointing in the direction opposite to that of the camera, marks the film's conclusion.

Both Brakhage and Baillie push in their later lyrical films toward cinematic visions of impersonal or unqualified consciousness. In films such as *Pasht*, *Fire of Waters*, and *Castro Street* they succeed in momentarily disengaging the self from vision. But that came only after they had invented and pursued a form that could articulate that complex relation for the first time in cinema.

7

MAJOR MYTHOPOEIA

The highest achievements of Brakhage's art since the spectacular series of lyrical films in the late 1950s and early 1960s have been three long or serial films, *Dog Star Man* (or in its expanded form, *The Art of Vision*), *Songs*, and *Scenes from Under Childhood* (itself the first part of a projected autobiography, *The Book of the Film*). Likewise Baillie had proceeded from lyric to epic with the making of *Quick Billy*, which holds a position in the evolution of his work comparable to that of *Dog Star Man* in Brakhage's.

The writing of *Metaphors on Vision* coincided with the shooting and editing of most of *Dog Star Man*. Brakhage seems to have started both around 1960. The book was published at the very beginning of 1964; the five-part film was completed by the end of that year and had its first screenings in 1965. Here more than at any other point in Brakhage's career his aesthetics throw light on the film. Nevertheless the critic must be careful not to let the film-maker's glosses completely dominate his viewing of the film. An over-subscription to Brakhage's paraphrases has blinded at least two published interpretations of the film to some of its complications.[1]

Dog Star Man elaborates in mythic, almost systematic terms, the world-view of the lyrical films. More than any other work of the American avant-garde film, it stations itself within the rhetoric of Romanticism, describing the birth of consciousness, the cycle of the seasons, man's struggle with nature, and sexual balance in the visual evocation of a fallen titan bearing the cosmic name of the Dog Star Man.

Brakhage has repeatedly disassociated his exegetical comments on his films from his aesthetics and statements on method. The former constitute critical insights for him, for which he rejects the authority of a privileged position; the latter are couched in the language of revelation. We first encountered this dichotomy in the passage quoted in the previous chapter on the nature of the artistic sensibility. "As you should very well know," he writes to the author, "even when I lecture at showings of past Brakhage films I emphasize the fact that I am not artist except when involved in the creative process AND that I speak as viewer . . . of The Work."

Despite the modesty of this disassociation, Brakhage is the most valuable guide we have to a reading of his films. But not so valuable that his word must be taken when the films contradict it. From two interviews, one published as the introduction to *Metaphors on Vision* and another unpublished one now in the Anthology Film Archives library, we can construct his argument for *Dog Star Man*:

> The man climbs the mountain out of winter and night into the dawn, up through spring and early morning to midsummer and high noon, to where he chops down the tree. . . . There's a Fall—and the fall back to somewhere, midwinter.
>
> I thought of *Dog Star Man* as seasonally structured that way; but also while it encompasses a year and the history of man in terms of image material (e.g. trees become architecture for a whole history of religious monuments or violence becomes the development of war), I thought it should be contained within a single day.
>
> I wanted *Prelude* to be a created dream for the work that follows rather than Surrealism which takes its inspiration from dream; I stayed close to the practical use of dream material. . . . One thing I knew for sure (from my own dreaming) was that what one dreams just before waking structures the following day. . . . Since *Prelude* was based on dream vision as I remembered it, it had to include "closed-eye vision."
>
> In the tradition of Ezra Pound's *Vorticism*, *Part One* is a *Noh* drama, the exploration in minute detail of a single action and all its ramifications. [Brakhage described the basic action of this section as "the two steps forward, one step backward" motion of the hero, which he related to the forward-backward motion of blood in the capillary system, the image of that part.]
>
> The heart had stopped in *Part One*, and, while we see an increasingly black and white image [of the man] that climbs up the mountain, there is a negative image of the Dog Star Man that is absolutely fallen at that instant.
>
> I had no idea what would happen in *Part Two*, except that it would be in some sense autobiographical; but I knew that the heart must start again in *Part Three*; and that it would be a sexual daydream, or that level of yearning, that would start the heart again.

The moment at which the man is seen both climbing and fallen is recapitulated in a way at the beginning of *Part Two*. . . . I reintroduced the man climbing both in negative and positive, superimposed. I had some sense that these twin aspects of the Dog Star Man could be moving as if in memory. . . . I realized that the man, in his fall and his climb in negative and positive, was split asunder and related either to himself as baby (those first six weeks . . . in which a baby's face goes through a transition from that period we call infancy to babyhood; . . . the lines of the face fill out what might be called a first mask or a personality, a cohesiveness which occurs in the facial structure or control of the face over those first six weeks) and/or to his child.

The whole idea of the baby's face achieving a solidity, or the first period of birth would relate metaphorically to spring, the springing into *per-son*. . . . At the end of *Part Two* a balance is achieved when the images return to the Dog Star Man in his fall. It was very important to me, too, that the tripod legs would show in the distance so that there is always some sense that this is a film-maker being filmed. . . . In no sense is it engaging or pulling in, precisely because in the plot level of the film the Dog Star Man is being engaged with his own childhood by his child. . . .

The images return to the Dog Star Man in his fall, in his jumps back down the earth, or his imagined fall. He's seen finally flat on his back on a rock ledge and the figure of the woman is collaged in.

Part Three has a "His, Her, and Heart" roll. . . . Female images are trying to become male and have not succeeded and the males are trying to become female and have not succeeded. . . . In the "Her" roll you see mounds of moving flesh that separate distinguishably into a woman's image, but then become very tortured by attempts to transform into male. It's very Breugelesque in a way; penises replace breasts in flashes of images; then a penis will jut through the eyes; or male hair will suddenly move across the whole scape of the female body. . . . At some point this ceases and this flesh becomes definitely woman. Then on the "His" roll . . . you have the opposite occurring: a male mound of flesh which keeps being tortured by a proclivity to female imagery; so that, for instance, the lips are suddenly transformed into a vagina. Finally the male form becomes distinct. Then, of course, these two dance together as they are superimposed on each other; you get this mound of male-female flesh which pulls apart variously and superimposes upon itself in these mixtures of Breugelesque discoveries, so to speak, or distortions. Finally toward the end, the male and female become separate so that they can come together.

Part Four begins with that man on the ledge as we found him at the end of *Part Two*. He rises up and shakes off the sexual daydream and becomes involved in shaking off every reason he might have for chopping that tree. . . . Finally, if looked at carefully, there is really no relevant, definite, specific reason given for that Dog Star Man to chop the tree as he does at the end of *Part Four*. . . . Finally the whole concept of the woodcutter gets tossed into the sky. . . . The axe is lifted up and the figure cuts to Cassiopeia's chair, which I suppose you can say is finally what Dog Star Man sits down into in the sky. . . . The whole film flares out in obvious cuts which relate in their burning out and changes of subtly colored leader to the beginning of the *Prelude*.

Brakhage's paraphrase suggests at times a narrative consistency which is not apparent in the film, while he omits other obvious connections. *Part One* clearly situates itself in winter, while *Part Four* begins with images of summer and proceeds along an alternation between summer and winter until its end. The seasonal system, as Brakhage outlines it, refers to the dominant metaphors of the parts, not to their visual presences. In *Part Two* we see the visual, aural, and haptic reactions of an infant (the mediator of spring) and in *Part Three* the superimposition of naked male and female bodies with a beating heart and paint splatter. *Part Three* is an erotic version of the myth of summer's richness. Finally, in *Part Four*, the images of the protagonist literally falling from summer work to winter desolation elliptically suggest the transitional season of fall and mimetically echo its processes in a reversing of the pathetic fallacy.

Yet more striking than the problem created by Brakhage's claims for the seasonal interpretation of the film is the difference between the actual function of *Parts Two* and *Three* in the film and in the film-maker's account of them. It is true that the heart slows down at the end of *Part One* (but it does not stop) and that it accelerates at the conclusion of *Part Three*. Yet the fallen Dog Star Man of *Part One* appears vigorously climbing upward again at the beginning of *Part Two*, and he is seen both climbing down and fallen at the end of that section. In fact, the opening and concluding climbs distinctly bracket the entire episode of the infant's sensibilities. Brakhage's reading of the film fails to account for this and substitutes in its place a much more obscure connection, that of the heart rates. Actually, *Parts Two* and *Three* have a dialectical relationship to each other. They are alternatives or aspects of the divided titan. He postulates two forms of privileged vision, the innocent and the orgasmic. In the earlier films, as we have seen, Brakhage describes the urgency of the need for unschooled vision and for erotic fulfillment, although not in a single film. In *Loving* there is a hint that the former can be born of the latter. With the idealization of the infantile and the orgasmic vision goes a severe skepticism about their adequacy.

It is at this point that Brakhage's perspective most closely coincides with Blake's, who at various moments in his development speaks of four realms or states of existence. The first, Beulah, or Innocence, encompasses the vision of the child; next Generation, or Experience, defines the adult world of titanic sexual frustration and circumscribed erotic fulfillment; only the minor appendages, the sexual organs, can unite in Blake's derisive vision, while the whole body cries out for a merging of male and female. Northrop Frye describes one relation of Innocence to Experience thus: "As the child grows up, his conscious mind accepts 'experience,' or reality without any human shape or meaning, and his childhood innocent vision, having nowhere else to go, is driven underground into what we should call the subconscious, where it takes an essentially sexual form."[2] The third and fourth states are respectively the damned and liberated alternatives to the two-fold opposition of innocence and experience. They are Ulro, the hell of rationalism, self-absorption, and the domination of nature; and Eden, the redeemed unity realm of "The Real Man, the Imagination."

The image of the child is complex in Brakhage's films. In *Anticipation of the Night* it evokes innocence lost, and the whole film alternates between the minor pastoral and the major elegiac. But *Dog Star Man* aspires to the more elaborate mentality of *Metaphors on Vision*, in which the child can be a guide, or a warning, but not an end. On the first page he writes:

> Once vision may have been given—that which seems inherent in the infant's eye, an eye which reflects the loss of innocence more eloquently than any other human feature, an eye which soon learns to classify sights, an eye which mirrors the movement of the individual toward death by its increasing inability to see.
>
> But one can never go back, not even in imagination. After the loss of innocence only the ultimate of knowledge can balance the wobbling pivot.[3]

Behind the puns, name-dropping, and quotations of "Margin Alien" rests the idea of an anagogic unity of literary and painterly imagery. In his writing and speaking about *Dog Star Man* there is a tension between the argument of the film as he conceived it before shooting, while making it, or after it was finished, and the aspects of the film which were revealed to him at any of these stages. That the outline changed during the seven years between its inception and completion he makes quite clear:

> I always kept the growth of *Dog Star Man* consonant with the changes in our living. I never let an idea impose itself to the expense of actually

being where I was when I was working on the film. I never built, or permitted any ivory tower to get built around myself so that I could pursue the original idea of *Dog Star Man* to the expense of keeping that work from changing in detail according to the life we were living.[4]

The dialectic between the clarity of design and the vicissitudes of the film-making process must be apparent to anyone who carefully studies the film. It accounts, in part, for the fact that someone as articulate and insightful as Brakhage could be blind to the way in which *Part Two* and *Part Three* of his film function as paired interludes in the texture of the work. In these two sections of almost equal length, which are visually distinct from the unity of *Prelude, Part One,* and *Part Four* (and different from each other), Brakhage, like Blake, describes the sources of renewal as an innocence of the senses and erotic union, and, again like Blake, suggests that alone each is insufficient and that together they open the still very difficult possibility of physical and spiritual resurrection.

The film is quite specific about that difficulty. After the interludes of *Parts Two* and *Three, Part Four,* which rushes to its conclusion in five minutes of very rapid montage on four layers of film, begins with the fallen figure and shows him alternately chopping the tree in the heat of the summer sun and wandering, stunned from his fall, through the winter forest of *Part One.* The resolution of the film is not a Blakean liberation into Eden and reunion of the imaginative and physical division. Brakhage at this point follows the post-Romantic substitution of tautology for liberation: in their major poems, *Un Coup de Dés* and *Notes Toward a Supreme Fiction,* Mallarmé and Stevens triumphantly proclaim the failure of the divine within or without man; instead they posit a teleology of poetry, and in their wake Brakhage ends his film with a naked affirmation of his materials and his mechanics. The images dissolve in projected light; the chopping of the tree becomes a metaphor for the splicing of film. The apotheosis which Brakhage describes (Dog Star Man assuming Cassiopeia's throne in the sky) appears but for a second on the screen and it is not the last image of that figure. We see him furiously chopping again, which qualifies the stellar image into an idea, a possibility, or a desire.

Prelude begins with a greenish-gray leader in which faint, shallow, shimmering changes of texture gradually appear. After a sudden flash of brightness a light weaves up and down once quickly on the screen. Out of this abstract chaos images of the sky, snow, fire, and streetlights emerge, sometimes slowly and sometimes suddenly. As the eye is teased by the speed and shifting focus of these initial elements, it becomes apparent that the montage is in the service of a double metaphor; the opening of the film seems like both the birth of the universe and the formation of the individual consciousness.

The entire film is formed of two superimposed layers of images, but at times, such as at the very beginning, there are visual silences on one or both layers which either allow one image to assume the presence it would on unsuperimposed film or present a vaguely lit visual field on the screen. For the most part the superimposition reinforces the basic flatness of the images in the *Prelude*; compositions-in-depth are extremely rare; and often Brakhage uses filters, distorting lenses, and a moving camera to create a two-dimensional space for his images. Finally there are numerous instances of painting or scratching over one or both layers, making the superimposition virtually three- or four-fold.

Early in the film shots of the bearded, long-haired Dog Star Man are glimpsed, along with fragmentary pictures of his dog and the moon. Within a few minutes the ambiguous faint textures on the screen (the initial chaos of the film) disappear permanently. In their place hand-painted lines, splatters of color, scratches on the emulsion, and a twisting plane caused by revolving an anamorphic lens[5] over an unidentifiable surface become the matrix out of which the brief specific images appear.

Both by superimposition and by montage Brakhage compares the movement of clouds with the flow of the blood in magnification. From this point on, a rhetoric of metaphor is established, mixing micro- and macrocosmic images with varying degrees of explicitness. The concrete images, no longer flashes within an abstract matrix, now dominate the film in different rhythms of elision and collision, from the extreme of leisurely reduplication (the same image on both layers), to sudden interjection (brief flashes interrupting a longer shot). A definite set of images will concentrate to form a thematic unit, which in turn will dissolve to be followed by a different theme.

In the first third of the film, after the initial movement of the consciousness in which images become more concrete and steadier on the screen, an evolving sequence concentrates on shots of the moon through a telescope and coronas of the sun, while the figures of the Dog Star Man and the woman are introduced as a theme of the development. Spectacular transformations of the moon into the sun are attended by subtler analogies of animal fur to fire and blood to emulsion scratches. As dramatic scratches echo and the flares off the sun paint smears over the image, earthly landscapes quickly pass; the sun is seen from the human perspective, and through montage the head of a penis seems to become the sun.

I could go on for pages enumerating the visual connections rushing by on the screen. What is most significant about them is their variety and the completeness with which the range of analogy spreads from microscopic cells to stellar eruptions. The forms of superimposition are numerous: explicit illusionism (the moon moving through the Dog Star Man's head); reduplication; conflicts of scale (the sun's corona over a lonely tree); conflicts of depth (the mask-like face of the hero over a deep image of a city street at night); color over black-and-white (bluish waves on the white moon); one distinct and one blurred figure; finally, the superimposition can recur synchronously, two images at a time, or, as is more usual, the alternations may be staggered, eliding the changes.

Dots, scratches, splattered paint, and cracked paint appear on the surface of the images. Often, colored filters render one or both images in a single hue. The gate may jump, causing an image to waver on the screen; the camera may shake, pan while the anamorphic lens is being twisted, or record in slow or fast motion.

The length of a shot can vary from a long hold on the moon or a leisurely change of focus on magnified bubbles to single-frame flashes. For the most part the montage establishes a synchronized rhythm between both layers of images, but there are occasional recurrent phrases of cutting on one level, as when streetlights alternate from left to right; or similarly, when the camera passes through mountains first in one direction, then another; or finally when the arc of the corona dances around the screen from top to bottom and from side to side. Each of these figures of montage posits an imaginary axis in the center of the screen around which the images turn.

Following the sun and moon sequence with its simultaneous introduction of the male and female figures, the images settle on earthly subjects. The mountains and a solitary house appear. In this central scene we see much more of the Dog Star Man himself. After an interlude of unraveling landscapes with expositions of internal organs, especially the heart, comes the most concentrated episode in the film: here we see the Dog Star Man struggling with the tree—the central act of the film according to the film-maker's argument. Significantly, this is the one important episode which occurs only in the *Prelude*. For the rest of the film, that moment of confrontation, hinted at here, is the central absent vortex around which the actions revolve. Actually Brakhage himself had not known that the struggle with the tree would occur only in the *Prelude* even after he finished that section in 1961. At that time he was talking as if it would be elaborated in the summer vision of *Part Three*, which he had not yet begun to structure.

As we watch the film the tree episode suddenly appears to crystallize within seconds, both layers seemingly devoted to its exposition. While he shakes the tree as if uprooting it, the camera zooms in again and again on the roots, comparing them once to a female crotch, and the immediately subsequent chopping of the tree repeats the rhythm of the zoom. Almost as suddenly as the scene materialized, it dissolves, and the idea of a family emerges, with shots of the Dog Star Man holding a baby and kissing the woman, and of her breast-feeding the baby.

In its final third, *Prelude* re-establishes its emphasis first on the sun, now seen with a tremendous eruption of surface scratches, imitating the flares; then the landscape variations reaffirm their presence, including now for the first time a burned forest with Greek columns superimposed (explicitly postulating the origin of that architectural development). A brief recapitulation of the tree scene, with another longer analogy between the roots and the female crotch, occurs just before the abrupt ending: mountains, fast-moving clouds, flowing blood, and the shadows of trees. Unlike most Brakhage films, including the other sections of *Dog Star Man*, *Prelude* has neither a climactic nor a *diminuendo* ending. The suddenness of the termination may be a concession to the structure of dreams that Brakhage says inspired the form of this film.

He has described how, after he shot what he thought would be all the material for the whole film, he did not know where to begin editing. He therefore pulled material willy-nilly from the unorganized rushes and edited thirty minutes by chance operations. Looking at this random film, Brakhage had a new insight into the material. He then consciously edited a parallel strip of film in relation to the original chance roll, as if commenting on it. When at times that method failed to produce a coherent vision, he re-edited a section of the randomly composed roll. Knowing this method, we better understand how the film moves in waves from closely knit forms to vague ones. The opening and the tree section seem to have been deliberately structured on both levels. The rising and falling of rhythms and clustering and dissolving of scenes must, then, be a function of the tension between the chance and conscious layers of the film.

Although the images of *Part One* proceed from *Prelude*, that section is formally antithetical to its predecessor. In *Prelude* Brakhage built a pyrotechnic, split-second montage with as much varied material as he could

force into half an hour. *Part One* is a *tour de force* of thematically constructed material stretched out to occupy the same amount of screen time.
The film organizes itself, not around a non-stop series of metaphors and
transformations, but in a number of more or less distinct paragraphs
(more distinct at the beginning and end, less so in the center) punctuated by an unusual number of faces for Brakhage.

Ezra Pound, in his book *Gaudier-Brzeska*, which Brakhage read and
identified as a primal source for this part, wrote:

> The image is not an idea. It is a radiant node or cluster; it is what I
> can, and must perforce, call a VORTEX, from which and through which,
> and into which ideas are constantly rushing.[6]
>
> . . .
>
> I am often asked whether there can be a long imagist or vorticist
> poem. The Japanese, who evolved the *hokku*, evolved also the *Noh* plays.
> In the best *Noh* the whole play may consist of one image. I mean it is
> gathered about one image. Its unity consists in one image, enforced by
> movement and music.[7]

The opening "paragraph" seems to both encapsulate and reorganize
the cosmology of *Prelude:* the first ten shots, generally much longer than
any in the former section, gradually define a particular point on the
earth's surface from the stellar perspective. Three long shots of the moon
partially obscured by moving clouds open the film. Then two shots of
clouds alone gradually reveal earthly mountains. Continuing the rhythm
but not the logic of the sequence, a white flame retreats into a burning
log, followed by a flash of whiteness, and then by a very slow shot of
frost disintegrating on a window pane into the shape of a hill or mountain as the image fades out. Finally a pulsating corona of the sun shimmers with explosions and issues a climactic burst. A very brief flash of
clear leader punctuates the transition to the next paragraph.

The effect of the opening is to move from a position beyond the earth
to a specific terrestrial location and then further to a synecdochic evocation of a dwelling (the window), which is also a metaphor for the hilly
terrain; then back out, even further than the starting point, beyond the
moon to the sun. Visually, the transitions are all consistent and smooth;
colors when they appear at all are washed out or subdued. Finally, the
entire texture of imagery familiar from the *Prelude* has a new presence
and grandeur because of its lack of superimposition—there is virtually
none in *Part One*—and the slowness of the montage.

The next grouping of eight shots introduces the Dog Star Man and the central action of the section: his arduous climb up a snow-covered mountain. A series of different tints—blue, pink, and brown—differentiates the essentially similar scenes of the hero carrying an axe, climbing, slipping, falling, getting up, struggling a little further. Of the eight takes, four end in long fades into blackness and one bleaches out to white, leaving only two direct cuts in the sequence. For the first time in *Dog Star Man* the camera is so placed as to articulate a depth on the screen. The protagonist climbs up along a slanted plane or moves diagonally upward across the screen against a background of distant trees and mountains.

These slants and diagonals create imaginary triangles within the rectangle of the screen. The precision of the compositions, their length of time on the screen, and their similarity of form, as if variations on a visual theme, bring the play of lines and planes to the fore. If such graphic coordinates determined the construction of *Prelude*, the speed of the images and the density of the metaphors obscured them; here their emphasis is part of the formal distancing or disengagement from the drama of the action visualized. Again Brakhage's mention of Gaudier-Brzeska proves a useful clue: his manifesto, *Vortex*, quoted in Pound's book, begins with "Sculptural energy is the mountain."[8]

Nowhere else in all of Brakhage's cinema is the antagonism of consciousness to nature so naked as in *Part One*. The mediator of this agon, the Dog Star Man, seems through most of the film to be defeated by the cold, the slope, and the tangles of trees in his way. Yet as the film progresses, the formal mechanics by which the myth is rendered come more and more to invade the metaphysics of the myth. First, without breaking the rhythm of the slow fades, the film-maker introduces a shot of the hero in greenish negative tossing as if in sleep, suggesting in a most tentative way that the climb itself might be a dream.

The sleeper fades into the arc of the moon, which in turn fades into the first section in which subjective camera positions occur, as if through the eyes of the climber in his struggle. Now hand-held shots of the sun, rushing water, and his hand gripping the snow as he slips are mixed with the filtered objective shots of him inching his way up the mountain. Amid pans of the landscape and blurs which begin to disrupt the even tempo of the opening topology appear images of blood, tissues, and internal organs—an exposition of what is inside the Dog Star Man.

As more and more impressionistic camera work is used, Brakhage achieves a uniquely cinematic tension. There is a dual realization that a particular shot is meant to suggest the Dog Star Man's state of mind or what he is seeing, and that the same shot is a camera trick. For instance, he sees mountains writhing against the sky. That effect is rendered by the flagrantly obvious twisting of an anamorphic lens. The paradoxical tension between mechanics and illusion is integral to the structure of the section and increases both in the rapidity of instances and the degree of obviousness as the film draws to its conclusion.

Several proleptic intrusions into the unity of the development seem enigmatic within the structure of *Part One*; they become clearer when repeated or reflected in *Parts Two, Three,* or *Four.* Yet they are plastically and rhythmically integrated within their immediate cinematic context. Such images are the birth of a child in reverse motion, the close-up of lovemaking with a triangle of light illuminating the couple, or the naked Dog Star Man writhing.

In the center of the film, shots become shorter, the phrasing by fades and leaders less frequent, and the non-objective blurs and flashes more regular. Brakhage even photographs previously articulate images of trees, falling snow, hair, and the body through a prismatic lens, blurring the distinction—originally so clearly delineated—between subjective and objective and establishing a metaphor between scenic views and stained-glass windows, which appear at times, recalling the parallel in *Prelude* between the trees of the burned forest and the marble columns.

The merging of perspectives and the acceleration of metaphor attend a flattening of the depth of the images and a general abstraction of all that we have seen so far. Pound defined Vorticism as follows:

> Every concept, every emotion presents itself to the vivid consciousness in some primary form. It belongs to the art of that form. . . . It is no more ridiculous that a person should receive or convey an emotion by an arrangement of shapes, or planes, or colours, than that they should receive or convey such emotion by an arrangement of music notes.[9]

He is approaching the concept of vortex as "the point of maximum energy. . . . There is a point at which an artistic impulse is visceral and abstract and can be realized in any of the arts."

The development gradually glides into the finale through a meditation on snow: the falling snow becomes the smoke of a forest fire; the hero shakes snow off branches as he clears his way with his axe; there is a single-frame animation of magnified snow crystals. As this section blends into the finale, the precision of the opening groupings returns. There are six separate phrasings of images in the finale of *Part One.* The first begins with the protagonist climbing up a slight incline with the dog moving easily by his side. As the finale progresses, the man seems to move slower and slower. Appropriately, by the end he has almost stopped. He climbs from the other side of the screen at the same incline and then falls. Brakhage shows flashes of his face in falling, followed by a shot of his heart. A black silence.

The second phrase is only two shots: the Dog Star Man climbing at a forty-five-degree angle, and a subjective shot of him falling. Then whiteness. The next section is again at a forty-five-degree angle; he falls. But the shot is cut short just as his dog begins to move in slow motion. Blackness follows, ending in internal tissues intercut with Greek columns. The fallen titan, in negative, struggles to get up amid flashes of orange.

The fourth paragraph is the most crucial in the finale. He makes his way up a sixty-degree incline. The angle is so steep it poses the question, is the mountain just the function of a tilted camera? The next shot, a seventy-degree angle, answers affirmatively; for the dog, with magnificent grace, easily glides up to his master's side, either defying gravity or demonstrating the tilt. Whiteness fades into black. At this point the terms of the opposition of nature and consciousness have been reversed. Although he is still defeated, the Dog Star Man is less the victim of nature than of his own or the film-maker's imagination. In the fifth grouping, he is lying in the snow, first in positive, then in negative. He pulls himself up a ninety-degree cliff. Having admitted the camera trick with the dog's leap, Brakhage triumphantly exaggerates it. Throughout the film, images of the protagonist's interior (heart, blood, tissues) and postulations of his "negative" self have become progressively more frequent and important. The final shot confirms the shift to an interior view: after a very long period of whiteness, the sixth phrase, a single shot, appears. It is a microscopic view of blood in a capillary vessel with its natural long push forward, short push back, long push forward motion.

Coming at this point the final shot illustrates the principle Brakhage derived from his study of idiotoxic disorders: that there is a physiological basis for a nexus of imaginative acts. Thus the rhythm of the blood corresponds to the winter rhythm of the Dog Star Man's struggle with nature.

I have already mentioned the bracketing device which frames *Part Two*; as if recapitulating and extending *Part One*, the film begins and ends with images of the Dog Star Man climbing and fallen. While the framing sequence is in progress the film-maker introduces the infant who will dominate the section in fragments and flashes.

Each of the parts of the film has as many layers of superimposition as its number; thus after the two-layered *Prelude, Part One* has one visual line, *Part Two* has two, *Part Three* three, and *Part Four* has four simultaneous layers of superimposition. At the beginning and end of *Part Two* the Dog Star Man appears on both layers, in positive black-and-white on one, in negative on the other. Their combination recalls the flashing effect of the monuments in *The Dead*.

At first he climbs downward away from the camera, then suddenly forward, up and beyond the camera. After the momentary introduction of the crying baby, he appears again, now in color, stumbling among mountainous rocks. As he gropes past one of them, the camera settles upon it. The surface of the rock becomes the first major element of the superimposition upon the baby. Texturally, the images of the baby are not like anything we have seen so far in this film. Brakhage originally intended to make a short film called *Meat Jewel* about the changes of expression in the face of his first son during the initial six weeks of his life. He employed the technique of *Mothlight* in constructing this film—that is, he punched holes in the images and carefully inlaid other film material, holding the mosaic together with a covering of mylar tape. As the child screams in black-and-white, the mouth cavity is replaced by fragments of colored film. At another point, his sense of hearing is emphasized by the insertion of a colored ear in the hole made by cutting out the black-and-white original.

The inspiration of this short film, which became fully incorporated into *Dog Star Man*, had been the film-maker's meticulous observation of the changes in facial structure of his first three children, all girls, and a poem, "The Human Face," by his friend Michael McClure, from which the working title was derived.

Brakhage zooms in repeatedly on the screaming infant as if moving the camera in sympathy with his cries. Later he concentrates on his blinking eyes and the twitching muscles of his face. As a development of this instance, he inlays the colored ear. Lastly, he watches the spasmodic movements of the feet and hands. The effect of these scenes is to present a catalogue of the senses: the birth of sight, of hearing, and the haptic complex evoked by the kicking feet and waving fists.

Superimposed upon the collaged images of the baby are a series of flat colored images, reminiscent of parts of *Prelude*, passing very quickly. The predominant object is the rock mentioned above. It is presented in a flickering light which emphasizes its porous texture and suggests the kind of pre-verbal cognition possible to the newborn child. Compared to the rock are the visual textures of light passing through trees, the sun seen through a gauze, rushing blood, and the flesh of a nipple. A striking metaphor occurs in the superimposition when the dripping milk from that nipple seems to be a tear in the baby's eye.

The end recalls the beginning, with superimposed solarized scenes of the hero climbing and colored shots of him fallen. As he lies on the ledge, a yellow, filtered shot of the nude woman is collaged over him, as if she were an emanation. The ragged edge of the inlaid material which is superimposed over him on the matching layer connotes the privileged status of the female aspect of his self—or his Emanation in Blakean terms—while at the same time reaffirming the illusory nature of the cinematic material.

The solid-color nude figure is familiar from the *Prelude*, but it is actually with *Part Three* that we associate these images; for that section, the most visually unique of the film, is composed entirely of colored nude images of parts of the male and female body superimposed over each other, while a heart and hand-painted smears (predominantly blue, green, and red) are superimposed over both. The combined effect is of a hermaphroditic sensuousness, rhythmically punctuated by the accelerated splashes of paint and beats of the heart. As the section moves to its end, the bodies become more abstract, as if the camera were very close to the flesh. The color changes become less intense, and thereby the presence of the heart, which had been minor at the opening, comes to predominate.

Here Brakhage's interpretative description of the film fails to illuminate what we see. The synchronous superimposition blurs any distinction between "a male level becoming female" and "a female level becoming male." We see, all at once, a thick interweaving of male and female bodies, and that's all. The occasional appearance of a hand fingering the penis fails to qualify the whole episode as a mediator's "sexual daydream" with any of the precision with which the first three sections were mediated.

Although *Part Three* does not function within *Dog Star Man* as the film-maker claims, that does not mean it is an artistic failure. It is the simplest and most direct portion of the film, and it functions within the whole, as I have already indicated, as an antithesis to *Part Two*—as experience's version of the sensual awakening. Within *The Art of Vision*, as we shall soon see, the same material may be experienced in a different way, perhaps closer to Brakhage's argument.

After the alternative interludes of *Parts Two* and *Three*, *Part Four* recommences from the action of the frames of *Part One* and *Part Two*.

This is the shortest (five minutes), most intricate, and most elliptical of the sections. The four layers of imagery provide an exceptionally dense viewing experience and make it difficult for the analyst to describe the film. Nevertheless Brakhage has often reduplicated his images two- and three-fold, creating an echo or fugue-like effect, in which one act repeats itself in different colors and at slightly asynchronic intervals. This somewhat eases the difficult problem of description. Finally, Brakhage deliberately makes use of imagistic and structural recollections of the previous parts of the film. Although they pass with exceptional rapidity, these allusions unmistakably register as formal, if not temporal, flashbacks even when they are narratively integrated within *Part Four*.

The film opens with several images, one on top of the other, of the Dog Star Man slowly rising from the supine position he was left in at the end of *Part Two*. Horizontal anamorphosis accentuates his outstretched body. His gestures, on the different levels, suggest both that he has risen from the dead and that he has awakened from a night's sleep. While he is still rising on some of the echoing layers, we see the first of many shots of him chopping the felled tree. This is clearly a midsummer image, as he perspires, wipes his forehead, and continues his vigorous chopping in the noon sun. The montage reinforces the notion of resurrection. As the film progresses the gesture of chopping will assume a series of different overtones. In fact, the core of *Part Four* is the transformation of associations we have acquired in the first seventy minutes of the film, through unanticipated juxtapositions and superimpositions.

One of the major motifs of *Part Three* had been a deep red shot of the full female figure, lying down and rising in one continuous movement. Brakhage triple-exposed this movement in the camera so that it appears on one layer of film. The woman seems to be rising out of herself in the composite. This shot had appeared proleptically in the *Prelude* and plays a significant role in the structure of *Part Three*. In its first appearance in *Part Four*, it reflects the rise of the hero, a sympathetic movement on the part of his female emanation; at the same time it introduces a very quick synecdochic narrative of lovemaking, conception, birth, and child-raising. The second figure in this sequence, a black-and-white image of bodies making love, also appeared in *Part One*, where it stood out as a rupture in the logic of the woodman's drama. There I called attention to an unexplained image of childbirth. In *Part Four* the birth scene, like the brief shots of the red-tinted woman, the genitalia, and the lovemaking, is presented very quickly and schematically, condensing the erotic and procreative cycle into a few seconds, but the visual echoes and metaphors make it perfectly clear what we are seeing. The occurrence of the shot of the Dog Star Man chopping wood early in this narrative renders that gesture a metaphor for lovemaking. Then a dynamic eruption of a solar corona, covered with emulsion scratches at the moment of the flame burst, symbolizes the orgasm. The whole movement from arousal, through copulation, labor, and birth to shots of breast-feeding and the dripping nipple which we recognize from *Parts Two* and *Three* takes less than a minute. The metaphors which accompany this sequence are too numerous to list here, and there are many images, not directly related to this development, which are interjected to extend or anticipate other significant moments in the film.

One related trope deserves analysis. During the birth, a vagina appears collaged into the texture of the images just as the yellow female figure had been at the end of *Part Two*. The allusion suggests a retroactive resolution of the ambiguity of the child in *Part Two*; here it is apparent that the child is not the Dog Star Man as an infant, but his child. Yet structurally it is important that this fact remain ambivalent and suspended while we watch the earlier section. At the same time Brakhage seems to want to indicate in the most indirect way an Oedipal equation of mother and lover.

The hand-made scratches also follow a sequence of significance. Early in the film they trace the shape of Ionic columns in a brief revival of the analogy between trees and temples, between leaves refracting light and stained-glass windows. The scratches draw imaginary roots soon after a revival of the metaphor of a tree's base and the female crotch, now extended to the male as well. When the sun-burst corresponds to an orgasm, the scratching emphasizes the connection. Finally, in the last moment of the film, a single scratch appears, the artist's mark on the celluloid.

The narrative of the child continues after a lacuna in which the emphasis changes from sex and birth to topology. From an airplane we look down on mountain peaks, while in superimposition the camera zooms in on a house. The elaboration of this movement from a panorama of mountains down to the isolated house gives rise to the most dramatic play of depth and flatness in the entire film. Structurally the montage recalls the opening of *Part One* with its movement inward from the cosmos to the point on the mountain where the hero is struggling. Here the range is limited to the terrestrial, but its formal dynamic turns upon the recurrence of a piece of discarded television footage the film-maker once picked

out of the garbage can at his laboratory. A hand with a pointer indicates the contour of a mountain. In the context in which Brakhage places this didactic fragment (perhaps of a weather report), it dramatizes the conflict of scale, of depth and flatness, and by implication of illusion and its unmasking, organized throughout *Dog Star Man*.

Originally the topological section of the film had been shot for a separate work, which like *Meat Jewel* was integrated into *Dog Star Man* and never completed in itself. This time another poet, Robert Kelly, had inspired Brakhage to make a landscape film by his use of the neologism "landshape." Its amalgamation into *Part Four* is yet another instance of Brakhage's proclaimed willingness to allow his film to develop as he edits it.

During the zooming movements on the house, flames appear in brief flashes, superimposed. Their locus becomes fixed in the family hearth as the virtual line from mountain to house extends inside, where we see the child, now several months old, crawling before a fireplace.

The crawling baby continues the haptic exploration of space initiated in the cradle of *Part Two*, while in superimposition the theme of the mountain develops. A third element in the combination, the protagonist on the mountain, once again compared to the baby as he feels his way around, sets up a metaphorical transformation: the fire before the baby evokes the corona of the sun, which in turn introduces a shot of the Dog Star Man looking up to the sun. He seems once again defeated, overpowered by the natural. He puts down his axe, and amid flashes of branches, the baby, flames, the corona, and white leader, he falls backward in slow motion down the mountain.

Again the film-maker introduces the triple exposure in red of the settling and rising female nude, now in ironic analogy to the falling hero. Then a sunset announces the time of the fall.

At this point the film tantalizes us with a premature movement toward a conclusion. The images dissolve in whiteness. But after a long pause they reappear, now in winter with the bruised and stunned hero on his knees in pain and groping through the snowy forest. As night comes on and stars begin to move quickly across the sky, the summer mid-day images of the titan chopping the tree suddenly return and take over the film until its end. As he chops there is a brief transition to negative, superimposed over moving stars, which in the film-maker's synopsis is the crucial moment of the conclusion. Within the rhythm of the film the negative image seems more a contingency than a true apotheosis, for the chopping continues after it in color. Intercut and superimposed with the regular gestures of the woodman appear splice marks, flares of film stock, and sprocket holes. In its final manifestation this often repeated image becomes a metaphor for the film-cutter. With the establishment of this connection the film evaporates in flares and leader.

In *The Art of Vision*, Brakhage presents all the layers of film which went into the making of *Dog Star Man*, individually and in superimposed combinations. The following schema shows the order of the film. The layers of a given section are identified by letters, so that, for instance, first the A layer of *Prelude* is seen, then the B layer, then the two together or the actual *Prelude* as it appears in *Dog Star Man*. Thus all of the shorter film is enclosed within the longer. In outline the form is:

Prelude	A	25 min.	
	B	25 min.	
	AB	25 min.	
Part 1	A	31 min.	(*Part One* is the only section without superimposition.)
Part 2	AB	6 min.	
	A	6 min.	
	B	6 min.	
Part 3	A	9 min.	
	B	9 min.	
	C	9 min.	
	AB	9 min.	
	AC	9 min.	
	BC	9 min.	
	ABC	9 min.	
Part 4	ABCD	6 min.	
	ABC	6 min.	
	ABD	6 min.	
	BCD	6 min.	
	AB	6 min.	
	AC	6 min.	
	AD	6 min.	
	BC	6 min.	
	BD	6 min.	
	CD	6 min.	
	A	6 min.	
	B	6 min.	
	C	6 min.	
	D	6 min.	

Originally Brakhage thought he would call this version *The Complete Dog Star Man*, but he changed his mind after showing it to Robert Kelly, before it had had a public presentation. Brakhage described his decision to alter the title in an unpublished interview with the author:

> Really when I had the sense of being finished with this work was when the four and one-half hour work got a title separate from the seventy-five minute *Dog Star Man* composite. That happened when I visited the Kellys. We looked at all that material in that order I had given it. The morning after we had seen the whole thing, Kelly said at breakfast: "It seems to me you ought to read a life of Johann Sebastian Bach." We took another couple of sips of coffee, and I thought, "Un-humm, well, that would be a good thing to do." Then suddenly he came out with: "Well, to get that sense of form whereby a whole work can exist in the center of another work, or spiral out into pieces in another work, as in Baroque music, and that second arrangement be another piece entirely." I said: "Well, you mean like—but that isn't exactly what happens in *The Art of the Fugue*, but something like that." Suddenly he came out with: "Why don't you call it *The Art of Vision?*" Immediately that seemed to me a completely perfect thing to do.[10]

He removed all the intermediary titles which announce the distinct sections of *Dog Star Man*. Two things immediately apparent from even a glance at the schema are that the present order elongates both the gradual concretion of the *Prelude* and the slow dissolution of *Part Four*, and that proportions of duration are radically altered. The longest section of *Dog Star Man, Part One*, becomes the second shortest in *The Art of Vision*. The material for *Parts Three* and *Four* grows from nine and six minutes respectively to 63 and 84 minutes.

Although not a single image actually changes, the experience of seeing *The Art of Vision* is considerably different from that of *Dog Star Man*. Aside from the obvious factor of duration, the longer version distinguishes itself by forcing an analytic procedure upon the viewer and by establishing a new sense of suspense in the combination or breakdown of superimpositions. Since the *Prelude* begins with its single layers, its colors are more vivid, not being cancelled out by the superimposition layer; its montage is more dynamic, without the elisions; and the visual pauses of black or white leader are more prominent. Since no title indicates the end of roll A and the beginning of B, only an experienced viewer can identify the transition. To a first viewer it would seem one continuous passage until the superimposition appears, but he would be aware of a formal and imagistic echoing of the first half hour of the film in the second. The eye, now familiar with the images in isolation, can discern the metaphors more surely and rapidly when in the third reel they arise through superimposition.

There is no difference between *Part One* in *Dog Star Man* and in *The Art of Vision* except the elimination of the titles, which makes the opening cosmology appear a direct continuation of the *Prelude* material. Yet despite the identity, their effect is slightly different. After almost an hour and a half of introductory and abstractly edited images, the structure of the mountain climbing sequence seems like a sudden narrative concretion. The absence of titles also makes the transition from *Part One* to *Part Two* less apparent, especially since the superimposition is withheld for a few moments. The breakdown of *Part Two*, unlike *Prelude*, decreates; in other words, the baby is divided from what he sees, suggesting that the object of the child's vision is the chaotic imagery of the opening hour and a half. The severing of the two layers, with the object of vision first, and the child later, intensifies the textural analogies between the flashing rock, the skin of the nipple, the internal organs, and the trees.

In *The Art of Vision* the yellow nude at the end of the second roll of *Part Two* smoothes the transition to the colored female nudes that begin *Part Three*, which gradually builds up its layers. The division of the first two layers into "Her" and "His" rolls is not as clear as the film-maker would indicate in his argument. Both begin with female predominance, although the second is swifter and surer in its shift to male. By itself, the C roll of heartbeats and hand-painting has an extraordinary beauty which the superimpositions diminish. In creating this image Brakhage was again deliberately trying to revitalize an outworn topos, the use of the heart as a symbol fc. love. In *The Dead* he had attempted the same kind of redemption of gravestones and the river as icons of death. The physical reality of the heart and its use as an orgasmic rhythm desentimentalize the symbol and make its use in this section potent. Finally, the extreme repetition of the layers of carnal images becomes itself an erotic metaphor.

Yet in the fourteen repetitions of the material from *Part Four* the effect is quite different. A total absence of narrative and the similarity of roll A to B in the previous permutations made the recurrences of *Part Three*'s material seem at times like one continuous film. Since *Part Four* was edited fugally with similar or identical images at significant points on all four layers, there can be no mistaking when one roll ends and the next begins. They all dissolve into flares, splices, and stars and begin again with the rising of the Dog Star Man. The form of the whole series reflects the dissolution within each of the variations as they reach their end.

Watching the final hour and a half of variations on *Part Four*, one is impressed by the idea of a cyclical order, which is immanent in *Dog Star Man* as a whole. In the insistent repetition of structures during these fourteen sequences, the cycle becomes a major concept.

Dog Star Man and *The Art of Vision* were made at the height of the mythopoeic phase of the American avant-garde cinema. Contemporary with their conception and presentation were Anger's *Scorpio Rising*, Markopoulos' *Twice a Man*, and Harry Smith's *Heaven and Earth Magic*, which I shall discuss in the next chapter. In Brakhage's film, perhaps more intensely than anywhere else, the strains of Romantic and post-Romantic poetry in American art converge with the aesthetics of Abstract Expressionism. The continuities and overlapping of artistic traditions make it difficult to pinpoint the specific vectors involved in the fusion of energies that went to make up the American avant-garde cinema between 1943 and 1970, but some points can be made.

The influx of masters of European modernism into America at the time of the Second World War was a catalyst for significant developments in both film and painting.[11] Yet those developments were not divorced from a native tradition, itself fed by European Romanticism, that can be seen in the poetry of Emerson, Whitman, Dickinson, Pound, Stevens, Crane, Williams, and Zukofsky. What we see today as the unified aesthetic of Abstract Expressionism was earlier a series of fiercely debated questions about form, procedure, and meaning. Although Maya Deren, for example, disassociates herself from the non-objective painters of the 1940s and attacks them in her *Anagram*, her polemic is infused with a rhetoric they shared, and one sees in her last film, *The Very Eye of Night*, a drift toward late Cubist space—a loss of depth, the breakdown of horizontal and vertical centrality (in this particular case through the rejection of gravitational coordinates), and the affirmation of the screen's surface, accompanied by an abstraction of the narrative tension which myth had given her earlier work. The visual texture and the structural principles of Sidney Peterson's cinema were pointing in the same direction when he turned away from the medium.

Markopoulos and Anger, more secure in their Romantic conventions, resisted both plastic and structural transformations until the very end of the sixties; Broughton continues to resist them. It was Brakhage, of all the major American avant-garde film-makers, who first embraced the formal directives and verbal aesthetics of Abstract Expressionism.[12] With his flying camera and fast cutting, and by covering the surface of the celluloid

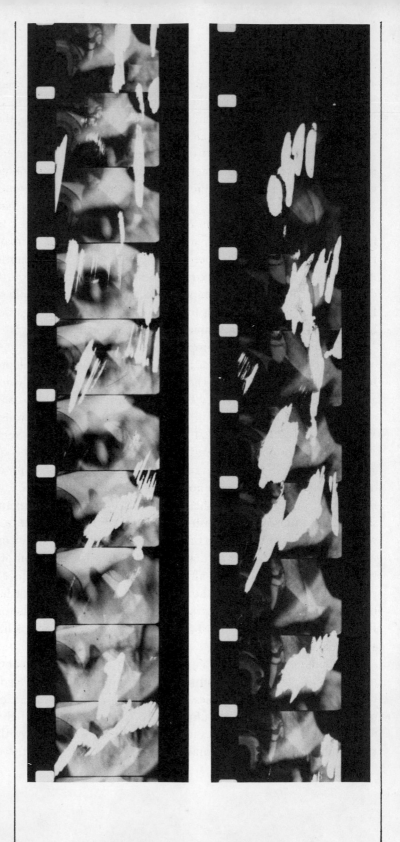

Abstract Expressionist play of positive and negative space: the filed-out image in Stan Brakhage's *Dog Star Man: Part 3* and the cut canvas of Jackson Pollock's "Cutout."

with paint and scratches, Brakhage drove the cinematic image into the space of Abstract Expressionism and relegated the conventional depth of focus to a function of the artistic will, as if to say "the deep axis will appear only when I find it necessary."

The language of revelation and of process which I have excerpted repeatedly from the film-maker's writings and speech recalls the statements of several painters. When asked if "there is no sort of preconception as to what the thing ought to be," Franz Kline answered:

> No. Except—except paint never seems to behave the same. Even the same paint doesn't, you know. . . . There are moments or periods when it would be wonderful to plan something and do it and have the thing only do what you planned to do, and then there are other times when the destruction of those planned things becomes interesting to you. So then it becomes a question of destroying—of destroying the planned form; it's like an escape, it's something to do; something to begin the situation. You yourself, you don't decide, but if you want to paint you have to find some way to start this thing off, whether it's painting it out or putting it in, and so on.[13]

That brings to mind Brakhage's statements on how he had to make a chance cutting of *Prelude* to get started on the organization of *Dog Star Man*. On the other hand, Jackson Pollock's statement on his process coincides with Brakhage's sense of artistic possession which recurs throughout *Metaphors on Vision*. Pollock wrote:

> When I am *in* my painting, I'm not aware of what I'm doing. It is only after a sort of "get acquainted" period that I see what I have been about. I have no fears about making changes, destroying the image, etc., because the painting has a life of its own. I try to let it come through.[14]

The connection between myth and Abstract Expressionism was not a simple matter to the artists involved. Mark Rothko said:

> If our titles recall the known myths of antiquity, we have used them again because they are the eternal symbols upon which we must fall back to express basic psychological ideas. They are the symbols of man's primitive fears and motivations, no matter in which land or what time, changing only in detail but never in substance, be they Greek, Aztec, Icelandic, or Egyptian. And modern psychology finds them still persisting in our dreams, our vernacular, and our art, for all the changes in the outward conditions of life.
>
> Our presentation of these myths, however, must be in our own terms,

which are at once more primitive and more modern than the myths themselves—more primitive because we seek the primeval and atavistic roots of the idea rather than the classical version; more modern than the myths themselves because we must redescribe their implications through our own experience.[15]

But Barnett Newman took a contrary position:

> We are reasserting man's natural desire for the exalted, for a concern with our relationship to the absolute emotions. We do not need the obsolete props of an outmoded and antiquated legend. We are creating images whose reality is self-evident and which are devoid of the props and crutches that evoke associations with outmoded images, both sublime and beautiful. We are freeing ourselves of the impediments of memory, association, nostalgia, legend, myth, or what have you.[16]

Ironically, Rothko gave formalistic titles to his canvases while Newman continued to label them with Biblical names ("Abraham," "Jericho"), religious associations ("The Stations of the Cross"), and Greek mythology ("Prometheus Bound"). Pollock vacillated between formalistic and mythic titles ("Lucifer," "Moon Woman Cuts the Circle," and "Cut-Out," "Number One") just as his art had its formalistic and psychological poles.

Brakhage is too eager a dialectician to have ignored this debate, both in its public and its interior forms. In "Margin Alien" he quotes tough-minded Clyfford Still (who persists in labeling his paintings by their dates of completion, e.g., "Painting, 1948-D"):

> We are committed to an unqualified act, not illustrating outworn myths or contemporary alibis. One must accept total responsibility for what he executes. And the measure of his greatness will be the depth of his insight and courage in realizing his own vision. Demands for communication are presumptuous and irrelevant.[17]

Even while he was making *Dog Star Man* Brakhage had inherited the Abstract Expressionist's uneasiness with mythical referents and structures, as the inclusion of this quotation shows. Yet for Brakhage, dialectical uneasiness is a source of strength. Immediately following the references to Still and Michael McClure, another anti-mythologist, Brakhage prints in corresponding columns excerpts from a statement on poetics by Charles Olson and bits of anti-aesthetics from John Cage. And throughout his writing Brakhage argues with himself and against the very need to write: "It is only as of use as useless."

The conception of *Songs* was a dramatic event in Brakhage's life. He had come to New York where he showed the completed *Parts Two* and *Three* of *Dog Star Man* with a vague idea of joining the New American Cinema Exposition then traveling in Europe. While in the city his 16mm equipment was stolen from his car. He collected enough money to get himself and his family back to Colorado, but he did not have funds for new equipment. With the twenty-five dollars paid by his limited insurance on the stolen equipment, he discovered he could buy an 8mm camera and editing materials. He did so. At least three factors were involved in the switch to 8mm, beyond what Brakhage would call the "magical" coincidence of finding the inexpensive equipment when he went looking to replace what he had lost.

In the first place, he wanted to get away from the giant form of *The Art of Vision* which had occupied him for seven years. Then, there was a definite economic advantage in making 8mm films: materials and laboratory prices were much lower than for 16mm work, and one could not be tempted into costly printing work (mixing layers of film, fades, etc.) simply because no laboratory undertook to do that in 8mm. All superimposition, dissolving, and fading had to be done in the camera. Finally, Brakhage saw a polemical advantage in the switch. Not only would his example dignify and encourage younger film-makers who could afford to work only in 8mm, but he would be able to realize, on a limited scale, a dream he had had for years of selling copies of his films, rather than just renting them, to people for home viewing. Since the early 1960s he had been prophesying a break-through for the avant-garde film-maker when films would be available for purchase like books, records, and painting reproductions and could therefore be owned and screened many times and at pleasure.

In the beginning Brakhage had no idea that *Songs* would become a single, serial work. Even after making the first eight sections he resisted that idea. But by the spring of 1965, with ten Songs finished in a little more than a year, he began to speak of the totality of the work in progress: "I think there will be more Songs. I do definitely see that they relate to each other. That is, practically every Song has images in it that occur in some other Song, if not in two or three others. The more remarkable thing is that each Song is distinct from each other; that holds them together in a very crucial kind of 'tension.' "[18] Within another year he was punning on the relation of a Song's number in the series to its subject (*XV Song Traits, 23rd Psalm Branch*); soon after that he was wondering when they

would end. They did conclude, with a dedication to the film-maker
Jerome Hill, after thirty Songs, or punning again, *American Thirties Song*,
in 1969.

Lack of space prohibits me from discussing each of the thirty Songs in
detail. Instead I shall sacrifice chronology to select sets of Songs for comparison and contrast in order to show how the series functions as a whole.
Brakhage's capsule descriptions, written for his own sales catalogue, describe with varying degrees of directness the subjects of the individual
Songs.

SONGS

"Go, little naked and impudent songs,
Go with a light foot!
(Or with two light feet, if it please you!)
Go and dance shamelessly!
Go with an impertinent frolic!
Greet the grave and the stodgy,
Salute them with your thumbs at your noses."

Ezra Pound, "Salutation the Second."

SONG I (1964); 4 min. Color. A portrait of a beautiful woman.

SONGS II & III (1964); 7 min. Color. An envisionation of fire and a mind's
movement in remembering.

SONG IV (1964); 4 min. Color. A round-about three girls playing with a
ball . . . hand-painted over photo image.

SONG V (1964); 7 min. Color. A child-birth song, . . . I think my best
birth film yet.

SONGS VI & VII (1964); 7 min. Color.

   VI: A song of the painted veil—arrived at via moth-death.

   VII: A San Francisco song—portrait of the City of Brakhage dreams.

SONG VIII (1964); 4 min. Color. A sea creatures song—a seeing of ocean
as creature.

SONG IX & X (1965); 10 min. Color.

   IX: a wedding song—of source and substance of marriage.

   X: a sitting around song.

SONG XI (1965); 6 min. Color. A black velvet film of fires, windows, insect life, and a lyre of rain scratches.

SONG XII (1965); 6 min. Black and white. Verticals and shadows—reflections caught in glass traps.

SONG XIII (1965); 6 min. Color. A travel song of scenes and horizontals.

SONG XIV (1965); 3 min. Color. A "closed-eye" vision song composed of
molds, paints, and crystals.

XV SONG TRAITS (1965); 75 min. Color. A series of individual portraits of
friends and family, all interrelated in what might be called a branch

growing directly from the trunks of SONGS I-XIV. In order of appearance: Robert Kelly, Jane and our dog Durin, our boys Bearthm and Rarc, daughter Crystal and the canary Cheep Donkey, Robert Creeley and Michael McClure, the rest of our girls Myrrena & Neowyn, Angelo diBenedetto, Rarc, Ed Dorn and his family, Myrrena, Neowyn, and Jonas Mekas (to whom the whole of the XVTH SONG is dedicated), as well as some few strangers, were the source of these TRAITS coming into being—my thanks to all . . . and to all who see them clearly.

SONG XVI (1965); 8 min. Color. A love song, a flowering of sex as in the mind's eye, a joy.

SONGS XVII & XVIII (1965); 7 min. Color. Cathedral and movie house—the ritual memories of religion—and then (in SONG XVIII) a portrait of a singular room in the imagination.

SONGS XIX & XX (1965); 8 min. Color. A dancing song of women's rites, and then (SONG XX) the ritual of light making shape/shaping picture.

SONGS XXI & XXII (1966); 8 min. Color. Transformation-of-the-singular-image was the guiding aesthetic light in the making of these two works. SONG XXI works its spell thru closed-eye-vision, whereas SONG XXII was inspired by approximates of "the dot-plane" or "grain field" of closed-eye-vision in textured "reality," so to speak. You could say that XXI arises out of an inner- and XXII into an outer-reality. These two works are particularly exciting to me because I at last accomplished something in the making of them that I had written hopefully to Maya Deren about years ago: films which could be run forwards AND backwards with equal/integral authenticity—that is that the run from end to beginning would hold to the central concern of the film . . . rather than simply being some wind and/or unwinding of beginning-to-ending's continuum. SONG XXII, additionally, can be run from its mid-point—the singular sun-star shape on water—in either direction to beginning or ending . . . thus film inherits the possibilities Gabrieli gave to music with his piece "My beginning is my ending and my ending is my beginning."

SONG XXIII: 23RD PSALM BRANCH (1966-67); 100 min. Color.

Part I—A study of war, created in the imagination in the wake of newsreel death and destruction.

 . . . We had moved around a lot and we had settled down enough . . . . so we got a TV. And that was something in the house that I could simply not photograph, simply could not deal with visually. It was pouring forth war guilt, primarily, into the household in a way that I wanted to relate to, if I was guilty, but I had feelings . . . of the qualities of guilt and I wanted to have it real for me and I wanted to deal with it.

And, I mean, it was happening on all the programs—on the ads as well as drama and even the comedies, and of course the news programs. And I had to deal with that. It finally became such a crisis that I knew I couldn't deal directly with TV but perhaps I could make or find out why war was all that unreal to me. . . .

Part II–A searching-into the "sources" of *Part I*, it is composed of the
following sections:
Peter Kubelka's Vienna, My Vienna, A Tribute to Freud, Nietzsche's
Lamb, East Berlin, and Coda.

SONGS XXIV & XXV (1967); 10 min. Color. A naked boy and flute song
and (XXV) a being about nature.

SONG XXVI (1967); 8 min. Color. A "conversation piece"–a viz-a-visual,
inspired by the (e)motional properties of talk: d:one, bird-like twitter-
ings, statement terror, and bombast.

MY MOUNTAIN, SONG XXVII (1968); 26 min. Color. A study of Arapahoe
Peak in all the seasons of two years' photography . . . the clouds and
weathers that shape its place in landscape—much of the photography
a-frame-at-a-time.

Rivers (1968); 36 min. Color. A series of eight films intended to echo
the themes of MY MOUNTAIN, SONG XXVII.

SONG XXVIII (1968); 4 min. Color. A song of scenes as texture.

SONG XXIX (1969); 4 min. Color. A portrait of the artist's mother.

AMERICAN THIRTIES SONG (1969); 30 min. Color. This film, preceded by
a portrait of the artist's father, is a long ode to the drives and driving-
spirit of the nineteen-thirties and of some of the shapes and textures
these energies created across the American landscape. This film is dedicated to Jerome Hill, whose image appears at the end of its "postlude."[19]

The scope of *Songs* ranges from the immediate recording of the objects
of a room by the film-maker sitting in a chaise-longue (*Song X*) to massive
meditations on war in two long parts, the second of which has six subdivisions (*23rd Psalm Branch*). But even that most complex of the *Songs*
contains moments and parts resembling the simplest. The persistence and
diversity of the simple strategies define the elusive unity of the serial work.
As far as Brakhage may go in forging a complex vision out of the reluctant
materials of 8mm, he always returns to the immediate, the sketch, the familiar—whatever risks being overlooked. The peripety of the thirty *Songs*
circumscribes Brakhage the lyricist and apocalyptic visionary while he
seeks to discover the limits of his new tool, the 8mm camera and film
surface.

Several of the *Songs* reconsider the questions, emotions, and situations
of his earlier films. *Song* V, punning on the birth of his fifth child, brings
to mind both *Window Water Baby Moving* and *Thigh Line Lyre Triangular*, without the drama of the first or the inwardness of the other.

In *Song* VI he looks again for an image of death while filming the last
moments of a moth against the background of flowered linoleum. Without the possibility of solarization (as in *The Dead*) or collage (as in *Moth-*

light), the film-maker must seek simpler means, and he develops a tension between the focus on the moth and the linoleum under him, visually incarnating Shelley's description of the filter between eternal and human life as a "painted veil."

In *Song XVI* he once again attempted to redeem a trite metaphor as he had previously done in *The Dead* and *Part Three* of *Dog Star Man*. Bracketed by shots of a misty landscape, the film compares flowers to sexual organs, and with its continual slow zooms on two layers of superimposition it evokes the rhythms of lovemaking. Often the erotic images are indistinct, but at the opening there are nipples, and then an erect penis is caressed. The film proceeds from the explicit to the suggestive. At the film's climax an orange fan of coral replaces the flowers. Then the end comes quickly: buttocks superimposed with other pieces of coral and starfish amid flares of orange. The transformation of the flowers into coral provides the film's finest moment; otherwise the flower imagery falls short of the film-maker's redemptive aspiration for it. The image is not as thoroughly divorced from conventional representation as the gravestones, the river, and the heart had been.

The unity of *Songs* as a whole does not depend entirely on the sometimes reassuring, sometimes startling reuse of specific images from earlier *Songs* in later ones. Even though 8mm superimposition must be done in the camera, which denies the frame-to-frame precision possible in 16mm dual-track editing, Brakhage makes extensive use of it. In numerous *Songs* there are isolated superimposed images cut into the texture of the film, but in the following films, superimposition is a major force shaping the totality: *I, II, V, VII, VIII, XII;* "Jane and the Boys," "Angelo," "Myrrena," and "Neowyn" from *XV Song Traits; XVI, XVII, XXII;* and "Nietzsche's Lamb" and the "Coda" from the *23rd Psalm Branch*.

Painting, scratching, and the laying of dots over the image appear periodically in the series, despite the immense difficulty of working on the surface of a film strip that has only one-fourth the area of 16mm. *Songs IV, XIV, XXII,* and the first part and "Nietzsche's Lamb" from the *23rd Psalm Branch* depend upon these techniques. Close in texture to the hand-painted *Songs* are the non-objective works (*XI, XX, XXI*), exhibiting for the most part patterns of pure light.

The divergence among the similar *Songs* is remarkable; here Brakhage is never satisfied with simple variation. Of the hand-painted and non-objective examples, *Song XI* exists completely on a flat plane. A round white light on the upper right of the black screen and two smaller yellow lights below it are the only fixed points. In the center tiny flecks of illumination appear as if highlighted off an indistinguishable figure.[20] Very quick, flame-like bursts of orange appear and disappear in different positions during the whole of the film. Four blue scratches can be seen after the first third of the film, vertically transversing the left side. But when the composition returns after a whitening flare-out, they are gone. Soon after, the Song ends.

In *Song XIV*, on the other hand, there are persistent hints and allusions to depth beyond the grainy painted surface. Sweeps of color change the dominant hue from green to orange to red and back to green again. At times faint underlying images of trees seem to support the pointillistic covering of paint, but it is not until the last seconds of the film, after a white section with dynamic splatterings of blue paint, that faded trees move past or cling to the edges of the overexposed screen, now free of paint. In *XI* the careful placing of surface scratches, lights, and indecipherable movements at different points in a black matrix forces all the visual material to occupy a single plane, while in *XIV* the play of paint and underlying image suggests more depth than actually appears on the photographed base.

Songs XX, XXI, XXII form an abstract series in themselves. In the first of them a central wavy red spot, perhaps a water reflection photographed through a filter, turns into a yellow fire and then flashes regularly in a montage of alternations with a forest steeped to abstraction in a blue fog. Gradually the metrical recurrences of the spot are suspended, as the surface of a lake, also in fog, provides a range of tones through the constantly shifting exposures from a deluging to a denying of light. Two-thirds of the way through the film the spot returns for just one frame. Soon after, it holds on the screen longer as the montage returns the original alternation and flares out.

XXI, like *IV*, involves overpainting. This time black dots and paint cover flowers while in the blackness cartoon-like scratches sketch flowery designs. The degree of blackness and range of overlaying change in waves which hint that the blackness is floating upward from below the screen. But before we can examine it carefully the black becomes blue; later it disappears in white. Then subdued amber, splattered like a Pollock, covers the whiteness, which in turn changes from a negative to a positive force, from base to surface, when with the return of black the whiteness seems like dots upon it. The transformations here are slower than in the other painted films; they happen by degrees. Finally the metamorphosis settles on a red circle which blazes away in flares of alternating red and yellow light.

That same circle begins the next film, which builds its structure on the interplay of long and close shots of sunlight reflected off a lake in clusters and lattices of bristling bright diamonds. Again the finale is a flare after several white-outs. Both XXI and XXII are meant for projection either from head to tail or from tail to head, but neither are palindromes. Their coupling brings us with the help of Brakhage's note to the subtle dialectic of the Songs as a whole. He tells us, "You could say that XXI arises out of an inner- and XXII into an outer-reality."

Despite the extreme mobility of the 8mm camera, the Songs depend less on camera movement than the earlier lyrical films. Brakhage's fight with the natural world seems at first to have quieted and his inwardness diminished. With couplings such as XXI and XXII and "Rivers" following Song XXVII: My Mountain, the opposition of consciousness to the natural world reaffirms itself; once again the accent is upon the visionary seer, not what he sees. In the light of the whole series, the opposition of early couplets such as II and III grows clearer. Again, the clues lie in the film-maker's notes: "An envisionation of fire and a mind's movement in remembering."

Song II shows air distorted by heat, as if just above a burning fire, and the sinking sun intercut with rapids of water. It invokes the concept of fire without showing a flame. In III, on the other hand, the same images of rushing water form a rhythmic montage, alternating directions, into which undistinguished shots of a street are injected and lost. Bits of an exceptionally grainy green leader, which at first divide the movements of water, eventually dominate the film. The displacement of emphasis reduces the water from presence to a metaphor for the eccentric movements of the grain. In the unpublished interview I have quoted before, Brakhage describes the making of this film:

> We were listening to Brahms' Third Symphony and became very tortured by the incredible beauty of its seeming to build up various kinds of tension and never breaking through any of them. I said, "That is a mind process: the way in which the mind gets hung up magnificently." It was such a disturbing moment that when we finished listening to it we were so excited and at the same time frustrated that Jane rushed out into the night to take a walk and I immediately picked up some green leader which had been baked in the sun . . . that seemed to stand for some basic impulse of mine. The question was what could I drop into that space? Water, of course, was there. Water shots relate to the grain.

I struggled to get something else in there by dropping in a photographic shot. I borrowed what had come with the little 8mm viewer I bought at this time. It was shot by the man who owned the camera store; some shots out of his window of a scene in Boulder. It was quite photographic; quite like a picture postcard with moving cars. It became possible by editing this green leader very carefully, so that it built a certain tension, to drop this scene into it via the water shots, which then could be drowned by water in another scene. That was a breakthrough which could make the leader relate to water and then fall back into being just the basic strata of mind movement.[21]

The laconic note for *Song XXV*, "a being about nature," refers to a natural landscape obscured by smoke, fog, and the distortion of heated air, as in *II*. There is a difficulty in writing about the dialectic of consciousness and nature in the *Songs* without reducing its complexity and ambiguity. The work spans five years with an order of composition in close approximation to the numbering of the pieces. Brakhage never made any changes in already finished *Songs* to bring them into a more explicit relationship with later ones. Some of the oppositions are obviously deliberate, such as *II* and *III*, *XXI* and *XXII*, and others less conscious. But there is no over-all antithesis, even of the most eccentric order. Instead of a center of gravity, *Songs* has a turning point in the *23rd Psalm Branch*, the longest and most intricate of the works. Here the repudiation of the physical world in favor of the poetic consciousness exceeds Brakhage's previous extremes, but two films later, in *Song XXV*, the vehemence is qualified and calmed.

Numerically, although not temporally, in the center of the thirty films are the *XV Song Traits*. The form of the portrait radiates through the *Songs*, including *I*, *XXIV*, and *XXIX* with fragmentary portraits worked into the first part of the *23rd Psalm Branch* and the end of the *American Thirties Song*. Superimposition and synecdoche are the predominant tropes of the film-maker's portraiture. *Song I* shows several full figures of his wife Jane in a striped robe reading and making gestures, whose individuality are emphasized by slightly fast-motion recording. In superimposition, passing boulders can be seen from a car, and toward the end of the film there are successive entrances of someone through a doorway. Brakhage defines "Robert Kelly" through close-ups of his hands, pointing and cutting cheese, with occasional reference to his face, but not full--figure. Again in "Jane and Durin," he gives us parts of the event without the wide view; the image will rest on his wife's ankle or on the dog's stomach as she scratches him. Only in the final and dedicatory portrait of Jonas

Mekas does he combine close-up gestures with characteristic movements of the whole body without recourse to superimposition.

Within the limits of the film-maker's conception of portraiture, the range of his formal invention is wide. That conception comes close to an older desire which he shared with Maya Deren and about which he corresponded with her—that of creating a cinematic haiku form. On the one hand, the simplified superimposition of 8mm may be compared to the haiku's juxtaposition of two isolated images. On the other hand, Brakhage also employs a two-part form in some of the simpler Songs. The synecdoches of Kelly, for instance, precede the appearance, fragmentation, and reappearance of a moving geometrical form resembling the diagram of electron orbits around a nucleus or planets around a sun, filmed off a television monitor. "The Dorns" contrasts snapshots of the poet Ed Dorn and his family with color-filmed images, as if the film-maker was looking at the photographs and remembering the moving scene.

Outside of the portraits, the two-part construction can be found in an extended form in Song IV, which is of three girls playing with a red ball and a painted-over street scene. The extension consists of prefacing the hand-painted part with a brief image of the ball game through a window and the rhythmic interruption of the game at the end with spaces of leader in grainy red and green (held over from the previous water meditation).

Synecdoche is crucial to all of Brakhage's cinema, but in Song XVIII it attains a prominence comparable to the portraits. The "portrait of a singular room in the imagination" consists of shadows, illuminated corners, bits of wall decoration, surfaces abstracted beyond identification, and a closing door. Critic Guy Davenport informs us that we are in a dentist's office in this film.[22]

The portrait of "Crystal," by way of contrast to the simple structures so far described, uses parallel montage as intricately as the most elaborate of the Songs except the 23rd Psalm Branch. Above all it recalls the play of diverse elements in the epithalamion Song IX. A very washed-out, dim shot of young Crystal Brakhage crying repeats itself amid images of snow outside a window, a canary in a cage, people and reflections at an airport (reminiscent of Song XII without quoting from it), children's drawings, horses in a blizzard, and changes of light intensity through a window. The movements of the camera and the elisions and collisions of the editing return to the visual rhetoric of Anticipation of the Night. The elements of the portrait combine to describe the anxiety of a child away from home, and the repeated emphasis on the cage and even more on looking out of the windows of the house raises the metaphor of the self as the center of both the house and the cage.

In *Song IX* similar camera movements and montage seem more spectacular because the images they fuse together are more disparate. A rhinoceros pacing back and forth in a cage with a patch of sunlight on his hide establishes the initial tempo, into which are cut shots of an outdoor wedding by moonlight, two naked children in sex play, a door opening on an empty room, and later a moving shot out of the same room with a young man silhouetted in it. The jittery dance of the moon over the wedding party makes specific the allusion to *Anticipation of the Night* which is felt in the construction. There also appears a brief quotation of a window by the sea taken from the beginning of *Song VII*. For Davenport, whose insights on the Songs are always valuable, the collision of the wedding party with the rhinoceros and the "nonchalantly and impudently naked" children make the film "a comic masterpiece. . . . Brakhage's sense of humor is the most difficult of his strategies," he tells us. "In an age of largely feminine humor, he remains doggedly masculine in his laughter."[23]

His point is well taken; for of the erotic Songs this is the only piece of ribaldry. In place of *Song XVI* which Davenport admires, I would propose *Song XIX* as the high point of sexual energy in the series. It does not relinquish its mystery in repeated viewings. The film centers upon slow and fast motion alternations of two women dancing. One appears to be the film-maker's wife, but it is difficult to be certain of identifications in the silhouette effect that their moving bodies create in the dim foreground with a bright window behind. The other, a younger girl, seems in her late adolescence. At first the camera picks out from their slow movements slow jumps of the feet or flights of arms. There is a vase of flowers in the overexposed window behind them; framed by its light, their silhouettes grow jagged edges, especially as they move faster. Sometimes only a corner or edge of the now blackened screen has a flickering image, a rhythmic synecdoche of the dance. As they accelerate to a humping motion, or so the camera makes them seem, the shadows merge their jagged edges in an erotic fusion. Through an open door, bright leaves can be seen blown by the wind and speeded up by the camera until their shimmering recalls the dancers. Another, younger, girl watches from the doorway as the blending of bodies becomes frantic, until the image burns out in flares.

With the return of a picture we see an altogether different couple, a man and a woman standing outside with their dog. The zoom slowly pulls back from this black-and-white image, returning inside by montage to the fast dance and dim colors several times. The zoom continues to the end of the film, revealing a house, then its grounds, a whole village, and finally an arid landscape of hills in which the village is situated. Night is falling. In a *diminuendo* of erotic tension the returns to the dance now show the smaller girl taking part accompanied by playful leaps of her dog.

Brakhage has said that this was filmed during a visit to the family of Robert Creeley in New Mexico. Presumably he and his wife were the figures before the house, and his two daughters were dancing with Jane Brakhage. Creeley had already appeared in the most exceptional of the portraits. As he sits and rises from a chair, he changes from positive to negative, an intensely subjective image with a presentiment of aging. This portrait and the following staccato pixilation of McClure putting on a beast's head were originally shot and edited in 16mm and reduced, to be included in *XV Song Traits* as well as released in 16mm as *Two: Creeley/ McClure*. The solarization of the Creeley portrait would be impossible in 8mm where there is neither negative film nor laboratory superimposition.

The furthest that Brakhage came in extending the language of 8mm cinema was his editing of the *23rd Psalm Branch*. Here he managed to create extended passages of dynamic montage out of two-frame (one-twelfth of a second) elements. He solved the problem of cluttering the screen with hundreds of splicing marks by introducing two frames of black leader between every shot, causing a rapid winking effect in the projection of the film but hiding the splices. He also succeeded in applying several sizes and varieties of ink dots to the surface of the 8mm image; at times hundreds seem to be clustered in the tiny frames.

The phenomenal and painstaking craftsmanship of this film reflects the intensity of the obsession with which its theme grasped his mind. In 1966, out of confusion about the Vietnam war and the American reaction to it, which he had to deal with in the question periods following his lectures on various campuses, Brakhage began to meditate on the nature of war. He amassed a collection of war documentaries and diligently studied newsreels and political speeches on television to the point of speculating on the significance of recurring clusters and shapes of the dots on the television screen; he read memoirs and battle descriptions, Gibbon's *Decline and Fall of the Roman Empire*, and at breakfast he claimed to read Tacitus instead of the daily newspaper because the intrigues were the same and better written in the first century historian's version. The fruit of his studies and thoughts was the longest and most important of the

Songs. A tour of lectures, in which he tried to express what could not be contained in the film was so confused and self-tortured in style that it approached madness.

If any of the earlier Songs seemed to assert the priority of nature over imagination, that impression has no place in the 23rd *Psalm Branch*; it is an apocalypse of the imagination. The consciousness of the film-maker moves between his idea of home and the self and his vision of war. A very fast pan of a passing landscape, as if shot from a car on a highway, stops short continually with the flashing interjection of dead bodies from stock black-and-white footage and of flickerings of solid colors. In the prolongation of this effect the short images of death are sometimes painted over.

The first release from this insistent prologue comes as the words "Take back Beethoven's 5th, then, he said" are scratched in black leader. They are the first of several quotations in the film. Another continuous pan follows, shot like the first but showing a deep passing land- and townscape rather than a moving flat blur. Into this lateral movement he first cuts a series of explosions, then explosions mixed with guns firing, the atomic bomb, a flood, cannon exploding, water leaping over a dam, tactical bombs, and burning buildings. At times the montage of horrors pursues its own split-second dynamic as if forgetting to relocate itself in the passing American landscape.

In his lectures at the time, Brakhage maintained a desperate fatalism. He spoke of war as a "natural disaster," assigning it an inevitable role like that of tornadoes or earthquakes. At times his audiences, and perhaps he himself, took this postulate to be a reconciliation with the fact of war, when within the film it was another, more vehement attack on nature.

A color flicker transfers us to a second text, a letter being written by the film-maker as he sits bare-chested in the sun. The speed of the panning makes it difficult to read. "Dear Jane," it begins, "The checker boards and zig-zags of man." On the next line we can only catch the crucial word "Nature." Turning from the letter, the camera shows us stones, fast movements over the ground, and flashes of a blue-tinted sun until a multicolored, hand-painted passage intrudes. It precedes a fast montage of images of the home, including visual quotations of the nude children from the "Neowyn" portrait and sledge riding from "Myrrena and Neowyn." The pace of the editing relaxes with shots of laundry on a wash line, a donkey, the sky. Airplane wings introduce a return to the letter, and the subsequent quick cutting of wings, clouds, and aerial views of the ground illustrate the expressions "zig-zags" and "checker boards."

After another color flicker and a passage of hand-painting, a third quotation, in the form of an open book of poetry, emerges. It is the beginning of the eleventh section of Louis Zukofsky's A:

> River, that must turn full after I stop dying
> Song, my song, raise grief to music
> Light as my loves' thought, the few sick
> So sick of wrangling: thus weeping
> Sounds of light, stay in her keeping
> And my son's face—this much for honor.

The second line is most readable in the camera's panning. "Song, my song, raise grief to music" defines the aspiration of the film and the cry of the film-maker. Another burst of explosions and bombs brackets a visual repetition of the poem.

Fast animation of children's drawings, also warlike, introduces a flickering alternation between them and the film-maker's face; and then the face alone flickers amid bits of blackness. The same fragmenting rhythm presents two warriors fighting in a print of a Hellenic vase, which disappears in red flares. Then, after a pause of blackness, the camera draws back from the face of the poet Zukofsky. His name on his book identifies him for those who do not recognize his rarely photographed face. Another zoom shows, dimly, his wife Celia. We see the poet only once more; that is after an exposition of colored frames mixed with the wrecks of buildings. But this time the movement away from his face leads to a series of Jews in concentration camps, as the film-maker considers what would have been the poet's fate had he lived in Europe thirty years before.

One of the conclusions which Brakhage reached in his study of newsreels, propounded in his lectures, was that crowds take a distinctive shape under the spirit of war. That shape, he held, defies the limitations of police restraint or topological constriction. Furthermore, the size of the crowd does not change the shape. Illustrating not this mysterious shape, but the identity of crowds, Brakhage cut another montage of equivalences out of his documentaries and placed it after the Zukofsky portrait. Here the lines of a parade and those of a procession within a cathedral do take the same linear shape, but then quick cuts of Hitler marching, numerous parades, religious processions, funerals, crowds cheering, tickertape celebrations, and crowds fighting police all flow together in a sustained explosion of mass frenzy.

From then until the scratched declaration several minutes later, "I can't go on," the pace of the montage generally maintains this intensity as the images shift slightly from crowds to a meeting of generals or the signing of a treaty, obscured by tiny ink dots which change their size and the direction of their drift across the screen continually. Color flickers and another comparison of crowds disappear as Churchill, Hitler, Mussolini, and Roosevelt are equated to each other and then blended into a climactic rush of chiefs of state, crowds, parades, official trains, tanks, airplanes, ships, disasters, and bombs.

But after the declaration Brakhage *does* go on, continuing for a short time the comparison of weaponry and moving the sequence toward the end with the slow fall into the sea of a single burning airplane, an action extended by progressively longer interruptions of black leader. From a last burst of explosions he returns to the letter by way of a split-screen effect I shall describe below. The speed of the cutting makes it difficult to be sure of the text. He writes, "I must stop. The war *is* as thoughts/ patterns are—as endless as . . . precise as eye's hell *is!*"

When 8mm films are prepared for multiple printing, a master is made on 16mm with two bands: on the right, half the film is printed from top to bottom; on the left, the other half is printed in the opposite direction. After the master is printed, a machine splits the double strip down the middle. Brakhage had an 8mm reduction made of the 16mm master. He thus had a copy of the film with four frames on the screen; a sequence of two on the left and two, upside-down, on the right. Before the last shots of the letter the film-maker provides us with a taste of his later recapitulation by introducing a piece from the middle of the master, but after we read Brakhage's handwriting, he starts from the beginning, including the titles with the fragmented and accelerated (since four frames pass at the rate of one) repetition. This tactic provides an alternative to the conclusion of *Dog Star Man/The Art of Vision*; it dissolves the tension of the film by suggesting that the events depicted are cyclic while it reduces the illusion to cinematic physicality.

Brakhage must have felt the cyclical and tautological conclusion insufficient for this film, since he followed it with a second part. There he reconsidered the idea of war in terms of what he saw in front of him as he traveled in eastern Europe. The whole reformulation is called "To Source" and opens with a short prologue of a lamp superimposed over a landscape and night lights. The first two subsections are obviously antithetical: "Of Peter Kubelka's Vienna" and "My Vienna." The former is a parallel montage of six elements: Kubelka playing his recorder, a view

of a building shot from below, "Stop" and "Go" traffic lights in alternation, Kubelka walking on the streets of Vienna with a young child, and a
statue in a public square.

"My Vienna" begins with Brakhage's vision of himself in a foreign city
and then moves from his thoughts of home to his imagination of war-time
Vienna, and ends with an ambiguous comparison of art to death.

The synecdochic opening shows a cigar in the film-maker's hand. Then
he rests his head upon the table and takes flickering shots of himself, apparently drunk. The camera explores the table and its dishes and shows a
horse in the snow before returning to the film-maker's self-portrait.

As he films images of falling snow from a Viennese window the scene
shifts to his home in Colorado; first to the window from Crystal's portrait, then to the sledges of "Myrrena and Neowyn" and the nude children of "Neowyn," all quoted from XV Song Traits. Still in Colorado, but
with unfamiliar shots, the door of his house opens, the fire burns in the
hearth, and Jane appears. This sequence has a red tone which elides with
the switch back to Vienna, where Brakhage, Kubelka, and a woman, all
toned red, are still at the table. Regular alternations move between
Vienna and Colorado until the film-maker's imagination of the past calls
up the image of Hitler from an old documentary. His marching is intercut
with the statue on the square from "Of Peter Kubelka's Vienna" and
with the Brakhage children returning home from school. From this point
until near the end there is no fixed locale into which the montage cuts or
from which it shifts, no distinction of tenor and vehicle. Each second
brings us to a different place and time. A fast movement through the
modern streets of Vienna, a white landscape through a Colorado window,
the rear-view mirror of a car, paintings in Vienna museums, children's
drawings from home, and bombs and fires destroying the streets of a city,
presumably Vienna during the war, are the elements of this confluence.
It resolves, and the film ends with the mixture of several artistic representations of Christ and documentary footage of dead bodies.

"My Vienna" restates the more complex dialectic of the whole of Part
One of this film. The transformation of apprehension into dreadful imag-
inings is clearly illustrated by the positing of the middle terms of association: Kubelka's family reminds Brakhage of his own; the streets of
Vienna bring to mind the damage to them during the war; the Christian
idealization of the suffering of Jesus makes him consider the inglorious
destruction of men by war.

The next three sections, "A Tribute to Freud," "Nietzsche's Lamb," and "East Berlin," gradually apply a brake to the dynamics of everything that preceded them. They are intellectually and formally the simplest of the subsections, although "Nietzsche's Lamb" must be characterized as the most complex of the three.

"A Tribute to Freud" not only pays homage to the father of psycho-analysis by recording a pilgrimage through Vienna to the house where he lived; it indirectly salutes the poet H. D. by borrowing the title of her memoir of Freud. The most striking image of this section occurs at the very end. It is a transparent group of female figures, like the Muses, on the glass of the door Freud must have moved through daily.

"Nietzsche's Lamb" combines images of an airplane flight (presumably the film-maker's return from Europe) with shots of a skinned lamb in a theatrical event by Hermann Nitsch. Montage at the beginning smoothed over and periodically almost obliterated by paint and dots becomes super-imposition in the second half of the film. The title puns on the happening-maker's name and that of the nineteenth-century philosopher, although it has been said that until after the film was released Brakhage was under the impression that Nitsch's name was actually Nietzsche.

Once before in the *Songs* Brakhage ended a film with the take-off of an airplane. *Song XIII*, describing the experience of travel, begins with trains, continues with automobiles, and ends in flight. In fact, the ultimate film of the series, *American Thirties Song*, extends the image of flight over most of its thirty minutes and thus concludes the *Songs*, except for a short dedicatory "Postlude."

There is an ambivalence in Brakhage's attitude toward Nitsch's Diony-siac art. He cannot disassociate it from the contexts of war and his im-pressions of Eastern Europe. Associated with the image of flight but ob-scured by the paint, we see documentary footage of boats which seem to be unloading refugees. At one point in the return, as the stewardess ap-pears in the aisle of the airplane, the film-maker very quickly imagines a bomb dropping from a cockpit. As he films the ground from above, zoom-ing down and back, he associates that vision with aerial maps of cities and a relief globe of the world. More enigmatic are two quotations from *Song XIX* of the dancing girl cut into "Nietzsche's Lamb," until we recall the ritual element in Brakhage's description of that film: the quotation is another pun, "a dancing song of women's rites." The theatrical ritual of the *Manifest Der Lamm* finds its counterpart in the spontaneous rite of *Song XIX*.

The last and most mysterious section of the film brings us back to Europe and "East Berlin." Both "Nietzsche's Lamb" and "East Berlin" seek to ground Brakhage's experience of Europe in "closed-eye vision." In the former he achieved this through painting over so that the maps, aerial views, boats, dances, etc., seemed to become concrete out of the cracks and colors of the paint, which at times completely obfuscated the image underneath. In "East Berlin" he transferred strategies from painting to combining flares, images only of lights against a black sky, and finally moving dots.

In making the 23rd Psalm Branch Brakhage was responding to the anxiety around him about the Vietnam war. In the terms which I have been using to discuss his vision, the force with which that war entered his thoughts challenged the metaphysical priority of the inner man. The finished film confirms the autonomy of the imagination and incorporates war through strategies of generalization, the dialectic of ideas and sights, contrasting subjective experiences of a single place, the oblique reference to the author of Civilization and Its Discontents, and finally closed-eye vision.

The "Coda" begins with a complete rupture from the images and techniques of the rest of the film and ends with a disquieting metaphor for the undefeatable impulse to war within the human spirit. This final image is all the more disturbing because it occurs in a joyous mood at the end of a brief pastorale. The "Coda" begins in the portrait style; first in a series of extreme synecdoches we see part of a man's face, his hands, a piece of amplifying equipment he holds (or the interior of a radio). From the glimpse of a keyboard and the rhythmical bobbing of his head, we deduce he is playing music. All this is in a blue tint; then a sudden switch to color, and soon after superimposition, shows first the tapping of a woman's bare foot, then her whole figure as she plucks a stringed instrument with a feather in the woods; over the image, hands strum a harp. These twin portraits of unidentified people lead without rupture to the final superimposition. A group of children play and dance in the woods at night waving burning sparklers while the image of a donkey fades in and out several times in superimposition. The terrible association of the sparkler dance with the Nazi Walpurgisnacht arise, perhaps the more dreadfully because Brakhage does not emphasize them with a montage of analogies. Thus this film, which had made an equation among parades, victory celebrations, street fights, and rallies, culminates in a cyclic vision and a discovery of the seeds of war in the pastoral vision.[24]

Song XXVII: My Mountain follows the structure of the *23rd Psalm Branch*: a long abstract presentation in the first part, then a second part of eight "Rivers" qualifying the first part in terms of the self. For approximately the first twenty minutes of the 26 minute-long first part, Brakhage presents shot after shot of a mountain peak, snow-covered throughout the change of seasons. Clouds and mists have a prominent role in this film; they can completely obscure the peak, sweep over it in fast motion, or begin a shot by blocking it, only to clear away, or the reverse; sometimes the film-maker even veers from the mountain to show cloud formations.

According to his statements, Brakhage was studying Dutch and Flemish painting while working on this film. He singled out Van Eyck for his attention to figures at the very edge of the composition. Brakhage did not use a tripod to film any of the images in *Song XXVII*, he claims. The laborious work of taking single frames of cloud movements must have been done while he was steadying the camera in his hands. This method causes slight movements on the edge of the frame which are almost unnoticeable when the eye fixes itself on the centered mountain peak. The illusion of fixity in the center and shimmering at the edges of the screen creates a visual tension which the film-maker felt would be lost if the viewer sensed the solidity of a tripod and the impossibility of variation.

The presence of the mountain in the far distance, emphasized by the occasional zooms and the sweeping of clouds forward over the space between the mountain and the camera, makes this the first of all Brakhage's films thoroughly to exploit the potential innate in cinema for the presentation of space in depth. The slow pace of the editing reinforces this. One of Brakhage's chief tactics for flattening space in his earlier films had been split-second montage.

If we recall that the lucid, even triumphal inwardness of the *23rd Psalm Branch* was exceptional within the *Songs*, we can see how the uneasy relation with the natural world, more characteristic of the series as a whole, reasserts itself in the first part of *Song XXVII: My Mountain*. With the change of techniques and the shift of the center of attention at the end of the film, Brakhage begins the undermining or subjectification of what had been the most self-enduring natural image in the whole of *Songs*.

In Romantic poetry the image of the mountain has repeatedly initiated a reaffirmation of the self and the imagination. In his study of landscape in Romanticism, Paul de Man quotes passages from Rousseau, Words-

worth, and Hölderlin on Alpine landscapes. "Each of these texts describes
the passage from a certain type of nature, earthly and material, to another
nature which could be called mental and celestial."[25]

The primary reflex of each of the "Rivers" is to move from an opening
shot of the mountain, or its clouds, to a more interiorized image. The eight
sections range between the explicit and the hermetic. In the first of them,
after a quick intercutting of the mountain and flames, Brakhage calls attention to the mechanism of the camera through a variation on the jumping image at the end of the first part. Here the distortion of the picture is
not complete; the loss of a loop in the camera resulted in a small fluttering, a ghost-like flickering above a more solid form. With this technique
he shows us parts of a small town: traffic lights changing color, a church
steeple. The section ends, without fluttering, in fast pans back and forth
over the mountain, undermining its presence and asserting that of the
film-maker.

In discussing the portrait "Crystal," the point was made that Brakhage
uses the mediation of a smeared, streaked, or dimly-reflecting window
while recording an outside view, as a metaphor for the circumference of
the self. In "Rivers" he makes extensive use of this trope. The sixth section, which like the first begins with an intercutting of mountain and fire,
quickly settles upon a long series of images of two horses in the snow.
They are seen through a window in which are reflected flames and sometimes shimmering patterns of light. The whole image is tinted yellow. In
this particular case, it is difficult to distinguish reflections on the window
from superimpositions, which may play a minor role here. The next part,
another portrait of Jane Brakhage, begins with her looking out of a window. The film-maker is outside filming in. From this image we can trace
the window trope back to Maya Deren and *Meshes of the Afternoon*. Like
the heroine of that film, Jane Brakhage mediates a subjective reflection;
with one splice we see her younger, with much longer hair, sitting outside
with her three daughters. They are dressed as they were in *Song IV* when
they played with a red ball. Although there is no direct quotation from
that Song, the material we see now looks so similar, with the same slightly
slowed motion, that it seems to have been made the same day. This is just
the beginning of the longest and most elaborate of the sections. In it we
see Jane playing the recorder and petting a goat, and the children playing
with a dog, then sleeping. In the middle of the film a composite use of the
window mediation appears when Brakhage films his daughters, now older
than when we first saw them, looking out of the window; he is shooting

from inside his car, whose windshield wipers cross the image.

The most explicit of the sections, "River 4," makes the fullest use of the window. Shot from one of the upper stories of Denver's largest hotel, it shows the neon and white lights of the city at night while in the foreground the standing nude body of the film-maker can be seen in the window's reflection. He concentrates on the reflection of his palm which leads immediately to shots of a frosted window intercut for several minutes with aerial views of mountain ranges, as if arising in the metaphoric imagination as he contemplates the lines of his hand.

Somewhat less emphatic is the conclusion of the second "River," which calls to mind closed-eye vision in the play, first of three white lights in the darkness, then of an illuminated bridge with flares. It concludes by integrating an image of the moon with the daytime sky, suggesting that the very heavens may be created by internal vision on the screen of the closed lid.

The fifth "River" is the most enigmatic. After the requisite opening shot of the mountain, it presents in superimposition a crane operating over pans of the mountain. A series of close-up, and often indistinguishable surfaces of flesh, oranges wrapped in cellophane, flowers, metalwork, a parking meter, and quick views of rapids ends, with an image of a rain-streaked window.

Brakhage subscribes to the belief, most forcefully put forward among his contemporaries by Charles Olson, that the artistic sensibility has privileged access to a holistic vision. In the *American Thirties Song* he explores the aerial view as a tool for discovering patterns not immediately visible to the grounded observer. From the aerial perspective he records the shape of farm lands and cities and the organization of residential blocks. From the title and from his notes we learn that he associates these patterns with American life in the 1930s, when he was born.

Before the titles, very fast blurred panning movements recall the opening of the *23rd Psalm Branch*. Out of these movements come quick, jittery glimpses of the face of Brakhage's father. The speed decelerates. An old woman is hanging out her wash. We see the old hands of Brakhage's father inside an automobile. After the title the portrait shifts to the more familiar, synecdochic style. In dim red outline we see the shape of the man's bald head, his shoes, his hands calling to mind the more sinister *Song XXIX*, and another dim red portrait of the film-maker's mother, who appears almost androgynous in her old age.

From the obscurity of the portrait the film moves to a short, bright movement of kitsch—flamingo designs in a bathroom, a few Roman Catholic household images, a picture of Jesus as a shepherd, an angel doll. As the *Songs* touch upon social behavior, Brakhage is careful not to use images in a strictly ironic manner; the visual studies of middle-class neighborhoods and decorating styles are presented in this film as fact, without condemnation by the film-maker. While he was making the *American Thirties Song*, Brakhage developed a passionate interest in American genre painting, which informs many aspects of this film.

Early in the film a car ride through a residential neighborhood with the camera jerkily recording passing trees and barely distinguishing the houses beyond them turns into an abstract metaphor: bluish trees become lines of water and a whirl of yellow lights.

The most striking of the interludes returns to the structures of *Song XIII*, the travel song, in the middle of the film which is itself largely an extension of that earlier Song. In a slightly elliptical sequence of shots a ferry or tourist boat docks at a pier in New York's Hudson River. Each shot in the sequence begins in an impressionistic blur as a mist quickly evaporates on the lens.[26] Then in superimposition he combines passing trains, or at times views from a moving train, with other harbor scenes in a smooth texture of elision. Ocean liners move on the river; isolated smokestacks gush up steam and smoke and cross the bottom of the frame. When the river scenes end temporarily, the train superimposition continues over a view from above of a city hotdog cart and its owner.

The last third of the film exclusively employs aerial imagery. From this there is a smooth transition to the dedicatory "Postlude." In synecdochic compositions and with short elliptical jumps, the film-maker shows an airport, the landing of a jet, the movement of a baggage wagon, the taxiing of the airplane, the fitting of the deboarding tube, and finally the emergence of the film-maker Jerome Hill among the passengers. A sweep of sprocket holes, a final reminder of the artifice of film, precedes the concluding signature.

Although there is a complete absence of mythological reference in the *Songs*, the series as a whole participates in the myth of the absolute film. One of the central aspirations of the avant-garde film has been the creation of an ultimate work: this aspiration has moved in two directions—toward purification, a reduction to the essence of cinema, and toward giant, all-inclusive forms. Both forms of absolutism can be traced through Brakhage's statements on his work. He has never addressed himself to a definition of the essence of his medium—although tautological references to the materials occur in most of his mature work—but he has referred to several of his shorter films at the time of release as "the most perfect" he has ever made.

In the expansive direction, *The Art of Vision* has been Brakhage's most ambitious attempt at an absolute structure. Yet he has predicted that *The Book of the Film*, his autobiography-in-progress of which at least the first part, *Scenes from Under Childhood* (1968-70), has been completed, will be more than twenty hours long. Extremes of duration are definitely a factor in the quest for the inclusive absolute film.

Songs began with the film-maker's attempt to move away from monumental forms and from the commitment to a single work over a number of years. It grew into a work longer than *The Art of Vision* and much more diverse in its materials. *Songs* presents an alternative to *The Art of Vision;* both have their origin in a concept of "dailiness" which Brakhage derived from his reading of Gertrude Stein; one approaches an epic of dailiness through organized mythopoeia, the other through a series of interrelated forms (fragments, essays, portraits, odes). In 1960 Brakhage presented a foundation with a project for "the dailiness film." The grant was rejected. In the synopsis printed in the chapter "State Meant" of *Metaphors on Vision* both long films have their roots. It begins:

> I am planning a feature-length film in which those commonplace daily activities which my wife and child and I share in some form or other with almost every family on earth are visually explored to the fullest extent of their universal meaning.
>
> . . .
>
> Having launched the ship of "the dailiness film," the title which I refer to the inspiration for this project, I can only exemplify certain possible developments for such a beginning [referring to possible images he had described], as it is essential to the integrity of such a project that its individual scenes arise out of the daily activities of our living and that these developing fragments inspired in the immediacy of life direct the form of the entire work. In the Mallarméan sense, the shadow between the white waves of these stapled pages is a better "hull" for the ship of the "dailiness film" than any number of words here written, for each state of this film must be realized in the drama of our living and visualized in the creative act, not predetermined by the literary form of this appeal.[27]

The years spanned by the making of *Songs* saw a number of collective morphological developments in the American avant-garde cinema that are reflected within the encyclopedic form of that work. In the first place, the

film diary began to emerge as a significant form during this period, and
will be more fully discussed in Chapter 11. Its origins can be traced back
to Marie Menken's *Notebook* and several films of Cornell (and indeed to
Cornell's attitude toward film-making as an extremely personal experience), with which both Brakhage and Jonas Mekas, the American avant-
garde cinema's major diarist, were very familiar.

The first series of film portraits was made by Andy Warhol in 1964
and 1965 (*Henry Geldzahler, 13 Most Beautiful Women, 13 Most Beautiful Boys*). Between 1964 and 1966 he made two long series of four-minute
portraits united by the title *50 Fantastics and 50 Personalities*. Independent of Warhol (although sometimes aggressively antagonistic toward his
work), Brakhage began the *XV Song Traits* in 1965. The next year Gregory
Markopoulos presented his first portrait collection, *Galaxie*. Subsequently
he has made *Political Portraits* (1969) and several uncollected portraits.

It is particularly surprising to find a version of the structural film (see
Chapter 12) within the *Songs*. The first part of *Song XXVII: My Mountain* suspends the film-maker's usual reliance on montage, metaphor, and
dynamic rhythm to concentrate on a single view. This happened at the
same time as George Landow, Michael Snow, and several others were employing similar strategies, but out of very different aesthetic promptings.
And there were similar preoccupations in the work of Gregory Markopoulos (*Gammelion*, 1968) and Bruce Baillie at this time.

In *Quixote* Baillie had brought his lyrical cinema to the threshold of
epic and mythopoeia. Although it seemed at that time that, like most of
the major avant-gardists, he would plunge into an extended mythopoeic
work, he resisted that drive, making instead his late lyrical and structural
films, *Tung, Castro Street, All My Life, Still Life*, and *Valentin de las
Sierras*. In 1967 he began an almost fatal bout with hepatitis which he recorded in his most ambitious film, *Quick Billy* (1971), a four-part, hour-
long essay in mythopoeia and autobiography. He presented the following
note with the film at its New York premiere at the Whitney Museum of
American Art:

> The essential experience of transformation, between Life and Death,
> death and birth, or rebirth. In four reels, the first three adapted from the
> *Bardo Thodol, The Tibetan Book of the Dead*. The fourth reel is the
> form of a black and white one-reeler Western, summarizing the material
> of the first three reels, which are color and abstract.
>   The work incorporates a large body of material dreams, the daily re-
> cording roll by roll of that extraordinary period of the filmmakers' life,

"the moment by moment confrontation with Reality," (Carl Jung, *The Tibetan Book of the Dead*). Each phase of the work was given its own time to develop, stretching over a period of 3½ years.

"The rolls," silent 3 minute rolls of films that came after the film itself, like artifacts from the descending layers of an archeological dig . . . numbered 41, 43, 46, and 47. Aesthetically complete, thus included (rent free option) as part of the total work. Reel 4 conceived by Paul Tulley, Charlotte Todd, and myself, with Debby Porter, Bob Treadwell and Kiro Tulley. Music by John Adams, titles by Bob Ross.

The "rolls" took the form of a correspondence, or theatre, between their author and Stan Brakhage, in the winter of 1968-69.[28]

Baillie's deepest debt to Brakhage, however, is not the encouraging letters he wrote in response to the four epilogue reels, which he saw out of context; it is rather to the opening of *Prelude: Dog Star Man* and to the whole of *Part Three* of that film.[29] The whole first three reels of *Quick Billy* hover on the edge of consciousness, mixing, blurring, and masking images so that they are rarely definable, even though within its own range of textures the film proceeds from the abstract to the relatively concrete and specific before leaping into the ironic narrative of the fourth reel. *Dog Star Man* had elaborated the possibilities of different densities of superimposition. Baillie's contribution to this rhetoric, which is particularly effective in the three areas of his concentration, the evocation of natal, thanatotic, and erotic consciousness, comes from his application of the processes of *Castro Street* to the materials of *Quick Billy*. He mixes his own superimpositions with complex masking, while Brakhage had worked in simple additive units (two to four layers). Furthermore, Baillie reinforces his visual mesh with an equally subtle fusion of natural noises, voice, and artificially altered sounds on the soundtrack.

Baillie has written, "All of the film was recorded next to the Pacific Ocean in Fort Bragg, California, from dreams and daily life there; all of it given its own good *time* to evolve and become clear to me. The Sea is the main force through the film. 'Prentice to the Sea!' was something I wrote to myself in those days."

For Baillie the complex texture of the first three parts of the film, which took their "own good *time* to evolve," incorporates a vestige of that temporality, just as the Église de St. Hilaire in Proust's Combray was a frozen monument to temporality in its succession of stylistic layers. That explains his use of the image of "an archeological dig" to describe the four "rolls" of unedited film which conclude *Quick Billy*. Like the different kinds of cinematic objects within Brakhage's *Songs*, the successive styles of Baillie's epic, represented by the first three reels, the fourth reel, and the "rolls" separately, define boundaries of visual experience—the oneiric and intellectual, the narrative and parodic, the immediate and retinal—but in their quest for origins, which Baillie associates, in his thirty volumes of notes and diaries relating to the film (in the Anthology Film Archives), with the "loss of innocence," he attempted to incorporate within the film the temporality of its creation, which Brakhage, in the simple chronology of his pieces, avoided. Later, making *Scenes from Under Childhood*, he began to take it into consideration. In his letter to Baillie about the last two "rolls" (46, 47), he describes the process in its full complexity, although he did not know at the time that the whole of Baillie's film would not be as immediate and unedited as the "rolls." (The italicizing of *as-photographed* and *imagines* are from Brakhage's text, in which the spelling, typographical errors and triple periods are preserved; the other italics are Baillie's.)

> Anyway, [*Scenes from Under Childhood*] is close to you work (& now, & from now on, as "in touch" as I am): and one of the most exciting approximations is this involvement with the-sceen-*as-photographed*, relatively free of Edit's Intellect and/or the SUPERimposition of the process of memory upon each instant of living: you, as I, seem to be taking strong advatage of *film's most unique possibility—preservation of the track of light* in the field of vision (thus the each move of the visionary) at the/each instant of photographing: I now find myself solidly See-er of my photography, rather than Editor thereOF it: but this inspiration—in the work process—exists in the incredible tension of my feeling an equal need to let Memory COLOR each unedited light track . . . via "B" and "C" rolls generally . . . and SHAPE both objects and spaces . . . by way of compounding pics./spaces, rather than superimposing upon them—again BC stuffing mostly: sometimes I even compress, by additives; and I do, then, tremble on the edge of superimposition: and, let's face it, sometimes I still just-plain-superimpose, as always, also: but the general DRIVE is one in honor of *the moment of photography*, so that there's very little shifting of the orders of shots within a sequence, and very little cutting of lengths of shot either. Actually, I've worked (more sub-consciously) in this area of direction many times before ("Desist-film"—THAT far back—"Daybreak & Whiteye," "Films by S. B.," the "T.V. Concretes," many "Songs" and many sequences of "Scenes From Under Childhood," Sec. #1): and it's coming to seem to me that "Scenes From Under Childhood" on its primary visual level IS a track of the evolution of SIGHT: thus its images flash out of blanks of color, thru fantastic distorts/twists of forms and orders (those fantasies wherein one *imagines* oneself: even suggesting those "pre-natal fantasies" wherein Freud, to his despair, finally found that unanalysable nest hatching all basic neuroses), space/shape absolutely *dominated by the rhythms of*

inner physiology, then shaking like jellied masses at first encounters with
outers, the beginning of The Dance, shattering OUT of even memory's
grip thru TO some exactitude of sight/light.[30]

His annotations on the entire correspondence relate Brakhage's expressions to his own readings in the *Tibetan Book of the Dead*. The words
"preservation" and "inner physiology" touch upon the central themes of
Quick Billy, although Brakhage could not have known it from the fragments he saw.

In the notebooks, Baillie once summarized the first three reels in eleven
sections:

I. Loss. II. The Beast III. Protection IV. cont. passage V. schism VI. White
Goddess VII. Male-Female Embrace VIII. High School Heroes IX. Wrath-
ful Deity/ Judgment X. Protecting Environment (birth?) XI. Sea/The
Father (Intelligence).

Yet even with the aid of this synopsis, and more detailed sub-headings, I
cannot isolate all the parts of the film. The imagery is often so abstracted,
and the elision of sections so smooth, that the whole film seems like a pulsating matrix, at first alternating between a consciousness of birth and one
of death, and later letting emerge, sometimes very briefly, the dream-like,
anamorphic image of a beckoning female (perhaps the White Goddess),
or evoking in sound and pictures physical lovemaking; and then pausing
meditatively over pictures from an album in which photographs of a high
school basketball team predominate.

All through the film are woven images of the sea, trees, animals—including the fearful symmetry of a dream-like tiger—fire, the sun, and the
moon. The superimposition with the textural masking blends these images
together and often keeps them at the threshold of recognition, as I have
said; it also creates mutations of form and color which give an aspect of
the monstrous to the imagery. Baillie originally planned to call the film
Feetfear. He told Richard Whitehall:

It's a name came to me in a series of dreams, and the film will try to film
those dreams I've had. There's a whole mythology of my own grown out
of there, and this is probably due to the craziness from hepatitis. This
chemical change in the brain operation. It's a little like being high on a
small amount of LSD. And I went up into the woods of Oregon and I
was terrified. The blackness. And I've had terrifying bestial dreams. They
work their way out into a lovelier meeting with Diana, the protectress of
men in the woods. I wrote them all down in detail, and I don't know

exactly what I'm going to work with, what I'm going to photograph.
Using Kodachrome because it's easy to keep it dark and non-grainy
around the edges when you're working in a low-level light. It would almost be more effective in animation. It's really the edges of shadows and
colors and working in a totally abstract way, and somehow realizing animal shapes out of it—almost the way one would impose an animated
figure into a photographed frame. The way Alexieff does it in *Night on
Bare Mountain*. In a way it grows out of the things that have been very
close to me over the past few months, a form of death. Using the real
animals as well as their shapes. Symbols. The word "symbol" is kind of
hard to use. But it really is symbols.[31]

In the same synopsis that I quoted, he tries to define the title *Feetfear* by
placing next to it the expressions, "Fear of leaving the beast/loss of innocence—'confronted by Reality.'" At that time he reserved the title *Quick
Billy* for the ironic fourth reel.

That parody, "set in Kansas in 1863," describes in ribald gags the arrival of an uncouth cowboy, played by the film-maker, who takes over a
Kansas farmhouse. His drunkenness and his rape of the farm girl parody
the states of marginal consciousness and the powerful erotic episode in the
earlier part, where Baillie, working with close and colored images of the
male and female body in a direct descent from *Part Three: Dog Star Man*,
succeeded in evoking the erotic experience as Brakhage never quite did,
either in *Dog Star Man*, the lyrical films, or in his two explicitly erotic series, *Lovemaking* and *Sexual Meditations*.

Baillie offers a cinematic and a literary analogy to the "rolls" in the
notebooks; they are "like chambers (episodes: e.g., Cocteau's hotel, or
Steppenwolf's magic theater)." They not only represent an early temporal
stratum in the composition of the film, they also locate in magical visions,
according to the analogies, the origins of the film, fix the place where it
was shot, show a prop for the fourth reel in its presence outside of the narrative, define the space of a breakfast scene that the film-maker had earlier described on the soundtrack. Thus, in one of the rolls the startling
face of the dying film-maker, which Brakhage accurately described to him
as staring into the camera as if into a mirror, identifies the maker, whom
we see otherwise in extreme body close-ups or in the cowboy *persona*. In
another, a giant Uncle Sam prop which had been used in the black-and-
white fourth reel moves along the seascape, which appears for the first
time without distortion, uniting the two earlier sections of the film. Finally, the slow pan around the kitchen shows the cabin where most of the
film was made and recalls in the silent images of an empty room the break-

fast, described in the longest passage of talk in the first three reels, of "hot pancakes and eggs and fresh bread and tea and honey" as they "sat in front of the window and watched the sea, where I shot all the film."

Baillie insists that *Quick Billy* be shown on a single projector, so that a pause would ensue between each of the reel changes. With the addition of the four "rolls," he then simultaneously returns his film from its temporal cross-references to its origins in an affirmation of "the moment of photography," and he reminds his audience that they are in front of a film, awaiting the change of reels. The first three reels had moved at once forward toward death and backward to adolescence and birth. In the fourth reel an arbitrary date in the past, 1863, began the film, and a projection into the future, the title "Ever Westward Eternal Rider!" ended it. After those allusions to temporal cycles, he rests on "film's most unique possibility—preservation of the track of light in the field of vision."

8

ABSOLUTE ANIMATION

Not all avant-garde film-making of the late 1950s utilized the trance form and psycho-drama. The graphic cinema offered a vital alternative to the subjective. This polarity (and the potential for its convergence) extends back to the origins of the avant-garde film in Europe in the 1920s. Through the examples of *Un Chien Andalou, Le Sang d'un Poète,* and *Entr'Acte,* a continuity has been suggested between the Surrealist and Dada cinema and the works of Maya Deren and Sidney Peterson. Another wing of the Dadaist cinema fused with filmic Cubism and Neoplasticism to produce films of equally major significance. In the 1920s the spectrum extending from Surrealism to Cubism in the cinema was continuous. But with the renaissance of independent film-making in America during and just after the Second World War, graphic and subjective film-making ideologically diverged and remained apart until their slow reconciliation in the early 1960s.

Hans Richter's *Rhythmus 21* (1921), Viking Eggeling's *Symphonie Diagonale* (1921), Marcel Duchamp's *Anemic Cinema* (1927), and Fernand Léger's *Ballet Mécanique* (1924) constitute the central works of the initial graphic cinema, and they span the scope of its variations.

Richter, who had been a painter and scroll-maker, took the primal conditions of black and white and the rectangular shape of the screen as the essential elements of his film. In sweeping movements which begin in the center of the screen and move out horizontally or vertically, the flat black space becomes white or vice versa. Within this matrix of fluctuating negative and positive space, white, gray, and black squares emerge from and recede into an illusory depth of the screen in a rhythmic pattern that grows increasingly more intricate until its sudden and short reversal to the elements of the black-and-white screen at the very end of the film.

Eggeling worked with Richter, and like him the urge to make films came from a desire to extend his work on scrolls into actual time. In his film *Symphonie Diagonale*, figures move along alternative diagonal lines crossing the screen from upper left to lower right and from upper right to lower left. At the same time they seem to move in depth from the surface of the screen to an imaginary receding point at its center, as Richter's squares had, and back again. Finally, Eggeling's shapes evolve in straight and elaborately curved lines while they pursue their diagonal and emerging-receding movements. The musicality of *Symphonie Diagonale* comes from its exhaustive use of reciprocal movements. An elaboration along one diagonal axis is mirrored immediately along the other; the growth at one end of a figure is matched by its disunion at another end; a movement into the screen precedes one out of it.

In *Anemic Cinema*, Duchamp alternates head-on views of his illusion-producing roto-reliefs with similarly turned discs of words, elaborate French puns printed spirally, creating a fluctuation of illusory depth within a very narrow spectrum (from the slightly convex or slightly concave illusions) to the flat readings. In this, his only film, Duchamp typically crystallized the significance of the graphic film. By virtue of its inheritance from still photography, the representation of space in depth comes naturally to the cinema, and the first films exploited it gloriously. The graphic film-maker deliberately rejected the illusion of depth built into the camera's lenses. He set out to re-establish virtual depth by manipulating the scale of flat plastic shapes (Richter and Eggeling), through the presenting and un-masking of simple optical illusions (Duchamp), and lastly with the obliteration of accustomed depth while retaining the traditional photographic images (as we shall see in various strategies of Léger).

The Surrealist cinema suddenly disappeared after Buñuel's *L'Age d'Or* (1930) to re-emerge thirteen years later in America, essentially transformed. The graphic cinema, on the other hand, continued its evolution with diminished force throughout the 1930s and 1940s. The coming of sound to film inspired several attempts to visualize music through cinematic abstractions and to synchronize visual rhythms to music.

The central figure in the transition from the European to the American graphic film was Len Lye. A New Zealander, Lye became intrigued with the kinetic possibilities of art when he was an adolescent, as he elaborates in an interview in *Film Culture 29*:

I had read that Constable had tried to paint clouds in motion and the Dadaists were experimenting with motion painting also. I had a paper route at that time, so I used to get up early and go off for a walk and try to sort out things about art. Then it hit me as I was looking at those darn sunrises, lit up clouds, why try to simulate motion in paintings of clouds or in after-image effects? Why not just do something that literally made movement?

Early in the 1920s he went to Australia to learn cartoon animation, but he did not make his first film until he moved to London in 1928. There he made *Tusalava* (Samoan for "things go full circle"), a black-and-white film combining his fascination with movement with a life-long involvement with the imagery of South Pacific primitive art. Yet cartoon animation has played a very small part in Lye's most important contributions to the graphic cinema. In fact, in the act of rejecting cartoon procedures, with which films such as Richter's and Eggeling's had been made, he became the first film-maker to paint directly on top of film stock, thus shortcutting the photographic process. Although *Colour Box* (1935) was the first result of this direct method, Lye's experiments in hand-painting film go back to Australia and the mid-1920s.

The direct application of paint to the surface of film transformed the dynamics of the graphic film. Color could be rendered more vivid than it could by the photographic process; the different kinds and densities of paint opened a range of texture hitherto ignored; and above all the problems of shape, scale, and the illusions of perspective which the early graphic film-makers inherited from the painterly and photographic traditions could be bracketed by an imagery that remained flat on the plane of the screen and avoided geometrical contour.

In *Colour Box*, a wavy, vertical line multiplies itself and interacts with circles and fields of dots against a background washed with paint. Although Lye avoids all indications of screen depth by having no movement into or out of the vanishing point, the lines and circles seem to move in front of the unshaped background paint, and both seem recessed slightly when stenciled letters, telling us to "Use parcel post," appear near the end and affirm a plane even closer to the literal screen than the painted plane. This use of block lettering recalls the similar employment of stencils in analytical cubism.

Apparently Lye was more interested in expanding a vocabulary of dynamic visual forms than in exploring the implications and possibilities of a cinema without photography; for in his next film, *Kaleidoscope* (1936) hand painting becomes less important than stenciling. Dots, complex patterns, circles, lines, and arabesques crisscross the screen in muted colors. Again the shapes and colors hug the surface of the screen with no indications of depth other than the shallow superimposition of some forms as they pass over one another.

Lye never completely abandoned working with the raw surface of unphotographed film, but his evolution as a film-maker did not occur along the lines initiated by this startling invention. In *Rainbow Dance* and *Trade Tattoo* (both 1936), he combined some of his surface techniques with photographed images of actuality. Although his reputation has been sustained by the invention of direct painting on film, Lye deserves equal credit as one of the great masters of montage. His specialty has been the jump-cut, an elliptical condensation of action achieved by elimination of middle shots so that the figure on the screen seems to jump forward along a prescribed course of action.

Along with the combination of elliptically edited scenes of elementary actions and surface lines, dots, and shapes, Lye began to develop techniques of color separation. Through an intricate process of masking and combining negative and positive images in the printing laboratory, Lye could make one figure in a photographed scene assume one pure color and another figure in that same originally black-and-white shot take on a different color. In doing so he achieved a strength of color his first films lacked, but only unhampered paint on film could create the lost textural range of the surface.

In his later works Lye moved away from both color and the synthesis of techniques. *Rhythm* (1953) shows the assembly of a Ford in one minute of hundreds of jump-cuts. The film is black-and-white without any abstract surface texture save white holes punched out of the opening and ending shots of the exterior of the Ford plant. Having created a film purely exploiting the jump-cut, he made another working only with the surface of unphotographed film. This time he scratched ideographic lines on black film stock. *Free Radicals* (1958) reduces and distills the dynamics of the hand-made film to a primitive kinetic dance of white lines and angles. The jaggedness of these meticulously executed scratches is an indexical evocation of the concentrated energy required to etch them onto film. The film-maker has described the quality of the movement as "spastic." Of his working method he has said:

> If I couldn't complete the etched line by forcing the needle to complete
> the design on the film, then the continuity of a dozen or so designs

which preceded it would be lost. So, I wriggled my whole body to get a compressed feeling into my shoulders—trying to get a pent-up feeling of inexorable precision into the fingers of both hands which grasped the needle and, with a sudden jump, pulled the needle through the celluloid and completed my design.[1]

When in the early 1940s Harry Smith made his first hand-painted films, he was unaware that the concept was not original with him; such is his claim, which the author believes. To the historian of cinema it would make little difference if Smith acted by invention or imitation, for his reputation is not bound to any proof of priority. The hand-painted films with which he began his career as a film-maker are the most remarkable ever achieved in that technique; and his subsequent films, both animated and photographed from actuality, sustain his presence as one of the central film-makers of the avant-garde tradition.

With characteristic self-irony and hermetic allusions, he composed the following notes on his work for the catalogue of the Film-Makers Cooperative:

> My cinematic excreta is of four varieties:—batiked abstractions made directly on film between 1939 and 1946; optically printed non-objective studies composed around 1950; semi-realistic animated collages made as part of my alchemical labors of 1957 to 1962; and chronologically superimposed photographs of actualities formed since the latter year. All these works have been organized in specific patterns derived from the interlocking beats of the respiration, the heart and the EEG Alpha component and should be observed together in order, or not at all, for they are valuable works, works that will live forever—they made me gray.
>
> no. 1: Hand-drawn animation of dirty shapes—the history of the geologic period reduced to orgasm length. (Approx. 5 min.)
>
> no. 2: Batiked animation, etc. etc. The action takes place either inside the sun or in Zurich, Switzerland. (Approx. 10 min.)
>
> no. 3: Batiked animation made of dead squares, the most complex hand-drawn film imaginable. (Approx. 10 min.)
>
> no. 4: Black-and-white abstractions of dots and grillworks made in a single night. (Approx. 6 min.)
>
> no. 5: Color abstraction. Homage to Oscar Fischinger—a sequel to No. 4. (Approx. 6 min.)
>
> no. 6: Three-dimensional, optically printed, abstraction using glasses the color of Heaven & Earth. (Approx. 20 min.)
>
> no. 7: Optically printed Pythagoreanism in four movements supported on squares, circles, grillworks and triangles with an interlude concerning an experiment. (Approx. 15 min.)
>
> no. 8: Black-and-white collage made up of clippings from 19th Cen-

tury ladies' wear catalogues and elocution books. The cat, the dog, the statue and the Hygrometer appear here for the first time. (Approx. 5 min.)

no. 9: Color collage of biology books and 19th Century temperance posters. An attempt to reconstruct Capt. Cook's Tapa collection. (Approx. 10 min.)

no. 10: An exposition of Buddhism and the Kaballa in the form of a collage. The final scene shows Aquatic mushrooms (not in No. 11) growing on the moon while the Hero and Heroine row by on a cerebrum. (Approx. 10 min.)

no. 11: A commentary on and exposition of No. 10 synchronized to Monk's "Mysterioso." A famous film—available sooner or later from Cinema 16. (Approx. 4 min.)

no. 12: A much expanded version of No. 8. The first part depicts the heroine's toothache consequent to the loss of a very valuable watermelon, her dentistry and transportation to heaven. Next follows an elaborate exposition of the heavenly land in terms of Israel, Montreal and the second part depicts the return to earth from being eaten by Max Muller on the day Edward the Seventh dedicated the Great Sewer of London. (Approx. 50 min.)

no. 13: Fragments and tests of Shamanism in the guise of a children's story. This film, made with van Wolf, is perhaps the most expensive animated film ever made—the cost running well over ten thousand dollars a minute—wide screen, stereophonic sound of the ballet music from Faust. Production was halted when a major investor (H.P.) was found dead under embarrassing conditions. (Approx. 3 hours)

no. 14: Superimposed photography of Mr. Fleischman's butcher shop in New York, and the Kiowa around Anadarko, Oklahoma—with Cognate Material. The strip is dark at the beginning and end, light in the middle, and is structured 122333221. I honor it the most of my films, otherwise a not very popular one before 1972. If the exciter lamp blows, play Bert Brecht's "Mahagonny." (Approx. 25 min.)

For those who are interested in such things: Nos. 1 to 5 were made under pot; No. 6 with schmeck (it made the sun shine) and ups; No. 7 with cocaine and ups; Nos. 8 to 12 with almost anything, but mainly deprivation, and 13 with green pills from Max Jacobson, pink pills from Tim Leary, and vodka; No. 14 with vodka and Italian Swiss white port.*[2]

---

* Of these films Nos. 6, 8, and 9 seem to have permanently disappeared. A section of No. 13 has been prefixed to a recently made film, shot through a kaleidoscope of the film-maker's construction, and called, at times, The Tin Woodsman's Dream. He has also shot a short animation of Seminole quilt designs. Now (1972) he is editing a cinematic version of the full opera "Mahagonny," which in part served as a soundtrack for No. 14. The dates assigned to the films in this note are unreliable, especially regarding the earlier films.

The continuity of Harry Smith's cinema is remarkable, all the more so because of its variety. The shifts in technique and the swerves in intention of each new film seem grounded in the principles of the previous film. After the initial attempt at a freely drawn hand-painted film (No. 1), he made two progressively more complex, batiked, geometrical animations (Nos. 2 and 3), colored by spray paint and dyes, also directly applied to the film. Then he began a series of photographed abstractions, first in black-and-white (No. 4), then in color (Nos. 5 and 7) with quantum leaps of intricacy at each stage. Nos. 10 and 11 integrate collage and fragmentary animated narrative into the spatial and color fields established in the earlier films. That narrative tendency expanded in No. 12 and would have reached an even greater elaboration had No. 13 been completed according to his plan. With the abandonment of that film, Smith turned from animation to the actual world for his imagery, but he maintained a plastic control over what he filmed by means of superimposition (No. 14) and the use of a kaleidoscope (The Tin Woodsman's Dream, second part).

The regular curve of this progression, describing in its course several versions of hermeticism from Neo-Platonic formalism through ritual magic to shamanism traces a graph of evolving concerns and reveals an amazing patience, at odds with the language but not the sense of the film-maker's comments on his work. Smith alone of the major American avant-garde film-makers who have more than two decades of work to their credit gives the illusion of having a plan to his films, which even his lost and aborted films do not spoil.

His insistence that the works be seen "together, or not at all," a condition which, by the way, he has relaxed since issuing that note in 1963, reaffirms the myth of the absolute film, which we have encountered in our discussion of Brakhage and which animates Smith's concerns about individual films (Nos. 12, 13 and the "Mahagonny" film in progress). Yet in Smith's case, that aspiration common to many avant-garde film-makers explicitly converges with the alchemical notion of the Great Work. Harry Smith is a practicing hermeticist. As much as his films share the central concerns of the American avant-garde cinema and incarnate its historical development, they separate themselves and demand attention as aspects of Smith's other work. He divides his time among film-making, painting (less in recent years), iconology (he has a formidable collection of Ukrainian easter eggs and has spent years practicing Northwest Indian string figures in preparation for books on these symbolic cosmologies), music (his reputation as an authority on folk music matches his reputation as a film-maker among experts), anthropology (Folkways will soon issue his record-ings and notes on the peyote ritual of the Kiowa), and linguistics (as an amateur, but with intense interest).

Since childhood Smith has sustained an interest in the occult and in the machinery of illusionism:

> My father gave me a blacksmith shop when I was maybe twelve; he told me I should convert lead into gold. He had me build all these things like models of the first Bell telephone, the original electric light bulb, and perform all sorts of historical experiments. . . . Very early my parents got me interested in projecting things.[3]

His father also initiated his interest in drawing by teaching him to make a geometrical representation of the Cabalistic tree of life. Smith even spoke of Giordano Bruno as the inventor of the cinema in an hilariously aggres-sive lecture at Yale in 1965, quoting the thesis of *De Immenso, Innumera-bilibus et Infigurabilibus* that there are an infinite number of universes, each possessing a similar world with some slight differences—a hand raised in one, lowered in another—so that the perception of motion is an act of the mind swiftly choosing a course among an infinite number of these "freeze frames," and thereby animating them. We see that Smith regards his work in the historical tradition of magical illusionism, extending at least back to Robert Fludd who used mirrors to animate books, and Atha-nasius Kircher who cast spells with a magic lantern.

This would not be worth mentioning were it not helpful in understand-ing Smith's aloofness from some of the vital theoretical issues facing film-makers today, who seek to define their art in terms of the essence of their materials and their tools. It puts into perspective as well the fact that he has repeatedly ventured into mixed-media presentations when the most important of his peers have firmly and at times vociferously rejected such excursions as irrelevant to the urgent problems of cinema. Yet his isola-tion is not complete and has tended to diminish in the last few years. In an interview in the *Village Voice*, he offered the following unexpected evaluation of his work as a film-maker among film-makers.

> I think I'm the third best film producer in the country. I think Andy Warhol is the best. Kenneth Anger is the second best. And now I've de-cided I'm the third best. There was a question in my mind whether Brakhage or myself was the third best, but now I think I am.[4]

The smoothness of the diachronic outline of Smith's development as a film-maker reflects the ease with which the formal and the hermetic poles meet in any given film along that graph. In the ensemble of his work, Neo-plasticism converges with Surrealism so undramatically that we are forced to see that the distances among the theosophy of suprematism, the Neo-platonism of Kandinsky and Mondrian, and the alchemical and Cabalistic metaphysics of Surrealism were not as great as among their respective spatial and tropic strategies. Harry Smith already occupied the new theoretical center where Neo-Plasticism and Surrealism might converge.

The hermetic artist is one who finds the purification, or the formal reduction, of his art coincident with his quest for a magical center that all arts, and all consciousnesses, share. The paradox of hermetic cinema which we encounter in the later films of both Kenneth Anger and Harry Smith is that the closer it comes to self-definition the further it moves from autonomy, the more it seems to involve itself in allusion, arcane reference, obscurity. While most of his contemporaries found first the dream and then the myth to be the prime metaphors for cinema's essence Smith, following the same path, posited a moving geometry as its essence before he joined the others in a move to mythopoeia.

He defined the geometry of cinema in terms of its potential for complexity rather than reduction to simplicity. His early films are progressively more intricate. Yet his first film is remarkably sophisticated in its range of tactics.

No. 1, the most eccentric of Harry Smith's animations, utilizes a principle of imbalance and unpredictability as a source of visual tension, which is reflected in several aspects of the film's imagery and form. Its freely drawn, Arp-like figures resist precise geometry, and the base itself, when it becomes solid, has a tendency to leave a band of a different color at the right edge of the screen. Hard-edged squares are integrated rather uneasily into this context of fluctuation and eccentricity. A vibration occurs when they appear at the beginning, in the middle, and just before the conclusion of the film.

Positions and colors alternate quickly, jumping within the frame, as two squares move toward each other along a virtual diagonal, as in Eggeling's film. Shapes change as soon as they are formed; amorphous circles turn into squares which open up to contain circles again. Only the original hard-edged squares resist transformation as they fall again in the middle of the film.

The instability of the base, which changes color, becomes texturally settled, and can dissolve into splatterings, reflects the ambiguity of the outlined forms which occasionally transform outside to inside. The film-maker's reference to "dirty shapes" in this film must refer to the vaguely phallic wedge in the middle of the film, which becomes a triangle with a hole through which a circle and a soft, again somewhat phallic rectangle pass. Once the ground turns into the figure in the manner of Richter's *Rhythmus 21*: a horizontal band expands in both directions, but before it wipes the previous base away it bends upon itself as if to become a new circle. As the outer shell dissolves, circles form within circles until the distinction between a circle and a square weakens. Four soft triangles, with holes in them, come together to suggest a rectangle. In the final appearance of the rigid squares, they again overlap to create a negative space, and they make the most complex set of variations in the film.

The difficulty of adequately describing *No. 1* reflects the excessive instability of its imagery. Changes continually occur on at least two levels, that of figure and that of base; there are often two or more simultaneous developments on both levels, with perhaps one point of synchronization between one figural and one base change, while all else is asynchronous. This instability, which always seems about to resolve itself on the level of the figure, actually finds its satisfying conclusion, its unexpected *telos*, in the two flashes, first eight frames long, then eleven, of the irregular yellow and red shape—the chromatic climax of the film—just before the end. For the viewer, the prolonged experience of irresolution might be a cinematic equivalent to atonal music; not the rigorous formalism of Anton Webern, but the witty imbalance of Charles Ives.

In *Nos. 2* and *3* Harry Smith abandoned the hand-drawn figure. He concentrated on the exhaustive use of the batiking principle by which he inserted the hard-edged squares into his first film. As he describes it in an interview in *Film Culture Reader*, that process involved placing "come clean" dots on 35mm film, spraying color on it, then covering the strip with vaseline before removing the dots. Another spraying will give two colors, one inside and one outside the circle. Of course the process can be multiplied with different colors.

This shift of technique implied a new dynamics for the films. In *No. 1* the film-maker recognized the essential instability of a drawn line which has to repeat itself twenty-four times a second. He elaborated the whole form of his film out of this basic instability, exaggerating it and mimicking it in structural and textural ways. The batiking process removed the essential vibration of line. Smith responded to this fact with more rigorous rhythmic form, a heightened centrality of imagery, a smoother balance of colors, and a strict reliance on basic geometrical figures. In *No. 2* in particular he explored the use of off-screen space implicit in the opening and in several moments of No. 1. By opening with and predominantly using motion from the top to the bottom of the screen, he introduced a sense of gravity around which the off-screen vectors are organized.

Several variations on the manifestation and rhythmic movement of the circle alternate through the film: 1) a circle defines itself out of the widening of a section by the expanding of two radii or disappears by inversion; 2) one circle or a phalanx of circles crosses the screen vertically or horizontally; 3) a circle collapses from its circumference inward or expands outward as far as or beyond the rectangle of the screen; 4) a circle splits into two semi-circles to reveal another circle behind it; 5) fixed concentric circles; 6) a small circle turns within a larger one with a continual tangency of circumferences.

After an opening of a circle expanding from a wedge, a welter of circles of different sizes and colors falls vertically across the screen. This is the only instance in the film of a mixed scale of circles; it is deliberately chaotic. In the penultimate image of the film these same circles rise again and pass out at the top of the screen.

The rhythmic pace seems measured and even throughout; the time required for a wedge to expand, for a circle to fall, for a dance of squares to occupy all four of its positions, or for the contraction, collision, or expansion of circles is equivalent. This metric regularity reflects the consistency with which the color changes at the entrance of each new circle or each sweep of a wedge into a full circle.

The reliance on primary colors emphasizes the purity and regularity of the film's form. By making this directly on film with the batiked process rather than animating it from drawings as is possible, Harry Smith maintained the vibrancy of directly applied color with its frame-by-frame fluctuations which otherwise would be lost. There is also a minimum of arbitrary blending and/or an absence of color at the points where the circles meet the base. This and a discreet amount of flaking, especially on the inlaid squares, give the film a textural immediacy. With the geometric regularity of the circles and the structural regularity of the film's construction, Smith has created a form in opposition to the color's irregularity. The result is more successful than the opposite tactic employed in No. 1.

When Smith says that "the action takes place either inside the sun or in Zurich, Switzerland," he is alluding to the hermetic source of the circle, the sun, and suggesting that the film might also take place in the mind of Carl Jung, then living in Zurich. His subsequent claim that No. 3 is the

most complex hand-painted film ever made is sustained by its comparison
with anything I have seen in this mode. The most ambitious aspects of
Nos. 1 and *2* are merely preludes to the textural, rhythmic, and structural
complexity of *No. 3*. It is not difficult to believe the film-maker when he
says that it took him several years of daily work to complete it.

It falls into three sections. In the first a hatch made of four bars (two
horizontal, two vertical, crossed over each other like a grid for playing tic-
tac-toe) gradually turns into a field of squares, which in turn reveal a
group of overlapping diamonds which are central to the second section.
There the diamonds undergo a number of changes amid expanding rectangles (characteristic of the first part of the film) and circles (characteristic of the last part). The final third uses the image of the expanding
circle to mount a spectacular climax integrating the previous strategies
and images of the film.

This time the film-maker makes little use of off-screen space; he organizes much of the movement within the film in terms of the illusionary
depth of the screen. Images recede into and explode out of a deep center.
Emphasis is placed on the relative positions of foreground and background
figures. The changes of color are more complex than in *No. 2*; solid hues
rest beside clearly defined areas of splattered paint and when figures overlap their common areas take on different colors. Finally, different rhythmic structures mesh with a complexity equal to the most elaborate
achievements of the entire graphic film tradition.

By the time he completed this film, Harry Smith had established con-
tacts with other film-makers, both in the San Francisco area where he was
working and in Los Angeles. It was at the same time that Frank Stauffacher and Richard Foster founded Art in Cinema, where avant-garde
films, both those from the Europe of two decades earlier and new works,
had their first rigorous screenings on the American West Coast. Although
Smith continued to paint throughout this period, he came to identify himself with the emerging cinema. In fact, when Stauffacher and Foster split
up and it looked as if Art in Cinema would fail (as it did), he tried for a
brief time to program new films for it. It is nearly impossible to pin Smith
down on specific dates within this period of the late 1940s and equally difficult to fix his movements precisely from other sources. Nevertheless we
know that he worked in San Francisco and Berkeley during this time and
that during this period he met John and James Whitney of Los Angeles,
who were to have a decisive influence on him and later on Jordan Belson.

Between 1943 and 1944 the Whitney brothers had made *Five Film*

Exercises on home-made animating and sound composing equipment. One of their highest ambitions was to produce "audio-visual music" or "color music" by the synchronization of abstract transformations to electronic sounds and by the utilization of basically musical forms for the overall construction of their films. In one article of 1944, they refer to Bauer, a source of inspiration they shared with Smith; in another of 1945 they speak of Mondrian and Duchamp (in so far as he urged mechanical reproduction over hand-made objects of art) as primary inspirations. Their early films show hard-edged or sometimes slightly out of focus figures in a state of continual transformation and movement about the screen. A shape that seems to curve three-dimensionally will change to make its flatness apparent (*Film Exercise 1*); the whole screen or half the screen will flash with color flickers (*Film Exercises 2 and 3*) and behind geometrical variations; a reciprocal play of movement into and out of screen depth will structure a film (*Film Exercise 4*); or a process of echo and recapitulation in different colors will be an organizing principle (*Film Exercise 5*). Their own notes for the catalogue of Art in Cinema most clearly define their aspirations:

FIRST SOUND FILM; COMPLETED FALL 1943:

Begins with a three beat announcement, drawn out in time, which thereafter serves as an imageless transition figure dividing the sections of the film. Each new return of this figure is condensed more and more in time. Finally it is used in reverse to conclude the film. . . .

This film was produced entirely by manipulation of paper cut-outs and shot at regular motion picture camera speed instead of hand animating one frame at a time. The entire film, two hundred feet in length, was constructed from an economical twelve feet of original image material.

FRAGMENTS; SPRING 1944:

These two very short fragments were also made from paper cut-outs. At this time we were developing a means of controlling this procedure with the use of pantographs. While we were satisfied with the correlation of sound and image, progress with the material had begun to lag far behind our ideas. These two were left unfinished in order to begin the films which follow.

FOURTH FILM; COMPLETED SPRING 1944:

Entire film divided into four consecutive chosen approaches, the fourth being a section partially devoted to a reiteration and extension of the material of the first and second sections.

SECTION ONE: Movement used primarily to achieve spatial depth. An attempt is made to delay sound in a proportional relationship to the depth or distance of its corresponding image in the screen space. That is, a near image is heard sooner than one in the distance. Having determined the distant and near extremes of the visual image, this screen space is assigned a tonal interval. The sound then moves along a melodic line in continuous glissando back and forth slowing down as it approaches its point of alteration in direction. . . .

SECTION TWO: Consists of four short subjects in natural sequence. They are treated to a development in terms alternately of contraction and expansion or halving and doubling of their rhythm. Sound and visual elements held in strict synchronization. . . .

SECTION THREE: A fifteen second visual sequence is begun every five seconds after the fashion of canon form in music. This constitutes the leading idea, a development of which is extended into three different repetitions. This section is built upon the establishment of complex tonal masses which oppose complex image masses. The durations of each are progressively shortened. The image masses are progressively simplified and their spatial movement increasingly rapid.

SECTION FOUR: Begins with a statement in sound and image which at its conclusion is inverted and retrogresses to its beginning. An enlarged repetition of this leads to the reiterative conclusion of the film.

FIFTH FILM; COMPLETED SPRING 1944:

Opens with a short canonical statement of a theme upon which the entire film is constructed. Followed by a rhythmical treatment of the beginning and ending images of this theme in alternation. This passage progresses by a quickening of rhythm, increasing in complexity and color fluctuation. . . .

A second section begins after a brief pause. Here an attempt is made to pose the same image theme of the first section in deep film screen space. As the ending image recedes after an accented frontal flash onto the screen it unfolds itself repeatedly leaving the receding image to continue on smaller and smaller.[5]

Harry Smith credits the Whitneys both with teaching him the techniques of photographic animation and with helping him to formulate a theoretical view of cinema.

He remained faithful to the circle, the triangle, and the square or rectangle as the essential forms of visual geometry. Before the black-and-white imagery of No. 4 begins, Smith pans the camera over a painting of his from the same period. The movements on the painting are in color. In contrast to his film work, the painting uses organic, bulb-like forms rather than rigid geometrical figures. In *Film Culture* he described this painting:

It is a painting to a tune by Dizzy Gillespie called "Manteca." Each stroke in the painting represents a certain note on the recording. If I had the record, I could project the painting as a slide and point to a certain thing.[6]

The possibility of translating music into images is another part of the hermetic world view. In practice Harry Smith's use of sound with film has been very problematic. The initial three painted films were made to be shown silently. After they were finished, the film-maker had the following experience: "I had a really great illumination the first time I heard Dizzy Gillespie play. I had gone there very high, and I literally saw all kinds of color flashes. It was at that point that I realized music could be put to my films." He claims that he then cut down No. 2 from an original length of over thirty minutes to synchronize it with Gillespie's "Guacha Guero." Neither the original long version nor the synchronized print survive.

Smith is notoriously self-destructive. The loss of several important films from his "Great Work" attests to this. He has proven in films like No. 11 and No. 12 that he can use both music and sound effects meticulously, and in the case of the later film, with genius. His elaborate preparation for the Mahagonny film indicates that again he will create a true sound and picture synthesis. His ability in handling sound makes all the more alarming the extreme casualness with which he put the Beatles' first album with an anthology of his early films, Early Abstractions, for distribution. It seems as if he wanted to obscure the monumentality of his achievement in painting and animating film by simply updating the soundtrack.

No. 4 combines camera movement with superimposition to create a dance of white circles and squares against a black background. Because of the absence of any perspective, the bobbing and swinging of the camera is translated by the eye into a movement of lights within or across the screen. By altering his speed of movement, the distance from the object, and the direction of the camera, he can elaborate a formal interplay of counterpoint, scale change, and off-screen orientation out of a simple grid of twenty-four white squares and a field of circular dots.

No. 5, entitled Circular Tensions, extends the use of the moving camera and superimposition into color and geometry. Against a black background a green square appears next to a red circle and triangle. Slowly they begin to move around and over one another. Then an eccentrically composed blue spiral appears dimly in superimposition, giving an illusory depth to the black space behind the geometrical figures. Numerous bright yellow lights sweep across the screen in different directions, leaving in their wake a bounding red circle. Its scale remains constant as the camera zooms in and out on superimposed rectangles.

In the late 1940s Harry Smith and Jordan Belson invited Hilda Rebay of the Museum of Non-Objective Art (now the Guggenheim Museum) to see their painting when she was in San Francisco. That visit ultimately resulted in a grant from the Solomon Guggenheim Foundation during 1951 for Smith to begin work on *No. 7*. When he moved to New York at the completion of the film, he was again helped by Hilda Rebay and given a studio in the Guggenheim Museum. At that time the Guggenheim Museum specialized in collecting the works of Kandinsky and Bauer. Of all of his films, *No. 7* comes the closest to animating a painting of Kandinsky in his geometrical style of the 1920s.

To make this film, Smith set up a primitive, back-screen projection situation that worked with astonishing precision. One machine projected black-and-white images on a translucent screen. On the other side of the screen a 16mm camera re-recorded them. A wheel of color filters in front of the camera was used to determine the hue of a figure or a background. By keeping an accurate record of where any pattern was recorded on the film strip, the film-maker could make elaborate synchronous movements by means of several layers of superimposition. Most of the visual tropes of *No. 7* derive from earlier animations of Smith's; but here they attain their apogee of intricacy and color control. No use is made of off-screen space. Illusory depth orients the entire film, but unlike the earlier films, there is a tension here between images which have their center of gravity in the absolute center of the screen and sets of images with two or more lateral centers.

The film-maker's note divides the film into four parts. In the first, if my division is accurate, the following tropes are dominant: 1) colored bars appear vertically, horizontally, or diagonally against the background and widen to the edges of the screen until they become the backdrop; 2) rings within rings of the same or different colors expand from the center of the screen; 3) two laterally placed circles, one larger than the other, emerge and recede alternately from two points of gravity, exchanging their relative scales in each alternation; 4) a central black circle enlarges with a vaguely defined red corona; 5) circles and rings, in different colors, come out of screen depth simultaneously, and the area of their overlapping takes on new colors; 6) an expanding square alternates between being black within against a diminishing colored space and colored within against a black space; 7) amid these intricate variations of orderly patterns, eccentrically placed squares, circles, and squares containing circles appear; 8) different parts of the screen change at different speeds. A deep red accents the first section. Yellow, pink, orange, reddish-blue, and of course

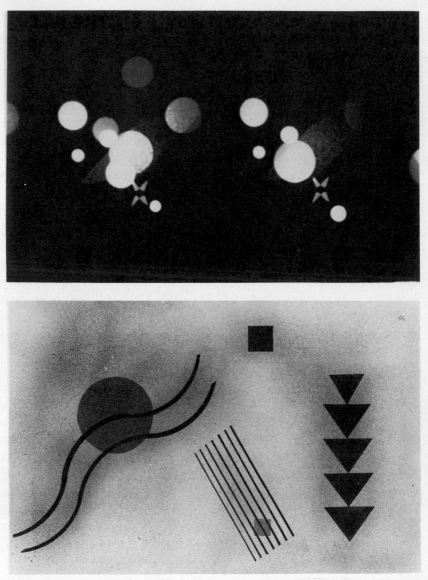

Geometrical abstraction in Harry Smith's *No. 7* and Wassily Kandinsky's "Loosely Bound."

black are predominant. In the second section the tonality shifts to a bluish-green with considerable use of red and white. Here the triangle makes its first appearance, initially in sequential sets of four wedges exploding outward, later with as many as sixteen wedges in eight concentric rings. Generally, the placement of figures is more irregular than in the earlier section and the rhythmic interactions even more complex, because the central organizing pulse itself can suddenly fluctuate.

When black circles with colored coronas appear, complex explosions of rings of wedges are syncopated within them. As the film progresses, the pace of the explosions increases. The section ends with a diminuendo of circular movements followed by sudden explosions of wedges as the surrounding corona turns from red to yellow.

In the third section the importance of the circle diminishes; it only appears at the end. The square and the rectangle take the center now. All over the screen there are squares, grids, and bars. There is no break in the continual blending of different kinds of grids and squares throughout this section. As in the previous part of the film, these processes overlap with different rhythms and in different scales. Numerous widening diagonals, which change the background colors, complicate the woven pattern of overlapping squares.

This is the most decentralized part of the film. Throughout it, there is a periodic but repressed background of exploding wedges. Towards the end of the section a dialectic establishes itself between eccentricity and centrality, in which the shift of axes of the wedges plays a decisive role.

The final quarter of the film derives its pulse from the continual expansion of rings from the center of the screen. In opposition to this dominant trope: 1) fast moving sets of radiating rings appear eccentrically; 2) circles grow out of pie-like sections (as in No. 2) and reduce themselves to sections; 3) squares emerge, turn into grids, and dissolve into blackness; 4) a single red triangle wanders around the screen and disappears in its center with an explosion of wedges; and 5) squares appear within squares.

After finishing No. 7, Harry Smith moved from San Francisco to New York. There he began to make collage films. Unfortunately, all we know of No. 8 and No. 9 are his laconic notes. By the time he made No. 10 and No. 11, which are versions of the same film, he had a highly developed collage animation technique in color. Many of the formal operations of the earlier films, especially No. 7, were incorporated into these two films. Of the several modes of tension in these works, the relationship between the screen as an enclosed world and off-screen space is particularly important. Similarly, the dialectics between a flat plane of action and illusory depth, between collage animation and abstract convulsions of the whole image, between gravity and the screen as an open field of movement, between sequences of transformation and abrupt change, derive from and elaborate upon the strategies of his earlier films.

Both *No. 10* and *No. 11* are pointedly hermetic. They describe analogies among Tarot cards, Cabalistic symbolism, Indian chiromancy and dancing, Buddhist mandalas, and Renaissance alchemy. The process of animation itself, with its continual transformations, provides the vehicle for this giant equation. Surrealism's version of the hermetic enters in at least twice, rupturing the logic of the occult analogies through unexpected and irrational juxtapositions. The first of these inclusions is a postman in a child's wagon, who plays an important role in the film because of his resistance to being transformed. The second is the comic appearance of a grimacing lady, looking out of a window near the end of both films. The presence of such imagery, which jars the consistency of the film, provides yet another dialectic and paradoxically enriches the hermeticism it is confounding by distancing it from the rational.

A detailed description of these films, shot as they are, would require a volume. So many of the fleeting collages are composed of internal subcollages, associating within a single shape the iconography of different cultures, that several pages would be needed to describe each one's presence, which lasts on the screen perhaps a second, before one could go on to the shape it changes into. Beyond that there is a welter of images and symbols moving around or behind the central image at many points in the film. In short, Harry Smith is utilizing cinema's potential, through its speed, to confound the perception of the spectator with a profusion of complex imagery. The language of James Joyce's *Finnegans Wake* has a comparable verticality. But in reading it, one adjusts by slowing down and analyzing. The speed of the film is fixed; the only recourse is to see it again and again at the same rate.

No. 10 begins with snow crystals falling through the frame. They become a molecular cluster with an abstract circumference of outward-pointing red wedges. The atoms of the molecule separate to become the tree of life, an outlined figure with ten points which is the central Cabalistic diagram. A bird lands on it, turning it into a skeleton with various totemic masks. At this point the flat background of expanding rings of wedges changes to radiating squares along a diminishing line of perspective, turning the plane of action into a field of depth. The most dynamic and most often employed illusion of depth in the film emerges from the creation of a recessed room or theater whose walls are receding planes of different colors. As on a stage, it looks as if a fourth wall had been removed so we can see within.

The first appearance of this theater coincides with the breakup of the skeleton and its reformation as a masked shaman, who floats upward through the ceiling and off-screen, leaving the space empty for a moment before it fades out. In rigid opposition to the illusion of depth, a flat field of colored dots fills the screen, but it quickly fades into another theater, out of whose floor comes a mask with six legs. As it circles the walls and ceiling, defying gravity and affirming the shape of the screen, an unsupported flame hovers in the center of the room. Soon an athanor (a basic piece of the alchemical equipment) encloses it. In the earlier films an act of enclosure, of circles within a square, for example, almost always initiated a chain of transformations of the forms within the framing device at a rhythm all its own. So too here, enclosures generate interior metamorphoses. The fire constantly changes its shape, becoming birds and alchemical symbols, while the legged mask continues to circle the stage. After the athanor breaks up, the mask descends to the center and is instantly turned into three images—a football, a tiny globe, and again a mask. When vertically aligned these three images become a goat-headed devil sitting on the earth, around which the serpent of the Aion has wrapped himself. At this point two illusions of depth are compounded as the squares radiate from the depth of the screen while everything remains situated within the theater.

A fire on the goat-devil's head becomes the bird which will carry him off-screen, while the snake unties himself from the earth. The theater dissolves into an expanding purple circle, but the snake and the globe remain in the foreground over changing flat patterns and exploding wedges only to disappear finally in a briefly appearing circle of spectrally diffused colors. But out of the center of that circle which obliterated him, the snake emerges slowly, with a string of beads and a child's doll for a body.

Against a black background an Indian dancer floats down from the top of the screen on a pill box. An entire constellation of symbols fuses into the back of a playing card. When the dancer crosses in front of it, she leaves her shadow on the card. Her dance is synchronously reflected in the shadow. Although she will soon be transformed, her image will reappear again, for she is the central female presence in No. 10.

Throughout the transformations of the dancer, her shadow remains on the back of the card. The shadow dances by itself, sending out a lightning stroke which creates a postman on a red wagon. He will become the central male figure of the film, the dancer's counterpart. At the completion of the dance the shadow becomes the dancer, and she and the postman, both inscribed in rings, orbit one another, while a series of rays emanate from the center of the screen.

The spatial dialectic of the film now becomes more intricate. Layers parallel to the plane of the screen tend to move or fracture to reveal another plane immediately behind it. This happens, for instance, when an object floats down-screen revealing the postman behind it. But when he tries to reach the dancer, the theater reconstitutes itself, now subdivided into barriers which frustrate his pursuit.

The moon descends from covering the whole screen to an arc with a black spot above it. From behind flies an orbiting planet, followed by a stork. Then a mushroom and the Rosetta Stone grow out of the moon. The dancer steps from in back of one stone; from the other the postman. They step behind these objects again and reappear as doubles: two identical dancers and two postmen.

The dancers and postmen join hands beside and on top of each other in chiastic order, while the moon descends, leaving them floating in space. In quick succession they change into a tree of life; a bird above three serpents holding the sun, the moon, and the earth; and a headless man, standing on the earth holding the sun and moon in his hands while small squares gush from his neck. He becomes a smaller version of the moon than the one that has just descended. A Tibetan demon appears behind that moon and carries it away in his mouth, while the couple float by on a cerebrum, leaving a conch, which turns into the end title.

Most of the imagery of *No. 11*, or *Mirror Animations*, is identical to that of *No. 10*. The film differs essentially in that it is carefully synchronized to Thelonius Monk's "Mysterioso." Most of the significant scenes of the earlier film recur here with slight variations; the dance of the Indian and her shadow, the pursuit within the subdivided theater, the chiromantic variations, and the grimacing woman in the window, which has become a picture frame all appear in approximately the same sequence. The tree of life, the snake, the symbols of the sun, moon, Hermes and Neptune within the pillbox, the Tarot cards, and the athanor present themselves in altered contexts. The Buddhist and Tibetan imagery, as well as the entire end of the film from the appearance of the moon on, are absent.

The most prominent innovation in *No. 11*, a priestess dressed in white who is created at the beginning of the film when lightning strikes a snow-flake, generates rhythmic and structural differences. Her priestly gestures are synchronized to the pulse of Monk's music. Her centrality at the beginning and end of the film finds reinforcement in regular movements of figures and triangles of light around all four sides of the screen. The transformations occur within the metrical pattern established by the movements of her arms, even when she is not on the screen. Her presence and the way she brackets the whole film diminish the roles of the dancer and the postman.

Despite some elaborations on the spatial strategies of *No. 10*, such as a scene in which the snake wraps itself around the back of the recessed theater and snatches a figure within it, *No. 11* underplays the dialectic of depth and plane, so important in the earlier film. There are less convulsive changes in the depicted screen space. The whole film seems to move slower, and the dazzling flood of imagery is somewhat chastened.

This chastening and the presence of the priestess as the mediator and controller of the operations of the film forecast the radical jump in style to *No. 12*. This film, sometimes called *The Magic Feature* or *Heaven and Earth Magic*, is Harry Smith's most ambitious and most difficult work. Although it is particularly difficult to assign dates to the animated films he made in New York, *No. 12* seems to have occupied him through most of the 1950s, especially toward the end of that decade.

The original conception of this film exemplifies the myth of the absolute film in its expansive form. The hour-long version that can be seen today is but a fragment of the original plan, but even so, it is among the very highest achievements of the American avant-garde cinema and one of the central texts of its mythopoeic phase.

In the interview published in *Film Culture*, the film-maker describes the plan for the whole film:

> I must say that I'm amazed, after having seen the black-and-white film (#12) last night, at the labor that went into it. It is incredible that I had enough energy to do it. Most of my mind was pushed aside into some sort of theoretical sorting of the pieces, mainly on the basis that I have described: First, I collected the pieces out of old catalogues and books and whatever; then made up file cards of all possible combinations of them; then, I spent maybe a few months trying to sort the cards into logical order. A script was made for that. All the script and the pieces were made for a film at least four times as long. There were wonderful masks and things cut out. Like when the dog pushes the scene away at

A

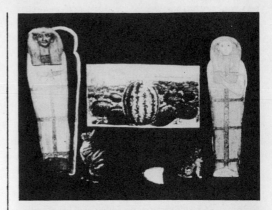

B

C

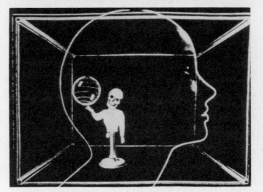

D

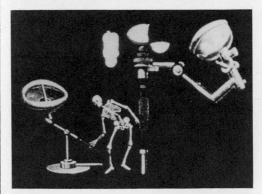

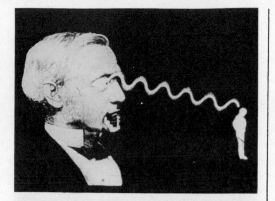

Harry Smith's No. 12:
(A) The initial scene.
(B) The ascent to heaven on a dentist's chair.
(C) The first tableau of heaven.
(D) The skeleton juggling a baby in the central tableau of heaven.
(E) Max Müller casts a spell on the Magus.
(F) The descent from heaven in an elevator.
(G) The return to the initial scene.

the end of the film, instead of the title "end" what is really there is a transparent screen that has a candle burning behind it on which a cat fight begins—shadow forms of cats begin fighting. Then, all sorts of complicated effects; I had held these off. The radiations were to begin at this point. Then Noah's Ark appears. There were beautiful scratch-board drawings, probably the finest drawings I ever made—really pretty. Maybe 200 were made for that one scene. Then there's a graveyard scene, when the dead are all raised again. What actually happens at the end of the film is everybody's put in a teacup, because all kinds of horrible monsters came out of the graveyard, like animals that folded into one another. Then everyone gets thrown in a teacup, which is made out of a head, and stirred up. This is the Trip to Heaven and the Return, then the Noah's Ark, then The Raising of the Dead, and finally the Stirring of Everyone in a Teacup. It was to be in four parts. The script was made up for the whole works on the basis of sorting pieces. It was exhaustingly long in its original form. When I say that it was cut, mainly what was cut out was, say, instead of the little man bowing and then standing up, he would stay bowed down much longer in the original. The cutting that was done was really a correction of timing. It's better in its original form.[7]

Although the film was shot in black-and-white, he built a projector with color filters that could change the tint of the images. Furthermore, the whole film was to be projected through a series of masking slides which would transform the shape of the screen. The slides take the form of important images within the film, such as a watermelon or an egg. Thus the entire movement would be enclosed within the projection of the slide. A different filter could determine the color of the surrounding slides. The whole apparatus functioned only once. In the late 1950s or early 1960s he presented the film for potential backers at Steinway Hall in New York. He would have liked to have installed seats in the form of the slide images —a watermelon seat, an egg seat, etc.—with an electrically controlled mechanism that would have changed the colors and the slides in accordance with the movements of the spectators in their seats. Lacking the extravagant means necessary to achieve this, he manipulated the changes by hand.

Despite the multiplicity of their references and obscure allusions Nos. 10 and 11 offer easier access to the viewer than No. 12. Here Smith avoids historical iconography, with the possible exception of the universally understood skeleton. The form of the film evokes hermetic maneuvers, which are all the more distanced because of their abstraction and lack of specificity. The tone of the film seems to call for a close reading which the form frustrates. Furthermore, the investigation of his sources, which he alludes to obliquely in his note on the film, opens up seemingly fruitful approaches to the film without ever providing satisfying insights.

The note veers from an elliptical description of the film's images to allusions about its sources. When he writes, "Next follows an elaborate exposition of the heavenly land in terms of Israel, Montreal and the second part depicts the return to earth from being eaten by Max Muller on the day Edward the Seventh dedicated the Great Sewer of London," he is deliberately obscuring the film with hints about it. By Israel he means the Cabala, particularly the three books translated by MacGregor Mathers as *The Kabbalah Unveiled*: "The Book of Concealed Mystery," "The Greater Holy Assembly," and "The Lesser Holy Assembly." Here the Cabalists interpret the tree of life in terms of the body of God, with intricate and detailed descriptions of features, members, configurations of the beard, etc.

The reference to Montreal, he later explained, indicates the parallel influence of Dr. Wildner Penfield of the Montreal Neurological Institute, whose extensive open brain operations on epileptics are described in *Epilepsy and the Functional Anatomy of the Human Brain* (Little, Brown, Boston, 1954). Several aspects of Penfield's book intrigued Smith: the hallucinations of the patients under brain surgery; the topology and geography of the cerebral cortex; and the distribution and juxtaposition of nervous centers. His occasional remark that No. 12 takes place in the fissure of Silvius, one of the major folds in the brain, is another allusion to Penfield.

A photograph of Max Muller, the nineteenth-century philologist and editor of *The Sacred Books of the East*, actually appears in the film. What Smith does not say is that this is the only face, out of several, which has a specific reference. Naturally, Smith's identification of this figure, which has a privileged place in the film, leads us to wonder, fruitlessly, who the other Victorian visages might be.

Finally, the allusion to the day the London sewers were inaugurated turns out to refer to the cover story of an illustrated magazine that provided many of the elements of the collage. The very choice of late-nineteenth-century engravings as the materials for his collage brings to mind the influence of Max Ernst's books, *La Femme 100 Têtes* and *Une Semaine de Bonté*. As we shall see, there are other, structural links with Ernst in this film.

The broadest outline of the "action" of No. 12 agrees with the film-maker's ironic note. As in No. 10, there are two main characters, a man and a woman; but here the man assumes the role of the priestess from No. 11, not that of the postman. Although Smith has described him as having the same function as the prop-mover in traditional Japanese theater, his continual manipulations in the alchemical context of No. 12, coupled with his almost absolute resistance to change when everything else, including the heroine, is under constant metamorphosis, elevates him to the status of a magus. According to the argument of the film, he injects her with a magical potion while she sits in a diabolical dentist's chair. She rises to heaven and becomes fragmented. The "elaborate exposition of the heavenly land" occurs while the magus attempts a series of operations to put her back together. He does not succeed until after they are eaten by the giant head of a man (Max Muller), and they are descending to earth in an elevator. Their arrival coincides with an obscure celebration, seen in scatological imagery (the Great Sewer), in which a climactic recapitulation of the journey blends into an ending which is the exact reversal of the opening shots.

The reader of Dr. Penfield might identify the injection of the heroine and the subsequent explosion of her cranium with the effects of open brain surgery on the conscious patient. Since the operation is painless, after a local anesthetic has been applied to the surface of the skull, Penfield had his patients talk while he probed their brains with his surgical needle. The visions, memories, sensory illusions, and motor reactions of individual patients when particular areas of their brains were touched are recorded by Penfield in numerous case histories.

A significant case of the fusion of a religious cosmology with mental disorder would be Daniel Paul Schreber's *Memoirs of My Nervous Illness*. Harry Smith first brought this book to my attention in a context unrelated to No. 12, but later he referred to the first tableau after the ascent as "Schreber's heaven." In the book, a well educated, influential German jurist vividly describes two periods of extreme paranoia in 1884 and 1893. The text is neither clinical nor apocalyptic. Although Schreber sees himself as mentally disturbed, he presents his fantasies as metaphysical revelations and himself as the privileged martyr to these insights. In essence, his thesis is that God attracts human nerves to the "forecourts of heaven." Among his numerous paranoid hallucinations were the ideas that he had contact on the nerve plane with other people, which they refused to admit in the flesh; that his stomach had been replaced with an inferior one; and that the boundaries of male and female were confused within him. Freud wrote a psychoanalytical study of the book, finding in it a psychosis based on homosexual fears. Harry Smith seems to be interested in it, as in all psychological phenomena, because of the quality of its imagination.

Schreber's father, Daniel Gottlob Moritz Schreber, was a physician and author of a very popular exercise book, *Medical Indoor Exercises*. From this book Smith took the character of the magus. By cataloguing the illustrations for the exercises, he collected a sequence of gestures which he animated into all the movements of the film's main character.

What makes No. 12 much more complicated than its argument and what obscures its outlines is the multiplicity of details filling the images and the refusal on the part of the film-maker to indicate levels of importance among these details. For example, before the dentist's chair can be used, it must be adjusted. A bird might lay an egg, out of which comes the hammer with which the magus can transform the dentist's chair. Other figures carry out bottles, mortars and pestles, and enema bulbs to prepare a liquid with which to oil the chair, and an almost identical set of operations is repeated for the preparation of the potion to be injected into the heroine. Since the viewer never knows the desired end of an operation or a series of operations, he must divide his attention evenly among these endless and varied procedures.

In addition to this, countless creatures and things are crossing the screen while these actions are going on—a dog, a cat, a skeleton horse, a walking house, a cow, a sheep, two spoon-like creatures, an homunculus, birds. At times they contribute to the operation at hand, but just as often their participation is deliberately obscure.

The technique of distancing the dramatic focus of a story behind a continual foreground of evenly accented detail is a literary tactic dating from the novels of Raymond Roussel, before the First World War, and periodically revived, most recently in the plays of Richard Foreman. In No. 12 Harry Smith has offered its hypostatic equivalent in cinema. His continual alternation of associative and disassociative sound effects underlines this distancing; for as often as he will synchronize the sound of a dog barking when the dog crosses the screen or of screams when the woman is being dismembered, he will connect mooings with a horse, suddenly inject applause, or preface or follow an event with the sound appropriate to it.

Perhaps even more disorienting than the pressure of detail or the dialectic of sound is the random combination of certain recurrent images. Like

Brakhage in *Prelude: Dog Star Man*, Harry Smith found a way of incorporating chance operations in his film without sacrificing its structure. In *Film Culture* he says:

> All the permutations possible were built up: say, there's a hammer in it, and there's a vase, and there's a woman and there's a dog. Various things could then be done—hammer hits dog; woman hits dog; dog jumps into vase; so forth. It was possible to build up an enormous number of cross references.[8]

> I tried as much as possible to make the whole thing automatic, the production automatic rather than any kind of logical process. Though, at this point, Allen Ginsberg denies having said it, about the time I started making those films, he told me that William Burroughs made a change in the Surrealistic process—because, you know, all that stuff comes from the Surrealists—that business of folding a piece of paper: One person draws the head and then folds it over, and somebody else draws the body. What do they call it? The Exquisite Corpse. Somebody later, perhaps Burroughs, realized that something was directing it, that it wasn't arbitrary, and that there was some kind of what you might call God. It wasn't just chance.[9]

> I never did finish that sentence about the relation of Surrealism to my things: I assumed that something was controlling the course of action and that it was not simply arbitrary, so that by sortilege (as you know, there is a system of divination called "sortilege") everything would come out alright.[10]

Smith's use of chance coincides with his idea of the mantic function of the artist. He has said, "My movies are made by God; I was just the medium for them." The chance variations on the basic imagistic vocabulary of the film provide yet another metaphor between his film and the Great Work of the alchemists. For the Renaissance alchemist, the preparation of his tools and of himself equalled in importance the act of transformation itself. Since every element in an alchemical change had to be perfect, each instrument and chemical had its own intricate preparation. Alchemical texts tend to read like endless recipes of purification, fire-making, etc. The commitment to preliminaries is so strong that in its spiritual interpretation, alchemy becomes the slow perfection of the alchemist; the accent shifts from goals to processes. The viewer of *No. 12* finds himself confronted with repetitive scenes of preparation—an egg hatches a hammer, which changes a machine, which will produce a liquid, etc.—toward a *telos* that brings us back to the beginning. The characters of the film end up precisely as they were at the beginning. Everything returns to its place of origin.

No. 12 shares with the mythopoeic cinema of Brakhage, Anger, and Markopoulos the theme of the divided being or splintered consciousness which must be reintegrated. As I have shown in the previous chapters, this theme is an inheritance from Romanticism. In Smith's version of the myth, heaven and the human brain are conflated. When the physically divided woman first arrives in heaven she is seen within the frame of a female head. Her release from the anxieties of selfhood comes at the end of the film when the elevator brings her back to earth, down through the titanic body of Max Muller, who is last seen circumscribed by the same female head. Her disappearance from the action of the middle of the film cannot be construed as an escape from her anxiety, which I have called selfhood; these are her moments of maximal fragmentation, when all of the magus' efforts are directed at bringing her back, or at least preparing the tools to do so.

All the movement in the film occurs along the plane of the screen. There are no actions into or out of the screen depth. In place of it, considerable attention is paid to off-screen space. While most of the off-movement involves the left and right sides of the image, following the law of gravity, there are occasionally descents and ascents from the top and bottom. At the very beginning of the film, Smith elliptically suggests that the magus has walked around the back of the screen: he pushes one sarcophagus on from the right; then without crossing the screen, he pushes another on from the left.

The absence of movement in depth draws the viewer's attention to subtle spatial illusions of foreground and background within the frontal plane. Figures do pass in front of or behind one another. Late in the film an elaborate chase occurs around a stone palace, with the magus rushing off and on screen, carrying the heroine, pursued by several figures. At each alternative sweep they pass in front of or behind the palace (through whose windows and arches they can be partially seen).

At one point in the film the whole plane of the screen splits laterally to show another plane on which a skeleton is operating a machine. The film-maker postponed the use of superimposition until the climax. At the end of the film, when the elevator lands on earth, transparent Greek statues pass in front of the action; somewhat later the major images are recapitulated in superimposition within a crystal ball.

Although there is no movement into or out of screen depth, various strategies are employed to suggest, at times, a recess of space there. The radiating balls, which help to create the illusion of ascent and descent to

A

B

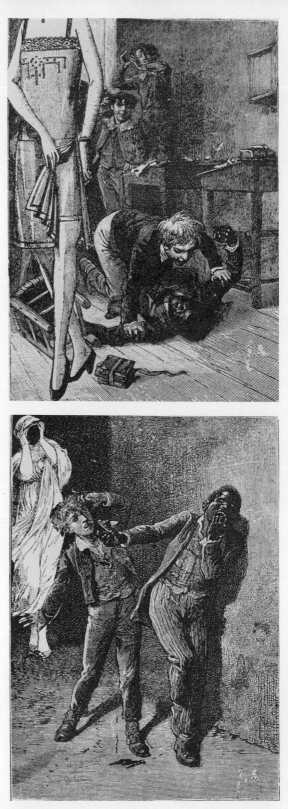

C

D

Max Ernst's *La Femme* 100 *Têtes*: a narrative se
quence (illus. A, B, C) and a collage of Fantomas, Dante, and Jules Verne from a later chapter of the book
(D).

VISIONARY FILM

and from heaven, are the first of these. A room or theater is suggested immediately afterward in the first of the heavenly landscapes. Finally, the image of the Great Sewer, the last backdrop of the film, gives the impression of a group of receding arcades.

Among the more interesting spatial strategies in *No. 12* are the sudden manifestations of the law of gravity. Through most of the film, figures simply move along virtual horizontal lines imagined within the black background. They do not need the support of a floor or structure to keep from falling out of the frame. But occasionally, as when the arch forms in the lower part of the screen, such support suddenly becomes necessary. The most dramatic use of this change of pace occurs during the episode in which a line of couches descends vertically down the screen. They create a void within the screen. The magus cannot pass without leaping on to one of the passing couches for support. His alternative, of course, is to float over the void by using the umbrella.

A related configuration of space within the black background would be the series of arches through which the magus walks or rides on the couch-boat. Normally, passage across the screen is smooth, along a single plane. When he begins to pass through arches by crossing in front of the right-hand pillar and behind the left-hand pillar of the arch, a sense of depth emerges without the illusion of diminishing into the vanishing point of the screen.

The circularity of the film's form, the use of nineteenth-century engravings, and above all the theme of the mutable woman recall Max Ernst's collage novel, *La Femme 100 Têtes* (1929), whose title in French puns as the woman with a 100 (*cent*) heads or the woman without (*sans*) heads. That novel, in collage pictures, begins and ends with the same image. Within it are sections and subsections built on varying degrees of thematic and narrative sequence. Whenever a series of plates has a specific narrative and therefore temporal logic, Ernst introduces another image or images into the collage which does not follow the same unity of time or scale.

The collages abound in complex machinery and scenes of violence and dismemberment. Studying the images in sequence, the reader experiences promises of narration which continually evaporate or transform into chains of metaphor. The ultimate unity of the book is that of the dream. Harry Smith has said that he let his dreams determine the filming of *No. 12*. According to his account, he slept fitfully in the studio where he was filming for the entire year in which the film was being shot. He would sleep for a while, then animate his dreams. The exact relation between his dreams and the structure of the film is ambiguous, unless we can suppose that he dreamed the life of the figures he had already cut out and assembled for his film. What is more likely is that he established an intuitive relationship between the structure of his dreams and the substructure of the film.

In 1971 at Anthology Film Archives Smith spontaneously delivered a lecture to a group of students he happened upon in that theater. As they were looking at a film, not by him, in the realist tradition—a film of photographed actuality—he said, "You shouldn't be looking at this as a continuity. Film frames are hieroglyphs, even when they look like actuality. You should think of the individual film frame, always, as a glyph, and then you'll understand what cinema is about."

It is certainly true that within Smith's own work the hieroglyph is essential. When he finally began to shoot actualities for No. 14 (1965), he translated the spatial and temporal tactics of his earlier films into superimposed structures. From an opening reel—for the film is made up of whole, unedited one hundred foot reels of film multiply-exposed in the camera—in which relatively flat and carefully controlled surfaces (a composition of a store window or animated objects) are laid upon images of depth (receding night lights or rooms), the film proceeds to more random conjunctions of autobiographical material, from interiors to exteriors, from richly orchestrated colors to washed-out browns. In the final reels, the film gradually retraces its formal course, returning to the animated precision, spatial dialogue, and surface texture of the opening. In the center of the film Smith himself gets drunk while discussing his project for a recording of the Kiowa peyote ritual with Folkways records, and after a passage of leader—he did not even cut off the head and tail leaders that were attached to the individual rolls—we see the Kiowa and their environment. It is as if he had opened up his hieroglyphic art to make a space for a limited self-portrait.

Later he managed to fuse animation directly to live photography when he combined "The Approach to Emerald City," the most complete of the surviving fragments of No. 13, with a sequence he shot in 1968 with a teleidoscope (a projecting kaleidoscope of his own construction) while making The Tin Woodsman's Dream. The temporal hiatus between the two parts of this film apparently means nothing to Smith, who sees the whole of his work, not just his cinema, as a single edifice.

Since 1969 he has been working on Mahagonny, for which No. 14 had been preparatory. Again he speaks of it in language appropriate to the myth of the absolute film. It will be, he forecasts, a work which will diminish all that preceded it, including his own films; it will coincide with, and perhaps instigate, a new American revolution. Again the proportions seem to be growing beyond the normal range of cinema. He considers the totality of the rushes to be a work in itself—as much a station in route towards the ultimate film as No. 14, its harbinger, had been—and he speaks of projecting them on a wall made of four specially designed pool table tops and prize fight rings, reflecting the central scene of Brecht and Weill's opera upon which it is loosely but devoutly based, as the Cabala is based on the words of the Bible.

Jordan Belson, Smith's closest associate in their early years in San Francisco, has made a contribution to the graphic film of comparable magnitude. Curiously, like Smith, he made a teleidoscopic film, *Raga* (1959), as well as at least one effort at dealing with actual surfaces with the control of an animator, *Bop Scotch* (1953). But proceeding from an attitude towards time and the working process diametrically opposed to Smith's, he has suppressed these films. In Belson's formulation of the absolute film, at least until 1970, the newest work is the only *present* film; it subsumes and makes obsolete his earlier achievements.

Belson is aware of the philosophical consequences of such a commitment to the all-consuming present. He is reticent about discussing his own past, and what he does say of it underlines his distance from it. Interestingly, that reticence extends to discussions of the "past" of the very films he willingly exhibits, particularly the techniques of their making. Yet he is eager to discuss the spiritual sources of his films. This is not inconsistent, as the films aspire to incarnate those source experiences and save them from time. They are transcendental, and their maker is a transcendentalist.

Jordan Belson too began his career as a painter and soon allied himself with Smith and the Kandinsky-Bauer tradition, although, to judge from his scrolls from the early fifties, he never committed himself to hard-edged geometry. Instead, he located his style in proximity to the later paintings of Kandinsky where the rigidly defined forms give way to a more atmospheric abstractionism and a painterly treatment of line and shape.

The few early films I have managed to see grow out of and inform the paintings, for there is an undisguised will toward movement in the scrolls. Belson graduated from the California School of Fine Arts in 1946 (just two years before Peterson gave his first film-making course there), and the next year, inspired by the screenings at Art in Cinema, he made his first film, *Transmutation* (1947), which is now destroyed. According to the film-maker, it was made under the immediate inspiration of seeing Richter's *Rhythmus 21*. *Improvisations* #1, from the following year, is also lost.

The earliest surviving films date from the beginning of the 1950s: *Mambo* (1951), *Caravan* (1952), *Mandala* (1953), and *Bop Scotch* (1953). The first three describe a gradual movement toward meditative imagery and rhythms. From the rather expressionistic oval forms, bright colors, and calligraphic designs of *Mambo*, which at times resembles the texture of William Baziotes' paintings, Belson refined his imagery in *Caravan*, emphasizing both the geometrical (radiating circles against moving backgrounds) and the biomorphic (serpentine and spermatoid shapes). Although the yin-yang emblem finds its way into *Caravan*, it is the subsequent film, *Mandala*, that definitively aspires to be an object of meditation in the oriental tradition, as its name indicates. The geometry of *Mandala* is even more emphatic than in the earlier film. The transformations are slower, and there are discrete jumps in positions. For the first time a discrete pulse gives a regular rhythm to the entire film.

After another period of concentration on his painting, Belson was led back to cinema after collaborating with the composer Henry Jacobs on the Vortex concerts of abstract and cosmic imagery with electronic sound at the San Francisco Planetarium (1957-9). Of the finished and abandoned films from this period, *Flight* (1958), *Raga* (1959), *Seance* (1959), *Allures* (1961), *LSD*, and *Illusions* (dates uncertain), the author has seen only *Allures* and the teleidoscopic film *Raga*. They represent the termination of his initial conception of cinema and forecast the transition to his mature style, which emerges after still another renunciation of cinema—this time in a profound despair over the value of art. Simply stated, the early films, up until and including *Allures*, are objects of meditation. The subsequent works, his nine major films, describe the meditative quest through a radical interiorization of mandalic objects and cosmological imagery.

Allures is actually the filmic result of Belson's experience with the Vortex concerts in the late fifties. Although it blends images of becoming and apperception (dissolving and congealing spheres, color flickers, hot spots of light) with its predominantly geometrical and mechanically symmetrical patterns, it comes short of delineating a perceptual process in its overall structure. These moments of organic metamorphosis bind together and bracket the electro-astronomical imagery (expanding rings, receding circles, emerging spirals, eclipses, oscilloscopic lines, dot grids, and spheres of orbiting pin-point lights) which forms the center of attention in the film.

Belson acknowledges a debt to James Whitney as his instructor in the mandalic potential of the graphic film. Aside from the film exercises he made with his brother John, James Whitney has made two films of his own, *Yantra* (1950-55) and *Lapis* (1963-66). The latter is the most elaborate example of a mandala in cinema. It utilizes a field of tiny dots, symmetrically organized in hundreds of very fine concentric rings, to generate slowly changing intricate patterns which are most precise in the center of the wheel, disintegrating at the outer rings. The film consists of movements into the center of this wheel of dots, which at first expands beyond the borders of the frame, and movements away from it, showing its circular boundaries. Changes of color, scale, speed, and dot pattern attend the visual movements, but they are orchestrated in time so as to suggest a formal circle, the opening images and color flicker being almost exactly repeated at the end. Both structurally and visually *Lapis* conforms to the circular form of the mandala; its elaborate movements belie a fundamental stasis.

None of Belson's early films are classical mandalas, but they all have the objective vehicles of meditation. According to the film-maker, they represent the "impersonal" phase of his career. That single word describes the fate of modernist geometrical art in the American avant-garde film. Like the trance film, the graphic film flourished in the first years after the war and then failed to sustain its vitality into the 1950s. We have seen how Harry Smith's art veered from the geometrical to the mythopoeic without abandoning animation, and in the next chapter I shall show how the graphic film was renewed in Europe by an American and an Austrian. Belson's successive resignations from film-making, James Whitney's retirement after *Lapis*, John Whitney's silence until the cybernetic alternative renewed his inspiration in the late 1960s, and Len Lye's fate, all attest the exhaustion of a formalist cinema in America.

When Belson gave up film-making in the early sixties, he diverted his creative energy to the practice of Hatha yoga. When the Ford Foundation offered him one of their coveted $10,000 grants in 1964, he turned them down. But after reconsidering, he accepted the money and reentered film-making with *Re-Entry*, the first of his "personal" films. For Belson the opposition of impersonal to personal art does not indicate an antithesis of geometrical formalism to Expressionism. As a yogi, Belson

seeks the transcendence of the self. His personal cinema delineates the
mechanics of transcendence in the rhetoric of abstractionism.

He has turned to yogic and Buddhist texts for guidance or confirmation
of his cinematic structures. Olaf Stapleton's science fiction novel, *Star
Maker*, also has the authority of a sacred text for Belson, and it provides
an alternative index to his vision. Stapleton's novel describes the cosmic
explorations of a man suddenly transported from his body as he sits in
contemplation behind his conventional British cottage. It is an odyssey
that proceeds from mildly Swiftean visions of life on planets similar to
Earth to an apocalyptic revelation of the hierarchical consciousness of
stars, galaxies, and the very cosmos, in stages that suggest a profound debt
on Stapleton's part to Hegel's *Phenomenology of the Spirit*. After attain-
ing the supreme moment of confrontation with the Star Maker, the consciousness of Stapleton's hero shrinks again into the spatial and temporal
coordinates of human perception and reanimates his body, as if no time
had passed. Although Stapleton, whose futuristic vision is fused with socialist utopianism, repeatedly discredits the meditative life within the
novel, Belson has obviously synthesized the psycho-theological elements of
this extraordinary novel with the Yogic diagram of the interior *chakras*—
or wheels—and other coordinates of Buddhist cosmology.

If one reads *Star Maker* with Belson in mind, it is difficult not to see
the circuitous astral journey of its protagonist as an allegory of his situation as an artist, withdrawing from art to discipline his meditation and
then returning to reveal in art the course of that meditation, as the narrator of the novel returns to his body to write the novel we have been
reading. Hearing the film-maker talk of this book, it becomes apparent
that he was not only greatly influenced by it but that it contained much
that he had independently come upon in his own speculations. Stapleton's
romance provided the scaffolding upon which he could organize some of
his perceptions, and perhaps most important of all, it offered a metaphysical diagram, comparable to what he discerned in Buddhist and Yogic
texts, but of a different order, so that by alternating intellectually between
the two he could maintain his independence from a religious orthodoxy
which might smother his art.

In *Re-Entry* he successfully synthesizes the Yogic and the cosmological
elements in his art for the first time by forcefully abstracting and playing
down both of them. The great advance of this film over all of his earlier
work consists in the organization of its images into an intentional structure. From an opening of symmetrically ordered dots, moving along the

plane of the flat screen and along illusionary lines of depth, the film moves, as if impelled by a directional force, through a fluid series of gaseous colors with a single metaphoric allusion to solar prominences. A second metaphor, the abstraction of a waterfall, focuses the amorphous bands of color into a series of vivid veils lifting to reveal the formation of a spherical vortex which congeals in the final moment into a planet, as if the whole thrust of the film had been towards this one point.

In his very useful description of this and the subsequent three Belson films, Gene Youngblood has to go to the vocabulary of the color chart to portray the changes within the film, from "pale manganese blue" to "cobalt violet" and "alizarin crimson." He also informs us, presumably on the film-maker's authority, that the twin sources of the film were John Glenn's first satellite voyage and the *Tibetan Book of the Dead*, and he interprets the structure of the film as "leaving the earth's atmosphere (death), moving through deep space (karmic illusions), and re-entry into the earth's atmosphere (rebirth)."

With the making of his next film, *Phenomena* (1965), Belson elaborated on the teleological structure. He gave it the same thrust towards its ending—a passage through gaseous space toward a climactic image—but he also elaborated an opening drive away from concrete imagery into the gaseous spectrum of the center. This time the flow of consciousness is not cyclic, as in *Re-Entry*; it is transcendent, from the phenomena of nature to the final apperceptive union of the planet with the pupil of the eye.

Youngblood quotes Belson, who described the film as

> an extremely capsulized history of creation on earth, including all the elements and man. It's the human sociological-racial experience on one level, and it's a kind of biological experience in the sense that it's physical. It's seen with the blinders of humanity, you know, just being a human, grunting on the face of the earth, exercising and agonizing. There's even a touch of the Crucifixion in there—a brief suggestion of a crown of thorns, a red ring of centers, each emitting a kind of thorny light cluster. The man and the woman are Adam and Eve if they're anyone. I see them as rather comic at that point. At the end of course it's pure consciousness and they're like gods. The end of the film is the opposite of the beginning; it's still life on earth but not seen from within, as *sangsara*, but as if you were approaching it from outside of consciousness so to speak. From cosmic consciousness. As though you were approaching it as a god.

The man and woman referred to are abstracted faces, possibly photographed through a stippled glass off a television screen near the beginning of the film. They are presented in a montage of colors, shapes, and textures unusually collisive for Belson, pulsating to a rock-like electronic beat. This frenetic and elliptical sequence is what he meant by the "capsulized history," although the two human figures are its only emblematic images. (The reference to the Crucifixion in the clusters of brilliant red sparks against a blue base is more a personal association than a factor in the force of the film.)

Sound plays a crucial role in accenting the changes in the film and in paragraphing phrases of its montage. Belson is not always as successful in his soundtracks as he is in *Phenomena*. Sound is crucial to his illusionism. He aspires to an absolute synthesis so that "you don't know if you're seeing it or hearing it." But in *Cosmos* and in *World*, one of his best films, the electronic scores he commissioned embarrass the imagery. He is close to Harry Smith in his flexibility. They both used jazz records as the backgrounds of their earliest films; later they proved they could be brilliant in handling sound (Smith in *No. 12*, Belson in *Phenomena* and *Chakra*), but they nevertheless continue to use the most mundane "accompaniment" on occasion. Belson is to some extent responsible for the unfortunate soundtrack of James Whitney's *Lapis*. He convinced him it needed sound, and the film-maker then banalized his vision with the use of excerpts from a raga.

However, in *Phenomena*, Belson supports the rhythm of his images by carefully selected and abstracted sound, and he also creates an audible movement from irony to purity. The opening abstraction of rock music is itself an element in the image of *sangsara*—the frantic vision of life from the perspective of a mind limited to following its appearances, the "phenomena" of the title. The soundtrack ends, appropriately, in applause.

In the rise beyond appearances, the echoing distortions of a passage of German lieder inaugurate a sequence of patterned imagery. The screen becomes grids of symmetrical cells, changing their vibrant colors in waves. The progressive dissolution of these geometrical fields, as the fragmented song becomes a buzz, extends the metaphor of a movement implicit in the succession of geometrical abstraction following the colliding textures and images. That movement reaches its end in the center of the film—the gases of pure color, which in turn begin their own intentional motion towards a new concretion. They pull first vertically, then horizontally across the screen until a central vortex forms. It crystalizes into a planetary sphere which in the final image becomes the negative center of the positive space around it—the teleological image of an immense eye. This meta-

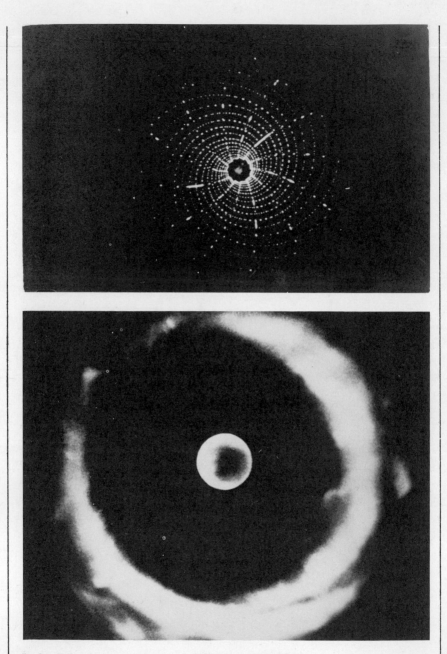

Jordan Belson's cosmic geometry in *Allures* and *Samadhi*.

phor is as close as Belson ever comes to the self-reflexive. Both his illusionism and his cosmology repudiate apperception. His films seem to postulate that once the consciousness begins its transcendental movement, the self upon which it might then look back vanishes; they do not accept the post-Romantic paradoxes which define the horizons of so many other films in the American avant-garde tradition, and this is both a weakness and a strength.

Even an art as deeply indebted to Eastern metaphysics as Belson's does not find its tradition in Eastern religious art, much as it might aspire to it and derive images or forms from it. The aesthetic use of oriental thought is a Romantic tradition, and a particularly fertile one in America. Belson is closer to the Emerson of *Circles* as an artist than to Ramana Maharshi or Tibetan iconographers. "The eye is the first circle; the horizon which it forms is the second; and throughout nature this primary figure is repeated without end. It is the highest emblem in the cipher of the world." These opening lines of Emerson's essay might be the motto of *Phenomena*. Some pages later, he forecasts the scenario of Belson's next film, *Samadhi*, writing, "Yet this incessant movement and progression of which all things partake could never become sensible to us but by contrast to some principle of fixture or stability in the soul. Whilst the eternal generation of circles proceeds, the eternal generator abides. That central life is somewhat superior to creation, superior to knowledge and thought, and contains all its circles."

Samadhi recapitulates the ending of *Phenomena* in its initial moments. (From this point on it will be an interestingly deliberate strategy of Belson's to begin a new film at the point where the previous one ends.) In the middle of *Phenomena*, the gases had briefly dissolved into a bumpy, concave field resembling rows of small translucent balls melted together or perhaps an abstraction of the furrows of the cerebral cortex. Belson begins *Samadhi* with this mysterious and haunting image in several forms, as colors sweep over a rippling surface. Then he repeats a figure-ground transition which turns a planetary circle into an eye.

From this point on the film sustains an unbroken intensity, engendering a chilling ecstasy. In the center of the screen circular forms undergo a chain of transformations. Large gaseous balls revolve; small distant spheres radiate rings of fire and fill the entire frame with their outpouring luminosity. A retarded breathing sound becomes an interiorized wind. By extending respiratory pace of the breathing into electronic pitches and percussive rhythms, the film-maker created an aural counterpart to the transitions from fluid or fiery balls to hard spheres which constitute the visual center of the film.

The gaseous forms seem to expand and the luminous balls fill the entire screen with their yellow or white light, while the static rigid circles and spheres, tiny in the dead center of the image, seem to recede. The continual, slow metamorphosis of images and the illusions of emergence and recession suggest a movement on the spectator's part into the depth of the screen. It is the movement of consciousness towards *samadhi*, the union of subject and object, or the fusion of *atma* (breath) and mind. This state, which reveals the pure white light of the force called *kundalini*, is one of the principal goals of Yogic meditation.

The statements that Youngblood quotes about *Samadhi* indicate as much as can be known at this time of Jordan Belson's theory of cinema. For him, as for almost all other film-makers within the American avant-garde, the cinema is an instrument of discovery, a means of coming to know more, or more clearly, what is most essential to him: "Early in life I experimented with peyote, LSD, and so on. But in many ways my films are ahead of my own experience."[11] He cites *Samadhi* as the single example of a convergence of a meditative vision with one arising out of the experience of film-making: "In fact *Samadhi* is the only one in which I actually caught up with the film and ran alongside of it for just a moment."[12] But he stresses the advantage of cinema for sustaining the mystic vision:

> The film is way ahead of anything I've experienced on a continuing basis. And the same has been true of my drug experiences. They somehow set the stage for insights. I had peyote fifteen years ago but I didn't have any cosmic or *Samadhic* experiences. That remained for something to happen through development of different levels of consciousness. The new art and other forms of expression reveal the influence of mind-expansion. And finally we reach a point where there is virtually no separation between science, observation, and philosophy. The new artist works essentially the same way as the scientist. . . . But at other times the artist is able to focus more in an area of consciousness and subjective phenomena but with the same kind of scientific zeal, the same objectivity, as scientists.[13]

The particular success of discovering in the filmic material the imagery of his privileged glimpses during Yogic trances led to his version of the myth of the absolute film:

I reached the point that what I was able to produce externally, with the equipment, was what I was seeing internally. I could close my eyes and see these images within my own being, and I could look out at the sky and see the same thing happening there too. And most of the time I'd see them when I looked through the viewfinder of my camera mounted on the optical bench. I've always considered image-producing equipment as an extension of the mind. The mind has produced these images and has made the equipment to produce them physically. In a way it's a projection of what's going on inside, phenomena thrown out by consciousness, which we are able to look at. In a way I'm doing something similar to the clairvoyant Ted Serrios who can project his thoughts onto Polaroid film. Only I have to filter my consciousness through an enormous background of art and film-making.[14]

The myth of the absolute film can have no more total expression than Belson's often repeated statement that he believed he would die after making *Samadhi* and he was surprised when he did not. With the remaining "momentum" of his energies he made *Momentum* (1969). That film literalized the metaphor of interior movement from *Samadhi*. In its opening shots a rocket blasts off in several different solid colors; following its trajectory, we focus on the center of the screen, where a series of enlarging circles being eclipsed and haloed by coronas suggests that the rocket's aim is at the sun. But rather than shoot into the explosive center of the image, which in its fullest magnitude fills the screen with spectacular radiations, we seem to veer over its rim, as larger and larger disks occupy the lower portion of the screen. The passage through gases, a typical feature of Belson's cinema, here takes the concrete form of movement through multicolored solar prominences.

Once past the sun, the film attains a new dimension. Structurally, it retraces the crescendo of the first half in a visionary or interiorized version of the trip to the sun. The central trope of the interiorization is the use of tiny, swarming dots in the re-enactment of the approach to the radiating sphere, which makes that spectacular image even more dynamic. At first the dots establish a difference of depth between the surface of the screen (the consciousness of the viewer-explorer) and the circular or gaseous figure in the distance (the object of that directional consciousness). This happens when white spots dance irregularly before the vague backgrounds. After they vanish, a new "sun" forms itself, even more radiant and explosive than the first. This time the consciousness, no longer mediated by the rocket ship, flows into its very center. In that movement the star itself becomes an organized haze of atomic points, like the specks of James Whitney's *Lapis*, radiating in rings out of the stellar crater, until in a final image of the starry sky, a bright central nova seems to have exploded.

Three central principles which Belson seems to have taken from Stapleton's *Star Maker* inform the cosmology of *Momentum* and the two films which follow it, *Cosmos* and *World*. They are that human consciousness, even when it believes itself to be exploring freely, is actually guided to its goal by a greater consciousness; that human consciousness transcends itself by merging with the object which magnetized it, without losing its awareness of its history as human; and that stars, galaxies, and the very cosmos are visible bodies of consciousness in a hierarchy.

Cosmos begins at the point where *Momentum* ends; zooming through layers of stars, it continues the earlier film's thrust. At the end, it fixes an image of a galaxy in which the atomic spots of the previous film now represent whole stars; a new stage has been reached in the quest for cosmic consciousness. But between the opening and closing sections Belson has elaborated a new kind of center.

Before he completed the film, he said that he was planning to rework the footage of his abandoned film, *LSD*, by means of a video tape transfer. In the long central section of *Cosmos*, the familiar transformation of gases and manifestation of circles occur in the much flatter, electrically frazzled rhetoric of video tape. It renders the ambiguous and hazy spaces of gaseous illusionism into a surface spread across the film screen, and at the same time the breakdown of the moulding line of photographed contours in the fluctuating grain of video transmission becomes an extension of the dot technique in the second part of *Momentum*.

Neither *Momentum* nor *Cosmos* has the strength or the purity of *Phenomena* and *Samadhi*. Belson invested deeply in the authority of his astronomical metaphor as imagery and as structure, but these films are limited by the failure of the emblematic stellar phenomena to define stations of an hierarchy of consciousness. When he uses the granular image as the metaphor for the subsuming of a seemingly infinite number of individual loci into a symmetrical organism or when he allows the tension between the flatness of video imagery and the depth of illusionary cinema to describe a passage between levels of consciousness, he is discovering the tropes of his vision in the texture of his materials; but when he simply ends a film with the icon of a galaxy, he is not.

However, in his third cosmic film, *World* (1970), Belson again attains the visual level of his very best work, even though the film is constrained, like the previous two, by a banal musical soundtrack. Here he is in better control of the video material, partially because he is no longer depending upon it to sustain the entire center of the film. The function that had earlier been fulfilled by emblematic astronomical imagery is more successfully managed in *World* by an abstract geometry reminiscent of *Allures*. In fact, the whole film looks back upon the formal coordinates of *Allures*, the mixture of symmetrical, exploding geometries and atmospheric spaces, and it includes such elements as color flickers, spiralling, comet-like shapes, oscilloscopic spheres, and expanding rings of dots in a work of architectural sophistication.

The transition between mechanical and organic forms is subtly managed by acts of enclosure and expansion which alternately seem to provide matrices for each other. The film has a crescendo-diminuendo shape which organizes its rhetoric of metamorphoses around the brilliant central image of a patterned sphere of complexly-orbiting white dots. The sphere, born of a solidification of grey gases, quickly changes into waves of expanding concentric rings. The skeletal sphere is disclosed, crucially, in the middle of the film, with the solemnity of a revealed arcanum; both the gaseous and the geometrical imagery seem to point towards it or emanate from it.

Meditation (1971) elaborates upon structures of the three films immediately preceding it, but it inscribes the astronomical metaphor within imagery of foaming water in slow motion and superimposition, flowing backwards. In *World* there had been a moment when video clouds blended briefly into such imagery, but it was not central to the film. In the opening of *Meditation*, the water anticipates the key moment of the plunge. Like *Momentum*'s beginning with the rocket as mediator, this film suddenly shows a diver, gliding horizontally across the screen, then plunging into the center. After a chain of metamorphoses, mixing the least literal video and granular techniques in Belson's vocabulary with the standard rhetoric of gas-sphere transitions, the human mediator re-emerges as a planet-eye. First the planet-eye is a circular hole in a black ground through which stars can be seen, but as it enlarges, the ground dissolves into more stars, leaving the circle to be defined by its red corona. The evaporation of that corona identifies the observing consciousness (the hole) with its object (the stars). From that point the film quickly moves to its end in a revolving galaxy which returns to water through a bridge of video clouds.

Chakra (1972) attempts to improve on his masterpiece, *Samadhi*, by restating that interior quest with accent on the barriers of the different stations passed through—the *chakras* of the title—rather than on the intentional movement which had been the dynamic of the earlier film. Belson achieves an interaction of continuous propulsion with discrete, discontinuous stages by using his sound track to isolate passages of the film. By extending strong and easily identifiable sounds across a section of visual transformations, those very transformations seem to occur within the bounded section; their propulsive energy seems directed at breaking through to the next stage, represented by the use of a new sound. The series of sounds itself (the buzz of bees, a motor, rain, high-pitched static, ocean, bells, the hum of a string instrument, drums, a flute, and music swelling to a climax) came from a sound chart in Mishra's *Fundamentals of Yoga,* just as the visual shapes correspond to the outline in Govinda's *Foundations of Tibetan Mysticism.*[15] Or perhaps it would be more accurate to say that they represent a reorganization of the imagery Belson uses in most of his films (swarming dots, a galaxy, circles and spheres, a video storm) to correspond to the sequence of shapes and images the Tibetan mystics saw while contemplating the progress of the *chakras* in their meditations. Belson has said that with *Chakra* the phase of his work that began with *Re-Entry* came to an end.

9

THE GRAPHIC CINEMA: EUROPEAN PERSPECTIVES

James Broughton, Kenneth Anger, and Gregory Markopoulos lived and made films in Europe during part of the 1950s. Their aesthetics had been moulded in the 1940s in America, and the change of place did not mean a fundamental change of style or vision, despite the radical division between American and European practical film theory at that time. The avant-garde tradition in film had broken down in the early 1930s, and despite sporadic and isolated efforts at independent film-making in several countries, the only continuous and sustaining force for ambitious cinema was at the margins of the commercial industries. All three film-makers returned to America to make their major works of the 1960s. When Anger and Markopoulos went back to Europe at the end of the decade, the situation there had been changed as a result of direct American influence.

Two important figures of the American avant-garde cinema, however, began to make their first films in Europe in the early 1950s. They are Robert Breer, an American, whose cinema grew out of the painting he was doing in Paris in the early 1950s, and Peter Kubelka, an Austrian who went directly into cinema but who did not find a significant context for his art until he came to America in 1965. Breer had resettled in Palisades, New York by 1959. Although their films are obviously very different and no influence can be traced from one to the other, both have their roots in the graphic cinema of Eggeling, Richter, Duchamp, and Lye without the mediation of the Abstract Expressionistic and mythopoeic phases that I have described in the previous chapters.

Both Breer and Kubelka were only marginally aware of the early graphic cinema. Nevertheless, they each took up its premises and reduced them to

a new essence after a hiatus of more than twenty years. The similarity of
their situations, if not of their films, has produced a number of related
(sometimes in likeness, sometimes in opposition) theoretical positions
and insights, which will become evident as I discuss their films and their
theories separately. Since they both came to America as fully mature
artists, their work and thought have been resistant to certain native patterns and will therefore offer an illuminating contrast within this book.

The two fundamental works of the graphic cinema from the 1920s
made without animation are Fernand Léger's *Le Ballet Mécanique* and
Marcel Duchamp's *Anemic Cinema*. By extending a metaphor from several of his paintings into film, Léger compared a universe of human actions and everyday objects to the functions of a machine. The movements of a woman on a swing, the loop of another climbing a flight of
steps again and again, the rapid alternation of a hat and a shoe through
montage, rhythmic flashes of street scenes, and periodic prismatic distortions are compared to the operations of gears, pistons, and flywheels.
Each of the movements of both the tenor and vehicle defines a shallow or
a flat space of performance. Even the loop of the woman climbing the
stairs with her wash confines her repeated efforts to the same two or three
steps in the flight, as if a very limited depth were open to her in the potential field.

Le Ballet Mécanique is a tour de force of rhythmic and spatial strategies. Two are particularly interesting within the scope of this chapter. It
was one of the first films to employ the rapid intercutting of static scenes
to give the impression of motion—a hat stretching out to a shoe or a
triangle jumping into the shape of a circle—and perhaps the very first to
combine fragments of actual motion into purely rhythmic figures. It was
certainly the pioneer in combining both these tactics to render three-
dimensional images flat to the eye by means of the speed with which they
pass on the screen. Both Breer and Kubelka are the heirs of this strategy
as much as of the formal intricacies of the films of Eggeling and Richter.

The second formal operation of importance to us derives from Cubist
painting. It is the incorporation of printed texts to present the literal flatness of reading within the framework of conflicting, diminished depths.
Clement Greenberg has described the function of printing within the
context of Cubist painting and collage:

> [Braque] discovered that *trompe-l'oeil* could be used to undeceive as
> well as to deceive with. It could be used, that is, to declare as well as to
> deny the actual surface. If the actuality of the surface—its real, physical

flatness—could be indicated explicitly enough in certain places, it would be distinguished and separated from everything else the surface contained. . . .

The first and, until the advent of pasted paper, the most important device that Braque discovered for indicating and separating the surface was imitation printing, which automatically evokes a literal flatness. . . . Only in the next year [1911] are block capitals, along with lower case numerals, introduced in exact simulation of printing and stenciling, in absolute frontality and outside the representational context of the picture.[1]

Léger introduced the same dimension to film when he showed a title, "ON A VOLE UN COLLIER DE PERLES DE 5 MILLIONS," which as we read it makes us forget the fact that it must have been placed a certain distance from the camera in order to be filmed. It seems as if the words lie on top of the actual screen. But when he swings the camera back and forth in front of the sign, we are forced to experience that depth.

Marcel Duchamp refined the same principle in his *Anemic Cinema* (1927). He slowly intercut centered shots of rotating wheels with spiral lines on them and wheels with puns printed spirally. The lines generated optical illusions of depth into and out of the screen surface when they turned. But the sentences remain perfectly flat because they are read.

Breer made very little use of printed texts for this purpose; Kubelka none at all. But later artists of the graphic film made it a cornerstone of the participatory film, an outgrowth of the structural film which often overlaps with the graphic.

Robert Breer's first film, *Form Phases I* (1952), comes directly out of the tradition of Richter and Eggeling. A black rectangle rests in the center of the screen with a white rim around it. All of the animation occurs within the black space. Lines appear, intersect, and spread to the edges of the blackness. A consistent rhythm of frozen and moving figures establishes the following pattern: the lines slowly move to a fixed form; then that form holds still for a few seconds and cuts abruptly to another frozen figure; after that is held the same amount of time, it slowly changes, freezes, cuts to another figure, etc. The alternation of changing lines with collisions of still shapes determines the structure of this very short film. In the course of its evolution the black rectangle loses its reductive shape; the changing lines leak over into the white border, diminish the edges of the rectangle into curves, and carve sections from it.

Breer described the background of his first film in an interview with Guy Coté:

First, I was a painter. In Paris, I was influenced by the geometric
abstractions of the neo-plasticians, following Mondrian and Kandinsky.
It was big at that time, and I began painting that way. My canvasses
were limited to ·three or four forms, each one hard-edged and having its
own definite color. It was a rather severe kind of abstraction, but already
in certain ways I had begun to give my work a dynamic element which
showed that I was not entirely at home within the strict limits of neo-
plasticism. Also, the notion of absolute formal values seemed at odds
with the number of variations I could develop around a single theme
and I became interested in change itself and finally in cinema as a means
of exploring this further. I wanted to see if I could possibly control a
range of variations in a single composition. You can see that I sort of
backed into cinema since my main concern was with static forms. In fact,
I was even a bit annoyed at first when I ran into the problems of
movement.[2]

Later in the same interview he unfolds the heart of his first film when he
says of all his work, "I'm interested in the domain between motion and
still pictures." The cuts of *Form Phases I* take place between still figures,
often the mirror images of each other, and the motion variations are
bracketed by the static poles of *arche* and *telos*, the beginning from which
and the end to which lines move. The realms between stillness and motion remain the object of almost all of Breer's explorations in cinema. He
came quickly to a heightened awareness of the operation of the single
frame as the locus of the tension between the static and the moving.

In *Form Phases II* (1953) the fastest shots are three frames long in a
color animation of evolving and freezing hard-edged shapes in both reciprocal and uncoordinated movements. Reversing and varying the reductive screen-within-the-screen of his first film, he placed a thin black
border, sometimes thicker on the left, sometimes on the right, around an
almost completely white rectangle in the center. In the middle of the film,
still another reduction of the screen shape, a small rectangle with blue
diagonal stripes, appears and enlarges to the edges of the frames as the
diagonals come loose and descend across the screen in waving blue lines.
The final and most interesting tactic for generating forms out of the given
shape of the screen is the use of a black dot which moves just within the
edges of the white, black-bordered space, defining its limits.

The following year he made a loop, *Image by Images I* (1954), composed entirely of shots only one frame long. Of course, every animated
film is made by shooting one frame at a time. But conventionally only tiny
variations in the shape and position of images are permitted by animators

to give the illusion of a continuous naturalistic motion. Breer's invention was to abolish all of the slight variations and to project a continuously repeating strip of film in which each frame was essentially independent of the others. Thus any sense of continuous movement would have to be replaced by a more general notion of rapid change, an affirmation of the static in the center of the greatest speed that cinema affords. Furthermore, the endless loop confirms the stasis of the individual frames by repeating them at fixed intervals.

The same year that he experimented with the loop of *Image by Images I*, Breer made his first collage film, *Un Miracle* (1954), in collaboration with Pontus Hulten. It animates Pope Pius XII in a gesture of benediction from the Vatican balcony so that first he seems to be juggling a series of balls and then his own head. The film is only thirty seconds long. It is, however, the first manifestation of a second strain in Breer's work which runs parallel to his formalism throughout the 1950s and dominates his work in the early 1960s—the humorous cartoon.

The first film (as opposed to a loop), in which he employed the single-frame changes of *Image by Images I* was *Image by Images IV* (1956). It is not a strictly single-frame film, as none of Breer's have been in toto since the original experiment: single-frame variations on line figures, both open and closed into geometrical shapes, numbers, and flickering colors collide with graceful continuous lines, with movements in clusters that are repeated several times with variations. Breer employs some interplay of positive and negative space—that is, ground becomes figure and the reverse—but it is not as prominent as in the earlier abstract films. There is also a certain amount of movement across and off the screen which punctuates the more important rapid exchange between centric circles and uncentered lines. For the first time, he gave this film a soundtrack: rapid sputtering noises similar to, if not actually sprocket holes passing the sound reader.

Retreating temporarily from his investigations of high-speed imagery, he made *Motion Pictures* (1956) the same year. In a filmography he described it as an "evolution of forms derived from the author's paintings." Against a black field, constantly changing colored strips of paper cross the screen, meet each other, and deflect at angles. Each encounter of two edges of the paper creates a possible transformation of direction, angle, color, and scale. At one point he modifies the texture of his materials by using a thick white paper towel. This time the soundtrack is made up of discontinuous sounds of a violin. *Motion Pictures* remained the most elaborate of Breer's achievements in the strict tradition of Eggeling and Richter.

With his next film, *Recreation I* (1956-57), Breer made his first major contribution to the alternative graphic film tradition, that of Léger and *Le Ballet Mécanique*. Here he elaborated the single-frame technique of *Image by Images I* and *IV* into a complex micro-rhythmic form, with the fastest possible stretches of imagery (single-frame sequences) interrupted by and evolving into just slightly longer shots of a few frames. The speed of the alternations tends to flatten the appearance of objects in the single-frame shots so that they expand into a somewhat deeper space when the merest extension of their duration occurs. Besides the hundreds of successive shifts in degrees of shallow depth, there is a coordinated tension between the stasis of the single frames and the minute, fragmented figures in motion when brief continuities occur.

Along with collages of colored paper, a moire pattern, and a piece of typewritten paper, *Recreation I* uses numerous solid objects of differing degrees of depth: buttons, a mechanical mouse, a jackknife, plastic film reels, a glove, a cat, string, the animator's hand, and most strikingly, a wad of paper expanding after compression. Almost all of the images appear twice, but not in a symmetrical pattern; often they are inverted and the number of frames allocated to them is not the same for each appearance. The effect of these numerous variations within a very limited range of depths and durations is to create a dense pattern of interlocking and incomplete rhythms accented by slight, discontinuous movements within the frame which the eye can organize into a complex unity.

Noel Burch, who wrote and speaks the run-on punning French speech which accompanies the film like a Dadaist commentary, accurately compared the total impression of this film to the collages of Kurt Schwitters.[3] Breer himself made a statement about the structure he generally prefers for his films, which is particularly appropriate here:

> I think of film as a "space image" which is presented for a certain length of time. As with a painting, the image must submit to the subjective projection of the viewer and undergo a certain modification. Even a static painting has a certain time dimension, determined by the viewer to suit his needs and wishes. In film, the period of looking is determined by the artist and imposed on the spectator, his captive audience. A painting can be "taken in" immediately, that is, it is present in its total self at all times. My approach to film is that of a painter—that is, I try to present the total image right away, and the images following are merely other aspects of and equivalent to the first and final image. Thus

the whole work is constantly presented from beginning to end and, though in constant transformation, is at all times its total self. Obviously, then, there is no denouement, no gradual revelation except for constantly changing aspects of the statement, in the same manner in which a painting is subjectively modified during viewing.[4]

In an article on the cinema, called "A New Realism—The Object," which equates "the realism of the cinema" with "the possibilities of the fragment or element," Fernand Léger calls for a new kind of film-maker:

New men are needed—men who have acquired a new sensitiveness toward the object and its image. An object for instance if projected for 20 seconds is given its full value—projected 30 seconds it becomes negative.[5]

In *Recreation I* Breer took up the challenge of Léger, but in a direction of heightened speed that the maker of *Le Ballet Mécanique* had not quite anticipated. In the same article, Léger said that "All current cinema is romantic, literary, historical-expressionist, etc." He is using the terms "romantic" and "expressionist" in a vague and popular sense, but they apply precisely when used to define his tradition, as Breer manifests it, in contrast to the late Romantic (and Abstract Expressionist) aesthetic I have mentioned in the earlier chapters of this book.

Although there is a concrete pattern in the development of Breer's work, it is not one that touches upon the trance film, the mythic film, or the structural film (even though—and this makes the matter complex—the structural cinema has been influenced by his achievements). The absence of these forms is not as significant as the absence of the aesthetic which generates them. The Romantic film-maker looks on the cinema as an instrument of self-discovery or mythopoeic discovery; the process of making a film becomes a quest for the film's often problematic content.

In terms of painting, both American and European art was irrigated by Cubism and neo-plasticism after the Second World War. In Europe, Surrealism died as a painterly force. The heirs of Mondrian and Kandinsky accepted their geometry but rejected the Neo-Platonic and theosophic framework in which it had been first expressed. In America, on the other hand, the Surrealist aesthetic merged with Cubism to influence the most Romantic school of twentieth-century painting, the generation of Pollock, Still, Newman, and De Kooning. Robert Breer's aesthetic was formed in Paris just after the war, within the sphere of post-Mondrian abstractionists.

In an interview Breer stated:

I started in Europe and I feel that my orientation was somewhat European. As a painter I was working out of Bauhaus traditions while Abstract Expressionism was getting going here, you know, coming out of Surrealism. . . . It's true that my films had their roots in European experimentation of the Twenties. . . . Another European aspect of my work might be that it is more conventionalized than that of the Americans. The Abstract Expressionists, and so forth, were working in a sort of anti-conventional way, trying for direct expression, while I was happy working out of conventions. I like this idea of limitations which you break all the time. The limitations have to be there, if they're self-imposed or if they come through some kind of historical inheritance, as mine are. I'd set up conventions on a film and then play with those within them.[6]

The first part of this statement is a lucid appraisal of the difference between his work and that of his American colleagues. His stance in regard to conventions has varied as his work has changed. The earliest films he made, between 1952 and 1957, grew out of the norms of geometrical painting into those of the graphic film, with important modifications of both. But beginning with *A Man and His Dog Out for Air* (1957), he made animated cartoons until 1964. They include *Inner and Outer Space* (1960), *Horse Over Teakettle* (1962), *Breathing* (1963), and the climactic *Fist Fight* (1964), in which cartooning broke up and led back to the fast motion cinema of his earlier works.

In the cartoon films there is a shift in his working process. Instead of creating the film directly in front of the camera as he was shooting it, he began to draw the lines and figures of individual frames on paper and cards. By flipping through the cards he could approximate the experience of the film. The actual shooting became more of an exercise in translation than creation. In an interview with Jonas Mekas, he spoke of *Recreation* as having been made

in a kind of deliberate feeling of wonderment: "What the hell will this look like?" you know, that kind of thing, and "I don't want to know . . . whether this is cinema or not; it doesn't matter." Then I would go back and try to incorporate some notions of control and construction.[7]

By introducing the middle step of creation on cards, he refined his animation but diminished the dynamics achieved in his first works.

In terms of the whole of Breer's work, the issue of conventions is less important than that of image content. It is there that he differs fundamentally from most of the Romantic film-makers. There is always a dis-

tance between him and the subjects of his films: he is an extreme formalist. He will choose the familiar—buttons, knife, string, a wad of paper; the
abstract—transforming geometrical shapes; the simple—a tangle of moving
lines eventually resolving into the cartoon of a man walking a dog; or conventional cartoon imagery—comic human figures and animals—as the object of his formal manipulations. The distance between his subjects and
the cinematic strategies he applies to them is neither ironic nor problematic. The weight of his interests as an artist lies in the creation and breakdown of illusions. This, he seems to believe, becomes clearest when the
materials of the illusions are depersonalized (and demythologized), or as
he has said, "conventional."

A letter about his undeveloped interests in three-dimensional films (inspired by a three-dimensional shadow play of Ken Jacobs) led to a discussion of his general aspirations in making art:

> It has to do with revealing the artifices instead of concealing them. The
> fact of that rabbit sitting inside the magician's hat is the real mystery,
> not how it's dissimulated. The hat should be transparent and show the
> rabbit.
> So it's again the threshold area that defines the form. Thresholds for
> my own exploration have been:
> 1. The fusion of stills into flowing motion and back again (flip cards,
>   collage film, sculpture).
> 2. Transition from literary convention to other—i.e., abstraction and
>   back again (collage films—Pat's B'day).
> 3. Transition from subconscious to conscious awareness—i.e., slow
>   motion sculpture, fast paced film.
> 4. Transition from 2D to 3D—transparent mutoscopes and cut out
>   sculpted mutoscopes—rotating bent wires.[8]

Naturally the notion of the "threshold" is more vital to Breer's aesthetic
than that of "conventions." Conventions are, in fact, a means for him to
come upon a threshold more immediately. Of the four realms of exploration, the first is the most important; for it extends throughout his work
and tends to encompass the other three. In *Jamestown Baloos* (1957) and
Eyewash (1959), he integrated the techniques of his earliest animations
with those of *Recreation I* in a process of questioning and defining the
boundaries between still and moving images, and the corollary distinction
between "actualities" and flat pictures.

Jamestown Baloos jarringly juxtaposes all of his previous techniques and
aesthetic strategies and invents a few more. The film has a triptych form
of two black-and-white sections with martial soundtracks bracketing a si-

lent one in color. In changes of tempo from very rapid to moderately slow and back again, he switches from the hand-drawn outline of a figure or an object to a magazine collage of that figure or the object itself. In all three parts he mixes satiric collages of Napoleon and the instruments of warfare with glimpses of landscapes and abstract textures and geometries, but he keeps the film in an unresolved suspense by subverting the viewer's psychological urge to fix one of these elements as the central theme and reduce the other two to sub-themes.

The transitions between themes within the three sections revolve around thresholds between motion and stillness. A series of watercolors, each on the screen for three or four frames, vibrates before the lens as if they were quickly shaken by hand. Collage gondolas move against static cityscapes of Venice. Then a barrage of single-frame landscapes by old masters rushes across the screen. They are arranged so that a tree or an image in one occupies approximately the same place in the next, giving a sense of continuity amid violent change. Finally Breer incorporates very short shots of actual landscapes, whose spatial expanses are revealed in fragmentation by a few panning frames after or before a brief hold. The mesh of flat work and photography in depth, with the pronounced accent on the former, is so fine and subtle that the film does not lose its carefully balanced tension in these transitions.

Most of *Eyewash* derives from photography of actual entities rather than from collages, drawings, or flat photographs. Reflections of light on water, blurred fast panning motions, passing trucks filmed through a telephoto lens, a rolling ball, single-frame street scenes, and a humorous and exciting shot of a workman just at the point of sawing through a blue plank, are the crucial images here. Breer cuts on motion, shifting depths, speeds, colors, and directions in the shot-to-shot junctures, while he organizes the whole film in terms of repeated images and waves of rhythmic intensity and relaxation. *Eyewash* anticipates many of Stan Brakhage's *Songs*, made a decade later, but it lacks the visionary coherence and passionate commitment that Brakhage with the advantage of ten years of development was able to bring to his materials. More than any other film of Breer's, this one recalls the strategies of *Le Ballet Mécanique*, especially when Léger moves out of his studio and organizes his glimpses of Paris into a chain of associations.

With *Eyewash* Breer ended his work in defining the threshold between flat animation and photographed actuality by means of freezes and movements fractions of a second long. He would return to the combination of both types of imagery in *Fist Fight* (1964) but through utterly different means. Most of his subsequent cinema has been flatwork, with two significant exceptions, *Hommage to Jean Tinguely's Hommage to New York* (1960) and *Pat's Birthday* (1962), both studies of the work of other artists for whom he has had an affinity, Jean Tinguely and Claes Oldenburg. After finishing *Eyewash*, Breer moved back to the United States. His return coincided with the decline of Abstract Expressionism as the dominant movement in American painting and slightly preceded the emergence of Pop Art.

Tinguely and Oldenburg are both makers of comic objects, toward which they maintain a psychological distance alien to the Romantic commitment of the Abstract Expressionist to his works. It seems natural then that they are the artists toward whom he would gravitate and with whom he would associate. The two films on these artists represent the severest deviation from his Parisian work. He had introduced cartoon elements into several of his early films, especially *Cats* (1956) and *Par Avion* (1957). But after his return to America the cartoon dimension grew as his concern with radical speed diminished but did not disappear. In *Horse Over Teakettle* (1962) he directly attacked the conventions of the cartoon while working within it. There he stuck to colored crayon drawings of a woman with an umbrella, a frog, and other easily identifiable creatures and objects. However, he transforms and moves these conventional figures within an intricate orchestration of expectations and surprises involving changes of scale, direction, virtual depth, and above all movement off the screen at all four edges.

Of the American films he made before *Fist Fight*, only *Blazes* (1961) touches upon his central concern with the border in cinema between motion and stillness. Here he painted one hundred cards with bold, free-drawn shapes and rough calligraphic lines; then he shuffled them and photographed them in irregular alternations of one and two frames each. With each shuffling he varied the rhythm of durations. There are short sections in which two images flicker between each other in single-frame changes; there are also single frames inserted after twenty of blackness, and some are held up to half a second on the screen. In the end he zooms in on a series of cards with three or four frames for each movement. A loud clicking sound gives an auditory equivalent to the rush of similar and recurrent designs before the eyes.

At the same time he translated his principles of animation into sculpture. By hand-cranking his mutoscopes of slightly varied cards, the observer

could control the degree of stillness or motion and thus provide himself
with the illusion of continuous change or destroy that illusion. The mutoscopes also provided a means of breaking down the theatrical situation of
cinema, which Breer has always held in suspicion. In two interviews he said:

> I got disoriented by the theatrical situation of film, by the fact that you
> have to turn out the lights and there is a fixed audience, and when you
> turn out the lights you turn on the projection light and you project the
> piece of magic on the wall. I felt that this very dramatic, theatrical situ-
> ation in some ways, just by the environment of the movie house, robbed
> some of the mystery of film from itself. The idea to make mutoscopes
> was to bring movies again into a gallery situation, where I can have a
> concrete object, which gave this mysterious result in motion.
>
> All my art ideas have to do with material I was using. . . . I wanted
> to examine it more closely, and bring it into the open, to expose it.[9]

In the middle of the decade, Breer's sculptural work shifted from
making mutoscopes to constructing objects that moved so slowly that
they would seem stationary when directly observed, but when ignored for
a period of time their shift of location would be obvious. At the same time,
the dimensions of the single frame re-emerged in his films with increased
vigor and purity.

Fist Fight, unlike any other of Breer's films, is autobiographical. In it he
contemplates and manipulates "still" images from his past in what is apparently a moving family album. Black-and-white photographs of his wife
as a girl, of himself at his work table, of children, a wedding party, and
many friends and personal scenes are scrambled together with fragments
of cartoons (including a quotation from *Horse Over Teakettle*), a handwritten letter passing too fast to be legible, fingers, a bare foot, a mouse in a
cartoon trying to turn on a lamp, and a real mouse falling through black
space—to isolate a few of the more striking images.

By treating the photographs as he had the geometrical shapes of his earlier animations, Breer seems to be trying to distance himself from these
images of his life. The personal material blends into the animations and
fragments without assuming a privileged emphasis. At times it seems as if
they were not personal pictures at all, but simply the most convenient
photographs for a film intensely determined to explore further ambiguities
of stillness and motion, painterly surface and illusory depth.

The film articulates itself in bursts separated by sections of blackness.
In each burst a technique or series of images may dominate or provide a
matrix, but all the elements (photographs, cartoons, abstractions) occur

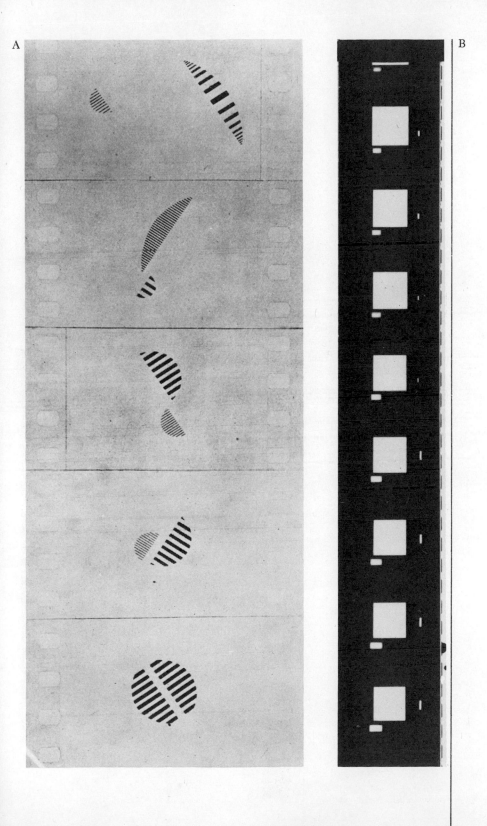

A   B

C

The graphic cinema:
sequential strips from
(A) Viking
Eggeling's *Symphonie Diagonale*
(not consecutive frames);
(B) Hans Richter's *Rhythmus 21*;
(C) Robert Breer's *69*; and
(D) Peter Kubelka's *Schwechater*.

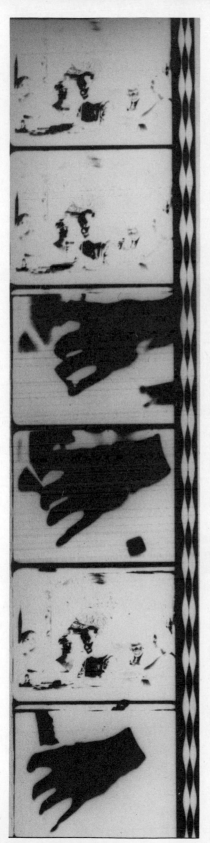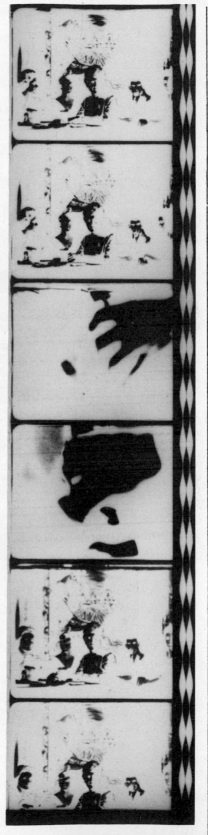

D

in each cluster. At first the flickering alternation of photographs and later the cartoon elements seem to be the center of concentration, yet the film resists giving a sense of development. In a note for *Pat's Birthday*, Breer had written, "Why things happen after each other in this film is because there isn't room for everything at once. But it's really a still picture and time is not supposed to move in one direction any more than it does in the other."[10] Although he does end that film with a recapitulation in brief shots of the actions already seen, *Pat's Birthday* follows the course of a day's outing, but in *Fist Fight* the tension between the human lives schematically depicted in the photographs and the recurrent bursts of images comes closer to the atemporality he claimed for the earlier film. Since *Fist Fight*, at eleven minutes, is the longest of Breer's films after the leisurely-paced thirteen minutes of *Pat's Birthday*, it takes on a quality of duration foreign to his earlier work; some of the image clusters seem as long and as integral as *Recreation* or *Blazes*.

Had Breer chosen to use the penultimate scene as the last, it would have resolved the tensions he elaborated earlier. In that section, he wrenched the camera off the animation table while it was still running. Then he walked out of his studio with it, filming the walls and his shoes as he went, until he was in the open and could photograph the sun. By returning to the bursts of animation and photographs after this gesture, he further maintained the equilibrium of the phrases and qualified the most expressionistic moment yet to occur in his cinema.

After *Fist Fight* Breer made three remarkably controlled animated films which return to the forms and themes of his earliest work but with more power and confidence than ever before. These three closely-related films, 66 (1966), 69 (1969), and 70 (1970), place Breer for the first time among the major colorists of the avant-garde. Each film sets itself a clearly-defined problem involving color, speed, illusion, and image-shape, and even though they are unquestionably units of a series, they do not overlap or borrow from each other. Each fully satisfies its own postulated conditions of operation; seen together they clarify the subtle problems the film-maker has posed for cinema.

In *Recreation* and *Blazes* the film-maker had explored the speeding up of perception through extended series of single frames of essentially different images strung together. In 66 he made the single frame seem to move faster by injecting it into a static, long-held, geometrical composition. When the eye is confronted by a cluster of different single-frame shots, it adjusts to seeing each of them. As the adjustment succeeds, the

$\frac{1}{24}$ of a second seems to grow longer. But when the eye relaxes on a continuous image, the sudden insertion of a single frame of something different seems much faster.

In 66 Breer deals with the problem of color in terms of the problem of speed by perception. He made a series of colored cards by cutting and applying shapes of zippetone, a highly reflective plastic tape. When filmed, the zippetone colors create evener and more vibrant hues than photographed surfaces that have been painted or colored by crayon. Breer's central strategy in this film was to place a colored shape with a white background on the screen for several seconds, then to interrupt it with another, usually smaller shape of a different color placed in what would be the background area of the initial image. The difference of color and the eccentricity of placement of the single-frame shot tended to cause a slight visual overtone when the first image reappeared.

For the most part 66 consists of a series of such images and their interruptions. Toward the middle of the film the interruptions become progressively more frequent; there are clusters of interruptions, flickering exchanges of two images, and even slight suggestions of movement in an otherwise completely static film. There are no illusions of depth or allusions to off-screen space. At the apex of speed in the middle of the film, two and sometimes even more shapes seem to move in different directions in flickering alternations. The movement seems to exist at this point to emphasize, by contrast and by the suggestion of its potential, the stasis upon which 66 is founded.

Breer's next film, 69, deals directly with depth illusions and achieves its color effects by almost completely reducing the film to black-and-white. The background for shapes is again white, except when the film slowly fades toward dark gray or tints the whole surface blue. Against this whiteness the outline figures of a hexagonal column, a wheel, a beam, and a door seem to sweep onto the screen from an off-screen axis and move through the screen's cubic space in depth. The column, which is the first and the pace-setting form, cuts through the lower left hand edge of the frame and disappears in depth as if it sliced through our field of vision for a section of its circular movement. The door appears to swing inward from a base at the bottom of the screen. The plank moves like the column, but outward, hinged at the lower right, and the wheel alone crosses the screen horizontally without emerging or receding in depth.

The film derives its major rhythm from the pacing of these four periodic movements. At first they are intercut in different combinations. At their most intense, all four flicker together with one frame apiece. This not only retards their motion by four times; it destroys the illusion of depth by permitting the eye to register each position as a flat drawing. The dialogue between the literal flatness of the screen and its illusory depth takes on a further dimension when a series of flat-line forms and simple shapes make rapidly disappearing configurations in the center of the screen while the three-dimensional illusions continue to operate from the edges. At his most complex, Breer lets us see smooth movements in depth and affirmations of the flatness of the screen at the same time in flickering changes and in juxtaposition.

The activity in the center of the screen creates the first counterpoint to the rhythmic succession and alternation of the solids. A second syncopation occurs from the fragmented manifestations of color in the film. The thin lines of the outlined solids may be suddenly replaced by equally thin colored lines without breaking the flow of movement. Even more strikingly the center of the outlines will be colored for a frame and will then be white in the next as the color switches to everything outside the figure. The flickering positive-negative changes of colored space continue at an even, fast rhythm while the colors being used change continuously.

Breer transformed the geometry and intensified the colors of 69 in his next film, 70. Here he used spray paint, which spreads over his white cards as a borderless affirmation of pure color, as well as bounded solid colors. He complemented the shapelessness of the sprayed cards with a play between hard-edged and soft forms throughout the film. In its first few seconds, he reveals his approach to color and shape separately. A series of sprayed cards passes in single-frame changes. Then, in two-frame shots, an amorphous shape, more like a hole, moves across the screen, alternately white on gray and gray on white. The pure colors pass again, this time in five-frame holds. Lastly, the hole reappears, constantly changing colors and switching whiteness from figure to ground.

Rotating tubes cut through sections of deep space; triangles and rectangles revolve, turning upon the upper and lower horizontals of the frame as axes. As they overlap, the areas they hold in common take on new colors at the same two-frame rate of change that rushes all shapes within the film through the spectrum. This illusory depth is complicated by the intermeshing of a second geometry of centric circles with their own color flicker.

The final part of the film returns to the amorphous shapes and the uneven application of color, now predominantly blues. As a tilted line, like a pitched horizon, slowly rises and falls on the frame, mirror images or complementary shapes move in the same or different directions above and below it, with positive-negative transfers of figure and color every two frames.

Solid colors in rapid alternation tend to lose their vibrancy. They blend toward whiteness. Breer utilized this paling effect in 69 where color intensities were low and subtle. In 70 he regained some of the saturation of 66 with the use of the spray paints and the two-frame, rather than single-frame rhythm. Furthermore, the five-frame holds of pure colors near the beginning of the film set up an anticipation of color textures which focuses the attention on both the rapid exchange of geometrical solids in the middle and the blue gradations of sprays at the end.

In these three films Breer for the first time joined Harry Smith, Jordan Belson, and Bruce Baillie as one of the chief colorists of the American avant-garde film. He did so by formulating in a new way, and out of impulses that extend back to his earliest films, a dialogue between color and shape, which, in the different ways I have noted, lies behind each of these film-makers' achievements in color film.

The film career of Peter Kubelka runs parallel to that of Robert Breer. There is no evidence that they knew of each other's work until the second Experimental Film Festival in Brussels (1958), by which time their basic approaches to film had crystallized. On the superficial level, these two film-makers seem to have very little in common. Breer has worked primarily in different forms of animation; Kubelka never has. Breer's cinema is intimately related to his work as a painter and sculptor; film-making is the only art Kubelka practices. Breer is not a polemicist; in his occasional interviews he is casual about theoretical concerns and exceptionally modest about his own films. Kubelka has become the most determined theoretician within the avant-garde cinema since Stan Brakhage; he is also a fierce exponent of his own originality, priority, and purity of influence (which, I must add, extends to a rejection as critical fantasy of any effort to compare him with Breer or any other avant-garde film-maker). Finally, Kubelka's films do not look at all like Breer's.

Their works quite unintentionally make two fundamental points: they define through their parallel careers the course of the late graphic cinema as it developed outside the evolution of the Romantic avant-garde film in America, and they provide a backdrop against which that evolution becomes clearer and more surely proven. Since they encountered the American avant-garde film as mature artists rather than in their formative peri-

ods, we would expect to see very little of its influence in their work. Yet
the existence of *Fist Fight,* Breer's most personal film, and Kubelka's
project-in-progress, *Monument for the Old World,* as well as his change
from being skeptical of all verbalization about film to becoming a professional lecturer and theoretician, are slight deviations in their careers which
can be accounted for by their contact with the Romantic autobiographers
and mythologists of consciousness in the American cinema.

Between 1954 and the present Peter Kubelka has finished five films
which together amount to a little more than a half hour of screen time.
The first, *Mosaik im Vertrauen* (1954-55) and the most recent, *Unsere
Afrikareise* (1961-66), bracket the three graphic films he made between
1957 and 1960. The first film is so closely related to the last, and rather
different from the middle three, that I shall postpone discussion of it until I have treated the graphic films.

Before he made *Mosaik im Vertrauen* he had attended a term at the
Centro Sperimentale di Cinematographia in Rome, and despite their con-
servatism and hostility to his work, he completed his studies there in the
mid-1950s. By 1963 he had become thoroughly familiar with the history
of the cinema. It was at that time that he founded the Oesterreichesches
Filmmuseum with Peter Konlechner, of which he has remained co-curator.
How conscious he was of the graphic film tradition of the 1920s, through
its major works or through its influences, is uncertain. Nevertheless, three
of his films—*Adebar* (1957), *Schwechater* (1958), and *Arnulf Rainer*
(1958-60)—respond with progressively severe reductions to the structure
of Eggeling's *Symphonie Diagonale* and the illusionist dialectics and handling of motion in Léger's *Le Ballet Mécanique,* Duchamp's *Anemic Cinema,* and above all in Len Lye's kinetic films.

For instance, Lye's *Rainbow Dance* utilized high-contrast freeze-frames,
which Lye used as color separators, and *Trade Tattoo* included brief figures of movement made abstract by ellipsis and cutting-on rhythm. Kubelka employs both of these strategies in a rigidly deductive form in *Adebar.* When he gave a seminar on his films at New York University in the
spring of 1972 (the most public and extensive expression of his theoretical position so far), he listed the following laws as the ordering principles
of his film: 1) each shot is 13, 26, or 52 frames long; 2) the first and
last frame of every shot has been frozen at 13, 26, or 52 frames; 3) there
is a change from positive to negative or the opposite at each splice; 4) the
sound is a loop of music made by Pygmies, with four phrases each 26

frames long; and 5) when every possible combination of shots has been exhausted, the film ends.

The subject matter of *Adebar* is dancing. In fact, like all of Kubelka's films, it was a commission; in this case as an advertisement for the Cafe Adebar in Vienna. The dancers were filmed against a white wall with strong back lighting, so that in the positive shots they seem like shadows. The only guide to their depth is the eclipsing of rear dancers by those in the foreground in the two shots perpendicular to the camera. Otherwise the images look almost flat.

I have been able to distinguish six movements: a couple dancing, a girl twirling under a man's arm, a mass of dancing legs, several people rocking with their hands at their hips, and two different shots of couples dancing along a line of depth from the camera. Furthermore, there are two still shots without any intervening movement, which are almost identical. They always appear juxtaposed with negative-positive alternations. When questioned by an attentive student about these repetitions, Kubelka said it was the exception to his rules and that the two still shots, each thirteen frames long, function as a single unit. There are 64 changes of shot in the film. If Kubelka means each of the three elements of a shot (freeze, action, freeze) in positive and negative must combine with every other possible element, there would have to be hundreds of shots in the film. Like Webern's densest compositions, this film of Kubelka's gives the impression of a strictly rational genesis, but it does not make its principles evident to the perceiver.

Here lies the fundamental distinction between the form of Kubelka's graphic films and the structural cinema, whose precursor he has claimed to be. In his films he hides his orderly principles by multiplying and interchanging them. The films move so fast and are so complex that the viewer perceives their order without being aware of the laws behind them. Thus for the viewer the experience of *Adebar*, *Schwechater*, or *Arnulf Rainer*, is on the formal level not fundamentally different from that of a Brakhage film, even though the principles governing Kubelka's editing are rational and Brakhage's subjective. The structural cinema, on the other hand, depends upon the viewer's ability to grasp the total order of the film—its shape—and the principles which generate it while he is viewing it, as will be illustrated in the last chapter of this book.

The result of *Adebar*'s laws is a form remarkably similar to Breer's *Form Phases*, where a design is frozen, slowly changed into a new frozen position, then jumps to a different static form and changes. Both films employ reverse field variations in some of the cuts between static holds. This similarity results from similar attempts at purifying the achievements of the early graphic cinema. Furthermore, both forms point to an aesthetic of the single frame as the crux of an investigation of the threshold between stillness and movement.

The fundamental principle of Kubelka's film theory is that there is no movement in cinema. Every frame is a still picture. In an interview with Jonas Mekas, he says:

> Cinema is not movement. This is the first thing. . . . Cinema is a projection of stills—which means images which do not move—in a very quick rhythm. And you can give the illusion of movement, of course, but this is a very special case, and the film was originally invented for this special case. . . .
> Where is, then, the articulation of cinema? Eisenstein, for example, said it's the collision of two shots. But it's very strange that nobody has ever said *it's not between shots but between frames*. It's between frames where cinema speaks. And then, when you have a roll of very weak collisions between frames—this is what I would call a shot, when one frame is very similar to the next frame.[11]

When he made *Adebar,* the film-maker had not yet clearly formulated this position. In that film the frozen image seems to act as a surrogate for the single frame, as he came to use it in his film of the following year, *Schwechater.*

The generative laws of *Schwechater* are much more complex. 1) The intercutting between black and images follows a repetitive pattern of one frame of black, one of an image, two black, two image, four black, four image, eight black, eight image, sixteen black, sixteen image; then it begins again with one black frame, etc. 2) There are 1440 frames in the film, equaling exactly one minute of screen time. 3) There are twelve passages of both image and leader tinted red for ninety continuous frames. These colored sections become progressively more frequent as the film moves toward its conclusion. 4) Two sounds, one low and the other high, occur only during the red passages. 5) There are four different images within the film: (a) a woman sitting at a table while a hand pours beer into a glass before her; (b) a side-view of that woman drinking; (c) a group of people in a restaurant; (d) beer foaming in a champagne glass. Every other time one of these images, or as little as one frame from them, appears on the screen, it is negative. 6) Shots (a) and (b) follow an exceptionally complex rule: (a) is thirty frames long, (b) is ninety frames. These frames are considered as numbered units. Whenever Kubelka wants to use a part of shot (a), he must use that number corresponding to what its place would be in the film if the film were a simple loop. For instance, he can use the thirtieth frame from (a) as the thirtieth, sixtieth, ninetieth, etc., frame of his film. He can use the last frame of (b) as the ninetieth, 180th, etc., frame. Furthermore, he can use a given frame from these two shots only once. Whether its use is positive or negative is determined by the previous image from the same shot sequence.

In his lectures at New York University, the film-maker did not indicate by what rules he inserted parts of shots (c) or (d) or frames of white leader into the film. Nor did he indicate any law which determined how many frames of any shot he would use in the spaces provided by the first law. I assume these were to be subjective decisions.

In *Schwechater* there are many single-frame shots. No image extends for more than nine frames of what he would call "weak articulations." What we experience then when we look at *Schwechater* is a flickering, pulsating fragmentation of related gestures and movements syncopated with differing rhythms of blackness and a superimposed redness that is accented by sound. According to Kubelka, he created the structural image of fire and of a running brook through the montage of this film without recourse to images of flames or water deflected by rocks.

The purpose behind the elaborate sixth law was to sustain a sense of two simultaneous loops, one three times as long as the other, pulsing throughout the film. Its effect, however, is not quite that of a loop. The pouring and the drinking in *Schwechater* become analyzed, simultaneous motions. By intercutting them and mixing the other shots and leaders with them, Kubelka pushes them toward the condition of stasis, of which the single-frame image is the ultimate reduction. Like Breer's much later intermeshing of rotating geometrical forms in 69, rapid intercutting both flattens, slows down, and even momentarily freezes each of the illusory motions.

However, in his third graphic film Kubelka reached the extreme of his reductiveness. *Arnulf Rainer* is a montage of black-and-white leader with white sound (a mixture of all audible frequencies) and silence. For the film-maker it is an evocation of the dawn, of day and night, of thunder and lightning. The formal laws which govern its construction are considerably more elaborate than those of either previous film, and they include a wide range of subjective decisions.

The composition of *Arnulf Rainer* is so complicated that none of its formal operations can be discovered by watching the film during a normal projection. Instead, one perceives an intricate pattern of synchronous clusters of flashes and explosions of sounds mixed with asynchronous patterns which evolve, recall, or anticipate other patterns on one of the two levels of sound and picture. At times the flickering of the black-and-white frames proceeds in silence, to be followed by the same or a similar rhythm on the soundtrack while the screen stays white or black. At a different moment the sound rhythm will forecast the visual pattern which appears in silence or with a different, and therefore not synchronized sound. The whole film is interwoven with such transfers of meter from sound to picture, or the opposite, in phrases that may be (according to Kubelka's notes) 288, 192, 144, 96, 72, 48, 36, 24, 18, 16, 12, 9, 8, 6, 4, or 2 frames in duration. There are 16 sets of phrases, each one 576 frames long (24 seconds). Within each of the 16 sections except one, the metrical patterns accelerate their changes as the phrases move from the longest to the shortest in fixed stages. Since there are no distinct, visible boundaries between the sections or the phrases inside of the sections, this structure is vaguely perceived as a seemingly endless series of irregular accelerations. A psychological aftereffect helps to emphasize the subdivisions. After each wave of acceleration a transparent halo-like square seems to hover off the screen for a fraction of a second. As the pattern of changes recommences, the floating image slowly (that is, slow within the terms of speed generated by the film itself) rejoins the actual screen. Many spectators find momentary illusions of color attend this effect. The force of the after-effect is to affirm the flatness and rectangularity of the screen almost every 24 seconds of the 6.4-minute film.

The one exception to this pattern is the sixth section, which is a black and silent pause for all 24 seconds. At first it seems as if the film has ended, but it recommences with full force. Kubelka proves here that even after an intense barrage of infinitesimal visual and aural variations, an extended series of "weak articulations" immediately begins to dissolve the heightened perception of frame-to-frame variations. In his criticism of Eisenstein's claim that the raw power of cinema resides in the collision between shots, Kubelka argued that the strongest collisions are between frames, that it is not the shots which collide but the last frame of one and the first frame of the other. He would have us dispense with the very notion of the shot. What we call shot, he points out, is a series of frames with weak articulations between them; that is, a frame is exactly or almost exactly like the previous one in a conventional shot. The illusion of a moving figure in a static field is a good example of weak articulation; the only difference between two frames is a slight change in the position of the figure. Thus for Kubelka film has an absolute limit of intensity: radical changes of picture and sound every $\frac{1}{24}$th of a second. This limit is one of the poles of *Arnulf Rainer*. The other is the long black pause, the extreme of weak articulation.

The film-makers who followed Kubelka in exploring the possibilities of the flicker film in either color or black-and-white have tended to conceive it differently. For Kubelka, *Arnulf Rainer* is the absolute film, the alpha and omega, which both defines and brackets the art. For the structural film-makers who use the flicker form, it is the vehicle for the attainment of subtle distinctions of cinematic stasis in the midst of extreme speed which can be presented so as to generate both psychological and apperceptive reactions in its spectators. Although Kubelka is not closing out the possibility of such reactions, he created his film as both a definition of cinema and a generator of rhythmical ecstasy.

The enigmatic titles, *Schwechater* and *Arnulf Rainer*, like *Adebar* before them, refer to the sponsors of the films. The former was originally commissioned as an advertisement for Schwechater beer. Kubelka even let the company dictate the images (the pseudo-elegant scene of models drinking beer as if it were champagne) in order to prove to them and to himself that cinema is not a matter of imagery but of frame-to-frame articulation. Arnulf Rainer, a Viennese painter and close friend of the film-maker, commissioned a portrait of himself and his work. In the course of making it, Kubelka became interested first in a film of pure colors, then one in black-and-white, sound and silence, alternations. He titled it as a dedication, and perhaps as an apology for not completing the commission for which he was paid.

Kubelka is the only film-maker I shall discuss in this book who affirms the absolute equality of importance between images and sound in cinema. Although the metrics of *Adebar* were determined by the fact that the sound phrases repeated in it are 26 frames long and although the sounds of *Schwechater* are skillfully and integrally utilized as structural elements, neither of those films quite lives up to the extreme demands of the film-maker's aesthetic. But with *Arnulf Rainer* he succeeded in making a graphic film which gave equal importance to sound and visuals. However, it is in his first film, *Mosaik im Vertrauen* and in his most recent, *Unsere Afrikareise*, that his theories of sound montage are most fully developed.

Both films are organized around "synch events," to use his phrase. In his lectures at New York University and at Harpur College he contrasted ritualistic "synch events" in primitive societies with their cinematic employment. He described his pleasure at witnessing an African festival in which a tribe silently watched the sun set. At the very instant that the red disk of the sun touched the horizon line, a drum beat broke the silence and the ritual festivities began. The film-maker, he admits, cannot compete with the ritual shaman in the "sensuality of his materials," the real sun and the silent community. He must make do with a pale mimesis of the sun by the white screen or with photographed, secondary imagery. His advantages over the tribal shaman, however, are two: he can speed up the "synch events" from a maximum of one a day to 24 each second; he can also combine the sound of one occasion with the image from another. The first of these advantages he explored in *Arnulf Rainer*; the second in *Mosaik*, and more radically in *Unsere Afrikareise*.

The two films have comparable structures. A number of isolated events are spread through them, sometimes as parallel montage and at other times with illusions of sequential and logical connections. In the earlier film, groups of images form short scenes every time they recur, but in the later one, each shot, in the traditional sense, tends to be independent of the one before and after it, except through connections which the film-maker invented with kinetic and sound montage. A set of two or three sequential shots with the same subject or location would be the exception in this film.

The suspended elements of *Mosaik im Vertrauen* (Mosaic in Confidence) are 1) a documentary of an historic crash on the Le Mans raceway that killed several people; 2) a bum who helps a girl take in her laundry and then spends the night talking with workers in a railroad yard; 3) an elegant model-type, Michaela, and her chauffeur; 4) a cocky young man standing in a doorway with the girl who had earlier taken in the laundry; and 5) railroad imagery. This list does not exhaust the pictorial elements of the film.

The film weaves among these fragmented scenes mixing prolepses, flashbacks, ellipses, and synecdoches with illusions of temporal and spatial interconnections in the following ways: very early in the film a single-frame flash of a figure straddling railroad tracks, bent over and staring through his legs, anticipates a later hold on that image. Toward the end of the film, a flashback recalls the speech of the cocky youth to the girl: "You will eventually fall for me," he says. In the initial presentation of the scene she answers, "Do you really think so?" Earlier she had used the same expression to the bum helping her take in her wash. The flashback follows a scene of the model getting out of her car, which has also been inserted earlier during the initial doorway presentation. When her elegant shoe touches the ground, the "synch event" is a direct cut to the sight and sound of the racecar crashing at Le Mans; she twists her hips to a carefully placed fragment of music followed by the key word from the youth's speech, "*verfallen.*" A repetition of that word brings with it a flashback to the couple in the doorway. The mesh of visual and aural associations in this brief section of the film is typical of its total construction.

Kubelka uses the off-screen look to connect disjunctive scenes. The chauffeur appears through montage to be watching the Le Mans disaster at one time, the bum at another. The first two or three times Kubelka cuts to the wash line scene, it seems to be a return to a temporal continuity, fragmented only by the interruptions of montage, but the next time he returns to it we find out from the conversation of the actors it is the next morning. The synecdochic introduction of the couple in the doorway is a comic highlight in the film. The camera cuts suddenly to a gaudy tie, accented by a thunderclap, then to the cigar in his mouth, his portable radio, and the girl's feet before presenting a total image of the young man. The first of six color inserts in the black-and-white film occurs when he suddenly switches off his radio; the music stops and he thrusts it under his arm. At this point the loud black-and-white radio makes a strong articulation to the silent bright red radio under his arm.

Not all the joinings are that forceful. He makes a transition at one point by gradually flashing single frames of the coming shot and then continuing frames of the previous shot. This isolated experiment in montage precedes Markopoulos' completely independent use of the same technique by almost a decade.

The fragmentation and intertwining of scenes give *Mosaik* a structure similar to two contemporary, late trance films in America, Brakhage's *Reflections on Black* and even more so its model, Christopher MacLaine's *The End*. On a purely formal level, the rhetoric of Kubelka's cinematic conjunctions, whereby diverse strands of themes are fitted together, evolved toward a language of metaphor precisely parallel to independent developments in America. The essential distinction between the American work and his is the intensified Romantic inwardness of the American film in contrast to Kubelka's perspective as "an anthropologist" of the "Stone Age" aspects of contemporary man, to use two of the film-maker's favorite expressions. In his skeptical naturalism, he refuses a privileged perspective for himself; the artist, according to his conception, shows to his contemporaries and to posterity what life is and was like in the dark ages of his own time. "We are in fact very near brothers of the animals (let's say the mammals); we have made a more complicated society, but in their lives and loves they are approximately the same," he told an interviewer. "When I was 19 or so," he added, referring to the time immediately before making *Mosaik*,

> I had a period when I was wary of being a part of humanity, and I symbolically signed a declaration of my resignation from humanity—"Peter Kubelka"—but in fact you cannot do it without staying still and dying. Despite the beautiful moments, it's a horrible situation—I mean, we are some sort of growing thing on a round ball in this ridiculous, black universe, there's no purpose—it's a joke, anyway.[12]

For *Unsere Afrikareise* (Our Trip to Africa) Kubelka recorded about ten hours of sound—talk, animals, noises, bits of radio music, all either separate or combined—and a few hours of images while in Africa. When he returned to Vienna, he transcribed all the sounds phonetically, using the techniques of symphonic scoring for passages of several kinds of sound. Then he memorized the book of his transcriptions. He also clipped three frames from every shot he had taken, mounted them on a card, and cross-indexed the cards in terms of rhythm, color, subject, and theme. The totality of pictures and sounds he collected he called his "vocabulary."

Like a poet he could then draw upon that vocabulary in the creative act of editing. One of Kubelka's fundamental principles is that a film must be reconceived between the shooting and the editing. The film-maker, he told his classes, should abandon any preconceptions he may have had while planning or shooting his film once it is shot. Then he must look freshly at his "vocabulary" to see what new form it might take. In the six years between shooting and finishing *Unsere Afrikareise*, that is what he did.

Kubelka isolated scenes with specific emotional vectors in order to reorganize them through sound and picture montage. He told Jonas Mekas:

> My films have a function (this goes for the African film)—I play with the emotions and try to tear the emotions loose from the people, so that

they would gain distance to their emotions, to their own feelings. This is one of my main tasks: to get distance to the whole existence, you see . . . I have a lot of distance. I always had it, and I have too much, so I feel very lonely and I want to communicate. You see, you have this whole range of emotions and these mechanisms, how the emotions are created. When you see certain images or hear certain sounds you have certain emotions. So I must always cry when I see moving scenes, when I see the hero getting the first prize for the biggest round and they play the national anthem . . . I have to cry . . . or when they bury somebody, I have to cry. At the same time, I am angry at myself, because I know that it's just the emotional mechanisms. So, with the African film, I do a lot of this, I trigger a lot of those mechanisms at the same time and create a lot of—at the same time—comic feelings, sad feelings.[13]

In this film Kubelka abandoned single-frame montage in order to create a seductive illusion of reality. He focuses the speed of perception on the instant-to-instant relationship between sound and image. Thus a passenger boat rising upward on the sea will be combined with a fragment of popular romantic music just long enough to initiate an emotional surge, or the movement of an insect among flowers will seem to dance when combined with a lively tune for a few seconds. He will synchronize a cliché of awe— "Die ganze Erde . . . Die Erde ist terra" (the whole earth . . . the earth is terra)—with a twist of the lens which radically shifts the focus from a close-up leaf to the full moon; a raucous explosion of laughter is joined to an image of a white woman mocking an African guard; the silent Sphinx seems to be wondering, "What did we shoot last Tuesday?" in a "synch event."

These synthetic fragments become the "words," according to the filmmaker's own simile, with which he writes his film. They are combined in numerous ways, among which the commonest are 1) analogical elision, in which the action of one shot seems to continue incongruously into the next, as when the hand of a snake charmer tapping a boa is meshed with the hand of a hunter lighting a pipe for a native girl; 2) emotional antithesis —for example, the combination of the sad gaze of a dying lion with the dance of the insect in a flower, previously mentioned; 3) visual illustrations of a continuous sentence on the soundtrack, as in the ironic sequence of a horsemen, flowing water, and a low aerial sweep over running animals accompanying the line, "We came by land, by ship, and by air"; 4) illusions of cause and effect, such as the hand of a hunter greeting Africans at screen right followed by a zebra's leg shaking toward screen left, as if the hunter were shaking hands with the fallen beast; and 5) the destruction of illusion, as in the following shot which shows why the zebra's leg was moving—it was being skinned.

Kubelka paid close attention to the slightest variations in rhythm within long shots, and he accented them by sound and editing. An example of this would be the African woman presumably pounding grain with a giant pestle. With each of her blows there is a synchronous groan. Sometimes he will let her establish a rhythm by making two or three blows without interruption; then he will cut at the very frame in which the pestle hits the block to the static head of a carcass, so that the groan seems to come from the skeleton as if it had been hit on the head by the pestle. Again, the music which turned the insect's movement into a dance lends a terrible grace to the subsequent shot of Africans lifting the dead lion on to a car because their heaves are in the same close synchronization to the music that the insect's bounces had been.

The illusions of *Unsere Afrikareise*—off-screen looks connecting disjunctive scenes, cutting to the firing of guns, fusions of music and movement —are more dynamic than those of *Mosaik im Vertrauen* because they look as if they were discovered within the action (as they were) rather than preconceived and imposed upon it (as had been the case in his first film). In a film whose junctures, however radical, are preconceived, the changes of shot tend to be telescoped to the viewer, if only at the horizon of his awareness. Once such a juncture occurs it has the satisfying look of preconception, but it also allows the attention to relax slightly until the next telegraphing and satisfaction. By cutting his film according to imminent junctures as Brakhage and Markopoulos also tend to do, Kubelka keeps the attention close to the threshold of the single-frame event, probing the instant-to-instant unrolling of the film for internal rhythms and metaphorical lines from which spring new connections.

10

APOCALYPSES AND PICARESQUES

The transition from the subjective and graphic cinema of the late 1940s to the mythopoeic cinema of the 1960s can be most clearly documented through the films of a number of independent film-makers working in relative isolation in the San Francisco area throughout the 1950s. The collapse of Art in Cinema meant, or at least coincided with, the dissolution of the community of film-makers. Where once films had been completed for the admittedly hostile audience of Art in Cinema at the San Francisco Museum of Fine Arts, now film-makers protected their isolation like hermits, often refusing to show their films to the few ephemeral groups that sprang up and soon disappeared throughout the country which were sincerely interested in viewing them. Both Harry Smith and Jordan Belson passed through periods of extreme artistic withdrawal, while Larry Jordan and Bruce Conner, significant figures of the subsequent generation, continue to hold ambivalent attitudes toward the exhibition and distribution of their films.

The rejection of the social aspects of film production might be seen as part of the Beat ethos which affected in one way or another most of the artists in San Francisco at that time. Yet despite the attitude of the artists, the continuity of an aesthetic tradition spans the decade. The ironic mode of Sidney Peterson and especially James Broughton persists in the work of most of the artists to be discussed in this chapter. Christopher MacLaine, Ron Rice, Bruce Conner, and Robert Nelson (but not Larry Jordan) found sufficient space within that ironic tradition to develop their unique styles. A persistent and pervading naïveté absent in the work of their predecessors often vitalizes their cinematic visions. Jordan, who shares a number of formal concerns with the four other film-makers listed above, has moved away from their oscillation between irony and apocalypse.

Christopher MacLaine's *The End* (1953) terminated the highly productive period of film-making in San Francisco that had begun with *The Potted Psalm*. When it was made, the avant-garde movement was already on the way to its first temporary dissolution. The film itself bursts with the rhetoric of finality; it is a deliberately conclusive work. Jordan Belson, who reluctantly photographed the film under MacLaine's direction, provides one link to the immediate cinematic past. The film leaves no room for the future. It forecasts the destruction of the world by atomic holocaust as the direct sequel to its projection.

The strident language of the narration of *The End* mixes the prophecy of immediate doom with nostalgia, as if the earth were already gone; descriptions of the film's characters which insist that these characters can never really be known (the phrase "for reasons we know nothing about" recurs periodically) shift to exhortations to the audience ("Ladies and gentlemen, we have asked you before to insert yourself into the cast. Now we ask you to write this story"). After a brief, frozen image of a mushroom cloud and the ironic opening title, "The End," the narrator expounds the thesis of the film as we sit in blackness:

> Ladies and Gentlemen, soon we shall meet the cast. Observe them well. See if they are yourselves. And if you find them to be so, then insert yourself into this review; for such it is, a review of things human, a view of things past, a vision of a world no longer in existence, a city among cities gone down in fire; for the world will no longer exist after this day.

In six sections of varying degrees of narrative coherence, we see, and above all hear about, MacLaine's possessed characters. The first, Walter, has been rejected by his friends. We see him running purposelessly through streets, parks, down flights of stairs, until he is shot, unexpectedly. "For reasons we know nothing about," the narrator tells us as we see an unknown hand holding a pistol, "just at that moment, another man decided to blow the head off the next person he saw. Our friend was that person." The scenes of Walter's running situate themselves in deep perspective, into which he flees or out of which he escapes. Often the empty staircase or street rests on the screen for a few seconds before the actor suddenly enters from an unanticipated direction to pursue his race along the receding line of perspective. Among these in-depth images of flight more enigmatic images are interspersed: street scenes, an arm with taut muscles, a tongue licking an ice-cream cone. Sometimes these shorter, intermediary images bear a direct or indirect relation to the narrative, as when the shadows of dancing people appear on a ceiling as the narrator refers to Walter's friends: "They went about their games . . . dancing the dance, and generally forgetting themselves quite admirably." But more often, these shots anticipate later episodes.

Synecdoche plays a major role in MacLaine's film, as does ellipsis. The combination of picture and sound at the conclusion of the next episode exemplifies the latter. Here Charles hides in doorways and fearfully makes his way through the city. We are informed that he has just killed his landlady and her daughter, and that he cannot bear to surrender himself to the police. The language of the section's end is vague: "Then he remembered a place he had often thought of before, and he walked toward it, still enjoying his walk. With his last dime, he removed himself from the threat of red tape and embarrassment, and the slate was already clean." Two elliptical images clarify this conclusion. First we see Charles pass through a ten-cent turnstile; then the camera pans up to the Golden Gate Bridge. In the combination of picture and sound, both indirect in themselves, we learn that he entered Golden Gate Park and jumped from the bridge.

Next, in presenting the suicide of John, a failed poet turned successful comedian, the film-maker uses several previously mysterious images as metaphors for his narrative. The texture of the metaphors is underlined by the arbitrary mixture of black-and-white shots in a predominantly color film. For instance, the black-and-white head of a sleeping bum is intercut with the color pictures of John's false friends, who calmly listen to his presuicide speech and applaud it as his best performance. When he leaves the room where, exclusively in close-ups, he had been talking and playing Russian roulette, the picture switches to black-and-white shots of hands playing a piano and a black man dancing. "Someone else took the floor, and John was forgotten. Applause went to the living." The suicide itself, before a brick wall on which "PRAY" has been painted, cuts from its colored details to these same black-and-white metaphors. The dying man's collapsing legs are compared to the dancer's; his dead body to that of the sleeping bum.

In the fourth section, in which Paul, a beautiful young man, decides to give himself to the ugliest of lepers to test the authenticity of love, color and black-and-white intermesh in the action itself. Scenes of Paul by the ocean are a mixture of both film stocks. The relationship between picture

and sound had become progressively more indirect in the three earlier
episodes, with more and more of the burden of action falling on the
words. Here we see Paul wandering by the sea in a garden of statues. He
is playing his flute, and he finally walks into a public building; we are told
that he will seek passage to a leper colony. But the apocalyptic vision of
the opening speech of the film returns when the narrator says, "He will
get about as far as the information desk. Then his time will be over, along
with ours."

The process of abstraction on the visual level of the film reaches its
apogee in the next episode. Here we are asked to create our own story.
"Here is a character." We see a man in a red shirt, played by the film-
maker, throwing a knife into a board. "Here is the most beautiful music
on earth." We hear Beethoven's Ninth Symphony. "Here are some pictures. What is happening?" The pictures include the façade of a house,
a monumental archway, the tensed arm we had often seen before, and
more shots of the man and his knife-throwing.

As if unable to tolerate the extremity of ambiguity with which he has
confronted us, he begins to make a story for us:

> He is a good boy, but somehow we feel he is up to no good. Someone
> has hurt him. But he has got his ego back, and he will assert himself
> now. Someone is in the house. Why is he hesitating? Why is he going
> into the house? No, he will enter and destroy, perhaps? Listen, I know
> no more about the story than you do, but I know that at this point he
> was suddenly both blind and dumb, and he takes this as a message from
> somebody he'd better accept as Master, and walks away from the house
> and its occupant. Then the world and its music come back to him, and he
> hums a little song and hears an echo.

The camera frames a cross in the lower left-hand corner of the screen.
Then as the Hymn to Joy from Beethoven's Ninth Symphony is heard,
we see puppets and human feet dancing to the music in images that had
been proleptic flashes earlier in the film.

The tactic of telling more than one promises to tell or more even than
one claims to know had been used earlier in the film toward a more pessimistic end. When the screen went black after the shooting of Walter, the
narrator said:

> If there were only more time, we could have the story of the unhappy
> young man who decided to blow Walter's brains out on *his* last day. We
> could follow him through his tribulations in the courthouse; could fol-
> low him into solitary confinement; could sit with him while his head

was being shaven as he lay whimpering and alone, confused and defeated. We could walk beside him down the gray and sanitary prison corridor toward the mercy we offer to those of us who run amok. We could watch through the window, when he strangles to death trying to catch a breath to say "mama." Well, we have not enough time for all of the stories. Let us go on. Maybe you will see yourself.

The narrator himself seems to be confused about whether there is not enough time to tell the stories or not enough time for the stories to happen; presumably Walter's killer will die with all of us in the immediate holocaust. The intentional confusion in the narrative reflects rhythmic alternations and paradoxes of gloom and optimism in the whole of the film. After the conversion in the middle of the fourth episode, the tone of the film suddenly becomes joyous. The final story, a pantomime of unsatisfied desire, does not end bitterly, nor does it have a verbal commentary. We see two figures on the beach—a young man trying to light a match as the waves are lapping over his hands, and a young woman who discovers two pipes which lose their bright colors as soon as she tries to puff on them. Eventually, they see each other and rush together, openarmed. But before they can make contact they fall next to each other writhing in the sand. This fable is resolved by the happy image of a girl riding a white horse in slow motion, intercut with a stream of water hitting a tree. The combination of these two images is the sensual climax of the film. It takes us far from the despair of the opening sections. But now that doom has been finally removed from the foreground of our attention, the atomic bomb explodes, a mushroom cloud rises, and the film ends in a shattering of the title, "The End."

The extraordinary ambition of *The End* looks forward to the great achievements of the mythopoeic film. MacLaine came to cinema a little too late to find conviction in the trance film. In *The End* he made his major statement through a form that could not contain it. Brakhage, during his first stay in San Francisco, saw *The End* in 1953, before it disappeared from sight for the next ten years. Two years later, perhaps under its influence, he too tried to get beyond the trance film by combining three episodes with a unifying theme in *Reflections on Black*. Later, after the first Film-Makers Cooperative was founded, Brakhage sought out MacLaine and helped put his films into distribution. The formal achievements which make *The End* a fascinating work—the combination of color and black-and-white, the proleptic use of metaphor, the dialectic of doom and redemption—can be found in a more integrated and fully-achieved way in Brakhage's *Dog Star Man*. Furthermore, in *Blue Moses* Brakhage refined some of the tactics of direct address and indirect narration which in MacLaine's original, although they are brilliantly employed, are drowned in the naïve urgency of his statement.

After a hiatus of five years, we encounter the next significant achievement in the complex ironic tradition that extends from James Broughton through MacLaine. Bruce Conner made *A Movie* in 1958 as an extension of his collage sculpture. Aside from the titles (which include a comically long hold on the film-maker's name), all the images of Conner's film were culled from old newsreels, documentaries, and fiction films. The natural irony of the collage film, which calls attention to the fact that each element quoted in the new synthesis was once part of another whole, thereby underlining its presence as a piece of film, creates a distance between the image depicted and our experience of it. Montage is the mediator of collage. Conner extends that mediated distance by introducing bits of blank film, academy leader, and stray titles ("End of part four" or "The End" near the beginning of the film), as well as reintroducing the title he gave the whole—*A Movie*—and his name at several points in the middle of the montage.

Unlike MacLaine, Conner is not naïve in his vision of doom. Everything he shows us has the primary actuality of the newsreel or the secondary reality of the images of violence we encounter in popular entertainment. Nor are the intellectual rhythms of *A Movie*, which move between the terrible and the ridiculous, part of a general interior drift, like the desperate but gradual postulation of hope before the finish of *The End*; Conner deliberately and carefully orchestrated the twists and changes of pace within his film. He is a master of the ambivalent attitude; it is the strength of his art and the style of his life. The sculpture with which he first presented *A Movie* brings nostalgic objects into violent fusions. His first film carries that principle to a radical extreme.

There is an early sequence which characterizes Conner's ambivalent manipulation of found images and which demonstrates his visionary stance at the same time. We see a submarine, the movement of whose periscope is intercut with a 1940s nudie film of Marilyn Monroe to suggest that the periscope operator is watching a peep-show. His excited reaction, which must originally have come while sighting an enemy ship, gets a laugh when we translate it to the voyeuristic context. The submarine fires a torpedo, continuing the sexual metaphor for comic effect while adding a hint of terror. The explosion of the torpedo becomes, through montage, an atomic bomb blast; the explosion puts the brake on our laughter with a moment of shock. The shock slowly wears off with the recognition of the visual grace of the mushroom cloud.

A sequence of dangerous stunts, which are comic because of their approach to disaster without actual hurt, precedes a sequence of battles which are shocking in their deadly activity. Graceful images which only indirectly suggest the possibility of death (a tightrope walker, descending parachutes) shift the tension after an onslaught of horror. The final sequence of the film, derived from a Cousteau underwater documentary, provides a symbol for ironies and ambiguities upon which the whole collage is organized. Symbolism becomes possible only when the intensity of irony diminishes by becoming a second-degree distancing—the irony of an irony. Within the space of this distancing, a mediating figure represents us, the viewers, within the film. First the camera follows a school of fish. Then we see that this shot had been from the perspective of a scuba diver, our mediator, who, leaving the fish, discovers a sunken ship. Its wreckage has become beautiful through a covering of barnacles. The narrativity and the mystery of this sequence partially derive from the interspersing of pauses of black leader between the shots. Both qualities can enter the film only when the ironic pressure of viewing the individual shots as film garbage suddenly diminishes. In the second-degree distancing, we simultaneously experience the mediation and realize we are watching film collage. The climax of the section creates a metaphor for this disjunction: as the diver descends into the hull of the ship the camera shoots upward at the sun reflected on the surface of the sea.

The rhythmic structure of A Movie depends on the internal dynamics of the shots, with the occasional help of interspersed leader. Conner tended to cut the disasters sharply at the point of maximal shock and to allow the antithetical, graceful movements a slower and more rounded development. The montage follows an ideological structure; it amasses images, contrasts them, or synthesizes them in an unexpected way. No attempt is made to control the overall metrics of the film through cutting.

Conner's subsequent film, Cosmic Ray (1961), emphasizes the dynamic integration of visual materials over ideological montage. The method of this integration is the imposition of a rhythmical pulse on all shots in the film; the shots include academy leader, end titles, flashes, phrases such as "Head" or "Start," a nude female dancer—often in superimposition with flashing lights—and bits of old films (advertisements, cartoons, and especially war documentaries). Ray Charles, singing "Tell Me What I Say," reinforces the tempo of the montage with a rock beat on the soundtrack.

No shot remains on the screen long enough for an internal development. Temporal logic plays no role in the succession of images, except in
the case of a cartoon which I shall discuss below. Nevertheless, the pacing
of the montage, coupled with the ironic symbolism of guns firing at the
climax, emphasized by the words of the accompanying song, suggest that
the entire film mimics the structure of a sexual encounter. Only gradually
does the visionary symbolism of the film disclose itself. Eventually we see
more and more shots of military parades, rockets, and bombs as the dancer
in a subtle, often barely noticeable way, reflects the action of those
glimpses in her dance.

Four fragments of an old Mickey Mouse cartoon frame the climax of
the film and provide its ironic center. The first image of Mickey gets a
laugh from its sheer incongruity in a film elaborating a metaphor of sex
and war. Next we see a huge cannon pointed at Mickey's head. When it
fires, Conner cuts rapidly to anti-aircraft weapons and cannon firing from
old documentaries. The phallic nature of all the guns is revealed by their
context in the montage and by the allusions of the song text. The barrages
of firing are the orgasmic center of the film. When the cartoon comes on
again, the cannon suddenly wilts like an exhausted penis as the song calls
out for "just one more time." As it began, *Cosmic Ray* ends in a welter of
leader and flashes.

With his next film, *Report* (1965), the longest of the three, Conner
returned to filmic assemblage (the dancer and the lights of *Cosmic Ray*
had been photographed by him) and to the intense ambivalence of his
first film at its privileged moments of secondary distancing. "Irony," according to Paul de Man, "engenders a temporal sequence of acts of consciousness which is endless."[1] *Report* begins in the ironical mode by seeming to be simultaneously about the assassination of John Kennedy and
about the media's reportage of it. Like Conner's first two films, it proceeds, again gradually, toward irony by incorporating collage elements
which reflect on the ambiguities of the initial situation.

Repetition, in the form of loop printing, is the dominant trope of the
film until its final expansion. Over and over again we see the motorcade,
the rifle carried through the police station, an ambulance, Jackie waving
as the soundtrack records a news broadcast consecutively from the time
of the shooting to the public announcement of death. The discontinuity
between narrative and image is the first of the second-degree ironies in
the film.

More than twenty countdowns of academy leader in a row in the middle of the film become a pivot around which the form turns. As the soundtrack repeats itself in scrambled time, the images become quicker, the looping ceases, and the film extends itself simultaneously into the realm of metaphor and the past of the President and the future of the assassination. A rodeo and a bullfight are intercut with shots of Kennedy meeting the Pope. The book depository and the killing of Oswald appear mixed with pieces of advertisements, more bullfighting, and the explosion of a bomb.

At unexpected points the seemingly extraneous material coincides with phrases from the soundtrack. When the newsmen report that the "doors fly open" on Kennedy's car, Conner cuts to refrigerator doors opening by themselves from a commercial. Mention of the President's steak dinner coincides with the death of the bull. In irony's hall of mirrors these are further reflections of the discontinuity which the progress of the film widens and never attempts to repair.

All three of Conner's films aspire to an apocalyptic vision by engendering in the viewer a state of extreme ambivalence. A *Movie* and *Cosmic Ray* achieve this by alternative gestures of attraction (humor, in the first, erotics in the second) and repulsion (violence in both). The change of pace tactic is not necessary for *Report*. The film utilizes the emotional matrix of the Kennedy assassination evoked by the newsreel material and above all by the verbal report, while establishing an ever-widening distance from it by means of the looping, the lack of synchronization with the sound, the metaphors, and the linguistic coincidences. It is the one film of the three that does not reverse its tone; it simply reveals itself more and more clearly as what it was at first.

The fables of *The End* and the ironies of Conner's first three films share an apocalyptical despair which will diminish, but not die out, in their immediate successors. Both film-makers extended the technical discoveries of their early works in films that were less ambitious and prophetic but no less exquisite. But I shall pass by those works in this schematic chapter in order to clarify the outline of a tradition which has not been defined before. Ron Rice and Robert Nelson, continuers in this line in the sixties, have simplified and elongated MacLaine's form, the picaresque. Nelson, as if to give his film more cohesion than Rice's, incorporated strategic elements from Conner's work.

Ron Rice's *The Flower Thief* (1960) is the purest expression of the Beat sensibility in cinema. It portrays the absurd, anarchistic, often infantile adventures of an innocent hero (played by Taylor Mead) while indirectly providing a portrait of San Francisco at the beginning of the sixties. The film-maker began his film with a myth about his working methods: "In the old Hollywood days movie studios would keep a man on the set who, when all other sources of ideas failed (writers, directors), was called upon to 'cook up' something for filming. He was called The Wild Man. *The Flower Thief* has been put together in memory of all dead wild men who died unnoticed in the field of stunt."[2]

The finished film seems to preserve the spirit of its making. The uneven lighting, a result of using outdated raw stock, the paratactic montage, which suggests that there was a minimum of editing after the film was shot, and the casual soundtrack create this impression. Although the film has a distinct beginning and end, one feels that the middle could be expanded endlessly. The sequence of its episodes is arbitrary. Rice described the action of the film in a note for its New York premiere at Cinema 16 (the spelling and punctuation are Rice's):

> The central character Taylor Meade a poet moves through a sequence of events. He steals a flower he enters The Bagle Shop, returns to his home, (an abandoned powerhouse), discovers a man hidden in the cellar with a childs teddy bear. He washes the teddy bear in the bathroom then discovers the room full of people, and is chased. He destroys a bull-shitting radio. The Beatniks carry on with spontaneous antics, reinacting the crucifistion, and changing the graphic meaning to the flag plainting at Iwo Jima. Telephone, pits, beats in lockers making love; a woman climbing monkey bars to reach her lover.
>
> The poet is searching, but he never finds love. The ending of the film suggests he finds something, but we do not know for he disappears into the sea. The audience must discover the "message" if one is demanded. Elements of Franz Kafka and Russian Humanism are there.[3]

Occasionally the soundtrack veers from random accompaniment to crude poetry: "The time man has spent in his brothers' prisons can now be measured in light years"; "Christ on opium, marijuana used in the past. . . . Peruvian civilization based on cocaine, America on coca-cola." Or to irony (an excerpt from *Peter and the Wolf* is heard while Mead picks flowers, *Alexander Nevsky* while he moves among fire trucks and tries to direct traffic).

Ron Rice's films contain mythic elements, but his heroes are neither the somnambulistic dreamers of the trance film in search of sexual identity nor the Romantic questers of the mythic cinema. They are complex mediators who move between realism and allegory within a single film in a chain of discontinuous roles. At times the poet of *The Flower Thief* becomes the impersonal victim of society, as when he is tried in a cardboard court, upon which is written Justice, for urinating in the park. But Rice also has an eye for the poetic particulars of naturalism: the poet's feeding his cat in the powerhouse by candlelight and a brief scene of a couple taking a shower are high points in his film.

Rice would have made another episodic film right after *The Flower Thief*; he even attempted two, one called *The Dancing Master* and another with his close friend the painter and film-maker Jerry Joffen. But he lost interest in them. According to a story he told in 1962, *Senseless*, finished that year, came out of a film he had planned to make of Eric Nord's island. Nord had been an actor in *The Flower Thief* and the proprietor of the Gaslight Cafe in Venice, California, who, as the story goes, purchased an island from the Mexican government with the modest intention of establishing a Utopia. Unfortunately he neglected to ascertain whether or not there was fresh water on his island. There was not, of course. So he and his pilgrims set up camp with army surplus parachutes for tents on the shores of Baja, California. When Rice and some other settlers arrived, Nord and his pioneers were gone. Unfurled lonely parachutes rocked with the breezes. Whether *The Dancing Master* was to be the Utopian film of Nord's island or whether Rice had planned to make an entirely different film on that terrestrial paradise, I do not know; nor does it matter much, since the nucleus of his projected film was gone either way. He had filmed the trip down to the camp and the deserted parachutes and whatever of the Mexican landscape interested him along the way. He and his friends stayed in Mexico, filming one thing and another as tentative films occurred to them.

When Rice got to New York he pooled the various episodes and studies together. Since there would be no plot, nor even the continuity of a single mediator, he pretended the film had been written by Jonas Mekas, who at that time was devoting many of his columns in the *Village Voice* to promoting the plotless film. On the screen he gives Mekas credit for "the script." It is a natural irony of circumstances that the resulting film of Rice's potpourri, *Senseless*, is by far the most carefully organized, formal film he left. (He died of pneumonia while in Mexico again at the end of 1964.) It is a film thematically constructed around a trip to and from Mexico, with recurrent images of cars and trains (they actually sold their car illegally and slipped out of the country on the train) and much pot smoking. The rhythmic intercutting of scenes gives the film its cohesion.

Back in New York, his home town, Rice brought together Taylor Mead and Winifred Bryan, a colossal black woman, to make *The Queen of Sheba Meets the Atom Man*. He did not live to complete the editing. He was constantly cutting it and adding new sequences. Bryan plays an alcoholic odalisque, and Mead much the same type as in the earlier film but now with overtones of a scientist. In the rough cut which Rice often screened to raise money to complete the film, there were two scenes of extended parody: a spoof on *Hamlet* with Jack Smith as the Prince, and a less direct take-off on Gregory Markopoulos' *Twice a Man*, which had been completed while *The Queen of Sheba Meets the Atom Man* was in production. In his tentative version Rice ended his film where Markopoulos' began, on the Staten Island ferry. According to Taylor Mead's notes on the production, the *Hamlet* spoof was to have been preceded by an excerpt from the Olivier film version, and another film quotation from Welles' *The Trial* was to have introduced still another satire.

The combination and intercutting of characters brought *The Queen of Sheba Meets the Atom Man* a step closer to the synthetic process of the mythic film, but at the same time the ironic gap between the actors as they appear on the screen and the roles they assume widened. In this enlarged space the film moves between epiphany and parody. The divorce between the subjective center of the film and the various forms it takes is reflected in Taylor Mead's encounter with many objects. Attracted to household products by advertisements, he does not understand their functions; so he will rub a box of cereal over his clothes or, with Chaplinesque inventiveness, insert the prongs of an electric plug in his nose in the hope of getting high. The subjectivity of the mythopoeic protagonist is grounded in his privileged contact with the primal rhythms and rituals of the universe, even when they defeat him. Rice concentrates on describing the estrangement of his heroes in terms of realities. Although he may suggest a deeper, alternative core of existence for the protagonist of *The Flower Thief*, he is more reluctant to do so for the figures of his later picaresque. When relieved of the immediate estrangement of the city, they manifest their subjectivity ironically: they engage in parodies.

A late example of the type of film being discussed is Robert Nelson's *The Great Blondino* (1967). In it, the picaresque and the mythic overlap, and irony, which is prevalent in many aspects of the film, ceases to play a structural role. In the previous chapters we have seen the applicability of Harold Bloom's analysis of Romantic mythopoeia to several major films of the American avant-garde, whose "myth, quite simply, *is* myth: the process of its making, and the inevitability of its defeat." Here the same pattern can be seen with somewhat diminished intensity. Blondino, the central character, a tightrope walker, wanders through the San Francisco townscape pursued by a detective from "the committee." In his gray clown suit, the alienated and naïve protagonist is the immediate heir of the flower thief and of MacLaine's figures, and more distantly but even more closely a reincarnation of the caged artist in pursuit of his eye in Peterson's *The Cage*. This connection, of which Nelson and his collaborator, the painter William Wiley, were unaware, is never so apparent as when Blondino pushes his ever-present wheelbarrow through crowded streets wearing a blindfold.

One debt to earlier films has been acknowledged by Nelson repeatedly: since his second film, *Confessions of a Black Mother Succuba* (1965), he has recognized his debt to Bruce Conner. From the very opening of *The Great Blondino*, his sixth film, the synthesis of Conner and Rice is evident. A white knight from a television commercial is transformed by a magical wand, also from a commercial, into the protagonist of the film, "a misfit, out of step," in the ironical language of one of the film's minor characters.

Until its last minutes the film has no narrative order. Scenes, which are too brief and dispersed to be called episodes, change and recur in rhythmic waves according to the logic of dream association. Several explicit scenes of the hero sleeping and even more references to dreams in the form of sawing wood or a line of "z's" flashing across the image can be meant either to frame a central portion of the dream or to implicate the entire film in a dream vision. At times, Blondino lapses into the passivity of a somnambulist from the trance film tradition. Then he mediates, as the dreamer, the disorienting encounter with collaged newsreels that the film-maker, again developing upon Conner's work, has built into the film. When Blondino is near the sea, a submarine, obviously from a newsreel, surfaces in the waters. Looking from his window, he sees an old strut airplane in operation.

Nelson suppresses the ironic presence of the quotations from newsreels and old films by meticulously integrating them into the spatial logic of his photographed scenes. Unlike Conner's collages, these images are not allowed to burst into the viewer's consciousness as affirmations of the materiality of the film as film. They are part of a strategy of careful disorientation which includes radical changes of scale. For instance, by super-

Conflict of scale in Robert Nelson's *The Great Blondino*.

imposition Blondino appears to dance in a frying pan, and later in one of the most memorable images in the film he climbs on a gigantic chair several times taller than a man, actually built for this effect, to watch a rhinoceros pacing in the distance. The effect of this latter disorientation is all the greater because the placement of the chair in the foreground of the shot makes it look optically rather than actually enlarged for a few seconds before Blondino enters the frame to provide a measure of comparison.

At the very end of the film there is a narrative attended by an ironical undercurrent reflexively attesting to the cinematic illusion. First the detective makes a statement of his function in the film: "When the committee heard about this fellow, we were quite sure that his operations were not in the national interest." Up to that point, his role had only been suggested by his costume, mimicry, and a musical motif underlining his periodic appearances. Following the detective's speech, Blondino attempts his fatal rope-walking. This is the climax of the film, but Nelson distances from it by cutting from the actor to his image on the tightrope, first projected on the screen of a movie theater, then on television. When he falls, subjective drama and the affirmation of material fuse: his descent is indicated by a fast montage of flashes, flares, and numbers from academy leader. Then, by metaphorical extension, his disaster is prolonged in a quotation from a science fiction film in which a giant octopus captures a man.

In the final ambiguous moment of the film, Blondino walks again on solid ground, pushing the wheelbarrow, in an image of prismatic distortion. This resurrection, like the quoted images preceding it, is nostalgic. In a note for the Experimental Film Festival of Knokke-le-Zoute at the end of 1967, the film-makers offered the following statement:

> This is a long film that uses no specific narrative development. Its coherence depends upon deeper non-verbal sensibilities. The great Blondino is a figurative allusion to the tightrope walker Blondin, who gained international fame in the 19th Century by walking many times across Niagara Falls on a tightrope. The film speaks about the level of risk at which we live and of the foolishness and beauty of our lives at the edge, where we confront that risk.[4]

Rather than speak of risk, the film longs for one. Its version of the process and defeat of mythopoeia is bound up with a temporal predicament of which the film-maker hardly seems aware. In this very controlled and well-integrated film, what is out of control and cannot be integrated is its elegiac mood, which ultimately undermines its mythopoeia.

Nelson's most sustained achievement so far, *Bleu Shut* (1970), found for itself a new form which could contain and derive energy from the contradictory tendencies of his fourteen earlier films. *Bleu Shut* is a prime example of the participatory film, a form which emerged at the end of the 1960s out of extensions of the structural film. If we survey these forms diachronically, it would seem that the great unacknowledged aspiration of the American avant-garde cinema has been the mimesis of the human mind in a cinematic structure. Beginning with an attempt to translate dreams and other revelations of the personal unconscious in trance films, through the imitation of the act of seeing in the lyric film and the collective unconscious in the mythopoeic film, this cinema attempted to define consciousness and the imagination. Its latest formal constructions have approached the form of meditation—the structural film—in order to more directly evoke states of consciousness and reflexes of the imagination in the viewer. The participatory films follow the direction established by the structural cinema in finding corollaries for the conscious mind.

In *Bleu Shut* Nelson proposed film-viewing as a testing experience. At the same time George Landow was making *Institutional Quality* from the same premise, while Hollis Frampton was presenting montage as a logical function and cinematic construction in general as a system of thought in his film *Zorns Lemma*. Each of these film-makers came to this point of formal evolution following clues in their own earlier works rather than from mutual interaction or from a common source of inspiration. For both Landow and Frampton that immediate past entailed an intense involvement with the structural film. Nelson's one structural film, *The Awful Backlash* (1967), a single shot for fourteen minutes of a hand untangling the snarled line of a fishing reel, does not represent a crucial moment in his evolution. For him the fixed camera was one of many contingent strategies explored in several short films made at the same time as *The Great Blondino*, which later would inform the synthesis of *Bleu Shut*.

In *The Great Blondino* the film-maker attempted to unite footage he collected from various sources with his own photography through a mythic narrative that could bridge both. In *Bleu Shut* he invented a form which would be capable of holding together many different kinds of film while maintaining their integrity as home movies, advertisements, quotations, etc. In Nelson's inflection of the participatory form, the very question of synthesizing the materials of the film is handed directly to the viewer. In the ironic structure he provides, all images share a relationship to one-minute subsections of the film. Screen time is affirmed in two ways. A small transparent clock appears in the upper right-hand corner of the screen, measuring the minutes and seconds throughout the film. That measurement is reinforced by a number which flashes briefly on the screen at the beginning of each new minute.

The film is ironically subtitled "(30 minutes)" and at the beginning a woman's voice tells us, "This film will be exactly thirty minutes long." But it is not. At the end of the half hour the cards indicating the minutes no longer appear, but the film continues for another four or five minutes, according to its own clock, as its maker, in negative, tests the sound system in preparation for a speech about the nature of cinema, which we never hear. The failure of the film to terminate at the exact instant predicted surprises us because all of the other promises heard at the beginning were precisely fulfilled. The woman's speech describes the future of the film:

> I'm now off-stage where Bob and Bill can't hear me. This is how its gonna be: This film is exactly thirty minutes long. The little clock in the upper right corner tells the exact amount of time that has elapsed from the beginning and the amount of time left. . . .
> At 5 minutes, 35 seconds comes the Johnny Mars Band.
> At 11:15, weiners.
> At 21:05, pornography.
> At 23:30, a duet.
> Watch the clock.

What she does not tell us is that most of the film's time will be occupied by a guessing game. For an entire minute a color photograph of a boat will appear on the screen with six possible names printed over it. The first time the choices are: Bodo, Moki-Moki, Heaven Sabuv, Vegas Vamp, Big Boy, and Sea Dancer. Off-screen, we hear two men, Bob and Bill (the film-maker and William Wiley), deliberating on which name they will pick. At the end of the minute they each make a choice; then the woman tells them the answer. This game is repeated eleven times at intervals of one minute. More often than not, both men guess wrong. Naturally the viewer of the film is drawn into the guessing game because of its duration, repetition, and the possibility of measuring his luck against that of the two guessers within the film.

In the minute-long intervals between the pictures of the boats, or in parts of those minutes, various collected and photographed images appear which invoke different problems in the perception of film. The naked film-maker, crawling through a cubicle of mirrors, creates a confusion of the actual with the reflected body. The image of a steaming hot-dog proclaims itself as a loop only when the viewer begins to perceive the repetitious pattern of a barely perceptible puff of steam, and then without any indication of a transition, the looping ends, and a fork severs the hot dog. A more obvious loop of a dog barking takes on an ambiguous dimension by the irregular alternation between silence and synchronized sound. The appearance of the frame line and surface dirt points out the filmic objectivity of an old pornographic film incorporated within *Bleu Shut*. Another allusion to the conventions of cinema is a Hawaiian number out of an old musical.

Each of these inserts, which are for the most part found objects, functions independently. There is no interweaving of imagery nor narrative continuity. Each elongates and divides the parts of the guessing game like advertising interrupting a television quiz show, but unlike advertisements, they do not have a distinctly negative relation to the game. They are of equal importance, simply reverse face. In fact, some of the intentional energy of the game carries over to the inserts, as if the audience were being called on to solve perceptual puzzles, to interpret them, and above all to construct a unity out of their diversity. *Bleu Shut* reverses the thrust of *The Great Blondino*. By fracturing the possible unities between found objects and filmed scenes and suggesting a field of cinematic perception without a center—or at best with a problematic center—it demythologizes its own ironies and at the very end almost throws the film-maker outside his own film (he does not fit within its "30 minutes"). *The Great Blondino*, on the other hand, had a mythic center where the ironies of the materials could mesh with the ironies of the narrative.

The movement between works which establish a tentative center and those which disperse or put into question their centers, observed in these two films by Nelson, characterizes all of the films I have grouped in this chapter. At times the desire for a central organization has been satisfied by a loose, picaresque development substituting for a mythic core, and just as often (but not in the case of *Bleu Shut*) the dispersed structure has been a metaphor for the apocalyptic intention of the film. Different dynamics and dimensions of irony in the films of MacLaine, Conner, Rice, and Nelson have intensified the formal alternations within individual films and within whole filmographies. These film-makers have been grouped here not to suggest that they form a school or exhibit a regional sensibility. Far from it. Bruce Conner and Ron Rice were very independent figures who began working in film in the late 1950s when the avant-garde cinema was at its least cohesive. They simply share in their works certain patterns of responding to the void. MacLaine was another isolated artist who came at the very end of a strong movement, whose major film pointed chaotically toward the forms of the later 1950s. Nelson, on the other hand, marks the end of that period. In his hand the picaresque and the centerless film becomes a deliberate strategy for making works which respond to the new cohesion of the national avant-garde cinema of the 1960s. An enclosed picture of the historical moment we have been considering calls for a discussion of the films of Larry Jordan, even though the ironic factor, a common denominator of those I have been discussing, plays a minimal role in both his films of photographed actuality and his animated collages. His materials, subjects, and forms coincide and envision a continuous world where strong or fragile moods are never ruptured. Yet despite these thematic differences, Jordan's isolation and his artistic responses to the situation of the 1950s draw him into consideration with the men I have been discussing.

Larry Jordan's formative period as a film-maker extends throughout the 1950s. He began to make films at approximately the same time as Stan Brakhage, with whom he went to high school in Denver. Jordan appears in Brakhage's Desistfilm (1953) and Brakhage in his Trumpit (1956), both psycho-dramas. Brakhage's approach to film-making and the energy with which he pursued it was unique in the 1950s. He moved between Colorado, New York, and San Francisco, often in pursuit of the vanished centers of late-1940s film-making. He continued making and extending the form of the trance film until he forged the lyric cinema described in chapter six. He not only avoided the kind of crisis most of his colleagues faced at that time, but he even managed to keep up a frail connection between the dispersed and sometimes retired film-makers he sought out in his cross-continental movements.

Jordan failed where Brakhage succeeded in finding a convincing form within the trance film. He matured as an artist and found his authentic voice in film by gradually withdrawing from the role of the film-maker that the previous generation of avant-gardists had established as a norm. As he lost interest in reconstituting the community of film-makers and in the politics of distribution and promotion toward the late 1950s, the distinction between a finished film and a work-in-progress seems to have dissolved for him. In its place came a gradual involvement with the possibility of cinema to testify to the processes of its own making and with films designed to celebrate a particular occasion. When he tentatively reemerged as a publicly exhibiting film-maker at the apogee of the revived interest in the avant-garde film around 1963, he had produced a substantial body of work, radically different from his early psycho-dramas, to which it is difficult to assign dates.

In those few years Jordan had become one of the few film-makers to develop confidence in the artistic validity of a less formal, more spontaneous cinema. Elsewhere in America, in similar isolation, a few other film-makers had come to the same position, as we shall see in the next chapter. Later, when Jordan briefly released the films he had been making without thought of public exhibition, he put them in groups, usually combining animations with actualities: e.g., *3 Moving Fresco Films* contained *Enid's Idyll* and *Portrait of Sharon*, both animations, and *Hymn in Praise of the Sun*, a series of "cine-portraits." Among his films are animated collages, pixilated actualities, portraits, superimposition films, and a hand-painted film. Some were edited within the camera. He described an aspect of his working process in *Film Culture*:

> [Making *Pink Swine*] I got very carried away with object animation, and combining layout animation and object animation. I was moving objects at all different rates; I was setting the camera; I wasn't hand-holding it; I was using it just like a musical instrument, like playing a saxophone, pushing the button on the camera and moving the objects in rhythm. All those films [in *Petite Suite*] were improvised; they're virtually as they came out of the camera. . . . I didn't want everything to move at one particular rhythm; it all depended on what the subject material was. But I wasn't planning it. I was just letting my mind go and see what could be done in 100 ft. [i.e., about three minutes of film]. I liked the 100 foot form. The film was done before you had time to change cameras; I don't remember whether it was one sitting or not, but it wouldn't have been more than two days. You can't do a dance, one dance, in two different days, and these films are essentially dances, you know.[5]

The oscillation between predetermined and spontaneous films set in motion a spiralling intensity in the investigation of the oneiric and metaphysical dimensions of Jordan's cinema. Curiously unlike MacLaine, Conner, Rice, and Nelson, that intensity paralleled a growing frailty, so that the extraordinary series of works which represent the climax of Jordan's career, *Duo Concertantes* (1962-64), *Hamfat Asar* (1965), *The Old House*,

Passing (1966), *Gymnopedies* (1968), and *Our Lady of the Sphere* (1969)—all animations of Victorian engravings except *The Old House, Passing*—occupies an exquisite space and time where reverie and dream meet, delicately poised between nostalgia and terror.

Duo Concertantes has two parts, *The Centennial Exposition* and *Patricia Gives Birth to a Dream by the Doorway*. Both *Patricia* and *Hamfat Asar*, the two most spectacular of his animations, operate against the backdrop of a fixed scene. In the former, it is a back view of a young lady framed in a doorway looking out upon woods and a lake; in the latter, Jordan uses an engraving of a seacoast with cliffs. Time and a change of culture have given a surrealistic and nostalgic aura to Victorian woodcuts, as Max Ernst and several collagists between him and Jordan have known for five decades. Where Ernst slammed together radically incongruent images from such found material and thereby released the terrors of monstrosities and the sensual depth of inconceivable landscapes, Jordan has chosen to refine their delicacy and to push his images almost to the point of evanescence—a limit represented in several collages by the reductive metaphor of a film within a collage-film flickering with pure imageless light.

The background picture of *Patricia* returns us to the moment when the American avant-garde film found its first image of interiority, that is, to the image of Maya Deren pressing her hands against the window in *Meshes of the Afternoon* to gaze inwardly upon a double of herself chasing the mirror-faced figure. The doorway in which Patricia stands is both the port of exchange and the barrier between the inner and outer worlds, as Maya Deren's window and before her Mallarmé's "Fenêtre" had been. Outside, tiny images descend from the top of the screen. First an elephant comes down and slowly sinks out of the bottom, but in his downward course he deposits an object which hovers on the horizon of the lake. The discontinuous power of that horizon line to hold objects from falling down the flat screen provides the film with a frail but finely conceived tension between two illusionary gravities, that of the actual theater in which we see the film where objects must fall from the top of the screen through the bottom as if to land on the floor under our feet and the represented gravity line, the horizon, within the engraving. The manifestation of objects and their movements within the film enumerate the variations possible between these two centers of gravity.

A hand appears in the upper frame; then a statue appears on the horizon like the spot to which the hand pointed. In the incessant materialization and disappearance off-screen or suddenly vanishing by moving of objects and creatures, the usual way of defeating the gravitational forces is by growing wings and flying off-screen, at the edges. At one point, an egg becomes a butterfly, which then breaks the hitherto established norm of separating inside from outside by flying inside the house and disappearing within.

The inside/outside distinction and its evaporation generates the central apperceptive metaphor of the film. A picture stand appears on the horizon. On its white screen a black-and-white flicker occurs; slides appear in sequence; then a bird flaps its wings in an evocation of the origins of cinema. It flies off the screen and into the illusory landscape surrounding it. In the final extensions of this trope, a swarm of bees appears on the little screen; some disappear as soon as they overreach its frame, but others escape into the landscape. These bees come inward, past the unmoving woman, and are lost within the house. To commemorate this triumph of the imagination, a star falls splashing into the lake, an egg takes wing, and Larry Jordan's most delicate film ends.

In *Hamfat Asar* (whose title joins a made-up word from Jordan's household, "hamfat," with an archaic name of Osiris, the Egyptian underworld god) the film-maker generates tensions similar to that of the discontinuous horizon in the earlier film by stretching a tightrope across his seascape. A figure on stilts crosses it repeatedly while creatures and objects float by in the background, manifest themselves, and obscure the foreground or cross and perch upon the tightrope. In the course of his crossings, he will become a bird, a train, a floating balloon.

Once, the entire picture bursts into actual flames. Later a star explodes, first whitening, then blackening out the whole image. When the landscape reappears, the tightrope is gone, but the man on stilts starts to cross, successfully, as if it were there. He does not complete the passage until, at the end of the film, a cloud floats by on which he can stand.

The Centennial Exposition, Gymnopedies, and *Our Lady of the Sphere* use with increasing complexity numerous backdrops which are connected by the continuous movement of a foreground figure from one to the next, although that figure tends to be undergoing its own continual metamorphosis. In *Gymnopedies* he tinted the entire film a pastel blue, and in *Our Lady of the Sphere* several solid screen colors and occasionally split-screen two-color moments have a structural function in the complex animation. He alternates zooming motions, accenting first movements on the left side of the image, then on the right, and he uses cubist superim-

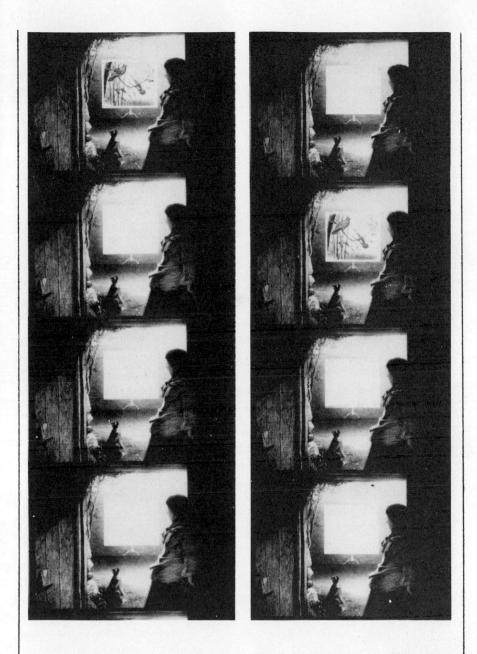

The flickering film-within-a-film:
Larry Jordan's *Patricia Gives Birth to a Dream by the Doorway*.

positions of a single figure out of phase with itself to represent new perspectives of space and depth in animation. He also uses montage to parallel interior scenes with those taking place on a moonscape. At its most complex, in a scene of circus acrobats turning into flashing stars, he employs hand-held backdrops and three different colors in superimposition with counterpointed movements on the different levels. In the middle of the film he shows a horse staring at an easel which becomes a film within a film, flickering and breaking the limits of its frame as had happened in *Patricia*. The elaborate techniques of *Our Lady of the Sphere* permit Jordan to break through the conventions of continuity he had created and then thoroughly explored in his earlier collage films. Yet he had to sacrifice the crucial tension of the slow and delicately elaborated imagery to gain the complex dynamics of the later film.

In *The Old House, Passing*, he resurrected a setting from the trance film, the mysterious house, to construct a radically elliptical narrative that attains a height of fragility comparable to the best of his animated films. According to the film-maker:

> It is a ghost-film wherein the central mood revolves *around* a plot, rather than moving straight along a plot line. Mood predominates over plot, but plot is always there before the eye, as well as behind and to the side of it. Within the meshes of the fabric an older woman has lost a man (husband?) and a child thru a mysterious accident or disappearance. Elements (a young man, woman and child) are drawn into her which release her from the past and the dark mysteries of the huge old house and the night-walking spirit of the departed soul.[6]

In this film Jordan translated the strategies of his animated films into events in actual space and time. By using prolepsis, repetition, and shifting perspective he keeps the relatively simple narrative in an elusive state of development throughout the film, as if he were extending the conventional opening of a mystery film into a total structure. The full disclosure of the narrative is suspended, hinted at, but never achieved. The situations of the film—a couple and their child spending a night in an old house and subsequently exploring it; the old woman who lives there watching them; the ghost of her dead husband watching her and them— give rise to an ambivalence in which the distinction between observation and fantasy breaks down, and past and present interpenetrate. The reveries of *Patricia Gives Birth to a Dream by the Doorway* have their narrative equivalents in the slow, formally composed, chiaroscuro images of shifting and overlapping explorations, discoveries, and encounters.

As the film proceeds toward its center in the scenes of the morning after the family has slept in the old house, the simple narrative begins to repeat itself. Emotionally charged instants, such as the pursuit of the ghost to the roof or the discovery of a child's skeleton in the fireplace occur in the undramatic texture of an increasing involvement in reverie.

Rather than reach a climax, the film simply shifts to a scene of exorcism. The family visits a cemetery, where we assume the ghost is buried, and in an act of deflating the mood of mystery, they blow soap bubbles through the graveyard and leave. But even that release is framed by the perspective of the ghost who watches their departure.

The Old House, Passing makes the temporality which is at the heart of all the films discussed in this chapter thematic. These film-makers of the fifties and sixties were perhaps the first to explore the fundamental disparity between the nostalgia of the photographic image and the "nowness" of projected film. Once this chasm began to open for them, they created an apocalyptic and a picaresque form that commented ironically on that temporality. It also sought to bridge that chasm with an ontology of terror (MacLaine's desperate men, Conner's disasters, the flower thief's paranoia, Blondino's tightrope walk, and the haunting of *The Old House, Passing*) which reaches its most diminished point in the experience of harmless risk (the games of *Bleu Shut*). Risk and terror (and in Jordan's case the threshold between terror and wonder) provide the healing moment in which cinematic time and the time of its perception would coincide.

In New York during the same years other film-makers were encountering the same temporal paradox, which they took as their theme in different personal ways, creating myths of recovered innocence and its failure.

11

RECOVERED INNOCENCE

When Ken Jacobs edited *Blonde Cobra* in 1963 out of footage his friend Bob Fleischner had abandoned and tapes Jack Smith had made, he had not seen, nor even heard of, Christopher MacLaine's *The End*, made exactly ten years earlier. Yet the two films are remarkably similar. They are both exaggerated expressions of suicidal despair whose formal structure metaphorically reflects their themes of self-destruction and disintegration. Although MacLaine combines the stories of several lonely people in his film and Jacobs presents only one—that of Jack Smith, himself a filmmaker—two structural similarities outweigh this difference. Long passages of spoken narration while the screen is black appear periodically, and black-and-white is regularly interwoven with color imagery. In both films these devices are used aggressively to rupture continuity and challenge the consciousness of the viewer. Even the distinction between the multiple perspective of *The End* and the single character of *Blonde Cobra* begins to break down. In the latter film Jack Smith assumes different roles (the lonely little boy, Madame Nescience, Sister Dexterity) and tells their stories, while in the earlier film the stories merge in the final montage.

Although the relationship between these two films is not genetic, they bracket an era of the American avant-garde contemporary with the Beat sensibility. They also bracket the country. Just as *The End* depends upon the cityscape of San Francisco, *Blonde Cobra*, even though it is shot almost entirely indoors, makes the presence of New York felt. Early in the film, as Smith nibbles on a clump of tile and cement in a sordid room, we hear a radio broadcast: "Twelve noon by the century-old chimes in historic City Hall. This is New York, the city of opportunity, where eight million people live in peace and harmony and enjoy the benefits of democracy." Near the end, Smith quotes himself: " 'Why shave? . . . when I can't even think of a reason for living?' Jack Smith. 1958. Sixth Street."

Jacobs insists upon the idea of a film as a dying organism throughout his works. *Blonde Cobra* breaks down before it can get started. After the first few tentative images, we hear Ginger Rogers sing one line, "Let's call the whole thing off," followed by a mess of scribbles on leader and a halting of the soundtrack. After two blasts of live radios in the theater and a change to color imagery and back to black-and-white, the character on screen says, "We will now start all over again." We see him writing out the film's titles.

The two false starts and the shock of the radios are the first challenges to the concentration of the viewer. The presence of the radios is incorporated within the film when the announcement, "Twelve noon," booms out on the soundtrack and again later when a single live radio plays, synchronized with a scene of Smith in baby clothes playing peek-a-boo and apparently listening to a radio. When the actor on screen smashes his radio's tubes with a hammer, the sound in the audience stops abruptly. It is only at this late point that the audience receives a sign that the interaction of picture and live radio is not arbitrary.

Even more unsettling is the duration of the black passages. At the beginning of the first story—the lonely little boy who waits all day for his mother to bring him candy ("She would give him some, but not much, just a little because she would save most of it for herself")—there are flashes of Smith miming the tale, promising the viewer a visualization which never materializes. That same promise is renewed when after several long minutes that story ends and we see Smith in drag as Madame Nescience. But he is on the screen less than a minute before blackness descends again, and the whole of her dream is told without illustration. By this time Jacobs has engendered a strong frustration of visual expectations. Another even briefer image appears, only to be followed by a repetitive, contradictory song ("God is not dead, he is just marvelously sick. . . . God is dead. . . .") through another long blackness. After these three central voids, Jacobs no longer uses this tactic, but the viewer who sees the film for the first time watches to the end under the threat of them. In fact, Jacobs momentarily teases us with the possibility of more. The screen briefly blackens and Smith quotes, " 'Life swarms with innocent monsters.' Charles Baudelaire." But this time the image returns immediately.

The narratives themselves are networks of ironies. The film-maker uses repetition to intensify the duration of the black passages. After a long de-

scription of the lonely little boy's day, Smith makes us fear an endless prolongation of the story by saying, "Next day, same thing all over again.
Mother . . . Mother . . . Mother." But rather than retell the empty
events he introduces a new trope by changing from the third to the first
person and closes the ironic distance between his story and himself:

> Then, and there was a little boy that lived upstairs . . . and one day
> the little boy found the other little boy that lived upstairs, the family
> who lived upstairs, in the upstairs floor, and the little boy who was less
> than seven, the lonely little boy, the lonely little boy was less than seven,
> I know that because we didn't leave Columbus until I was seven, I know
> it, I was under seven and I took a match and I lit it and I pulled out the
> other little boy's penis and I burnt his penis with a match!

At the moment of transition to the first person, the narrative tone changes
to a rapid, hysterical confession which mounts in intensity until the last
word, which ends both the story and the blackness.

A comparable shift of narrative levels occurs in the subsequent story.
First he establishes the character of Madame Nescience, then he describes
her sadistic dream in which she becomes a Mother Superior. He repeatedly confuses the roles while relating the dream. At one point, while
imitating the voice of Sister Dexterity, he addresses the Mother Superior
as if she were the dreamer: "Madame Nescience—I mean, Mother Superior!" and excuses his lapse by saying "you see this is a dream." But after
that he continues to call the nun by the dreamer's name without correcting himself.

The space through which the characters move is cluttered and cramped.
The camera hovers close to them, often shifting slightly to follow their
movements. Even when they dance to the Astaire and Rogers' duet, "Let's
call the whole thing off," the camera cannot get a shot of their whole
bodies. It must pan down to their feet. Generally the footage looks like
what it is, fragments of two abandoned films, with little concern for composition within the frame or spatial elaboration. Yet within the ironic
structure Jacobs made for this material, its fragmentation and lack of composition become positive qualities.

In the fifth catalogue of the Film-Makers Cooperative, Jacobs describes
the genesis and the theme of the film:

> Jack [Smith] says I made the film too heavy. It was his and Bob's
> [Fleischner] intention to create light monster-movie comedy. Two com-
> edies, actually two separate stories that were being shot simultaneously

until they had a falling out over who should pay for the raw stock destroyed by a fire when Jack's cat knocked over a candle. Jack claimed it was an act of God. In the winter of '59 blue Bob showed me the footage. Having no idea of the original story plans I was able to view the material not as exquisite fragments of a failure, of two failures, but as the makings of a new entirety. Bob gave over the footage to me and with it the freedom to develop it as I saw fit.

. . .

Silly, self-pitying, guilt-strictured and yet triumphing—on one level—over the situation with style, because he's unapologetically gifted, has a genius for courage, knows that a state of indignity can serve to show his character in sharpest relief. He carries on, states his presence for what it is. Does all he can to draw out our condemnation, testing our love of limits, enticing us into an absurd moral posture the better to dismiss us with a regal "screw off."[1]

What is the precise nature of the triumph of which Jacobs speaks? Surely it is not the qualified optimistic moment of the apocalyptic and picaresque films discussed in the previous chapter: the moment of forgetting doom just before the end of *The End*, the final mystery of *A Movie*, the scattered ecstasies of *The Flower Thief*, Blondino's resurrection, or the exorcism that concludes *The Old House, Passing*. There is a moment in *Blonde Cobra* when Jerry Sims collapses in a dance and Smith continues the number by himself that hints at release. In the scene immediately following, the penultimate of the film, there is the structural possibility of such a vision, but it is deliberately made ironic. Smith in baby clothes plays peek-a-boo with the camera to the accompaniment of a live radio in the audience. The potential energy for making this scene a triumph—a willful deepening of Smith's infantilism—begins when he smashes the radio on screen, at which point the radio in the audience stops, as already noted. Baby music from a child's record comes on. He seems to have defied the radio's interruption of his fantasy. But then he undermines this moment by smoking a cigarette and burning holes with its tip in the piece of gauze between the camera and himself. This act, which had occurred before in the film, characterizes the scene as another sordid episode in this mock quest for sexual identity.

Jacobs hated the trance film when he began to make cinema. At the time, he has said, it seemed "precious" and "narcissistic" to him. Although he eschewed its form and conventions, he borrowed its central theme in *Blonde Cobra*. The individual scenes and stories provide an ironic series of sexual options. Transvestism also pervades the film; most of the time he is on the screen, Smith wears drag. The one sustained episode in color has a masochistic climax: Sims, imitating a thirties gangster, enters the room where Smith and another man are puffing smoke at each other and burning a necktie with their cigarettes. Sims stabs one man to death and then attacks Smith with his knife. He cringes and grimaces in fear. Then he mumbles, "Sex is a pain in the ass," and the camera pans up Smith's body to show the knife inserted in his buttocks.

The last station of this sexual odyssey is the very infantilism which had inflected the manner in which all the other sexual options were portrayed. But within *Blonde Cobra* this is not a resolution of the sexual problematic. In the final scene, Smith chants in desperation, "A mother's wisdom had dragged me down to this! a crummy loft! a life of futility! hunger! despair!" He puts a toy gun to his head. The image of a graveyard, first seen when the radio announcer described New York in the first part of the film, appears. Then Smith collapses to the floor revealing Sims behind him holding a card reading FIN. As the film runs out, we hear Smith crying "What went wrong? What went wrong? What went wrong?" referring both to the failed suicide and the end of the film.

The triumph to which Jacobs alludes is not within the film. It is the triumph of the ironical mode which brackets dreams within stories, confuses a character with the actor portraying it, and reveals a sexual despair while mocking sexual despairs. The folding over of guises and revelations deprives the film of a fixed point of reference, the solid presence of content, and makes it into a film object, which fitfully starts and after almost expiring several times, dies with an unanswered question, "What went wrong?"

The style and the form of *Blonde Cobra* were developed over a number of years. Throughout the late 1950s Jacobs had been shooting and editing a vastly ambitious film, *Star Spangled to Death*, which he still promises to complete. I have seen ninety silent edited minutes of this work, which will be three hours long with sound if Jacobs finishes it according to his plans. Before 1964 the longer version had been completely edited, but in order to raise money to pay for its soundtrack he shortened it for a benefit screening. The money was not forthcoming. What remains now for him to do is restore the original editing and construct the soundtrack.

In conceiving and making *Star Spangled to Death* Jacobs developed his aesthetic of failure. The hour and a half of material that he removed for the benefit screening consisted for the most part of found objects (a softcore pornography reel, home movies, a national anthem film), passages of leader, and several early "failed" films of his own. In an unpublished interview, Jacobs described his ambitions for this film and its structure:

> I had a terrific bent toward a barren dynamic perfection. I was leaning in every possible way toward a work like Mondrian would make. At the same time, these perfect structures, I knew, were not right. I felt that their destruction revealed more of a truth than their standing perfection. [For *Star Spangled to Death* I was] days ahead of time setting up very involved sets and situations for Jack and Jerry to wander into, situations which they could break up.
>
> I would just move toward some ordered situation and then introduce Jack or Jerry to break up its pattern or to create some new possibilities of patterns that my mind would not have come up with. I felt the chaos of those two individuals and my penchant for a pattern clarified each other; the patterns became clearer because of the chaos, in the midst of the chaos; these two bodies of chaos became clearer because of the pattern.
>
> I was very interested in combustion. There was even a long destruction sequence in which thing after thing was broken. . . . Just watching things break, and in their breaking reveal their structure, had the most vibrant moment of life, all the clarity of their being made, like explicitly for their moment of destruction. I was interested in revealing things in their breaking and I wanted *Star Spangled to Death* to be a film that was constantly breaking.[2]

In talking about his film Jacobs is careful to distinguish between the "collapse of order" he wanted to achieve and "pure disorder." The relationship between order and its collapse recalls Stan Brakhage's use of chance operations within a controlled editing situation. Jacobs seems to have translated this interplay to the shooting stage by allowing the unpredictable character of his two chief actors to transform the structure of his fixed and very intricate compositions. Both formulations of this aesthetic have their roots in Abstract Expressionism. Jacobs' comes directly from it without the mediation of contemporary American poetics; he studied painting with Hans Hofmann at the Art Students League and in Provincetown in the late 1950s before devoting his energies completely to cinema. In the same interview, he compares the sudden shifts of meaning he wanted to have in *Star Spangled to Death* to Abstract Expressionist painting:

> All your preconceptions of Jack or Jerry could be just turned around any moment. You'd have to rethink who they were again. I was interested in painting that could constantly make you reconceive the entire work.

You'd think it was *this* kind of painting, or this kind of spatial development; and then you hit a point in the painting when you realize that this thing was not behind that.[3]

In a much later structural film, *Soft Rain* (1968), Jacobs would bring this painterly adventure of perception to cinema. In his notes for the fifth Film-Makers Cooperative catalogue he is the film's best analyst:

> Three identical prints of a single 100 ft. fixed-camera take are shown from beginning to end-roll light-flare, with a few feet of blackness preceding/bridging/following the rolls. View from above is of a partially snow-covered low flat rooftop receding between the brick walls of two much taller downtown N.Y. loft buildings. A slightly tilted rectangular shape left of the center of the composition is the section of rain-wet Reade Street visible to us over the low rooftop. Distant trucks, cars persons carrying packages, umbrellas sluggishly pass across this little stage-like area. A fine rain-mist is confused, visually, with the color emulsion grain.
>
> A large black rectangle following up and filling to space above the stage-area is seen as both an unlikely abyss extending in deep space behind the stage or more properly, as a two dimensional plane suspended far forward of the entire snow/rain scene. Though it clearly if slightly overlaps the two receding loft building walls the mind, while knowing better, insists on presuming it to be overlapped by them. (At one point the black plane even trembles). So this mental tugging takes place throughout. The contradiction of 2D reality versus 3D implication is amusingly and mysteriously explicit.[4]

In this superbly detailed description of the phenomenological reading of his own film, Jacobs omits saying that the black rectangle registers as a shade between the camera and the view described as soon as it trembles. In turn this gives rise to the unresolved possibility that we may be looking through a window. He continues:

> Filmed at 24 f.p.s. but projected at 16 the street activity is perceptibly slowed down. It's become a somewhat heavy laboring. The loop repetition (the series hopefully will intrigue you to further run-throughs) automatically imparts a steadily growing rhythmic sense of the street-activities. Anticipation for familiar movement-complexes builds, and as all smaller complexities join up in our knowledge of the whole the purely accidental counter-passings of people and vehicles becomes satisfyingly cogent, seems rhythmically structured and of a piece. Becomes choreography.[5]

There he ends. Although the loops are identical, the image leaves us unsure of that until we can identify and match one of the movements. Once

the looping is confirmed, we wonder how many times we will see it. Un-
noted by the film-maker is the interesting relationship between the purely
linear graphic grid of the composition (the wall of one building forming a
perfect diagonal to the center of the screen, the black rectangle coming
exactly half-way down from the top) and the eccentric juxtaposition of
these elements as volumes.

Jacobs' formal description of *Soft Rain* is evidence of the "bent for barren dynamic perfection" he spoke of in relation to *Star Spangled to Death*.
In the ninety-minute version of that film, formal composition makes visual
geometry out of junk and garbage, a back alley, and cluttered rooms.
Gauzes, curtains of cellophane, and projecting bamboo poles delineate
planes of depth in which complex, orchestrated movements harmonize or
conflict, elaborate a deep space, or call attention to off-screen areas. The
variety of spatial and editing strategies is considerable: color scenes are
mixed with black-and-white; the texture of the imagery ranges from high
contrast to practically washed out; a series of very careful compositions in
which parts of an actor's body are framed at the edge of the screen will be
interrupted by jerky camera movements; switches to negative, punch
holes, and flares will disrupt a composition or break up an edited sequence. Individual shots often embody the tension between order and
chaos that Jacobs described as his ambition, as if Jack Smith or Jerry
Sims were suddenly to appear and disrupt the quiet of *Soft Rain*. But
like *Blonde Cobra* and unlike *Soft Rain*, human actions dominate the
film. Although there are moments of quiet and rest, the chaotic over-
whelms the ordered in the experience of the film.

According to the film-maker's description, *Star Spangled to Death* will,
when its soundtrack is completed, relate the "mock allegory" of Jack
Smith as "the Spirit Not of Life But of Living" and Jerry Sims as "Suffering." The myth that Jacobs proposes is not an ordered story to be
broken down, subverted by the form of the film; it is an abstraction of
that form itself. For the myth is without a dramatic focus until Sims decides to renounce his role and thus ceases to be the metaphysical embodi-
ment of Suffering. Smith and other minor characters convince him to re-
sume, to be "a person whom suffering has taken over like a disease," and
as a reward for doing so they allow him to destroy a Rockefeller-for-
Governor poster. When this ritual is over, the film ends in a cast party
photographed with a hand-held moving camera. The film is so slow starting, has so many false beginnings, undeveloped lines, digressions, and
abrupt breaks that it is almost half over before the allegorical person-

alities are defined. By the time the two central roles are clear, Suffering has decided to abdicate. The second part of the film describes in fragmentary narratives the reversal of this decision. The filming of lunch breaks, rests in the shooting, and the inclusion of bad takes increase the deliberate confusion of actor and role which is the ultimate subject of the allegory itself.

The making of *Star Spangled to Death* took most of Jacobs' artistic energies between 1957 and 1963. Since then he has done very little with it. It is a work of such scope and ambition that despite its negativity and its aesthetic of failure it participates in the myth of the absolute film. He once described a screening of a Ron Rice film at the Film-Makers Cinemateque at which a reel of film fell from a table near the projector and rolled across the balcony floor, through a partition in the rail, and down to the seats below without harming anyone. He would have liked to have such an ending for the projection of *Star Spangled to Death*. He is aware too that his seeming inability to complete the film is bound up with its aesthetic.

In addition to *Blonde Cobra*, Jacobs completed *Little Stabs at Happiness* (1959-63) as a by-product of, or "a true breather" from, his long film. Except for the addition of titles which identify the four sections of the film and the use of 78 rpm records and a short monologue on the soundtrack, the film is exactly as it came out of the camera, with no editing. Both Smith and Sims appear in it. The first episode shows Smith and a girl sitting in a dry bathtub playing with dolls. At one point he tries to eat the crotch of a doll between puffs on a cigarette. The camera moves casually, often resting on a bare lightbulb or another static element in the room.

Each part of the film (they are all in color) is a separate moment without narrative causality. Each is immediately present. But as if he were unable to bear the unqualified presence of his images, in the second section Jacobs himself intrudes on the soundtrack, apologizing for his monologue by saying that he wanted some sound other than music to relax the audience's restlessness at this point. He then launches, in the most casual manner, a full-scale attack on the presence of his film. First he undermines the temporal integrity of the visual episode; then he attempts to involve us in the lives of the people we see on the screen. He tells us what time it is, 12:28, the moment of his recording the soundtrack. He brings the clock nearer to the microphone so we can listen to it tick. He plays a few notes on an organ before telling us he wants to use it in a future film. He even inserts a lacuna in the soundtrack itself: "I've just played that back," he says, "and I like it. It's vague." Meanwhile, on the screen two girls have been sitting on chairs on a roof. The camera pans slowly from the shoes of one to those of another. A series of leisurely, careful compositions shows them rocking before a brick wall. After the lacuna, Jacobs tells us that he no longer sees anyone in the film. He begins by describing how the two girls have disappeared from his life and goes on to describe his broken relationships with Jerry Sims and Jack Smith. The nostalgia of this monologue transforms our perception of the songs in the later sections. As dated pieces, they now carry a sense of pastness which spreads over to the images as well. But unlike *Blonde Cobra* and *Star Spangled to Death*, the immediacy of the visual is much stronger than the verbal undermining.

As soon as the speech ends, the scene changes without the introduction of a new title. Fast moving, fragmented shots of shadows on a wall prepare for a montage of the orange pipes which cast the shadows. Amid that montage he injects brief shots of someone jumping around on the roof and a girl hiding her face from the probing camera behind an old felt hat. The sequence passes in silence.

The next section, "It Began to Drizzle," also has a silent epilogue. But first, to music, Jacobs presents fixed-frame compositions of Jerry Sims and a woman sitting outside in a light rain. A table and chairs have been set up on cobblestones. The shots shift in a geometrical elaboration of the space between the two unspeaking actors. Often one occupies the extreme foreground while the other sits in the distance. At the end of this sequence, there is a brief silent scene of Jacobs himself drawing chalk figures on a sidewalk among Chinese children.

Jack Smith, as "the Spirit of Listlessness" dressed in a clown suit, plays and lounges on a roof. He sucks at colored balloons, flashes light into the camera with a mirror, and almost seems about to take flight to the song, "Happy Bird."

Smith himself made his own first film, *Scotch Tape* (1962), during the shooting of *Star Spangled to Death*. That day Jacobs had assembled his cast in a destroyed building or a section of a junk yard. Rusted cables in great tangles and broken slabs of concrete were all about. Smith borrowed the camera and filmed a dance of people exuberantly hopping around and under the cables. The area of wreckage was so extensive that he could film his dancers either from a few feet away or from hundreds of feet above them. Only by the size of the human figure is the scale of the shot perceptible. Occasionally panning but usually with a fixed frame, he mixed shots of nearness with extreme distances. In the longest shots he framed his group of actors in a corner of the cluttered image; then he positioned them under a covering slab of concrete so that in the brief duration of the shot the viewer must seek out the dancers in the visual field. In the closer shots he makes use of a green artificial flower under which they dance or which some of them hold in their teeth while jumping about. Once, the flower rests statically in focus while the blurred bodies vibrate in the background.

Scotch Tape is only three minutes long, in color, and appears to have been constructed in the camera without much subsequent editing, if any. It takes its title from a triangular wedge of dirty Scotch tape along the right side of the image. Since Jacobs seldom had enough money to develop his rushes from *Star Spangled to Death*, he had shot several rolls of film before he realized that the tape had gotten caught in the camera. Rather than let this accident ruin his film, Smith capitalized upon it in his title. Fortunately its fixed position offers a formal counterbalance to the play of scales upon which the shot changes are based.

Jonas Mekas hailed *Blonde Cobra, Little Stabs at Happiness*, and *Scotch Tape* as opening a vital new direction in the American cinema. On May 2, 1963, he wrote in his column "Movie Journal," in the *Village Voice*:

> Lately, several movies have appeared from the underground which, I think, are making a very important turn in the independent cinema. As *Shadows* and *Pull My Daisy* marked the end of the avant-garde experimental cinema tradition of the 40's and 50's (the symbolist-surrealist cinema of intellectual meanings), now there are works appearing which are marking a turn in the so-called New American Cinema—a turn from the New York realist school (the cinema of "surface" meanings and social engagement) toward a cinema of disengagement and new freedom.
>
> The movies I have in mind are Ron Rice's *The Queen of Sheba Meets the Atom Man;* Jack Smith's *The Flaming Creatures* [sic]; Ken Jacobs' *Little Stabs at Happiness;* Bob Fleischner's [sic] *Blonde Cobra*—four works that make up the real revolution in cinema today. These movies are illuminating and opening up sensibilities and experiences never before recorded in the American arts; a content which Baudelaire, the Marquis de Sade, and Rimbaud gave to world literature a century ago and which Burroughs gave to American literature three years ago. It is a world of flowers of evil, of illuminations, of torn and tortured flesh; a poetry which is at once beautiful and terrible, good and evil, delicate and dirty.
>
> *Blonde Cobra*, undoubtedly, is the masterpiece of the Baudelairean

cinema, and it is a work hardly surpassable in perversity, in richness, in beauty, in sadness, in tragedy. I think it is one of the great works of personal cinema, so personal that it is ridiculous to talk about "author's" cinema. I know that the larger public will misinterpret and misunderstand these films.[6]

No artist within the American avant-garde film has equaled the influence of Jonas Mekas as a polemicist. That influence was at its height in 1963 when he proclaimed the birth of the "Baudelairean cinema." He couched his evaluation in terms of a historical perspective quite different from that of this book. I would like to interrupt my discussion of Jacobs and Smith at this point to analyze and trace the history of Mekas' position.

In January 1955, Mekas published the first issue of his magazine, *Film Culture*. He had arrived in New York six years before as a displaced person along with his brother Adolfas. They both immediately began to learn the techniques of film-making, although Jonas continued to write poetry in his native Lithuanian. In that first issue they included an article by Hans Richter, their teacher at the Film Institute of City College of New York. "The Film as an Original Art Form" affirmed an essentially avant-garde stance. Nevertheless, the editorial position of the magazine represented in that first issue by Edouard de Laurot's "Toward a Theory of Dynamic Realism" was severely critical of the American avant-garde cinema. In the third issue, Mekas published "The Experimental Film in America," an attack in the guise of a survey with subsections entitled "The Adolescent Character of the American Film Poem," "The Conspiracy of Homosexuality," "The Lack of Creative Inspiration: Technical Crudity and Thematic Narrowness." He concluded, "The image of the contemporary American film poem and cineplastics, as briefly presented here, is decidedly unencouraging. . . . To improve the quality of the American film poem, experiments should be directed not so much towards new techniques but toward deeper themes, toward a more penetrating treatment of the nature and drama of the man of our epoch." Significantly, he calls for more attention to these film-makers as a way of encouraging their improvement. Stan Brakhage has described an emergency meeting of the film-makers called by Maya Deren and Willard Maas at the time of the publication of this article to discuss the possibility of a lawsuit. Nothing came of it. Two and a half years later (November 1957), Mekas turned over half the magazine to "The 'Experimental' Scene," in which film-makers themselves contributed articles. There were no more attacks.

With its nineteenth issue in 1959, *Film Culture* established the Independent Film Award to mark "the entrance of a new generation of film-makers in America." In the editorial for that issue, Mekas proclaimed the death of Hollywood. While describing the avant-garde cinema of the 1950s as a "degeneration," he gave those film-makers credit for having "kept the spirit of free cinema alive in America." The first flowering of that spirit was, according to him, the recipient of the first Independent Film Award—John Cassavetes' *Shadows*. In the next three issues, spread over two years, awards were given to Robert Frank and Alfred Leslie's *Pull My Daisy* and Richard Leacock's *Primary*. And, as the editorials became longer, more credit was given to avant-garde film-makers. Furthermore, since 1958 a feature article on a major avant-gardist by Parker Tyler had been part of every issue.

In the editorials between 1959 and 1961, one can see the tremendous impression *nouvelle vague* in France had on Mekas' thinking. It seemed to him that there had been a fundamental revolution in film-making, which he optimistically saw spreading to England and Poland as well as America. At the same time he was discovering an indigenous realist cinema in the work of Jerome Hill, Lionel Rogosin, and Morris Engel. With feature films in production by Shirley Clarke, Robert Frank, and numerous lesser-known independent directors who have not subsequently developed, it looked to Mekas as if the economics of American film-making had shifted from lavish Hollywood productions to more modest 35mm and even 16mm films. He interpreted this as the end of the "experimental" film of the 1940s and 1950s and the beginning of a more socially committed, more publicly oriented, independent cinema. Once he began thinking of the early avant-garde cinema as the forerunner of the movement of which he was the champion, he gradually began to see more in the films he had previously rejected.

In retrospect this is not at all surprising. Mekas' sensibilities are those of a Romantic. In three of his films he portrays himself reading books; in *Guns of the Trees*, it is Shelley's *Prometheus Unbound* that opens and closes the film; throughout the abandoned *Rabbitshit Haikus* (1962-63), which he made while on the set of his brother's *Hallelujah the Hills*, he is reading Blake; in *Diaries, Notes, and Sketches*, subtitled *Walden*, it is Thoreau. The Romantic phenomenology was difficult to perceive in the avant-garde cinema of the 1940s and 1950s, but easier when the mythopoeic cinema in the early 1960s manifested itself. Jonas Mekas was there to recognize it and celebrate it. In 1958, he had been named the film critic of the *Village Voice*. By the early 1960s the paper had grown from local to

national circulation with particular influence in the arts. Thus by the time
he became the champion of the New American Cinema, Mekas was one of
the most powerful film critics in America. The first clear sign of a shift in
his attitude toward the older avant-gardists was his choice of Maya Deren
as his substitute critic at the *Village Voice* in the summer of 1960 when he
took time off to concentrate on the shooting of *Guns of the Trees.*

Had he confined his activities to writing and making films, Jonas Mekas
might not have been quite as powerful as he was to become in the early
1960s. On September 28, 1960, he called the first meeting of the New
American Cinema Group, 23 independent film-makers of whom only one,
Gregory Markopoulos, aside from Mekas himself, falls within the scope of
this book. Of the several points outlined in their manifesto, one was to
have revolutionary significance but not as envisioned by that group. The
sixth point of the manifesto called for the foundation of "our own cooperative distribution center."

For a year Emile de Antonio tried to distribute a handful of 35mm
short and feature films theatrically before a true film-makers' cooperative
could be founded. While this unsuccessful effort was in operation, Mekas
accepted the position of organizer of a series of special screenings, most of
them on weekend midnights, at the Charles Theater on New York's
Lower East Side. There he initiated a number of one-man shows for
avant-garde film-makers whose work had never been completely shown in
New York. He followed this up with an article on the film-makers in the
Voice. He also began the tradition of open-house screenings to which film-
makers brought unknown works, rushes, and works-in-progress. It was at
such an open-house that he discovered Ken Jacobs, who was screening
parts of *Little Stabs at Happiness.*

In the fall of 1961 Maya Deren died. Stan Brakhage happened to be in
New York at that time, holding a series of screenings of his recent films at
the Provincetown Playhouse. Since *Reflections on Black* (1955), Cinema
16, the only distributor of avant-garde films in the 1950s, had refused to
handle his work or even to show it in their yearly programs devoted to the
"experimental" film. When Mekas saw the ensemble of work Brakhage
had produced between 1958 and 1961, he was sensitive to its quality. He
awarded Brakhage the fourth Independent Film Award (*Film Culture*
24) for *The Dead* and *Prelude: Dog Star Man.* Since then the award has
gone exclusively to avant-gardists: Jack Smith, Andy Warhol, Harry Smith,
Gregory Markopoulos, Michael Snow, Kenneth Anger and Robert Breer.

In 1962 Mekas himself took over the film distribution project. By this

time the initial experiment at the Charles Theater had grown into a series
of screenings, at first weekly and later daily, in various rented theaters
around Manhattan. By 1962 the group of film-makers who had anticipated
a radical change in the production and distribution of feature films in
America had given up that idea. Yet Mekas realized that an outlet was
needed for the films of Brakhage, Markopoulos, Menken, Jacobs, Smith,
etc. He appointed the young film-maker David Brooks as manager of the
cooperative. Its first catalogue contained only *Guns of the Trees, Pull My
Daisy*, and the films of Gregory Markopoulos out of the list originally proposed by the group. Cassavetes' *Shadows*, Clarke's *The Connection*, and
even Adolfas Mekas' *Hallelujah the Hills* were being distributed com-
mercially.

It would be several years before the rental fees of the Film-Makers Cooperative and the income from the Film-Makers Showcase, later called the
Film-Makers Cinematheque, would produce income of even a thousand
dollars a year for the film-makers. Yet they provided a center where film-
makers could see each other's work; and *Film Culture* and the *Village
Voice* brought news of this activity around the country. On the model of
the Film-Makers Showcase, Bruce Baillie founded Canyon Cinema outside San Francisco in 1962 and soon after that moved it to Berkeley. By
1963 there was a Canyon Cinema Cooperative.

In "Notes on the New American Cinema" (*Film Culture* 24, 1962),
Mekas attempted a comprehensive synthesis of the realist and visionary
tendencies within the independent cinema. He speaks of Morris Engel,
Lionel Rogosin, John Cassavetes, Shirley Clarke, Sidney Meyers, Rickey
Leacock, as well as Stan Brakhage, Robert Breer, Ron Rice, Marie Menken, Stan Vanderbeek, and several others, but in the polemical sections of
the essay, "Part Two: A Few Statements on the New American Artist as a
Man" and "Part Three: Summing Up, Connecting the Style with Man,"
he employs the language of Romantic and Abstract Expressionist aesthetics (the essay opens with quotations from De Kooning and Shelley):

> The new artist, by directing his ear inward, is beginning to catch bits
> of man's true vision. By simply being *new* (which means, by listening
> deeper than their other contemporaries), Brakhage and Breer contribute
> to the liberation of man's spirit from the dead matter of culture; they
> open new vistas for life. In this sense, an old art is immoral—it keeps
> man's spirit in bondage to Culture. The very destructiveness of the
> modern artist, his anarchy, as in Happenings, or, even, action painting,
> is, therefore, a confirmation of life and freedom.[7]

In the notes on "Improvisation," "The Shaky Camera," and "Acting," he makes it clear that he is less interested in the realistic world view of Engel, Clarke, Rogosin, and Leacock than in the way they substitute a kind of spontaneous performance for classical acting.

Mekas' involvement with a theory of acting extends back almost as far as his involvement with Romantic poetry. Before they left Lithuania, he and Adolfas had set up a regional theater. Later in a German camp for displaced persons they studied with Ippolitas Tvirbotas, a teacher of the Stanislavsky method. But it was the transformation of acting into performance, or the breakdown of the difference between the performer and his role, that seems to have particularly interested him in the late 1950s and early 1960s. The first four Independent Film Awards, for instance, show a progressive preference for the reality of performance. In *Shadows*, actors play in a spontaneous and improvising manner; in *Pull My Daisy*, non-actors—poets and a painter—play themselves; in *Primary* the performers are Senators Kennedy and Humphrey, playing for the Presidency as filmed with Leacock's passionate detachment. Finally, in the Brakhage films, the film-maker makes himself, his family, indeed his life, the subject of his film; it is passionate self-involvement.

Although this sensitivity to a philosophy of performance is only part—and not a dominant part—of his aesthetic, it accounts for some positions and tendencies in his criticism. If we reconsider his text on the "Baudelairean cinema" in this light, the principle underlying its historical schema reveals itself. Time soon proved him wrong in announcing the death of "the symbolist-surrealist cinema of intellectual meanings." Within a year *Twice a Man, Scorpio Rising, Heaven and Earth Magic*, and much of *Dog Star Man* would be publicly screened for the first time; Ken Jacobs was about to begin shooting his most explicitly symbolical and mythopoeic film, *The Sky Socialist*. The fundamental change of the early 1960s within the avant-garde film, as I have shown in several places, was the emergence of the mythopoeic film, a direct descendant of the trance film, which had undergone a gradual but fragmented evolution in the 1950s.

From the vantage point of almost a decade since the "Baudelairean cinema" article, it seems to me that Mekas mistook a flurry of contemporary activity for the avant-garde tradition. He also seems to have equated the somnambulistic performances within the trance films with their total meaning while astutely sensing that the magnification of symbolism and the image of the possessed quester were intimately intertwined. What he did not foresee was a new form which could be even more symbolically and intellectually complex without the somnambulist.

To Mekas' credit one must add that in the early 1960s a dimension of social criticism entered at least some of the avant-garde films. The previous chapter touches upon some manifestations in California. Mekas' own film, *Guns of the Trees*, which is formally closer to *The End* than to the films of Cassavetes, Clarke, Rogosin, or Engel, was a social protest. *Scorpio Rising* can be viewed in this way. The films from this period by Stan Vanderbeek, Richard Preston, and of course Jacobs' *Star Spangled to Death* and *Blonde Cobra* attack aspects of American society.

Jacobs, in his own highly personal view of the history of the avant-garde film, used the term "underground film," which became a journalistic commonplace after 1962 and which Stan Vanderbeek seems to have invented in 1961 (*Film Quarterly*, XIV, 4) to describe the period from the late 1950s until the mid-1960s, including his own films, Smith's *Flaming Creatures*, the earliest Warhol films, and others. Interestingly, Jacobs claims that period ended when avant-garde films became "fashionable." He partially blames Mekas for contributing to its end by "promoting a star system." It is true that an issue of *Film Culture* (Summer 1964) had a center section of photographs of "Stars of the New American Cinema," and, perhaps more to the point, Mekas dismissed the scope of *Star Spangled to Death* with a discussion of Smith's performance:

> I recently saw a rough cut of Jacobs' new film, *Star Spangled to Death*, a three-hour movie he has been shooting for the past seven years, and I was surprised to find in it the beginnings of *Scotch Tape* and *Blonde Cobra* and the beautiful earliest work of Jack Smith where he does as good a job as the early Chaplin—which I know is a big statement, but you'll see someday it's true.[8]

This again is the manifestation of a sensitivity to performance and an excitement over new possibilities in acting. But neither the transition Mekas proposes from symbolist-surrealist to disengaged and free or that of Jacobs from "narcissistic" to Underground to "fashionable" transcends Mekas' or Jacobs' sense of himself at the center of things. When he made the "Baudelairean cinema" statement, Mekas obviously saw himself on the side of the free, looking backwards; Jacobs uses the underground platform to look in both directions.

Jonas Mekas' theoretical interest in performance had a more profound effect upon his criticism and his film-making when it intersected with his poetics. The concept of the self is the locus of that intersection. The title of Stanislavsky's book, as Mekas once pointed out to a group of young film-makers, is *The Actor Works Upon Himself*. In "Notes on the New American Cinema," he says "Improvisation is the highest form of condensation; it points to the very essence of a thought, an emotion, a movement." What had been a method of preparing actors to perform roles in plays becomes, in Mekas' transformation, the central process of the imagination:

> Improvisation is, I repeat, the highest form of concentration, of awareness, of intuitive knowledge, when the imagination begins to dismiss the prearranged, the contrived mental structures, and goes directly to the depths of the matter. This is the true meaning of improvisation, and it is not a method at all; it is, rather, a state of being necessary for any inspired creation. It is an ability that every true artist develops by a constant and life-long inner vigilance, by the cultivation—yes!—of his senses.[9]

Jonas Mekas, following the initial efforts of Maya Deren, has devoted much of his time and resources in the last twelve years to sustaining a "visionary company"[10] of film-makers through his criticism and his organization of the Film-Makers Cooperative, the Film-Makers Cinematheque, the Friends of the New Cinema (which gave small grants to approximately twelve film-makers each year between 1964 and 1971), and Anthology Film Archives. Although his work is the most spectacular example of commitment to the vision of a community of film-makers, it is supported and reflected in similar but less sustained efforts by many of the film-makers I have been considering: Maya Deren as the first propagandist for the American avant-garde film and the founder of the Creative Film Foundation, Frank Stauffacher as founder of Art in Cinema, Bruce Baillie as founder of the Canyon Cinema Cooperative, Peter Kubelka as designer of Anthology Film Archives' Invisible Theater, and Stan Brakhage as a lecturer and enthusiast, sometimes in the guise of a Savonarola, attempting to bridge the generations and geographical isolation of film-makers. To this list should be added Ken Jacobs as the first director of The Millennium Film Workshop between 1966 and 1968 which made equipment and instruction freely available to aspiring film-makers in New York.

But to return to the films of Ken Jacobs and Jack Smith, it is necessary to consider first a film-maker who exerted a considerable influence on both of them, as well as on Stan Brakhage, Larry Jordan, and Jonas Mekas. He is Joseph Cornell. I have already discussed Brakhage's encounter with Cornell at the turning point of his style. After years of correspondence, Larry Jordan spent several weeks during the summer of 1968 at Cornell's home in Queens, New York, assisting him in his well-known work as a collagist and box-maker. He also photographed, under Cornell's direction, a very evocative film of a trip to a graveyard, which has not yet been shown publicly. Cornell gave him three related collage movies which he had been working on for several years with instructions on how to complete them. In 1970, under the sponsorship of Anthology Film Archives, where Cornell's films have been made available to the public for the first time, Jordan completed all three—*Cotillion, The Midnight Party*, and *The Children's Party*.

Cornell's first collage film, *Rose Hobart* (later tentatively renamed *Tristes Tropiques*), was made in the late 1930s and first shown at Julien Levy's art gallery in New York. It represents the intersection of his involvement with collage and his love of the cinema, for Cornell had been for many years a collector of films and motion picture stills. *Rose Hobart* is a re-editing of Columbia's jungle drama, *East of Borneo*, starring Rose Hobart. It is a breathtaking example of the potential for surrealistic imagery within a conventional Hollywood film once it is liberated from its narrative causality. In reducing the feature film to approximately fifteen minutes and replacing the soundtrack with music, he concentrates on the moods and reactions of the heroine. Since he often does not show to whom she is talking or to what she is reacting, her fears and anxieties seem to be in response to the very mystery which the collagist's editing has made of the film. Two men—an Oriental in a turban and an American—and two women appear fleetingly throughout the film without revealing their roles.

Among his tactics to intensify fragmentation are cutting to a scene just before it fades out, combining in rapid succession a series of similar encounters, intercutting two scenes from different times as if they were simultaneous, and showing the closing or opening of a door without the person entering or leaving. Because of this fragmentation, certain images take on surrealistic dimensions, such as the natives driving crocodiles into the river with poles or a curtain pulled to reveal a belching volcano.

By the radical employment of hysteron-proteron which alters the logical order, the film-maker gives the impression of repetition and ruptures linear time and attendant causality. For instance, he shows Rose Hobart leaning over a balcony early in the film. When she looks down, he intercuts a slow-motion shot of ripples in a pool, one of two images that possibly were not part of the original Columbia footage. Shortly afterward he shows her approaching the same balcony in a piece of film that must have immediately preceded her leaning over, but now the intervening shots have given her act a new context. Several times he cuts from the dying or dead man with a turban to shots of him fully alive. At the end of the film, he dies metaphorically; as Rose Hobart stands before his bed or his bier, the sun quickly passes through a full eclipse, and then, by a skillful joining of shots, seems to fall from the sky like a pebble into the pool we had seen before and disappear under a surface of slow-motion ripples. She lowers her head, as if reacting to his death in the final shot.

Ken Jacobs, who worked very briefly for Cornell while he was making *Star Spangled to Death*, borrowed *Rose Hobart* to study and to show to Jack Smith. He described his reaction to the film:

> I was seeing Jack again and I told him, "Jack, you've got to see this movie." We looked at it again and again, and we were both knocked out. Jack tried to act at first like a little bit removed, like I was overstating it, and then he broke down and said, "No, it's very good." We looked at it in every possible way: on the ceiling, in mirrors, bouncing it all over the room, in corners, in focus, out of focus, with a blue filter that Cornell had given me, without it, backwards. It was just like an eruption of energy and it was another reinforcement of this idea I had for making this shit film [*Star Spangled to Death*] that would be broken apart and then again there would be an order.[11]

Although Jacobs describes his reaction to *Rose Hobart* in terms of the film he was making then, its influence extended to his most recent film, *Tom, Tom, the Piper's Son*. There he transformed an old Hollywood film into a modernist work, not by re-editing and showing it through a filter but by rephotographing it at different speeds, accenting the grain, and indeed performing a series of operations on it similar to the variations with which he had projected Cornell's film.

In his later films—both those photographed by Rudy Burkhardt, Stan Brakhage, and Larry Jordan and the collage films which Jordan completed —Joseph Cornell describes the marginal area where the conscious and the unconscious meet. These are films which affirm a sustained present moment in which a quality of reminiscence is implicated. Frequently, they share the themes of his boxes and collages and make allusion in their titles or their imagery to Romantic and symbolist poetry, which has been a continual source of inspiration to him. An exceptionally subtle fluctuation of consciousness between present observation and reminiscence occurs in the interplay between a formal and a thematic strategy. Formally, many of Cornell's films show the trace of his method of making them: the camera moves as if to catch something another man (Cornell) is pointing out. Thematically, there are figures within each of the films who are proposed as tentative mediators, through whose consciousness these camera movements might be experienced. The degree of mediation, in which the filmmaker and his stand-in in the film approach unity, varies considerably between the films and even within them. Often the conditional consciousness is that of a passing child, but birds and even statues (explicitly in *What Mozart Saw on Mulberry Street*, implicitly in *Angel*) can assume it.

In *A Legend for Fountains* there are three levels of mediation (a woman, children, birds). The first section, called "Fragments," establishes a series of motifs upon which the second section, without a title, elaborates. A young lady slowly descends a dark staircase, passes through a hallway and out into the street. Looking down the same hallway, we immediately see her returning with the same slow pace. As if to record the time lost in that elliptical jump-cut, the camera shows "fragments" of her walk: she stares through the windows of a sandwich shop and a toy store; she hurries around a corner and rests against a wall covered with graffiti; her breath condenses in the cold air. The camera dwells on children that she sees playing in the street; it slowly explores the graffiti and finally follows the flight of birds among the buildings above her.

The second and somewhat longer section repeats and extends the imagery of the first, beginning with the moments before she left the building. An opening title, ". . . your solitude, shy in hotels . . . ," quotes a source of inspiration in the film, Garcia Lorca's "Tu Infancia en Menton," from which the title also comes. The young lady sits by a window stroking a black cat. The camera observes her silhouette from inside and her face can be seen under the reflections on the glass from without. When she leaves the building, the image fixes upon the reflections on the window of the moving door, as in the opening of Brakhage's *Anticipation of the Night*. Outside, the attention shifts between her, the birds on top of the buildings, the graffiti on the walls, and the children playing amid trashcans.

Whenever he is asked about the relationship between his films and his boxes and collages, Cornell denies that there is any. The films, he sometimes says, "never got off the ground." Nevertheless, they share a number of recurrent themes with the boxes: the child, the aviary, the hotel, and of course the window. The bits of letters and newspapers pasted to the back wall of some of his boxes function similarly to the graffiti-covered surfaces of *A Legend for Fountains*.

The window as a veil in Joseph Cornell's *A Legend for Fountains* and in his *Medici Boy Box*.

The serial structure, involving a return to and a reorganization of elements in two or more related works, which unites many of his boxes and collages, extends to his films. The double structure of A *Legend for Fountains* is one example. The most mystifying transformation by variation that he achieved in film was in making *Gnir Rednow*. He reversed left to right and printed backwards the film he had commissioned from Stan Brakhage, *Wonder Ring*, and in so doing, he introduced a differential which made the film characteristically his own. In the three collage films that Larry Jordan completed, the serial structure is very apparent. All three involve the re-editing of a film about a children's party that the film-maker found. He creates three related contexts of the child's consciousness by combining the dancing, feasting, and games of the party with circus acts, telescopes, constellations of stars, Zeus throwing thunderbolts in a primitive film, and windows.

What Jack Smith gained from seeing Cornell's first collage film remains a matter of speculation. Although his first long film, *Flaming Creatures* (1963), does not contain collage material, it involves the transformation and "liberation" of Hollywood stereotypes in an ironical recreation of the pseudo-Arabian world of Maria Montez films. His unfinished *Normal Love* (1963-   ) also draws upon the mythology of the conventional movies for its pantheon of monsters. In *No President* (1969), which was shown once and then dismantled, he incorporated a found documentary on the life of Wendell Willkie into a film of his own.

In 1963 and 1964 Smith published two articles in *Film Culture* which outline the way he views the cinema. The first was on Maria Montez and the second on Josef von Sternberg. Both of them assert that the essence of cinema is the visual in opposition to the narrative, which retards comprehension.

> People never know why they do what they do. But they have to have explanations for themselves and others.
> So Von Sternberg's movies had to have plots even tho they already had them inherent in the images. What he did was make movies naturally—he lived in a visual world. The explanations plots he made up out of some logic having nothing to do with the visuals of his films.[12]

He argues for an appreciation of Maria Montez films as pure cinema, once the narrative line is ignored:

> These were light films—if we really believed that films are visual it would be possible to believe these rather pure cinema—weak technique, true, but rich imagery. . . .

The primitive allure of movies is a thing of light and shadows. A bad film is one which doesn't flicker and shift and move through lights and shadows, contrasts, textures by way of light. If I have these I don't mind phoniness (or the sincerity of clever actors), simple minded plots (or novelistic "good" plots), nonsense or seriousness (I don't feel nonsense in movies as a threat to my mind since I don't go to movies for ideas that arise from sensibleness of ideas). Images evoke feelings and ideas that are suggested by feeling.[13]

Visual truth, for Smith, reveals more than acting intends:

But in my movies I know that I prefer non actor stars to "convincing" actor stars—only a personality that exposes itself—if through moldiness (human slips can convince me—in movies) and I was very convinced by Maria Montez in her particular ease of her great beauty and integrity.[14]

Applying the same perspective to von Sternberg, he discovers not only a plastic play of light and shadow but a revelation of sexual presence:

His expression was of the erotic realm—the neurotic gothic deviated sex-colored world and it was a turning inside out of himself and magnificent. You had to use your eyes to know this tho because the sound track babbled inanities—it alleged Dietrich was an honest jewel thief, noble floosie, fallen woman, etc. to cover up the visuals. In the visuals she was none of those. She was V.S. himself. A flaming neurotic—nothing more or less— no need to know she was rich, poor, innocent, guilty, etc. Your eye if you could use it told you more interesting things (facts?) than those. Dietrich was his visual projection—a brilliant transvestite in a world of delirious unreal adventures. Thrilled by his/her own movement —by superb taste in light, costumery, textures, movement, subject and camera, subject camera/revealing faces—in fact all revelation but *visual* revelation.[15]

Nowhere has Jack Smith spoken as well about himself as in this passage allegedly about von Sternberg's Dietrich. *Flaming Creatures* deliberately manifests what he finds implicated in Maria Montez's and von Sternberg's films, and without the interference of a plot. When he brings to the fore what has been latent in those films—visual texture, androgynous sexual presence, exotic locations (the Araby of Montez' films or the Spain, China, and Morocco of von Sternberg's)—and at the same time completely discards what held these films together (elaborate narratives), he utterly transforms his sources and uncovers a mythic center from which they had been closed off. Ken Kelman, in the first article on *Flaming Creatures* in *Film Culture,* found that it "echoes with ancient ritual chant,

with Milton and with Dante . . . for the very scope and scale of sin becomes demonic in a Miltonian sense, and *Flaming Creatures* might be
subtitled *Pandemonium Regained,* a paean not for the Paradise Lost, but
for the Hell Satan gained."

Although Jack Smith dispenses with plot, he retains the structure of the
scene in his film. There are ten scenes which blend into one another with
deliberately obscured boundaries. Their sequence, for the most part, seems
determined by rhythm and dramatic effect rather than by narrative. The
move toward and away from a central core of three episodes in which the
flaming creatures die in an orgy and after an interlude are reborn gives a
centripetal form to the cyclic myth. The style of photography changes
with the scenes, orchestrating them as if they were movements of a musical work.

At the very beginning of the film a voice tells us that "Ali Baba comes
tonight," but he never arrives. The Arabian harem of men and women en-
acts, instead, its regular ritual of orgasmic death and regeneration. Each
of the scenes has its own piece of music, sound effects, or speech, but unlike *Scorpio Rising,* the sound does not rigidly define the extension of the
episode. Like the scenes themselves, the sound of one blends into the next,
a silent interlude marks their transition, or they are intercut as one scene
tries fitfully to get started before the previous has quite ended.

Smith first encountered the use of outdated raw film to produce washed
out or high contrast textures in Jacobs' *Star Spangled to Death,* but it was
seeing Rice's *The Flower Thief* that convinced him of its possibilities. In
Flaming Creatures he far exceeds either of these films in the employment
of murky, burned out, or high contrast textures to create different depths
and ranges of space. In the first scene, as figures pass back and forth in
front of a poster on which the credits of the film have been ornately written, the gray, washed out picture quality gives the impression that he was
filming in a cloud. The narrowing of the tonal range obscures the sense of
depth, which Smith capitalizes on by cluttering the panning frame with
actors and with details of limbs, breasts, a penis, and puckered lips so that
not only depth disappears but the vertical and horizontal coordinates as
well.

By way of contrast, the subsequent scene takes place in the clearly defined space before a painted backdrop of a large white bush in a white
flowerpot. This simple setting, as well as the use of a suspended lantern
later as the background for several very diverse scenes, recalls classical Jap-

anese theater. Like that theater, Smith also makes strategic use of a back-drop without anything in front of it.

In the second scene he placed before it a transvestite in a white dress sniffing white flowers and a woman in a black nightgown. They flirt; she wiggles to the Spanish music playing throughout the scene; the transves-tite waves a gloved hand; they meet, kiss, and pose together. The camera remains stationary, occasionally cutting to a closer shot, isolating just one of them.

Before their relationship develops the scene temporarily shifts to a group of creatures putting on lipstick in panning, mostly aerial views. The sound becomes the voice of an advertisement for "a new heart-shaped lipstick that stays on and on." When the film-maker's voice interrupts the advertiser to ask, "Is there a lipstick that doesn't come off when you suck cock?" he calmly answers, "Yes, indelible lipstick." Smith seems uncon-vinced. He asks, "But how does a man get lipstick off his cock?" to which the advertiser tartly replies, "A man is not supposed to have lipstick on his cock." Then he continues his unctuous pitch for the lipstick. The adver-tising voice is so authentic that there is a shock when he first answers the question. Before that, it might have been recorded directly from radio or television.

While the speech continues, the camera wanders over a tangle of nude and half-nude bodies so intertwined that they seem a single androgynous figure of many heads (all applying lipstick, including bearded men), breasts, and penises. But after two brief transitional tableaux—a group of creatures falling down in slow motion and a group composition with the sole of a dirty foot projecting out at the camera—the attention returns to the couple before the flowerpot backdrop. They chase each other back and forth off-screen to the left and right. The camera rests on the empty scene as one or the other rushes across the screen. There is no logic to the direction or sequence of their chase; the woman might move from right to left, her pursuer in the opposite direction; once they even cross paths. But eventually the transvestite captures and throws the woman in black to the floor.

Then the camera begins to vibrate, blur, and participate as the new scene, the orgy, commences. The creatures immediately converge upon their victim, strip her, smell her armpits, poke her genitals, and crawl over her. This rape sets in motion a general orgy which the camera, now wildly shaking, glimpses without making specific. Initially, faint screams grow so loud that they drown out the music at the very moment when the orgy either sets off or coincides with an earthquake. The whole set goes into spasms; the lantern sways frantically; plaster falls from the ceiling on the writhing creatures, who seem to have intensified their frenzy in the knowledge that this might be their final bacchanal.

Their death evokes the myth of the seasons. Leaves fall upon their scattered bodies. Towards the end of the orgy the raped woman had staggered to her feet, but she collapsed and was dragged off by a second transvestite, past the dead and dying creatures. But when the now slow moving camera returns to her, she and her abductor are also dead. The earthquake as a cosmic orgasm turned the *sparagmos* of the victim into the *sparagmos* of the bacchantes.

Amid passages of silence and bits of very low violin music, Smith dwells upon the empty scene. A bit of gauze blows before the familiar backdrop; the lantern lies broken on the floor; for a long time the image settles on a fly and his shadow on the white cloth of the backdrop. With a sudden burst of dated honky-tonk music, the lid of a coffin begins to move. But Smith cuts away to the void, and silence ensues, as if this shot had been premature. The proleptic image and its sound makes the empty shots that follow it all the more barren.

The myth of the vampire is invoked when Smith finally returns to the coffin scene. A transvestite Marilyn Monroe rises from it in a white burial gown, holding lilies. To the honky-tonk song, she stretches and surveys the dead bodies and debris; then she chooses a corpse to attack. Aroused in this act, she lifts her dress and begins to play with her penis. It is not her being a vampire but her sexuality that signals the rebirth of the creatures. The lantern hangs again from the ceiling. Beneath it, the creatures dance —first the Monroe figure and her victim, then others as they revive and join in.

The concluding three scenes of the film are a sequence of ecstatic dances. In the first, all the creatures in white costumes dance together. The burned out photography presents a dazzling effect of white on white and a depth of figure behind figure twirling and swaying in the crowded arena before the backdrop. Then a Spanish dancer in black drag with a rose in her teeth does a mad solo whirl to bullfight music. Finally, as if not to be upstaged, the Monroe figure appears puffing on a cigarette, filmed through the lantern. With the sound of the dated rock and roll record, "Be-bop-alula," she performs the final dancing rites intercut with a tableau of an odalisque, one breast exposed, surrounded by Arabs, one of whom points to her nipple.

The final third of *Flaming Creatures* is a continuous surge toward the ecstatic. The camera alternates between static and slowly panning shots of the dancing crowd and disorienting aerial views. The visual poles of black and white which the pursuing transvestite and the woman in the nightgown represented in the first half of the film are transposed to the white Monroe figure and the dark Spanish dancer in the second half.

To see *Flaming Creatures* is to understand some of Jack Smith's dissatisfaction with the way Ken Jacobs portrayed him or allowed him to reveal himself in *Blonde Cobra*. "Jack says I made the film too heavy," Jacobs says in his note for the fifth Film-Makers Cooperative catalogue. The infantilism, cruelty, transvestism, and irony that contribute to the tragedy of delusions in *Blonde Cobra* reappear as factors in a myth of recovered innocence in *Flaming Creatures*, where the triumph may be ironic, but it is not at all problematic.

A triumph, in the sense of a triumphal march, is the subject of the film Jack Smith began to film immediately after finishing *Flaming Creatures*. In fact, he called it *The Great Pasty Triumph* before changing the title to *Normal Love*. In the rough cut that he exhibited in 1964, it was a paratactic parade of episodes describing a pantheon of monsters from horror films: the Mummy, the Werewolf, the Mongolian Child, the Spider, as well as the Mermaid, Cobra Woman, and assorted creatures more or less derived from the stock mythology of Hollywood. The projection of the rushes of these scenes throughout 1963 at midnight after the programs of the Film-Makers Cinematheque or at Ron Rice's loft was the occasion for important meetings of film-makers, actors, and critics. Each episode was a self-contained, sensuous exploration of a simple event structured by scene, photographed on outdated color stock that produced ravishing expanses of pastel greens, pinks and blues.

Of all the major film-makers of the mythopoeic stage of the American avant-garde film, Jack Smith was perhaps the most gifted with imaginative powers. Each sequence of *Normal Love* as it was serially unveiled demonstrated the sureness with which Smith could transform his creature-actors and the landscape in which he placed them into elements of a mythic vision of redeemed innocence and heightened sensuality. In slow, steady shots one could see the green Mummy wading after a nude girl in a pond of waterlilies; the Mermaid taking a milk bath or having a mud-throwing

fight with the Werewolf; a pier covered with the bodies of dead or sleeping transvestites in pink gowns projecting into the azure sea; the emerald
Cobra Woman exploring a dark cave; a watermelon feast; a giant pink
birthday cake with half a dozen creatures dancing on it, including a very
pregnant woman.

Romantic mythology, whose chief theme is the dialectics of consciousness, frequently centers on the vision of childhood, lost and regained.
Flaming Creatures and *Normal Love* are curiously free of dialectical form.
The constrictions of the self, the tension between the film-maker and the
film, and the circuitous journey from innocence as ignorance to a redeemed innocence are absent in these films. They begin as if the Romantic quest were already behind them; they are visions of a liberated consciousness. Only in *No President* does Smith use the failed Promethean
hero in his mythology, although in a very ambivalent manner, by intercutting the documentary on Wendell Willkie's life with the erotic tableaux
of his creatures.

Richard Foreman was the first to observe, to the best of my knowledge,
a different level of dialectic in every presentation by Smith. His plays,
slide shows, and even film screenings, especially of works-in-progress, in-
variably start late, break down several times, and involve Smith himself
rushing out, instructing actors, fixing equipment, and suddenly changing
the course of the work, until these activities assume the center of attention
and the work which initially attracted the audience seems one prop among
others, mostly junk. The most convincing text on this fusion of the work
of art with its maker and the situation in which it is presented is Jonas
Mekas' long article, "Jack Smith, or The End of Civilization," from the
Village Voice, July 23, 1970. It would seem, then, that the cinematic object for Smith loses its absolute integrity and becomes a privileged part
of the dialectical work which is the performance. This may account for his
refusal definitely to complete a film since *Flaming Creatures* (he has even
attempted to change, and very possibly destroy, that film in recent years).
The question that his performances provoke is how conscious is he of
turning these apparently neurotic activities into an aesthetic strategy? The
very title of his disorganized play for Film-Makers Cinematheque's month
of expanded cinema events in 1965, *Rehearsal for the Destruction of Atlantis*, indicates that he is aware of the effect of his methods.

Other film-makers, impressed by Smith's imaginative faculties, have
thought of making use of his imagery. Ron Rice often accompanied
Smith as he was shooting *Normal Love*. They tended to return to his loft

with most of the cast, still in their costumes, after the day's filming. At first Rice made some casual film studies of the actors swinging on the hammocks in his loft. Later he expanded them into the production of *Chumlum* (1964).

The texture and structure of Rice's film is altogether different from Smith's. Throughout *Chumlum* there are usually at least two layers of moving imagery in superimposition. The compounding of figures, costumes, swinging movements, and the simultaneous fusion of side and aerial views flatten the space, thicken the pastel tones in deep and muddled colors, obscure the individual roles, and fragment the actions. *Chumlum* seems a continuously even, unaccented web of visual textures. The smoothness of the visual mesh is supported by the drone-like music of Angus MacLise on the chumlum, from which the title comes.

The fragmentation of events and the tactics suppressing internal modulations give Rice's film a sense of temporal suspension. The inclusion of punch-holes that usually are to be found at the beginning and end of a hundred foot strip of raw film and the apparent minimum of editing (the enjambment of different layers of superimposition suggests this) indicate that *Chumlum* is made up of approximately ten rolls of film composed in the camera. Unlike Harry Smith with *Late Superimpositions*, which was shot the same way, Rice did not accent the difference between the whole rolls in assembling them.

At the end of the film he shifts from indoor scenes, all shot in his studio, to an outdoor section. But he underplays this change by using a reel superimposing both indoors and outdoors at the very beginning. Within the center of the film, he seems to have subverted the natural order of the reels (that of the shooting) so that actions would appear inconclusive and repetitive. Toward the middle, he shows Jack Smith in an Arabian costume with a fake mustache, smoking hashish. The film becomes his reverie in which time is stretched or folded over itself.

In the outdoor conclusion, which intensifies the play of color and repetition, he shows the actors, still in their costumes, walking to a log house in the woods, their gowns and feet tangled in briars. He filmed this moment twice in superimposition, slightly out of synchronization, as a resolving metaphor for the "folded" temporality of the whole film. If there is a development or progress in the film, it is from indoors to outdoors, from swinging, crawling, and dancing in the harem to dancing in the sky over Coney Island (through superimposition)—an image which recalls the end of *The Flower Thief* where Taylor Mead dissolves into the sea.

Chumlum and *Late Superimpositions* belong with *Little Stabs at Happiness*, some of Larry Jordan's films, Brakhage's *Song V*, and Markopoulos' *Galaxie* and *Ming Green* as manifestations of the growing confidence in the early 1960s in the process of composing a film within the camera. This direct method found its spokesman and one of its leading practitioners in Jonas Mekas as he came to devote more and more of his energies to his film diary.

Unlike the literary diary, the film diary does not follow a day-by-day chronology. Structurally, it corresponds more to a notebook, but in its drive towards a schematic or fragmented expression of the totality of the film-maker's life, it is more like a diary, perhaps one in which the entry dates have been lost and the pages scrambled. Mekas and younger diarists such as Andrew Noren and Warren Sonbert devote their creative energy to shooting, constructing, and revising their filmed lives.

Mekas' *Diaries, Notes and Sketches* (1964-69) and *Reminiscences of a Journey to Lithuania* (1971) are exercises in Romantic autobiography. Mekas constantly weaves together celebrations of the present moment, immediately and unironically present on the screen, with elegiac and ironic allusions to a presence that is forever absent to the camera lens: the vision of nature and of his childhood. Like all of the films brought together in this chapter, Mekas' two diaries are versions of the myth of lost innocence and the failed quest for its recovery. The credo of his commitment to the Romantic dialectic is an article from 1964, "Notes on Some New Movies and Happiness," in which he combines observations on the films of Ken Jacobs, Ron Rice, Joseph Cornell, and others with thoughts on happiness and sadness from his childhood memories. He writes:

> It is neither a coincidence nor anything strange that exactly the same men who have tasted a fool's happiness, give us also the deepest intuitions of the tragic sense of life.

> Imitation of the true emotion. Sentimentality. No oneness. No true peace. (Who knows what true peace is?) Nostalgia of things of nature. Or are we going into neo-Romanticism? And what does it mean? Or am I going into neo-Romanticism? And this essay is nothing but pieces of my own new film? Perhaps.[16]

That new film was *Diaries, Notes and Sketches*. Mekas presented an extended synopsis on a giant sheet of paper to all the viewers at its premiere, prefaced by these remarks:

> This film being what it is, i.e., a series of personal notes on events, people (friends) and Nature (Seasons)—the Author won't mind (he is

almost encouraging it) if the Viewer will choose to watch only certain parts of the work (film), according to the time available to him, according to his preferences, or any other good reason. . . .

A note in the beginning says, that this is the First Draft of the Diaries. Why should the Author permit then, one may ask, the unpolished or half-polished edition to come out? His answer is, he thought that despite the roughness of sound and some parts of the images, there is still enough in them—he felt—to make them of some interest to some of his friends and a few strangers. In order to go to the next stage of polishing, he felt, he had to look at the footage as it is, many many more times, and gain more perspective to it—that's why this edition.

For a screening of this film at the Museum of Modern Art, Mekas wrote:

Since 1950 I have been keeping a film diary. I have been walking around with my Bolex and reacting to the immediate reality: situations, friends, New York, seasons of the year. On some days I shot ten frames, on others ten seconds, still on others ten minutes. Or I shoot nothing. When one writes diaries, it's a retrospective process: you sit down, you look back at your day, and you write it all down. To keep a film (camera) diary, is to react (with your camera) immediately, now, this instant: either you get it now or you don't get it at all. To go back and shoot it later, it would mean restaging, be it events or feelings. To get it now, as it happens, demands the total mastery of one's tools (in this case, Bolex): it has to register my state of feeling (and the memories) as I react. Which also means that I had to do all the structuring (editing) right there, during the shooting, in the camera.[17]

In this text, which unites the return of "improvisation" with film construction, the film-maker is forgetting or underestimating the importance of editing and even more of sound in his own film. It is true that within an episode he sticks to the material as the scene was shot without restructuring except for inserting titles. When he says, a little later, that the materials were "strung together in chronological order," he is taking liberties; there were no violent disruptions of chronology, but some events were reshuffled. Of this I can be certain because my family and I appear in it achronologically. The very use of *Walden* as a structural element attests the editing architecture of the film.

The pixilated imagery, blazing by in extremely fast motion, provides the central and most often repeated metaphor for the temporality of the present moment. The nostalgia for a deeper and more authentic nature is invoked in the passages of speech and the titles "I Thought of Home" at

Peter Kubelka in pixilated sequence from Jonas Mekas's *Reminiscences of a Journey to Lithuania.*

the beginning and end of the film and "*Laukas*, A Field, as Wide as Child-hood" in the first reel. The distance between the present moment and the nostalgia is repeatedly mediated by the text of *Walden,* for in *Diaries, Notes and Sketches* the language of the text, the titles, and the film-maker's voice is the sole vehicle of reconciling the exiled past—the author's childhood in Lithuania—with the film camera's dependence on the here and now of its visual substance.

In his next film, *Reminiscences,* he uses the occasion of his first return to Lithuania in twenty-seven years to construct a dialectical meditation on the meaning of exile, return, and art. The film is in three parts. In the first, he put together all the footage he had made since he first bought a camera in 1950 of his early life in New York, concentrating on the gath-erings of Lithuanian exiles, who "looked to me like strange, dying ani-mals, in a place they didn't belong to, in a place they didn't recognize," as the film-maker says in his commentary within the film. In the center of the film is the movement of return in the form of "one hundred views" of Lithuania, the film-maker's mother, his family. The elegiac tone of the opening part, accented by the space of twenty years between the photog-raphy and the editing, and the commentary by the author, disappears in the middle ode, which accepts the inability of a return in space (to Lithua-nia) as well as in time (to childhood).

He resolves the contradictory movements of the first and second parts by celebrating the present with renewed vigor on the return trip via Vienna. There he shows us the lives of artists and thinkers (Hermann Nitsch and his castle, Peter Kubelka and the cellar where he makes wine, Wittgenstein's house, and the Americans Ken Jacobs and Annette Mi-chelson, both visiting at the same time) whom he calls "Saints" in the identifying titles. By ending the film journal of his early years in New York and his long awaited return to Lithuania with portraits of his artist friends, one "pursuing his vision, without giving an inch, and heroically," another "who had the courage to remain a child in the purity of his see-ing and his ecstasies," he defines his own triumph as an artist. In the last minutes he tells us, "I begin to believe again in the indestructibility of the human spirit."

"A child in the purity of his seeing" is not the most accurate expression Mekas could have found for Ken Jacobs' visionary stance. Ken Jacobs too has a dialectical relationship with the myth of recovered innocence. His most direct attempt at the mythopoeic film, *The Sky Socialist,* which was shot between 1965 and 1967 and has been left unedited since then, grew out of his urge to address a monumental work to the Brooklyn Bridge, which he could observe from his loft window and roof in lower Manhattan. Like Hart Crane, whom he has not seriously read, he posited from his contemplation of the sheer magnificence of the bridge and the aspiration of the Roeblings, its builders, an eccentric form which weaves through history and invokes a sense of the divine in a world bereft (as far as Jacobs sees it) of divinity. In Crane's words,

> O Sleepless as the river under thee,
> Vaulting the sea, the prairies' dreaming sod,
> Unto us lowliest sometime sweep, descend
> And of the curveship lend a myth to God.

The inversion of a classical invocation, in which the bridge is asked to "lend a myth to God," is precisely the theme of Jacobs' film.

After a proem of zooming and sweeping pans of the bridge, the action settles for three hours—with occasional revisits to the bridge and the river, which the film-maker calls "choral interludes"—on the roof, where two people "stand in for" (rather than act the roles of) the dead Anne Frank and Isadore Lhevinne, the author of two obscure American novels, *Ariadne* (1928) and *Napoleons All* (1932), influenced by Symbolist prose. Despite the continual discouragement of Maurice, a fictive incarnation of the principle of despair, Isadore and Anne fall in love and marry.

It is impossible to determine what character this romance will have until the film is finished, if it ever is. Jacobs says he will narrate the essential actions and speeches in "a conversational tone" on the film as well as tell the story of how the Roeblings, father and son, built the bridge and of the socialistic vision which inspired it. "Roebling is the Sky Socialist," Jacobs has said, "and so am I as the maker of the film."

The sparse narrative is typically problematical. For the film to have a happy ending and thus reverse historical fact, the film-maker brings "The Muse of Cinema to the Rescue," as a chapter title in the film informs us. As a reel of film is running out in front of the camera, she cuts it off and splices on the happy ending. When Jacobs equivocally describes the Muse as "showing off," "possibly a failure" in her "self-indulgent" granting of the happy ending, he is part of a tradition extending from the dark muses of Blake and, with diminished terror, through Shelley, Keats, and Yeats,[18] although, unaware of his Romantic predecessors, he thought he was inventing the dialectical acceptance of her intercession. Other chapters include "The Retribution of Anne Frank," in which she symbolically revenges her death upon a Nazi officer, "The Wedding Breakfast," and "Isadore's Transmogrification." The last of these ends the film in a slow ritual of purification with a glass of water that represents both the sexual consummation of the marriage (there is an art-deco nude on the glass) and the cinema (the glass becomes a distorting lens, a theater of reflections).

The pace of *The Sky Socialist* is very leisurely; its movements are choreographed in a clearly defined deep space. In Jacobs' subsequent film, *Tom, Tom, the Piper's Son*, that space contracts to the grainy screen of rephotography and its time becomes an involuted version of the structural film.

Tom, Tom begins and nearly ends with an old film of the same title made in Hollywood in 1905, quoted entirely both times. For approximately ninety minutes (the original lasts about ten minutes), Jacobs gives us his variations on the images and movements of that film. His *Tom, Tom*, as opposed to the original, has a grainy, pointillist texture (an inevitable result of filming off a screen or a home-made optical printer, which the structural cinema has capitalized on) and a compressed sense of space. In transposing, he changed the time of the original with slow motion, the scale with close-ups of background detail, the sequential order with repetitions and backward movements, and above all the kinesis by radically retarding the narrative of the original. Here the principle of elongation finds its clearest demonstration, which the structural cinema affirms in strong contrast to the beloved condensation of such film-makers as Anger, Brakhage, Belson, Markopoulos, Kubelka, and Breer. It is almost as if the film, in its aggressive didacticism, intended to prove once and for all the postulates of Russian formalist criticism, where the theory of the structural cinema has its historical origins. Victor Shklovsky writes in *Art as Technique* (1917):

> We find everywhere the artistic trademark—that is, we find material obviously created to remove the automatism of perception; the author's purpose is to create the vision that results from that de-automatized perception. A work is created "artistically" so that its perception is impeded and the greatest possible effect is produced through the slowness of perception.
>
> The technique of art is to make objects "unfamiliar," to make forms difficult, to increase the difficulty and length of perception because the process of perception is an aesthetic end in itself and must be prolonged. *Art is a way of experiencing the artfulness of an object: the object is not important.*[19]

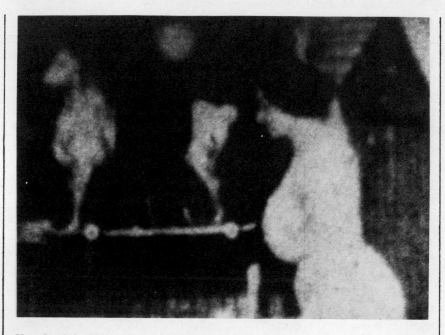

Ken Jacobs's *Tom, Tom, the Piper's Son:* flatness and grainy texture achieved through rephotography.

Jacobs' film is didactic in a specifically modernist tradition. In the first place, it is sublime film criticism, revealing the intricacy of the original by literally transforming it. Stravinsky did the same for Pergolesi; Robert Duncan "set Shelley's *Arethusa* to new measures." In addition Jacobs reveals a nexus of composition and imagery latent in the film akin to Seurat and Manet. He has recovered the graphic genius of the original film's source for at least the first and last of its eight tableaux—Hogarth's *Southwark Fair*; for it is the imagery and backgrounds of this etching that the anonymous film-maker transposed to film. We see a sensual tightrope walker whirling a hoop in slow motion, a hunchback rolling over and over, a crowd falling one by one out of a barn, and almost floating into a haystack. There are intimations of Picasso's harlequins as well.

Because of the directness of the mechanism he employs, *Tom, Tom* must be grouped with the structural films I shall discuss in the next chapter, despite Jacobs' tendency to rupture the forms of all of his films. In the three versions of the film I have seen, there is a marked difference of architecture. They each violate symmetry by appending a series of slow motion details after the second presentation of the original film. The second version, however, introduces color inserts of a shadow play (another mixed form which Jacobs practices, especially in three-dimensional stereoscope) which violently interrupt the continuity of the black-and-white film. Visually they are relaxing (so the film-maker describes their function), but structurally they are extremely disorienting. More in keeping with the texture of the film, but nevertheless digressive, is a passage in the second and third versions in which the film-maker literally lifts away the screen off which the original is being "copied," and we are confronted with a flicker of the bare projector bulb behind the screen.

In the third version an even more aggressive passage shows an image jumping in the projector gate to the point of indecipherability by vertical distortion. Audiences seeing this for the first time do not know if the projectionist has misthreaded or if what they are seeing is part of the film itself. He has thus incorporated within the film an aggressive factor similar to the use of the two radios in *Blonde Cobra*. As the jumping continues (and it continues for a very long time, seeming as if it were about to rectify itself only to jump again) it becomes evident that the strategy is deliberate.

To the film-maker himself, *Tom, Tom, the Piper's Son*—a filmed nursery rime—is an exercise in "folded" temporality, and an attempt to recover an innocence in the childhood of the medium itself:

Ghosts! Cine-recordings of the vivacious doings of persons long dead. The preservation of their memory ceases at the edges of the frame (a 1905 hand happened to stick into the frame . . . it's preserved, recorded in a spray of emulsion grains). One face passes "behind" another on the two-dimensional screen.

The staging and cutting is pre-Griffith. Seven infinitely complex cine-tapestries comprise the original film, and the style is not primitive, not uncinematic but the cleanest, inspired indication of a path of cinematic development whose value has only recently been rediscovered. My camera closes in, only to better ascertain the infinite richness (playing with fate, taking advantage of the loop-character of all movies, recalling with variations some visual complexes again and again for particular savoring), searching out incongruities in the story-telling (a person, confused, suddenly looks out of an actor's face), delighting in the whole bizarre human phenomena of story-telling itself and this within the fantasy of reading any bygone time out of the visual crudities of film: dream within a dream!

And then I wanted to show the actual present of film, just begin to indicate its energy. A train of images passes like enough and different enough to imply to the mind that its eyes are seeing an arm lift, or a door close; I wanted to "bring to the surface" that multi-rhythmic collision-contesting of dark and light two-dimensional force-areas struggling edge to edge for identity of shape . . . to get into the amoebic grain pattern itself—a chemical dispersion pattern unique to each frame, each cold still . . . stirred to life by a successive 16-24 f.p.s. pattering on our retinas, the teeming energies elicited (the grains! the grains!) then collaborating, unknowingly and ironically, to form the always-poignant-because-always-past illusion.[20]

STRUCTURAL FILM

The most significant development in the American avant-garde cinema since the trend toward mythopoeic forms in the early 1960s has been the emergence and development of what I have called the structural film. The pattern which operated within the work of Maya Deren was echoed, as I have shown, in the entire thrust of the American avant-garde cinema between the late forties and the middle sixties; on the simplest level it was a movement toward increased cinematic complexity. Film-makers such as Gregory Markopoulos, Sidney Peterson, Kenneth Anger, Stan Brakhage, and Peter Kubelka, to name a few of the most conspicuous, moved toward more condensed and more complex forms.

Since the middle sixties a number of film-makers have emerged whose approach is quite different, although dialectically related to the sensibility of their predecessors. Michael Snow, George Landow, Hollis Frampton, Paul Sharits, Tony Conrad, Ernie Gehr, and Joyce Weiland have produced a number of remarkable films apparently in the opposite direction of that formal thrust. Theirs is a cinema of structure in which the shape of the whole film is predetermined and simplified, and it is that shape which is the primal impression of the film.

A precise statement of the difference between formal and structural organization must involve a sense of the working process; the formal film is a tight nexus of content, a shape designed to explore the facets of the material—the very title of Kubelka's first film, *Mosaik*, is an expression of this conscious aspiration. Recurrences, prolepses, antitheses, and overall rhythms are the rhetoric of the formal; in its highest form, the content of such films would be a mythic encounter.

The structural film insists on its shape, and what content it has is minimal and subsidiary to the outline. Four characteristics of the structural film are its fixed camera position (fixed frame from the viewer's perspective), the flicker effect, loop printing, and rephotography off the screen. Very seldom will one find all four characteristics in a single film, and there are structural films which modify these usual elements.

If, as I have claimed, the great unacknowledged aspiration of the American avant-garde film has been the cinematic reproduction of the human mind, then the structural film approaches the condition of meditation and evokes states of consciousness without mediation; that is, with the sole mediation of the camera. The trance film's somnambulist, the mythopoeic film's heroes and gods, and the picaresque wanderer had been the primary mediators of the earlier stages of the avant-garde film.

What then would be the difference between the lyrical film I have described and the structural film? What would be their relationship? The lyrical film too replaces the mediator with the increased presence of the camera. We see what the film-maker sees; the reactions of the camera and the montage reveal his responses to his vision. In the opening sequence of Hammid and Deren's *Meshes of the Afternoon*, we found the roots of first-person cinematic consciousness. They filmed the first approach and exploration of the house from the point of view of the puzzled participant. But they immediately qualified—or mediated—that forceful opening by showing the figure of the protagonist in subsequent variations. In creating the lyrical film, Stan Brakhage accepted the limitations of that opening sequence as the basis for a new form. Out of the optical field and metaphors of the body's movement in the rocking gestures of the camera, he affirmed the film-maker as the lyrical first person. Without that achievement and its subsequent evolution, it would be difficult to imagine the flourishing of the structural film.

The four techniques are the more obvious among many subtle changes from the lyrical film in an attempt to divorce the cinematic metaphor of consciousness from that of eyesight and body movement, or at least to diminish these categories from the predominance they have in Brakhage's films and theory. In Brakhage's art, perception is a special condition of vision, most often represented as an interruption of the retinal continuity (e.g., the white flashes of the early lyric films, the conclusion of *Dog Star Man*). In the structural cinema, however, apperceptive strategies come to the fore. It is cinema of the mind rather than the eye. It might at first seem that the most significant precursor of the structural film was Brakhage. But that is inaccurate. The achievements of Kubelka and Breer and before them the early masters of the graphic film have done as much to inform this recent development. The structural film is in part a synthesis of the formalistic graphic film and the Romantic lyrical film. But this description is historically incomplete.

By the mid-1960s the contributions of the lyrical and graphic cinema had been totally assimilated into avant-garde film-making. They were part of the vocabulary a young film-maker acquired at the screenings of the Film-Makers Cinematheque or the Canyon Cinema Cooperative. They were in the air. The new film-makers were not responding to these forms dialectically, because they situated themselves within them, no matter which films they preferred and which they rejected.

The major precursor of the structural film was not Brakhage, or Kubelka, or Breer. He was Andy Warhol. Warhol came to the avant-garde cinema in a way no one else had. He was at the height of his success in the most lucrative of American arts—painting. He was a fully developed artist in one medium, and he entered another, not as a dabbler, but with a total commitment. He immediately began to produce major cinema. For years he sustained that production with undiminished intensity, creating in that time as many major films as any of his contemporaries had in a lifetime; then, after completing *The Chelsea Girls* (1966), he quickly faded as a significant film-maker.

Warhol began to take an interest in the avant-garde film in 1963 when it was at the height of the mythic stage. He quickly made himself familiar with the latest works of Brakhage, Markopoulos, Anger, and especially Jack Smith, who had a direct influence on him. On one level at least— and that is the only level of importance to us—Warhol turned his genius for parody and reduction against the American avant-garde film itself. The first film that he seriously engaged himself in was a monumental inversion of the dream tradition within the avant-garde film. His *Sleep* was no trance film or mythic dream but six hours of a man sleeping. (It was to have been eight hours long, but something went wrong.) At the same time, he exploded the myth of compression and the myth of the film-maker. Theorists such as Brakhage and Kubelka expounded the law that a film must not waste a frame and that a single film-maker must control all the functions of the creation. Warhol made the profligacy of footage the central fact of all of his early films, and he advertised his indifference to direction, photography, and lighting. He simply turned the camera on and walked away. In short, the set of concerns which I have associated with the Romantic heritage of the American avant-garde film were the object of Warhol's fierce indifference.

Stephen Koch has something to say on this subject:

> The Duchampian game in which objects are aestheticized merely by turning to them with a certain glint in your eye, does have continuing value, though not as the comical anti-art polemic so often ascribed to it. . . .
>
> It is possible to understand this rather specialized aesthetic experience as a metaphor, in consciousness, for the perception of things at large, in which the unlike things compared and fused are the self and the world. . . . It is a major modernist procedure for creating metaphors, and an antiromantic one, since it locates the world of art's richness not in Baudelaire's "Elsewhere" but in the here and now. At least almost.
>
> Warhol goes further. He wants to be transformed into an object himself, quite explicitly wants to remove himself from the dangerous, anxiety-ridden world of human action and interaction, to wrap himself in the serene fullness of the functionless aesthetic sphere.[1]

Warhol defines his art "anti-romantically." Pop art, especially as he practiced it, was a repudiation of the processes, theories, and myths of Abstract Expressionism, a Romantic school. Warhol's earliest films showed how similar most other avant-garde films were and, to those looking closely, how Romantic. Yet whether or not the anti-Romantic stance can escape the dialectics of Romanticism is an open question. Koch seems to think it cannot:

> Transforming himself into the object celebrity, Warhol has made a commitment to the Baudelairean "resolution not to be moved"—an effort to ensconce himself in the aesthetic realm's transparent placenta, removed from the violence and emotions of the world's time and space. So he turns out to be a romantic after all.[2]

The roots of three of the four defining characteristics of the structural film can be found in Warhol's early works. He made famous the fixed-frame in *Sleep* (1963), in which a half dozen shots are seen for over six hours. In order to attain that elongation, he used both loop printing of whole one hundred foot takes (2¾ minutes) and, in the end, the freezing of a still image of the sleeper's head. That freeze process emphasizes the grain and flattens the image precisely as rephotography off the screen does. The films he made immediately afterwards cling even more fiercely to the single unbudging perspective: *Eat* (1963), forty-five minutes of the eating of a mushroom; *Empire* (1964), eight continuous hours of the Empire State Building through the night into dawn; *Harlot* (1965), a seventy minute tableau vivant with off-screen commentary; *Beauty #2* (1965), a bed scene with off- and on-screen speakers lasting seventy minutes. Soon afterwards, he developed the fixed tripod technique of reconciling stasis to camera movement. In *Poor Little Rich Girl: Party Sequence* (1965), *Hedy* (1966), and *The Chelsea Girls* (1966) he utilized camera movements, especially the zoom, from the pivot of an unmoving tripod without stopping the camera until the long roll had run out. Yet Warhol as a pop artist is spiritually at the opposite pole from the structural film-makers. His fixed camera was at first an outrage, later an irony, until the content of his films became so compelling to him that he abandoned the fixed camera for a species of in-the-camera editing. In the work of Michael Snow and Ernie Gehr, the camera is fixed in a mystical contemplation of a portion of space. Spiritually the distance between these poles cannot be reconciled.

In his close analysis of Warhol's early work, Koch views these films with the kind of intensity and perspective that the structural film-makers brought to them. He sees in them the framework of an apperceptive cinema. In the end of *Haircut* (1963), in which someone in a barber's chair, after a long stare into the camera, breaks into unheard laughter as the final roll of film flares up in whiteness, he sees "the cinematic drama of the gaze, reaching its final and reflexive development":

> The moment is a gently felt turn of self-consciousness suggesting the gentlest of put-ons—a put-on not in the sense of artistic fraud but that implied by a kind of Prosperolike cadenza (if I may compare great to small), a breaking of the spell. With it we realize that, like all the other early films, *Haircut* is about the hypnotic nature of the gaze itself, about the power of the artist over it.[3]

Koch sees that beyond the obvious aggressions and ironies of the early Warhol films—and perhaps because of them—there is a conscious ontology of the viewing experience. What the critic does not say is that these apperceptive mechanisms are latent or passive in Warhol's work. To the film-makers who first encountered these films in the mid-sixties (those who were not threatened by them), these latent mechanisms must have suggested other conscious and deliberate extensions: that is, Warhol must have inspired, by opening up and leaving unclaimed so much ontological territory, a cinema actively engaged in generating metaphors for the viewing, or rather the perceiving, experience.

Thus the structural film is not simply an outgrowth of the lyric. It is an attempt to answer Warhol's attack by converting his tactics into the tropes of the response. To the catalogue of the spatial strategies of the structural film must be added the temporal gift from Warhol—duration. He was the first film-maker to try to make films which would outlast a viewer's initial state of perception. By sheer dint of waiting, the persistent viewer would alter his experience before the sameness of the cinematic image. Brakhage had made a very long film in *The Art of Vision*, but he was apologetic about its four hours; it had to be that long and not a minute longer, he would claim, to say what it had to say. Ken Jacobs had been bolder or more honest in describing the endless and perpetually disintegrating experience of his projected *Star Spangled to Death*. But that too would have been a perversely orchestrated experience from beginning to end.

Warhol broke the most severe theoretical taboo when he made films that challenged the viewer's ability to endure emptiness or sameness. He even insisted that each silent film be shown at 16 frames per second although they were shot at 24. The duration of his films was one of slightly slowed motion. The great challenge, then, of the structural film became how to orchestrate duration; how to permit the wandering attention that triggered ontological awareness while watching Warhol films and at the same time guide that awareness to a goal.

Not all of the structural films respond to the severe challenges of their form. Those instances of structural cinema in the filmographies of men who had worked successfully in other modes tend to use the frozen camera, loop print, the flicker effect, and rephotography to open up new dimensions within the range of concerns that they pre-established in their earlier works.

Just why, at approximately the same time, Stan Brakhage, Gregory Markopoulos, Bruce Baillie, and Ken Jacobs began to extend their art in this direction is difficult to determine. Warhol's sudden shock-blow to the aesthetics of the avant-garde film was a factor, just as it was to film-makers like Michael Snow, Paul Sharits, George Landow and Hollis Frampton whose whole work lies within the domain of the structural film.

Michael Snow, the dean of structural film-makers, utilizes the tension of the fixed-frame and some of the flexibility of the fixed tripod in *Wavelength*. Actually it is a forward zoom for forty-five minutes, halting occasionally, and fixed during several different times so that day changes to night within the motion.

A persistent polarity shapes the film. Throughout there is an exploration of the room, a long studio, as a field of space, subject to the arbitrary events of the outside world so long as the zoom is recessive enough to see the windows and thereby the street. The room gradually closes up its space (during the day, at night, on different film stocks for color tone, with filters, and even occasionally in negative) as the zoom nears the back wall and the final image of a photograph upon it—a photograph of waves. This is the story of the diminishing area of pure potentiality. The insight that space, and cinema by implication, is potential is an axiom of the structural film.

In a note for the fourth International Experimental Film Festival, where it won first prize, Snow described the film:

> Wavelength was shot in one week Dec. '66 preceded by a year of notes, thots, mutterings. It was edited and first print seen in May '67. I wanted to make a summation of my nervous system, religious inklings, and aesthetic ideas. I was thinking of planning for a time monument in which the beauty and sadness of equivalence would be celebrated, thinking of trying to make a definitive statement of pure Film space and time, a balancing of "illusion" and "fact," all about seeing. The space starts at the camera's (spectator's) eye, is in the air, then is on the screen, then is within the screen (the mind).
>
> The film is a continuous zoom which takes 45 minutes to go from its widest field to its smallest and final field. It was shot with a fixed camera from one end of an 80 foot loft, shooting the other end, a row of windows and the street. This, the setting, and the action which takes place there are cosmically equivalent. The room (and the zoom) are interrupted by 4 human events including a death. The sound on these occasions is sync sound, music and speech, occurring simultaneously with an electronic sound, a sine wave, which goes from its lowest (50 cycles per second) note to its highest (12000 c.p.s.) in 40 minutes. It is a total glissando while the film is a crescendo and a dispersed spectrum which attempts to utilize the gifts of both prophecy and memory which only film and music have to offer.[4]

He simplified the essential ambiguity in the film by describing one of the events as a death. The order of the actions is progressive and interrelated: a girl supervises the moving in of a bookcase; later she returns with another girl; they listen to the radio (a few phrases from "Strawberry Fields," pop culture's version of ontological skepticism) without talking; so far we are early in the film, the action appears random; mid-way through, a man breaks glass (heard off-screen) to get in an unseen door and climb the stairs (so we hear); he enters the studio and collapses on

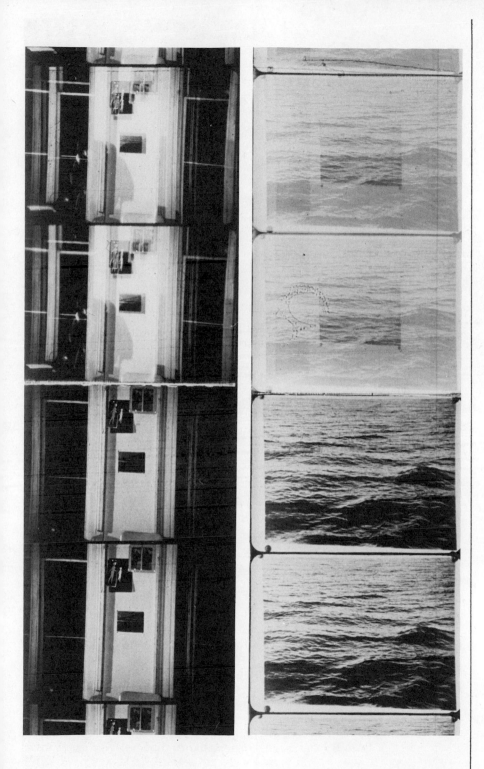

Three strips from Michael Snow's *Wavelength*.

the floor, but the lens has already crossed half the room, and he is only glimpsed; the image passes over him. Late in the film, a girl returns, goes to the telephone which, being at the far wall, is in full view, and in a dramatic moment which brings the previous events of the film into a narrative nexus, calls a man, "Richard," to tell him there is a dead body in the room. She insists that the man does not look drunk, but dead, and she says she will wait downstairs. She leaves.

Had the film ended at that point, the image of death would have satisfied all the potential energy and anticipation built up through the film. But Snow prefers a deeper vision. We see a visual echo, a ghost image in black-and-white superimposition of discontinuous flashes of the girl entering, turning toward the body, telephoning, and leaving. Then the zoom continues, as the sound grows shriller, into the final image of the static sea pinned to the wall, a cumulative metaphor for the whole experience of the dimensional illusion in open space.

The events of *Wavelength* occur first as discrete actions or irreducible performances. But the pivotal telephone call bridges the space between their self-enclosure and the narrative. Snow exposes his cinematic materials in *Wavelength* (even more so in his later film, whose title is the mark ←→) as momentary states within the work. The splice marks, flares of light, filters, different film stocks, and the focal interests of the room (the yellow chair against the far wall especially) create a calculus of mental and physical states, as distinguished from human events, which are as much a part of the body of the film as the actions I have dwelt upon. Things happen in the room of *Wavelength*, and things happen to the film of the room. The convergence of the two kinds of happening and their subsequent metamorphosis create for the viewer a continually changing experience of cinematic illusion and anti-illusion.

Annette Michelson finds this film a metaphor for consciousness itself. Her eloquent paraphrase reveals its relation to phenomenology:

> We are proceeding from uncertainty to certainty, as our camera narrows its field, arousing and then resolving our tension of puzzlement as to its ultimate destination, describing in the splendid purity of its one, slow movement, the notion of the "horizon" characteristic of every subjective process and fundamental as a trait of intentionality. That steady movement forward, with its superimposition, its events passing into the field from behind the camera and back again beyond it, figures the view that "to every perception there always belongs a horizon of the past, as a potentiality of recollections that can be awakened; and to every recollection there belongs as an horizon, the continuous intervening inten-

tionality of possible recollections (to be actualized on my initiative, actively up to the actual Now of perception." [Husserl, *Cartesian Meditations*] And as the camera continues to move steadily forward, building a tension that grows in direct ratio to the reduction of the field, we recognize, with some surprise, those horizons as defining the contours of narrative, of the narrative form animated by distended temporality, turning upon cognition towards revelation.[5]

The very unsteadiness of the forward movement and its perceptible tiny jolts forward confirm Michelson's analysis. One of Snow's most interesting tactics is the superimposition of the forthcoming, slightly forward position on the one we are looking at, giving us for the length of that superimposition a static image of the temporal process. Its most effective employment is at the very end of the film when, after a long-held wide shot, the photograph of the waves, surrounded by a border of the wall to which it is pinned, suddenly shares its screen space with a view within the photograph. We anticipate, and when the older layer dissolves we experience, the illusory depth of the receding line of sight extending over the static sea.

Wavelength tightly coheres to Michelson's phenomenological analogue, but it also summons up the empty rooms of Mallarmé's most ambitious writing, the photograph providing the metaphoric reverberations of the poet's omnipresent mirror: "Certainement subsist une présence de Minuit. L'heure n'a pas disparu par un miroir, ne s'est pas enfouie en tentures, évoquant un ameublement par sa vacante sonorité." (Certainly a presence of Midnight continues. The hour has not disappeared through a mirror, is not hidden in the curtains evoking furniture by its empty sonority.) This is the beginning of *Igitur*. Snow, of course, was guided neither by Husserl nor Mallarmé. He has referred to Vermeer and Duke Ellington as sources of his film. Still, Symbolism is relevant here. The structural film—and *Wavelength* may be the supreme achievement of the form—has the same relationship to the earlier forms of the avant-garde film that Symbolism had to its source, Romanticism. The rhetoric of inspiration has changed to the language of aesthetics; Promethean heroism collapses into a consciousness of the self in which its very representation becomes problematic; the quest for a redeemed innocence becomes a search for the purity of images and the trapping of time. All this is as true of structural cinema as it is of Symbolism.

For Snow making a film is a matter of "stating the issues about film." In an interview he said:

I thought that maybe the issues hadn't really been stated clearly about film in the same sort of way—now this is presumptuous, but to say—in the way Cézanne, say, made a balance between the colored goo that he used, which is what you see if you look at it that way, and the forms that you see in illusionary space. . . . I was trying to do something very pure and about the kinds of realities involved.[6]

And in a letter following up the interview he added:

I mentioned Cézanne in a comment about the illusion/reality balance in art in painting. Tho many other painters have worked out their own beautiful solutions to this "problem," I think his was the greatest and is relevant because his work is representational. The complicated involvement of *his* perception of exterior reality, his creation of a work which both *represents* and *is* something, thus his balance of mind and matter, his respect for a lot of levels are exemplary to me. My work is representational. It is not very Cezannesque tho. *Wavelength* and ←→ are much more Vermeer (I hope).[7]

Had the discourse of comparison been poetry, he would have had to substitute the name of Mallarmé for Cézanne.

The conceptual origins of Snow's mature work can be found in an early film of his, *New York Eye and Ear Control* (1964). Numerous dualities make the film cohere. The cutout figure of the Walking Woman, an obsessive image from his paintings and sculpture, at times white, sometimes black, recurs throughout the film, which has two parts. In the first half, the flat cutouts contradict the deep space of the landscapes, rockscapes, and seascapes in which they are placed. The second half occurs indoors, within a small unoriented space, where people (black and white) pose in relationship to the cutouts and their negative molds.

New York Eye and Ear Control suggests a declension of ideas, of black and white, flat and round, statis and ebullience, silence and sound. But despite the film-maker's articulate description of the overall construction in conversations, it is architectonically naive. Snow's primary weakness here is the central strength of his later work—the discovery of a simple situation permeated by a field of rich philosophical implication which duration elaborates.

Snow considers the primary historical contribution of *New York Eye and Ear Control* to be its direct confrontation with aesthetic endurance. If this was his intention, he has been more successful in a later film, *One Second in Montreal* (1969), where more than thirty still photographs of snow-covered parks are held on the screen for very long periods. The shape of the film is a crescendo-diminuendo of duration—although the first shot is held very long, the second stays even longer, and so on into the middle of the film, after which the measures begin to shorten.

One Second in Montreal is one of several structural films that encroach upon the domain of the graphic cinema. It can be said that Wavelength bridges the distance between the subjective and the graphic poles by zooming the depth of the loft into the flatwork of the photograph. Paul Sharits, Ernie Gehr, George Landow, and Hollis Frampton have deliberately made the distinction between these categories of film-making problematic in their recent works. In One Second in Montreal Snow inverted the micro-rhythmic preoccupations of Kubelka and Breer by organizing his film around temporal differences that are barely perceptible because the attention of the viewer is permitted to wander and to change during the long holds.

In ←→ (1969) and The Central Region (1971) the film-maker elaborated on the metaphor of the moving camera as an imitation of consciousness. The central fact of ←→ is velocity. The camera perpetually moving, left-right, right-left, passes a number of "events" which become metaphors in the flesh for the back-and-forth inflection of the camera. These events suggest the elements of contemporary dance. Each activity is a rhythmic unit, self-enclosed, and joined to the subsequent activity only by the fact that they occur in the same space. They provide a living scale for the speeds of camera movement, and they provide solid forms in the field of energy that the panning makes out of space.

The overt rhythm of ←→ depends upon the speed at which the camera scans from side to side or up and down. Likewise, the overt drama of Wavelength derives from the closing-in of space, the action of the zoom lens. The specific content of both films is empty space or rooms. It is the nature and structure of the events within the rooms which differentiate the modes of the films.

In the letter quoted earlier, Snow described ←→, which he was completing at the time:

> As a move from the implications of Wavelength ←→ attempts to transcend through motion more than light. There will be less paradox and in a way less drama than in the other films. It is more "concrete" and more objective. ←→ is sculptural. It is also a kind of demonstration or lesson in perception and in concepts of law and order and their transcendence. It is in/of/depicts a classroom. I think it will be seen to present a different, possibly new, spectator-image relationship. My films are (to me) attempts to suggest the mind to a certain state or certain states of consciousness. They are drug relatives in that respect. ←→ will be less

comment and dream than the others. You aren't within it, it isn't within you, you're beside it. ⟷ is sculptural because the depicted light is to be outside, around the solid (wall) which becomes transcended/spiritualized by motion-time whereas in *Wavelength* it is more transcended by light-time.[8]

In the film the camera pans back and forth outside a schoolroom while a janitor crosses, sweeping, from right to left. The remainder of the film, which is fifty minutes long, takes place within that room. For the first thirty-five minutes the camera repeatedly sweeps past events or "operations," to use the vocabulary of contemporary dance, usually separated from each other by passages of panning the empty room: a girl reads by the window, a class takes place in which the title symbol appears on the blackboard, a couple pass a ball, the janitor sweeps the floor, two men playfully fight, someone washes the window from outside, and a policeman looks in. The speed of the moving camera varies in relation to each event, sometimes to underline and sometimes to obscure the rhythm and axis of the activity; furthermore actors enter either by the door or suddenly appear and disappear through editing.

Midway through the film the event series ends. The camera accelerates, blurring the objects of the room, until the depth of space, which had been significantly asymmetrical—the camera being nearer one wall than the other—flattens into the two-dimensional. At the point of maximal speed the direction changes to the vertical and gradually slows to a stop. The film seems to have ended; the credits appear. Then the substance of the film is recapitulated in a coda.

The incessant panning of the camera creates an apparent time in conflict with the time of any given operation. In the film's coda, which is a recapitulation of all the events out of their initial order and in multiple superimposition, the illusions of temporal integrity dissolve in an image of atemporal rhythmic counterpoint as all the directions and parts of the film appear simultaneously.

In the letter I have quoted, Snow wrote: "If *Wavelength* is metaphysics, *Eye and Ear Control* is philosophy and ⟷ will be physics." Later he explained what he meant by these analogies. For him *New York Eye and Ear Control* analyzes modes of action, philosophy being a curriculum extending from ethics to logic, but excluding metaphysics (for Snow, the religious and apperceptive dimension and the locus of paradoxes) which is the specific domain of *Wavelength*. Michelson's brilliant analysis of the film does not account for its transcendental aura, which emerges, I believe, from the tension between the intentionality of the movement forward and the superhuman, invisible fixity of the tripod from which it pivots. That tension is in turn reflected and intensified by the corresponding opposition of the natural sounds to the electronic crescendo. And that tension climaxes in the final eerie plunge from the flat wall into the illusionary depth of the motionless seascape. Snow writes that he placed his camera and tripod on a pedestal to get a view of the street beyond the window, and he "discovered the high angle to have lyric God-like above-it-all quality."

The nearly mechanical scanning movement of ⟷ (he experimented with a machine that could swing the camera back and forth) takes a module of human perception and moves it in the direction of physical law, which denies to the human events it scans the internal cohesion of narrative, so that they in turn withhold from the camera the privilege of a fictive or transcendental perspective. Thus the film-maker compares the manifold to physics, or he can say, "You aren't within it; it isn't within you; you're beside it." Yet that does not exclude the possibility of an internal development within the film itself. In a text on *The Central Region*, he repeats and expounds his analogies:

> I've said before, and perhaps I can quote myself, *"New York Eye and Ear Control* is philosophy, *Wavelength* is metaphysics and ⟷ is physics." By the last I mean the conversion of matter into energy. $E=mc^2$. *La Région* continues this but it becomes simultaneous micro and macro, cosmic-planetary as well as atomic. Totality is achieved in terms of cycles rather than action and reaction. It's *above* that.[9]

I take the analogy of "the conversion of mass into energy" to be a description of the climax of ⟷ when the acceleration of the camera allows for a transition from the horizontal to the vertical and ultimately for simultaneous spaces and events in the superimposed coda.

The Central Region reconciles the structural metaphors of *Wavelength* and ⟷. The central region of the title is a nearly barren plateau, void of people or any signs of their existence, and this region is also the sky above it, which the camera sweeps in 360 degree circles, explores in expanding or contracting spirals, and crosses in zig-zagging pans, focusing on the ground around its base in flowing close-ups and the distant horizon in zooming telephoto shots; but it is also the invisible spherical space which the camera, despite its miraculous equatorial mount which can mechanically perform more motions than the subtlest of film-makers holding his camera by hand, cannot see because it is itself. The whole visible scene, the hemisphere of the sky and the ground extending from the camera mount (whose shadow is visible) to the horizon, becomes the inner circumference of a sphere whose center is the other central region: the camera and the space of its self.

By programming the movements of the camera in advance, Snow and his crew were able to have themselves dropped by helicopter on the plateau for several days and hide out of view while the individual takes of the film were being made. The complete absence of humans, combined with the panoramic and visibly mechanical movement of the camera, gives the cinematic image a terrible autonomy. Annette Michelson observed that *Wavelength* was a film devoid of metaphors which was itself a grand metaphor for the activity of consciousness. *The Central Region* carries that limitation of metaphor even further; nothing the camera passes acknowledges its existence, however tangentially; yet the film as a whole metaphorically describes the Romantic estrangement from nature; all of its baroque motions vainly seek an image in the visible central region that will illuminate the invisible one.

Curiously, this very unique film recapitulates the quests of two very different film-makers, Stan Brakhage and Jordan Belson. In its imagery and in its dynamics, *The Central Region* looks back upon *Anticipation of the Night*, in which Brakhage's shadow self becomes the shadow of the camera mount. His exploration there through the moving camera of the child's awakening consciousness has its corollary in the opening spiral of Snow's film where the space which the viewer must study for the next three hours gradually discloses itself as the image feels its way from close, out-of-focus ground to horizon. Their imagery coincides in visions of "moonplay"; the camera movement in both films makes the moon dance in the night sky. Brakhage ends with a defeating dawn; Snow includes a beautiful *aube* in the middle of his film. In many ways it is the most spectacular of the sixteen different sections, which vary from about three minutes to a half hour in length and are clearly punctuated by a glowing yellow x against a black screen. In the dawn scene, the slowly seeping light very gradually clarifies the landscape and at the same time allows us to perceive the camera movements.

Brakhage's probing camera, unlike Snow's, is completely humanized. Its irregularities of movement are indices of the fictional self behind it. In its disembodied perspective the motion of *The Central Region* recalls that of *Samadhi* or *World*. Belson probably found a metaphor for his cinema when he read in Stapleton's *Star Maker*, "Miserably I tried to shut out the immensities by closing my eyes. But I had neither eyes nor eyelids. I was a disembodied, wandering view-point."

The crucial issue that separates Snow's disembodied viewpoint from Belson's is, of course, illusionism. Snow always incorporated an apperceptive acknowledgment of the cinematic materials and circumstances in his film. In the article on *The Central Region* he wrote:

> Most of my films accept the traditional theater situation. Audience here, screen there. It makes concentration and contemplation possible. We're two sided and we fold. . . . The single rectangle can contain a lot. In *Région* the frame is very important as the image is continually flowing through it. The frame is eyelids. It can seem sad that in order to exist a form must have bounds, limits, set, and setting. The rectangle's content can be precisely that. In *La Région Centrale* the frame emphasizes the cosmic continuity which is beautiful, but tragic: it just goes on without us.[10]

Belson's art seduces us away from the immediacy of the materials—the rectangular screen, the tripod, the focusing lenses—into an illusionary participation, while Snow's transcendentalism is always grounded in a dialogue between illusion and its unveiling.

The metaphysical culmination of *Wavelength* had been the moment of breaking through the photographic surface; the "physical" turning point of ⟷ was the conversion of space into sheer motion. A similar conversion occurs in the last section of *The Central Region*. The camera circles so quickly that the motion is no longer read as camera movement and the landscape itself seems to fly. As the speed accelerates, the earth it photographs forms a spinning ball and the last image of the film defines the central region as a planet in space, recalling the same metaphor for consciousness in most of Belson's work.

Paul Sharits' films are devoid of mystical or cosmological imagery, but they aspire to induce changes of consciousness in their viewers. Writing about his most successful flicker film, N:O:T:H:I:N:G (1968), he uses the language of Tibetan Buddhism:

> The film will strip away anything (all present definitions of "something") standing in the way of the film being its own reality, anything which would prevent the viewer from entering totally new levels of awareness. The theme of the work, if it can be called a theme, is to deal with the non-understandable, the impossible, in a tightly and precisely structured way. The film will not "mean" something—it will "mean," in a very concrete way, nothing.

The film focuses and concentrates on two images and their highly linear but illogical and/or inverted development. The major image is that of a lightbulb which first retracts its light rays; upon retracting its light, the bulb becomes black and, impossibly, lights up the space around it. The bulb emits one burst of black light and begins melting; at the end of the film the bulb is a black puddle at the bottom of the screen. The other image (notice that the film is composed, on all levels, of dualities) is that of a chair, seen against a graph-like background, falling backwards onto the floor (actually, it falls against and affirms the edge of the picture frame); this image sequence occurs in the center, "thig le" section of N:O:T:H:I:N:G. The mass of the film is highly vibratory color-energy rhythms; the color development is partially based on the Tibetan Mandala of the Five Dhyani Buddhas which is used in meditation to reach the highest level of inner consciousness—infinite, transcendental wisdom (symbolized by Vairocana being embraced by the Divine Mother of Infinite Blue Space). This formal-psychological composition moves progressively into more intense vibration (through the symbolic colors white, yellow, red and green) until the center of the mandala is reached (the center being the "thig le" or void point, containing all forms, both the beginning and end of consciousness). The second half of the film is, in a sense, the inverse of the first; that is, after one has passed through the center of the void, he may return to a normative state retaining the richness of the revelatory "thig le" experience. The virtual shapes I have been working with (created by rapid alternations and patterns of blank color frames) are quite relevant in this work as is indicated by this passage from the Svetasvatara Upanishad: "As you practice meditation, you may see in vision forms, resembling snow, crystals, smoke, fire, lightning, fireflies, the sun, the moon. These are signs that you are on your way to the revelation of Brahman."

I am not at all interested in the mystical symbolism of Buddhism, only in its strong, intuitively developed imagistic power. In a sense, I am more interested in the mantra because unlike the mandala and yantra forms which are full of such symbols, the mantra is often nearly pure nonsense—yet it has intense potency psychologically, aesthetically and physiologically. The mantra used upon reaching the "thig le" of the Mandala of the Five Dhyani Buddhas is the simple "Om"—a steady vibrational hum. I've tried to compose the center of N:O:T:H:I:N:G, on one level, to visualize this auditory effect.[11]

Kubelka has posited *Arnulf Rainer* as the absolute pole of "strong articulations," the split-second collision of opposites, black and white, silence and white sound. In *The Flicker*, Tony Conrad extended that technique to an area of meditative cinema by orchestrating smooth transitions between white dominance and black dominance and by keeping his piercing soundtrack at an even level. Lacking the internal modulation of *Ar-*

nulf Rainer, The Flicker uses the aggressive speed of the flicker effect to
suggest a revelatory stasis or very gradual change.

When Paul Sharits made the first color flickers—*Ray Gun Virus* (1966)
and *Piece Mandala/End War* (1966)—he further softened the inherent
strong articulations. Pure colors when rapidly flashed one after the other
tend to blend, pale, and veer toward whiteness. By the time he made
N:O:T:H:I:N:G he had learned how to control these apparent shifts and to
group his color bursts into major and minor phrases with, say, a pale blue
dominant at one time, a yellow dominant at another. From the very beginning the screen flashes clusters of colors, while the sound suggests a
telegraphic code, chattering teeth, or the plastic click of suddenly changing television channels.

In the middle of the chain of color changes he shows us an image interlude of a chair animated in positive and negative. It floats down the
screen, away into nothing, or the near nothing of the mutually exterminat-
ing colors. The interlude is marked by the sound of a telephone. From
early on, the film is continually interrupted for short periods by the two-
dimensional image of a light bulb dripping its vital light fluid. From the
first occurrence of this image until the last drop of bulb fluid has leaked
out, a series of static beeps is heard, gradually spaced further and further
apart. In the end we see only long passages of color clusters whose dominants are synchronized to the mooing of cows.

Sharits molds the viewer's attention and punctuates it by incorporating
into his seemingly circular flicker films (the mandala is his chosen shape)
linear signs for determining how much of the film's time has expired, how
much is yet to come. The dripping bulb is one such clock; we anticipate
that the film will end when it does. Ken Jacobs shows us the original *Tom,
Tom, the Piper's Son* first so that we can gauge the development of his
variations, only to trick us at the end, as Nelson does when he lies about
the time of *Bleu Shut*. Sharits, however, seems to be interested in maintaining the purity of the relation between the duration of his films and the
internal expectations and milestones they generate.

In T,O,U,C,H,I,N,G (1968) he spells the title out, letter by letter, beginning with the T and ending the film with the G. Here still images begin to
assume equal weight with the color flicker. Single frame shots of a shirt-
less young man flash in positive and negative, both color and black-and-
white. In some of the shots he holds his tongue in a scissors as if about
to cut it off; in others a woman's fingernails are scratching his face. Two
different stills of the scratching, in quick succession, test the spectator's

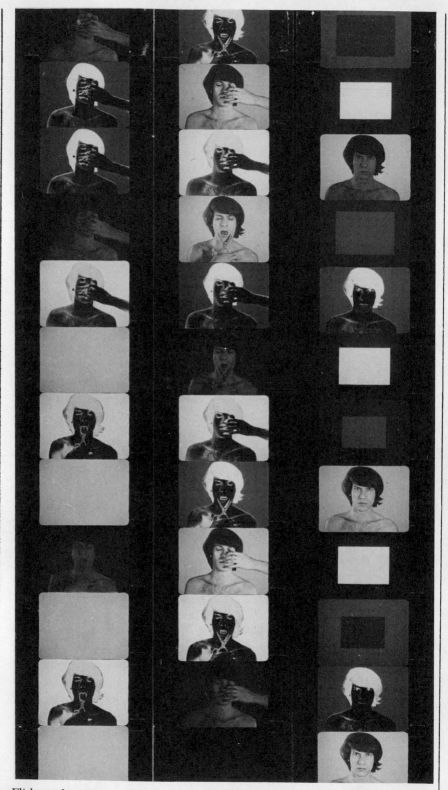

Flicker and sparagmos: Paul Sharits' *T,O,U,C,H,I,N,G*.

tendency to elide them into an illusion of movement. Mixed with these icons of violence are a photograph of an operation in color and a close-up of genitals in intercourse in black-and-white. All through the film the word "destroy" is repeated by a male voice in a loop. Eventually the ear refuses to register it, and it begins to sound like other words.

He makes similar use of the word "exochorion" in his subsequent film S:TREAM:S:S:ECTION:S:ECTION:S:S:ECTIONED (1970), this time spoken fugally with similar words by female voices. On the screen we see, for the first time in a Sharits film, a moving image—flowing water.

While the cycles of water current three times decrease in layers of superimposition from six to one, the number of vertical scratches on the film steadily increases in increments of three. The viewer clocks the film in relation to his expectation that when there is no more room for three additional scratches the film will end.

The multiple superimposition of water flowing in different directions initially presents a very flat image in the opening minutes of the film. But the subsequent scratches, which are deep, ripping through the color emulsion to the pure white of the film base and often ploughing up a visual residue of filmic matter at the edges, affirm a literal flatness which makes the water seem to occupy deep space by contrast.

The dilemma of Sharits' art has turned on the failure of his imagery to sustain its authority in the very powerful matrix of the structures he provides. His search for metaphors and icons for the particular kind of cinematic experience that his films engender has not been as successful as his invention of markers to reflect the duration of his films. In N:O:T:H:-I:N:G the off-balance, empty chair and the draining light bulb allude to the floating, almost intoxicating experience the seated viewer feels after extended concentration on flickering colors, pouring from the projector bulb. The metaphors of T,O,U,C,H,I,N,G totalize the suicidal and sexual inserts of *Ray Gun Virus* and *Piece Mandala/End War* and represent the viewing experience as erotic violence. Curiously in s:s:s:s:s:s he represents, unwittingly of course, the metaphor Kubelka is so fond of elaborating for the structure of *Schwechater*; in his lectures he always compares that film to the flowing of a stream. In Sharits' film too, the complexly deflected water flows are like the illusory movement of cinema. However, these metaphors either lack the immediacy of the color flickers or the scratches around them, or they overpower their matrix, as in T,O,U,C,H,I,N,G, and instigate a psychological vector which the form cannot accommodate as satisfactorily as the trance film or the mythopoeic film.

It is precisely such a gift for finding the apperceptive trope that distinguishes George Landow's films. His first film, *Fleming Faloon* (1963), is a precursor of the structural tendency. The technique of direct address is at the center of its construction. The film begins with two amateurs reciting "Around the world in eighty minutes"; then it contains jumpcuts of a TV newscaster and image upon image of a staring face, sometimes full screen, sometimes as the object of a dollying camera with the face superimposed upon itself. At other times the film splits into four images (unsplit 8mm photography in which two sets of two consecutive images appear in the 16mm frame). Televisions, mirrored televisions, and superimposed movies are interspersed.

In *Film in which there appear sprocket holes, edge lettering, dirt particles, etc.* (1966), he derived his image from a commercial test film, originally nothing more than a girl staring at the camera, in which a blink of her eye is the only motion, with a spectrum of colors beside her. Landow had the image reprinted so that the girl and the spectrum occupied only one half of the frame, the other half of which is made up of sprocket holes frilled with rapidly changing edge letters, while on the far right, half of the girl's head appears again.

When the strip was to become *Film in which*, Landow instructed the laboratory not to clean the dirt from the film and to make a clean splice that would hide the repetitions. The resulting film, a found object extended to a simple structure, is the essence of minimal cinema. The girl's face is static—perhaps a blink is glimpsed; the sprocket holes do not move but waver slightly as the system of edge lettering flashes around them. Deep into the film the dirt begins to form time patterns, and the film ends.

Bardo Follies (1966) describes a kind of meditation and refers in its title to the *Tibetan Book of the Dead*. The film begins with a loop-printed image of a water flotilla moving past a woman who waves to us at every turn of the loop. After about ten minutes (there is a shorter version too) the same loop appears doubled into a set of circles against the black screen. Then there are three circles for an instant. The film image in the circles begins to burn, creating a moldy, wavering, orange-dominated mass. Eventually the entire screen fills with one burning frame which disintegrates in slow motion in an extremely grainy soft focus. Another frame burns, and the whole screen throbs with melting celluloid. Probably this was created by several generations of photography off the screen—its effect is to make the screen itself seem to throb and smolder. The anticipatory tension of the banal loop is maintained throughout this section in which the film stock itself seems to die. After a long while it becomes a split screen of air bubbles in water filmed through a microscope with colored filters, a different color on each side of the screen. Through changes of focus the bubbles lose shape and dissolve into one another, and the four filters switch. Finally, some forty minutes after the first loop, the screen goes white. The film ends.

Structurally it is the gradual abstraction of a single image (originally emphasized by loop-printing) through burning and slow motion rephotography off the screen. The final images of air bubbles are metaphorical extensions of the process of abstraction. The entire opus is open to the interpretation suggested by the title—the pursuit of the pure light from the "follies" of daily life. The viewer comes to see not the images of the earth—the girl and the flotilla—but the colors and tones of the light itself in a chain of purification.

In *The Film that Rises to the Surface of Clarified Butter* (1968), Landow extends the structural principle of the loop into a cycle of visions. Here we see in black-and-white the head of a working animator; he draws a line, makes a body; then he animates a grotesque humanoid shape. In negative a girl points to the drawing and taps on it with a pencil. This sequence of shots—the back of the animator, the animation, the negative girl looking at it—occurs three times, but sometimes there is more negative material in one cycle than in another. Next we see the animator, this time from the front; he is creating a similar monster; he animates it. Again we see him from the front; again he animates it. Such is the action of the film. A wailing sound of Tibet accompanies the whole film. The title as well is Eastern: Landow read about the film that rises to the surface of clarified butter in the *Upanishads*.

The ontological distinction between graphic, two-dimensional modality (the monsters) and photographic naturalism (the animators, even the pen resting beside the monsters as they move in movie illusion), which is used as a metaphor for the relation of film itself (a two-dimensional field of illusion) to actuality, is a classic trope implicit since the beginning of animation and explicit countless times before Landow. Yet this is the first film constructed solely around this metaphor.

Landow's structural films are all based on simple situations: the variations on announcing and looking (*Fleming Faloon*), the extrinsic visual interest in a film frame (*Film in which there appear sprocket holes, edge lettering, dirt particles, etc.*), a meditation on the pure light trapped in a ridiculous image (*Bardo Follies*), and the echo of an illusion (*Film that*

Rises to the Surface of Clarified Butter). His remarkable faculty is as maker of images, for the simple found objects (*Film in which* and the beginning of *Bardo Follies*) he uses and the images he photographs are radical, super-real, and haunting.

Several film-makers extended their aspirations for an unmediated cinema which would directly reflect or induce states of mind and which first generated the structural film, into a participatory form which addressed itself to the decision-making and logical faculties of the viewer. George Landow and Hollis Frampton were the most significant film-makers to span the transition from structural to participatory modes. This shift marks an evolution within the structural film. It does not arise from a revolution as fundamental as that of other historical moments I have been discussing, such as the trance film, the lyrical film, the mythopoeic film, or the structural film itself.

Institutional Quality (1969), *Remedial Reading Comprehension* (1971), and the series-in-progress *What's Wrong with This Picture?* (1972-   ) constitute Landow's contribution to this development. As in all his previous films the form of *Institutional Quality* is closed and more or less dominated by a single image. In this case it is a school marm, administering to the viewer experience reminiscent of childhood psychological perception tests and the television series *Winky Dink and You*, in which children were encouraged to draw upon a transparent sheet over the television screen, guided by an instructor on the air. Landow's teacher instructs us, "There is a picture on your desk," and we see a bourgeois living room whose only sign of motion is the banding fluctuation of its television screen. The instructions of the teacher remain accurately within the rhetoric of testing instructions, but the montage of the film and the apperceptive condition of the viewer make these instructions ironic. After calling our attention to the picture of the living room, she says, "Do not look at the picture," an order that the film spectator must blatantly ignore. At the end when she says "Now write your first name and your last name at the bottom of the picture," the image flares to white before we see that the film-maker has written his name at the end of his picture: "By George Landow."

When the voice instructs the viewer to put the number 3 over the object one would touch to turn on the television, a hand as big as the whole living room appears and pencils a three on the television screen, which destroys our illusion of scale and indicates the literal flatness of our own

motion picture screen. Throughout the film the voice continues these instructions, and whenever the living room is visible, the hand obeys. There
is no let-up in the voice, but more and more the image cuts away from
the middle-class living room to pictures and questions about 8mm and
16mm films. The numbering of the objects in the room is reflected in
the printed numbers over the picture of a projector indicating its operating parts. In a final didactic gesture, titled "A Re-Enactment" in letters
printed over the image, an embarrassed and giggling girl demonstrates
the threading procedure for loading an 8mm projector. "A Re-Enactment"
is itself part of the television rhetoric used to describe the dramatization
of the comparative testing of similar products within a commercial.

The fumbling and embarrassed performance of the demonstrator points
up Landow's growing concern with facsimiles and counterfeits. In the
second part of *What's Wrong with This Picture?* he remade an instruc-
tional film about civic ethics, with slight flaws. The shaky superimpositions and the quality of performance in the demonstration of equipment
in *Institutional Quality* participate in this aesthetic of faulty facsimiles.

In *Remedial Reading Comprehension* he repeats and varies many of
the tactics of the previous film, but this time he includes an actual found
object along with his counterfeits. A speed reading training film flashes
short phrases from a sequential text. The whole of *Remedial Reading
Comprehension* is a film of short phrases in an ambiguously didactic sequence. Dream inspiration and academic education are conflated in an
opening that cuts from a sleeping girl to a classroom, expanding from a
corner of the screen above her as if it were a "balloon" until it fills the
screen, blotting her out. At the cry of "lights," a faked commercial for
rice appears, contrasting a grain of brown rice with one of converted rice.

The act of reading is amplified by bracketing two images of the film-
maker running in flattened space created by rephotography off a screen;
over his doubly superimposed picture appears the statement, "This Is A
Film About You." (This is one of two direct addresses in the film. The
other, "Suppose your name is Madge and you have just cooked some rice,"
occurs in the commentary of the advertisement.) When the running image returns, the sentence concludes, "Not About Its Maker."

Landow has referred to these films as an autobiography. It is an autobiography, or more exactly a *bildungs-roman*, devoid of psychology, moving in an elliptical leap from childhood and grammar school to college.
Hollis Frampton too has used the participatory film for the indirect and

serial "autobiography," *Hapax Legomena,* a title derived from classical philology, referring to those words of which only one instance survives in the ancient texts.

Just before embarking on the serial film, Frampton completed his major work to date, *Zorns Lemma* (1970). This film is divided into three sections: an initial imageless reading of the *Bay State Primer;* a long series of silent shots, each one second of photographed signs edited to form one complete Latin alphabet; and finally a single shot of two people walking across a snow-covered field away from the camera to the sound of a choral reading.

The first of several intellectual orders which Frampton provides as structural models within the film is, of course, the alphabet. *The Bay State Primer* announces, and the central forty minutes of this hour long film elaborates upon it. Within that section a second kind of ordering occurs; letters begin to drop out of the alphabet and their one-second pulse is replaced by an image without a sign. The first to go is X, replaced by a fire; a little later Z is replaced by waves breaking backwards. Once an image is replaced, it will always have the same substitution; in the slot of X the fire continues for a second each time, the sea rolls backwards at the end of each alphabet once the initial substitution occurs. On the other hand, the signs are different in every cycle.

The substitution process sets in action a guessing game and a timing device. Since the letters seem to disappear roughly in inverse proportion to their distribution as initial letters of words in English, the viewer can with occasional accuracy guess which letter will drop out next. He also suspects that when the alphabet has been completely replaced, the film or the section will end.

A second timing mechanism exists within the substitution images themselves, and it gains force as the alphabetic cycles come to an end. Some of the substitution images imply their own termination. The tying of shoes which replaces P, the washing of hands (G), the changing of a tire (T), and especially the filling of the frame with dried beans (N) add a time dimension essentially different from that of the waves, or a static tree (F), a red ibis flapping its wings (B), or cat-tails swaying in the wind (Y). The clocking mechanism of the finite acts is confirmed by the synchronous drive toward completion which becomes evident in the last minutes of the section.

In an elaborate set of notes on the film and its generating formulas, Frampton even describes its structure as autobiographical, the three parts

George Landow in *Remedial Reading Comprehension*: the text declares the participatory film's paradoxical inversion of the trance film.

corresponding to his Judeo-Christian upbringing, his development from
being a poet to a film-maker while living in New York City, which is the
background of the signs and replacements, and finally a prophecy of his
move to the country. He lists the criteria for choosing the replacements as:

1. banality. Exceptions: S, C (animal images);
2. "sculptural" as distinct from "painterly" (as in word-images) work
   being done, i.e. illusion of space or substance consciously entered and
   dealt with, as against mimesis of such action. Exceptions D, K (cutting cookies, digging a hole);
3. Cinematic or para-cinematic reference, however oblique. To my mind
   any phenomena is para-cinematic if it shares *one* element with
   cinema, e.g. modularity with respect to space or time.

Consider also the problems of alternating scale, and maintaining the
fourfold HOPI analysis: CONVERGENT VS. NON-CONVERGENT/RHYTHMIC VS.
ARHYTHMIC.[12]

In the final section the visual pulse shifts to the aural level as six
women recite the translation of Grosseteste's "On Light, or the Ingres-
sion of Forms" in phrases one second apiece. His decision to allow one
second to be the pulse of his film attempts to replace Kubelka's reduction
to the metric of the machinery (the single frame) with an arbitrary tempo.
This is one of several totalizations and parodies of the quests of the
graphic film in *Zorns Lemma*. The blank screen of the opening section
had been one; secondly by mixing flat collages with the actual street signs
in the middle section, he compounded the paradoxes of reading and depth
perception that the graphic film inherited from Léger, and which Landow explored in his participatory film.

In *Zorns Lemma* Frampton followed the tactics of his two elected literary masters, Jorge Luis Borges and Ezra Pound. From Borges he learned
the art of labyrinthine construction and the dialectic of presenting and
obliterating the self. Following Pound, Frampton has incorporated in the
end of his film a crucial indirect allusion; it is to the paradox of *Arnulf
Rainer*'s reduction. In Grosseteste's essay, materiality is the final dissolution, or the point of weakest articulation, of pure light. But in the graphic
cinema that vector is reversed. In the quest for sheer materiality—for an
image that would *be,* and not simply *represent*—the artist seeks endless
refinement of light itself. As the choral text moves from Neo-Platonic
source-light to the grosser impurities of objective reality, Frampton slowly
opens the shutter, washing out his snowscape into the untinted whiteness
of the screen.

Zorns Lemma takes its title from set theory, where it seems that "every partially ordered set contains a maximal fully ordered subset." The units of one second each, the alphabets, and the replacement images are ordered sets within the film. Our perception of the film is a participation in the discovery of the ordering. Other Frampton films derive their titles from specialized disciplines—physics in the case of States (1967/1970), Maxwell's Demon (1968), Surface Tension (1968), and Prince Rupert's Drops (1969), and philology in Palindrome (1969)—and take their structural models from the academic disciplines.

A film such as Zorns Lemma must come about from an elaborate preconception of its form. That kind of preconception is radically different from the organicism of Markopoulos, Brakhage, Baillie, and indeed most of the film-makers treated in the early and middle chapters of this book. In the elaborate chain of cycles and epicycles which constitutes the history of the American avant-garde film, the Symbolist aesthetic which animated the films and theories of Maya Deren returns, with a radically different emphasis, in the structural cinema. Although dream and ritual had been the focus of her attention, she advocated a chastening of the moment of inspiration and a conquest of the unconscious, a process which she associated with Classicism. The film-makers who followed her pursued the metaphors of dream and ritual by which she had defined the avant-garde cinema, but they allowed a Romantic faith in the triumph of the imagination to determine their forms from within. From this aesthetic submission grew the trance and the mythopoeic film. When the structural cinema repudiated the credo that film aspires to the condition of dream or myth, it returned to the Symbolist aesthetic that Deren had defined, and in finding new metaphors for the cinematic experience with which to shape films, it reversed the earlier process so that a new imagery arose from the dictates of the form.

NOTES

MESHES OF THE AFTERNOON

1. Salvador Dali, *The Secret Life of Salvador Dali* (Vision, London, 1968), trans. Haakon Chevalier, p. 212.
2. Luis Buñuel, "Notes on the Making of *Un Chien Andalou*," *Art in Cinema*, ed. Frank Stauffacher (San Francisco Museum of Art, 1947), pp. 29-30.
3. Maya Deren, *Notes, Essays, Letters,* in *Film Culture,* 39 (Winter 1965), p. 1.
4. Luis Buñuel, *L'Age d'Or and Un Chien Andalou* (Villiers, London, 1968), trans. Marianne Alexandre, p. 90.

RITUAL AND NATURE

1. Parker Tyler, *The Three Faces of the Film* (Yoseloff, New York, 1960), picture caption opp. p. 96.
2. *Ibid.,* picture caption opp. p. 96.
3. Deren, *Notes,* p. 30.
4. Maya Deren, "Chamber Films," *Filmwise,* 2 (1961), pp. 37-38.
5. P. Adams Sitney, "Imagism in Four Avant-Garde Films," *Film Culture,* 31 (Winter 1963-4).
6. Deren, *Notes,* p. 18.
7. Deren, "Chamber Films," pp. 38-39.
8. Deren, *Notes,* p. 31.
9. *Ibid.,* p. 13.
10. *Ibid.,* p. 17.
11. Maya Deren, *The Divine Horsemen: Voodoo Gods of Haiti* (Chelsea House, New York, 1970), pp. 5-6.
12. Deren, *Notes,* p. 27.
13. Maya Deren, "Cinematography: The Creative Use of Reality," *Daedalus* (Winter 1960), pp. 154-55.
14. *Ibid.,* pp. 156-57.
15. Maya Deren, "Cinema as an Art Form," *Introduction to the Art of the Movies,* ed. Lewis Jacobs (Noonday, New York, 1960), p. 258.
16. Deren, "Cinematography," p. 167.
17. Deren, "Cinema as an Art Form," p. 262.
18. Deren, *Notes,* p. 65.
19. *Ibid.,* p. 63.
20. *Ibid.,* p. 74.
21. *Ibid.,* p. 30.
22. *Ibid.,* p. 70.
23. *Ibid.,* p. 70.
24. *Ibid.,* p. 70.

THE POTTED PSALM

1. Sidney Peterson, *"The Potted Psalm,"* in *Art in Cinema*, pp. 61-62.
2. René Clair, "Picabia, Satie, et la Première *Entr'Acte*," *L'Avant-Scene*, 86 (Nov. 1968), trans. Kate Manheim, p. 5.
3. *Ibid.*, p. 11.
4. Unpublished notes deposited at Anthology Film Archives, New York.
5. Interview with the author, recorded in July and August 1970.
6. Sidney Peterson, "Cine-Dance," *Dance Perspectives* 30 (Summer 1967), p. 16.
7. *Ibid.*, p. 16.
8. *Ibid.*, p. 16.
9. *Ibid.*, p. 19.
10. Parker Tyler, *"The Lead Shoes,"* Cinema 16 program notes (New York, April 21, 1954).
11. James Broughton, "What Magic in Lanterns?", unpublished manuscript at Anthology Film Archives.
12. Sidney Peterson, "A Note on Comedy in the Experimental Film," *Film Culture*, 29 (Summer 1963), p. 28.
13. Broughton, notes at Anthology Film Archives.
14. Maya Deren, Parker Tyler, Dylan Thomas, Arthur Miller, Willard Maas, "Poetry and the Film: A Symposium," *Film Culture*, 29 (Summer 1963), p. 29.
15. *Ibid.*, pp. 56-57.
16. *Ibid.*, p. 59.
17. Broughton, notes at Anthology Film Archives.
18. *Ibid.*

THE MAGUS

1. Tony Rayns, "Lucifer: A Kenneth Anger Compendium," *Cinema*, 4 (London, Oct. 1969).
2. Lewis Jacobs, "Avant-Garde Production in America," *Experiment in the Film*, ed. Roger Manville (Grey Walls, London, 1948), p. 136.
3. Kenneth Anger, "Filmography," *Film Culture*, 31 (Winter 1963-4), p. 8.
4. *Ibid.*, p. 8.
5. Kenneth Anger, *Magick Lantern Cycle* (Film-Makers Cinematheque, New York, 1966), p. 4.
6. Rayns, p. 29.
7. Anger, *Magick Lantern Cycle*, p. 3.
8. Kenneth Anger, *"Inauguration of the Pleasure Dome,"* Cinema 16 Film Notes (April 4, 1956).
9. Bruce Martin, Joe Medjuck, "Kenneth Anger," *Take One*, vol. 1, no. 6 (1967), p. 13.
10. Kenneth Anger, "Aleister Crowley and Merlin Magick," *Friends* (September 18, 1970), p. 16.
11. Anger, *Magick Lantern Cycle*, pp. 3-4.
12. Rayns, p. 30.
13. Anger, *Magick Lantern Cycle*, p. 11.
14. René Wellek, *Discriminations* (Yale University Press, New Haven, 1970), p. 113.
15. Kenneth Anger, *"Invocation of my Demon Brother,"* *Film Culture*, 48-49 (Spring 1970), p. 1.
16. Rayns, p. 24.

FROM TRANCE TO MYTH

1. Gregory Markopoulos, "Psyche's Search for the Herb of Invunerability," *Filmwise*, 3-4 (1963), p. 7.
2. Unpublished notes, originally intended for Cinema 16 Film Notes, now in Anthology Film Archives.

3. *Ibid.*
4. *Ibid.*
5. Donald Weinstein, "*Swain:* Flowers and Flight," *Filmwise*, 3-4 (1963), p. 28.
6. Charles Boultenhouse, "*Serenity*," *Filmwise*, 3-4 (1963), p. 41.
7. Gregory Markopoulos, "From *Fanshawe* to *Swain*," *Film Culture*, 41 (Summer 1966), p. 19. Many of Markopoulos' articles have been collected in *Chaos Phaos* (Temenos, Florence, 1970), 4 vols.
8. Gregory Markopoulos, "Excerpts from a Tentative Script for *Twice a Man*," *Film Culture*, 29 (Summer 1963), p. 14.
9. Gregory Markopoulos, "The Driving Rhythm," *Film Culture*, 40 (Spring 1966), p. 33.
10. Gregory Markopoulos, "Towards a New Narrative Film Form," *Film Culture*, 31 (Winter 1963-4), p. 11.
11. *Ibid.*, pp. 11-12.
12. Gregory Markopoulos, "The Film-maker as the Physician of the Future," *Film Culture*, 44 (Spring 1967), p. 61.
13. *Ibid.*, p. 61.
14. Robert Lamberton, "*Himself as Herself*," *Link* (Spring 1967), p. 17.
15. *Film-Makers Cooperative Catalogue*, 4 (New York, 1967). p. 17.
16. "Special Events Program," Radio Free Europe, May 10, 1966, transcription in Anthology Film Archives.
17. Gregory Markopoulos, "The Event Inside the Camera," *Retrospective Gregory Markopoulos*, catalogue of Undependent Film Center (Munich, 1970), pages unnumbered.
18. Unpublished notes, Anthology Film Archives.
19. Film-Makers Cinematheque program notes, April 18-30, 1968.
20. Letter to Stan Brakhage, July 20, 1963.
21. Harold Bloom, "The Internalization of the Quest-Romance," *Romanticism and Consciousness*, ed. Harold Bloom (Norton, New York, 1970), p. 6.
22. Gregory Markopoulos, "Projection of Thoughts," *Film Culture*, 32 (Spring 1964), p. 3.
23. Gregory Markopoulos, "Institutions, Customs, Landscapes," *Film Digest*, 23-4 (1967). Reprinted in *Chaos Phaos*, vol. 3, pp 83-84.

LYRICAL FILM

1. Bloom, "The Internalization of the Quest-Romance," p. 7.
2. The thirty Songs themselves have several subdivisions: *15 Song Traits*, *23rd Psalm Branch*, and *Song XXVII: "My Mountain" and Rivers* contain parts which might be considered as individual works. In fact, Brakhage does list the 16mm film *Two: Creely/McClure*, which is incorporated in 8mm in *15 Song Traits*, as a separate item in his filmography.
3. Stan Brakhage, "On *Anticipation of the Night*," *Filmwise* (1961), pp. 19-20.
4. Gertrude Stein, "Miss Furr and Miss Skeene," *Selected Writings of Gertrude Stein* (Random House, New York, 1962), p. 564.
5. Stan Brakhage, *Metaphors on Vision*, in *Film Culture*, 30 (Autumn 1963), p. 25. Although the pages are unnumbered, I have numbered them for convenient reference.
6. *Ibid.*, p. 23.
7. *Ibid.*, p. 59.
8. Bloom, "The Internalization of the Quest-Romance," p. 6.
9. *Metaphors on Vision*, p. 26.
10. *Ibid.*, p. 19.
11. *Ibid.*, pp. 9-10.
12. *Ibid.*, p. 14.
13. *Ibid.*, p. 80.
14. *Ibid.*, p. 77.

15. An unpublished interview with the author in the spring of 1965. A transcript is in the library of the Anthology Film Archives.

16. *Canyon Cinema Cooperative Catalogue*, 3 (Sausalito, 1972), p. 19.

17. Richard Whitehall, "An Interview with Bruce Baillie," *Film Culture*, 47 (Spring 1969), p. 19.

18. Richard Corliss, "Bruce Baillie: An Interview," *Film Comment*, vol. 7, no. 1 (Spring 1971), p. 31.

19. *Film-Makers Cooperative Catalogue*, 5 (New York, 1971), p. 23-24.

MAJOR MYTHOPOEIA

1. Dan Clark, *Brakhage* (*Film-Makers Cinematheque Monograph Series*, 2) (New York, 1966), and Fred Camper, "*The Art of Vision*: A Film By Stan Brakhage," *Film Culture*, 46 (Autumn 1967).

2. Northrop Frye, "The Keys to the Gates," in *Romanticism and Consciousness*, p. 237.

3. *Metaphors on Vision*, p. 25.

4. Interview with the author, Spring 1965.

5. This is the very lens Sidney Peterson used so often a decade earlier. He presented it to Brakhage after he had given up film-making.

6. Ezra Pound, *Gaudier-Brzeska: A Memoir* (New Directions, Ney York, 1960), p. 92.

7. *Ibid.*, p. 94.

8. *Ibid.*, p. 20.

9. *Ibid.*, p. 81.

10. Interview with the author, Spring 1965.

11. See Clement Greenberg, *Art and Culture* (Beacon, Boston, 1965), esp. the article, " 'American-Type' Painting," pp. 208-29.

12. The link between Abstract Expressionism and Brakhage was first examined by Charles Boultenhouse in "Pioneer of the Abstract Expressionist Film," *Filmwise*, 1 (1961), and it was elaborated and made to encompass the aesthetics of the American avant-garde cinema as a whole by Annette Michelson in "Film and The Radical Aspiration," *Film Culture*, 42 (Fall 1966).

13. David Sylvester, "Interview with Franz Kline," *Living Arts*, vol. 1, no. 1 (Spring 1963), reprinted in *Readings in American Art Since 1900: A Documentary Survey*, ed. Barbara Rose (Praeger, New York, 1968), p. 156.

14. Jackson Pollock, "My Painting," *Possibilities*, 1 (Winter 1947-48), and in *Readings in American Art*, p. 152.

15. "Art in New York," Radio Program, WNYC, Oct. 15, 1943.

16. "A Statement," *Tiger's Eye*, vol. 1, no. 6 (Dec. 15, 1948), and *Readings in American Art*, pp. 159-60.

17. *Metaphors on Vision*, pp. 72-73.

18. Interview with the author, Spring 1965.

19. The notes on *Songs I-XXII* are drawn from *The Film-Makers Cooperative Catalogue*, 4 (1967), pp. 25-27. The notes on the following Songs are drawn from the catalogue, *Brakhage Films*, issue undated (Jane Brakhage, Rollinsville, Colo.).

20. Guy Davenport, "Two Essays on Brakhage and his *Songs*," *Film Culture*, 40 (Spring 1966), p. 11, informs us that the subject is an infant breast-feeding.

21. Interview with the author, Spring 1965.

22. Davenport, p. 12.

23. *Ibid.*, p. 11.

24. None of the close viewers of this film have felt the dreadful overtones which I have experienced, watching the conclusion over a hundred times. In *Film Culture*, 46 (Autumn 1967) three opinions are gathered on the *23rd Psalm Branch*: Jerome Hill finds the "Coda" ecstatic, "a peaceful close" (p. 15). For Robert Lamberton, it recalls *Anticipation of the Night*: "The grace and joy of the movement of the children is beautifully and terribly a part of the thing, a part of despair and the beginning of

hope" (p. 15). Finally Fred Camper believes Brakhage has reconciled the violence of the whole film in this image: "And then, we are confronted with an image that at once suggests harmony and violence, or the harmony *of* violence; an image that also suggests the cyclical nature of human history" (p. 18).

25. Paul de Man, "Intentional Structure of the Romantic Image," in *Romanticism and Consciousness*, p. 75.

26. In the *Songs* Brakhage has been exceptionally inventive in improvising effects and techniques for 8mm where specialized equipment does not exist. In *Song VII* he masked the images in numerous ways by placing his fingers in different positions over the lens. The anamorphosis of *Song VIII* was created by a glass ashtray held and revolved before the lens. As I have already said, the split-second montage of the *23rd Psalm Branch* was made possible by the inclusion of two black frames between every change of shot. I suspect the mist effect here was made by the film-maker breathing on the lens before each shot.

27. *Metaphors on Vision*, pp. 47-48.

28. Program notes of the Whitney Museum of American Art, "New American Film-Makers Series," March 25-31, 1971.

29. It is a coincidence that *Quick Billy* resembles the first part of *Scenes from Under Childhood* more than any other Brakhage film. They were both made at the same time. From Baillie's notebooks on deposit at Anthology Film Archives it is clear that he came to certain crucial decisions, such as including a section of photographs from his youth, before he could have seen how Brakhage did the same.

30. Stan Brakhage, letter to Baillie, Jan. 15, 1969.

31. Whitehall, p. 20.

ABSOLUTE ANIMATION

1. Unpublished annotated filmography, Anthology Film Archives.
2. *Film-Makers Cooperative Catalogue*, 3 (1965), pp. 57-58.
3. P. Adams Sitney, "Harry Smith Interview," *Film Culture*, 37 (Summer 1965), p. 5.
4. Jonas Mekas, "Movie Journal," *The Village Voice* (June 3, 1971).
5. John and James Whitney, "Film Notes," in *Art in Cinema*, pp. 61-62.
6. Sitney, "Harry Smith Interview," p. 9.
7. *Ibid.*, pp. 10-11.
8. *Ibid.*, p. 10.
9. *Ibid.*, p. 10.
10. *Ibid.*, p. 12.
11. Gene Youngblood, *Expanded Cinema* (Dutton, New York, 1970), p. 168.
12. *Ibid.*, p. 174.
13. *Ibid.*, p. 174.
14. *Ibid.*, p. 173.
15. Rammurti Mishra, *Fundamentals of Yoga* (Lancer, New York, 1959), p. 195; Lama Anagarika Govinda, *Foundations of Tibetan Mysticism* (Weiser, New York, 1970), p. 184.

THE GRAPHIC CINEMA: EUROPEAN PERSPECTIVES

1. Greenberg, pp. 72-73.
2. Guy Coté, "Interview with Robert Breer," *Film Culture*, 27 (Winter 1962-3), p. 17.
3. Noel Burch, "Films of Robert Breer," *Film Quarterly*, vol. 11, no. 3 (Spring 1959).
4. Coté, p. 18.
5. Fernand Léger, "A New Realism—The Object," *Introduction to the Art of the Movies*, p. 97.
6. Unpublished interview. Anthology Film Archives.
7. Jonas Mekas, P. Adams Sitney, "Interview with Robert Breer," *Film Culture*, 56-57 (Spring 1973), p. 44.

8. Robert Breer, "Letter," *Film Culture*, 56-57, p. 70.

9. Mekas, Sitney, "Interview," p. 40; Charles Levine, "An Interview with Robert Breer," *Film Culture*, 56-57, pp. 58-59.

10. Robert Breer, "What Happened?" *Film Culture*, 26 (Fall 1962), p. 58.

11. Jonas Mekas, "An Interview with Peter Kubelka," *Film Culture*, 44 (Spring 1967), p. 45.

12. Peter Kubelka, "Working for the Next 1000 Years," *Cinema*, 9 (1971), pp. 29-30.

13. Mekas, "An Interview with Peter Kubelka," p. 43.

APOCALYPSES AND PICARESQUES

1. Paul de Man, "The Rhetoric of Temporality," *Interpretation*, ed. Charles Singleton (Johns Hopkins, Baltimore, 1969), p. 202.

2. *Film-Makers Cooperative Catalogue*, 5 (1971), pp. 270-71.

3. Ron Rice, "*The Flower Thief*," Cinema 16 film notes (April 25, 1962).

4. *Fourth International Experimental Film Competition*, catalogue, (Cinémathèque Royale de Belgique, Brussels, 1967), p. 80.

5. P. Adams Sitney, "Larry Jordan Interview," *Film Culture*, 52 (Spring 1971), p. 80.

6. *Canyon Cinema Cooperative Catalogue*, 2 (1969), p. 55.

RECOVERED INNOCENCE

1. *Film-Makers Cooperative Catalogue*, 5, pp. 165-66.

2. Unpublished interview, Anthology Film Archives.

3. *Ibid.*

4. *Film-Makers Cooperative Catalogue*, 5, p. 166.

5. *Ibid.*, p. 167.

6. Jonas Mekas, "Movie Journal," *The Village Voice* (May 2, 1963).

7. Jonas Mekas, "Notes on the New American Cinema," *Film Culture*, 24 (Spring 1962), p. 15.

8. Jonas Mekas, "Movie Journal," *The Village Voice* (Oct. 23, 1963).

9. Mekas, "Notes," p. 15.

10. See Harold Bloom, *The Visionary Company* (Doubleday, New York, 1961).

11. Unpublished interview, Anthology Film Archives.

12. Jack Smith, "Belated Appreciation of V.S.," *Film Culture*, 31 (Winter 1963-4), p. 4.

13. Jack Smith, "The Perfect Filmic Appositeness of Maria Montez," *Film Culture*, 27 (Winter 1962-3), p. 31.

14. *Ibid.*, p. 32.

15. Smith, "Belated Appreciation," pp. 4-5.

16. Jonas Mekas, "Notes on Some New Movies and Happiness," *Film Culture*, 37 (Summer 1965), pp. 18-19.

17. Program notes of the Museum of Modern Art Department of Film (June 23, 1970).

18. See Harold Bloom, *Yeats* (Oxford University Press, New York, 1970).

19. Victor Shklovsky, "Arts as Technique," in *Russian Formalist Criticism*, ed. Lee Lemon and Marion Reis (University of Nebraska, Lincoln, 1965), p. 12.

20. *Film-Makers Cooperative Catalogue*, 5, p. 167.

STRUCTURAL FILM

1. Stephen Koch, *Stargazer* (Praeger, New York, 1973), pp. 22-23.

2. *Ibid.*, p. 23.

3. *Ibid.*, pp. 54-55.

4. *Film Culture*, 46 (Autumn 1967), p. 1.

5. Annette Michelson, "Toward Snow," *Artforum* vol. 9, no. 10 (June 1971), p. 31.

6. Jonas Mekas, P. Adams Sitney, "Conversation with Michael Snow," *Film Culture*, 46 (Autumn 1967), p. 3.

7. Michael Snow, "Letter," *Film Culture*, 46, p. 5.

8. *Film-Makers Cooperative Catalogue*, 5 (1971), p. 301.

9. Michael Snow, "On *La Région Centrale*," *Film Culture*, 52 (Spring 1971), p. 61.

10. *Ibid.*, p. 62-63.

11. Paul Sharits, "Notes on Films," *Film Culture*, 47 (Summer 1969), p. 15.

12. Hollis Frampton, unpublished notes, Anthology Film Archives.

INDEX

Absolute film, 258-9, 272, 287, 300, 308-9, 337, 376

Abstract Expressionism, 54, 80, 180, 186-8, 190, 233-7, 313, 319-20, 323, 373, 382, 410

Aeschylus, 166; *Prometheus Bound*, 165, 170

Anger, Kenneth, 85-6, 93-135, 153-4, 174-5, 193-4, 233, 273-4, 295, 313, 381, 403, 407, 409; *Drastic Demise*, 93, 96; *Eaux D'Artifice*, 26, 94, 102-4, 106, 129; *Escape Episode*, 93, 95-7; *Fireworks*, 21, 65, 93-5, 97-103, 106, 115, 118-19, 129, 136, 174; *Hollywood-Babylon*, 93, 95, 115; *Inauguration of the Pleasure Dome*, 56, 92, 94, 104-15, 118-19, 124, 129-31, 134, 164; *Invocation of My Demon Brother*, 94, 128-35, 201; *Kustom Kar Kommandos*, 94, 124-8, 153; *Lucifer Rising*, 94, 117, 128-30; *Prisoner of Mars*, 93, 96; *Puce Moment*, 105, 112, 124, 128; *Rabbits' Moon (La Lune des Lapins)*,104, 128; *Scorpio Rising*, 93-4, 101, 115-25, 129, 131, 152-4, 233, 383-4, 392; *The Nest*, 93, 96; *Tinsel Tree*, 93, 96; *Who Has Been Rocking My Dream Boat?* 93, 95

Anthology Film Archives, 212, 262, 299, 385-6

Antonioni, Michelangelo, 202

Arp, Hans, 274

Art in Cinema, 47, 48, 51, 68, 85, 205, 277-8, 300, 343, 385

Baillie, Bruce, 174, 201-11, 260-65, 331, 382, 385, 412, 435; *A Hurrah for Soldiers*, 202-3; *All My Life*, 207, 260; *Castro Street*, 207-10, 260-61; *Have You Thought of Talking to the Director?*, 202-3; *Mass*, 202-5; *Mr. Hayashi*, 202; *Quick Billie*, 206, 211, 260-65; *Quixote*, 202, 204-5; *Still Life*, 207, 260; *To Parsifal*, 202, 204, 208; *Tung*, 207, 260; *Valentin de las Sierras*, 207, 260

Balzac, Honore de, *Le Chef d'oeuvre Inconnu*, 69-74; *Séraphita*, 157-9

Barker, George, 36, 84

Baudelaire, Charles, 369, 378-9, 383, 410

Bauer, Rudolf, 278, 281, 300

Baum, L. F., 123-34

Baziotes, William, 301

Belson, Jordan, 277, 280, 300-312, 331, 343-4, 403, 422-3; *Allures*, 301-2, 306, 311; *Bop Scotch*, 300-301; *Caravan*, 301; *Chakra*, 305, 312; *Cosmos*, 305, 310; *Flight*, 301; *Illusions*, 301; *Improvisations #1*, 301; *LSD*, 301, 310; *Mambo*, 301; *Mandala*, 301; *Meditation*, 311; *Momentum*, 309-11; *Phenomena*, 304-5, 307, 310; *Raga*, 300-301; *Re-Entry*, 302-4, 312; *Samahdi*, 306-10, 312, 422; *Seance*, 301; *Transmutation*, 301; *World*, 310-11, 422

Blake, William, 110, 186-8, 215-16, 225, 380, 402

Bloom, Harold, 170, 174, 187, 354

Borges, Jorge Luis, 434

Boultenhouse, Charles, *Handwritten*, 26

Brakhage, Jane, 185, 189, 198, 245, 256

Brakhage, Stan, 29-30, 62, 68-9, 85-7, 89, 103, 136-7, 154, 170, 174-201, 203, 206-8, 210-64, 273, 295, 331, 333, 342, 347, 361, 373, 379, 381-2, 385, 387, 403, 407-9, 412, 422, 435; *Anticipation of the Night*, 89, 180-86, 188, 191, 195, 201, 215, 246-7, 388, 422; *Blue Moses*, 201-2, 348; *Cat's Cradle*, 188, 197-8; *Daybreak and Whiteye*, 176, 181, 262; *Desistfilm*, 175-6, 179, 262, 361; *Dog Star Man*, 26, 29, 89, 124, 152, 153, 169, 185, 188, 193, 196, 199, 211-38, 242, 251, 261, 264, 294, 348, 381, 383, 408; *Fire of Waters*, 188, 199-201, 210; *Flesh of Morning*, 65, 99, 176, 179; *In Between*, 176; *Lovemaking*, 264; *Loving*, 179, 181, 183, 197, 214; *Metaphors on Vision*, 180, 183, 185-7, 191, 196-7, 211-12, 215-16, 236, 259; *Mothlight*, 169, 188, 196, 224, 241-2; *Nightcats*, 179; *Pasht*, 188, 198-9, 210; *Reflections on Black*, 20, 176-8, 339, 347, 381; *Scenes from under Childhood*, 211, 259, 262-3; *Sexual Meditations*, 264; *Sirius Remembered*, 188, 191-3, 195; *Songs*, 174, 184, 211, 238-62 (I, 239, 242, 245; II, 239, 242, 244-5; III, 239, 244-5; IV, 239, 242-3, 246, 256; V, 239, 241-2, 398; VI, 239 241-2; VII, 239, 242, 247; VIII, 239, 242; IX, 239, 246-7; X, 239, 241; XI, 239, 242-3; XII, 239, 242, 246; XIII, 239, 253, 258; XIV, 239, 242-3; XV *Song Traits*, 238-40, 242, 245-6, 252, 260; XVI, 193, 240, 242, 247-8; XVII, 240, 242; XVIII, 240, 246; XIX, 240, 247-8, 253, 257; XX, 240, 242-3; XXI, 240, 242-4; XXII, 240, 242-5; 23rd *Psalm Branch*, 238, 240-42, 245, 248-55, 257; XXIV, 241, 245; XXV, 241, 245; XXVI, 241; XXVII: *My Mountain*, 241, 244, 255-57, 260; XXVIII, 241; XXIX, 241, 245; *American Thirties Song*, 241, 253, 257-8); *The Art of Vision*, 188, 211, 255, 230-34, 238, 251, 259, 412; *The Dead*, 188, 191, 193-5, 224, 232, 241-2, 381; *The Way to Shadow Garden*, 21, 176-7; *Thigh Line Lyre Triangular*, 188-91, 241; *Two: Creeley/McLure*, 248; *Vein*, 188; *Wedlock House: An Intercourse*, 189; *Window Water Baby Moving*, 188-9, 197-8, 241; *Wonder Ring*, 179, 180-81, 390

Braque, Georges, 314-15

Brecht, Bertolt, *Mahagonny*, 271, 300

Breer, Robert, 156, 313-32, 381-2, 403, 409, 419; *A Man and His Dog Out for Air*, 320; *Blazes*, 323-4, 328; *Breathing*, 320; *Cats*, 323; *Eyewash*, 321-3; *Fist Fight*, 320, 323-4, 328, 332; *Form Phases I*, 315-16, 333; *Form Phases II*, 316; *Hommage to Jean Tinguely's Hommage to New York*, 323; *Horse over Teakettle*, 320, 323-4; *Images by Images I*, 316-18; *Image by Image IV*, 317-18; *Inner and Outer Space*, 320; *Jamestown Baloos*, 321-2; *Motion Pictures*, 317-18; *Par Avion*, 323; *Pat's Birthday*, 321, 323, 328; *Recreation (I)*, 318, 320-21, 328; *70*, 328, 330-31; *69*, 326, 328-31; *66*, 328-9, 331; *Un Miracle*, 317

Brooks, David, 382

Broughton, James, 47-51, 57, 60-65, 69, 79-83, 85-92, 123, 175-6, 233, 313, 343, 348; *Dreamwood*, 62, 64, 87, 90-92; *Four in the Afternoon*, 64, 82-3, 85; *Loony Tom, the Happy Lover*, 64, 85; *Mother's Day*, 60-65, 88-89, 138, 154; *Nuptiae*, 86-7, 89-90; *The Adventures of Jimmy*, 64-5; *The Bed*, 86-7, 89-90; *The Pleasure Garden*, 86-7;

The Golden Positions, 87-9; *This Is It*, 87, 89
Bruno, Giordano, 273
Buñuel, Luis, *L'Age d'Or*, 267; *Un Chien Andalou*, 3-6, 11-15, 18-19, 25, 47-8, 53, 57, 266
Burch, Noel, 318
Burckhardt, Rudy, 387
Burroughs, William, 294, 378
Byron, [George Gordon], 119

Cage, John, 237
Canyon Cinema, 202, 205, 305, 382
Canyon Cinema Cooperative, 206, 382, 385, 409
Cassavetes, John, 382-3; *Shadows*, 378, 380, 382-3
Cézanne, Paul, 418
Chaplin, Charles, 51, 85, 384; *City Lights*, 61
Christopoulos, George, *The Death of Hemingway*, 144
Cinema, 16, 47, 76, 83-4, 102, 107, 146, 271, 352
Clair, René, *Entr'acte*, 47, 57-9, 66, 266
Clarke, Shirley, 380, 382-4; *The Connection*, 382
Claudel, Paul, 142
Cocteau, Jean, 64; *Le Jeune Homme et al Mort*, 104; *Le Sang d'un Poète*, 18, 21, 33-4, 36, 91-2, 133, 149, 264, 266
Coleridge, S. T., "Kubla Khan," 104
Collins, Jess, 176
Conner, Bruce, 343, 348-51, 355, 360-62, 367; *A Movie*, 348-9, 351, 371; *Cosmic Ray*, 23, 129, 349-51; *Report*, 350-51
Conrad, Tony, 407; *The Flicker*, 424-5
Constable, John, 268
Corliss, Richard, 207
Cornell, Joseph, 177, 179-80, 260, 386-90, 398; *A Legend for Fountains*, 388-90; *Angel*, 388; *Centuries of June*, 179; *Cotillion*, 386, 390; *Gnir Rednow*, 390, *Rose Hobart*, 386-7; *The Children's Party*, 386, 390; *The Midnight Party*, 386, 390; *What Mozart Saw on Mulberry Street*, 388
Coté, Guy, 315
Crane, Hart, 170, 233; *The Bridge*, 402
Creative Film Foundation, 40, 170, 385
Creeley, Robert, 240, 248
Crowley, Aleister, 94, 104, 106-8, 111, 113, 115-16, 123, 130-31, 134
Cubism, 73, 197, 233, 266, 268, 314, 319

Dada Movement, 57, 66, 266, 268, 318
Dali, Salvador, 3, 15; *Un Chien Andalou, see* Buñuel
Davenport, Guy, 246-7
De Kooning, Willem, 190, 319, 382
DeMille, Cecil B., 81; *King of Kings*, 120-21
Deren, Maya, 3, 6-7, 20-48, 64-6, 69, 79-80, 83-5, 103, 134, 154, 170, 175, 189, 202-3, 205, 240, 246, 266, 379, 381, 385, 407, 435; *An Anagram of Ideas on Art, Form, and Film*, 28, 41-6, 233; *A Study in Choreography for Camera*, 24-9, 31, 75, 86-7, 103; *At Land*, 21-5, 28, 30-31, 45; *Meditation on Violence*, 26-9, 31, 39, 45; *Meshes of the Afternoon*, 6-16, 18-19, 21-5, 28-31, 33, 36, 45, 47, 55, 57, 85, 123, 136, 256, 363, 408; *Ritual in Transfigured Time*, 28, 30-33, 35-7, 39, 45, 69, 91, 99, 123-4; *The Divine Horsemen*, 28, 37; *The Very Eye of Night*, 28, 40, 45, 107, 123-4, 233
Desnos, Robert, 19
Dickinson, Emily, 40, 179, 233
Doolittle, Hilda (H. D.), 253
Dorn, Ed, 240, 246
Duchamp, Marcel, 57-8, 278, 313, 410; *Anemic Cinema*, 266-7, 314-15, 332
Duncan, Robert, 176, 197, 405
Dunham, Catherine, 7

Eggeling, Viking, 313, 315, 318; *Symphonie Diagonale*, 47, 266-8, 274, 325, 332
Eisenstein, Sergei M., 29, 81, 116, 155-6, 334; *Potemkin*, 47
Eliot, T. S., 116
Ellington, Duke, 417
Emerson, Ralph Waldo, 40, 233; *Circles*, 307
Engel, Morris, 380, 382-4
Epstein, Jean, 29
Ernst, Max, 363; *La Femme 100 Têtes*, 166, 291, 296-8; *Une Semaine de Bonté*, 291
Euripides, 147, 150; *The Bacchae*, 81
Experimental Film Festival, 86, 104, 152, 169, 331, 357, 413
Expressionism, 6, 25, 154, 175, 302, 319

Fellini, Frederico, 202
Feuillade, Louis, 117
Film Culture, 379-80, 385
Film-Makers Cinematheque, 104, 376, 382, 395-6, 409
Film-Makers Cooperative, 93-4, 198, 204, 206-7, 270-71, 347, 370, 374, 382, 385, 395
Firbank, Ronald, *Valmouth*, 103
Fischinger, Oscar, 270
Fleischner, Bob, 368, 370-71, 378; *Blonde Cobra, see* Jacobs
Ford, John, 81
Foreman, Richard, 293, 396
Foster, Richard, 277
Frampton, Hollis, 156, 407, 412, 419, 430-35; *Hapax Legomena*, 432; *Maxwell's Demon*, 435; *Palindrome*, 435; *Prince Rupert's Drops*, 435; *States*, 435; *Surface Tension*, 433; *Zorns Lemma*, 358, 432, 434-5
Frank, Robert, and Alfred, Leslie, *Pull My Daisy*, 378, 380, 382-3
Frazer, Sir James George, *The Golden Bough*, 147, 149
Freeman, Robert C., Jr., 136, 144, 147
Freud, Sigmund, 14, 31, 81-2, 153, 175, 184, 241, 253-4, 262; *Civili-sation and Its Discontents*, 254
Frye, Northrop, 215

Gehr, Ernie, 407, 411, 419
Geldzahler, Henry, 161
Gillespie, Dizzy, 279-80
Ginsberg, Allen, 294
Godard, Jean-Luc, 202
Goncourt, Edmond and Jules, *Mannette Salomon*, 79
Gracq, Julien, *Le Château d'Argol*, 171
Graphic Film-Making, 43, 266-343, 409, 419, 434
Greenberg, Clement, 314-15
Griffith, David Wark, 163
Grosseteste, Robert, 434

Hammid, Alexander, 3, 7, 9-10, 33; *Bezucelna Prochazna (Aimless Walk)*, 10, 23; *Meshes of the Afternoon, see* Deren
Harrington, Curtis, 103, 107, 111, 144, 157, 174; *Fragment of Seeking*, 21, 136; *Picnic*, 21
Hawthorne, Nathaniel, *Fanshawe*, 144, 146
Hegel, Georg Wilhelm Friedrich, *Phenomenology of the Spirit*, 303
Heyman, Hella, 22
Hill, Jerome, 239, 241, 258, 380
Hirsch, Hy, 52, 54, 68
Hoffman, Hans, 373
Hogarth, William, "Southwark Fair," 405
Hölderlin, Friedrich, 256
Honegger, Arthur, 142
Hulten, Pontus, 317
Husserl, Edmund, 417

Imagism, 25-7, 29, 31, 103
Independent Film Award, 380-81, 383
Ito, Teiji, 40
Ives, Charles, 275

Jacobs, Henry, 301
Jacobs, Ken, 321, 368-79, 382, 384-5, 387, 398, 401-6, 412; *Blonde Cobra*, 368-72, 375-9, 384, 395, 405; *Little Stabs at Happiness*, 376-

8, 381, 398; *Soft Rain*, 374-5; *Star Spangled to Death*, 372-8, 384, 387, 392, 412; *The Sky Socialist*, 383, 401-3; *Tom, Tom, the Piper's Son*, 387, 403-6, 425
Jacobs, Lewis, 95
Joffen, Jerry, 353
Jordan, Larry, 343, 361-7, 385-7, 390, 398; *Duo Concertantes*, 362-6; *Enid's Idyll*, 362; *Gymnopedies*, 363-4; *Hamfat Asar*, 362-4; *Hymn in Praise of the Sun*, 362; *Our Lady of the Sphere*, 363-4, 366; *Patricia Gives Birth to a Dream by the Doorway*, 363-6; *Pink Swine*, 362; *Portrait of Sharon*, 362; *The Centennial Exposition*, 363-4; *The Old House, Passing*, 362-3, 366-7, 371; *Trumpit*, 361
Joyce, James, 69; *Finnegans Wake*, 284
Jung, Carl Gustav, 31, 82, 142, 153, 276

Kafka, Franz, 352
Kandinsky, Vassily, 274, 281-2, 300, 316, 319
Keaton, Buster, 51
Keats, John, 402
Kelly, Robert, 196, 200, 229, 231, 240, 245-6
Kelman, Ken, 391-2
Kircher, Athanasius, 273
Kline, Franz, 236
Koch, Stephen, 410-11
Konlechner, Peter, 332
Kubelka, Peter, 68, 156, 241, 251-2, 313-15, 327, 331-42, 385, 400-401, 403, 407, 409, 419, 434; *Adebar*, 332-4, 337; *Arnulf Rainer*, 332-3, 335-8, 424-5, 434; *Mosaik im Vertrauen*, 332, 338-40, 342, 407; *Schwechater*, 327, 332-5, 337, 427; *Unsere Afrikareise*, 332, 338, 340-42

Lachman, Harry, *Dante's Inferno*, 104-5, 112, 131
Lamberton, Robert, 158-9
Landow, George, 260, 407, 412, 419,

428-31, 434; *Bardo Follies*, 428-30; *Film in Which There Appear Sprocket Holes, Edge Lettering, Dirt Particles, Etc. . . .* , 428-30; *Fleming Faloon*, 428-9; *Institutional Quality*, 358, 430-31; *Remedial Reading Comprehension*, 430-31, 433; *The Film That Rises to the Surface of Clarified Butter*, 429-30; *What's Wrong with This Picture?*, 430-31
Langdon, Harry, 51
Laurel, Stan, and Oliver Hardy, 51
Laurot, Edouard de, 379
Lautrémont, Comte de, 123; *Les Chants de Maldoror*, 104
Leacock, Richard, 382-3; *Primary*, 380, 383
Ledoux, Jacques, 86
Lee, Francis, 84
Léger, Fernand, 319, 434; *Ballet Mécanique*, 25, 266, 314-15, 318-19, 322, 332
Levy, Julien, 386
Lhevinne, Isadore, *Ariadne*, 402; *Napoleon's All*, 402
Lloyd, Harold, 51
Locke, John, 186, 188
Lorca, Garcia, 388
Louys, Pierre, *Psyche*, 137, 140, 142
Lovi, Steven, *A Portrait of the Lady in the Yellow Hat*, 195
Lumière, Auguste and Louis, 81-2, 180
Lye, Len, 267-70, 302, 313, 332; *Colour Box*, 268-9; *Free Radicals*, 269-70; *Kaleidoscope*, 268-9; *Rainbow Dance*, 269, 332; *Rhythm*, 269; *Trade Tattoo*, 269, 332; *Tusalava*, 268
Lyrical Film, 174-211, 244, 260, 358, 361, 408-9, 412, 430

Maas, Willard, 36-7, 83-4, 115, 180, 379; *Geography of the Body*, 36, 84; *Image in the Snow*, 84; *Narcissus*, 36, 124
Maclaine, Christopher, 51, 343-8, 355, 360-62, 367; *The End*, 64, 339, 344-8, 351, 368, 371, 384

Maclise, Angus, 397
Magritte, René, 15, 17, 66-7
Mallarmé, Stéphane, 259, 363, 418;
    Igitur, 417; Un Coup de Dés, 216
Man, Paul de, 255-6, 350
Man Ray, 57-8; Étoile de Mer, 18-19
Manet, Édouard, 405
Markopoulos, Gregory, 30, 40, 62,
    134, 136-75, 206, 233, 295, 313,
    339, 342, 381-2, 403, 407, 409,
    412, 435; "Angelica Clamores,"
    163; Bliss, 171; Chaos Phaos, 153;
    Charmides, 143, 163; Eldora, 146;
    Eros, O Basileus, 160, 165, 169,
    171, 173; Flowers of Asphalt, 146;
    Galaxie, 157, 173, 260, 398; Gam-
    melion, 137, 139, 171-3, 260; Him-
    self as Herself, 139, 157-61, 163,
    165, 173; Lysis, 137, 142-3, 163;
    Ming Green, 157, 161-2, 171, 398;
    Psyche, 136-43, 145-7, 149, 152,
    172, 174; Serenity, 139, 146, 170-
    71; Swain, 21, 65, 99, 136, 139,
    143-7, 152, 163, 172; The Illiac
    Passion, 92, 107, 110, 124, 139,
    163-71, 173; Through a Lens
    Brightly: Mark Turbyfill, 157, 161;
    Twice a Man, 124, 139, 146-58,
    161, 163, 167, 172-3, 182, 198,
    233, 354, 383
McClure, Michael, 119, 224, 237,
    240, 248
Mead, Taylor, 352, 354, 397
Mekas, Adolfas, 379, 383; Hallelujah
    the Hills, 144, 380, 382
Mekas, Jonas, 41, 93, 159, 161, 206,
    240, 245-6, 260, 320, 334, 340,
    353, 378-84, 396, 398-401; Diaries,
    Notes and Sketches, 380, 398-401;
    Guns of the Trees, 380-82, 384;
    Rabbitshit Haikus, 380; Reminis-
    cences of a Journey to Lithuania,
    398, 400-01
Méliès, Georges, 123, 162
Melville, Herman, 40; "The Light-
    ning Rod Man," 201
Menken, Marie, 36, 84, 115, 180,
    382; Notebook, 180, 183, 260;
    Visual Variations on Noguchi, 180
Meyers, Sidney, 382

Michelson, Annette, 401, 416-17,
    420, 422
Millennium Film Workshop, 385
Miller, Arthur, 83
Milton, John, 170, 392
Mondrian, Piet, 3, 274, 278, 316,
    319, 373
Monk, Thelonius, "Mysterioso," 271,
    286-7
Montez, Marie, 390-91
Moore, Ben, 36
Muller, Max, 271, 289, 291-2, 295
Mythopoeic Film, 30-31, 40, 90-92,
    107, 121, 123-4, 152, 154, 172,
    188, 211-65, 274, 287, 295, 302,
    313, 319, 343, 347, 352-3, 357-8,
    380, 383, 395, 401, 407-9, 427,
    430, 435

Nelson, Robert, 51, 82, 343, 351,
    354-62; Awful Backlash, 358; Bleu
    Shut, 358-60, 367, 425; Confes-
    sions of a Black Mother Succuba,
    355; The Great Blondino, 354-8,
    360, 367
Neoplasticism, 266, 274, 316, 319
Newman, Barnett, 237, 319
Nietzsche, Friedrich, 246, 252-3; The
    Birth of Tragedy from the Spirit of
    Music, 46
Nitsch, Hermann, 253, 401
Noren, Andrew, 398

Oldenburg, Claes, 323
Olson, Charles, 231, 257

Panofsky, Erwin, 25
Participatory Film, 172, 201, 315,
    358, 430, 431, 433-5
Penfield, Dr. Wildner, 291-2
Peterson, Sidney, 47-57, 59-60, 65-
    81, 154, 171, 175, 233, 266, 300,
    343, 407; Mr. Frenhofer and the
    Minotaur, 52, 65, 69-74, 78, 134;
    The Cage, 52-9, 65, 134, 355; The
    Fly in the Pigment, 54; The Lead
    Shoes, 52, 65, 75-9; The Petrified
    Dog, 52, 65-9; The Potted Psalm,
    48-55, 57, 59, 64, 66, 344

Picabia, Francis, 47, 57-8; *Entr'acte,*
  see Clair
Picasso, Pablo, 69-74, 77, 405
Poe, Edgar Allan, 40
Pollock, Jackson, 235-7, 243, 319
Pop Art, 323, 410, 411
Pound, Ezra, 212, 233, 434; *Gaudier-
  Brzeska,* 220-22; "Salutation the
  Second," 239
Preston, Richard, 384
Proust, Marcel, 166, 261
Psychodrama, 18, 33, 45, 64-5, 99-
  100, 136, 265, 361-2

Rainer, Arnulf, 337
Rayns, Tony, 95, 103, 122, 131
Reage, Pauline, *The Story of O,* 115
Rebay, Hilda, 280
Reinhardt, Max, *A Midsummer
  Night's Dream,* 94, 103, 116
Resnais, Alain, 202
Rice, Ron, 51, 82, 343, 351-5, 360-
  62, 376, 382, 395-8; *Chumlum,*
  397-8; *Senseless,* 353-4; *The Flower
  Thief,* 64, 351-3, 355, 367, 371,
  392, 397; *The Queen of Sheba
  Meets the Atom Man,* 354, 378
Richter, Hans, 313, 315, 318, 379;
  Rhythmus 21, 47, 266-8, 275,
  301, 325
Rilke, Rainer Maria, 172
Rimbaud, Arthur, 378
Robbe-Grillet, Alain, 160
Rogosin, Lionel, 380, 382-4
Romanticism, 45-6, 55, 89, 100, 110,
  119, 128-30, 134, 170-71, 186-8,
  211, 233, 255-6, 295, 307, 319-20,
  323, 331, 340, 352-5, 380, 382-3,
  387, 396, 398, 402, 410, 417, 422,
  435
Rothko, Mark, 236-7
Rousseau, Henri, 73
Rousseau, Jean-Jacques, 255
Roussel, Raymond, 293

Sade, Marquis de, 378
Satie, Erik, 47, 57-9, 208
Schneemann, Carolee, 197-8
Schreber, Daniel Gottlob Moritz,
  293

Schreber, Daniel Paul, *Memoirs of
  My Nervous Illness,* 292
Schwitters, Kurt, 318
Sennett, Max, 59
Serrios, Ted, 309
Seurat, Georges, 405
Shakespeare, William, 84, 117, 170;
  A Midsummer Night's Dream,
  116; *Hamlet,* 354; "Venus and
  Adonis," 168
Sharits, Paul, 407, 412, 419, 423-7;
  N:O:T:H:I:N:G, 423-5; *Piece Man-
  dala/End War,* 425, 427; *Ray
  Gun Virus,* 425, 427; *S:S:S:S:S:S,*
  427; *T,O,U,C,H,I,N,G,* 425-7
Shelley, P. B., 242, 382, 402; "Are-
  thusa," 405; *Prometheus Bound,*
  110, 170, 380
Shklovsky, Victor, 403
Simms, Jerry, 371, 373, 375-7
Smith, Harry, 40, 270-77, 279-300,
  302, 331, 343; No. 1, 270-72, 274,
  276-7; No. 2, 270-72, 275-7, 280,
  283; No. 3, 270-72, 275-7; No. 4,
  270-72, 279-80; No. 5, 270-72, 280;
  No. 6, 270-71; No. 7, 270-72, 281-
  3; No. 8, 270-71, 283; No. 9, 271,
  283; No. 10, 271-2, 283-8, 290;
  No. 11, 271-2, 280, 283-8, 290;
  No. 12 (*Heaven and Earth Magic*),
  124, 233, 271-2, 287-99, 305, 383;
  No. 13, 271-2; No. 14 (*Late Superimpositions*), 271-2, 299-300, 397-
  8; *Mahagonny,* 271-2, 280, 299-
  300; *The Tin Woodman's Dream,*
  271-2, 299
Smith, Jack, 157, 354, 368-79, 382,
  387, 390-97, 409; *Flaming Creatures,* 152, 378, 384, 390-96; *No
  President,* 390; *Normal Love,* 153,
  390, 395-6, *Rehearsal for the Destruction of Atlantis,* 396, *Scotch
  Tape,* 377-8, 384
Snow, Michael, 29, 260, 382, 407,
  411-23; *New York Eye and Ear
  Control,* 418, 420; *One Second in
  Montreal,* 418-19; *The Central Region,* 419, 421-3; *Wavelength,* 412-
  23; ←→, 416, 418-21, 423
Sonbert, Warren, 398

Sparagmos, 81-2, 92, 113, 122, 394, 426

Spenser, Edmund, 170

Stanislavsky, Constantin, *The Actor Works Upon Himself*, 385

Stapleton, Olaf, *Star Maker*, 303, 310, 422-3

Stauffacher, Frank, 60, 277, 385

Stein, Gertrude, 182, 191, 259

Steiner, Ralph, H_2O, 25

Sternberg, Joseph von, 138, 390-91

Stevens, Wallace, 186, 233; "An Ordinary Evening in New Haven," 187; *Notes Toward a Supreme Fiction*, 216

Still, Clyfford, 68, 237, 319

Stravinsky, Igor, 405

Stroheim, Eric von, 157

Structural Film, 31, 172, 201, 207, 260, 315, 319, 333, 337, 358, 361, 374, 403, 405, 407-35

Suprematism, 274

Surrealism, 3, 6, 11, 14-15, 43-5, 51, 54, 60, 66-7, 84, 117, 177, 179, 212, 266-7, 274, 284, 294, 319-20, 363, 378, 383-4, 386

Symbolism, 130, 387, 417, 435

Tenney, James, 197-8

Thomas, Dylan, 83

Thoreau, H. D., 165, 380; *Walden*, 399

Tibetan Book of the Dead (Bardo Thodol), 260, 263, 304, 424, 428

Tinguely, Jean, 323

Trance Film, 11, 18, 23, 25, 30-31, 64-5, 91-2, 99-101, 103, 123, 136, 144, 147, 152-3, 172, 176, 179-80, 268, 284, 302, 319, 339, 347, 352, 355, 358, 366, 371, 383, 408-9, 427, 430, 433, 435

Tyler, Parker, 10, 61, 76-8, 83, 179, 380; *The Three Faces of the Film*, 20-21, 36

Upanishads, 424, 429

Vanderbeek, Stan, 382, 384

Van Meter, Ben, 131

Vermeer, Jan, 417-18

Vertov, Dziga, 29, 155

Vogel, Amos, 146

Wagner, Richard, 162

Warhol, Andy, 164, 168, 273, 381, 384, 409-12; *Beauty # 2*, 411; *Eat*, 410-11; *Empire*, 411; *50 Fantastics*, 260; *Haircut*, 411; *Harlot*, 411; *Hedy*, 411; *Henry Geldzahler*, 260; *Poor Little Rich Girl*, 411; *Sleep*, 409-10; *13 Most Beautiful Boys*, 161, 260

Watson, J. S., *The Fall of the House of Usher*, 47; *Lot in Sodom*, 47

Webber, Melville, *see* Watson, J. S.

Webern, Anton, 275, 333

Weiland, Joyce, 407

Weinstein, Donald, 145-6

Wellek, René, 129

Welles, Orson, *Citizen Kane*, 15, 138; *The Trial*, 354

Whistler, J. M., 130

Whitehall, Richard, 205, 263

Whitman, Walt, 40, 233

Whitney, John and James, 277-9, 302; *Five Film Exercises*, 277-9

Whitney, James, *Lapis*, 302, 305, 310; *Yantra*, 302

Wiene, Robert, *The Cabinet of Dr. Caligari*, 21, 25, 111, 144, 203

Wiley, William, 355, 359

Williams, W. C., 233

Wittgenstein, Ludwig, 193, 401

Wordsworth, William, 174, 255-6; *The Prelude*, 187

Yeats, W. B., 402

Youngblood, Gene, 304, 308

Zukofsky, Louis, 233, 250; *A*, 250